SuSE® Linux

INSTALLATION AND CONFIGURATION HANDBOOK

WITHDRAWN

que®

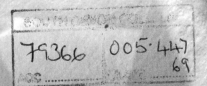

SuSE® Linux
INSTALLATION AND CONFIGURATION HANDBOOK

**Nazeeh Amin El-Dirghami and
Youssef A. Abu Kwaik**

 A Division of Macmillan USA
201 West 103rd Street, Indianapolis, Indiana 46290

SuSE® Linux Installation and Configuration Handbook

International Standard Book Number: 0-7897-2355-7

Library of Congress Catalog Card Number: 00-100074

Printed in the United States of America

First Printing: May 2000

02   01   00   4   3   2   1

Trademarks

Warning and Disclaimer

ASSOCIATE PUBLISHER
Tracy Dunkelberger

ACQUISITIONS EDITOR
Gretchen Ganser

DEVELOPMENT EDITOR
Maureen A. McDaniel

TECHNICAL EDITOR
Brian Schau

MANAGING EDITOR
Matt Purcell

SENIOR EDITOR
Susan Ross Moore

COPY EDITOR
Megan Wade

INDEXER
Kevin Kent

PROOFREADERS
Juli Cook
Heather Hiatt Miller

TEAM COORDINATOR
Cindy Teeters

MEDIA DEVELOPER
Craig Atkins

INTERIOR DESIGNER
Anne Jones

COVER DESIGNER
Anne Jones

COPY WRITER
Eric Borgert

LAYOUT TECHNICIANS
Stacey Richwine-DeRome
Heather Hiatt Miller
Ayanna Lacey
Mark Walchle

Contents at a Glance

Table of Contents

About the Authors

Nazeeh Amin El-Dirghami graduated with a degree in computer science from the American University in Cairo, where he installed and configured multiple Linux servers throughout the Computer Science Department. He has written a series of Arabic articles about Linux, which were the first ever to provide an in-depth introduction of Linux to the Arab world. He currently works as a software developer at ITWorx, developing software for Corel Linux.

Youssef A. Abu Kwaik graduated from the American University in Cairo, majoring in economics and minoring in computer science. He has installed SuSE Linux for the weather forecasting ministry in Egypt and written a series of Arabic articles about Linux for the prominent Arabic magazine *Computer Publishing*. He started using SuSE Linux when version 4.3 was released and has enjoyed the art of scripting that SuSE Linux offers ever since. He currently is a software developer at ITWorx, where he develops software for Corel Linux.

Dedication

I would like to dedicate this book to my family. My father for getting me hooked on computers very early in my life, and for being such a great dad! My mother for being the light of my life; everything that I am is because of her. My little brother for being so understanding and nice to me, even though he would never admit it!

Nazeeh Amin El-Dirghami

To my father for spending his life making me what I am. To my mother for enlightening my life. To my brother and sisters for being who they are.

Youssef A. Abu Kwaik

Acknowledgments

The authors would like to thank the following people and entities for making this book happen.

We would like to thank God for making all this happen, and for giving us the knowledge and the ability to project it to others.

We would like to thank our parents, brothers, and sisters for being there for us throughout our lives. Youssef especially would like to thank his mother for going through the trouble of waking him up at night to work on the book. Nazeeh would like to thank his parents for enduring having to live without seeing him for days because he was busy working on the book.

We would like to thank the SuSE team for creating such an amazing distribution. We had a lot of fun using and studying it. Again, thanks SuSE, we owe you a lot!

We would like to thank the whole Macmillan team for making this book possible—Gretchen Ganser for contacting and pushing us to get this book out on time; Maureen McDaniel for her amazing development abilities that taught us so much; Brian Schau for his excellent technical remarks (there was always something to learn from them); Megan Wade for her superb editing—she will probably fix this sentence for us; and Susan Moore for being so nice about late chapters.

We would like to thank all our friends for still wanting to know us even though we haven't gone out with them for months. We also would like to thank all the people at ITWorx, you guys are great!!

Nazeeh would like to thank the following people:

- Nenad Andjelic (did I spell it right, Ned?) for introducing me to Linux. Thanks a lot, Ned!
- Hazem Nassef for teaching me so much about Linux and UNIX in general. I owe you a lot of what I know.
- Dr. Mohy Mahmood for teaching me so much about computer science.
- Dr. Amr El-Kadi for increasing my interest in Linux even further.
- Youssef for believing me when I told you about Linux—we make the best team ever!
- Metallica, Megadeth, WASP, Blind Guardian, Amorphis, and Yngwie J. Malmsteen for making such excellent music!

Youssef would like to thank the following people:

- Sally El-Ogueil for standing by me and supporting me every minute of the day.
- Dr. Mohy Mahmood for standing by me when I needed help. Thanks, Doctor!
- Dr. Amr Goneid for pushing me to challenge myself.
- Peter Norton for being my idol in programming.
- Nazeeh for introducing me to Linux and for making the best partner ever!
- Manowar and Meat Loaf for making such good music!

We would also like to thank Linus Torvalds for creating Linux, and the whole GNU/Linux community for teaching us the art of sharing. We owe so much to everyone who ever wrote a piece of documentation for Linux—thank you. We also would like to thank the StarOffice team—this whole book was written on it.

Thank you Blizzard for creating StarCraft; we never enjoyed a game so much!

Finally, we would like to thank Microsoft for making Windows the way it is. If it weren't for that, we never would have looked at Linux.

Tell Us What You Think!

As the reader of this book, *you* are our most important critic and commentator. We value your opinion and want to know what we're doing right, what we could do better, what areas you'd like to see us publish in, and any other words of wisdom you're willing to pass our way.

As a Publisher for Que, I welcome your comments. You can fax, email, or write me directly to let me know what you did or didn't like about this book—as well as what we can do to make our books stronger.

Please note that I cannot help you with technical problems related to the topic of this book, and that due to the high volume of mail I receive, I might not be able to reply to every message.

When you write, please be sure to include this book's title and author as well as your name and phone or fax number. I will carefully review your comments and share them with the author and editors who worked on the book.

Fax: 317.581.4666

Email: quetechnical@macmillanusa.com

Mail: Tracy Dunkelberger
         Associate Publisher
         Que Corporation
         201 West 103rd Street
         Indianapolis, IN 46290 USA

What Is Linux?

You can't open a magazine or go to a large computer exhibition these days without seeing or hearing something about Linux. It seems to be the buzzword these days—Linux this, Linux that, and so on. A lot of people still do not know what exactly Linux is. Is it just another power application? Is it a new paradigm of software applications? Is it a new and cool game?

Linux is an operating system that runs on a variety of hardware architectures ranging from the Intel x86 to PowerPCs. An *operating system* is the software responsible for controlling your hardware resources and organizing how your applications will use them. Without an operating system, your machine would just sit there doing nothing. You would have invested in the most expensive and technically advanced paperweight ever.

The operating system brings life to your machine by controlling every aspect of your hardware. The operating system controls how your CPU, RAM, hard drive, sound card, video card, modem, networking card, and so on are used. The operating system also gives application developers the required interfaces they need to access their hardware. This eliminates having to worry about what hardware you have and having to communicate with it using its rather complex protocols. The operating system completely shields users from this by giving them a unified interface to all the different types of hardware and performing the task of talking to the hardware directly.

Several types of operating systems exist in today's market, such as the tried and trusted UNIX system, along with its variants; the popular MS Windows, along with all its various versions; the MacOS for Macintosh computers; the IBM OS/2; and so on. Because Linux was developed in the image of UNIX, it greatly resembles it in every aspect.

UNIX is one of the most popular operating systems worldwide. It was originally developed at AT&T as a multitasking system for minicomputers and mainframes in the 1970s, but has since grown to become one of the most widely-used operating systems anywhere[md]despite its sometimes confusing interface and lack of central standardization. In the almost 30 years that it has been around, UNIX has thoroughly been tested and proven to be a very stable system. Currently, UNIX machines run the foundation of the Internet, which is a huge but stable network. This is attributed to the well-designed and highly stable UNIX systems that control it.

Linux was developed using the same design standards as UNIX. Therefore, Linux has inherited the rock-solid nature of its parent, UNIX. However, Linux is a modern UNIX; it has support for new technologies that have not existed on UNIX flavors before. Bringing these technologies to the world of UNIX is just one way Linux has paid back UNIX for its stable nature.

One characteristic that Linux hasn't inherited from UNIX, though, is its price. UNIX has always been quite expensive. Linux, on the other hand, is absolutely free of charge. You do not have to pay a dime for it; it is freely available on the Internet for you to download. To understand why this is the case, let's look at Linux's history.

Linux started off originally as a hobby project for the young Linus Torvalds. Torvalds was inspired by a very small UNIX link operating system called Minix, which was developed by Andrew Tannenbaum. Torvalds wanted more out of Minix, so he began to think about developing his own UNIX-like operating system.

Right around this time, Intel released a new line of processors, the 386. These processors had new features that were specific to task switching and multitasking. Torvalds started his project by experimenting with this new interface provided by the 386 processor. He coded a simple task swapper using assembly code. Soon enough, though, he started writing code in C, which made things much easier and sped up development.

Around late August 1991, Torvalds had a *very* basic operating system. It had a very buggy floppy disk driver that worked for his machine and a small filesystem. Torvalds released his code to the public as version 0.01. This version was not even executable, and it required a running Minix system with which to experiment. By this point, Torvalds was totally committed to improving Minix.

On October 5, 1991, Torvalds released version 0.02 of his operating system along with an official announcement on Usenet. By then, his operating system was capable of running the Bash shell and Gnu C Compiler (gcc). His announcement read as follows:

> "Do you pine for the nice days of Minix-1.1, when men were men and wrote their own device drivers? Are you without a nice project and just dying to cut your teeth on an OS you can try to modify for your needs? Are you finding it frustrating when everything works on Minix? No more all-nighters to get a nifty program working? Then this post might be just for you.

> "As I mentioned a month ago, I'm working on a free version of a Minix-look-alike for AT-386 computers. It has finally reached the stage where it's even usable (though may not be, depending on what you want), and I am willing to put out the sources for wider distribution. It is just version 0.02...but I've successfully run bash, gcc, gnu-make, gnu-sed, compress, etc. under it."

Several hackers responded to this announcement and started helping Torvalds by working on different parts of the operating system. The version number moved to 0.03 and then jumped to 0.10. By March 1992, Torvalds set the version to 0.95, which denoted that the system was almost ready for an official first release.

Currently, Linux is one of the most powerful operating systems for the PC, and is giving the commercial operating systems a real run for their money. The current version is 2.2.14, with version 2.4 expected very soon (it should be out by the time you read this). Linux is considered to be the most successful free software project ever. Currently, it still is completely free and is maintained by Linus Torvalds, along with hundreds of other developers on the Internet.

Advantages of Using Linux

Linux is currently one of the most stable operating systems available for the PC. The operating system has many advantages; let's look at some of them.

Linux is a true 32-bit operating system, all the way to its internals. Therefore, it uses your processor with maximum efficiency because all processors today are 32-bit oriented. In contrast, some of the commercial operating systems still use 16-bit code.

Just like UNIX, Linux is a complete multitasking, multiuser operating system. This enables many users to log in to and run programs on the same machine simultaneously. After all, Linux began as a task swapper on the 386 processor.

Linux is fully compatible with UNIX standards, meaning it inherited its design and philosophy. Some hackers believe UNIX to be the Real Thing—the one true operating system. Linux is in most ways a UNIX operating system, but Linux adds a bit of its own functionality as well. This compatibility with UNIX has made it very easy for developers to port UNIX software on the Linux platform.

The Linux kernel is capable of emulating the 387-FPU instructions for systems without a math co-processor. This enables it to run programs that require floating-point math capability.

Linux has support for a wide variety of filesystems. It has support for Microsoft filesystems such as FAT, VFAT, FAT32, and NTFS; CD-ROM filesystems; Amiga filesystems; Apple Macintosh filesystems; and others. It also has good support for network filesystems such as NFS and CIFS/SMB. It is very unlikely that you will come across a filesystem for which Linux does not have support.

Linux, being a UNIX-like operating system, has well-built networking support. It supports virtually all the networking protocols used on the Internet. It has full support for TCP/IP along with the complete range of software for it. It has support for ethernet, PPP, SLIP, CSLIP, IPX, AppleTalk, and so on. In addition, device drivers for the most commonly used networking adapters are available.

Linux has versions of all the popular networking applications available for UNIX. It has the popular Apache Web server, the sendmail e-mail server, ftp servers, news servers, proxy servers, the file and print sharing server for MS Windows machines, and so on.

To achieve maximum memory usage and efficiency, the Linux kernel uses virtual memory and paging. This enables the system to run many more programs than the physical RAM can hold. This is accomplished by saving processes that aren't currently running to disk to make room for others that need to be run.

The Linux filesystem uses file and directory permissions to restrict user access, making Linux a secure system in multiuser environments. The availability of the entire source code for the operating system makes it easy for anyone to locate and fix security bugs.

Virtually all the common UNIX utilities and commands are available under Linux. Any UNIX user will feel right at home with Linux. These utilities include all the popular editors such as vi, Emacs, pico, and so on.

Linux also uses the GNU versions of the UNIX utilities and commands. These are usually more advanced than the older UNIX commands, but they are fully compatible with them.

Linux has a wide variety of shells that you can use, too, including bash, tcsh, ksh, zsh, and others. Each one has support for powerful shell scripting and commands.

A very powerful, network transparent graphical windowing system is something else that Linux has. This system, called the X Window System, has been around for years on UNIX systems and is very well structured and designed. A free port of the X Window system is installed by default on Linux. Graphical desktops already exist for Linux, with KDE and GNOME being the biggest and most complex of them.

Despite the common perception that Linux does not have office programs, it actually has several. You can use the powerful and well-structured LaTex system. Or, if you prefer graphically-based programs, you can use Sun's StarOffice—a complete office suite available free of charge. Corel has released a free copy of its WordPerfect word processor to the Linux community, which will soon be followed by a version of Corel WordPerfect Office 2000. Other projects are developing their own integrated office suites, such as Koffice for KDE and GNOME Office for GNOME.

Linux comes with a full set of development tools that are both free and powerful. These tools include a full range of compilers for several programming languages, such as debuggers, profiling tools, code versioning systems for team development, scripting tools, GUI libraries, threading libraries, and networking libraries. If you are planning to port MS Windows applications, you can use the WINE library, which provides Windows API compatibility for Linux.

Disadvantages of Using Linux

Even though Linux has many advantages, it still has a few disadvantages. For starters, it is not as user-friendly as the other commercial operating systems. Linux was developed by programmers for programmers. The entire Linux movement concentrated heavily on making the operating system as stable as possible, so there wasn't much attention paid to making it user-friendly. It takes a while to get used to Linux, but after you do, you won't have any problems. With the goal of making Linux stable having been achieved, developers have turned their attention to building a user-friendly desktop.

Linux does not have as much software as other commercial operating systems, especially in the area of games. But, this is changing now as more companies are interested in porting their games to the Linux platform.

Linux also does not support as much hardware as the commercial operating systems support. This is because most of the device drivers required by hardware devices are written by individuals on the Internet. Whereas, in the case of the commercial operating systems, the manufacturers of the hardware devices make the device drivers available. However, this too is changing as more and more hardware manufacturers are providing device drivers for their products on the Linux platform.

Another disadvantage of Linux is that non-UNIX users can find it a bit difficult to understand at first. The main reason for this is that Linux uses a different system of operation from the one these users are used to. This difficulty, however, tends to go away with time as the user becomes more familiar with the system.

The filesystem permissions system also tends to confuse new users in the beginning because they are used to single-user operating systems that do not have such restrictions. But, after the user becomes familiar with the concept of a multi-user system, she will not have any problems.

One final disadvantage of Linux is that most of its configuration requires users to know how to use the command line. This tends to make new users a bit uncomfortable if they are used to a graphically based configuration.

Why SuSE Linux?

Linux is available on the Net for free; you can download it at your convenience. But, it will be very difficult for you to assemble the whole system by yourself. That would require you to build the filesystem, install the kernel, and build the rest of the system by compiling it from scratch. This is obviously more work than anyone would want to do, which is why distributions came into being.

A *distribution* is a fully working and structured Linux package that has an installation program that helps you install it. So, all you need to do is to grab a distribution from the Internet and install it using the installer. Voila! You have a running Linux system without any effort.

SuSE Linux is a distribution put together by S.U.S.E. and is one of the best distributions available on the market and the Internet today. Let's look at some of the features of SuSE Linux.

SuSE Linux takes the difficulty out of installing Linux thanks to its graphically based YaST2 installation program. SuSE Linux installs on any system by using a graphical installation program that asks you a few questions. Then, based on your answers, it installs and configures the system automatically.

Linux always has been known to be difficult to configure. Words such as *cryptic text files* have been used to describe the process. SuSE Linux's YaST makes it very easy for you to configure and maintain your Linux system without having to deal with the configuration files directly. Instead, everything is configured through the user-friendly dialog of YaST.

Most of Linux's functionality is achieved through the use of scripts. The SuSE team members are professionals when it comes to scripts. The scripts that run the system are masterpieces in shell scripting. They run the system in top-notch shape and with maximum efficiency.

SuSE Linux is available in two versions, a small snapshot version and a full six-CD version that's for sale. Both versions are available for download on the Internet, and the full version is bundled with tons of applications and utilities. A full installation exceeds 6GB of hard disk space, but you end up having basically every single program that is available for Linux. The snapshot version is good for smaller installations. It does not have as many packages as the retail version, but it still has the benefits of YaST.

The SuSE team has fully documented most of the configuration files on the system, making it easy for anyone to understand the structure of the configuration file. Sample configurations also are available to ease the process of installation.

SuSE installs the two most famous and easy-to-use desktop environments available for Linux: KDE and GNOME. Both are fully configured and ready to run out of the box. In addition, hundreds of applications for each desktop environment are bundled with SuSE Linux.

Another advantage of SuSE Linux is that it's structured to be used as both a desktop and server operating system. You can set the security level of the system to match the network you are in.

SuSE Linux bundles StarOffice 5.1, which is considered one of the best office suites available today. A collection of other commercial software is available for you to try, including a demo of Applixware office, several games, and some development tools.

SuSE bundles several emulators you can use to run programs that are not Linux native. These emulators include the DOS emulator that runs MS DOS applications and WINE, which is still in the alpha stage but runs some MS Windows applications.

SuSE Linux has been certified by Oracle to run their Oracle database for Linux. This enables users to install the Oracle database on SuSE Linux and have it up and running with the least amount of effort.

The SuSE team always provides the latest kernel with their distribution. This kernel is usually modified by the SuSE team to include extra functionality they deem important. This new functionality, if implemented by SuSE, is given back to the Linux community to integrate into the official Linux kernel. For example, SuSE, in cooperation with Siemens, developed a patch to the kernel to enable it to use up to 4GB of RAM.

In addition, the SuSE team has developed some X servers that support video cards not supported by the XFree86 project. Again, all the X servers are given to the XFree86 group to integrate into their official branch.

Bottom line, SuSE Linux is not just a professional distribution, it is complete Linux satisfaction.

Who Should Buy This Book

The first thought that a person might have when they pick up a book is "Is this book right for me?" Well, is this book you are holding now right for you? Yes, it is! This book has been written to help various levels of users. If you are a person who has never worked with Linux before and would like to try it, you will find this book very easy to read and understand. If you are already a Linux user and would like to learn more about SuSE Linux or Linux in general, you will surely find useful information in this book.

Linux, in general, is not very easy to configure for most new users. When we started using it, we were faced with quite a few problems, as was almost everyone. This book is the result of our experiences, the problems we faced, and the solutions we came up with. Topics are explained quite thoroughly because we truly believe that it is important for the user to understand what they are doing instead of just following steps. To truly feel at ease with Linux, you should understand it, not memorize it. There are several ways to configure the same part of Linux, so if you don't understand what you are configuring, you might get stuck and not know what to do. Speaking of problems, every chapter ends with a troubleshooting section that covers most of the common configuration problems and pitfalls.

This book is not all theory, though; it uses a practical approach to the topic. Every chapter attempts to explain to the reader what she is about to configure and why she should configure it. Then, the reader is led, step-by-step, through the configuration process. This enables the reader to not only understand what she is configuring, but to actually configure it as she learns. We've been careful to use fairly general examples to enable the reader to apply them to different situations with little modification.

What This Book Covers

This book covers the whole process of installing and configuring a SuSE Linux distribution. It takes you from installing the system to configuring a full-fledged network server or desktop workstation. The information found in this book covers the most recent version of SuSE Linux (6.3), but is applicable to older versions as well.

Chapter 1, "Pre-Installing SuSE Linux," begins with a step-by-step guide to preparing your system for a SuSE Linux installation. This includes everything from partitioning your hard drive without destroying your currently installed operating systems to installing SuSE Linux. Chapter 2, "Installing SuSE Linux," thoroughly explains the two modes of installation, the new graphical YaST2 and the old text-based YaST1. You will learn how to boot the installation and how to install SuSE Linux from local media and from network via FTP or NFS.

To complete the installation, Chapter 3, "Installing the X Window System," explains how to install and configure the X Window System with the least amount of effort. This will enable you to have a graphical desktop at a very early stage of the installation.

Chapter 4, "Managing Users and Groups," teaches you how to effectively control your users and place restrictions on them. Topics such as filesystem quotas, process limitations, and memory limitations are thoroughly covered in Chapter 5, "Managing Filesystems." System maintenance and configuration topics are discussed in Chapter 6, "Backing Up the System," and Chapter 7, "System Upgrade."

The process of configuring a Linux kernel is one of the most important things a user should learn. Chapter 8, "Installing a New Kernel," discusses how to configure and recompile your kernel. You will learn about all the options you can set and how to maintain your kernel. When you are finished with this chapter, you should never have a problem configuring and compiling your kernel again.

Chapters 10, "Sound Card Configuration;" 11, "Printing;" and 12, "Configuring Peripherals," teach you how to install and configure most of your hardware. Topics covered include installing printers, sound cards, CD-Writer, DVD, fax, scanners, and TV capture cards.

Even if you don't want to use SuSE Linux as a network server, you will probably need to know how to configure it in a networked environment. Part III, "Network Configuration," covers several networking-related topics with extensive information and guides. You will learn how to effectively integrate your SuSE Linux machine with different types of networks. For example, you will learn how to communicate with MS Windows machines using the famous Samba package, with UNIX flavors using NFS, with Apple machines using AppleTalk, and with Novell NetWare networks. Your SuSE Linux will be able to talk to any machine on the network using its own native language.

Part III also covers setting up a SuSE Linux server. Topics such as setting up an email server, a Web server, and an FTP server are discussed. You will learn how to set up these services and understand how they work.

If you are planning to use SuSE Linux in an ISP, you will find the information you need in Part III, as well. Topics covered include dial-in servers and DNS, along with other networking topics.

The desktop user will also find this book very helpful. Chapter 24, "Configuring the Desktop," thoroughly explains how to install and configure the two most famous desktop environments available for Linux today, KDE and GNOME. For all your office needs, you can read Chapter 25, "Installing and Configuring StarOffice," and Chapter 26, "Installing and Configuring WordPerfect." Chapter 28, "Installing and Configuring Netscape Communicator," will have you up and surfing the Net in no time.

Two of the most famous database engines for Linux are covered in Chapter 29, "Configuring MySQL," and Chapter 30,"Installing and Configuring Oracle." These two chapters will teach you how to install and configure both of these databases through easy-to-follow steps.

To use Linux effectively, you must know how to use the shell. Chapter 31, "Using the Shell," teaches you how to use it efficiently. The famous Midnight Commander is thoroughly explained as well, encompassing all your file manager needs in the console.

Part V, "Appendixes," contains a lot of useful information. Appendix A, "Getting More Information," explains where to find proper documentation for all the software discussed in this book. Appendix B, "Hardware Compatibility List," provides a list of all the available supported hardware. Appendix C, "YaST," explains the tool that has become *the* key configuration tool in SuSE Linux. Appendix D, "Tips and Tricks on Tuning Your Linux Box," offers additional information on how to tweak your system. Appendix E, "Various Utilities," discusses tools that can be used with SuSE Linux for added functionality.

Overall, you will find this book very useful and easy to read. Installing and configuring SuSE Linux will be not only easy, but also fun (a lot of fun).

Installation

1

Pre-Installing SuSE Linux

In this chapter

Preparing for the Installation

Before you start installing SuSE Linux, you should take some precautionary steps. There are many things that you have to keep in mind before you start the actual installation process and reach the point of no return. The most important fact that you have to keep in mind is that there is nothing as precious as your data. Back up any important data that you have. Second, do not start the installation until you have read and understood what you will see. We strongly recommend reading this chapter along with the following chapter before you actually start the installation.

Prepare Yourself

The first thing you need is patience. Installing a new operating system you have never seen before is not easy. The SuSE Linux team has done their best to make the installation process as simple as possible. However, installing a new operating system means that your PC will speak a new language, which you might not understand. SuSE Linux is easy to install after you understand the terms and the Linux vocabulary and philosophy. Understanding requires patience.

Hardware Requirements

Unlike some operating systems that require super-qualified hardware, SuSE Linux will install and run on system configurations that you previously considered junk. Of course, the better the hardware configuration, the better the performance. Still, SuSE Linux can be installed on 386 systems with 8MB of RAM. If you want to check whether SuSE Linux supports your hardware, read Appendix B, "Hardware Compatibility List." The supported hardware list at the end of this book applies to SuSE Linux 6.3 and above. Newer hardware also might be supported. We highly recommend that you visit the following Web site to check whether your hardware is supported or not: http://cdb.suse.de/cdb_english.html.

NOTE　The hardware list in Appendix B contains information available at the time of this book's writing. An up-to-date supported hardware list is available at http://cdb.suse.de/cdb_english.html.

Linux developers add support to new hardware all the time. Hardware companies have started to release drivers for Linux. Therefore, there should not be any problems in hardware support in the near future. ■

Hardware Requirements for Installation

SuSE Linux can be installed several different ways. SuSE Linux can be installed from the installation DVD or CDs. It also can be installed over NFS or FTP. Another way to install it is to copy the CD contents to an existing directory and start installing.

The factors affecting the hardware requirements for installation are the method by which you install SuSE Linux and the display card you have.

To install SuSE Linux using the installation DVD disk or the installation CDs, you should have the appropriate drive that is capable of reading such disks. If you are planning to install it over a network or by using the CD contents you have copied to the directory, you will not need any other drive to install SuSE Linux.

For SuSE Linux 6.3, the installation process can be performed using YaST2. YaST2 carries a fully graphical installation that is said to be simplicity itself. For YaST2 to work, you need a display card that supports Vesa 2.0. If you do not have one, you can always use the normal text mode YaST to install SuSE Linux. The CD accompanying this book uses YaST to install SuSE Linux and runs on all systems.

Yes, You Can Have Both Linux and Windows Together

One question that immediately will come to your mind is "Can I have SuSE Linux and Windows 9x or NT on the same system?" Yes, you can. If you tell it to, SuSE Linux will detect your existing Windows partitions and will be able to read and write to them. During the installation, if you use YaST2, a boot manager will be installed and automatically set up. However, if you use YaST, you will have to set it up manually through an easy-to-use interface. A *boot manager* is a program that runs when your system starts and asks you which operating system to boot for the current session.

N O T E   SuSE Linux can coexist with Windows 9x and Windows NT. You will not lose any of them if
you install SuSE Linux properly. Although you will be able to access the Windows 9x and
NT partitions from SuSE Linux, you will not be able to access the Linux partitions from Windows. ▪

Space Requirements

Before we start discussing the hard disk space requirements for the SuSE Linux installation, we should note that SuSE Linux can be separated into partitions. Therefore, when we talk about the space needed for the SuSE Linux installation, we're talking about the size of a *complete* partition. This chapter discusses how to split a big partition into two partitions to help you free up disk space. In addition, a number of commercial packages can be used to resize hard disk partitions to make some space available for SuSE Linux to install. We expect that a partition resizer module will be integrated in YaST2 in the coming SuSE Linux versions.

SuSE Linux can be installed in a variety of ways. Table 1.1 shows the space required if you launch the installation using YaST2. Note that YaST2 was designed to make the installation process simple for newbies. Thus, customization is not performed per package but per category.

Table 1.1   Hard Disk Space Required if You Install SuSE Linux Using YaST2

Installation Method	Space Required
Minimal	150MB + swap
Default	500MB + swap
Almost everything	More than 6GB +swap

A swap partition with a size of double your RAM size or more is recommended. A swap partition size depends on how your SuSE Linux will be used.

Having a swap partition will increase the usability of your system. Linux uses your swap partitions to extend your memory by making the swap partition a virtual memory.

If you use the Minimal or Default installation method, you will be installing the SuSE Linux system and its base applications. You will need more space if you decide to install any of the packages listed in Table 1.2.

Table 1.2   Extra Packages and Environments

Package	Required Space
KDE	180MB
GNOME	100MB
Netscape	35MB
StarOffice	150MB
Applixware	400MB
Oracle8	600MB
Development tools	200MB

On the other hand, if you choose to install SuSE Linux using YaST, you will have more customization options. This will indeed give you better control over the space required for the installation. For a good configuration that is suitable for a normal home user, you can probably set up a system that requires a range of 500MB–1.2GB. The CD that comes with this book can guarantee setting up a highly advanced operating system for almost all users and will not require more than 1.5GB if you install all the packages. We highly recommend giving SuSE Linux no less than 2.0GB if you are planning to use it extensively or if it will be used by multiple users. If the system will be running as a print or file server, we recommend using more than a hard drive to balance the load on the system and give better performance. The ultimate load on any machine is running a database server. In this case, you should have large hard drives with high disk space available on them. Refer to your database manuals for more information on customizing systems for best performance.

Disk Partitioning from DOS

Several factors will determine whether your installation goes smoothly. One of these factors is whether the disk space you assign to SuSE Linux is free space (in other words, unpartitioned). If it is, YaST and YaST2 will detect the existence of this unpartitioned space and attempt to use it, if you tell them to. For example, assume you have a 4GB hard drive partitioned in two partitions—C: and D:. If you decide you want to give SuSE Linux 2GB instead of D:, you would follow these steps:

> **CAUTION**
>
> The following steps are only for illustration. They might not apply to all cases. Do not attempt to follow these steps without reading the rest of this section, or you might end up losing your partitions.

1. Copy all needed data from D: to C:.
2. Exit Windows and start your computer in DOS mode.
3. Start the fdisk utility. Fdisk usually comes with DOS 6.2 and below in the `C:\DOS` directory. And, it usually comes with Windows 9x in the `C:\Windows\command` directory.
4. Press 3 to delete a partition or logical disk drive.
5. Press 3 again to delete a logical DOS drive in an extended partition.
6. You will be prompted for the drive letter you want to delete. Type `D:`.
7. To ensure that you are not deleting a wrong partition, fdisk will ask you to enter the label of this partition to delete it. After you have entered the correct label, the partition is deleted and 2GB of disk space is available to SuSE Linux.

NOTE When emptying space for SuSE Linux to install, you will have to ensure that the space is put together in one piece. If you do not find two adjacent partitions that can fit the space you require for SuSE Linux, you can delete nonadjacent partitions and use presizer to move the partitions and create one large piece of free space. ∎

Primary, Extended, and Logical Partitions

Hard drives can have up to four primary partitions. This restriction has resulted in the use of extended partitions. You can think of *extended partitions* as containers that were made to hold partitions within themselves. Partitions contained within extended partitions are called *logical partitions*. Figure 1.1 shows a hard drive with one primary partition, one extended partition, and four logical partitions in the extended partition.

FIGURE 1.1

The dotted area represents the whole hard drive. The dashed box represents an extended partition. Each box inside the dashed box represents a logical partition with its corresponding drive letter under DOS.

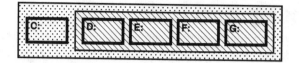

Note that the extended partition does not have a drive letter under DOS and Windows.

CAUTION

Although you can have more than one primary partition on one hard drive, some operating systems—including Windows 9x—have great difficulty understanding this fact. If you want Windows to function properly and show all your partition tables, you must have only one partition table, and in most cases, only one extended partition. In the extended table, you can have as many logical partitions as you want. Linux does not have this drawback and will understand any partition configuration you might have.

Now that you understand the differences between the three types of partition tables, go back to the example in the previous section and read it again. If you want to delete one partition that you have, you now know which one to delete.

CAUTION

Be very careful when using fdisk. You might lose important data if you delete the wrong partition. Check the drive letter you want to delete carefully. Take more than one look and be sure that you are deleting a partition from the correct hard drive if you have more than one hard drive. You have been warned!

CAUTION

For people with hard drives larger than 8GB, make sure that the space you empty is within the 8GB range. BIOS restrictions make it impossible to boot partitions that are beyond this boundary. Some work is being done to solve this problem through software, but SuSE Linux 6.3 will not be able to boot if it goes beyond this boundary. If you cannot get enough empty space to install SuSE Linux before this boundary, be sure you empty at least 100MB within this boundary to use it only for booting. Also, you should empty enough disk space to install SuSE Linux after this boundary. You will learn how to use a separate partition for booting SuSE Linux in Chapter 2, "Installing SuSE Linux."

Using FIPS to Split Your Partitions

A very important utility that comes with SuSE Linux and runs under DOS is FIPS. *FIPS* can split a partition in two. You will appreciate this important feature if you have a big partition and you want to use a part of it to install SuSE Linux. SuSE Linux needs a partition for itself, so you must split your big partition and use one of the new ones to install SuSE Linux.

What FIPS Does

To get the best results from FIPS, you need to understand how it works. FIPS will check how much space is left at the end of a partition. This space is the maximum you can tell it to use as a new partition. If you have files that reside at the end of a partition, you will not be able to split the partition, even though the partition has enough disk space. Figure 1.2 explains such a dilemma.

FIGURE 1.2
If you try to use FIPS to split the D: drive, you will be able to get only 500MB at maximum. You will not be able to split the E: drive, even though it has 1GB of free space. This is because the data lies at the end of the partition.

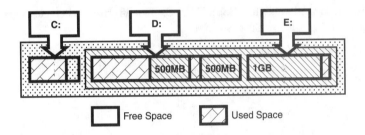

Preparing for FIPS

Before you use FIPS, you will need to do some preparation. If you were to prepare the D: and E: drives shown in Figure 1.2, you would perform the following steps:

1. Choose which partition you would like to split.
2. Consider the amount of space you will cut off this partition.
3. Run a disk check utility on this partition. Microsoft Windows comes with a ScanDisk utility that will do the job. Click Start, Accessories, System Tools, ScanDisk to start the ScanDisk utility.
4. Run a disk optimization utility on this partition. The disk optimization utilities have the advantage of moving all the used disk space to the beginning of the partition. Microsoft Windows comes with Disk Defragmenter. Click Start, Accessories, System Tools, Disk Defragmenter to start the Disk Defragmenter utility. Click the Setting button and check the Rearrange Program File So My Programs Start Faster check box.

Now the partitions should look like Figure 1.3.

FIGURE 1.3
After defragmenting
the partitions, you can
split the whole space
left on them using
FIPS.

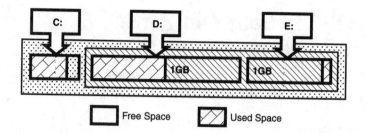

Some programs, such as Norton Image, image the disk partitions so they can be restored if damage occurs. These programs store the image files in the last sector of the partition, which can't be split unless these files are deleted.

FIPS in Action

FIPS is located in the first SuSE Linux CD in a directory called `dosutils\fips`. To start working with FIPS, follow these steps:

1. Make a bootable disk.
2. Unzip the FIPS program to the disk.
3. Boot using the disk.
4. Start FIPS and split your partitions.

FIPS comes with very good documentation that explains how it handles special cases, such as the use of double spaces and other utilities.

> **CAUTION**
>
> Do not attempt to run FIPS from within Windows. FIPS will tell you that you should not run it from within Windows and prompt you to quit using FIPS.
>
> Do not use FIPS while using smartdrv or any disk caching utility. If you do so, you risk losing your whole partition table.

When you first start FIPS, it will ask which drive you want to partition. Choose the drive number on which you want to split partitions.

TIP You can quit FIPS at any time before it starts splitting the partition by using the Ctrl+C combination.

Next, FIPS will ask you which partition you would like to split. Note that FIPS will list only partition numbers and not drive letters. You can map the partition numbers yourself or run FDISK to check the drive letters that exist on each drive. FIPS will suggest the partition numbers that FIPS can split—for example, Which Partition Do You Want To Split (1/2)? (see Figure 1.4).

TIP You can use FDISK to check the drive letters that exist on each physical drive. Run FDISK and press 5 on the keyboard to select the drive number. After you have selected the drive number, press 4 on the keyboard to view the drive letters on the physical drive.

FIGURE 1.4

FIPS enables you to choose the partition number you want to split. You should worry about only the partition number and the space on it. Do not pay attention to columns you do not understand in this screen.

For safety reasons, FIPS will ask you whether you want to make a backup copy of the root and boot sectors before proceeding. Answer yes if you want to play it safe. If anything goes wrong, you will be able to use this backup to restore your partitions.

N O T E If you decide to make a backup of your root and boot sectors, you will have the opportunity to restore them using the `restorrb` command that comes with the FIPS zip file. It is highly recommended that you back up your root and boot sector. ■

After FIPS makes the backup copy, it will let you use the cursor keys to change the size of the new partition. Use the up and down arrow keys to resize in large amounts (10 cylinders) and the left and right arrow keys to resize in small amounts (1 cylinder).

Getting and Using Partition Resizer (PRESIZER)

Partition Resizer is more advanced than FIPS because it can resize and move partitions. Partition Resizer also can change the size of an extended partition. You can find partition resizer on the CD that comes with this book or you can directly obtain it from the author's Web site at `http://members.xoom.com/Zeleps/`. Partition Resizer offers a graphical view of the partitions, but control lies in the keyboard.

Partition Resizer has the same constraints that FIPS does. Read the previous section "Preparing for FIPS" for more details on these constraints. You cannot shrink a partition after there is used space.

To run Partition Resizer, make a bootable disk, unzip the contents of the presizer zip file to the disk, and boot from the disk. After you have booted, run presizer.

When Partition Resizer starts, it will scan for the available hard disks you have and check the partitions on each disk. It will then give you the following options:

- 1- Resize/Move a partition
- 2- Change a FAT16 partitions's cluster size (Destructive)
- 3- Partition information
- 4- Exit

By pressing 1, you will get a list of all the available partitions on all your disks. The list has the following format:

- **(No.)**—The number you type to choose to resize or move this partition.
- **Flags**—The flags set to this partition. The list of flags is written at the same screen.
- **System Type**—The filesystem in which the partition was formatted. Partition Resizer can resize only FAT16 and FAT32 partitions.
- **Letter**—The drive letter of the corresponding partition.
- **Serial Number**—The serial number of the partition.
- **Size**—The current size of the partition.

If you type in the number of the partition you want to move or resize and press Enter, you will move to the Partition Resizer resize/move screen.

 TIP To move to the previous screen in any screen of Partition Resizer, you can use the ESC button.

Partition Resizer Controls

While in the resize/move mode, you can resize or move the partition you selected in the previous step. The following are controls you can have over this partition:

- **Tab key**—The tab key changes the mode from resize to move or vice versa. Partition Resizer starts in resize mode.
- **Arrow keys**—While in resize mode, the arrow keys are used to change the size of the partition. Alternatively, while in move mode, the arrow keys are used to move the partition. The left/right arrow keys will resize/move in small increments, whereas the up/down keys will resize/move in large increments.
- **Spacebar**—The spacebar is used to show/hide the extended partition boundaries. If you are resizing/moving a logical partition, you can't exceed the extended partition boundaries.

Use the previous controls to change the size of the selected partition. When you are finished, press Enter for the changes to take effect. If you want Partition Resizer to perform a surface check, you can press Y when it prompts you. Surface checks causes Partition Resizer to quit if it finds any bad sectors on your partition.

> **CAUTION**
>
> Partition Resizer does not have a utility that restores your partition table in case of damage. You have to use an external application to do so. We recommend that you run FIPS to make the backup for you and then quit it before it applies changes to the partition table. This way, you will have a backup of your partition table that can be restored using the `restorrb` command. Try to keep the operation as simple as possible. In other words, make the resize operation one step and the move operation another step. Then, after each operation, perform a backup. This way, you can always be sure that any damage will be minimized.

Mission: Disk Space

Put on your military clothes and start scheming for the best plan to get the required disk space for SuSE Linux. Your main tools will be FDISK, FIPS, and PRESIZER. FDISK will be used primarily to delete and create FAT and FAT32 partitions, while FIPS will be used to split the partition in two. The newly created partition will be empty, which means it can be safely deleted and used by SuSE Linux. PRESIZER can move and resize partitions, so we can stack together the unpartitioned space that will be used by SuSE Linux. However, PRESIZER can't resize NTFS. So, if you have an NTFS partition, you'll have to make do with it as is. The only thing you can do with an NTFS partition is move it from one space to another. It is highly recommended that you back up all the important data on the NTFS partitions, especially if it is the one from which NT boots. If NT boots from a specific partition, we recommend that you do not touch the partitions lying before it or this specific partition. Now, get a piece of paper and a pen and start outlining what you will do in steps.

For example, suppose that you have a hard drive with three partitions—C:, D:, and E:. You do not want to touch C: because all your important data is on it and it boots Windows. D: has a free space of 1GB, and so does E:. You want to give SuSE Linux 1.5 GB. (Refer to Figure 1.3.)

You can follow these steps:

1. Copy all data from drive E: to drive D:.
2. Use FDISK to delete E: and reboot.
3. Use FIPS to split 500MB of D: and generate a new drive E: with 500MB. Reboot.
4. Delete the new E: drive and reboot.

When you are finished with this scheme, you will not have a drive letter E:, and all the data that was on this drive will have been copied to the D: drive.

Alternatively, you can use these steps:

1. Use FIPS to split 600MB of D: and generate a new drive E: with 600MB. Your old E: becomes F:. Reboot.
2. Use FDISK to delete E:. Now your drive letters return as they were, and your old E: drive restores its name. Reboot.
3. Use PRESIZER to move E: through the 600MB unpartitioned space. Reboot.
4. Use FIPS to split 900MB of E: and generate a new drive F: with 900MB. Reboot.
5. Use FDISK to delete F:. Reboot.

In fact, you can perform all the steps using the PRESIZER that comes with this book. If you do not want to use FIPS and want to use PRESIZER instead, you can perform the following steps, letting PRESIZER do all the work:

1. Use PRESIZER to resize D:, leaving out 600MB.
2. Move E: through the unpartitioned space and stack it next to D:.
3. Resize E: and leave out 900MB.

The next section of this chapter discusses other software you can use to resize and move partitions. Now you are ready to design your plan and then implement it.

Other Commercial Software

Some commercial software packages can resize and move partitions without any of the problems or restrictions you might find in FIPS and Partition Resizer. One of the most famous and powerful of these software packages is Partition Quick Magic. The features of this package include the capability to identify, move, and resize a large number of filesystems. It even includes the Linux filesystem support that can be used to resize and move the Linux partitions. The package uses a fully graphical interface featuring mouse interaction and runs under DOS, Windows 9x, and Windows NT. You can buy the package from http://www.powerquest.com.

Troubleshooting

I can't start the programs described in this chapter from my Windows OS.

You should not start any of the programs mentioned in this chapter from within Windows. This will only lead to losing data on your hard drives.

Partition Resizer does not show a graphical representation of my partition table. It shows garbage instead.

Try to start Partition Resizer using the /text mode.

Partition Resizer does not allow me to resize a partition and FIPS will not allow me to split a partition.

Check whether you have enough empty space on the partition you want to split or resize. If you have space, check whether you have files laying on the last sector of the partition. Some programs such as Norton Image create a small file at the end of the partition. Delete this file.

Where should I look for more information on Partition Resizer and FIPS? I have a problem that is not listed in this chapter.

Both FIPS and Partition Resizer come with carefully maintained troubleshooting documentation files. We encourage you to read those files along with the documentation that comes with them before you start modifying your partition table. ●

Installing SuSE Linux

In this chapter

Installation Basics

When you install SuSE Linux, you must also install a new operating system. A flawless installation without destroying or losing your existing data should be your main objective. The three main worries for novice users are the following: Did I miss anything? Did I install what I need? and Am I installing more than I need?

As mentioned in Chapter 1, "Pre-Installing SuSE Linux," SuSE Linux is easy to install if you understand the terms and vocabulary this operating system uses. During the installation procedures this chapter discusses, you will learn most of the terminology used in device naming in SuSE Linux. At the end of this chapter, we will guide you through most of the conventions and the SuSE Linux philosophy to prepare you for your first steps into the wonderful world of SuSE Linux.

What You Need

SuSE Linux comes in two forms:

- **SuSE Linux - Snapshot**—This edition fits on one CD and is distributed freely. You can download the ISO image from the SuSE FTP site to make a copy for yourself. This book comes with the SuSE Linux 6.3 snapshot.

- **SuSE Linux - Full version**—This edition is a full, sophisticated edition with 1,500 applications and 60-day installation support. It comes in two forms:
  - Six CDs
  - One DVD disk

SuSE Linux can be installed over a directory on your Windows partition, FTP, or network. The easiest way to install SuSE Linux is to use the SuSE Linux installation CDs or DVD disk. We strongly recommend you get the full SuSE Linux version if it is going to be widely used for multiple purposes.

Installing from the SuSE Linux Installation Media

If you are going to install SuSE Linux using the SuSE CDs or DVD disk, you need only one of the following:

- If you can boot your computer from your CD-ROM/DVD drive, you don't need anything.

- If you have Windows 9x or DOS running and you are able to access your CD-ROM from within one of them, you can use the setup.exe program to set up your SuSE Linux.

- If you can't boot your computer from your CD-ROM/DVD drive, you need two empty floppy disks. Make sure that no bad sectors exist on the floppy disks. You will learn how to prepare those disks in the following section.

Installing from a Directory

If you are going to install SuSE Linux from a directory, all you need to do is to copy the installation media contents to this directory. To do this, you will need one of the following bootable disks:

- **A DOS bootable floppy**—Using this disk, you can start the `setup.exe` installation program.
- **A Linux bootable disk**—Using this disk, you can start the installation program that will launch SuSE to your system. You will learn how to create this disk in the section "Preparing the Disks" later in this chapter.

Installing Through NFS or FTP

Using NFS or FTP is one of the most important methods that can be used to install SuSE Linux. As a matter of fact, this method enables you to install SuSE Linux even if you do not have any installation media in hand. All you need is a shared NFS directory that contains the SuSE Linux installation files you want to install. If you will be installing through FTP, you need only a working FTP connection over an Ethernet card.

You also will need two empty floppy disks to start the installation process. Preparing the disks is discussed in the following section.

Preparing Your System

Each of the installation procedures requires some special preparation in order to start the SuSE Linux installation. In this section, you will learn how to prepare for each of the installation methods.

CD-ROM/DVD

If you are going to install SuSE Linux using the installation media and your system can boot from the CD-ROM/DVD drive, you should set up your BIOS to load the operating system from the CD-ROM/DVD. Figure 2.1 illustrates a phoenix BIOS that will boot from a CD-ROM if a CD is inserted in the CD-ROM drive when the system is booted.

Preparing the Disks

You must prepare a boot disk and kernel modules disk if you are going to install SuSE Linux under one of the following scenarios:

- You want to install SuSE Linux using the installation media on a system that can't boot from a CD-ROM.
- You are going to install SuSE Linux from a directory.
- You are going to install SuSE Linux through NFS.
- You are going to install SuSE Linux through FTP.

Part
I
Ch
2

FIGURE 2.1

The easiest way to set up SuSE Linux is to set up your BIOS to boot from a CD-ROM. Insert the SuSE Linux CD/DVD in the CD-ROM/DVD drive and restart your system. To set up your BIOS to boot from a CD-ROM, if it supports it, press F2 or DEL while starting the system.

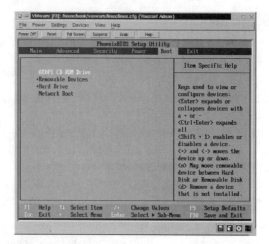

N O T E   If you have a working Internet connection, you don't have to worry about having the SuSE installation media to prepare the disks. You can get the disk images from the SuSE FTP site and start preparing the disks. ▨

The RaWrite Utility

To create the disks required for the SuSE Linux installation, you use a utility called RaWrite. RaWrite comes with SuSE Linux and is located in CDROM:\dosutils\rawrite. If you want to get this utility through FTP, you can get it from the SuSE FTP site at ftp://ftp.suse.com. The RaWrite utility runs under DOS. An example of running RaWrite is illustrated in the following command (the bold text indicates text that you enter):

```
D:\>CD \DOSUTILS\RAWRITE
D:\DOSUTILS\RAWRITE>RAWRITE
RaWrite 1.2 - Write disk file to raw floppy diskette
Enter source file name: IMAGEDISK
Enter destination drive: A
Please insert a formatted 1.44M diskette into drive B: and press -ENTER- :
Writing image to drive A:
```

In the previous example, you created a disk from a disk image file called IMAGEDISK. The image was written to floppy disk in the A: drive.

Using the RaWrite Utility to Create the Disks

Now that you have learned how RaWrite works, it's time to put it into practice. The images for the disks you need to create are located in the CDROM:\disks directory. The disk images in this directory are as follows:

- **bootdisk**—Standard bootdisk. You need this boot disk to use YaST for installation. If you want to install your SuSE Linux using YaST2, you don't have to create this image.

- **eide**—Bootdisk with support for special EIDE adapters. You need this disk image only if the first one doesn't work for your hard drive controller.

- **laptop**—If you are planning to install SuSE Linux on a laptop with the floppy on a USB port, you must have this disk image.

- **yast2**—You must create an image of this bootdisk if you want to install SuSE Linux using YaST2.

- **rescue**—This disk contains a rescue disk from which you can fix problems with the existing SuSE Linux installation or boot problems.

- **modules**—Special kernel modules that might be needed during the installation process. You need this disk only if you are planning to install SuSE Linux over NFS or FTP or your system needs special kernel modules to detect hardware during installation.

The following example explains how to create two floppy disks for the YaST2 and kernel modules. In this example, we assume that D: is your CD drive and that the first SuSE CD is inserted in the CD-ROM drive.

Insert an empty formatted disk in your A: disk drive and issue the following commands:

```
D:\>cd \disks
```

```
D:\DOSUTILS\RAWRITE
RaWrite 1.2 - Write disk file to raw floppy diskette
Enter source file name: yast2
Enter destination drive: A
Please insert a formatted 1.44M diskette into drive B: and press -ENTER- :
Writing image to drive A:
```

Now, replace the disk with another empty formatted one and issue the following commands to create the kernel modules disk.

```
D:\DOSUTILS\RAWRITE
RaWrite 1.2 - Write disk file to raw floppy diskette
Enter source file name: modules
Enter destination drive: A
Please insert a formatted 1.44M diskette into drive B: and press -ENTER- :
Writing image to drive A:
```

Congratulations, you now can proceed to the next section in which you will learn more about what you should expect from the SuSE Linux installation process.

Preparing Yourself

In this section, you will learn some conventions you might encounter during the installation process. Bear in mind that YaST2 gives you the option of Automatic Installation in which you won't have to suffer the pain of navigating new territory. However, if you install SuSE Linux through the Guided Installation option when installing using YaST2 or if you are planning to use YaST, you will have to learn some of the conventions in this section.

Multiuser Environment

SuSE Linux is a multiuser environment. In a *multiuser* environment, the system can be used and shared by many users while retaining the settings each user has configured for herself. If the machine on which SuSE Linux will be installed is on a network, users can connect to the SuSE Linux box through many networking facilities provided by SuSE Linux. The space provided to each SuSE Linux user is located in the /home/username directory. No normal user can control system settings or alter system configurations unless allowed to by the system's top-level user, called *root*. The root user is the default user for the system and can control and set up the system. Because you will be installing SuSE Linux, you will be root during the installation process. You should not use the system as root after you have installed it. You should log in as the root user only when you are modifying the system settings.

Each user on the SuSE Linux system has a username and password. During the installation process, you will be asked to enter the root password. You should enter a password that is not easy to guess and that you will not forget. You also will be prompted to create a new user for the system. You should create this user so you can log in to your system as a normal user, not as root.

Disk Partitions in SuSE Linux

Disk partition naming in SuSE Linux has a completely different convention from that of MS-DOS or MS Windows. There is nothing called C: or D: for disks. Rather, there are mount points and a filesystem. The *filesystem* is made up of the physical devices, such as hard disk partitions, floppy disks, CDs, zip drive disks, and so forth. Alternatively, a *mount point* is a directory in which you mount those filesystems. A mount point makes the connection between you and the physical device.

In addition, you still can arrange your files in directories. Note that your only restriction is that all your directories will reside in /home/<username>. No other user on the system will be able to see your files unless you allow him to.

During the installation, you will be asked where to install SuSE Linux. Table 2.1 details the mapping you can use to understand the filesystems about which YaST or YaST2 will ask you.

Table 2.1   Linux Partition Map

Disk/Partition	Convention Used in Linux
First partition on first IDE	/dev/hda1
Second partition on first IDE	/dev/hda2
Extended partition on first IDE	/dev/hda5
First logical partition of first IDE	/dev/hda6
Second logical partition of first IDE	/dev/hda7
First partition of first SCSI (follows the same conventions as in the IDE examples)	/dev/sda1
First partition on second IDE (follows the same conventions as in the IDE examples to access other partitions)	/dev/hdb1
First partition on third IDE	/dev/hdc1
First partition on second SCSI (follows the same conventions as in the IDE examples to access more SCSI drives and partitions)	/dev/sdb1

YaST Versus YaST2

The release of YaST2 has enabled SuSE Linux users to use new graphical (and easy-to-use) installation methods prepared for them by the SuSE team. YaST2 doesn't ask as many questions as its predecessor YaST. But, package customization in YaST2 is not as powerful as it was in YaST. Also, in YaST2, you cannot perform most of the partitioning management that you could in YaST.

If you are installing SuSE Linux for the first time with no experience in SuSE Linux or Linux, you should use YaST2. If you are going to use the partitioning system provided by YaST, you should use YaST to install your SuSE Linux. Also, if you are familiar with SuSE Linux or Linux, you should use YaST because it gives you more control over the installation process.

Users installing SuSE Linux using NFS or FTP have no choice but to install SuSE Linux using YaST.

Quick Installation Using YaST2

YaST2 provides an easy way to install SuSE Linux with a minimum number of questions you have to answer. It is bliss for SuSE Linux beginners!

N O T E   In SuSE Linux 6.3, you can install SuSE Linux using YaST2 only if you have the installation media. You cannot use YaST2 to install SuSE Linux through a directory, FTP, or NFS. ■

Part

I

Ch

2

Starting the Installation Process

You should be able to boot the system using either the installation media itself or the boot-disks you prepared in the previous section "Preparing Your System." When you boot using one of these methods, the first thing you see is a welcome message from the SuSE team. It then starts to boot the Linux kernel and starts an X Window session in which YaST2 will run.

After the welcome screen, YaST2 starts, and you will see the first screen of the YaST2 installation.

The Basic Configuration

The first screen in the installation process using YaST2 is the Basic Configuration screen as shown in Figure 2.2. In this screen, YaST2 asks you about your choice of language, keyboard layout, and time zone. You should make your selections based on your preferences. Note that if you change the language, YaST2 will automatically change the interface language, which means that the rest of the installation process will change to your language and that your SuSE Linux default language will change to the selected language.

FIGURE 2.2
The first YaST2 window enables you to change the settings for the language, keyboard layout, and time zone. Because this is the first screen, any changes you make here will be applied during the installation.

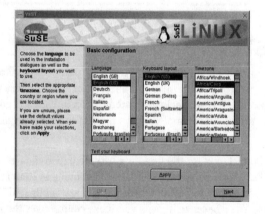

Your keyboard layout will be used to determine the keyboard mapping that SuSE Linux will use. To test your keyboard layout, select the keyboard layout from the list and click Apply. After you click Apply, type any string in the Test your keyboard field. If it doesn't work, try another mapping.

The Timezone list box is used to determine your time zone. This sets the time on your SuSE Linux to your correct time zone. Search for your time zone in the list and select it.

N O T E Do not worry if your mouse doesn't work in this dialog. You can use the Tab key to move between lists in the dialog. The up and down arrows move the selection highlight and pressing the spacebar when you are on a button clicks the button. ▪

Mouse Configuration

The mouse configuration dialog lets you specify your mouse type from a large list of mice (see Figure 2.3). Highlight the mouse type that applies to your mouse and press the Next button when you are finished. YaST2 will activate the mouse settings you made and then will continue. You should not exit the list without selecting the correct mouse type. If you select an incorrect mouse type, you should use the keyboard to get back and correct the mouse type; otherwise, you will not be able to use the mouse during the rest of the installation process.

Part

I

Ch

2

FIGURE 2.3
By selecting the mouse type from the available list, you will be able to use your mouse during the installation process. It also will be applied to SuSE Linux after it is installed.

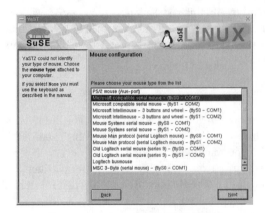

Installation Method

In this dialog, you will determine which installation method you will use. The dialog lists two installation methods (see Figure 2.4):

FIGURE 2.4
YaST2 asks you about the installation method you will use during the installation process. Select Automatic installation for easy installation with few questions or Guided installation for easy installation with more control.

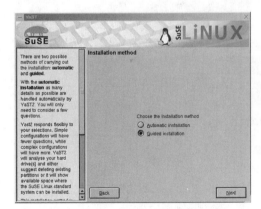

■ **Automatic installation**—In this installation method, YaST2 will ask you as few questions as possible. The default settings will be used for any decision YaST2 makes. You will be asked only information that can alter your system settings or critical information that you have to enter.

Output of this installation method is the following:

- Installing LILO on your MBR
- Standard package installation
- Three partitions for SuSE Linux: /boot, a swap partition, and a root partition

■ **Guided installation**—In this installation method, YaST2 will be more interactive when performing any operation. No hard questions will be asked, though; you will be able to customize only your system. A novice user can install SuSE Linux using this method with no trouble.

Installation Target

YaST2 will prompt you about the drive on which you will be installing SuSE Linux in case you have more than one drive (see Figure 2.5). If you have only one drive, it will prompt you for the partitions on which you want to install SuSE Linux. YaST2 will recognize and use the free space on your selected hard drive. If you choose any other partition, the partition will be formatted by YaST2 to be used by SuSE Linux. Be careful when selecting the partitions that will be used by SuSE Linux (see Figure 2.6).

> **CAUTION**
>
> After a partition has been formatted by YaST2, there is no way to restore its contents if you do not have a complete backup of its contents. Be very careful when selecting which partitions you would like SuSE Linux to use.

FIGURE 2.5
YaST2 will prompt you to select your target hard drive in case you have more than one drive.

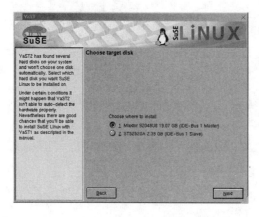

FIGURE 2.6
You will be able to select which partitions of the target hard drive you want to use by checking the box that applies to each partition.

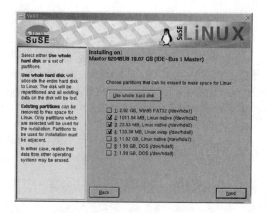

Selecting Software

YaST2 enables you to select the software you want to install using a default packaging system. The SuSE team has provided the following selections:

- **Minimal**—This will install your SuSE Linux to a fully functional console-based SuSE Linux system. This option uses as much as 150MB.

- **Default**—This selection will install SuSE Linux to a fully functional X Window-based SuSE Linux system. This option requires that you have at least 500MB.

- **Almost Everything**—You need to install this option only if you are sure that you will be using a wide range of the software that comes with SuSE Linux. This options will use as much as 6GB.

You also can choose to install other packages that come with SuSE Linux, which are listed in the checkbox list. To make a selection, just check the box that applies to your choice. Figure 2.7 illustrates the Software selection dialog.

FIGURE 2.7
YaST2 offers an easy method of package selection that should apply to a wide range of tastes. Select the base system you prefer and then check the box that corresponds to the software you will be using.

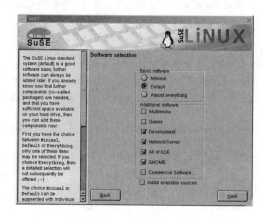

LILO Installation

LILO (Linux Loader) is the boot manager that boots SuSE Linux when it's installed over a system. In the LILO Installation dialog, you can configure where LILO should be placed (see Figure 2.8). LILO installation on the MBR does not damage your currently installed operating system. For example, if you install LILO on the MBR, it will not damage Windows 95, 98, or NT. If you want to use another boot manager and tell it to invoke LILO, you can install LILO on the /boot partition and configure your boot manager to use it. You also could install LILO on a disk you can use to boot SuSE Linux. See Chapter 9, "Configuring the System Boot Up Sequence," for more information on the SuSE Linux boot operation.

FIGURE 2.8
You can set up the LILO within YaST2, which enables you to keep your old operating system bootable while adding the capability of booting SuSE Linux.

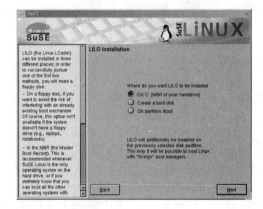

Creating a System User

As noted before in this chapter, you should use the root user only when modifying system settings. In the Personify dialog, YaST2 enables you to create a user who will be the first system user after the root user (see Figure 2.9). After you enter your name, you can let YaST suggest a username for you. Fill in your password and verify it so that you can move on to the next step.

Securing Your SuSE Linux with a Root Password

A secure SuSE Linux system must have a password that is hard to guess and is known only to the root user. The root user has many capabilities in the SuSE Linux system. See Chapter 4, "Managing Users and Groups," for more information on user management in SuSE Linux. For now, make sure that you enter a password that is unique to you and is not easy to guess in the Root Password dialog (see Figure 2.10).

FIGURE 2.9
YaST2 enables you to personify your first user account on SuSE Linux to have a non-root login on your first SuSE Linux start.

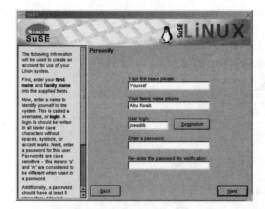

CAUTION

Do not choose passwords that are real words, such as *secret*, *password*, *pass*, *magic*, or *root*. Do not choose a password that's the same as your login name or is a person's name. These types of passwords are the easiest to crack because they are stored in dictionaries, which some programs use to crack into systems.

FIGURE 2.10
Enter and verify the root password in this dialog. You should choose a password that is hard to guess.

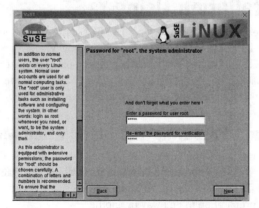

Confirmation

Now that you have completed all the YaST2 preparations, YaST2 will confirm what you have selected throughout the preparation process so that you can confirm your settings (see Figure 2.11). You can save your settings to a floppy disk for use in the future. If you want to make any modifications to the configuration, press the Back button.

To start the actual process of installation, press the Next button, and YaST2 will start the installation.

FIGURE 2.11
If you confirm the settings in this dialog, which lists all the selections you have made in the previous YaST2 dialogs, the installation will start immediately.

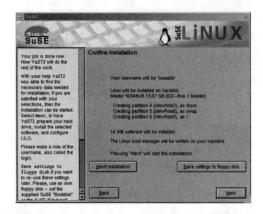

After the SuSE Linux system has been installed, you next must complete the system configuration process, which is explained in the following section.

SuSE Linux Installation Using YaST

The installation process consists of four steps. The first step is the selection and preparation of the installation medium. The second step is deciding how you are going to boot the actual installation program. The third step is linuxrc, which is a program that runs to prepare the system for the installation. The final step is YaST, which handles all the installation after the system has been prepared by linuxrc. Let's look at the required steps.

Step 1: Selecting and Preparing the Installation Medium

The installation medium is the medium off of which you will install SuSE Linux. SuSE Linux is extremely flexible when it comes to the medium from which you want to install it. You can install it from CDs, a DVD, a hard drive, another computer on the network, and FTP. Each of these requires some preparation in one way or another.

Installing from a CD-ROM If you are planning to install from a CD-ROM, you do not need much preparation. All you need to do is to set your computer to boot from a CD-ROM as described in the previous section "Preparing Your System." If your system does not have support for booting from a CD-ROM, you can use boot disks instead to boot the installation and then use your CD-ROM afterwards.

Installing from a Hard Drive In some cases you might be installing SuSE Linux on a PC that has no CD-ROM drive. In this case, you can install SuSE Linux from the hard drive. This, however, requires you to prepare your hard drive, which consists of just a simple file copying process.

The basic idea is that you want to copy the contents of the SuSE Linux CDs onto the hard drive. Please note that you will need quite a bit of hard drive space to do this. To prepare the hard drive to be an installation medium, follow these steps:

1. Create a directory on your hard drive and call it anything you want, such as `suseinst`. Inside that directory, create another directory that must be called `suse`. You should end up with a directory name similar to `/suseinst/suse`.

2. You will need to create the following three directories under `/suseinst/suse/`:

   - `a1`
   - `images`
   - `setup`

3. Now, you should start copying files from the CD to these directories. Copy all the contents of `/suse/a1` on the CD to `/suseinst/suse/a1` on your hard drive.

4. Copy a suitable kernel from `/suse/images/` to `/suseinst/suse/images`. If you are not sure which one to choose, we suggest you read the `readme.dos` file that is found in the same directory. You *must* copy a kernel image here. If you have adequate hard drive space, copy all the files in `/suse/images` to your local hard drive.

5. Next, copy `/suse/images/initdisk.gz` to `/suseinst/suse/images/`.

6. Copy the files in `/suse/setup/` to `/suseinst/suse/setup/`.

7. So far you will be able to install only a very basic system. If you want to install more software, you should copy all the contents of `/suse/` to `/suseinst/suse/`. This is the entire contents of the CD, which is around 650MB of space. However, it will give you a fuller installation. If you are low on hard drive space, you don't have to do this now. You can install the basic system and then add to it later.

Installing from NFS   If your PC does not have a CD-ROM but has a network card and is part of a network, you can use a CD-ROM on another machine for the installation. This is done by using a Network Filesystem (NFS). This is an advanced subject and we strongly recommend that you have someone proficient with Linux/UNIX around to help you. You will need the following information:

- Your IP address
- Your netmask
- Your gateway
- The IP of the NFS server
- The directory or server on which the SuSE installation files reside

The basic idea is that you want to mount the SuSE CD on that machine and make sure that it is exported to others. The information you need is both the IP of the machine that is acting as the NFS server and the mount point of the CD-ROM.

Installing from FTP   If you don't have SuSE Linux on CDs or a hard drive and still would like to install it, you can do so by installing it over the Internet. This requires you to have a network card and a running network to which you are connected. The information you will need is as follows:

- Your IP address
- Your netmask
- Your gateway
- The IP of your name server
- The IP of the FTP proxy, if you have one
- The address of the FTP server to connect to (usually `ftp.suse.com`)

You can get this information from your system administrator.

Step 2: Booting the Installation Program

In this step you must decide how you are going to boot the installation. You have three choices: you can boot from MS DOS, you can boot from a boot disk, or from the CD-ROM directly.

Booting from MS-DOS   To boot from MS-DOS, your CD-ROM drive must be initialized and running under DOS. You cannot use Windows 95 for this—you must be running under MS-DOS, not in a DOS window inside Windows 95. To boot, follow these steps:

1. Change to your CD-ROM drive letter and run the `setup.exe` program.
2. The program will ask you to choose the language with which you want to work. Select the language with which you are most comfortable and press Enter.
3. You now are asked to enter the drive letter of your CD-ROM. The program will attempt to guess it for you. Press Enter to continue.
4. The program displays a welcome screen; press Enter to continue.
5. You are given the option of using loadlin or a floppy. Choose loadlin and press Enter.
6. The program asks you how much RAM you have. It attempts to guess that value for you and sets it as the default. If it is incorrect, change it to the correct value and press Enter.
7. The program asks you whether you want to use the CD or hard drive. Choose CD and press Enter.
8. You have to select a kernel with which to boot. Highlighting a kernel will display a short brief on what it supports. Select one that has good support for your hardware and press Enter.
9. If you want to enter any extra options for the kernel, you can enter them in this screen. You probably won't need to unless you have a lot of experience with SuSE Linux. Press Enter to continue.

10. The program will ask you whether it should install loadlin on your hard drive. Answer No and press Enter.

11. You are prompted to save the current setup. You don't really need to, but you can if you want.

12. Finally, you are ready to boot the installation. Press Load Linux now to start.

Booting from a Boot Disk   You can boot the installation program from a Linux boot disk. This disk is easily prepared using the setup.exe program from Step 2. Instead of choosing loadlin, choose floppy disk and press Enter. The program will prompt you to insert a disk in your drive; insert an empty disk and press Enter. The program will format the disk and create a boot disk on it. This is the disk you can use to boot the installation program.

This disk also can be created using RaWrite as explained in the previous section "Preparing Your System."

Booting from a CD-ROM   You can boot directly from the CD-ROM if your PC supports it. To learn how to set up your system to boot from a CD-ROM, refer to the previous section "Preparing Your System." In SuSE 6.3, you will boot from the second CD, not the first. The first CD boots into YaST2, whereas the second boots into YaST.

Step 3: Linuxrc

Now you are all set to start the installation. You have prepared your installation medium and boot method, so now you can start booting the installation program. When your system boots up, the first screen that appears is a welcome message from the SuSE team. Press Enter to continue. This will load the first part of the process, which is controlled by a program called linuxrc. Linuxrc does some preliminary preparations to your system to pave the way for YaST to start.

The first screen of linuxrc is the language selection (see Figure 2.12). This is the language YaST will use to speak to you throughout the installation process. You should be careful at this point because the language you select here will be used throughout your use of SuSE Linux until you change it again from YaST. You select the language by highlighting it using the arrow keys and pressing Enter.

FIGURE 2.12
Select the language you want to use for the installation.

NOTE   Navigation throughout the installation process is very easy. Use the arrow keys to highlight the list item you want and press Enter to choose it. You can press the Tab key to move between the different fields and buttons on the screen. ■

The second screen asks you whether you have a color or monochrome monitor. Make your selection and press Enter to continue. At the next screen, linuxrc asks you to choose your keyboard mapping. This is the way in which YaST will interpret the keystrokes from your keyboard. Make sure you pick the correct layout, or else YaST, and in turn your whole Linux system after it's fully installed, will misinterpret most of the keystrokes. Linuxrc displays a thorough list of preconfigured keyboard layouts that match most keyboards. Find the one that matches your keyboard and press Enter to continue.

You now are taken to the linuxrc main menu (see Figure 2.13). The first option in the menu is Settings. This gives you access to all the screens you have just been through in case you need to change any of the settings you configured in them. The second option is System Information, which shows you information about your system and any hardware that was successfully detected by the Linux kernel. The third option is Kernel Modules; you would need to use these only if you have SCSI hardware that is not compatible with Adaptec 2940, or if you are planning some kind of network installation that requires your network card to be up and running. The fourth option is Start Installation / System, which simply exits linuxrc and starts YaST. Finally, the last option is End / Reboot, which enables you to quit the installation process.

FIGURE 2.13
The main menu of
linuxrc.

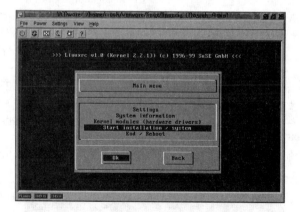

The following section explains kernel modules and their role in the installation process. You should read this section if you are planning a network installation. Otherwise, skip to the section "Step 3: Linuxrc Continued."

Kernel Modules   We need to take a minute here to explain what kernel modules are. The SuSE installation program attempts to detect most of the commonly used hardware on boot up. If your system uses a SCSI adapter other than Adaptec 2940, or if you are planning to install the system over NFS or FTP, you need to load the proper drivers for your SCSI controller and network card. These drivers are also called *modules*. To load these modules, you highlight the third option in the linuxrc menu, Kernel Modules, and press Enter.

Linuxrc loads the Kernel Modules menu (see Figure 2.14). You have seven options in this menu. The first four are related to loading SCSI, CD-ROM, network card, and PCMCIA modules. The fifth option shows you all the currently loaded modules. The sixth option is used to unload modules and the last option causes linuxrc to attempt to autodetect the devices.

FIGURE 2.14
Use this menu to load special drivers for your hardware.

To load a module, just highlight the device type you want to use and press Enter. Linuxrc will show you a list of all the supported models of this device. Find the one that matches your device and press Enter to load it and activate the device. You should try the Autoload of Modules option first because it can automatically locate and configure your devices for you.

Step 3: Linuxrc Continued

We now resume our discussion of linuxrc. To start the installation, choose Start Installation / System and press Enter. The Start installation screen pops up, as shown in Figure 2.15. At this point you can start YaST by choosing the Start Installation list item.

The remaining options are not really installation-related but are more like emergency tools. For example, you can boot an already installed system by using the Boot Installed System option. In addition, you can start a rescue system that can help you troubleshoot and fix an already installed but corrupted system by using the Start Rescue System option. Finally, you can start the Live CD using the Start Live CD option.

To start YaST, which will guide you through the rest of the installation process, highlight the Start Installation list item and press Enter.

Part

I

Ch

2

FIGURE 2.15
The Start Installation menu.

As you can see in Figure 2.16, linuxrc asks you to choose the source media. This is precisely what we have been preparing for, provided that you read the previous steps. At this point, you should know exactly what you will use and already have it prepared. You have four choices: to install from CD-ROM, to install from network (NFS), to install from network (FTP), and to install from hard disk.

FIGURE 2.16
Pick the installation medium you want to use.

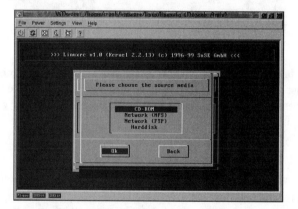

Installing from CD-ROM To install from CD-ROM, highlight the CD-ROM list item and press Enter. Make sure that your SuSE CD number 1 is in the drive before you press Enter. Don't get confused here—you boot from CD number 2 but install from CD number 1.

Installing from Network (NFS) Linuxrc will ask you for some information about your network. It will ask you for your IP, the other machine's IP, the gateway, and the mount point where SuSE Linux exists. All this information should be available to you, provided that you prepared for it earlier. Just enter that information and linuxrc will attempt to contact the other machine and read the SuSE Linux files.

To install from network via NFS, make sure that your network card is already detected and running. If you have not done that, use the Tab key to highlight the Back button and load the card's module from the Kernel modules menu. After your network card is all set, highlight the Network (NFS) list item and press Enter to start the installation.

Linuxrc will ask you whether you will use bootp to configure your network. If you will, answer Yes; otherwise answer No. If you answer No, linuxrc will then ask you for your IP. Enter it and press Enter. Next, linuxrc will ask for the netmask, which is usually 255.255.255.0. If you need a gateway to access the NFS server, enter it in the following screen; if you don't need one, just enter your IP again. Linuxrc now will ask you to enter the IP of the NFS server and the directory where the SuSE Linux files reside. When you enter that information, linuxrc will attempt to connect to the server and mount the remote directory.

Installing from Network (FTP)   If you don't have SuSE Linux on CDs or hard drive, you can still install it via FTP. To install from FTP, make sure that your network card is already detected and running. If you have not done that, use the Tab key to highlight the Back button and load the card's module from the Kernel modules menu. After your network card is all set, highlight the Network (FTP) list item and press Enter to start the installation.

Linuxrc will ask you whether you will use bootp to configure your network. If you will, answer Yes; otherwise, answer No. If you answer No, linuxrc will then ask you for your IP. Enter it and press Enter. Next, linuxrc will ask for the netmask, which is usually 255.255.255.0. If you need a gateway to access the NFS server, enter it in the following screen; if you don't need one, just enter your IP again.

Linuxrc asks you whether you want to use a name server (DNS); if you need one, enter its IP and press Enter. You probably will need a name server if you are going to install from a site and you know only its name and not its IP. Linuxrc will ask you to enter the address of the FTP server from which to install; enter it and press Enter. In the next screen, linuxrc asks whether you want to use a username and password to log in to the FTP site rather than using anonymous login. If you have a username and password for the FTP site, answer Yes and enter them. Otherwise, answer No to use anonymous login. Linuxrc will ask whether you want to use an FTP proxy; if you do, answer Yes and enter its IP address. Linuxrc will now attempt to connect to the FTP site for the installation.

Installing from Hard Drive   If you have prepared your hard drive to have a copy of the SuSE Linux installation files, you are all set. If you haven't then you should refer to the previous section "Step 1: Selecting the Installation Medium."

To install from a hard drive, highlight the Harddisk list item and press Enter. Linuxrc will ask you to enter the hard drive partition that contains the files; type it in and press Enter. Linuxrc then will ask you to enter the name of the directory where you have the files. If you prepared your copy like we did, it should be /suseinst.

Step 4: YaST

Now that you have booted the installation program, configured the system using linuxrc, and selected the source medium, you are ready to install the actual system. This is where YaST takes over from linuxrc to guide you through the installation process. The first screen you see from YaST is the Type of Installation screen (see Figure 2.17). YaST gives you the following four options:

- **Install Linux from scratch**—This performs a full, new installation of SuSE Linux on your machine. This is the option recommended most for new users because it takes care of most of the process's internals automatically.

- **Update existing Linux system**—If you are upgrading from an older version of SuSE Linux, you should use this option. Usually, it is preferable to reinstall SuSE Linux than to update an older installation. Just back up your files, remove the old Linux, and install Linux from scratch. If you are a real expert, you can update the system and fix any problems that might arise.

- **Installation using Expert mode**—This mode of installation is preferred by expert Linux users. We do not recommend that you try this mode if you have never installed Linux before. This step heavily assumes that the user has installed Linux before and is quite familiar with the process.

- **Abort - no installation**—If you have suddenly decided that no you do not want to install now, you can easily and safely exit the process from here.

FIGURE 2.17
The available installation modes in YaST.

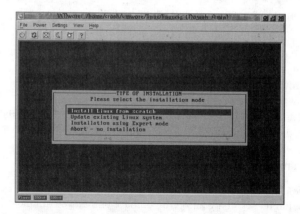

The two modes of installation are the install from scratch and expert modes. Installing from scratch is recommended for most users, whereas the expert mode should be attempted only by experts.

Installing Linux from Scratch   The installing Linux from scratch mode is relatively straightforward and easy. The first screen asks you about partitioning your hard drive. (We are assuming you have read and applied the steps in Chapter 1 and have free unallocated space on your hard drive.) Use the Tab key to highlight the Partitioning button and press Enter.

If your PC has more than one hard drive, YaST will ask you to select the one on which you want to install SuSE. If that hard drive has free unallocated space on it, YaST will automatically detect that and suggest the hard drive be used for the installation (see Figure 2.18). This is the preferred choice because YaST will take care of all the partitioning for you.

FIGURE 2.18
YaST has detected free space on the hard drive.

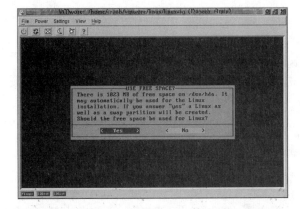

If YaST does not find free space on the hard drive, it will suggest that it either uses the whole hard drive or that you partition it manually, as shown in Figure 2.19. Partitioning the hard drive manually is discussed in the section "Installing Linux Using Expert Mode" later in this chapter. Using the whole drive means that YaST will wipe out any existing data and operating system that might be installed on your drive and install SuSE Linux on the entire hard drive. If this is really what you want to do, select Whole Hard Disk and press Enter.

FIGURE 2.19
YaST asks you whether you want to partition manually or have YaST use the whole hard drive.

CAUTION

Choosing Whole Hard Disk in the previous step will completely erase your hard drive. Any other operating systems and data you have on the hard drive will be gone forever. Please make sure that this is *really* what you want to do. Otherwise, you will end up with absolutely nothing but SuSE Linux on the hard drive.

YaST now partitions and prepares your hard drive for SuSE Linux. This process might take some time depending on the size of the space YaST has to work with. YaST will create the following three partitions on your hard drive:

- **/boot partition**—This partition is where your boot files will be kept. This partition is usually very small in size.

- **/ partition**—This is the root partition where all your systems will be installed. This partition takes the most space from your hard drive.

- **Swap partition**—This partition is used as virtual memory by Linux. Linux uses swap partition instead of files for its virtual memory. This partition is usually twice as big as the amount of RAM you have, with a maximum size of 128MB.

When YaST is finished preparing your hard drive, it will take you to the package selection screen (see Figure 2.20). This is where you will select which packages to be installed by SuSE Linux. At this point, you have two choices: You can either select one or more of the preset package configurations (recommended) or manually select the packages you want to install (not recommended if this is your first time through the installation process).

FIGURE 2.20
YaST's package selection/configuration menu.

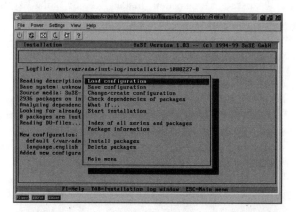

To select one of the package configurations, highlight the first option in the menu, Load Configuration. As you can see in Figure 2.21, YaST will display a list of common configurations and the approximate amount of hard drive space that each will use. Any configuration that has an asterisk (*) next to it is selected by default regardless of whether you select it. For example, SuSE Minimum System is selected by default because it is a subset of any other configuration you could select. To select a configuration, highlight it and use the spacebar to mark it. A configuration is selected if it has an [X] next to it.

FIGURE 2.21
SuSE has prepared various system configurations you can use instead of selecting the packages manually.

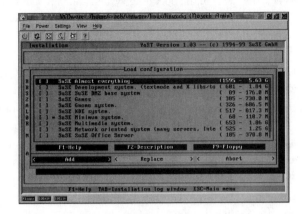

Press the Enter button to exit this screen and return to the main menu. You are now ready to install the system with the selected configuration. To start the installation, highlight Start Installation and press Enter. YaST will initiate the package installation sequence, which first checks that all packages have their dependencies resolved and then installs all the packages. The installation process takes a while to complete depending on the size of the configuration you selected. YaST shows you a progress indication for every package it is installing as well as how many packages are left to install (see Figure 2.22).

FIGURE 2.22
YaST shows you detailed information about the installation progress.

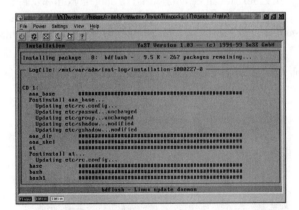

When YaST is finished installing all the packages, you are returned to the previous screen, the main menu. Your system is now installed and ready to be started and configured for the first time. To boot your system for the first time, highlight the Main menu list item and press Enter. YaST now starts to configure your system.

Booting and Configuring SuSE Linux   Now that your system has been successfully installed by YaST, it will configure it. The first screen in the configuration series is the kernel selection screen. The kernel is the heart of the operating system and is responsible for running and managing your hardware and system resources. YaST allows you to pick from a selection of kernels so that you can have the best kernel for your system. YaST gives you the following five kernels from which to choose:

- **Kernel with support for various EIDE controllers**—If your system is based on IDE devices then this kernel is a good choice.

- **Kernel built for i386 processors (also used for 486)**—If your machine is a 386 or 486 then you should use this kernel because it is better tuned for these processors.

- **Kernel with APM-support**—This kernel has support for Advanced Power Management (APM). If you are installing on a notebook PC, this kernel is good because it will activate and use the power management features of your notebook.

- **Standard kernel (Pentium optimized)**—If your machine runs on a Pentium processor or AMD K6/K3 then this kernel is good for you because it uses certain Pentium processor optimization.

- **Kernel with SMP-support**—This kernel should be used on systems that have more than one processor.

Use the arrow keys to highlight the kernel you want to use and press Enter to have YaST install it for you.

The next step is configuring LILO, which is the program that will be installed on your hard drive to boot SuSE Linux. It can be configured to boot any other operating systems on your system, as well. We highly recommend you install LILO on your system. YaST asks you whether you want to install it; answer Yes by using the Tab key to highlight the button and pressing Enter.

YaST will display the LILO configuration screen (see Figure 2.23). Filling out this form is explained in detail in the section "The Linux Loader" in Chapter 9.

FIGURE 2.23

The Linux Loader configuration screen.

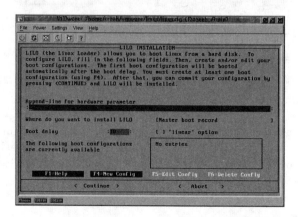

The next screen is the Timezone Configuration screen. As you can see in Figure 2.24, YaST gives you a list of all the time zones in the world. Find yours and press Enter to continue. YaST then will ask you whether you want to set the time according to GMT or local time. Use the Tab key to highlight the button you want and press Enter to continue. In most cases, you probably will want to use local time rather than GMT because local time sets the system clock to your time zone, whereas GMT sets it to Greenwich Mean Time.

FIGURE 2.24

Selecting the time zone.

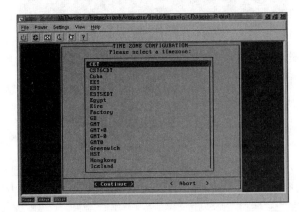

The next screen is the hostname selection screen. Here you will enter the name you want to give to your machine and the domain to which it belongs (see Figure 2.25). Even if you are not on a network, you should type something here—just make up something because your machine really should have a name. If you are on a real network then you should enter the correct domain name and use a hostname that is unique to your machine.

FIGURE 2.25

Setting up your host-name and domain name.

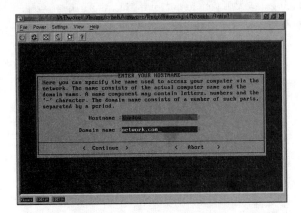

YaST then asks you what type of networking you want to set up. In Linux, your system should have some networking capabilities even if it's not on a network. As you can see in Figure 2.26,

YaST gives you two options, Loopback Only and Real Network. If you are not connected to a network, you should choose Loopback Only; otherwise, choose Real Network.

FIGURE 2.26

You can configure your system to be on a real network or to use loopback for stand-alone machines.

If you opted to configure a real network in the previous step, YaST will ask you whether you want to use Dynamic Host Configuration Protocol (DHCP). If you use DHCP, your network settings will be automatically configured when your machine boots. This requires your network to be running a DHCP server. If your network does use DHCP, you should answer Yes. Otherwise, answer No to manually configure the network. If you are not sure whether your network supports DHCP, consult your network administrator.

If your network does not use DHCP, YaST will configure your network with your help. YaST asks you to enter the required information for your network (see Figure 2.27). You need to know the IP of the machine; the netmask, which is usually 255.255.255.0; and the IP of the network's default gateway. If you do not know this information, you should get it from your network's administrator. Fill in the information and press Continue to proceed.

FIGURE 2.27

Setting up the network manually.

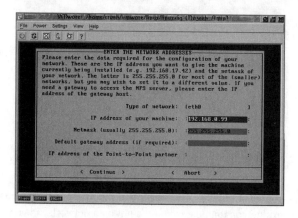

YaST now asks whether you want to enable others to connect to your machine via telnet, finger, and FTP. If you are planning to run a very secure system, you should answer No now and then turn them on later at your convenience. If you are not too worried about security, you can enable them by answering Yes.

 TIP

Telnet enables people to remotely use your machine as if they were physically sitting in front of it. FTP enables remote file transfers to and from your machine. Finger enables people to remotely probe which users are currently logged on and which users are not on your machine.

Next, YaST asks whether you want to enable portmap. If you are planning to use your machine as an NFS server or for NIS services, you should answer Yes. If you did not understand what the previous sentence was about, you don't need portmap, so answer No.

If you choose to start portmap, YaST asks whether you want to use your machine as an NFS server. If you do, answer Yes; otherwise, answer No.

 TIP

NFS (Network File System) enables people to remotely access parts of your local filesystem on their machines. It is not recommended that you enable it unless you have some experience doing so. A badly administered NFS server can be a big security hole on your system.

YaST now prompts you for the text that will be used in the "from" field of your news system. This is useful if you are planning to run a Usenet news server on your machine. YaST will enter a default string, which is usually correct. Press Continue to accept it and move on. This won't affect your system even if you are not planning to run a news server.

Next, YaST asks whether you want to access a name server. A name server is necessary if you are on a network that is connected to the Internet. Domain Name Server (DNS) is required to resolve fully qualified domain names to IP addresses. If your network is connected to the Internet, answer Yes.

Next, the Name Server Configuration screen pops up (see Figure 2.28). Enter the IP of the name server you want to access. If you use more than one, you can enter the other(s) separating each by a space. Enter the name of your domain in the domain list. If you are not sure about what to enter in this form, consult your network administrator.

In the next screen, you configure the networking device (see Figure 2.29). YaST asks you about your networking device and shows you a list of supported network cards. Select your card from the list and press Enter for YaST to configure it.

YaST now attempts to configure your mail system. SuSE Linux installs sendmail as the default mailing system. As you can see in Figure 2.30, YaST gives you the following five common sendmail configurations from which you can choose:

FIGURE 2.28
Configuring your name servers (DNS).

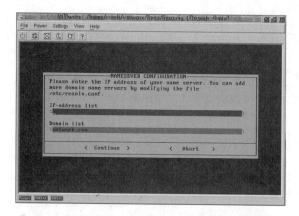

FIGURE 2.29
Selecting your network card.

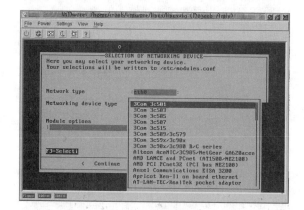

FIGURE 2.30
The sendmail configuration choices.

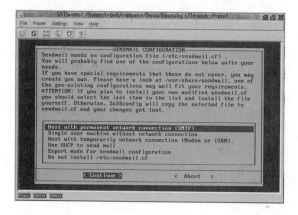

- **Host with permanent network connection (SMTP)**—You can use this if your system has a permanent connection to the Internet.

- **Single user machine without network connection**—Use this option if your machine doesn't have a network connection. You might be wondering why in the world you would set up a mailing system if you didn't have a network connection. Several of your applications send you internal mail messages to report progress and errors. Remember, even when Linux is not connected to a network, there is a network inside it.

- **Host with temporarily network connection (Modem or ISDN)**—Use this configuration if you have a dial-up connection. This enables you to use your machine as a mail server, and when you connect, your email will be sent.

- **Use UUCP to send mail**—If you will be connecting to a network, choose this configuration so you can send email.

- **Expert mode for sendmail configuration**—Proceed with caution when choosing this configuration; it should be used only by experts.

Use the arrow keys to highlight the configuration you want to use and press Enter to continue.

YaST now takes over completely and starts to configure your system based on your answers to the previous questions. YaST launches SuSEConfig, which configures your system for you (see Figure 2.31).

FIGURE 2.31
YaST launches SuSEConfig to configure your system.

When SuSEConfig is finished, press Continue to proceed. YaST tells you that your system is now installed successfully and will be started (see Figure 2.32). Press Enter to start your system for the first time.

The system boots up directly with no computer restart necessary. Figure 2.33 shows a system booting up for the first time.

FIGURE 2.32

YaST announces that your system has been installed successfully.

FIGURE 2.33

SuSE Linux booting for the first time.

When the system boots up, it will ask you to enter a password to use for the root user. If you do not want to have a password for the root user, which is *not* recommended, just press Enter.

SuSE Linux starts YaST again to complete the rest of the configuration process. YaST first asks whether you want to create an example user. We recommend you create a user for yourself. Answer Yes and press Enter.

As you can see in Figure 2.34, creating a user is very simple. You just need to specify the name of the user and the password. Press Continue when you are finished.

Next, YaST asks whether you want to set up a modem. If you have a modem installed, answer Yes. If you have a modem, YaST will prompt you to choose the COM port of the modem from a list. Highlight the correct one and press Enter to continue.

FIGURE 2.34

Creating an example user for the first time.

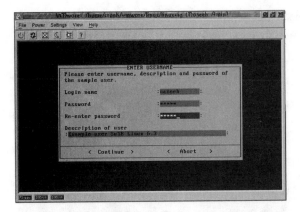

YaST asks whether you want to configure your mouse. If you have a mouse attached to your machine, answer Yes. YaST gives you a list of the supported mice (see Figure 2.35). Highlight your mouse type and press Enter to continue. YaST will ask you to choose the COM port on which your mouse runs if it is not a PS/2 mouse. Highlight the correct COM port, usually COM 1, and press Enter.

FIGURE 2.35

Mouse configuration in YaST.

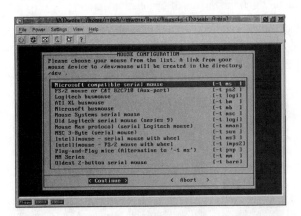

YaST now asks whether you want to use gpm with your mouse. This program enables you to use the mouse in the console to copy and paste text. This is usually a pretty handy feature to have, so answer Yes to enable it. YaST will then activate your mouse to test it. If you can see and move the mouse cursor on the screen, choose Keep; otherwise, choose Change Configuration to reconfigure your mouse.

SuSEConfig is launched again to continue configuring your system. Some scripts will be started to configure your system for the very first time. This might take some time depending on the speed of your system. Press Enter to start them; they will be running in the background as your system continues to boot.

As you can see in Figure 2.36, your newly installed SuSE system is now up and running and waiting for you to log in. Congratulations, you have successfully installed SuSE Linux!

FIGURE 2.36

SuSE Linux waiting for you to log in.

Installing Linux Using Expert Mode   By selecting the expert mode to install SuSE Linux, you will have a wider variety of options you can configure when installing SuSE Linux. We will concentrate on the Adjustments of Installation option.

When you select the expert mode for installation, YaST runs in full-feature mode (see Figure 2.37). From the YaST menu, select Adjustments of Installation, Configure Hard Disk Partitions to partition your hard disk manually from within YaST.

FIGURE 2.37

Expert mode installation.

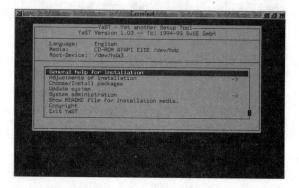

Configuring Hard Disk Partitions   In the partition table editor provided by YaST, you can create and delete ext2 and Linux swap filesystems. These two types of filesystems can be used by SuSE Linux when it is installing. Note that the YaST partition editor also can delete foreign filesystem partitions. You can use the partition editor with the following guidelines:

■ **Delete**—To delete a partition, highlight the partition to be deleted by using the arrow keys and then press F4. When prompted to delete the partition, choose Yes.

■ **Create**—To create a partition, press F5. You will be asked whether this new partition is a primary partition or an extended partition. For more information about primary and extended partitions, refer to Chapter 1. Choose the type of partition you want to create and press Enter. In each case, you will be prompted to choose the partition number and size. YaST will guess the starting and ending cylinder for you using the full space available on the device. If you want to specify the space to allocate to this partition (other than full space), you should enter this space manually. The created partition type will be set to Linux native by default.

Part

I

Ch

2

Hint

You do not have to specify the disk space using the cylinder measurement. It is sufficient to enter a plus sign (+) followed by the number of megabytes you want to allocate to this partition. For example, the following code shows how you can allow a partition to have 2GB of disk space:

```
+2000M.
```

■ **Change**—To create a swap partition, you must create a Linux native partition and press F3 to change its type to Linux swap. When you change the type of a partition to a Linux swap, you will be prompted to format this partition. You should choose Yes if it is the first time you have changed the type of this partition to a swap partition.

Setting Up the Target Filesystem   To complete the expert configuration branch of the SuSE Linux installation, you should set up the target filesystem configuration. This is done through the YaST menu. Select Adjustments of Installation, Setup Target Filesystems.

In this dialog, you can prepare the mount points you should set to each partition you have created using the partition editor. In addition, you can create mount points to all the available filesystems on your system to access them from your SuSE Linux (see Figure 2.38).

FIGURE 2.38
Partitions layout example.

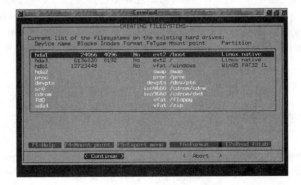

You should create at least one mount point, which is the root filesystem mount point : /. To create a mount point, select the partition you want to mount and press F4. This will bring up a list of the default mount points. Select a default mount point to which to set the partition or specify a new mount point name. You can create a new mount point by selecting the Other Entry item. If the partition already has a mount point and you do not want to assign a mount point to this partition, select the No entry option.

After you have assigned a mount point to a filesystem, you can format the partition if it was not previously formatted. Note that you should check the format flag next to each partition before you proceed. You could end up formatting your system partitions if you set this flag to a wrong partition or to all the partitions.

If the system on which you want to install SuSE Linux has a previous installation of SuSE Linux or any other Linux flavor that was originally partitioned, you can use the previous partitioning schema by pressing F7. This causes YaST to read the previous filesystem settings and apply them to the list.

CAUTION

Do *not* press the Continue button before you ensure that the format flag is set only to the partitions you want to format. If the format flag is set to partitions you do not want to format, change it by pressing F6 when the partition is selected. Be vigilant about checking the format flag because you can lose precious data if it's set to the wrong partition(s).

Select the Packages   After you have made changes to your filesystem, you can select the packages you want to install to your SuSE Linux. From the YaST menu, select Choose/Install packages, which will open the Package Installation dialog. Select Change/Create Configuration to select packages individually.

YaST shows you a list of all the series found on your SuSE distribution. Packages are ordered according to series—for example, the Apache Web server package is found under series N (network). To select a package, highlight the series to which it belongs and press Enter to enter that series. Find the package with which you want to work. The package can have one of the following two states:

- [ ]—Means it is not selected for installation on your system.
- [X]—Means the package is now selected for installation on the system.

You can change the state of a package by pressing the spacebar to cycle through the two states.

To exit from a series, press F10; the same applies if you want to exit the whole module. Next, you should install the packages by choosing the Start installation option from the main menu and pressing Enter.

The rest of the installation process is identical to the previous section "Installing Linux from Scratch." Just follow the steps in that section to complete the installation process. ●

## CHAPTER 3

Installing the X Window System

In this chapter

History

The *X Window System* is an advanced graphical windowing system for UNIX-based systems. The X Window System enables you to have a graphical desktop that uses icons, windows, menus, and so on. If you have worked on the Macintosh operating system or Microsoft Windows, you are already familiar with what a windowing system is.

The X Window System, herein referred to as *X*, was initially developed in the laboratory for computer science at the Massachusetts Institute of Technology (MIT). It was part of a collaborative effort between MIT and DEC—a project called Athena. The X Window System was first released in 1984 and its origins were heavily based on the "W" windowing package that was developed by Paul Asente at Stanford.

In September of 1987, the first version of X, known as X11, was released by MIT. This release is the same X that we know and use today. By the second release of X, X11R2, X was no longer maintained by MIT. Control passed to the X Consortium, which was formed in January 1988.

The origins of X date back to the 1970s, when the first ideas of a windowing system were born. These ideas were the result of research carried out in Xerox Corporation's Palo Alto Research Center (PARC). During the late 1970s, they were working on the Parc and Star computers. These computers never really made it to market and instead became research material. Xerox used them to demonstrate a window system built to run Smalltalk 80. The idea of a window system took people by surprise and changed their view of using computers. The WIMP (Windows, Icons, Menus, Pointer) interface that Xerox introduced started a revolution in the world of computing.

The primary development on X is currently being done by the X Consortium. Liberal licenses permit other entities to develop their own versions of X, such as the XFree86 effort. This is a collection of X servers designed to work for the Intel x86 platform. This is the release that is bundled with SuSE Linux.

Installing the X Window System

SuSE Linux packages the latest copy of the X Window System as released by the XFree86 project. Before you rush into installing X, you first should know which type of video graphics card you have and whether it is supported. To find out which card you have, refer to your card's manual for the exact specifications. You should find out which chipset the card uses—for example, whether it is based on the 3Dfx Voodoo chip or the NVidia TNT family of chips. XFree86 has good support for most video graphics cards. You can check the list of cards in Appendix B, "Hardware Compatibility List," to find out whether your card is supported. The following are the minimum required packages.

Package requirements:

Series x:

- ifnteuro
- oldlib5
- oldlibs6
- xaw3d
- xdevel
- xf86
- xfnt100
- xfntbig
- xfntscl
- xfsetup
- xpm
- xshared

Series xsrv: (You should choose the server that matches your card from the following list.)

- x8514—Server for 8514-based cards.
- xagx—Server for agx cards.
- xfbdev—X server for the vesa frame buffer device.
- xglint—Accelerated server for GLINT/PERMEDIA cards.
- xi128—Server for Number Nine Imagine 128 graphic cards.
- xi810—Server for i810-based cards.
- xmach32—Server for Mach32-based cards.
- xmach64—Server for Mach64-based cards.
- xmach8—Server for Mach8-based cards.
- xmono—X monochrome server.
- xp9k—Accelerated server for P9000-based cards.
- xrush—Hardware accelerated 3D X Server for 3Dfx cards.
- xs3—Server for S3-based cards.
- xs3v—Server for S3 ViRGE cards.
- xsis—Alpha quality server for SiS 530 and 620 cards.
- xsvga—Server for svga cards.
- xvga16—Server for vga cards (16 colors). You must install this one along with the server for your card.
- xw32—Server for W32 cards.

When you are finished installing the X Window System, you are ready to start configuring it.

Configuring the X Window System

Configuring your X Window System is the next step after installing it. The configuration process has a reputation for being quite difficult and complicated. A while ago it would have taken you quite a bit of reading and trial and error to get X up and running. But this is no longer the case; the XFree86 team developed two programs that aid the configuration of X. The first is a text-based configuration tool called xf86config; the second is a graphically-based tool called XF86Setup. Both tools do the job pretty well, but the ultimate configuration tool has been developed by the SuSE team—SaX.

SaX is a graphical configuration tool that is very user-friendly and intelligent at the same time. SaX attempts to detect most of your configuration for you, narrowing down your role to mere supervision rather than total configuration. We will explain how to configure X using all three tools, so you can then choose the one with which you are most comfortable.

SaX

SaX is an intelligent piece of software. It will try to minimize the time it takes to configure X using other X configuration programs. It has a large database containing information about most of the graphic cards currently available on the market. It also has a large database of monitors, which makes it easy for a novice user to select a monitor type without having to know detailed information about his monitor.

You can run SaX in two ways. The first way to launch SaX is by typing sax on the command line. The second way is by using YaST to configure your X server. If you try to start SaX while you are in normal user mode, it will ask for the root password. Enter the root password and SaX will start.

To start SaX using YaST, choose System Administration, Configure XFree86. In the confirmation dialog, select SaX.

When SaX starts, it will try to probe your system for your correct display card. If it fails to detect it, it will try to use the VGA mode to start in 16-color mode. If SaX fails to start because of an incorrect VGA card detection, you might have to start it using a special parameter, -s. Using the -s parameter, you specify to SaX which X server to use. An *X server* is a convention used to describe your display driver on the SuSE Linux operating system. If SaX doesn't start because it fails to find your graphic card, try using the following command to start it. This command specifies that SaX should start in VGA 16-color mode, which should run on all graphic boards:

```
bash#sax -s /usr/X11/bin/XF86_VGA16
```

Mouse Configuration Using SaX The first dialog that appears after you start SaX is the mouse configuration dialog. The mouse configuration dialog is pretty self-explanatory (see Figure 3.1). You only have to enter the advanced tabs in specific cases in which you want to modify certain settings that apply to your mouse. The following steps will configure your mouse.

FIGURE 3.1

When SaX first starts, it needs to know some information about your mouse. This will help you use your mouse throughout the SaX configuration process.

The first mouse configuration dialog in SaX helps you configure your mouse to be used within SaX. You still need to perform the same mouse configuration again for the X server. To do so, follow these steps:

1. Select your mouse type from the protocol box. From the Device group, select the mouse device. If you have configured your mouse using YaST before, the mouse device should be `/dev/mouse`.

2. Click Apply to test the mouse setting you configured. If the mouse works fine, click OK.

3. If the mouse does not work after you have clicked Apply, use the Tab key to select the combo box. After it is selected, use the up and down arrows to change the settings in the combo box to your correct mouse settings. Click Apply and try again. If the mouse works, click OK to move on to the next step.

Now that you have prepared your mouse to be used with SaX, you must configure your mouse to be used within the X server (see Figure 3.2). Select your mouse vendor from the Vendor list and select your mouse type from the Name list. You also should select the mouse port that SaX shows in DOS style ports, such as COM1, COM2, and so forth. The last step is choosing the number of buttons your mouse has. If your mouse has three buttons, check the 3 Buttons radio button in the Buttons group.

FIGURE 3.2

SaX provides an easy-to-use mouse configuration dialog. Remember to test your settings by clicking Apply before clicking the Next button. You still can use the keyboard if anything goes wrong while configuring the mouse.

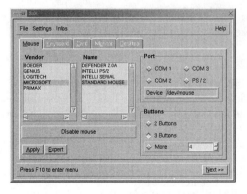

NOTE Your mouse may have only two buttons. However, because the X Window System uses the third mouse button for many operations, primarily the paste operation, you should activate the third button emulation. To do so, click Expert, select the Options tab, and check the Emulate 3 Buttons checkbox. This enables you to generate a third button click by clicking both the right and left mouse buttons at the same time. ■

When you finish filling in the information about your mouse, the Next button will be activated, enabling you to move on to the next step in configuring your X Window System. Click Next to continue.

Keyboard Configuration Using SaX The next step in the SaX configuration process is to configure your keyboard (see Figure 3.3). SaX does not detect your keyboard automatically, so you will have to do it yourself. SaX starts off by preselecting a standard keyboard in the Model list. If you have a different keyboard model, scroll through the list to select your keyboard. After you have selected the model, you can select the keyboard language by highlighting the language you prefer from the Language list.

If you're happy with your settings, click Apply and test your keyboard by typing anything in the line edit field. If your keyboard works fine, move on to the next step by clicking Next. If the keyboard settings do not match your expectations, try other configurations of the model and language.

FIGURE 3.3
You can select your keyboard model and language from the keyboard configuration tab within SaX. Click Apply and test the settings in the test field before you move on to the next step.

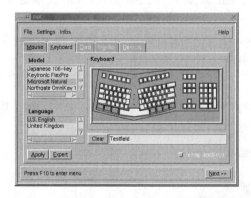

Card Configuration Using SaX After you have configured your keyboard, you should configure your display card. SaX will show you two lists, the Vendor list and Name list (see Figure 3.4). SaX uses the following three methods to configure the card:

■ **Autodetection**—In this method, SaX will try to figure out the card and its settings.

■ **Per card setting**—In this method, you must find your card in the list by selecting the vendor name from the Vendor list and then selecting the card name from the Name list.

■ **By X server**—In this method, you select the X server you want SaX to use by selecting Generic from the Vendor list and the X server you want from the Name list.

FIGURE 3.4

SaX provides the easi-
est way to configure
your display card
through the autodetec-
tion option.

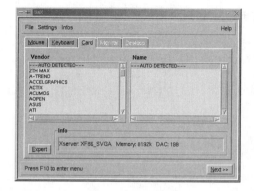

In all cases, you can still enhance the performance of your display by clicking the Expert button and applying advanced changes to the settings made by SaX. Note that you should have
sufficient knowledge of the capabilities of your display card and the X Window System before
you attempt to do so.

N O T E   If SaX fails to detect your display card memory, you should click the Expert button and
change it manually from the Server-Settings tab. In some graphic cards, you might have
to turn on the software cursor if the cursor shape is missing while using X. To enable the software
cursor, click the Expert button and open the Options tab. Select the sw_cursor option and click the
Run test button to ensure that it works on your system (see Figure 3.5). Note that you should use
this option only if the shape of your mouse cursor is not correct in X. ■

FIGURE 3.5

By selecting the
sw_cursor option, you
force the X Window
System to draw the
cursor using software
options, thus overrid-
ing any hardware bugs.

Monitor Configuration Using SaX   You can select your monitor from a wide database of
monitor vendors and models. If you do not know the monitor model or vendor, you can select
your monitor from a VESA list in which you must supply your monitor information (see
Figure 3.6).

CAUTION

Unless you know what you're doing, do not try to change the settings in the Expert mode of the monitor
settings. You might harm your monitor if you enter an incorrect value.

FIGURE 3.6

If you do not know the monitor model or your monitor is not listed, you can choose the resolution your monitor supports at the correct refresh rates from the VESA list.

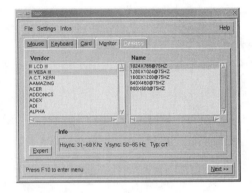

Desktop Configuration Using SaX   Using the Desktop configuration tab, you can set up the X Window System resolutions you will be using. If you are going to use only one resolution, you can configure your desktop by following these steps:

1. Select the color depth you want to use from the Colors combo box (see Figure 3.7).
2. Select the resolution you want to use from the Resolution combo box.
3. Click Configure this mode to start the SaX resolution configuration program.

FIGURE 3.7

You can quickly set up the color depth and resolution you want to use in your X sessions from the Desktop tab in SaX.

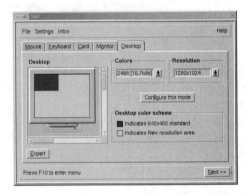

Alternatively, if you want to use more than one resolution when using the X Window System, you must configure it using the Expert mode. Click the Expert button to open the Expert mode dialog and perform the following steps (see Figure 3.8).

1. Select the color depth you want to use.
2. Click the |>> button to add any resolutions you want to be able to use. Remember, your monitor should be capable of using the resolutions you select.
3. Click the up and down arrows to manage the arrangement of the resolutions. X will start off with the first one in the list.

4. Click OK when you're satisfied with your settings. In the main window, click Next to start configuring the resolutions you have selected.

FIGURE 3.8

While using the X Window System, you can use the Ctrl+Alt and the + or – (on the numeric keypad) combinations to change the screen resolution, but only if you set up more than one resolution when you configured X.

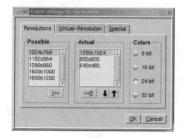

Resolution Configuration Using SaX   While configuring the resolution mode, you have the ability justify your desktop to your optimal setting without having to worry about making any screen adjustments. Use the arrow buttons to put the screen in place. Note that the screen edges are marked with blocks, except the upper-left corner, which contains the screen title. These blocks ensure that you can see the whole screen width and height. Make sure that the three blocks and screen title are visible. Use the stretch buttons to stretch your screen, and when you're satisfied with your screen position, save your settings. If you have chosen to use more than one resolution, click the Configure next mode button until you have configured all the resolutions you selected. After you have completed this whole process, click Save and Exit to save your X configuration file.

N O T E   If your screen does not show anything or goes black, you should use the Ctrl+Alt+Backspace key combination to stop the X server from being tested. After the test stops, you return to SaX. Fix any configuration problems and then test your configuration again. The problem could be one of the following:

- Resolution is not supported by monitor.
- Color depth is not supported by monitor.

In addition, any card setting problems will cause the test to exit to SaX automatically. ▨

XF86Setup

The X Window System comes equipped with a powerful tool that helps you configure the X Window System without having to perform configuration file editing. You can start the XF86Setup from the command line while running as root or from YaST. To start XF86Setup from bash, enter the following command:

```
bash#XF86Setup
```

Part

I

Ch

3

Or, to start XF86Setup using YaST, choose System Administration, Configure XFree86. In the confirmation dialog, select XF86Setup.

When XF86Setup starts, it brings up a welcome message from the XFree86 group (see Figure 3.9).

FIGURE 3.9

The XF86Setup program that comes with the X Window System enables you to configure your X. While it does not perform any detection of your card, other utilities that come with X do that for you.

Mouse Configuration Using XF86Setup   Although you can access all the tabs in the XF86Setup program in any order, we will discuss the tabs starting from left to right. The first tab on the left is the Mouse tab, which you can access by pressing Alt+M on the keyboard or by clicking the Mouse tab. The Mouse tab is shown in Figure 3.10.

FIGURE 3.10

Using XF86Setup, you easily can select your mouse from a wide variety of mice supported by X.

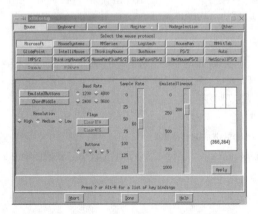

You can change the settings for your mouse by selecting the mouse protocol and mouse button number. If your mouse has only two buttons, you should click the Emulate three buttons button or press e. If your mouse does not work, you can use the arrow keys to move between mouse protocols to select the one that applies to your mouse. After you have selected a correct mouse protocol, press a on the keyboard to apply the settings. Or, you can click the Apply button if your mouse is functioning.

After you have ensured your mouse is functioning properly, click the Keyboard tab and move to the next section to learn how to configure your keyboard.

Keyboard Configuration Using XF86Setup   Keyboard configuration using XF86Setup is as easy as selecting the configuration of two combo boxes. Select the keyboard model from the Model combo box and the keyboard language from the Layout (language) combo box (see Figure 3.11). Click Apply to apply your settings. Most people do not need to set up the advanced functions on the right side of the screen because these are used to map keys for special keyboards.

FIGURE 3.11
Keyboard configuration using XF86Setup.

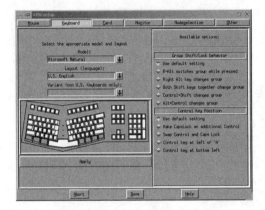

Part
I
Ch
3

Card Configuration Using XF86Setup   Display card configuration using XF86Setup can be performed in the following two ways:

- **Detailed Setup**—Before using the detailed setup in Figure 3.12, you should have some knowledge of the X Window System servers. You should select the X server for your display card using the buttons at the top of the screen. You also should configure the appropriate settings for your X server. You can specify options for the X server using the Options combo box, which enables multiple selections. You can click the Card List button to select your card from a large list of cards, which takes less time than guessing which settings apply to your display card.

- **Card List**—In the Card List mode, all you have to do is to search for your display card in the card list (see Figure 3.13). After you have selected your card, you can move on to the next step or you can press the Detailed Setup button to add options to the settings that were applied when you selected the card.

N O T E   We recommend you specify the memory manually rather than making the X server probe for it. Use the Detailed Setup to specify the memory on your graphic card. In some graphic cards, you might have to turn on the software cursor if the cursor shape is missing while using X. To enable the software cursor, click the Options combo box and select sw_cursor. You should use this option only if the shape of your mouse cursor is not correct in X. ▪

FIGURE 3.12
Configuring a graphic card using Detailed Setup enables you to set up options for your graphic card.

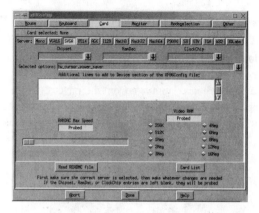

FIGURE 3.13
Using the Card List mode, you can select your card from the card list without having to perform any manual configuration.

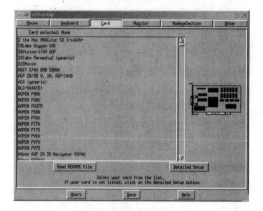

Monitor Configuration Using XF86Setup   You must configure the X Window System to properly use your monitor using the Monitor tab, which contains a list of preconfigured settings that apply to a large number of monitors (see Figure 3.14). We advise you to have your monitor handbook nearby to check the refresh rate your monitor supports so you can be sure to choose the correct monitor configuration. You can modify the settings by editing the Horizontal and Vertical Sync fields to fit your monitor. However, this can be dangerous—do not enter incorrect values because they can harm your monitor. Make sure that the values you enter are the correct values you got from the monitor handbook.

Mode Configuration Using XF86Setup   Mode configuration is important when it comes to configuring the color depths and resolutions you want to use during an X session. In the Modeselection tab, you will find a list of the color depths and modes you can select (see Figure 3.15). Select the color depths you want to use by clicking the color depth button and then choose the modes you want to use by clicking them.

FIGURE 3.14
Monitor configuration in XF86Setup enables you to choose the correct refresh rate for your monitor.

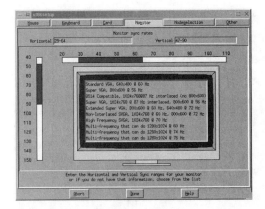

FIGURE 3.15
You can choose the resolution modes and color depths you want to use in X using the Modeselection tab.

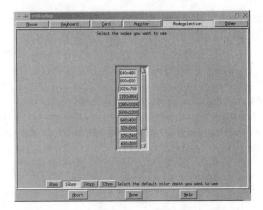

Part

I

Ch

3

Other Configurations Using XF86Setup   XF86Setup enables you to configure advanced options you want the X server to use. As shown in Figure 3.16, the settings are as follows:

- **Allow server to be killed with hotkey sequence (Ctrl-Alt-Backspace)**—If you check this option, you will be able to close the X server using this combination. It is a good idea to turn on this option.

- **Allow video mode switching**—This option enables you to use the Alt+Ctrl+(+) and Alt+Ctrl+(-) key combinations to switch between video modes.

- **Don't Trap Signals**—Uncheck this option if it is checked.

- **Allow video mode changes from other hosts**—Uncheck this option if it is checked.

- **Allow changes to keyboard and mouse settings from other hosts**—Uncheck this option if it is checked.

FIGURE 3.16
On the Other tab, you can set up server-specific operations.

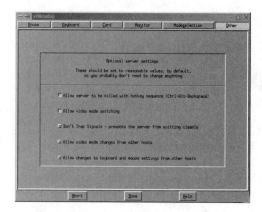

Mode Tuning Using xvidtune Now that you have completed all the steps of configuring XF86Setup, you should put it into practice. Click the Done button to apply the changes. Then, when XF86Setup asks for confirmation, click the Okay button to configure the position of your screen on each of the resolutions you have selected using the xvidtune program.

N O T E If your screen does not show anything or goes black, you should use the Ctrl+Alt+Backspace combination to stop the X server. After you have killed the X server, restart the XF86Setup and go through the whole configuration again. This time, try to select different monitor configurations.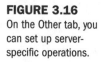

xf86config

The last tool you can use to configure your X Window System is xf86config. This tool is text-based and pretty old, but it is very good at configuring X. Very seldom will this tool fail in configuring X; even if all the others fail, you can still count on this one to succeed. That is, of course, provided your card is supported by X; if it isn't, nothing can help you.

To configure X using xf86config, follow these steps:

1. Log in as root.

2. Run xf86config by typing the following on the command line:
   `#xf86config`

3. The screen scrolls with introductory text about xf86config. When you finish reading that introduction, press Enter to continue and start the actual configuration process. If you want to quit at any point in the program, just press Ctrl+C.

4. The program will warn you that you have a directory called /usr/X386/bin, which means you have an older version of X installed. Don't worry about this warning—you do not have an old version of X, this directory exists only for compatibility reasons. Press Enter to continue.

5. The first menu you see is the mouse type menu, which enables you to choose the type of your mouse. If you have a two-button mouse, you should select the first option, Microsoft-compatible (2-button protocol). Enter the number that corresponds to your mouse or one that is compatible with it and press Enter.

6. The program asks you whether you want to enable ChordMiddle. If your mouse is a three-button mouse, you should answer yes here to enable the third mouse button. Otherwise, answer no. Enter y for yes or n for no and press Enter to continue.

7. The next question asks you whether you want to enable Emulate3Buttons. If your mouse does not have three buttons, you can emulate a third button by pressing the two mouse buttons simultaneously. To enable this, answer yes to this option. Enter y for yes or n for no and press Enter to continue.

8. Now, the program asks you about the mouse device, which is the device file for the mouse under /dev/. This should be /dev/mouse, which is the default answer to this question. Press Enter to accept this default and continue.

9. Next is the keyboard type configuration. The program asks you whether you want to use XKB. XKeyboard is a new extension that was added to X to manage the keyboard layout. It is highly recommended that you use XKB, so answer yes here. Enter y for yes or n for no and press Enter to continue.

10. An introductory message will be displayed. It tells you that you will now be presented with a list of preconfigured keyboard layouts. Press Enter to continue.

11. The program will give you a list of keyboards you can use. Find the keyboard that matches yours and enter its number. You probably will choose the second one because it's the standard these days. Enter the number of the keyboard that matches yours and press Enter to continue.

12. The next section concerns your monitor. The program shows you some introductory text on the subject. Press Enter to continue.

13. You will be shown a list of monitor settings supported by XFree86. Before you attempt to select any of these, you should try to find the technical specifications of your monitor in its manual. Then, select the one closest to yours. The sixth setting works with most monitors because it uses conservative settings. If you cannot find your manual, you might want to choose this setting. If you know the exact numbers for your monitor, you can enter them by choosing the eleventh choice.

14. If you have chosen any setting other than the eleventh, skip this step. The eleventh option is where you enter your monitor's settings manually. The program will ask you for the Horizontal Sync range. Enter it as written in your manual. Press Enter to continue.

15. The program will now ask you for the Vertical sync range of your monitor. You should get this information from your monitor's manual. If you can't find the manual, you should select a conservative choice—the third one works for most monitors. If you know the exact numbers for your monitor, choose the fifth option to enter them manually.

Part

I

Ch

3

16. If you have picked any setting other than the fifth, skip this step. The program will now ask you to enter your monitor's Vertical Sync range. Enter it as written in your manual and press Enter to continue.

17. The program asks you to enter some descriptive names for your monitor. These will not affect your configuration in any way at all. They will be used only in the configuration file to name the sections properly. These strings are as follows, in the order in which they are requested by the program: Identifier of the monitor, vendor name of the monitor, and model name of the monitor. You can press Enter for every one of them to accept the defaults.

18. The program now enters the video card configuration section, in which you will choose your video card. The program displays some introductory text; at the bottom of the text it asks you whether you want to look at the card database, you should answer yes to this. Enter y for yes and press Enter to continue.

19. The program will give you a list of all the cards supported by the current version of XFree86. To scroll through the list, press Enter. After you find your card, enter its number in the list and press Enter to continue.

20. The program will display the option you selected to confirm it. Press Enter to continue and accept it.

21. The program now will ask you to choose a server to use for this card. You have five options: the XF86_Mono, which is a monochrome server; the XF86_VGA16, which supports only 16 colors; the XF86_SVGA, which supports 256 colors but is accelerated on some cards and can support high colors; the accelerated servers; and choosing the server from your cards definition. The fifth option is recommended because it selects the server based on which card you selected in the previous step. Type 5 and press Enter to continue.

22. The program now will ask you whether it should create a symbolic link to the X server. Answer yes by typing y and pressing Enter.

23. The program then asks whether you want that symbolic link to be created in /var/X11R6/bin. Answer yes by typing y and pressing Enter.

24. The program needs to know how much memory is on your cards. You are given a list from which to choose. If your card has more than 4MB of memory, select choice number six to enter the amount of RAM manually. The value should be in KB, so if your card has 8MB, you would enter 8192, which is 8×1024K.

25. The program asks you to enter some descriptive names for your video card. These will not affect your configuration in any way at all. They will be used only in the configuration file to name the sections properly. These strings are as follows, in the order in which they are requested by the program: Identifier of the video card, vendor name of the video card, and model name of the video card. You can press Enter for every one of them to accept the defaults.

26. The program then asks you enter your Clockchip setting. This enables XFree86 to program your card's clock. Most cards do not support this, but if yours does, you should select it from the list. Otherwise, press Enter to disable Clockchip.

27. Next, the program asks whether it should attempt to probe your card's clock settings. The program asks "Do you want me to run 'X -probeonly' now?" The answer to this question lies in the line that appears onscreen above this question. In most cases, this line is "The card definition says to NOT probe clocks." If this is the case, you should answer no; otherwise, answer yes. Enter y for yes or n for no and press Enter to continue.

28. Now, it's time to set the resolutions you want to use. The program enables you to configure the resolutions you want to use per color depth. You can change the resolutions for 256 color mode, 32k/64k color mode, 24 bit color and packed pixel mode, and 24 bit color mode. The program will show you the current settings for each color mode at the top of the screen—for example, "640×480" "800×600" "1024×768" for 8bpp. This line means that the X server, when run in 8bpp (256 colors) mode, will start off in 640×480. Pressing Ctrl+Alt+PlusKey(+) will switch the resolution to 800×600 and then to 1024×768. If you like the current settings, choose the fifth option and then press Enter.

29. If you picked the fifth option in the previous step, skip this step. Choosing any other option but the fifth one means you want to manually configure this color mode. The program will display a list of all the resolutions it can support. Enter the numbers of all the resolutions you want to use for this color mode. For example, entering 42 means the X server will start with 1024×768 initially, and when you press Ctrl+Alt+PlusKey(+), it will switch to 800×600. The program then asks whether you want to set a virtual screen that is larger than your desktop. Press y for yes or n for no and press Enter to continue.

30. Finally, the program asks whether you want to save your configuration. Press y for yes or n for no and press Enter to continue.

31. That's it. You are finished configuring your XFree86.

You can now test your configuration by running X:

```
$ startx
```

If you configured your X properly, it should start without any problems.

Setting Up XDM/KDM

If you hate to start your SuSE Linux in console mode and instead want SuSE Linux to start using a graphical login, you can make this happen by configuring XDM. If you have KDE installed, you can use KDM instead, which provides a powerful graphical login.

Part

I

Ch

3

To set up XDM or KDM, start YaST and follow these steps:

1. Choose System Administration, Login Configuration. The Configure Login GUI dialog will pop up (see Figure 3.17).

2. In the Configure Login GUI dialog, select Login GUI for a graphical login, instead of ASCII.

3. If you have KDE installed, you will be able to select KDM in the Display manager field; otherwise, it will be disabled and you will be able to use only XDM. Choose KDM, if available. You can learn more about configuring KDM in Chapter 24, "Configuring the Desktop."

4. Select the Shutdown Behaviour of KDM for all. This will enable anyone to shut down the system by clicking shutdown and confirming the shutdown. You can learn more about this option in Chapter 24.

FIGURE 3.17
You can use YaST to configure the system to start in GUI login mode.

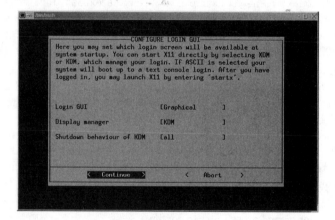

Setting Up Frame Buffer Device X Server

The Frame Buffer Device that comes with the kernel version 2.2.x is a blessing for those who have cards not currently supported by X. The only constraint is that the card should support VESA version 2. You need to prepare some settings for the frame buffer device X server to work:

■ **Kernel Preparation**—You do not have to recompile the kernel to prepare it for the frame buffer device X server unless you are using a kernel you recompiled previously. The kernel that comes precompiled with SuSE Linux is equipped with frame buffer support. If you want to recompile the kernel by yourself, you should include the following three options in the kernel:

- Console drivers
- Video mode selection support
- Support for frame buffer devices

You also might want to include support for your card if it's found in the Kernel support list under the frame buffer devices. If you can't find your card, use the VESA VGA graphics console option.

■ **LILO Preparation**—To start your system in frame buffer mode, you must pass some parameters to the kernel using LILO on system startup. You can do so by passing the parameter VGA=mode. You can set the mode to VGA=ask if you want to be asked which mode you want to use each time you start the system. The modes for the VESA frame buffer are listed in Table 3.1.

You can set up LILO using YaST. Start YaST using the --mask lilo parameter as follows:

```
bash#yast --mask lilo
```

In the Append-line for hardware parameter, add the following text to start your system in 32k-color depth and 1024×768 resolution:

```
vga=0x116
```

Table 3.1 VESA Mode Numbers

Colors	640×480	800×600	1024×768	1280×1024
256	0×301	0×303	0×305	0×307
32k	0×310	0×313	0×316	0×319
64k	0×311	0×314	0×317	0×31A
16M	0×312	0×315	0×318	0×31B

The frame buffer device X server easily can be configured using SaX. Follow the same procedures described in the previous section "SaX" until you reach the Card configuration. In the Card configuration tab, select the Vendor Generic Server Selection. From the Name list, select the Framebuffer server. Continue with the steps in setting up your X server.

X Display Tips

This section deals with some X Window System tips for novice X users.

Tip #1: Adding Hosts to the Access Control List

Suppose you're in an X session and you want to start an X program as root. The message you get will be something like the following:

```
Error: Can't open display
```

This is because the restrictions made by X allow only the user who started X to start X-based applications. In this case, you should enable the host who will be starting the application by using the command xhost. To enable a host to start X applications on the server, use the following command:

```
bash$xhost + hostname
```

The previous command adds the hostname of the host who's allowed to connect to the X server. To allow users connecting from the localhost, use the following command:

```
bash$xhost + localhost
```

Users connecting from the localhost will be able to start X programs if they exported the correct DISPLAY environment variable.

Tip #2: Exporting the *DISPLAY* Environment Variable

After you have added the localhost to the control access list, the root user must export the correct DISPLAY environment variable to connect to the X server. This can be done as follows:

```
bash#export DISPLAY=:0
```

Tip #3: Starting X Programs on Other Servers and Exporting the *DISPLAY* Variable to Your X Server

Let's suppose you want to access some X programs on another machine and want to see them on your X server. If your IP is 192.186.186.5 and the machine from which you want to start the program is 192.186.186.6, you can do the following:

1. Log in to the 192.186.186.6 server using telnet.
2. On your machine, allow the 192.186.186.6 to connect to your X server by issuing the command xhost + 192.186.186.6 in another xterm.
3. On the telnet window, issue the command export DISPLAY= 192.186.186.5:0.
4. Start the program, which will show up on your X Window System.

Troubleshooting the X Window System

My card is not supported by X, what should I do?

You can either use the Frame Buffer Device X Server if your card supports VESA version 2, or you can buy another one that is supported.

Whenever I try to configure the X Window System, I get a server not found in SaX and XF86Setup.

You did not install the package that contains your X server. Check the list of system requirements in the section "Installing the X Window System" previously in this chapter.

The X Window System starts in a different mode than the one I want, what should I do?

If you have used SaX to configure your X Window System, make sure you arranged the resolutions you want. The mode on top will be the first to be used. If you have used XF86Setup, make sure you added the following line in the Screen section of /etc/XF86Config:

```
DefaultColorDepth
```

When I set up XDM/KDM, the system keeps flashing and I can't access the system.

This occurs if you start to use XDM/KDM without first performing a complete test of a working X system. Try to reboot the system either by holding the Ctrl+Alt+Del combination until it catches the reboot signal or by telnetting to the system and rebooting it. At the lilo prompt, enter linux 2. When the system starts in console mode, reconfigure the X Window System and make sure it works. If it does not work, use YaST to start your system in ASCII login. ●

Part

I

Ch

3

System Administration

Managing Users and Groups

Linux: A Multiuser Operating System

Linux is a multiuser operating system, which means that it can service more than one user at a time. This ability to fully utilize your system to service as many users as possible is one of the advantages of multiuser operating systems. Most multiuser operating systems accomplish this by using the concept of user accounts.

A common multiuser operating system employs user accounts to allow more than one person to use the system at the same time. Different users are grouped under different groups. This enables the system administrator to easily control how the system is used and optimally utilized.

What Is an Account?

In order to have a multiuser operating system, you should have user accounts. An *account* is a logical partition on your system. Each user who will use your system will have such a logical partition or an account. An account can act like a cubicle for that user. The user has his own space and he can share the tools that are available in the vicinity—not all of which he may be allowed to use. Users are not allowed to see what others have in their space unless the other users permit it. Resources are controlled among the users by a more superior user who is the administrator or root.

Now that you know the logic behind an account, you need to know what an account is—*physically* speaking. An account starts by giving the user both a username and a password, which enables them to *log in* to the system. Users have to log in so that they can use the system. Usernames and passwords help control who is supposed to use the system and who isn't. When a user logs in to the system, he is positioned inside what is called his home directory. In a typical Linux/Unix system, you will have a directory called /home. Inside that directory you will find several other directories named after the users in the system. Each user has his own /home/username directory. For example, a user named John would have his home in /home/john, and if there is another user named Mary, her home would be /home/mary.

The idea of giving each user a directory of her own is very helpful. Each user stores her files inside that directory. Users usually are not allowed to write anywhere else on the whole system apart from their home directory and the /tmp directory.

When you have users, you need to have a way to control them. That is where the root account comes in. Every Linux system has a default and critical account called the root account. The root account belongs to the person who will administer and control the whole system.

The root account should never be shared with other people; it is the most powerful account on the whole system. As root, you can do anything you want to the system. You can create files anywhere regardless of permissions, as well as add, remove, and modify users. The purpose of having the root account is maintenance and upgrading of the system. For example, to install an application that will be shared by all users, you have to log in as root. To be able to totally destroy the system, you have to be logged in as root. That is why it is very dangerous to be root—one mistake and you easily can wipe out the whole system. Although being root might feel nice, in a real-world multiuser system, it's the worst job ever. You have a lot of responsibility.

Working with Users

Managing your users is a very simple process, and is even simpler thanks to SuSE YaST. YaST offers a very simple interface to managing users. You can use it to add, modify, and delete users all from one place.

Adding New Users

To add users to your system, you use YaST. Remember, because you are maintaining the system you have to be logged in as root. For example, to add a user named John Gear, who has the username john, follow these steps:

1. To run the User administration module of YaST you either navigate to it by choosing System Administration, User administration; or run YaST to load the users module directly:

   ```
   # yast --mask user
   ```

2. The User Administration module loads up (see Figure 4.1).

FIGURE 4.1
YaST uses a very friendly and easy interface for managing users.

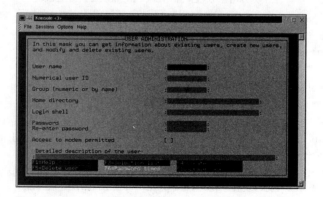

3. In User Name, enter john and press Enter.

   Notice how YaST has filled in most of the remaining fields for you. YaST uses default values for them.

4. The next field is Numerical User ID, which is a unique number assigned to every user. This is an important number because the system never really deals with usernames; it instead uses numerical IDs to identify users. Leave this field as is.

5. The next option is the Group this user will be a member of. The default is `users`; accept it. More on groups will be discussed later.

6. The next field, Home Directory, is the path to the user's home. This is where that user will be positioned after he or she logs in. Common practice is to include the username in the home directory's name. In this case, it will be `/home/john`.

7. In the next field, you see the Login Shell. A *shell* is a command interpreter that reads and executes commands from the user. In Linux, you have a wide variety of command interpreters, or shells. Press F3 to see a list of the available shells. The most common and recommended shell to use is bash (Bourne Again Shell).

8. Next, you have to enter the Password for that user. This is important. However secure your system is, it is only as secure as the passwords that you use. A good password is one that is a mixture of characters and numbers that are not directly relevant to that user.

CAUTION

Linux passwords are only eight characters long; anything longer than eight characters will be discarded. Passwords are case sensitive, which means that *password* is not the same as *PaSswOrD*. A common mistake is to recklessly enter a password, ignoring the case, and then fail to log in because you cannot remember how you entered it.

---

9. Enter the password again in the Re-Enter Password field to confirm it.

10. The next choice is whether you want that user to have access to your modem. This is a new parameter that was introduced in SuSE 6.2. If the user will need to use the modem, then check that option; otherwise, leave it unchecked.

11. The final field is where you enter a brief Description of the User. In this case, enter `John Gear`.

12. That's it. Now look over all the values you entered, and if you are happy with them press F4 to create that user.

13. In SuSE 6.3, you can set some extra parameters for the password by pressing F6. As you can see in Figure 4.2, a new dialog pops up. You use this dialog to further tune the restrictions on that account. For example, you can set the number of days before the password expires, the maximum number of days for the same password, and so on. Note that the default values are pretty lean, so if you like being strict, change them. When you are done, click Continue to exit to the previous dialog.

14. To exit the User Administration mask, press F10 or Esc.

FIGURE 4.2
You can set extra parameters for the password using this dialog.

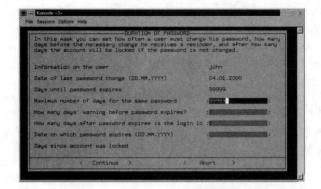

To test whether the user was created or not, switch to a login session and attempt to log in with the username john. If you are able to log in, you were successful.

Modifying a User

Now that you have added a user, what happens if you would like to modify that user's settings? Easy, you use the exact same mask you used to add the user:

1. Run YaST again:

   ```
   # yast --mask user
   ```

2. YaST User Administration starts with a blank form. To load the data for the user you want to modify, you simply press F3 in the User Name field. You will get a list of all the users currently registered in the system. Use the arrow key to locate the user you want to modify and press Enter to accept.

3. Now the form has all the data regarding that user. Use the arrow keys or Tab to move from one field to another, changing any values you want.

4. When you are satisfied with the changes, press F4 to apply those changes.

5. Press F10 to exit the User Administration mask.

Deleting a User

To delete a user, you need to use YaST again:

1. Run YaST in the User Administration mode:

   ```
   # yast --mask user
   ```

2. YaST User Administration starts with a blank form. Press F3 in the User Name field to load the data for the user you want to delete. Use the arrow key to locate the user you want to delete and press Enter to accept.

3. Now the form has all the data regarding that user. To delete that user, simply press the F5 key. YaST will ask you if you really want to delete that user. If you do, answer Yes.

Part

II

Ch

4

4. The user was deleted from the system's list of users allowed to log in. But her home directory and files still remain. That is why YaST asks you if you would like to remove the files and subdirectories contained in the user's home directory. If you want to totally remove that user from your system, then answer Yes.

> **CAUTION**
>
> When you delete a user's account, there is no way to restore the deleted files—the user is gone forever—so you might want to back up her home directory in case that user might return.

Disabling a User's Account

You have seen how you can delete a user, but what if you just want to disable that user's account for a while? It would be a bit drastic to delete his account, and then re-establish it once you want him to be able to log in. There is a much easier approach to disabling an account.

To disable an account, you can use the `passwd` command. To lock an account, you type the following:

```
# passwd -l john
```

And to unlock it, enter the following:

```
# passwd -u john
```

The account will only be disabled, not removed. All that will happen is that John will not be able to log in to the system until you decide to unlock the account.

Working with Groups

Users in Linux can be assigned to different groups. Groups are created to logically divide users for better organization and control. In a common system, you will find a group for root and a group for users; other groups exist to organize files. But why would you want to bother with creating other groups?

Take this scenario as an example: Say that you are going to set up your server in a university. In a common university, you have different groups of people—you have students, faculty members, administration staff, computer support staff, and so on. Each of those groups has a different set of demands from the system:

- Students might just need to use the system for email.
- Faculty might need to use it for email and sharing of files like exams and paper.

- Administration might need to use the system to run administrative programs.
- Computer science people might need to use it for programming.

It would be difficult to keep track of all these different demands if there was no way to organize the different categories of users. That's where groups come in handy. By creating a group for each category of users, you easily can organize and control them. For example, you can create the following groups:

- students (for all the students)
- faculty (for the faculty members)
- admin (for the administration personnel)
- cs (for the computer science users)

Now you can start adding users to the relevant groups. Your users are neatly organized thanks to the use of groups. But groups can do even more! Because the students want to use only email, there is no reason to allow them to use any other software on the system. Therefore, using permissions, you can deny students the ability to execute any software other than email.

The same concept can be applied to other groups. Faculty members, for example, can be the only group allowed to have access to the /exams directory on the system. cs can be the only group that has access to the compilers and development tools available on the system.

Groups help you organize your users, as well as control them. This way you can ensure the system has better security and more efficiency.

Creating a Group

To create a new group, follow these steps:

1. Run YaST in the Group Administration mode, either by running YaST and then navigating to it (System Administration, Group Administration) or by typing the following:

   ```
   # yast --mask group
   ```

   When the module is loaded, you see an empty form. This is similar to the adding user process.

2. The first field is the Name of Group field, where you enter the name of the group you want to create—for example, students. Press Enter to move to the next field.

3. The next field is the Numeric Group ID. This is similar to the idea of numerical IDs for users. As far as Linux is concerned, a group is nothing but a numeric ID. YaST entered a default numeric ID for you. Press Enter to move on.

4. The next field is the Password to access that group. It is important to have a group password. If you don't put a password on a group, anyone can simply run the command newgrp groupname and be able to be a member of that group. This is a matter of security and is very important to not ignore!

TIP Group passwords are meant for the people who will not be members of that group. Let's say that John is a member of the group users, while Rob is a member of the group faculty. Rob happens to be sitting with John and needs to access some of the files that belong to faculty through John's account. If Rob tries to do that, and the files are only viewable by faculty, he will get a permission denied error. He could view the files by logging in with his account, but that is not convenient. Instead Rob could switch John's group to faculty for a temporary amount of time using the command newgrp:

```
$ newgrp faculty
```

The system will ask for a password, which is the password that was entered to guard that group at the time of creation. Now Rob can access any files under the faculty group using John's account. When Rob is done, he types logout, which reverts the effect from John's account and puts it back to normal. Thanks to this command, Rob did not have to log in using his account and waste time; he simply opened a gate to the group for some time.

5. Re-enter the password to confirm it. Press Enter to move on to the last field.

6. This field is where you specify which users are allowed to access your group. This is convenient because you can add people from different groups to your group's access list. For example, you are creating a group called faculty, and John is from the group users. If you add John's name in this field, he will be able to access the group faculty as well as his own group, which is users. This way you can have a user be a member of more than one group.

7. To add the users, you can either enter their usernames separated by a comma or press F3 and pick the users one by one from the list of available users on the system.

8. When you are done, go over the values in the form and press F4 to create that group.

9. Finally, press F10 to exit the group administration mask.

Modifying a Group

You have created your group and want to modify it—how do you do that? By using the exact same mask in YaST:

1. Run YaST:

   ```
   # yast --mask group
   ```

2. YaST starts with the Group Administration module. To select the group that you want to modify, press F3 in the Name of Group field.

3. Use the arrow keys to find the name of the group and press Enter to select it.

   The form will show all the values for that group.

4. Use the arrow keys to move from one field to the other and change the values that you want.

5. When you are happy with the changes, simply press F4 to apply that changes.

6. Finally press F10 to exit the group administration mask.

Deleting a Group

In the case that you want to delete a group, here's how you do it:

1. Run YaST:

```
# yast --mask group
```

2. YaST starts with the Group Administration module. Press F3 in the Name of Group field to select the group you want to delete.

3. Use the arrow keys to find the name of the group and press Enter to select it.

   The form should have all the values for that group.

4. To delete that group, press F5.

5. YaST will confirm your request to delete the group; if you are sure, select Yes.

6. Press F10 to exit the Group Administration mask.

Managing Home Directories

Home directories are one of the most important parts of your system. If they are handled incorrectly, you might have to face a group of angry users. This is why you have to be very careful with the directories. As we said earlier, the home directories are where all the users in the system keep their files. All their application settings and preferences are stored there, and email is saved in folders inside the home directory.

Considering this, we can understand why users will be very unhappy if something happens to their home directories.

Setting Global Preferences for Your Users

A good practice is to create a good configuration for most applications and apply that configuration to all the users. This way you save users the time of configuring their applications. But how do you propagate such a change? This is a step you should do before you start adding users to your system.

To fully understand how this works, let's see what happens when you create a user. Upon the creation of a user, a few things happen automatically by the system:

1. The system user's database is updated with the name and password of the new user.

2. A /home/username directory is created.

3. All the contents of /etc/skel are copied to /home/username.

4. The ownership of /home/username is changed to the new user.

There it is! Our key to global configuration—the third step. We observe that the system copies the contents of the directory /etc/skel to the newly created home directory. /etc/skel is simply a home skeleton, which contains all the files and subdirectories that a new home directory will have.

Now that you know this, you can easily customize that directory. All that you have to do is create a test user. Run all the applications you want to customize and save the preferences. Create any subdirectories you might need and tweak anything you want. When you are done and you have the perfect account (in your opinion), simply switch to root and replace the contents of /etc/skel with the contents of your test account. Then change the ownership of all the files to user root and group root:

```
# chown root.root /etc/skel -R
```

> **CAUTION**
>
> You should be careful when you perform global configuration. Some programs tend to save their preferences, including the user's name. If this happens, when you copy that program's preferences to all users, it won't work correctly because it has been saved for a specific user. Check your programs for that before attempting to include their preferences.

That's it! Start creating your users, and with each user created, the new /etc/skel will be copied to that user's home directory. Global configuration has been accomplished.

Protecting Home Directories

Protecting home directories is an important step. You have to protect them from being lost. System crashes in Linux are not likely to happen, but that is not an excuse to not protect your system. Hardware crashes might destroy files and directories, including the home directories.

Performing regular backups of the /home directory is a very good practice. Scheduling a weekly or monthly full backup of this directory can save you from a lot of complaints in case something happens. If your system is a very busy one, back up daily. Better safe than sorry!

Controlling Your Users

When you have a system with more than one user, you will eventually find the need to control how they use, or maybe abuse, your system. There are a lot of different aspects that you can control for your users. These range from the amount of memory users are allowed to use to the amount of hard disk space they are allowed to have.

But before you learn how you can control those aspects, you should learn about a few concepts. When a user logs in to the system, some environment variables are automatically set for her. Among these are the user ID and group ID. The user ID is declared in a variable called $UID and the group ID is declared in $GROUPS. Another important concept you need to know is that upon log in, the contents of the script /etc/profile are executed automatically by the shell. This information might sound irrelevant now, but it will be of great help in a while.

Controlling the System Resources Available to Users

To control the system resources available to users, you use a command in bash called ulimit. To learn more about this command, read the man page for bash (man 1 bash).

The following are the various parameters you can set using ulimit:

- The maximum size of core files created (ulimit -c)
- The maximum size of a process's data segment (ulimit -d)
- The maximum size of files created by the shell (ulimit -f)
- The maximum size that might be locked into memory (ulimit -l)
- The maximum resident set size (ulimit -m)
- The maximum number of open file descriptors (ulimit -n)
- The pipe size in 512-byte blocks (ulimit -p)
- The maximum stack size (ulimit -s)
- The maximum amount of cpu time in seconds (ulimit -t)
- The maximum number of processes available to a single user (ulimit -u)
- The maximum amount of virtual memory available to the shell (ulimit -v)

Let's see how you can set these limits for your users. The file you want to edit is /etc/profile. Open the file using your favorite editor. You have to be root to write to this file. The first section of the file has the following:

```
# /etc/profile

PROFILEREAD=true


umask 022

# adjust some limits (see bash(1))
#ulimit -c 20000        # only core-files less than 20 MB are written
#ulimit -d 15000        # max data size of a program is 15 MB
#ulimit -s 15000        # max stack size of a program is 15 MB
#ulimit -m 30000        # max resident set size is 30 MB

ulimit -Sc 0            # don't create core files
ulimit -d unlimited
```

Part

II

Ch

4

Because this file is executed upon every log in, anything you type here will be set for the user. You can even decide whether you want users to be able to set any of the limits. This is done by setting both a soft limit and hard limit for the parameter you are setting. A hard limit cannot be exceeded by users, whereas a soft limit can be exceeded by users up to the hard limit. For example, say you do not want users to be able to run more than 50 processes, but you know that some of them might need to run up to 70 processes. To set a hard limit, just put an *H* before the option you want to set, and to set a soft limit, put an *S* before the option. If you do not put either one, the value you assign will be both the hard and soft limit. For example:

```
ulimit -Hu 70       # set the hard limit to be max 70 processes.
ulimit -Su 50       # set the soft limit to be 50.
```

This will give users 50 processes to run. If they need more, they can use the ulimit command to increase that limit to the maximum 70 processes, as in the following example:

```
$ ulimit -u 60      this will work
$ ulimit -u 80      this will fail since it exceeds the allowed amount.
```

Now that you know how to set user limits, what if you need a little more flexibility? What happens if you want to assign different groups of users different settings? The method used in the preceding example sets the same limits on all the users regardless of their group. You might want the CS group to be able to run more processes than the students group, for example. To do this, you have to resort to some logic, which happens to be pretty easy to do.

As mentioned before, upon login, the shell declares two important variables for you. These variables are $UID (user ID) and $GROUPS (group ID). The logic here is for you to check those variables and, based on their values, assign different settings. Let's see how you can do that.

Say that you have two groups, one called students and the other called users. You want to set different settings for each group. The first thing you will need to do is get the group ID for each one. Follow these steps:

1. Run YaST in the Group Administration mode:

   ```
   # yast --mask group
   ```

2. Press F3 in the Name of Group field.

3. Use the arrow keys to navigate through the list of group names until you find the group users, and then press Enter.

4. Now the form fills up with all the data relevant to the group users. You are only interested in the group ID, which in this case is 100.

5. Do the same for the group students, which has a group ID of 104.

6. Take note of those numbers.

You need to write a small piece of scripting code that checks the value of the $GROUPS variable and sets the correct settings for each of the two groups. You want the students group to be able to run no more than 10 processes and the users no more than 50. Let's see how you can do this. Insert the following somewhere in the beginning of /etc/profile:

```
# first we check if that user belongs to the users group
if test "$GROUPS" = "100" ; then
        #ok.. he is.. start setting the limits!

    ulimit  -u
fi

# Now we check if that user belongs to the students group
if test "$GROUPS" = "104" ; then
        #ok.. he is.. start setting the limits!

    ulimit  -u
fi
```

Using this simple logic, you can set different settings for each group, thus achieving the optimal system usage. No group has more than it should need. Of course, the same thing can be applied to the user level. In case you want one of the users to have a little more capability than others, just replace the $GROUPS with $UID, check for the user's numerical ID, and set the limits for that user.

Controlling How Much Hard Disk Space Your Users Are Allowed to Have (Quota)

One of the most frustrating aspects of administrating a multiuser system is having users realize that they are not the only ones on the system. Users have a tendency to forget that, and they hardly take it into account when they use the system resources. So far you have learned how to control how users are going to use the system's processing and memory resources, but what about storage space? Any administrator will tell you that hard disks, unfortunately, do not grow on trees.

Users tend to fill their accounts with lots of files and programs without regard to how much hard disk space is available. Thus, one user can take up enough space to accommodate two users. This is not fair, and certainly some control is required here. This is where hard disk quota comes in handy.

Quota is a means of controlling how much hard disk space is available for a user. Using quota you can, for example, limit users to only 10 MB of hard disk space. If they attempt to exceed that, the system will not allow them to. This way you can be sure that no one is abusing the system resources. Quota is not new technology at all—it has existed since the day Unix surfaced—and it is an important tool for user control.

Preparing to Use Quota Support Before you use quota, you need to prepare your SuSE Linux system. Quota support is composed of two parts: a kernel and a set of software tools. You need to have both of them to use quota.

Reconfiguring Your Kernel   To use quota on Linux, your kernel must be configured to include quota support. This usually requires a kernel compilation. We say usually because if you have not changed anything in the kernel that has been installed by SuSE Linux, it already has support for quota built in. And in that case, you can simply skip this section and move on. But if you have changed your kernel in any way, you might have turned off support for quota. In that case, you will need to recompile your kernel after configuring it to include quota support. Detailed instructions on how to build the kernel can be found in Chapter 8, "Installing a New Kernel." To recompile your kernel to include quota support, just follow these quick steps:

1. First, log in as root.

2. Change your current path to /usr/src/linux:
   ```
   #cd /usr/src/linux
   ```

3. To configure your kernel, run the kernel's configuration module by typing the following:
   ```
   #make menuconfig
   ```

4. A menu driven dialog pops up. Navigate to Filesystems using the arrow keys and press Enter.

5. A new dialog pops up. The very first option in that dialog is Quota Support. If that option does not have an asterisk next to it, press the space bar to mark it to be included in the kernel. An asterisk denotes that this feature is to be built in the kernel. If you find that it is already marked, you already have support for quota in your kernel and you do not need to be doing all this. In that case, use Esc to quit your way out of the kernel configuration dialog and skip to the next section.

6. Now that you have marked quota to be included in the kernel, use the Esc key to quit the kernel configuration module. It will prompt you to save the new settings; choose Yes.

7. You have configured the kernel; now you need to compile it. To compile the kernel, type the following commands in this order:
   ```
   # make dep
   # make clean
   # make bzlilo
   ```

8. Each step will take some time to finish executing. You will see a lot of text scrolling by, which is normal. After all the steps are complete, you need to reboot for the changes to take effect.

That's it. You should now have support for quota in your kernel. If you encounter any problems with the previous steps, read Chapter 8 for complete detailed information concerning compiling a new kernel.

Installing the Software   Now you need to make sure that you have the required software to use quota. To install the software, use YaST to install the package called `quota` from the series AP1. To install it, follow these steps:

1. Log in as root.
2. Make sure that your SuSE installation CD is inserted in the CD-ROM drive.
3. Run YaST and choose Install.
4. A new menu loads. Choose Change/Create Configuration.
5. Choose series AP.
6. Look for a package called `quota`.
7. If you have an `i` next to it, you're fine. If not, then press the space bar to mark the package for installation.
8. Press F10 to exit.
9. Press Start Installation.
10. YaST will start to install the package for you.
11. When done, just exit from YaST and you're done.

Modifying Your System to Run Quota Support   The next step is telling SuSE Linux which filesystems to monitor for quota. Quota only works on the second extended filesystem (ext2). This is the filesystem that is used by Linux by default. To mark a filesystem for monitoring by quota, you need to edit `/etc/fstab`.

`/etc/fstab` is the file that contains the information about your filesystems. Open the file in any editor. It should look something like this:

```
/dev/hda7       swap                            swap        defaults    0
/dev/hda6       /                               ext2        defaults    1
/dev/hda5       /boot                           ext2        defaults    1
/dev/hdc        /cdrom                          iso9660     ro,noauto,user 0
/dev/fd0        /floppy                         auto        noauto,user 0
none            /proc                           proc        defaults    0
# End of YaST-generated fstab lines
```

Your system might show something different than this, which is ok. You can see here that you have two `ext2` filesystems—the root (/) and the boot (/boot). You are more interested in the root (/) because it is the one that contains the /home directory. You want to control the filesystem that has your users' homes. To enable quota support on a filesystem, add the option `usrquota` to the fourth field, and to enable group quota, add the option `grpquota`. For example:

```
/dev/hda7       swap        swap        defaults                        0
/dev/hda6       /           ext2        defaults,usrquota,grpquota      1
/dev/hda5       /boot       ext2        defaults                        1
/dev/hdc        /cdrom      iso9660     ro,noauto,user                  0
/dev/fd0        /floppy     auto        noauto,user                     0
```

```
none              /proc          proc          defaults                0
# End of YaST-generated fstab lines
```

You have now enabled both user and group quota on the / filesystem.

Creating Record Files   For each filesystem for which you are going to use quota support, you need to create record files on its root.

Using the preceding example, you need to create those files on /. You will need to create a file called quota.user (for user quota) and another called quota.group (for group quota). To create those files, use the touch command:

```
# touch /quota.user
# touch /quota.group
```

You have to make those files read/write to user root only:

```
# chmod 600 /quota.user
# chmod 600 /quota.group
```

If your /home is a partition of its own, and you want to set quota on it, you will create those files under /home. Now it's time to reboot for all these changes to take effect.

Assigning Quota for Users   To start assigning quota for users, use the edquota command. Before starting to use this command, you might want to set your $EDITOR variable to an editor of your choice, for example pico. This is a good idea because the default editor is vi, which is hard to use for most people. Enter the following:

```
# export EDITOR=pico
```

Say you want to set the quota for user John. You run edquota like this:

```
# edquota -u john
```

This will open the editor with the information regarding John's quota:

```
Quotas for user john:
/dev/hda6: blocks in use: 1325, limits (soft = 5000, hard = 6500)
        inodes in use: 156, limits (soft = 1000, hard = 1500)
```

Using quota you can limit the space used by a user, which is the blocks, and the number of files the user can own, which is the inodes. This particular user has used 1325 KB of space and is allowed a soft limit of 5000 KB and a hard limit of 5000 KB. As for the number of files, he has 156 files, with a soft limit of 1,000 and a hard limit of 1,500.

When setting the quota for a user, you can set both a hard limit and a soft limit. If the user exceeds the soft limit, she will be warned by the system, and if she attempts to exceed the hard limit, the system will not allow her.

To set the quota for John, simply edit the numbers to your desire, save, and exit. That's it, it's done.

Assigning Quota for Multiple Users   You learned how to set the quota for one user, but are you going to do this for every user on the system? That's not very practical. You can automate this by using a script. All you have to do is set the quota for one user and have the system copy the settings to all other users. To do that, you enter the following command:

```
# edquota -p john `awk -F: '$3 > 499 {print $1}' /etc/passwd`
```

This command duplicates the setting for the user John to all the users in the system whose ID is greater than 99. On most systems, group users get IDs starting from 500 and up, but check your system. The `awk` command reads those usernames from the password file `/etc/passwd`. That's it; you have set the quota for all your users.

Assigning Quota for Groups   To set the quota for a group, you use the same procedure as for a single user. If you want to set the quota for the group `students`, set `$EDITOR` to your favorite editor (if you haven't already done so):

```
# export EDITOR=pico
# edquota -g students
```

pico will open with the relevant information for the group `students`:

```
Quotas for group games:
/dev/hda6: blocks in use: 6325, limits (soft = 18000, hard = 30000)
           inodes in use: 2114, limits (soft = 5000, hard = 7000)
```

Edit the values for the limits, save, and exit.

Part

II

Ch

4

Setting the Grace Period   You have seen that you can have two limits, the soft limit and hard limit. We said that when the user exceeds the soft limit, the system warns him. But what happens if the user continually exceeds the limit? That's the grace period. Here you set a time for which the system allows the users to exceed the soft limit before enforcing it. This can be set in seconds, minutes, hours, or days.

To set the grace period, use the `edquota` command:

```
# edquota -t
Time units may be: days, hours, minutes, or seconds
  Grace period before enforcing soft limits for users:
  /dev/hda6: block grace period: 7 days, file grace period: 7 days
```

In this example, we have set the grace period at seven days for both the files and blocks soft limits. You can set it to any value you want.

Updating Your Settings   Now that you have changed so much in your quota settings, you need to update the quota system. Simply run the command `quotacheck -a`.

This command runs automatically at startup. However, if you do not want to reboot the system for changes to take effect, simply run this command manually or set it to run on a regular basis every week using `cron`.

Viewing the Status of Your Quota   To check the current state of your system's quota, you can run the command repquota. This command will print out information about all the users on your system and how they are using their storage limits. You can run the command to report on either one filesystem or all the filesystems that have quota support.

The following will report on the / filesystem only:

```
# repquota -u /          This is for user quota.
# repquota -g /          This is for group quota.
```

The following will report on all the filesystems that have quota support:

```
# repquota -ua           This is for user quota.
# repquota -ga           This is for group quota.
```

For more information, you can view the man pages for all of these commands.

Turning Quota On and Off   If you want to turn quota support off or on, run the quota script in /etc/rc.d. This is very simple.

To stop quota support, enter the following:

```
# cd /etc/rc.d
# ./quota stop
```

To start quota support, enter the following:

```
# cd /etc/rc.d
# ./quota start
```

Troubleshooting

I added a user but I can't seem to log in using that user's account, but it works when I reboot—why?

This happens with the evaluation version of SuSE 6.2. YaST does not restart the nscd program after it adds a user. All you have to do is restart it manually:

```
# cd /etc/rc.d
# ./nscd restart
```

This will solve the problem, and you won't need to reboot. Update your YaST for the fixed version.

I added a new group, but the system cannot use it unless I reboot.

Again, this is the exact same problem as the previous one. The same solution will work here, too.

Quota does not work!

Well, are you sure your kernel is compiled with quota support? Check for that and recompile if necessary. Do you have all the tools for quota? If not, install the quota RPM from your AP series on your SuSE CD. Did you create the `quota.user` and `quota.group` files? Are these files readable and writeable by root only? Did you mark the filesystem on which you want to use quota? Is quota support on? If not, check the previous section on starting and stopping quota support. ●

Part

II

Ch

4

Managing Filesystems

Understanding Filesystems

The filesystem is one of the most important components of an operating system. The filesystem handles how you use your storage media. All day long you open files, save files, delete files, and so on, and you never really think about how it happens. Every operation you perform on files goes through the filesystem.

The filesystem is a layer of logical organization between you and the hardware on which you are storing your data. Take a hard drive, for example—when you first buy it, it is completely useless to you unless you format it in some way. Before you can use that hard drive, your operating system must build a filesystem on it. The filesystem organizes how your data will be placed on the drive. It enables you to use filenames to name your files and directories to organize them. Just imagine if you could not use directories; all your files would be in one place with absolutely no organization whatsoever. Without a filesystem, working with computers would be almost impossible.

The filesystem is a part of the operating system. All requests from applications and the user to access files use the filesystem portion of the operating system. Trying to access the actual media directly instead would prove to be quite a complex process.

Currently a lot of different filesystems exist. Each operating system tends to come up with its own filesystem. Microsoft uses filesystems based on FAT (File Allocation Table) technology as well as NTFS, which is used by Windows NT/2000. The Amiga uses FFS (Fast Filesystem); OS/2 uses HPFS (High Performance Filesystem); Linux uses ext2 (Second Extended Filesystem); and so on. Whereas these are operating system–specific filesystems, media-specific filesystems also exist. CD-ROMs are one example of media-specific filesystems. They use a filesystem called ISO9660.

Filesystems can do the same basic job of storing files, but they differ in other features. Some filesystems such as MS FAT are very simple—they store files and directories. The early versions of FAT were unable to store more than 11 characters for a filename. Other filesystems have more powerful features such as long filenames and file permissions for security. Some filesystems deal very well with system crashes, whereas others have a tendency of getting corrupted.

Different operating systems cannot read each other's filesystems. This is one reason why CD-ROMs use their own filesystem; this way you can read them on different operating systems. Linux is extremely flexible when it comes to filesystems because it can read all the previous filesystems and more.

Linux initially used the same filesystem used by Minix (a small Unix clone operating system). But Linux soon needed a more powerful filesystem, so the extended filesystem (ext) was born. Shortly after that it was upgraded to the second extended filesystem (ext2), which is expected to be followed by a newer version soon.

Mounting and Unmounting Filesystems

In Linux and Unix, generally the filesystem is the mother of all components. The whole philosophy of the operating system is built around the filesystem. Almost everything is a file in Linux. All devices are files on the filesystem, and all drives are directories on the filesystem. You even can create network sockets on the filesystem.

When you use Microsoft operating systems, you'll notice that your drives are labeled A:, B:, C:, and so on. In Linux this is not the case at all. Your drives become part of the filesystem when you use them. For example, to use a floppy disk in the A: drive, you instruct the operating system to make the contents of that disk available under /floppy. This way the disk appears as just another directory on your system. The same concept applies to other partitions on the same hard drive or on another drive altogether. After you are finished using those drives, you have to instruct the operating system to release them from the filesystem.

In order to access the files on a different drive or partition, you have to issue a mount command. The command has a basic structure:

```
mount device mount-point -t filesystem
```

You have to specify at least two parameters—the device you want to use and the mount point. The mount point is the directory under which you want the contents of that device to appear. This can be any directory that you create. Common practice is to use /mnt/drive (for example, /mnt/floppy for the floppy disk). There are no restrictions on the directory you want to use, it's up to you to use whichever directory you want as long as it is empty.

The device option is easy to figure out. All the devices available on your system have a corresponding filename under the directory /dev. The following are the most common ones:

Physical Drive	Linux /dev File
Floppy Drive A:	/dev/fd0
Floppy Drive B:	/dev/fd1
Drive on IDE 1 Connector 0 (Usually Drive C:)	/dev/hda
Drive on IDE 1 Connector 1 (Usually Drive D:)	/dev/hdb
Drive on IDE 2 Connector 0 (Usually Drive E:)	/dev/hdc
Drive on IDE 2 Connector 1 (Usually Drive F:)	/dev/hdd
SCSI Drive 1	/dev/sda
SCSI Drive 2	/dev/sdb

The last parameter, which is the filesystem parameter, might be a bit confusing to most people. Like we said before, Linux can read a lot of filesystems. When Linux is about to mount a disk, you should tell it what filesystem exists on that disk so that it can translate it to its own filesystem (ext2). This way all the files on the disk get treated as if they were a true part of your local filesystem. You might not always need to give the name of the parameter to mount because it attempts to correctly guess it, but if it doesn't, you should provide it.

As you can see, it's pretty easy and organized. As an example, to mount a floppy disk in drive A, enter the following command:

```
# mount /dev/fd0 /mnt/floppy -t vfat
```

This instructs the operating system to mount the disk in drive a: (/dev/fd0) under the directory /mnt/floppy using Windows VFAT as the filesystem (use Virtual FAT to ensure that long filenames display correctly). To see the contents of the disk, go to /mnt/floppy.

If you are going to mount a CD-ROM, it's the same process as mounting the floppy disk. All you need to know is where on your IDE your CD-ROM is connected. You can do this by either physically looking at your hardware or observing the kernel's boot messages. When the kernel boots up, it displays the hardware it found and the corresponding /dev/ file for it. If you missed it when the kernel was booting, type dmesg to see it again. The line you are looking for will look something like this:

```
hda: WDC AC26400B, ATA DISK drive
hdb: Maxtor 91303D6, ATA DISK drive
hdc: TOSHIBA DVD-ROM SD-M1212, ATAPI CDROM drive
hdd: ZIPCD 4x650, ATAPI CDROM drive
```

This system has two CD-ROM drives—a Toshiba DVD-ROM, which is /dev/hdc, and a ZIPCD 4x650 at /dev/hdd. To mount either of them, use its device name:

```
# mount /dev/hdd /mnt/
```

This mounts the CD in the ZIPCD drive under /mnt. Notice how you did not use the -t option. This is because mount will correctly guess that the filesystem is iso9660.

When you want to mount other partitions or hard drives you have to specify the partition number you want to mount. For example, if your hard drive has an MS Windows partition on it, you have to specify where it is when you mount it. To specify the partition you want to mount, insert its number after the device. For example, the first partition on the first drive would be /dev/hda1, the second one would be /dev/hda2, and so on. If you are not sure on which partition your MS Windows is installed, you can always use the command fdisk to see the partition table. Follow these steps:

1. Run fdisk as root, and specify the drive you want to see:
   ```
   # fdisk /dev/hda
   ```

2. fdisk loads up and presents you with a command prompt. Enter p to display the partition table:
   ```
   Command (m for help): p
   ```

3. fdisk will display all the partitions found on that drive:
   ```
   Disk /dev/hda: 255 heads, 63 sectors, 784 cylinders
   Units = cylinders of 16065 * 512 bytes
      Device Boot    Start     End   Blocks   Id  System
   /dev/hda1   *         1     530  4257193+  83  Linux native
   /dev/hda2           531     547   136552+  82  Linux swap
   /dev/hda3   *       548     775  1831410   c   Win95 FAT32
   ```

4. Look for a partition that has `Win95` in the system field.

5. `/dev/hda3` has `Win95 FAT32` in the system field.

6. Enter `q` to quit `fdisk`.

Now you know that MS Windows is installed on `/dev/hda3`. To mount it, enter the following:

```
# mount /dev/hda3 /mnt/ -t vfat
```

Again, all the contents of that partition will be displayed under `/mnt`.

Now you know how to mount another filesystem, but how do you unmount it? It's easy; you use the `umount` command as follows:

```
# umount /mnt
```

The `umount` command takes either the name of the device or the mount point as a parameter. You have to issue this command before you attempt to remove the medium from the mounted drive. In most cases, you won't even be able to remove the medium unless you unmount it (the CD-ROM is such an example). The `umount` command ensures that all changes to the files on the mounted medium have been saved.

Understanding /etc/fstab

Mounting and unmounting filesystems can become quite tedious, especially if you do it on frequently used drives or partitions. Linux has a special configuration file for mounting filesystems, `/etc/fstab`. `fstab` stands for Filesystem Table, which is the file that maintains the most common mount configurations on the system. To further understand this file, let's look at a sample `/etc/fstab` file:

```
/dev/hda1      /boot    ext2     defaults 1
/dev/hda2      swap     swap     defaults 0
/dev/hda3      /        ext2     defaults 1
proc    /proc  proc     defaults 0
```

This file is read by several programs on the system that need to know about the mount points of the various filesystems. When the system boots up, it identifies the root partition of the system from this file, in this case `/dev/hda3`. Let's look at the format of this file.

This file defines each partition or drive in one single line. The fields are separated using whitespaces. The first field is the device field, which is where you put the name of the device that you want to mount. For example, for a CD-ROM the first field would be `/dev/cdrom`.

The second field is the mount point for that device. This is where you want the device to be mounted on your local filesystem. So for a CD-ROM, the second field would be `/cdrom`.

The third field is the filesystem type with which you want to mount this device. You can use any of the types available to the `mount` command: `minix`, `ext`, `ext2`, `xiafs`, `msdos`, `vfat`, `hpfs`, `iso9660`, `nfs`, `swap`, and `auto`. Using `auto` will tell `mount` to attempt to automatically figure out the filesystem type. For a CD-ROM, the third field would be `iso9660`. Auto will work as well, but there is no need to let `mount` guess when we know what it is.

The fourth field is the options you want to pass to the `mount` command. Again, you can use anything that `mount` accepts. For a detailed list of these options, check `man mount`. The following are the most common options:

- `defaults`—The default options are: `rw`, `suid`, `dev`, `exec`, `auto`, `nouser`, and `async`.
- `auto`—Mount this filesystem automatically on system boot up.
- `noauto`—Do not automatically mount this filesystem on boot up.
- `noexec`—Do not allow execution of binaries.
- `exec`—Allow the execution of binaries from this filesystem.
- `user`—Allow a normal user to mount this filesystem at will.
- `nouser`—Do not allow a user to mount this filesystem.
- `ro`—Mount the filesystem as read only.
- `rw`—Mount the filesystem as read/write.

In the case of the CD-ROM, you would probably want a normal user to mount it and execute binaries from it. So, the options are `user`, `exec`, and `noauto`. Note that you should use the `noauto` option if you don't want the system to attempt to mount the CD-ROM drive on boot up.

The fifth field is specific to the `dump` command. This command backs up a second extended filesystem. If you want to use this command, you should enter a 1 in this field; otherwise, enter a 0. Note that the filesystem should be of type ext2 for `dump` to be used. In the case of the CD-ROM, you would enter a 0.

The sixth and final field is read by the `fsck` command. This command checks the integrity of the filesystem. If you enter a 1 in this field, `fsck` understands that it should check this filesystem for errors when necessary; if you enter a 0, it won't. For ext2 filesystems, and especially the root filesystem, enter a 1. For the CD-ROM, enter a 0.

So, now you understand the format of `/etc/fstab`. And you learned how to add a new entry for your CD-ROM. The entry in its final form looks like this:

```
/dev/cdrom    /cdrom    iso9660    user,noauto,exec 0
```

Now any user easily can mount the CD-ROM by typing one of the following:

```
$mount /dev/cdrom
```

```
$mount /cdrom
```

The `mount` command will read the `fstab` file and understand what to do automatically. Very convenient, isn't it?

CAUTION

Please note that /etc/fstab is used by several programs on your system. This means that it has to be correct in format. You should make sure that you don't change the permissions of this file. This file should be readable by everyone on the system, but only writeable by root. YaST eventually will warn you if the file's permissions are incorrect.

Creating and Formatting Filesystems

It is inevitable that at some point you will need to create or format a filesystem. This might be because you get a new hard drive or free up another partition due to limited space. To be able to use that new space, you will have to format it. You should format this new space to use the second extended filesystem because this is the default filesystem used by Linux.

The method you need to follow to format a new partition or drive depends on what was on that space before. In most cases, this will be a new hard drive that is blank. In other cases, it could be a hard drive or partition that has another operating system installed on it. In the first case, you will need to partition the new drive. In the second case, you will need to modify the partitioning of the drive. Let's see how you can do both.

Formatting a New Drive or Partition

Suppose you are planning to add more space to your SuSE Linux system by throwing in an extra hard drive or partition. If it's a new hard drive, the first thing you want to do is create a new partition table on it.

To create a new partition table for your new hard drive, you will use YaST. This is a pretty safe procedure because YaST does not apply any change unless you confirm it. To create your new partition table, follow these steps:

1. Run YaST.
2. Navigate to Adjustment of Installation, Configure Hard Disk Partitions. Press Enter.
3. YaST will ask you to select the hard drive that you want to partition. Select your new hard drive.
4. Select Partitioning and press Enter.
5. YaST displays your new hard drive. It should read No Partitions Available because this is a new hard drive.
6. You want to create one or more partitions on this drive, so press F5.
7. YaST asks you whether you want a Primary Partition or an Extended Partition. Choose Primary Partition.

Part
II

Ch
5

8. Now YaST displays all the possible primary partition names that you can have on the drive. Pick the one you want—we recommend that you pick the first one. It should be something like /dev/hdb1.

9. Now it's time to tell YaST how much space this partition should take up. By default, YaST takes all the available space on the drive. You can accept that or tell it the size by writing it in the End of partition field. To specify the size, enter a + before it. For example, 400 MB would be entered as +400M. Press Continue when you are done.

10. YaST shows your new partition table with the newly added partition.

11. Be sure that the new partition is of type Linux Native. You can change it by pressing F3.

12. You can repeat the same process to add more partitions.

13. When you are done, press Continue to have the changes take effect. If you press Abort, you will lose all the changes.

These were the steps for creating a new partition table altogether. If you are simply going to add a new partition that already exists for another operating system, you can use almost the same procedure. All you have to do is follow the same steps and when YaST displays your partition table, find the partition you want to use and change its type to Linux Native, or if you have free unallocated space, create a new partition.

Now that you have the partition all ready to use, you have to format it. This is the easy part. You will use the mkfs (make filesystem) command. To create a second extended filesystem on your new partition—for example, /dev/hdb1—run the command like this:

```
# mkfs -t ext2 /dev/hdb1
```

mkfs takes two parameters, the filesystem type and the partition to format. This will take a short while, and when it is done, your new partition will be ready for use. You now can update your /etc/fstab file and add a new entry for this partition in it.

Creating a New Swap Partition

To create a new swap partition, you use the exact same procedure as the previous one. You might need to create a new swap partition if your system needs more virtual memory. To do that, simply repeat the previous steps and pick Linux Swap as the partition type. When you format the new partition, use the following command:

```
# mkswap /dev/hda2
```

In your /etc/fstab add a new entry for the new swap partition like this:

```
/dev/hda2        swap     swap     defaults 0
```

Be sure that you put the correct device in the entry. To activate the swap partition immediately, use this command:

```
# swapon /dev/hda2
```

That's all. The swap partition will be activated on every boot up automatically.

Checking Your Filesystem

To maintain your filesystem at top performance, you should check it periodically for errors. Fortunately, the system does that for you after a fixed amount of reboots and when the system shuts down incorrectly. But you might need to check your filesystem manually. How you do so depends on the filesystem you want to check. Please note that you can check only ext2 type partitions. Other types should be checked using their respective operating systems.

To check a partition, you first should unmount it. If this partition is not your root partition, this will be easy. Just follow these steps:

1. Unmount the partition with the umount command.
2. Run the fsck command:
   ```
   #fsck /dev/device
   ```
3. The command will check the filesystem on this device and report any errors found. You then can choose to have it fix them or not.
4. When finished, simply mount the partition again and you're done.

To check your root partition, you have to do a little more than this. Follow these steps:

1. Switch to single-user mode:
   ```
   # telinit S
   ```
2. Remount the root filesystem as read-only:
   ```
   # mount -n -o remount,ro /
   ```
3. Check the filesystem using the fsck command:
   ```
   # fsck /
   ```
4. When finished, remount the filesystem as read/write:
   ```
   # mount -n -o remount,rw /
   ```
5. Switch the system to normal mode:
   ```
   # telinit 3
   ```
6. You're done!

When checking partitions, be sure you do not check a filesystem that is mounted read/write. If you can't unmount it then remount it as read/write and then check it. If your system is used by a lot of people, it would be a good idea to switch it to single-user mode before you check the filesystems.

Part
II

Ch
5

Understanding the Network Filesystem

So far you have learned how to mount drives that are connected to your machine. Mounting, however, can do a lot more than that. You can even mount drives that exist on remote machines. This is accomplished using the Network Filesystem (NFS). NFS enables you to give others the right to mount your filesystem on their machines across a network.

You might have already used NFS when you installed SuSE Linux. When you install SuSE, you have the option of installing via NFS. This enables you to install from another machine on the network that has a CD-ROM to a machine that does not. The whole process uses NFS to mount the other machine's CD-ROM on your local filesystem and treat it as a part of your machine. All of this happens transparently to you. You don't do anything different from what you would do if you had the CD-ROM on your local machine.

Your machine can be set up to be an NFS client, an NFS server, or both. If you are planning to only mount remote filesystems then you will be interested in being an NFS client only. If you want to allow people to mount your filesystem remotely, you will need to set up your machine as an NFS server.

Preparing to Use NFS

Before you can start using NFS, you have to configure SuSE Linux for NFS. There are two things you have to configure, the kernel and YaST.

The first thing you want to configure is your kernel. You need to turn on NFS support in the kernel. If you have not modified the kernel that was installed by SuSE, you don't have to worry about this step at all—skip to the next step.

Now you will configure the kernel for NFS. If you are not sure about how to do this, read Chapter 8, "Installing a New Kernel," for more information on the subject. The parameter you want to enable in the kernel is in Filesystems, Network File Systems, NFS Filesystem Support. You can install it either built in or as a module. If you will not be using NFS a lot, we recommend installing it as a module; otherwise, install it built in.

Now your system is configured as an NFS client. This means you can mount remote filesystems. If you are planning to use your own system as an NFS server, you have to configure it to do so using YaST. Follow these steps:

1. Run YaST as root.

2. Navigate to System Administration, Network Configuration, Configure Network Services.

3. YaST will ask you a series of questions. The first one is whether you want to start inetd at boot time. Choose Yes or No. If you want people to be able to telnet or FTP to your machine choose Yes. (This question is not really related to what you are trying to do now, so don't worry about it.)

4. The second question is a part of what you want. Should `portmap` be started at boot time? Choose Yes here because the NFS server needs this to function.

5. The third question is should your computer be started as an NFS server? The obvious answer here is Yes. This will allow people to mount your filesystem remotely.

6. The last question asks you what you want to have posted in the `from` line of your new system. Your hostname should be good enough here. Again, this has nothing to do with NFS so don't worry about it.

7. That's it. You're all set now to use NFS.

Now that you know how to set up your machine to be both an NSF client and server, it's time to see how to actually use NFS.

Using NFS (Client-Side)

Using NFS as a client is simple. It is exactly the same idea as mounting local drives. In order to mount a remote filesystem you need to know the name or IP of the NFS server and the name of the directory you want to mount.

The IP of the machine can be substituted with its name on the network. Ask your network administrator for that information if you don't know it. You also should know the name of the directory that you are going to mount. But if you don't, you can use the `showmount` command to obtain a list of the available directories on the server. To do that, run `showmount` with the name or IP of the server as a parameter:

```
# showmount -e hostname
```

This will give you a list of all the directories available for remote mounting on this server.

To actually mount a remote directory on your local machine, you issue a `mount` command. For example, if you are trying to mount a directory called `/files` on a machine with the IP 192.168.0.25 under `/mnt` locally, the command would look like this:

```
# mount 192.168.0.25:/files /mnt
```

 TIP

A good mount option to use is the `hard,intr` option. This helps in NFS server crashes. Say you are mounting a remote directory, and a program is using a file from that directory. Suddenly, the NFS server on the remote machine crashes, which will cause your program to fail. However, if you supply the mount option with `hard,intr`, the program will hang for a while until the NFS server is back up and running; then it will continue to do what it was doing. So, the `mount` command would be as follows:

```
# mount 192.168.0.25:/files /mnt -o hard,intr
```

That's it. Pretty simple, isn't it? And of course, to unmount it, just issue an `umount` command:

```
# umount /mnt
```

Using NFS (Server-Side)

Using your own machine as an NFS server is pretty easy. First, you have to make sure that you set it up to do so. If not, refer to the "Preparing to Use NFS" section for instructions on how to do so.

After you have NFS up and running, all you need to do to allow people to remotely mount directories on your machine is edit a file called /etc/exports. This file is read by the NFS server when it starts and tells the server which directories to export to remote users.

The format of the file is very simple. For example, if you want people to be able to remotely mount a directory called /files, you would enter the following line in /etc/exports:

```
/files (ro)
```

That's all. The (ro) means they can only mount it read only. If you want them to be able to write to it, you can replace it with read/write ((rw)):

```
/files (rw)
```

As you can see, this is pretty much an open policy. Anyone can simply mount that directory. But what if you want to restrict things a little bit? What if you want only people coming from the machine named friends.network.org to be able to mount that directory? No problem, just specify it in your command:

```
/files friends.network.org (ro)
```

There, anyone not from friends.network.org will not be allowed to mount this directory. You also can replace the name with the IP of the machine. You can even use wildcards or the question mark (?) to allow groups of machines the right to mount the directory. For example, to allow everyone from network.org to have access to that directory, use this command:

```
/files *.network.org (ro)
```

For every directory you want to export to others, insert a similar line for it in /etc/exports. But, after you change that file, you have to tell the NFS server that you did so. To do this, type the following command:

```
# /sbin/init.d/nfsserver reload
```

This command will instruct the running NFS server to re-read the /etc/exports file.

Troubleshooting

I tried to mount a device but mount failed with an error message.

Well, are you sure that you specified the partition you want to mount? If you are trying to mount drive /dev/hda, you can't just say mount /dev/hda .... because this does not work on hard drives. You have to specify the partition you want to mount. So, the command would be something like mount /dev/hda2 .... You can run fdisk /dev/hda to view the partitions that exist on this drive.

I followed your solution to the previous problem, but I still get an error message.

This depends on the message; if it says something about being unable to find super block, the device is not formatted properly. If it is complaining about the filesystem type, you have entered a wrong type. Try using -t auto as your option if you are not sure of the filesystem that is on that device. Finally, the device could be already mounted, or the mount point could be already mounted by another device.

I cannot unmount a device.

mount does not unmount a device if any program is using it. So, if you have a shell open for any other program that is working inside the mount point, close it. Then try to unmount it, which should work. You can find out the PID of the processes that are using the filesystem by using the lsof command. For example,

```
#lsof /home
```

The command will show you a list of all the processes currently using /home. You then can either shut them down or kill them using the kill command. To kill a process, enter the following:

```
# kill process_pid
```

process_pid is the PID number of the process; you can get that from the lsof listing.

My CD-ROM won't eject. What happened?

There is nothing wrong with your CD-ROM. Linux locks the CD-ROM drive when you mount it. The eject button is totally useless unless you unmount the CD-ROM.

I can't mount a network filesystem.

Make sure that you configured your system correctly and that your machine is allowed to mount the remote network filesystem. Check the other machine's /etc/exports file.

People can't mount my network shares.

Again, check your configuration. Make sure you turned on NFS support in YaST. And check your /etc/exports file. If you changed it, make sure you notify the NFS daemons using the exportfs script. ●

Part
II
Ch
5

Backing Up the System

In this chapter

Backup, Backup, Backup

This chapter is based on the famous saying "Better safe than sorry!" Backing up is one of the most important operations that system administrators and users will perform. If SuSE Linux is used as a server, the system administrator is in charge of making sure that his users do not lose data due to system failure. *Data* in this context is defined as any service the SuSE Linux server offers. This includes files on FTP, documents in the users' home directories, users' special settings, and email. If SuSE Linux is run as a server, the backup operation should be automated to be done in specific periods to ensure that the backup is always up to date.

If you are running SuSE Linux as a desktop, you also should consider performing backups because it's always a good idea to have a backup of the system settings. In most cases, having a good backup can restore your system to the way it was in case a system failure occurs.

Software Requirements

This chapter discusses three important packages widely used as backup tools.

Package Requirements:

Series a:

- tar
- cpio
- YaST

What You Should Back Up

It is essential that you know what you need to back up before you start the actual backup process. To know what you should back up, you first must consider what SuSE Linux is used for. SuSE Linux was designed to fulfill both the desktop as well as the server environments. In both cases, you should back up the system configuration files so that you can restore the system easily. The most important configuration files for the system reside in the /etc directory.

TIP Even if you are not running SuSE Linux in a mission-critical environment, you should always have backups of the /etc directory. This directory contains the key configurations you made to the system. You can spare yourself reconfiguring the systemwide settings by having a backup of this directory.

Table 6.1 contains the default configuration directories and corresponding package that uses this configuration on SuSE Linux.

Table 6.1   Important System Directories

Directory	Description
/etc/	The systemwide configuration directory. It contains all the important settings. This directory is a must-have when backing up.
/opt/kde/share/config	The default configurations for KDE. The per-user .kde directory is more important than this one.
~/.kde	The per-user .kde configuration directory. If you use KDE as your main desktop environment, you should back up this directory to save your settings.
~/.gnome	The per-user GNOME configuration directory. If your main desktop environment is GNOME, you should back up this directory.
/opt/www	You should back up this directory if your SuSE Linux is a Web server.
/usr/src/linux/.config	This file contains your SuSE Linux kernel configuration. You should back up this file only if you have applied special settings to your kernel and recompiled it. It will save you a lot of time reading the kernel options help.
/usr/share/	Many packages have their configuration files in this directory. This is where you should look for the packages with settings that need to be backed up.
/usr/X11/share	Some X-related packages keep their configuration files in this directory.
/usr/X11/lib/X11 /app-defaults	Default interface settings for many X applications are kept in this directory.
/usr/local/etc	Although the default SuSE Linux installation does not use this directory to keep configuration settings, programs specific to this server might be installed in /usr/local and thus keep their configuration files in /usr/local/etc.

Planning a Backup Strategy

When planning a backup strategy you must consider how important your data or your users' data is to you. In fact, the efficiency of a backup can be measured by two factors:

■ **Availability of the system**—It is important that you restore the system to what it was as quickly as you can. A good system configuration backup should do this in almost no time.

■ **Reliability of the system**—Reliability means that you also can restore the data that was lost. In mission-critical servers, you should have a mirroring system that mirrors the important data files to another hard drive. You might need to make daily or weekly backups depending on how critical the data your server serves is.

As a normal home user, you should back up any important data that is unique to you. In most cases, backing up your home directory is enough unless you have installed files outside your home directory.

The Backup Drawing Board

After you have a good system configuration, you should back up the /etc and /usr/local/ etc directories. Even if you have made changes to the configuration using YaST, backing up /etc and /usr/local/etc will save you the time you would spend watching YaST prepare the packages and update the SuSE reference database files.

If your system works as a server, you should back up the files accessed by users. In most cases, backing up only the /home directory is sufficient.

 TIP Even if you are a lucky person, you should have more than one backup of a multiuser system. Do not overwrite the old backup with a newer one unless you have another copy of the backup. Imagine that a system failure occurs while you are performing the backup. You might end up losing your backup and your system. Better safe than sorry!

Back Up Using YaST

YaST is an excellent choice for people who want to restore a full system with little command-line use. YaST offers a full backup system with excellent reliability and can do the following for you:

■ Check which packages you have on the system. If you have made changes to any package, the changes will be saved.

■ Check the changes you have made to the system. Only the files you have changed will be backed up. The default settings will be restored from the original setup.

■ Check whether you have added new software to the system. New software will be added to the backup.

■ Optionally, it can check whether you have modified or added any files to the system. Those files will be added to the backup, too.

■ It offers the capability to include directories that you want to add to the backup or exclude directories you do not want added to the backup.

■ After the search operation is finished, you can choose not to back up some files through a list YaST prepares of the files it checked and found modified or added.

Invoking the YaST Backup Module

To start the YaST backup module, you must log in as root and start YaST. Choose System Administration, Create Backups. Alternatively, you can run YaST using the backup mask, which will start YaST in the backup mode immediately. Use the following command to start YaST in backup mode:

```
bash#yast --mask backup
```

Selecting Directories

At the main backup screen YaST enables you to choose which directories you want YaST to check for creating an optimal backup (see Figure 6.1).

FIGURE 6.1

You can optimize the backup operation YaST performs by selecting on the right side of the screen the directories YaST should look in. You also can specify that YaST not check mounted devices of the types listed in the left side of the screen.

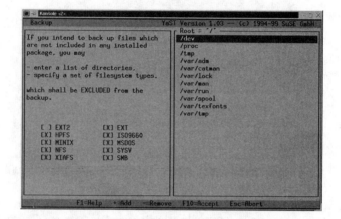

In some cases, you might have directories that are mount points to other filesystems. For example, say you are mounting a CD-ROM or Windows share. If you do not want YaST to back up the contents of this mount point, you would check the boxes that correspond to the filesystem you do not want YaST to check or include in the backup.

The directory listing on the right side of the screen contains the directories YaST will check for modifications. You can add a directory by pressing the plus (+) key. You wil be prompted to enter a path to the directory you want YaST to include in the scan for modifications operation. To remove a directory from the list, highlight it by moving the cursor and pressing the minus (-) key.

Part

II

Ch

6

N O T E If you do not optimize the directory listing in which YaST will scan for changes, the search time for changes will be dramatically high. Be sure that the paths YaST will look in are really things you want to back up.

There is no point in backing up the following directories: /tmp, /dev, and /proc. Unless you know what you're doing, do not back them up. ■

After you have finished the preparation for the backup, press F10 to start the search.

YaST will start collecting the information about the packages installed on the system. If you have installed a large number of packages, the operation can take a few minutes. Throughout the package search operation, YaST will notify you with the number of files that have been changed in the packages and the total size of the changes if you select to back up the modified files.

After YaST has searched through the default package changes, it will ask you whether you want to check for new files that have been added to the system (see Figure 6.2). If you want to, answer Yes; otherwise, to make a backup of only the system changes, answer No.

FIGURE 6.2
After YaST finishes searching through the changes you made to the default packages, it asks you whether you want to search for new files you added to the system. If you want to back up only the system settings you made, answer No; otherwise, answer Yes.

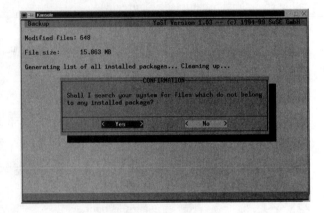

According to your answer to the previous question, YaST will either search your system for additional files and move on to the file selection window, or move directly to the file selection screen.

In the file selection screen, you can have YaST back up the files marked with X and ignore the unchecked files (see Figure 6.3). Select the files you want to back up and press F10 to move to the next step.

FIGURE 6.3
By checking an X next to the file in this list, you tell YaST to back up this file. If you do not want YaST to back up the file, clear the checkbox. All files are checked by default.

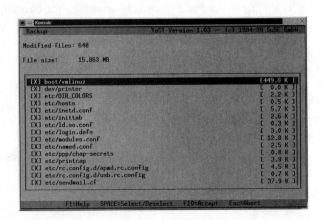

In the last step of the backup procedure, you should specify the archive name. If you choose, you also can specify the options for the archive and the file listing file path (see Figure 6.4). The following are the options for the archive:

FIGURE 6.4
You can specify archive-specific information by filling in the information required in this screen. The information you supply to YaST in this dialog will be passed to the `tar` command to generate the archive.

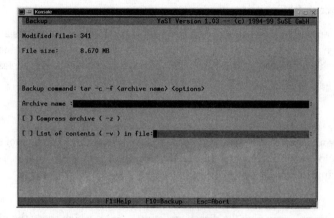

- **Archive name**—This is the name of the archive that will be created in the absolute path. Archive names usually end with a `.tar` extension, or `.tar.gz` if you choose the Compress Archive option. You can specify the archive to be saved on a tape by passing `/dev/tape/archivename.tar`, which tells YaST to make the archive on tape.

- **Compress archive**—This option tells YaST to compress the archive. You can decrease the space needed for the archive by using this option.

- **List of contents**—When checked, YaST will be verbose when adding the files to the archive.

- **List of contents**—When checked, you should enter a filename in the in file field. YaST will save a list of the filenames archived to this file.

After you have filled in the values, YaST will start backing up the files to the archive name you selected.

Restoring Files

To restore files from a tarball backup file, you should use the `tar` command. In the following example, we assume that the archive is located on `/dev/tape`. The following command restores all the files from the tape to their original location:

```
bash#tar xvf /dev/tape -C /
```

If the stored archive is a compressed archive, you should use the following command instead:

```
bash#tar xzvf /dev/tape -C /
```

If a system failure occurs in which you have to reinstall the whole system, the previous method works best. If you want to be selective when choosing files to restore out of an archive, you can learn more about `tar` in Appendix E, "Various Utilities."

Part
II

Ch
6

Using cpio to Back Up Your Files

YaST isn't the only utility you can use to perform the backup operations described in the previous section "Back Up Using YaST." SuSE Linux offers another important tool with a large degree of scalability: cpio.

cpio is famous for its ease of use and archiving capabilities. It supports archiving and extracting large numbers of archive formats. *cpio* is short for Copy In/Out, which describes the program behavior. In fact, cpio can be used to copy pass data, which is typically the same as mirroring a directory tree from one path to another.

Out Mode

When you back up your data, you need to use cpio's out mode. Think of cpio as a pipe you use to pipe your data in so that it goes out the other side as an archive. Consider the following example:

```
bash#ls |cpio -ov >backup.cpio
```

In this example, you pipe the directory listing to cpio, which reads the files, generates an archive, and redirects the output to a backup.cpio file. The -o option tells cpio to generate an archive of the listing sent to it. The -v option tells cpio to be verbose when adding files.

The way files are passed to cpio might seem odd to you, but, after you've used it a while, you will realize the power it gives you. In fact, with some knowledge of shell scripting, you can create a selective archive using cpio. Consider the following command:

```
bash#cd /home;find . -print -depth| cpio -ov > home.cpio
```

This command will back up the /home directory into home.cpio.

In Mode

To restore the data you back up using cpio, you should use cpio's in mode. The -i option tells cpio to restore the data out of the archive and in the location specified. For example, to restore the home.cpio file, enter the following command:

```
bash#cpio -idvu < home.cpio
```

The -d option tells cpio to create subdirectories when required. The -u option tells cpio to overwrite files in the directory if files with the same name exist. You should use this option with caution.

Other Backup Software

If SuSE Linux is running important databases based on advanced products such as Oracle or Informix databases, you might want to increase the security of your backups by using advanced backup packages.

One of the most famous packages SuSE recommends to use in mission-critical systems is Time Navigator by Quadratec (`http://www.quadratec-software.com`). Time Navigator is an advanced package that can be used to integrate and back up giant databases on SuSE Linux. Visit their Web site for more information on the availability of the package. ●

Part

II

Ch

6

System Upgrade

Upgrading Your Linux

SuSE Linux comes with so many packages and applications, one may never need to look elsewhere. The question here is, are you going to need to upgrade any of its components? Well, that depends on how you use your SuSE Linux. If you use it as a server for a small network or small number of users, you might never need to touch it after it's up and running. If you are using it as a server for a large network, you might need to upgrade a few packages to fix security or performance bugs, or to get new features. If you are using it on a desktop computer, then you might want to upgrade a lot of your applications as newer versions are released. The key is to only upgrade when you need to.

Precautions Prior to Package Installations

If you are running SuSE Linux as a server that handles users, then you have to be very careful when upgrading packages—both in the decision to upgrade and the actual process of upgrading. Before you decide to upgrade a package, you have to read about all the changes that this new version will bring and make sure that it does not break any existing data files. If, for example, you are upgrading your mail reader and the new version is not compatible with the old version's configuration files, then your users will be very upset when they find out that they have to reconfigure their software. But, if you have to upgrade to this version, for instance for security reasons, then at least inform your users of this upcoming change beforehand.

Another consideration is the actual upgrade process. You don't want to upgrade a package of applications when you have users connected. A user might be using that application now, and this might conflict with your upgrade process. Some applications you can upgrade with users logged on, for example, applications that are used only by root.

So, how can you make sure that you do not have users logged on while you are upgrading your packages? Unplugging the network cable is one way; but there are less physical methods of achieving the same goal. You can switch Linux to single-user mode or just turn off the network.

Turning off the network will stop any users from being able to log on the machine. To do this, simply go to /sbin/init.d/ and execute the following commands:

```
# cd /sbin/init.d/
# ./network stop
```

Now the network is down. Just make sure that you inform your users beforehand that the server will be down for a while. After you are done with your upgrades, you can bring the network back up:

```
# ./network start
```

Now that the network is back up, users can start to log on to the system again. For major system upgrades, you might want to switch Linux to single-user mode. To do this, run the following command:

```
# telinit S
```

This command will switch Linux to single-user mode. To get back to a multiuser system with the network, enter the following command:

```
# telinit 2
```

Or if you want to go back to multiuser mode with the network and xdm/kdm, enter this command:

```
# telinit 3
```

More information on telinit can be found in Chapter 9, "Configuring the System Boot Up Sequence."

Upgrading SuSE Linux

SuSE constantly upgrades its packages as new versions are released. The new packages might contain important bug and security fixes. SuSE prepares those new releases in RPM packages that install flawlessly on your system. They also provide the source RPMs if you want to compile the packages yourself. Source RPMs are good because SuSE fine-tunes them to work best on their distribution.

So, how do you know if there is a new set of updated packages for your system? Well, you can find this out in many ways. You can start by checking the SuSE Web site at http://www.suse.com. Follow these steps:

1. Start your browser at this address.

2. Click Updates. You will be taken to a page that organizes the available updates by distribution version.

3. Click your version. You will be taken to another page that lists all the available new updates for your distribution along with a fairly detailed description of each one. The packages are listed by series.

Installing New Packages from Your Hard Disk

Now that you know there are new updated packages, you can start to install them right away. This is easy; just follow these steps:

1. Click the packages' names (while holding down the Shift key if you are using Netscape Navigator) to start downloading them to your hard disk.

2. When you have all the packages you want on your hard disk, you can install them using one of two methods—YaST or manually. Both are easy to perform. Let's start with the manual method.

Part

II

Ch

7

Installing Packages Manually   To install the packages manually, all you have to do is issue the rpm command. For example, let's say you downloaded all the packages in a directory called /tmp/updates. Follow these steps:

1. Log in as root.
2. Turn off the network if you do not want to have users logged on while you perform the upgrade.
3. Change the current path to the directory that has the RPMs you want to install:

   ```
   # cd /tmp/updates
   ```

4. Then, use the following rpm command to install them all in one run:

   ```
   # rpm -Uvh *
   ```

If rpm finds an old version of one of the packages, it will upgrade it; if not, it will install the new package. rpm will go through all the new packages and install them.

Installing Packages Using YaST   If you do not want to use the manual method, you can always use YaST to install the new packages. Follow these steps:

1. Run YaST, choosing Choose/Install Packages.
2. Now that you are in the Installation Menu, choose Install packages, as in Figure 7.1.

FIGURE 7.1
YaST installation menu.

3. Tell SuSE where to get your packages. At the Source: (None) field, press Enter to get a list of the installation sources YaST can use, as shown in Figure 7.2.

FIGURE 7.2
Installation sources
YaST can use.

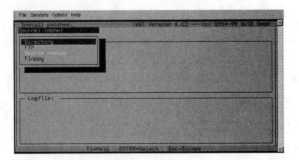

4. Choose Directory, and type in the path to the directory that contains your new RPMs, which in this case is /tmp/updates. YaST will load the names of all the RPMs it finds in that directory.

5. To install an RPM, simply mark an X next to its name using the spacebar.

6. Press F10 to start installing the RPMs.

Updating SuSE Using the Internet

In the previous two methods, you downloaded the RPMs to your hard disk and then started to install them using RPM or YaST. If you have a fast Internet connection, you can easily use YaST to download and install RPMs in one shot. The idea is to have YaST connect to the SuSE FTP site and download and install the RPMs from there. Follow these steps:

1. Run YaST and choose Choose/Install packages.

2. At the Source field, press Enter. Choose FTP—notice that YaST put the correct URL for the FTP site in the address field. You can change that of course, but in our case, this will be fine. Press Enter.

3. YaST attempts to connect to the FTP site, and if it succeeds, it will list the available directories (see Figure 7.3). The list is organized in series just like the SuSE Installation CDs.

FIGURE 7.3
Using YaST to install from FTP.

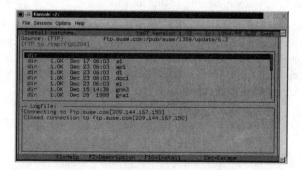

4. Press Enter to view the contents of each series.

5. Mark the packages you want to install using the spacebar, as Figure 7.4 shows.

FIGURE 7.4
Select the files you want to install by marking an X on the file.

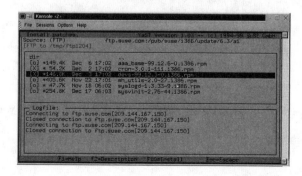

Part
II

Ch

7

6. Press F10 to install the packages.

Please note that YaST will not remember your choices if you exit from a series to see another series. You have to press F10 and install all the packages you want from the current series before you can switch to another series.

Upgrading Your X Window System

The X Window System, as we all know, is the main application responsible for supplying Linux with a graphical interface. X Windows is the layer that interfaces with your graphics hardware and enables GUI applications to use it.

Upgrading your X Windows is an important issue. There are multiple reasons to upgrade it. If you are running your system as a server, security becomes a top concern, and a new version of X Windows might have security bug fixes, for example.

Another reason might be if you installed a new graphics card, and your current version of X Windows does not support it, but a newer version out there does. Finally, you might just want to upgrade for better performance.

How do you find out if there is a new version available for X Windows? The first place to look is the home of X Windows, `http://www.xfree86.org`. Whenever there is a new version for X Windows available, you will be sure to find an announcement and a download link on this site.

Another question that you might have is how do I know whether I need to upgrade? Or how do I know whether the new version supports my new card? The answers to these questions are in the Release Notes that are issued with every new version. The announcement itself usually includes highlights for the new version. For example, the current version of X Windows, 3.3.5, was announced like this:

```
XFree86-3.3.5
[August 1999]
XFree86-3.3.5 is now available!
     This is a full release, that completes the missing
 pieces from the somewhat less optimal 3.3.4 release in
July 1999. If you are having problems with a
 prior release, please
try XFree86-3.3.5 first before asking for help.
     Highlights of the new release include
          DG/ux ix86 support was added
          QNX support was added
          Linux/x86-only S3 Savage4 driver was added (provided from S3)
          Fixes for SiS 530/620 (provided from SiS)
          Fix Mach64 server to support Rage LT and LT Pro
          PAM support
          Misc bug fixes for several drivers
          Misc fixes for security problems and other bugs
```

You easily can see the new features and additions in this version, but you might want to read the Release Notes for the full information.

Obtaining the Latest Version of X Windows from SuSE

The easiest way to upgrade your X Windows is to get the latest RPMs from SuSE directly. You should find binaries that are ready to run on your system with minimal effort. To check whether or not SuSE has the new RPM, follow these steps:

1. Go to `http://www.suse.com` and click Updates.
2. When the Updates page loads, find your distribution version and click it.
3. Check whether they posted RPMs for the new version of X Windows. If they did, then you can easily download and install them using YaST.

You can use the exact same procedure as in the previous section to update your X Windows. Using SuSE's FTP site to update your X Windows is part of updating your SuSE.

Obtaining X Windows and Installing It

Occasionally it might take some time for SuSE to have the RPMs for the new version of X Windows on its FTP site. In this case, you will need to download it from the XFree86 site directly.

All you have to do is download the appropriate binaries and unpack them in the proper place. That's all it takes to upgrade your X Windows. The key is choosing the correct packages to get. This depends on what you want to gain from upgrading your X Windows. If you are upgrading to get support for a new card, you can just download the server that works for that card. If you are upgrading for bug fixes, then you should get the whole thing. In most cases, it's better to get the whole version to make sure that everything works properly.

Before you start downloading the latest version of X Windows, you need to know which files to get. The Release Notes has a section about installing Xfree86 that contains information about the required files to upgrade your X Windows. These files are as follows:

`preinst.sh`	Pre-installation script
`postinst.sh`	Post-installation script
`extract`	XFree86 extraction utility
`Xbin.tgz`	Clients, runtime libs, and app-defaults files
`Xdoc.tgz`	Documentation
`Xlib.tgz`	Data files required at runtime
`Xman.tgz`	Manual pages
`Xset.tgz`	XF86Setup utility
`Xjset.tgz`	XF86Setup utility (if you prefer the Japanese version)
`XVG16.tgz`	16-color VGA server (XF86Setup needs this server)
`X****`	The server for your card

Part

II

Ch

7

Okay, now you know what files you need to get. Use an FTP program to download those files. The URL is `ftp://ftp.xfree86.org/pub/XFree86/3.3.5/binaries/Linux-ix86-glibc`. Start to download the preceding files to a directory on your hard disk. When you're finished, download the correct server for your card from the `Servers` directory.

Now that you have all the files, you will need to install your new X Windows. This is a simple step. After you have downloaded all the files in `/update/X`, follow these steps:

1. Make the file `/update/X/extract` executable. Enter the following command:

   ```
   # chmod +x /update/X/extract
           # chmod +x /update/X/preinst.sh
           # chmod +x /update/X/postinst.sh
   ```

2. Change your path to `/usr/X11` with the following command:

   ```
   # cd /usr/X11
   ```

3. Before you actually unpack your files, you have to run the script called `preinst.sh`:

   ```
   # sh /update/X/preinst.sh
   ```

   This script needs to perform some tasks to prepare for the installation of the new version of X Windows.

4. Unpack all the packages in the right place, which is `/usr/bin/X11`. The files are all `*.tgz`. You might be tempted to use `gzip` and `tar` to unpack them, but XFree86 strongly recommends using the `extract` utility they provide to unpack the files.

   The unpacking is done with one command:

   ```
   # /update/X/extract /update/X/*
   ```

5. `extract` will begin to unpack all the packages, placing the contents of the files in their correct places. This might take some time depending on the speed of your system. After the unpacking is complete, you will need to run the `postinst.sh` script:

   ```
   # sh /update/X/postinst.sh
   ```

6. The script will ask you a few questions; accepting the default answers works just fine. When the script is finished, you are ready to use the new version of X Windows. If you upgraded to install a new graphics card, proceed from here to Chapter 3, "Installing the X Windows System," to find out how to set up your card.

Installing X Windows from Source

This is quite a complex process. You might never need to do this, but if you want to fine tune your X Windows to the source, you will have to compile it for yourself. The first thing you need to do is to get the source packages for XFree86; these can be found in `ftp://ftp.xfree86.org/pub/XFree86/3.3.5/source`. In this section, you will compile only the X Servers, X library, and toolkits. To do this, you need to get only the file `X335src-1.tgz`. The rest of the files are fonts and contribution software—you won't need to recompile those. So, download the file `X335src-1.tgz` (notice that it's around 17MB).

After you have the file, grab a cup of coffee or something. This is going to take some time:

1. Create a directory to use for the process, making sure that you have enough disk space for this. The unpacked files take up 70+MB, and when compiled, might need 100MB more. For this example, create a directory called /compile.

2. Unpack the file with the following command:

   ```
   # tar xvfz X335src-1.tgz -C /compile
   ```

   When done, you should have a directory called xc under /compile. This is where all the files are stored. Now you are ready to start the process.

3. Everything you need to know about how to do this is in the file called INSTALL.TXT— read this file! The file has full instructions on how to compile X Windows. Explaining how to compile X Windows in detail is out of the scope of this book. We will, however, explain a quick method to do this. We are assuming that if you are about to compile X Windows to fine tune it, you have enough knowledge to understand the INSTALL.TXT file.

4. After you read the INSTALL.TXT file and configure X Windows, you are ready to start compiling it. To do this, run a make command in /compile/X/xc:

   ```
   # make World >& world.log
   ```

   This will start the compilation process and will save all the messages coming from make to the file world.log.

CAUTION

Unlike most compilations, make will not stop compiling if an error is encountered. You have to check the file world.log when make is done to ensure that you actually got everything to compile. To check, just look for any error messages in the file; if you find none, then you have everything. Now you need to install X Windows. A note of caution here—after you install the compiled version, it will replace a lot of the configuration files for your current X Windows, so you might want to back them up first. Just to be safe, you really should backup your /usr/X11R6 directory. Just copy all of its contents to another temporary directory. This way, if things don't work right for you, you can copy it back.

5. To install X Windows, run a make install in /compile/X/xc with this command:

   ```
   # make install
   ```

6. Install the man pages with the following command:

   ```
   # make install.man
   ```

That's it—you are done. You have compiled your X Window System.

Part

II

Ch

7

Upgrading Your KDE

The K Desktop Environment (KDE) is the main graphical desktop environment for SuSE
Linux. It offers a very powerful and integrated desktop using a vast set of applications and
utilities. KDE is currently at version 1.1.2 (code name Kolor). New versions of KDE are
released every few months depending on how stable they are. The upcoming version is KDE
2.0, which promises to be very powerful and complete, with a whole new set of components
and applications. Upgrading your KDE is a simple process once you know what you have
to do.

Checking Your KDE Version

Before you start checking for a new version of KDE, you will probably need to check the version of the one you have installed now. If you have SuSE 6.2, then you have KDE 1.1.1. You
can check the version number by running the KDE Control Center. Simply launch an xterm
and type kcontrol. The first window that appears should contain your current KDE version.
Figure 7.5 shows the start screen of the KDE Control Center and the current KDE version.

FIGURE 7.5
KDE Control Center
start screen.

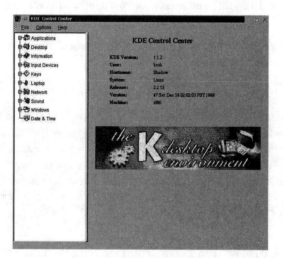

Checking for a New Version of KDE

Now that you know which version you have, you should check if there is a newer version.
One way is to check the SuSE update page as described previously. SuSE has built a great
site that offers the latest RPMs of KDE and KDE applications compiled for your SuSE. This
is the first place you will want to check for any new KDE packages at http://www.suse.de/
en/support/download/LinuKS/index.html. Figure 7.6 shows you the site. You can download

the packages that are appropriate for your distribution version and install them in the same way you updated your SuSE Linux in the previous section.

FIGURE 7.6
SuSE KDE packages
Web site.

Sometimes KDE releases are so new that SuSE doesn't synchronize with them. In that case you will want to check the home of KDE itself for the latest releases. Start your browser at http://www.kde.org—new versions of KDE are announced on the front page, as shown in Figure 7.7. Here you can see that the latest version is KDE 1.1.2. If you find out that a newer version of KDE is available, but is not yet packaged by SuSE, you have two options. You can either get it from KDE or wait for SuSE to package it and post it on its site. If you decide to wait, which we must say will not be a long wait, download the latest RPMs and install them using the same method described in the previous section "Upgrading Your Linux." If you decide you just can't wait, read on to find out how you can get the latest version yourself.

CAUTION

You have to remember that SuSE does not compile KDE out of the box. In most cases, the SuSE team adds or modifies the KDE source code before compiling it. In some cases the modified code does not work with some of the current KDE applications. In that situation you might want to get the original KDE code and compile it.

Part
II

Ch
7

FIGURE 7.7
The KDE Web site's
announcement
section.

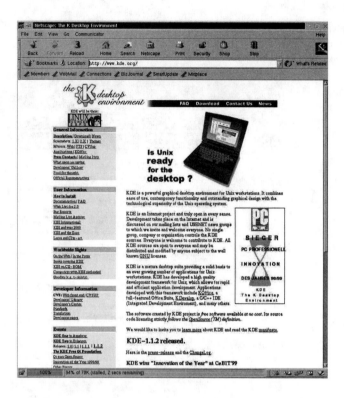

Getting the Latest KDE from *kde.org*

The main FTP site for KDE is `ftp://ftp.kde.org`. When new versions are released, this site usually has a lot of traffic and might not be easy to access. In that case, you will want to use a mirror site. A list of all the mirror sites is at `http://www.kde.org/mirrors.html`. Choose the mirror site that is geographically closest to you for maximum transfer speed. In our case, we will choose `ftp.kde.org`. Follow these steps:

1. Using your favorite ftp program, connect to `ftp.kde.org`. KDE packages are usually found in a directory called `/kde/stable/latest/distribution`.

2. Inside that directory you will see four directories, `deb` (for Debian Linux), `pkg` (for Solaris Unix), `RPM` (for Red Hat and SuSE), and `tar` (generic format). The first thing you will want to check is the `RPM` directory in case you find RPMs for SuSE. At the time of this writing, RPMs for SuSE were already built and are found in the `RPM` directory. All you have to do is download and install them using either YaST or RPM directly.

But what happens if you do not find RPMs for SuSE? In that case you might need to build KDE from source. This is a simple process, but it does take some time. The sources for KDE are found in `/pub/kde/stable/1.1.2/distribution/tar/generic/source/bz2`. This directory contains a lot of files, and some of them you might not really need. The following table lists all those files and tells you whether you really need this package or not.

Package Name	Package Description	Required/ Optional
kdeadmin-1.1.2.tar.bz2	System Administration programs	Optional
kdebase-1.1.2.tar.bz2	Part of the KDE core	Required
kdegames-1.1.2.tar.bz2	Games for KDE	Optional
kdegraphics-1.1.2.tar.bz2	Graphics programs for KDE	Optional
kdelibs-1.1.2.tar.bz2	KDE libraries, part of KDE core	Required
kdemultimedia-1.1.2.tar.bz2	KDE multimedia applications	Optional
kdenetwork-1.1.2.tar.bz2	KDE network applications (mail, news readers, and so on)	Optional
kdesupport-1.1.2.tar.bz2	Libraries required to compile and run KDE	Required
kdetoys-1.1.2.tar.bz2	KDE toy applications	Optional
kdeutils-1.1.2.tar.bz2	KDE utility applications	Optional
korganizer-1.1.2.tar.bz2	Organizer/ scheduler for KDE	Optional
qt-1.44.tar.bz2	GUI toolkit used to build KDE	Required

As you can see from the previous table, there are only four packages that are required to upgrade your KDE. If you are just upgrading, you can download `kdebase`, `kdelibs`, `kdesupport`, and `qt`. These are the files that include the bulk of the updates; the rest of the applications do not change drastically. In your case, you will compile all the packages.

Part
II

Ch
7

Compiling KDE

Download the packages to a directory, for example `/install`. After you have all the files, start to unpack them. If you have a lot of free disk space, you can unpack all of them at once. If you don't, just unpack the package you will compile, and when you are done remove its files. The order in which you compile the packages is important; the following is the correct order:

1. `qt`
2. `kdesupport`
3. `kdelibs`
4. `kdebase`

From here on, you can compile the rest of the packages in whichever order you want; it won't matter.

To compile a package, it's good practice to read the README file that comes with the package. For `qt`, you won't really need to compile it if you installed SuSE with KDE. You should, however, make sure that you installed the `qtdevel` package in the `xdev` series. If you haven't installed that RPM, please take a moment to do so now.

Compiling a package is a very simple process. It is a series of steps:

1. Change your path to the directory where you downloaded the files. Enter the following command:

   `#cd /install`

2. Unpack the package you want to compile with the following command:

   `# tar xvfI package.tar.bz2`

   This will create a directory named after the package's name. For example, if you are unpacking `kdesupport-1.1.2.tar.bz2`, a directory called `kdesupport-1.1.2` will be created.

3. Change your path to the newly created directory:

   `# cd kdesupport-1.1.2`

4. Run the auto-configuration script with the following command:

   `# ./configure`

KDE source packages are not hardwired to any platform; they are meant to compile on several different platforms. When you run the configure script, it will check the platform it is currently running on and start gathering important information about it. This information is used to create the appropriate files for your compilation to succeed.

Start the compilation process by entering the following:

`# make`

This will take quite a bit of time, depending on your machine's speed and amount of RAM. You should see lines scrolling by, which are source files being compiled to build KDE. After the lines stop scrolling and you are back at the prompt, and there were no error messages reported, you can start installing the package.

Install the package with the following command:

```
# make install
```

This will take some time, but not as much as the previous step. You will see lines scrolling very quickly this time. Your package is being installed in the default place for KDE, which is /opt/kde. This is okay because it's where SuSE puts KDE by default. It is good practice to run the command ldconfig after every compilation to make sure that any new libraries have been registered with Linux:

```
# ldconfig
```

That's all! The package is compiled and installed. You can remove the source directory now and start with another package. When you are done with all the packages, your new KDE will be ready to run. From then on, when you start KDE, it will tell you that a new version has been installed and that it will synchronize its files with it.

Upgrading GNOME

GNU Network Object Model Environment (GNOME) is another powerful desktop environment similar to KDE. GNOME offers the user an attractive desktop, full of eye candy. The SuSE 6.2 full version comes with GNOME, but the evaluation version does not. SuSE offers RPMs for GNOME through its site for those who want to install it.

Checking Your Version of GNOME

As with KDE, the first thing that you need to do is check the version of GNOME that you are currently running. To do that, simply click About in the GNOME menu. A window appears with information about the currently installed version of GNOME.

SuSE offers packages for GNOME. If there are any newly updated packages, you should be able to find them by following the instructions in the section "Upgrading SuSE Linux" at the beginning of this chapter. To check for the absolute latest version of GNOME, you will probably need to check its site at http://www.gnome.org. The GNOME site is very well-organized so it is easy to find what you want. If there is a new version of GNOME, you can find out by opening the page, as shown in Figure 7.8.

Part
II

Ch
7

FIGURE 7.8
The GNOME start
page.

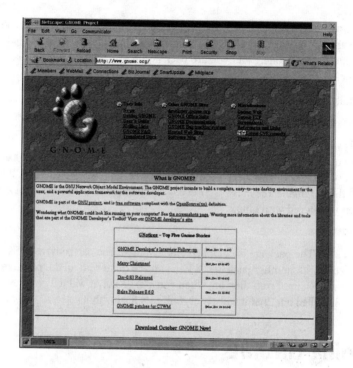

Obtaining the Latest Version of GNOME

To get the latest version of GNOME, all you need to do is set your browser to
http://www.gnome.org and click Getting GNOME. You should find links to the different distributions supported.

In your case, click the fourth link, which is for SuSE packages. This takes you to the page
where you can download the packages. GNOME is made up of a lot more packages than
KDE, so this might take a while to download. But, before you start downloading all the packages, you should decide which ones you really need. It is recommended that you install all of
them if you have the bandwidth to download them all. GNOME is very sensitive with respect
to its components. Therefore, it's better to get all the files for one release and install them to
make sure that it will work properly. The packages are as follows:

Package Name	Package Description	Required/ Optional
audiofil-0.1.9-1.i386.rpm	Package used for sound file processing	Required
chkfontpath-1.5-1.i386.rpm	Package used by the fonts subsystem of GNOME	Required

Package Name	Package Name Description	Required/ Optional
ee-0.3.11-2.i386.rpm	Image viewer	Optional
esound-0.2.15-1.i386.rpm	Sound daemon used by GNOME	Optional
gdm-2.0beta4-2.i386.rpm	GNOME login manager	Optional
glib-1.2.6-1.i386.rpm	Library of useful functions, such as trees and linked lists	Required
gmc-4.5.40-1.i386.rpm	GNOME Midnight Commander (file manager)	Required
gnaudio-1.0.0-1.noarch.rpm	Audio files used by GNOME	Optional
gncontr-1.0.51-1.i386.rpm	GNOME Control Center	Required
gncore-1.0.53-2.i386.rpm	GNOME core	Required
gngames-1.0.51-1.i386.rpm	GNOME games	Optional
gnlibs-1.0.53-1.i386.rpm	GNOME libraries	Required
gnmedia-1.0.51-1.i386.rpm	GNOME multimedia applications	Optional
gnpim-1.0.50-1.i386.rpm	Personal information manager for GNOME	Optional
gnpimd-1.0.50-1.i386.rpm	Used by gnpim	Optional unless you installed gnpim
gnprint-0.9-1.i386.rpm	Printing support for GNOME	Optional
gnumeric-0.38-1.i386.rpm	Spreadsheet for GNOME	Optional
gnutils-1.0.50-1.i386.rpm	Utilities for GNOME	Optional
gtk-1.2.6-1.i386.rpm	GIMP Tool Kit (GUI toolkit)	Required
gtkeng-0.8-1.i386.rpm	GTK Themes Engines	Optional
gtkmm-1.0.3-1.i386.rpm	C++ wrapper library for GTK	Optional
gtop-1.0.5-1.i386.rpm	Processes viewing program	Optional
icepref-0.11-1.noarch.rpm	Configuration panel for ICE window manager	Required (unless you are not using ICE WM)

continues

Part

II

Ch

7

Package Name	Package Name Description	Required/ Optional
`icewm-0.9.48-10.i386.rpm`	ICE Window Manager	Required (unless you are using another WM)
`imlib-1.9.7-1.i386.rpm`	Image manipulation library	Required
`imlibcfe-1.9.7-1.i386.rpm`	Imlib configuration panel	Required
`libglade-0.7-1.i386.rpm`	Library for loading GUIs at runtime	Optional
`libgtop-1.0.5-1.i386.rpm`	Library for monitoring various system properties	Required
`libxml-1.7.3-1.i386.rpm`	XML support library	Optional
`mc-4.5.40-1.i386.rpm`	Midnight Commander for the console	Required
`mcserv-4.5.40-1.i386.rpm`	Server for the Midnight Commander network file management system	Required
`orbit-0.5.0-1.i386.rpm`	ORB support for GNOME	Required
`urw-fonts-1.1-8.noarch.rpm`	Fonts	Optional
`xchat-1.2.1-1.i386.rpm`	IRC chatting program	Optional
GNOME development package downloads	All the following packages are required if you want to compile your own GNOME applications	Required for compiling GNOME apps; not required for RPMs
`glibdev-1.2.6-1.i386.rpm`	Development for GTK/Glib	
`gncontrd-1.0.51-1.i386.rpm`	Development for the GNOME Control Center	
`gncored-1.0.53-2.i386.rpm`	Development for the GNOME core	
`gngamesd-1.0.51-1.i386.rpm`	Development for the GNOME games	
`gnlibsd-1.0.53-1.i386.rpm`	Development for GNOME libraries	

Package Name	Package Name Description	Required/ Optional
gnprintd-0.9-1.i386.rpm	Development for the printing support	
gtkdev-1.2.6-1.i386.rpm	Development for the GTK	
gtkmmdev-1.0.3-1.i386.rpm	Development for the GTK--	
imlibdev-1.9.7-1.i386.rpm	Development for imlib	
libgladed-0.7-1.i386.rpm	Development for Glade	
libgtopd-1.0.5-1.i386.rpm	Development for libgtop	
libxmld-1.7.3-1.i386.rpm	Development for XML	
orbitdev-0.5.0-1.i386.rpm	Development for ORBit	
pygnome-1.0.50-1.i386.rpm	Development for GNOME using Python	
pygtk-0.6.3-1.i386.rpm	Development for GTK using Python	
pygtk-libglade-0.6.3-1.i386.rpm	Development for Glade using Python	

To install those packages, download them into a directory and use either YaST or RPM to install them. For example, we downloaded them in a directory called /tmp/gnome, and using rpm we installed them with the following:

```
# cd /tmp/gnome
# rpm -Uvh --nodeps *
```

After rpm is finished, your GNOME is now upgraded to the latest version. Simple, isn't it?

CAUTION

The --nodeps switch should not be used if you did not download *all* the packages. If you downloaded some of them, install them without the --nodeps switch to see if your system is missing any necessary packages. If RPM reports that you are missing a package, you will need to download that package and install it first. If you downloaded *all* the packages, you can use the --nodeps switch for fast installation.

Part

II

Ch

7

Upgrading GNOME from Source

This process is similar to the one used with KDE, except for a few slight differences. One difference is that you have a lot more packages to compile. When you attempt to compile GNOME from source, it is advisable to remove the current version of GNOME if it was installed using RPM. So, the first thing you will want to do is use YaST to uninstall all the packages for GNOME from your system.

Installing GNOME from source is a bit more complicated than KDE. If you are not using the correct versions of all the libraries, GNOME might not compile or might act funny. This is why if you are doing this for the first time, it is advisable to download all the required packages and compile them. Then, when you do this again, you will know what you have on your system and can decide what to compile again.

You can get the source packages for GNOME from their site at http://www.gnome.org. Click Getting GNOME and then click Installing From Tarballs. The following are the absolute minimum required files:

- audiofile
- esound
- glib
- gtk+
- imlib
- gtk-engines
- ORBit
- gnome-libs
- libgtop
- control-center
- gnome-core
- mc

These are the absolute minimum packages you will need to compile to have a running GNOME system. You will need more packages as you attempt to compile more components. If you have a previous copy of GNOME installed on your system via RPM, please remove any RPM files for the above files before you compile them to avoid conflicts. The order in which you compile GNOME is very important. You have to compile the files in the same order as they are shown in the preceding list.

Compiling GNOME is no different from compiling KDE. Be sure you read the README files for every package for installation instructions. You use the exact same procedure—follow these steps:

1. Unpack the package with the following command:

```
# tar xvfz package.tar.gz
```

2. Change the path to the newly created directory. Enter this command:

```
# cd package_name/
```

3. Configure the source for your platform:

```
# ./configure
```

4. Compile the code by entering the following:

```
# make
```

5. Install the package with this command:

```
# make installation
```

6. Finally, run `ldconfig`:

```
# ldconfig
```

Repeat these steps for all the packages. This will take a lot of time, so be patient. Make sure you watch for errors in compilation before proceeding to the next package. When you are finished compiling all the packages successfully, you are ready to run your new version of GNOME.

Installing a New Library

Linux applications tend to use a lot of libraries. Libraries in Linux are just like Dynamic Link Libraries (DLLs) in Windows. This means that at some point in time, you might need to install a new library for some new application to run. This is usually a fairly easy task to do.

The reason for installing a new library is usually to run a new application that requires it. The most common scenario is that you download an application you want to run and it tells you that it needs a specific library to run. You will want to check whether you have that library or not. The easiest way to do that is by running `ldconfig -v`. For example, if your application says it needs a library called gtk, then you will want to run `ldconfig` like this to check:

```
# ldconfig -v | grep gtk
```

This command will list the names of all the libraries on your system that have gtk as part of their name. If you have the library, you are fine, if not, you will have to get it and install it.

To get a library you don't have, go to the site where you downloaded the application. It will most likely have a link you can use to get the required libraries. If you find such a link, download the library from it—this is the most secure method. If the site does not provide a link, you can search for that library on the Internet using http://www.freshmeat.net or http://www.filewatcher.org. Both of these sites are good starting points for your search. After you find the library, make sure it's the correct version that you need (a higher version will also work, but a lower version won't).

Part

II

Ch

7

When you finally find the library you need, try to find an RPM version of it. If you do find one, download that and install it using `rpm` by entering the following:

```
# rpm -Uvh library.rpm
```

If that fails to install for any reason, RPM will tell you why. You might need to install more packages for this library to work. In that case, you will have to find those and install them. If RPM does not fail, then you should test the library by running your application. If it works, you are all set. If it doesn't work, then you probably need another version—uninstall the library and start over again.

If you did not find any RPMs, you will definitely find the source package. Download that and read the README file to make sure you are not missing anything. The procedure we are explaining here does not apply to all packages, but it does apply to most:

1. To start compiling the library, you first have to unpack it with the following command:
   ```
   # tar xvfz library.tar.gz
   ```

2. This will unpack it in a directory of its own. Switch to that directory and start to configure the source for your system by running the auto-configure script:
   ```
   # ./configure
   ```

3. If the `configure` script executes successfully, then you are all set to start compiling the library. Enter the following command:
   ```
   # make
   ```

4. This might take some time. After it successfully completes, you will have to install the library with the following:
   ```
   # make install
   ```

5. Run `ldconfig` to register it with Linux:
   ```
   # ldconfig
   ```

That's it. You are done installing the library. Test it by running the application.

Upgrading an Existing Library

To upgrade an existing library you can get either the RPM for it or compile it from source. This is almost exactly the same procedure as the previous section's. The main difference is if the library you are upgrading was installed using RPM, and you are going to upgrade it by compiling the new version, you should remove the old library first. This way you can avoid conflicts between the two versions if they install in different places on your system. Apart from that, it is the same process as in the previous section.

Upgrading Your *glibc*

The GNU C Library (glibc) is the main library that your whole Linux depends on. This is the core of the system. If this library gets corrupted or deleted, nothing will work—and we mean nothing. Your whole system will just sit there. This is why this is a risky procedure and if you can avoid it, you should.

Another word of warning regarding glibc versions. Before you decide to upgrade your glibc to a newer version, you have to ask yourself a few questions:

- Why am I doing this?
- Do I need this upgrade?
- Is it critical to upgrade? (For example, will this fix security problems?)
- And the most important question of all: Will this upgrade break some of my applications?

That last question is very important. For example, upgrading from glibc 2.0 to glibc 2.1 might break some applications and libraries, causing you to have to recompile them all to work again. Upgrading your glibc can be a very simple process or can turn into days of work. Be sure you know what you want.

So, how do you answer these questions? Well, first you will want to check all the documents that come with the new version of glibc. They should tell you about any problems you might encounter. Announcements of new versions of glibc usually have that information available. Another thing you should do is to contact SuSE technical support to make sure it will be safe to upgrade.

Okay, enough warnings, let's get down to business. The actual process is fairly simple. First, you need to get the source files for the new version of glibc. These are found in ftp://ftp.gnu.org/gnu/glibc. You will need to get four files:

- glibc
- glibc-linuxthreads
- glibc-localedata
- glibc-crypt

Download all those files in one directory, for example, /tmp/sources. Next, unpack them. Follow these steps:

1. You have to unpack linuxthreads, crypt, and localedata inside the glibc directory. Enter the following:

```
# tar xvfz glib.tar.gz
# cd glibc
# tar xvfz ../glibc-linuxthreads
# tar xvfz ../glibc-crypt
# tar xvfz ../glibc-localedata
```

Part

II

Ch

7

2. Now you must prepare for the compilation. You should create a directory called `compile` inside the `glibc` directory with the following command:

```
# mkdir compile
```

3. Proceed to configure the source with the following:

```
# cd compile
# ../configure --enable-add-ons=linuxthreads,crypt,localedata
```

4. This will start checking your system's configuration. When it is done, run a `make`:

```
# make
```

5. This will take some time. When it is finished, you are ready to install it. This is it, the moment of truth, the point of no return. Enter the following command:

```
# make install
```

6. Run `ldconfig` to register it with Linux:

```
# ldconfig
```

Ok, try to run anything, `ls` for example. If it works, you are fine. Start testing your system and see how it feels after the upgrade. If it doesn't work correctly, reinstall the A series from your SuSE CD to correct the situation.

Upgrading Your GCC

The GNU C Compiler (GCC) is your compiler package. The compilers that come with SuSE 6.2 are very good and recent. You might never need to upgrade your compiler. Currently, the latest version of GCC is 2.95. Note that this version is not a good one to have if you are going to be compiling your kernel.

It is best to upgrade your compilers through SuSE. When new versions of your compiler are released, SuSE will package them for you. This is the safest way to do this. To download the latest compilers from series D on the SuSE FTP site, follow the instructions at the beginning of the chapter in the section "Upgrading SuSE Linux."

If, however, you need to compile from source, you will have to download the latest version of GCC from GNU. The latest compilers are found in `ftp://ftp.gnu.org/gnu/gcc`. You will find several files there. You can download either the whole package or just the components you need (C++ or C compiler). In this case, download the whole thing (`gcc-2.95.1.tar.gz`, which is around 17MB). To compile it, follow these steps:

1. Unpack the package to start compiling it with the following command:

```
# tar xvfz gcc-2.95.1.tar.gz
```

2. This will create a directory that has all the source files for the `gcc` package. The compilation process is quite similar to that for `glibc`. Please read the files in the `install` directory for detailed information about compiling `gcc`.

3. Next, create the `compile` directory by entering the following:

   ```
   # mkdir compile
   ```

4. Configure the source files with the following:

   ```
   # ../configure
   ```

5. Compile the package:

   ```
   # make bootstrap
   ```

6. Or, if you are low on disk space, enter the following:

   ```
   make bootstrap-lean
   ```

This will take a while to finish, especially if you issued a `make bootstrap-lean`. After it completes, you are ready to install the new compilers. Before you do that, though, if your previous compiler was installed using RPM, make sure you remove it using YaST before you install the new compilers to avoid a conflict.

To install the compiler, enter the following command:

```
# make install
```

That's it, GCC is installed. To check, enter this command:

```
# gcc --version
```

This will output the version number of the current compiler, which should be the new one. If you have any problems and you would like to revert to the old compiler rather than uninstall the new one, enter the following:

```
# make uninstall
```

Then, install the compilers from the SuSE CD series D again.

Troubleshooting

The compilation breaks with errors.

Check what the error is; it might be due to libraries not found on your system or not properly installed. Check your libraries.

KDE does not compile.

Did you compile the packages in the correct order? Do that.

GNOME does not compile.

This is largely caused by incompatible libraries. Download the libraries that are available with the current distribution of GNOME to be safe. Remove the old ones before installing the new ones. Having multiple copies of a library can really mess up GNOME.

Part
II

Ch
7

GNOME now acts weird after I upgraded it.

Remove your local setting by deleting the .GNOME directories in your home directory. Try again.

The configure script fails and I am not sure why.

Check the message it failed with, and if you still don't know why, read the contents of the file config.log. Everything the configure script does is reported in that file.

Ok, I fixed the problem with the configure script, but it still fails.

Remove the file config.cache and try again.

Some applications don't run anymore now that I upgraded one of my libraries.

Read the README file that came with the libraries to see whether it says anything about broken applications. Recompile the applications that don't run.

The kernel won't compile after I upgraded my GCC.

Well, if you upgraded to GCC 2.95, this is expected. Revert back to the old one or compile the kernel on a different machine. ●

## CHAPTER 8

Installing a New Kernel

Defining the Kernel

Some Linux professional users like to think that you aren't a Linux user unless you have recompiled your own kernel. Although this might be very true for them, it is not really a fact. You might never really need to recompile your kernel; it all depends on the requirements of your system. SuSE Linux specifically attempts to provide a ready-to-use kernel for several system configurations, so you can simply install one of them and start working without having to recompile your own kernel. But, of course, sometimes you will need to recompile. Reasons for this can be if you are upgrading your kernel to a newer version that offers better performance or fixes a bug you were experiencing, or if you added a new piece of hardware that needs a special driver or parameters to be built in to the kernel.

The kernel is the heart or core of the operating system. The kernel is the layer that separates the hardware layer from the applications layer. Applications that need to access the hardware do so through calls to the kernel services. The kernel then communicates or "talks" to the hardware and returns results and messages back to the application. This way, applications do not have to worry about directly talking to the hardware in its native and complex protocols; the kernel simplifies all that for the application. The kernel manages all the system resources, such as memory and CPU time. Another very important role for the kernel is to control the execution of programs (or processes) and schedule them in an efficient manner to accomplish multitasking.

Why Should I Install a New Kernel?

The most common case in which you might want to install a new kernel is to install a new driver or component on the system. For example, if you have just purchased a new SCSI hard drive, and you never had SCSI devices on your system before, you will need to install the device driver in order for the SCSI interface to use your hard drive. This is done by configuring the kernel to include the correct SCSI interface for your hard drive and recompiling the kernel to activate that driver.

Another reason to install a new kernel is if a new release of the kernel is out and it has better performance or fixes bugs that you are experiencing. In this case, you would download that new kernel and install it on your system. And last but not least, some of us like to install new kernels just for the sake of compiling a new kernel!

Installing a Precompiled Kernel Versus Compiling Your Own

Before you attempt to install a new kernel, you have to make an important decision. Do I have to compile my kernel? Or can I get away with a precompiled one? This is an important decision to make because your choice will dictate the process you have to go through to reach your goal. To make such a decision, you will need to have sufficient background information.

Installing a new kernel can be done in one of two ways. You can either get a precompiled kernel that suits your needs, or if you can't find one you will have to configure and compile your own. The first choice requires much less time than the second one, because a precompiled kernel just needs to be installed and the system rebooted. If you chose to compile your own kernel, you will need to spend some time configuring it and compiling it.

The answer to this question depends on the reason you are installing a new kernel. If you are looking to support a device or service that your current kernel does not, you can start by looking for a precompiled kernel that has that support. If you did not find a precompiled kernel that meets your needs, or if you want to upgrade to a newer kernel version, you will probably need to compile your own. Take your time making this decision; we will discuss both methods in this chapter. Let us start off by installing a precompiled kernel.

Installing a Precompiled Kernel

The fastest method of installing a new kernel is by using a precompiled one. A precompiled kernel is a kernel that was configured, compiled, and packaged by SuSE for easy installation by the user. SuSE attempts to provide a precompiled kernel for most common hardware and service configurations. If you are looking for support for common hardware and services, chances are that you will find a precompiled kernel good enough for you. The more uncommon the configurations you want, the less your chances are.

There are two ways you can get a precompiled kernel from SuSE: the SuSE CDs and from their site on the Internet. SuSE CDs have different configurations of the same kernel. On the other hand, the Internet site will have just one configuration but for a newer kernel version than the one you are currently running. So if your aim is to just upgrade to a newer version of your kernel, you will probably want to get it from the Internet site. You can configure it yourself and recompile it to fine-tune it to your exact needs later.

Installing from SuSE CDs

SuSE CDs have a wide variety of precompiled kernels that support a range of different devices and services. These kernels are easy to install. All you need to do is pick the one that fits your needs, install it, and reboot your machine. When your machine boots again, it will be booting the new kernel.

You use YaST to browse the list of precompiled kernels and install any of them. Follow these steps:

1. Run YaST and choose System Administration, Kernel and Boot Configuration, Select Boot Kernel.

2. YaST then displays a list of the available kernels that you can install right away (see Figure 8.1).

FIGURE 8.1

This menu presents all the available kernels that you can install right away.

3. Look through the kernels and see whether any of them support the hardware and services you are looking for. Use F1 to have YaST show you a more detailed description about the currently selected kernel.

4. When you find a kernel that meets your needs, press Enter to install it. YaST then proceeds to install the new kernel and asks you whether you want to replace the already existing .config file. This file holds the configuration of the kernel that is currently running; choose Yes to overwrite it with the configuration of the new kernel you are about to install.

5. Next, YaST will ask you if you want YaST to run LILO on your system. Choose Yes to have LILO (Linux Loader) boot your new kernel.

6. That's it, reboot and your new kernel will boot.

Downloading a Precompiled Kernel from the Internet

SuSE regularly updates its distribution by putting new RPMs on its FTP site. You can use YaST to download and install those files. You always can check the FTP site to see whether there is a new version of the kernel available that is packaged and ready to run on your version of SuSE. Follow these steps:

1. Run YaST and pick Choose/Install packages. The installation menu appears.

2. Choose Install packages (see Figure 8.2).

FIGURE 8.2

YaST is ready for you to tell it the source of the packages it will install.

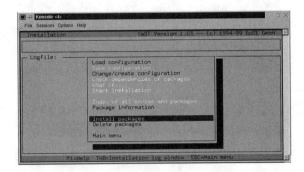

3. Next, you tell SuSE where to find the packages. You can do this in two ways. If you are connected to the Internet and have a fast connection, you can have YaST download and install the Kernel RPM directly from the FTP site. If you have a slow or no connection, you might want to download the kernel manually from the SuSE FTP site and put the RPM somewhere on your hard disk and have YaST install it from there. For this example, use the Internet method.

4. At the Source field, press Enter.

5. Choose FTP. Notice that YaST put the correct URL for the FTP site in the address field (see Figure 8.3). You can change that, but in this case, this will be fine. Press Enter.

FIGURE 8.3
YaST automatically inserts the correct URL for the SuSE updates FTP site.

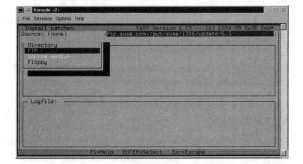

6. YaST attempts to connect to the FTP site, and if it succeeds, it will list the available directories.

7. You want a new kernel, so look in d1 (see Figure 8.4). At the time of the writing of this book, a new version was not available for SuSE. If there was, it would have been called `1x_suse_2.2.x.i386.rpm`. If you have a file like that, simply press the spacebar next to it to mark it with an X.

FIGURE 8.4
Updates are organized in series just like the SuSE CDs.

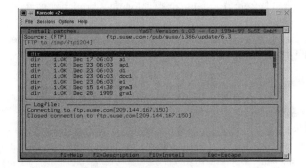

8. Now press F10 to start downloading and installing the RPM. When finished, you will have installed a new kernel. You might need to configure it and reinstall it again to further meet your needs.

9. Reboot the machine for the new kernel to boot.

Read on to learn how to download, configure, and install your own kernel.

Installing a Kernel from Source Code

Installing a kernel from source code is a relatively easy process; it just requires time and patience. There are a lot of reasons for doing this:

- You tried to find a precompiled kernel that meets your needs but none were available.
- You would like to fine-tune your kernel for maximum performance.
- A device or service you need is not available in your current version of the kernel, but is part of a new version.
- A new version of the kernel fixes bugs that you were experiencing, especially security-related bugs.
- A new version of the kernel has better performance than the one you are running now.
- You just want to try it!

To be able to perform this interesting process, you need to be equipped with the relevant knowledge and tools. The first thing you need to understand is how to read kernel versions.

Reading Kernel Versions

The kernels come in two branches, namely the stable branch and the development branch. The *stable* branch series is meant for users to install; they are stable enough to be relied on. The *development* branch is meant more for developers, not users. Development kernels might not be stable because they are constantly being worked on and new code and features are usually added to it. When the development kernel is stable, it becomes the next stable branch, replacing the current one.

But how do you know which one is which? The kernel has a version number that is represented by three numbers separated by dots, for example 2.2.10. The first number is the kernel major version, this identifies the generation of the kernel. The second number indicates whether this kernel is from the stable or development branch. An even number means it belongs to the stable branch, an odd number means it belongs to the development branch. The third and last number is the patch level or minor version. So, currently the stable branch is 2.2.x and the development is 2.3.x.

CAUTION

It is recommended that you stay away from development kernels, especially if you need a reliable system. There are situations, however, in which you might find the need to use them—for example, if they have a driver for a device that is so new it is not in the stable kernels yet. Even in that case, we recommend you wait until that driver is integrated in the stable kernel rather than risk the chance of corrupting your system.

Checking Your Kernel's Version

Now that you know how to read a kernel's version properly, how do you find out the version of the kernel you are running now? This piece of information might come in handy if you want to know whether there is a newer version of the kernel than yours. The most obvious way is to read it off the login prompt of your Linux machine. If you have configured your Linux to boot in console mode, you will spot the version of the kernel just above the login prompt. Another method you could use is by running the uname command like this:

```
$ uname -r
2.2.13
```

The uname utility, when run with the -a switch, outputs information about the version of the kernel currently running on the system. Here you see that my system is called mymachine and is running kernel 2.2.13. Thanks to your newly acquired knowledge you can quickly tell that this is a stable kernel.

Checking for the Latest Version of the Kernel

You now know how to read a kernel's version, and you know how to check the version of the kernel you are running. Next, you should know how to check whether you have the latest version of the kernel or if there is a newer one. There are many ways to find this information; major Linux sites announce the release of a new kernel as soon as it happens. These sites even list the new features and drivers included with the new release. Freshmeat (http://www.freshmeat.net) and Linux Today (http://www.linuxtoday.com) are just two of many sites that announce new kernel releases.

Another way you can instantly check for the latest version of the kernel is by using the finger command like this:

```
$ finger @ftp.kernel.org
[linux.kernel.org]

        The latest stable version of the Linux kernel is:      2.2.13
        The latest beta version of the Linux kernel is:        2.3.23
        The latest prepatch (alpha) version *appears* to be:   none
```

From this information along with the output of the uname command, you can tell that you are not running the latest version of the kernel.

TIP   Most users, upon finding out that a new kernel has been released, rush off to install it. Always remember the golden rule for this: If it's working fine, leave it as is. In other words, if you don't need to upgrade, don't upgrade.

Kernel Compilation Checklist

To compile a kernel, you need to have a few things. You will need the following:

- Kernel sources (series D, package `lx_suse`)
- C compiler—GCC 2.7.2.3 or up (series D, package `gcc`)
- C Library—Glibc 2.x—included with SuSE (part of the A series)
- Patch program, if you are going to patch the kernel (series D, package `patch`)
- About 80MB of free hard disk space
- Patience

Downloading and Unpacking a New Kernel

You are now all set to start the process of configuring and compiling your own kernel. There's just one last step before you do so—downloading the kernel's source code. This step is necessary only if you are upgrading to a newer version of the kernel. If you are going to compile the kernel currently on your system, you may go straight to the section "Configuring Your Kernel;" otherwise, read on.

Getting the actual code for the kernel is a simple downloading process (a bit time-consuming, though, depending on the speed of your connection). The kernel is usually above 10MB in size. The official place to get the kernel is `ftp.kernel.org`. But please use a mirror that is geographically close to you. To do that, download from `ftp.`*`xx`*`.kernel.org`, where *xx* is your country code. For example, to download from a mirror in the United States, download from `ftp.us.kernel.org`. Use the common FTP command to log in anonymously to `ftp.us.kernel.org`:

```
nazeeh@linux:~ > ftp ftp.us.kernel.org
Connected to ftp.us.kernel.org.
220 elijah.nodomainname.net FTP server (Version wu-2.5.0(1) Wed Aug 25 14:13:56
EDT 1999) ready.
Name (ftp.us.kernel.org:nazeeh): ftp
331 Guest login ok, send your complete e-mail address as password.
Password:
230-Welcome to the FTP site of NoDomainName Networks! Look in /pub for
230-all available downloads, including mirrors of RedHat, the Linux
230-Kernel archives, Internet RFCs, the Interactive Fiction archive, and
230-the GNU Project, as well as software from NoDomainName Networks.
230-
230-You are user 19 out of 100.
230-
230 Guest login ok, access restrictions apply.
Remote system type is UNIX.
Using binary mode to transfer files.
```

The kernels are found under /pub/linux/kernel/. For the kernel you want you will go to /pub/linux/kernel/v2.2, which is where you can find the 2.2.x series. Now you are faced with two options, you can download the whole kernel source, or just a patch to upgrade your kernel to the new one. This depends on the version of the kernel you have. If, for example, you have kernel version 2.2.10 and you want to upgrade to 2.2.11, it would be safe to just download the patch-2.2.10-2.2.11.gz file, which is a patch to your kernel. If you want to upgrade from 2.2.1 to 2.2.13, it makes more sense to get the whole kernel rather than the patch. The reason for this is that you will have to download all the patches from 2.2.2 all the way to 2.2.13, because you cannot just apply the 2.2.13 patch to a 2.2.1 kernel; it can be applied only to 2.2.12.

TIP You will find two copies of each file on the FTP directory where you're downloading the kernel: one ending with *bz2* and the other with *gz*. These are two different programs used to compress the source code for the kernel to make its size smaller for downloads. In most cases it is recommended you get the bz2 (bzip2) copy because it will be smaller in size than the gz (gzip).

Unpacking the Kernel Source

After you have downloaded the kernel, you will want to unpack it and start to compile it. To do that you have to know where to unpack it. At this point we need to note that you have to be logged on as root to do the following. The kernel is usually located in /usr/src/ under a directory called linux. The linux directory is a symbolic link to the actual directory that contains the kernel, which is usually named linux-x.x.x to denote the version. You will need to replace that kernel. You have to first delete the symbolic link. Then you unpack the kernel in that directory, and create a new symbolic link to point to your kernel's directory. So, you do the following:

1. Enter the compile directory, /usr/src/. Then remove the symbolic link with the following command:

   ```
   # rm linux
   ```

2. Unpack the kernel (gz version):

   ```
   # tar xvfz /path/where/you/downloaded/the/kernel/linux-2.2.13.tar.gz
   ```

3. Unpack the kernel (bz2 version):

   ```
   # tar xvfI /path/where/you/downloaded/the/kernel/linux-2.2.13.tar.bz2
   ```

4. The kernel unpacks under a directory called linux, so you need to rename it to something a little more understandable:

   ```
   # mv linux linux-2.2.13
   ```

5. Next you point to it with a symbolic link called `linux`:

```
#ln -s linux-2.2.13 Linux
```

6. Finally, if you are upgrading from an old kernel, it is useful to import the previous kernel's configuration to your new kernel. The kernel's configuration is saved in a hidden file called `.config`.

   To import the old kernel's configuration, simply copy that file from the old kernel's directory to the new kernel's directory. For example, if your old kernel was 2.2.10 and you are upgrading to 2.2.13, you would have the following two directories:

```
/usr/src/linux-2.2.10
usr/src/linux-2.2.13
```

7. To copy the configuration, you issue the following copy command:

```
# cp /usr/src/linux-2.2.10/.config   /usr/src/linux-2.2.13
```

Upgrading the Kernel Using a Patch

Sometimes it's easier to upgrade your kernel using a patch. A *patch* is a file that contains the difference between two versions of the kernel. When you apply a patch to a kernel, that patch edits your kernel's files with the differences found in the new kernel, thus upgrading it. A patch is usually considerably faster than downloading the whole kernel.

To apply a patch, use the utility called patch. Patches usually come compressed either by gzip (`*.gz`) or bzip2 (`*.bz2`). Follow these steps:

1. The first thing you need to do is move the patch into the `/usr/src` directory and unpack it:

```
linux:/usr/src # cp /path/to/patch/patch-2.2.x.gz /usr/src/
linux:/usr/src # gzip -d patch-2.2.x.gz
```

2. Now that you have unpacked the patch, you should apply it. This is easy with the following command:

```
linux:/usr/src # patch -p0 < patch-2.2.x
```

The program will apply the patch to the kernel, and status messages will be scrolling very quickly. It is a good idea to apply the `-s` option to the patch so that it reports only errors rather than everything. After it completes, the kernel has been upgraded to the next version. Of course, all of this could be done in one step—or as UNIX gurus like to call it, a one-liner:

```
linux:/usr/src # gzip -c /path/to/patch/patch-2.2.x.gz | patch -p0 -s
```

This command decompresses the patch and pipes it to the patch program on the fly.

What if you want to reverse a patch? This is done using the same patch program. To reverse the effects of a patch and restore your original files, run patch with the -R option:

```
patch -R < patch-2.2.x
```

This will revert the effect of the applied patch.

That's it! You unpacked the kernel in the correct place and imported your old configuration. Now you are ready to start configuring and compiling your kernel.

SuSE Specific Changes

If you have downloaded a kernel from somewhere other than SuSE, you will need to make a small modification to one of the kernel files—the makefile. Follow these steps:

1. Use your favorite editor to open the file /usr/src/linux/makefile.
2. Locate a line that says INSTALL_PATH=/boot. The line will be preceded by a hash mark (#).
3. Remove that hash and make sure that the line says INSTALL_PATH=/boot.
4. Save the file and exit. Now the kernel is ready to install on SuSE.

Now it's time to do the real thing, configure the kernel.

Configuring Your Kernel

This is the most important step of the process, the kernel configuration step. It's not very difficult; it just requires concentration. Now that you have unpacked the kernel and placed it in the right location, it's time to configure it. To do this you run the kernel configuration utility.

The kernel comes with three different versions of the configuration utility, two text-based and one graphical (GUI). The one that is the most user-friendly is the graphical one, followed by the menu-based text version, and then the fully–text-based version. All three have exactly the same set of options to configure for the kernel; it's just that each one displays them differently.

Before we go on and explain how to run and use each of the three different utilities, we'll provide a quick overview of the whole process of configuration/compilation.

Kernel Configuration/Compilation Quick Start

These are the steps for configuring and compiling the kernel:

1. Log in as root.
2. Decide whether you will use the graphical or text-based utilities. If you choose the graphical version, then run X Windows. If you want to use the text-based version, then you don't have to run X Windows. But it won't hurt if you do because you can run the text-based utilities from an X terminal.

3. Enter the following directory with the kernel sources:

```
# cd /usr/src/linux
```

4. Run the configuration utility with one of the following:

- `# make xconfig` for the graphical utility
- `# make menuconfig` for the menu-based utility
- `# make config` for the fully text-based, no menus utility

5. Configure the various kernel parameters.

6. Save the configuration and then exit the utility.

7. Start to compile the kernel by executing the following commands in sequence or in one line separated by a semicolon:

```
# make dep
# make clean
# make bzlilo
# make modules
# make modules_install
```

8. Reboot the system for the new kernel to load.

And you're done. Now for the detailed version....

Running the Graphical Kernel Configuration Utility

SuSE Linux comes with an excellent utility that enables you to configure, compile, and install the kernel with the least amount of effort. This utility is called `susewmif`. Please note that this utility is no longer supported by SuSE 6.3. To compile the kernel using this utility you have two choices. If you are running KDE, you can access it from the KDE menu, which is found in SuSE, Everything, System Tools, Compile Kernel. If you are not running KDE, you can still execute it by calling `susewmif` yourself from a command terminal by typing the following:

```
$ susewmif kernel
```

After the command is executed, a red-colored terminal window will be opened prompting the user for the root password (see Figure 8.5).

FIGURE 8.5
Enter your root password here.

After you enter your root password, `susewmif` will start the kernel's graphical configuration utility (see Figure 8.6). After you are finished configuring your kernel's options, click Save and Exit, which prompts you that you are now done with the configuration process and should proceed to the compilation process.

FIGURE 8.6

The kernel's graphical configuration utility is very user-friendly.

After you click OK to acknowledge the message, a new window appears. This is the Options for Kernel Compiling window (see Figure 8.7). The options it displays follow:

- **Build Kernel (`make bzImage`), recommended**—This option instructs the program to actually compile the kernel, so keep this one checked.

- **Build Modules (`make modules`), recommended**—If you have some components of the kernel marked as modules, you will have to check this option so that the program will compile these modules.

- **Install Modules (`make modules_install`), recommended**—If you have modules in your kernel, you will want to check this option to have the program install them for you.

- **Setup LILO (`make zlilo`)**—This option is a bit sensitive because it will install the new kernel as your default boot up kernel. If you are sure that you know what you are doing, then check it. If you are in doubt that the configuration you built might not boot correctly, you should not check this option and you should read on to learn how to install a kernel for testing rather than the default one.

- **Check Dependencies (`make dep`), recommended**—This option instructs the program to check that you have all the files required to successfully compile the kernel. Check it.

- **Remove Object Files Before Compiling (`make clean`), recommended**—This option removes all the files generated by a previous compilation. Checking it will make the compilation time longer but will ensure that you get a whole new kernel rather than using previously compiled components.

- **Clean Everything, Even Configuration Data (`make mrproper`), not recommended**—This option is rarely used because it totally reverts the kernel to its defaults, thus deleting all traces of your personal configuration. You might want to use it if you misconfigured the kernel somehow and would like to start again from scratch.

FIGURE 8.7
The final options for
the compilation
process.

Okay, you are almost done! To start compiling the kernel, press the Quit and Compile button, grab a cup of coffee, and relax as the kernel compiles. This might take somewhere from seven minutes to more than an hour depending on your processor's speed. After the compilation completes, if you have chosen the Setup LILO option, you will need to reboot for the new kernel to load. Otherwise, continue reading to learn how you can test your newly compiled kernel before actually installing it as your default.

Running the Text Menu-Based Kernel Configuration Utility

Now that you know how to run the graphical configurable utility, let's see how you can run the text menu-based one. You might need to use it if you do not have X Windows available on your machine (even though you can run it from within X Windows through an X terminal). Follow these steps:

1. The first thing you need to do is make sure that you are running as root. You can do that by either logging in as root or, if you are already logged in as a normal user, switch to root by running the command su and entering the root password, as in the following example:

   ```
   crash@linux:~ > su
   ```

2. Now enter your password at the following prompt:

   ```
   root@linux:/home/crash >
   ```

3. Now that you are root, you are permitted to run the configuration utility, which you can do by changing your current path to the kernel's directory:

   ```
   root@linux:/home/crash > cd /usr/src/linux
   root@linux:/usr/src/linux >
   ```

4. Type the command that runs the utility:

   ```
   root@linux:/usr/src/linux > make menuconfig
   ```

5. The program runs several commands of its own to prepare the menu-based configuration utility and then displays it (see Figure 8.8).

FIGURE 8.8
The kernel's menu-based configuration utility is very well organized.

This program is very easy to use. You use the arrow keys to navigate the menus, press the Enter key to enter a submenu, and use the highlighted letters as navigation shortcuts. For example, you can go to the Loadable Modules Support page by pressing the L key and then Enter. To exit a menu and go to the previous one, press the Esc key twice.

When it comes to choosing components, pressing Y includes that component, N excludes it, and M includes it as a module. You can use the spacebar to cycle through these options instead of using the appropriate letters. Components that have <> around them can be made into a module. [*] or <*> indicates that this component will be built in the kernel, <M> means that this component will be built as a module, and [ ] means that this component will not be built.

When you are done configuring the kernel via this program, chose Exit from the main menu. The program asks "Do you wish to save your new kernel configuration?"; choose Yes. Now you are ready to compile the kernel. To do so, you have to execute a few commands in the correct sequence. You can either enter them one by one or just put them all on one line separated by semicolons (;) and wait until it's finished. The commands in the correct sequence are as follows:

- **make dep**—This command checks that you have all the required files to compile the kernel.

- **make clean**—This command removes all traces of a previous compilation. It slows down the compiling process, but it ensures a clean kernel that is based solely on your configuration.

- **make bzImage**—This command compiles the actual kernel.

- **make bzlilo**—This command installs the kernel as your default. Use with caution! If you are not sure you want to install this kernel, don't run this. Read on to learn how to install a new kernel for testing purposes.

- **make modules**—If you have some components that are modules, you need to run this to compile them.

- **make modules_install**—If you have modules, run this to install them.

Or as a one-liner, enter the following:

```
root@linux:/usr/src/linux > make dep; make clean; make bzImage; make bzlilo;
    make modules; make modules_install
```

Now might be a good time for you to grab a cup of coffee because this is a lengthy process. It can take anywhere from seven minutes to over an hour depending on your hardware. When it is finished, if you have executed the `make bzlilo` command, you will need to reboot for the new kernel to load. Otherwise, read on to learn how to test the new kernel before installing it as your default.

Running the Text-Based Kernel Configuration Utility

Last but not least, you learn how to use the ancient method of configuring the kernel, the text-based utility. Follow these steps:

1. The first thing you need to do is make sure that you are running as root. You can do that by either logging in as root or, if you are already logged in as a normal user, switch to root by running the command `su` and entering the root password as in the following example:

   ```
   crash@linux:~ > su
   ```

2. Enter your password at the following prompt:

   ```
   root@linux:/home/crash >
   ```

3. Now that you are root, you are permitted to run the configuration utility. To do so, change your current path to the kernel's directory with the following command:

   ```
   root@linux:/home/crash > cd /usr/src/linux
   root@linux:/usr/src/linux >
   ```

4. Type the command that runs the utility:

   ```
   root@linux:/usr/src/linux > make config
   ```

5. This process is time-consuming. You are presented with every option of the kernel in a question form with the available options in brackets. For example:

   ```
   *
   * Code maturity level options
   *
   Prompt for development and/or incomplete code/drivers (CONFIG_EXPERIMENTAL)
   [Y/n/?]
   ```

   In this example, you are asked if you would like to be prompted for development and/or incomplete code/drivers. The options you have are Y for yes, which is the default one now; n for no; and ? for help on that option.

6. Proceed to configure the kernel by answering the questions.

When finished, continue compiling the kernel by executing a few commands in the correct sequence. You can either enter them one by one or just put them all on one line separated by semicolons (;) and wait until it's finished. The commands in the correct sequence are as follows:

- **make dep**—This command checks that you have all the files required to compile the kernel.

- **make clean**—This command removes all traces of a previous compilation, which slows down the compiling process but ensures a clean kernel that is based solely on your configuration.

- **make bzImage**—This command compiles the actual kernel.

- **make bzlilo**—This command installs the kernel as your default. Use with caution! If you are not sure you want to install this kernel, don't run this. Read on to learn how to install a new kernel for testing purposes.

- **make modules**—If you have some components that are modules, you need to run this to compile them.

- **make modules_install**—If you have modules, run this to install them.

Or as a one-liner, enter the following command:

```
root@linux:/usr/src/linux > make dep; make clean; make bzImage; make bzlilo;
    make modules; make modules_install
```

Now might be a good time for you to grab a cup of coffee because this is a lengthy process. It can take anywhere from seven minutes to more than an hour depending on your hardware. When it completes, if you have executed the make bzlilo command, you will need to reboot for the new kernel to load. Otherwise, read on to learn how to test the new kernel before installing it as your default.

Testing a Kernel Before Installing It

This is an important issue because if you are not sure that your new kernel will boot properly, there is no need to have it installed as the default kernel without testing it first! This happens to be a simple process. Instead of executing the make bzlilo step, replace it with make bzdisk and make sure you have a floppy disk in your A: drive.

This will install the kernel on the disk so that you can test it. Reboot the computer and it will boot from that disk. If all goes well and the kernel runs correctly, you can install it by running make bzlilo. If something goes wrong, remove the disk and reboot the computer to boot your old kernel.

But what if you don't have a disk drive? No problem—you can configure LILO to boot more than one kernel. Skip the make bzlilo step and use YaST to set up LILO to have an option to load your test kernel. Run YaST as root:

```
root@linux:/ > yast
```

Next, from the menu choose System Administration, Kernel and Boot Configuration, LILO Configuration. Or, to go directly to the LILO configuration, you can run YaST like this:

```
root@linux:/ > yast --mask lilo
```

Now you are ready to configure LILO (see Figure 8.9). Follow these steps:

FIGURE 8.9

LILO is very easy to configure using YaST.

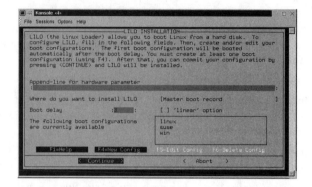

1. The first thing you need to do is create a new configuration for your test kernel. Press F4.

2. For the configuration name, enter test and press Tab to move on to the next field.

3. Choose Boot Linux for the Which Operating System option. YaST then should automatically fill in the (Root) Partition to Boot option with the correct partition; just check it to make sure.

4. As for the Kernel to be Booted by LILO Option, press F3 to get a file selection box.

5. Browse over to /usr/src/linux/arch/i386/boot/ and choose bzImage (see Figure 8.10).

FIGURE 8.10

Select the kernel to boot.

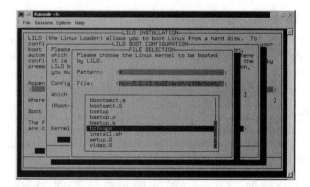

6. Save and exit.

7. You should now have a new entry called test. Press Enter to save the LILO configuration and exit.

Now you are ready to test your new kernel. Reboot the computer and at the LILO prompt, enter the word test. This will load your new kernel. If everything works correctly, run the make bzlilo command to install the new kernel as your default. Otherwise, reboot and load Linux as you normally would to revert back to your previous kernel.

Getting to Know the Various Important Configuration Parameters

Now that you know how to compile a kernel, let's have a look at the configuration parameters available. It will be very helpful to be familiar with the most common ones.

Code Maturity Level Options

Some parts of the kernel are still under development; hence, they are not stable enough for everyone to use. This happens even in the stable kernels. Developers like to encourage testing, so if you would like to see those options and drivers that are still in development and therefore not fully stable, you should say yes to this option. Saying no will make them invisible. Most people say no here, but if you *really* want a specific driver that is still experimental, then say yes here to be able to choose it. But be wary, it might not work as intended—that's why it is called experimental.

Processor Type and Features

This is where you pick the parameters for your processor:

Processor Family:	Here you will see a list of the various processor families supported, such as 386, 486/Cx486, Pentium, and so on. If you have a Pentium II or above, you should choose the Ppro/6x86MX option.
Maximum Physical Memory:	This options enables you to set the maximum size of memory your system has. You can set it to 1GB or 2GB of RAM.
Math Emulation	If your processor does not have a math coprocessor, you can have the kernel emulate one for you. All processors 486 DX and above have a math coprocessor, so you might not need kernel emulation.
MTRR (Memory Type Range Register) Support	This feature is only available for P-II and AMD-K6-2 Stepping 8 and above. These are special registers that might be used to control processor access to memory ranges. It is very useful if you have a PCI/AGP VGA card. By enabling this option and configuring X-Windows to use it, you can speed up your graphics by 2.5 times. If your processor supports this, enable it.
Symmetric Multi-processing Support	If you have more than one CPU in your machine, enable this option to have the kernel use all the available processors.

Loadable Modules Support

A loadable module is a part of the kernel that is not built inside the kernel; it is built as a separate object that is loaded when needed. Modules are very efficient in the sense that they make the size of the kernel smaller. Modules enable device drivers to be configured dynamically as they are loaded, in contrast to having to recompile the whole kernel to reconfigure one of the device drivers.

This is where you choose support for your modules:

Enable Loadable Modules Support	To enable the use of modules, say Y. This option is recommended.
Set Version Information on All Symbols for Modules	If you say Yes here, modules are built with the kernel version included. This way modules have to match the kernel version in order to be loaded. Saying No relaxes this constraint but might not be very safe in case one module is designed for a specific version of the kernel. No is safe to say here.
Kernel Modules Loader	Enabling this will autoload the modules on demand. Disabling this will cause modules to be loaded manually. Yes is a good choice here.

General Setup

This section includes most of the options that are common to most machines. Let's look at some of the important options:

Networking Support	You should say Yes here, even if you don't have a network. Some programs need to use the networking services even when running on a stand-alone machine. Say No only if you *really* know what you are doing.
PCI Support	If you have a PCI bus, say Yes.
System V IPC	IPC stands for Inter Process Communication. This option is very important to have because a lot of programs make use of System V IPC to communicate. Say Yes.
Kernel Support for a.out Binaries	a.out was the old format for executable files. It has been replaced with the new ELF format. You would be better off building support for a.out as a module because it's unlikely that you'll need it on a regular basis.
Kernel Support for ELF Binaries	Say Yes here. It's very important to have this because all programs are now in ELF format.
Parallel Port Support	Say Yes here if you want to use your parallel port with Linux. Can also be a module.

PC-Style Hardware	Say Yes here to have a PC-style parallel port.
Advanced Power Management BIOS Support	Say Yes here if your motherboard supports power management. This will enable features such as automatic power off on shutdown. Choose the power management features you need from the list that follows this option.

Plug-and-Play Support

Linux still lacks serious plug-and-play support. The plug-and-play support currently present in the kernel is for parallel devices only.

Block Devices

This section is where you define your block devices. Block devices are floppy disk drives, IDE device support, and so on. Let's look at the most important options here:

Normal PC Floppy Disk Support	Say Yes here if you have a floppy disk drive.
Enhanced IDE/MFM/RLL disk/ cdrom/ Tape/Floppy Support	If you have IDE devices, say Yes to enable them.
Include IDE/ATA-2 this is Disk Support	If your system is IDE-based, make sure that built in and is not a module. If your main hard disk is SCSI, you can have this as a module. The key point here is to make sure that you have built-in support for the hard drive that boots Linux.
Use DMA by Default When Available	Most of the current hard drives support Ultra DMA technology. This speeds up the performance of the hard drive. Saying Yes here will make Linux turn on this feature automatically. But beware, some hard drives fail when this option is on.

Networking Options

This section is where you set up your networking options. Most system administrators will need to set this up. The following are some of the important options:

TCP/IP Networking	You'd probably want to have this. Most of today's networks use this protocol to communicate. Even if you are not connected to a network, some programs use this protocol to communicate.

The rest of the options depend on your network's setup and are discussed later in other chapters.

SCSI Support

If you have any SCSI devices, this is where you configure them:

SCSI Support   Say Yes here to enable SCSI.

SCSI Disk Support   If you have a SCSI hard drive, say Yes.

SCSI CD-ROM Support   If you have a SCSI CD-ROM, say Yes.

Next, you will need to choose the appropriate device driver from the SCSI Low Level Drivers section.

Network Device Support

This is where you specify the networking devices present on your system:

Network Device Support Say Yes here to enable network device support.

Dummy Net Driver Support This is most commonly used by PPP and SLIP connections. Including it as a module is not a bad idea.

PPP Support Say Yes here if you will be needing PPP support, for example, if you need to connect to an ISP. You might want to make it a module.

SLIP Support Say Yes here if you will be needing SLIP support, for example if you need to connect to an ISP. You might want to make it a module.

Amateur Radio Support

If you would like to connect your Linux to an amateur radio, you will need to enable this option.

IrDA Subsystem Support

If you have a laptop that uses infrared wireless communication devices, you will need to enable this option to be able to use these devices.

ISDN Subsystem

If your machine has an ISDN modem, then you will need to enable this option.

Old CD-ROM Drivers (not SCSI, not IDE)

If you have an old CD-ROM that does not use SCSI or IDE, this is where you need to look for drivers for it.

Character Devices

Character devices include your terminal, mouse, printer, and so on. Let's look at some of the options you have here:

Virtual Terminal	This is the terminal that you see when your system boots up. It is virtual in the sense that you can have more than one running at the same time. Say Yes.
Support for Console on Virtual Terminal	This works with the virtual terminal; say Yes here.
Parallel Printer Support	If you want to use a printer with Linux, say Yes here.
Mouse Support (Not Serial Mice)	If you have a PS/2 or a non-serial mouse, you have to enable this option.

Video for Linux

This is where you should go if you have any video devices installed on your system, such as a QuickCam.

Joystick Support

If you have a joystick or gamepad, this is where you configure it.

Filesystems

This is one of the most important subsystems of the kernel configuration. This is where you define which filesystems you want your Linux to support. You will probably want to include most of these as modules because they are not used all the time by the kernel:

Quota Support	If you would like to enforce a disk space quota on your users, you need to enable this option.
Kernel Automounter Support	If you are a part of a large distributed network, you will want to enable this feature. It allows you to automatically mount remote filesystems on demand. If you have a small or no network, say No here.
DOS FAT fs Support	If you would like to deal with Microsoft FAT filesystem (DOS, Windows), you will need to enable this option. If you have Windows installed, say Yes.
VFAT (Windows 95) fs Support	Say Yes here to enable Linux to read the long filenames of Windows 9x.

ISO 9660 CDROM Filesystem Support	CD-ROMs use a filesystem called ISO 9660, so to be able to read your data CDs, you will need to have this option enabled.
Microsoft Joliet CDROM Extensions	This is an extension that Microsoft added to the ISO 9660 to enable it to use long filenames. Most CDs now use this extension, so you might want to have this option enabled.
Minix fs Support	This was the first filesystem used by Linux. You may never need to use it, but having it as a module won't hurt.
NTFS Filesystem Support (Read Only)	NTFS is the filesystem used by MS Windows NT and Windows 2000. If you have a partition with either of these two operating systems installed, enable this option to be able to read those partitions. You may read but not write on them. This is mainly for security reasons.
OS/2 HPFS Filesystem Support (Read Only)	HPFS is the filesystem used by OS/2. If you have OS/2 installed, you should enable this option to be able to read the OS/2 partition. Again, it's read-only.
/proc Filesystem Support	This is an important filesystem. Enabling this creates a directory called /proc that is not physically there. This directory acts like a control and information center for the kernel. You can read/change kernel parameters while it's running through this directory. Enable this.
UFS Filesystem Support	This is the filesystem used by SunOS and FreeBSD. If you have either of them installed, enable this to be able to read those partitions.

Network Filesystems

This is where you configure your network filesystems. Network filesystems enable you to share files over a network transparently:

Coda Filesystem Support	Coda is a very advanced network filesystem. It enables you to share files over a network as if they were on your local machine. It acts like NFS but is superior. It has support for laptops and disconnected machines.
NFS Filesystem Support	NFS allows you to share files with other UNIX machines over a network by mounting those terminals on local directories. If you have other UNIX machines, enable this.
SMB Filesystem Support	SMB is the protocol used by Window machines to communicate over a network and share files and printing. If you need to share files with Windows machines, enable this.

Sound

If you have a sound card and you want to be able to use it with Linux, this is where you need to configure it:

Sound Card Support In most cases you will need to enable this as a module. This way you can experiment with the parameters passed to the module to get your card working. If you have a Plug and Play sound card, you will have to set this as a module. If your sound card is not PnP, then you can set this to Y and configure your card as built-in.

OSS Sound Modules OSS sound modules are the most common sound modules. They have support for most sound cards, such as Creative Labs Sound Blaster. If you have a PnP card, set this to a module and configure your sound card using `isapnptools`.

Kernel Hacking

If you are interested in kernel development, you will want to enable this option. This option enables you to have control over the system even when it crashes. More information about this is found in the `documentation/sysrq.txt` file in your kernel directory `/usr/src/linux`.

Behind the Scenes

So, now you know almost everything there is to know about configuring, compiling, testing, and installing a kernel. But, have you ever wondered what really happens when you configure a kernel? Where is the configuration saved?

The kernel configuration utilities you used saved the kernel's configuration in a file called `.config`. Yes, it's the file you copied from your previous kernel to the new one so that you preserved your old configuration. This is a text file that has a simple format. Every option you configure is in that file in the following format:

`CONFIG_OPTION = y,m`

`OPTION` is the option you are configuring and `y` and `m` stand for Yes and *module*. If a line is preceded by a hash mark (#), that option is not included or is a No.

Let's have a look at what a common `.config` file looks like in real life:

```
#
# Automatically generated by make menuconfig: don't edit
#
#
# Language for Kernel Configuration
#
```

```
CONFIG_CONFIGLANG_ENGLISH=y
# CONFIG_CONFIGLANG_GERMAN is not set
#
# Code maturity level options
#
# CONFIG_EXPERIMENTAL is not set
#
# Processor type and features
#
# CONFIG_M386 is not set
# CONFIG_M486 is not set
CONFIG_M586=y
# CONFIG_M586TSC is not set
# CONFIG_M686 is not set
CONFIG_X86_WP_WORKS_OK=y
CONFIG_X86_INVLPG=y
CONFIG_X86_BSWAP=y
CONFIG_X86_POPAD_OK=y
CONFIG_MATH_EMULATION=y
CONFIG_MTRR=y
# CONFIG_SMP is not set
```

As you can see, the file is very simple to understand. Although it says at the beginning of the file not to attempt to edit it, if you know what you are doing, you can go ahead and edit the file yourself. There is little need to edit it yourself, but sometimes if you just want to turn on or off one option, it can be faster to just do it by editing that file manually rather than loading one of the configuration utilities. But, just in case, back up that file before attempting to tamper with it manually—better safe than sorry.

Troubleshooting

There are a few common problems that can occur when compiling the kernel. The following is a short list of these, along with suggested remedies:

When I run `make bzlilo`, it says something about the image being too big or something like that.

This is a fairly common error, specifically with the 2.2.x series of kernels. This is usually caused by having a lot of the options built in the kernel and not having them as modules. Built-in options increase the size of the kernel; so it is better to have most of the options as modules because this keeps the kernel small. So go through your kernel's configuration and see which options you can set as modules—the more the better.

The kernel acts weird (crashes, exhibits I/O problems).

This is usually caused by forgetting to run a `make clean` and `make dep` command. Running them and recompiling usually solves the problem. Another cause for this could be the version of the compiler that you are using to compile the kernel. SuSE comes with the appropriate compiler for the kernel. If you have upgraded your compiler to GCC 2.95, you might experience problems with your kernel. Linux uses GCC 2.7.2.3, and SuSE uses EGCS 1.1.x, which works fine. GCC 2.95 is not very kernel-friendly, so avoid it for kernel compilations.

My kernel takes forever to compile! And I have a fast machine.

This is due to having a lot of options in the kernel set. Any option you set in the kernel will take compiling time. And if you are compiling a kernel that was configured by SuSE, you will find a lot of options set that are unnecessary for your system. SuSE kernels try to include as many device drivers and options as possible so that they run on the largest number of configurations. A lot of these device drivers and options might not apply to your system, so there's no point compiling them. Again, go through the kernel configuration carefully and remove anything that does not apply to your system.

The kernel is slow.

Again, this is a problem with having a large kernel. Try using more modules, and removing options that you do not need.

The kernel compilation fails.

This is not supposed to happen. The kernel rarely fails a compilation, but if you have applied a patch to your kernel, it might happen. Sometimes patches fail to upgrade a kernel correctly. In that case, download the full kernel source, which should solve the problem. In the very unlikely event that a *stable* kernel release does not compile, be sure that it will be fixed by the time you discover this. Development kernels might not compile all the time, which is why they are in development.

Another cause could be your GCC version. Make sure that you are using the correct version. The one that comes with SuSE is guaranteed to compile kernels correctly. If you have attempted to upgrade your compiler, check your upgrade. Incorrect include files or paths might cause compilations to fail. One quick remedy is to reinstall the compiler rpms that came with SuSE.

Compilation aborts with some message about `internal compiler error`.

This is a tricky one. This error is *generally* associated with hardware problems. These hardware problems are usually faulty RAM or processor overheating. For the RAM, you can check this by clearing the contents of the RAM to enable a new copy of GCC to load, thus replacing a possibly corrupted memory image. To do this, use the `dd` command:

```
dd if=/dev/zero of=/dev/null bs=1024k count=64
```

This command will transfer 64MB of garbage to `/dev/null`, which is basically nowhere. Replace the number after counting the amount of RAM you have. This will clear the RAM for you. Now try to compile the kernel again, and if the same problem persists, then it could be faulty RAM or CPU overheating.

For CPU overheating, make sure that the heat sink is firmly attached to your CPU and that your PC is properly ventilated. If the CPU overheats, it starts to act weird, showing up most commonly in compilations. Cool down your CPU by powering the PC off for 30 minutes or so. If it compiles the kernel after that, then you have a problem with CPU overheating. Deal with it as soon as possible. For more information regarding this problem, check the site `http://www.bitwizard.nl/sig11`.

I compiled the kernel, but when I rebooted the system, I am still running my old kernel.

Did you run `make bzlilo`? If not, then do that. Another solution is to check your LILO configuration to make sure that it is correct. Finally, run LILO again.

I can't seem to compile anything after I installed my new kernel.

The most common mistake here is that after you compiled your kernel, you decided that the source files were taking up way too much space, and you deleted them. The kernel source files include header files that are crucial for almost all compilations, and if they are not there, a lot of things won't compile. To solve the problem, unpack the kernel source files again and run a quick `make config` just to make sure that all required links are created. ●

## CHAPTER 9

Configuring the System Boot Up Sequence

In this chapter

Understanding the Boot Up Process

It is important to know how Linux boots up. It helps when you want to customize the system further. The way Linux boots up can be divided into two major steps, the Linux Loader (LILO) and the runlevel scripts. Understanding how each of these parts works can help you control exactly how you want SuSE Linux to boot.

The Linux Loader

To understand what the Linux Loader (LILO) is, you need to know what happens when your computer is turned on. When you turn on your PC, the basic input/output system (BIOS) executes what is called a *power on self test* (POST). This test counts the amount of RAM you have and performs various tests on the system to ensure it is functioning properly. When this test completes, the BIOS reads the first sector on your hard disk and loads its contents into memory. Then, the BIOS transfers CPU control to that area in the memory to execute the code. This code loads your operating system.

From this information, you know that you want to place your operating system loader on the first sector of your hard disk—and this is precisely where LILO is. The BIOS loads LILO into memory and control is passed on to it. Then LILO starts to execute in the manner in which it was configured, loading the operating system into memory and passing control to it. Thus, the system boots up.

 TIP The following is the boot scenario:

You turn on your PC, BIOS loads and executes the POST, and then it loads LILO from the first sector of your hard disk. LILO loads the Linux kernel and passes control to it.

Configuring LILO

LILO has such a simple job, you might be wondering what there is to configure about it. Actually, LILO is a highly configurable and flexible multi-operating system loader. Even though it is called the Linux Loader, LILO can load several different operating systems other than Linux. This is why you can easily dual boot Linux with another operating system on the same machine. You configure LILO to give you the option of which operating system to load at boot up. (You may have already done this in the initial install process.)

YaST can be used to configure most of LILO's common options. Other more uncommon options require you to manually configure LILO yourself, which is a very simple task.

Using YaST to Configure LILO

YaST offers a very simple-to-use interface to configure LILO. To fully utilize the interface, you have to be familiar with its various options. Run YaST, navigate to System Administration, Kernel and Boot Configuration, LILO configuration. You can have YaST load directly into the LILO configuration screen by typing the following:

```
# yast --mask lilo
```

Figure 9.1 shows the LILO Installation screen that appears when YaST is loaded. Let's walk through the options on this screen to understand them; use the Tab key to cycle through them.

FIGURE 9.1

LILO setup using YaST.

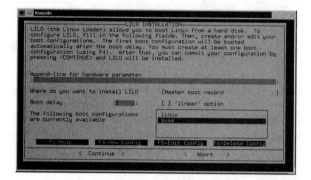

The first option is called Append-Line for Hardware Parameter (look ahead to Figure 9.2). When the kernel loads, it attempts to auto-detect the configured system resources used by most of the hardware. This can be the Ethernet card, the sound card, and so on. If the kernel is unable to automatically detect the resources used by these devices, you can tell the kernel what these resources are. To do so, you put them here, and when LILO boots the kernel, it will pass them to the kernel. Which parameters you put here depends on the device you are trying to configure.

The next option is Where Do You Want to Install LILO. You get the following four options here:

- **Master Boot Record**—This will make LILO the first thing executed after the BIOS. This is recommended for most configurations because you can configure LILO to give you the option of which operating system to boot.

- **Boot Sector of the Root Partition**—This will place LILO on the boot sector of your root partition. This way LILO should be called by another boot manager. You might want to use this if you are using another boot manager, such as the NT Loader, to boot Linux. Remember, you will always need to use LILO to load Linux.

- **Boot Sector of the /boot Partition**—This will do the exact same thing as the previous option, but will install LILO on a partition you created for the /boot directory.

- **On Floppy Disk**—This will install LILO on a floppy disk. This disk is good for emergencies because you can use it to boot your PC.

CAUTION

On some old systems, the BIOS was unable to see past cylinder number 1024 of the hard disk. Because LILO uses the BIOS to load the operating system, if the operating system was placed *after* cylinder number 1024, LILO would fail to boot it. Therefore, you might need to create a separate partition for /boot somewhere before cylinder number 1024. The /boot directory contains all the files required to boot Linux. Thus, by placing it before cylinder 1024, you should have no problems booting Linux. After Linux boots, you don't have to worry about that BIOS problem anymore. Please note that this problem exists in old hardware and if you have a Pentium class PC and up, chances are great that you don't have that limitation. However, if you need to use any BIOS extension software, you will likely experience this problem. In that case, you will need to consult your hard disk manufacturer to obtain these BIOS extensions. Another solution of course is to try and place your installation before the 1024 cylinder.

The next option, the Boot Delay, is the number of seconds that LILO should wait before proceeding to execute the first boot configuration. You can have LILO wait for you to pick an operating system to load, and then when it times out, it will load the first operating system on its list.

The Linear option is a fix for a problem with the BIOS not being able to handle disk geometry gracefully. Setting Linear to on can avoid problems caused by the BIOS.

The last option lists all the boot configurations that are currently available. The first one on the list is the default.

Adding a New Boot Configuration to LILO   To have LILO boot an operating system, you need to add it to the list of boot configurations. This is easy to do once you have all the information you need. This information depends on the boot configuration that you are trying to build. You can use LILO to either boot a different kernel for your SuSE Linux system, or load a different operating system altogether.

You might want to have LILO boot a different kernel for your installed Linux system for testing purposes. For example, say you installed a new kernel and you want to test it before you actually use it as your default. In this case, you can use LILO to load it upon demand. All you will need to know is the full path of the new kernel.

If you want to use LILO to load a different operating system, you will need to know on what partition that operating system lies. For example, if you have Window 98 installed on your machine along with Linux, you need to know where Windows is installed. This is easy to do using fdisk—follow these steps:

1. Log in as root.
2. Open an X terminal if you are using the X Window System.
3. Start fdisk, passing your hard disk as a parameter:
   ```
   # fdisk /dev/hda
   ```

4. Type p to have `fdisk` show you all the partitions on your hard disk.

5. To find where Windows is installed, you should use a line such as this:

   ```
   /dev/hda2    256   1997   13992615   f   Win95 Ext'd (LBA)
   ```

   From the file system type at the end of the line, you can tell that this is a Windows 9x partition.

6. Now that you know the partition you want is `/dev/hda2`, type q to quit `fdisk`.

You can use LILO to boot this partition.

TIP You can use LILO to boot another installation of Linux. Yes, you can have another partition with SuSE Linux on it and have LILO boot it. In this case, you will need to know the name of the partition on which this second SuSE Linux installation lies. Why would you want to do this? If you want to test something and you are too worried you might corrupt your main SuSE Linux installation, you can have another one to test.

Now that you have the information you need, you can create a new boot configuration for LILO:

1. Run YaST in the LILO configuration mode:

   ```
   # yast --mask lilo
   ```

2. Press F4 to add a new configuration for LILO to load.

3. In the Configuration Name option, type the name you want to use to load this configuration. For example, if this configuration is going to load Windows 98, a good name might be win.

4. Press the Tab key to move on to the Which Operating System option. Here you have three choices from which to pick:

   - **Boot Linux**—Choose this option if you want to boot another kernel for your system.

   - **Boot DOS/Win**—Choose this option if you want to boot a Windows- or DOS-based partition. This option should be used if you want to boot any other operating system, including another Linux partition.

   - **Boot OS/2**—Choose this option if you want to boot OS/2.

5. The next option is (Root-) Partition to Boot. This is where you specify to LILO the partition to boot. YaST will attempt to guess the correct partition to boot according to what you picked for an operating system. Correct it if it's wrong. (To see a list of partitions that fit your operating system choice, press F3.)

6. The Kernel Optional option is activated if you pick Boot Linux. This option is useful if you are testing a new kernel. When you check this option, LILO will never complain if it can't find the test kernel.

Part
II

Ch
9

7. The Kernel Optional option again is only activated if you choose Boot Linux. This is where you tell LILO the exact path to the kernel it should boot. Press F3 to get a window with a list of all the directories that you have on your hard disk. Navigate to where your kernel is and press Enter to pick it. The default kernel location is the /boot directory if you used a SuSE pre-compiled kernel, whereas it is the / directory if you downloaded and compiled a new kernel.

8. Press Tab to highlight the Continue button and press Enter to save your boot configuration.

9. YaST returns to the LILO Installation window—notice how your boot configuration was added to the list. Figure 9.2 shows the boot configuration setup by YaST.

FIGURE 9.2
New boot configuration added to LILO setup in YaST.

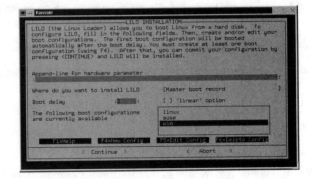

10. Press Tab to highlight the Continue button and press Enter to save this configuration to LILO.

11. YaST runs LILO to apply the changes. The result of the operation is shown in a small window. Figure 9.3 shows a successful LILO installation message.

FIGURE 9.3
YaST runs LILO to install a new MBR. The result is either a success or failure. In all cases, YaST will tell you the result.

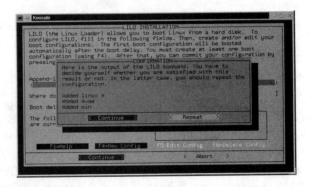

12. Press Enter to quit.

TIP When you download a Linux kernel and recompile it, the kernel is installed in the root directory (/) by default. However, you might want it to be installed in the /boot directory. To do so, you just have to edit the makefile of the kernel and change the line that says:

```
INSTALL_PATH=/
```

to

```
INSTALL_PATH=/boot
```

This way, when you compile and install the new kernel, it will be installed in the /boot directory.

Editing and Removing a Boot Configuration   If you want to edit one of the currently available boot configurations, you can do so using YaST. Follow these steps:

1. Run YaST, entering the following command:

    ```
    # yast --mask lilo
    ```

2. Use the Tab key to move to the list of available boot configurations.
3. Select the one you want to edit.
4. Press F5 to edit it or F6 to remove it.
5. When done editing, press Continue to exit.
6. Press Continue to save and quit.

Advanced LILO

YaST is perfect if you want to quickly configure LILO's most common options. But LILO has more options than YaST shows, and the only way to set those up is by directly manipulating LILO's configuration file—/etc/lilo.conf. A common LILO configuration file is made up of two sections.

The first section is the Global section, where you put all the options for LILO, as well as any options that apply to all the boot configurations.

The second section is the Boot Configurations section, where you have the settings for all the boot configurations. You can give each configuration its own set of options that apply only to it.

A basic lilo.conf file looks something like this:

```
# Start LILO global Section
boot=/dev/hda
#compact          # faster, but won't work on all systems.
vga=normal
read-only
prompt
timeout=100
# End LILO global Section
other = /dev/hda1
```

```
    label = win
    table = /dev/hda

image = /boot/vmlinuz
  root = /dev/hda6
  label = linux
other = /dev/hda1
  label = win2
  table = /dev/hda
```

The first option is the boot option, which tells LILO where to install itself. In this case, it's /dev/hda, which tells LILO to install itself on the Master Boot Record of the hard disk. If you use /dev/hda1, LILO will install itself on the boot sector of that partition.

The second option, compact, makes LILO load more quickly. (But this does not work on all systems.) This is useful when LILO is installed on a floppy disk, but if you are installing on a hard disk, the speed difference is not significant.

The vga option tells LILO which screen mode to start with. You can set the resolution of the screen in text mode using this option. Setting it to normal is recommended because it works on all systems. To have LILO give you a list of the available modes at boot up, enter vga=ask.

The read-only option is kernel-specific. It tells the kernel to mount the root filesystem as read-only. Later, as the system boots up, it will be mounted as read-writeable.

The prompt option tells LILO to wait for you to make a choice. This option works with the timeout option. If you have a prompt and don't have a value for timeout, then it will wait forever. This is not recommended because you will never be able to remotely reboot your system since it will stop at the LILO prompt waiting for input.

The timeout option is the number of tenths of a second that LILO should wait before timing out on any keyboard input operations, including the prompt operation.

The next section defines the boot configurations that LILO will handle. Every configuration has to start with either image or other. Use other if you will boot a different operating system or a different installation of Linux. Use image if you want to boot another kernel. Other takes the partition to boot as a parameter, while image takes the path to the kernel to boot as a parameter.

The label option receives the name of the configuration as a parameter. This is the name you would enter to boot this configuration.

The table option comes with the other option. It tells LILO on which device this partition is located. For example, if the partition is /dev/hda1, then the device is /dev/hda.

The root option comes with the image option. This takes the partition to boot as a parameter. This is usually the partition on which your SuSE Linux is installed.

In summary, if you want to create a boot configuration for booting Windows 98 on `/dev/hda1` and you want to call it `win98`, it would look like this in `lilo.conf`:

```
other = /dev/hda1
label = win98
table = /dev/hda
```

Now all you have to do is save `lilo.conf` and run `/sbin/lilo` to apply the changes. When you use YaST, it runs `/sbin/lilo` for you—that's why when you manually manipulate `lilo.conf`, you have to run `/sbin/lilo` yourself.

Part
II

Ch

9

Other options of interest that you can use include the `password` option. This is a particularly useful option when it comes to security. You can use it to put a password on either LILO as a whole or just on a boot configuration. This way you can block unauthorized people from accessing your whole PC or just from booting a specific operating system.

To put a password on LILO as a whole, just put the option somewhere in the `Global` section like this:

```
password=mypc
```

This will set the word `mypc` as a password to LILO as a whole. If you want to set a password for a particular boot configuration, just put it with the parameters for that configuration—for example:

```
other = /dev/hda1
label = win98
table = /dev/hda
password=runwin
```

Now, whenever you run the boot configuration `win98`, you will be prompted to enter a password. You have to take care of something, though. If you are going to use the `password` option, you have to set `lilo.conf` to be readable only by root. This is for security because the password is in plain text.

Another option of interest that belongs in the `Global` section is the `message` option. The `message` option takes a path to a file as a parameter. LILO will display the contents of this file when booting up, so you can put any message you want in here and it will show up when LILO loads. You have a maximum of 64 KB for this file. You will have to run `/sbin/lilo` to apply that change.

LILO has a lot of other options that you can use. You can find information about them by reading the man page for `lilo.conf`.

Uninstalling and Reinstalling LILO

If LILO has been installed on your master boot record (MBR), situations might arise in which you need to remove it or even reinstall it.

If you install or reinstall Windows 9x, it will overwrite your MBR and thus remove your current installation of LILO. The only way to fix this is to boot your installed Linux system from either your SuSE installation CD or a boot disk, reconfigure your LILO, and then reinstall it. If you don't need to reconfigure LILO to boot the newly installed MS Windows 9x, for example, then you just need to run /sbin/lilo to reinstall LILO on the MBR.

If you need to remove LILO, you need to overwrite your MBR. This can be done using Microsoft's fdisk utility. Either create an MS-DOS boot disk and copy fdisk.exe on it, or boot into Windows 9x and run fdisk from it. The command to remove LILO is as follows:

```
C:\> fdisk /mbr
```

This will replace your MBR with a DOS-based MBR and LILO will be removed.

LILO Error Interpretation

This section deals with interpreting the errors generated by LILO. LILO does not generate errors in the form of messages because of space limitations. Error messages require space and LILO is limited to just the boot sector. Thus, the error messages that LILO generates are in the word LILO itself. When you start your PC and you see the word LILO, you might think that LILO writes it all at once. What actually happens is that LILO writes it letter by letter after each boot stage is accomplished. The following are the various ways in which LILO gives you an error message:

- **Nothing appears when you start your system**—LILO isn't installed on the system or it isn't written on the boot sector. You might want to reinstall it again.

- **The letter *L* appears**—LILO is installed, but it cannot continue functioning. It's probably a media failure or incorrect geometry specified in the configuration file.

- **The letters *LI* appear**—Either the same as the preceding or the file /boot/boot.b does not exist. This error message might also occur if you have an old BIOS in which the boot directory exceeds the 1024-cylinder boundary. However, this situation is very unlikely nowadays.

- **The letters *LIL* appear**—Probably a geometry mismatch or media failure.

- **The letters *LIL?* appear**—It's likely the same problems as when *LI* appears.

- **The letters *LIL-* appear**—This is a case of geometry mismatch or the file /boot/map not existing.

- **The letters *LILO* appear**—You're not facing a problem with starting LILO. It should be starting up.

Reconfiguring LILO solves all these problems. If you run into any of these problems, all you have to do is reconfigure LILO to use the correct settings.

Another problem you might face is when you type in the OS you want to load but it doesn't load. If LILO complains about the OS not existing or problems of this kind, you should set up LILO one more time because this indicates that you didn't specify a correct partition.

init and Runlevels

Recall how you learned that the booting process has two major parts—the first being LILO loading the kernel? Now you get to discover the second phase of the boot up process—init and runlevels.

When LILO boots Linux, control is transferred to the kernel. The kernel boots, initializes the system, installs device drivers for the various hardware you have, and so on. When the kernel is finished, it executes init. init is a program responsible for creating the operating environment. What is meant by *operating environment*? Let's explain that. When the kernel loads, it prepares the machine to run programs by managing the various resources for them.

init starts a series of other programs that together make up the working environment for the user. These programs include filesystem-checking utilities, network initialization, login prompts, and so on.

init Scripts

But how does init know what to run? init initializes your whole system using scripts that are called *init scripts*. These scripts are executed by init one by one; each of them is responsible for preparing a part of the system. For example, the network script handles initializing the network for the system.

init scripts are found under /sbin/init.d/. This directory holds all the scripts that initialize the system. The following are the most common scripts:

boot	This is the first script that init executes. It checks your filesystems for errors, cleans up the system, and so on.
boot.local	This script gets called from within boot. It has nothing in it by default. If you want something to be executed when boot is being run, put it in here.
apache	This script starts the Apache Web Server.
cron	This script starts the cron scheduler daemon.
dhclient	This script initializes your network using DHCP.
firewall	This script puts up your firewall.
gpm	This script sets up mouse control in the console.
halt	This script gets called when you halt the system.

halt.local	Put anything here you want executed just before you halt your system.
hylafax	This script sets up HylaFax for Linux.
i4l	This script is for ISDN for Linux.
inetd	This script runs the inet daemon, which is responsible for setting up network services such as ftp and telnet.
network	This script brings up your networking capabilities.
nfs/nfsserver	These scripts are for NFS.
nscd	This script is responsible for the name switch daemon, which handles logins to the system.
pcmcia	This script initializes your PCMCIA devices.
powerfail	If your UPS tells Linux that a power fail is happening, this script gets called.
route/routed	These two scripts handle the kernel's routing tables.
rpc	This script is for Remote Procedure Calls (RPCs) under Linux.
sendmail	This script handles sendmail.
serial	This script initializes your serial ports.
single	This script takes your system to single-user mode.
smb	This script initializes Samba for MS-Windows connectivity.
xdm	This script brings up the graphical login manager.
skeleton	You can use this script as a starting point to create your own init script. Just fill in the commands you want to run.

As you can see, each of these scripts has a well-defined purpose. By using these scripts, you can start and stop any of these services without having to reboot. Each of these scripts takes four possible command-line arguments—start, stop, restart, and status. To start a service, simply type its name followed by the word start. For example, to start the network, enter the following:

```
bash#/sbin/init.d/network start
```

To stop the network, enter this:

```
bash#/sbin/init.d/network stop
```

Pretty simple, isn't it? The same applies to all the scripts.

Runlevels

Another parameter that init uses is the runlevel number. Runlevels are used by init to bring the system to different states of operation. By telling init to move from one runlevel to another, you are taking your system from one configuration to another. SuSE Linux comes with six runlevels:

- runlevel 0 is halt.
- runlevel S is single-user.
- runlevel 1 is multi-user without network.
- runlevel 2 is multi-user with network.
- runlevel 3 is multi-user with network and xdm.
- runlevel 6 is reboot.

Runlevels 4 and 5 are left empty so that you can edit them yourself. Now the whole picture should be clearer. If you want to switch your system from runlevel 3 (multi-user with network and xdm) to runlevel S (single-user), all you have to do is tell init to do that. This is simply done by running the command:

```
# telinit runlevel
```

To switch to single-user, enter the following:

```
# telinit S
```

Runlevels are directories that hold the scripts required to bring the system to the configuration specified by the runlevel. Each runlevel has its own directory that contains symbolic links to the appropriate links in /sbin/init.d. Runlevel directories are found in /sbin/init.d/. Each runlevel has its own directory named rcX.d, where X is the number of the runlevel. So runlevel 3 is rc3.d.

Most of the time the order in which you call the scripts is important, which is why you can number them for init. If you look at any of the runlevel directories, you will see half the links start with *SXXname* and the other half with *KXXname*. S indicates that the script is to be run when starting the runlevel and K indicates a script that runs when killing the runlevel. The *XX* is a number that denotes the order of that script, starting from 01. For example, S06firewall is linked to /sbin/init.d/firewall, and means that this script is to be run as the sixth script.

When init is starting a runlevel, it calls all the links that start with *S*, with the start parameter as a command-line argument. This starts the correct scripts to bring the system up in a particular configuration. And when init switches runlevels, it first calls all the scripts that start with *K* in the current runlevel with stop as a command-line argument. init then calls the scripts of the new runlevel with start. This happens when you reboot or halt your system; remember that reboot and halt are runlevels as far as Linux is concerned.

Switching runlevels is done using the telinit command. Run telinit with the number of the runlevel you want to switch to as a command-line argument. For example, to switch to runlevel 2, you would enter the following:

```
bash#/sbin/telinit
```

This will tell `init` to start executing all the K scripts in the current runlevel and then all the S scripts in runlevel 2. No reboot is necessary.

Booting to a Different Runlevel Using LILO

`init` reads the number of the runlevel to boot into by default from `/etc/inittab`. The line for this is the following:

```
# default runlevel
id:3:initdefault:
```

The default runlevel to boot into is 3. If you want to have `init` act otherwise, you can either replace this number with the runlevel you want, or have LILO tell `init` which runlevel to boot into.

LILO can tell `init` which runlevel to start. This can be helpful if you are having problems booting your Linux and you can't change the default value in `inittab` to another one that works. You have LILO tell `init` which runlevel to execute for now until you can change it later or fix the problem. To have LILO do that, pass the runlevel number to LILO after the name of the image to load, as in the following example:

```
LILO BOOT: Linux
```

This causes Linux to boot in runlevel 2. Simple, isn't it? But remember, this is only temporary; next time you reboot, it will boot into the default runlevel in `inittab`.

Modifying the Runlevels

You can modify which scripts are to be executed for each runlevel by using YaST to turn off the services these scripts execute. YaST will then modify the scripts to reflect that change for you.

Another way you can do this is by simply editing the YaST generated script configuration file. This file is located in `/etc/rc.config`. You will find the names of all the services represented by your scripts in that file. A `yes` in front of the name allows that script to be executed, a `no` does not execute it.

One way you can do this, which we don't really recommend, is by removing the links to those scripts from the respective `rcX.d` directories. This way these scripts won't be executed in this runlevel.

Adding Your Own Script to the *init* Scripts

Adding your own script to the `init` scripts is not hard to do. But before you decide to create your own script, you might find it easier to edit `boot.local` instead. To create your own script, do the following:

1. Copy `/sbin/init.d/skeleton` to a new file named after the script you want to create:

   `#cp skeleton myscript`

2. Open `myscript` using your favorite text editor.

3. Find the text `start)`.

4. Put the commands you want your script to start here.

5. Put the commands you want to be executed when your script is called with `stop` after the `stop)` text.

6. Do the same for `restart)` and `status)` if you find it useful. You don't have to use them.

7. Save the script.

8. Make the script executable:

   `#chmod +x myscript`

9. Now you need to add that new script to your runlevel. You use the `rctab` command to do that:

   ```
   #ln -s Smyscript ../myscript
   #ln -s Kmyscript ../myscript
   ```

10. Run the following command:

    ```
    #export EDITOR=pico
    #rctab -e
    ```

11. The command will start the pico editor with a file that looks very much like this:

    ```
    #
    # Generated by rctab: Thu Jan  6 20:39:41 PST 2000
    #
    #  Special scripts
    #
    #  halt   -- only for runlevel 0
    #  reboot -- only for runlevel 6
    #  single -- only for single user mode
    #
    #  Remaining services
    #
    # apache apmd argus arkeia at atalk autofs boot.setup cron dhclient dhcp
    # dhcrelay dummy gpm halt.local hylafax i4l i4l_hardware identd idled ijb
    # inetd inn ipcmdrd ircd kbd kerneld ldap lpd mysql named nazeeh network
    nfs
    # nfsserver nisplus nscd ntopd nwe pcmcia pcnfsd quota quotad radiusd
    random
    # rinetd route routed rpc rwhod scanlogd sendmail serial smb smbfs
    snifflic
    # snmpd squid svgatext syslog usb webgw wwwoffle xdm xntpd ypclient
    yppasswdd
    # ypserv ypxfrd
    #
    Runlevel:1  Runlevel:2    Runlevel:3    Runlevel:4  Runlevel:5
    ```

kerneld	kerneld	kerneld	-	-
serial	serial	serial	-	-
pcmcia	i41_hardware	i41_hardware	-	-
dummy	pcmcia	pcmcia	-	-
syslog	dummy	dummy	-	-
boot.setup	dhclient	dhclient	-	-
random	i41	i41	-	-
svgatext	network	network	-	-
apmd	route	route	-	-
gpm	rpc	rpc	-	-
kbd	argus	argus	-	-
-	nfs	nfs	-	-
-	scanlogd	scanlogd	-	-
-	syslog	syslog	-	-
-	boot.setup	boot.setup	-	-
-	nisplus	nisplus	-	-
-	routed	routed	-	-
-	named	named	-	-
-	quota	quota	-	-
-	quotad	quotad	-	-
-	random	random	-	-
-	yppasswdd	yppasswdd	-	-
-	ypserv	ypserv	-	-
-	ypxfrd	ypxfrd	-	-
-	ypclient	ypclient	-	-
-	autofs	autofs	-	-

12. Your file may look a bit different, but should have the same format. To add your new service to a runlevel, simply write its name under it. For example, to add your script to runlevel 3, add its name under the column titled Runlevel 3.

13. When done, simply exit the editor. rctab will then process your changes and update the runlevels accordingly.

That's all it takes. Just make sure that your script has all the proper commands and nothing extra. If you need help, you can always see how any of the other scripts works. You can get quite a lot of ideas from reading other scripts.

Troubleshooting

I added a new service to the runlevels, but it doesn't work.

Are you sure that it has executable permissions? If not, run a chmod +x script command to fix that. ●

Sound Card Configuration

Linux and Sound: A Brief History

As we all know, in the early stages of Linux development, most of its users were programmers. These users didn't care for multimedia as much as memory management and process scheduling. Thus, for a long time Linux existed with no support for sound or sound applications. It was only when a company specializing in the implementation of UNIX multimedia decided that this OS needed some help with sound. The company's name was 4Front, and the project was Open Sound System support for Linux. Open Sound System (OSS) is considered the first project to unify a standard for UNIX sound systems on all UNIX architectures.

Support for Linux was important for both Linux and OSS. Linux found a standard sound system that had existed for a long time, was reliable, and contained sound applications that used OSS. OSS also gained a lot by supporting Linux. With the large number of Linux developers and the large number of applications they wrote using the OSS API, OSS ensured its existence as a standard for UNIX sound systems and expanded the support for sound cards to the standard PC sound cards.

OSS comes in two versions:

- A full commercial version that supports a large number of sound cards
- A lite GPL version that supports a small number of standard cards

It wasn't until recently that a group of Linux programmers decided to begin work on a new sound drivers project: Advanced Linux Sound Architecture (ALSA). The project aims to build a new standard and a full list of supported sound cards, and at the same time keep backward compatibility with the OSS standard. This step will ensure that the present sound programs that rely completely on OSS will work, and it also presents a new standard with new APIs.

Only a few months ago manufacturers began to realize that Linux has become a power in the operating systems market and started writing drivers for Linux. 4Front offers a fully functioning OSS version for a trial period of seven days; this will be referred to in this chapter as *OSS demo*. The full registered version of OSS will be referred to as *OSS*, while the GPL'd version that comes with the kernel will be referred to as *OSS/lite*.

What SuSE Linux Offers

SuSE Linux is an extremely helpful distribution. If you have the full version of SuSE Linux, you also have a full OSS version (3.8.1) and the demo version of OSS (latest on 4Front FTP). The difference between the two versions is that the commercial version does not include support for some ISA sound cards. On the other hand, the demo version supports some PCI cards. SuSE assumes that you do not redistribute the registered OSS version. You should read the license agreement file located in `/usr/lib/oss`. The package is found in series pay/oss.

Many sound cards are supported by the three sound card drivers—OSS/lite, OSS (commercial), and ALSA. In this case, we recommend using the ALSA drivers. This is because ALSA keeps backward compatibility with OSS API, thus enabling you to run the applications that require OSS, while also running the applications that use ALSA.

Software Requirements

The software requirements for this chapter are unique in style. The following are the general software requirements that are needed for sound to run. If you are going to use OSS/Lite, OSS, or ALSA, you will have to use the software listed in the following list along with the software specified in the section of the driver you are going to use:

Package Requirements:

Series a:

- isapnp (for Plug-n-Play cards)
- pciutils (for automatic configuration of Plug-n-Play cards)

Series snd:

 TIP From the packages listed here, you can pick up what you like. They are not essential for configuring the sound card, but we recommend the following.

- audiofil
- esound
- sox
- xmix

Series pay:

 TIP Only if you are planning to use OSS should you select only one of the following. Those packages are not included in the snapshot version of SuSE Linux.

Kernel Requirements:

Sound:

- Sound core support (as module)

Part
II

Ch
10

Setting Up Hardware

This process is rather long, so be patient. In this process you will be checking whether your sound card is configured through DIP switches/jumpers or through PnP. Most of the new sound cards are PnP; so, if you have a new sound card, it's probably PnP. Linux support for PnP devices is not performed by the kernel (2.2.x series). This does not mean that you won't be able to use your sound card, though. Thanks to the `isapnptools` package, you can configure your PnP devices and use them with no trouble.

Searching for the Proper Resources

In all cases, you must search for the proper resources for the sound card. In this part you will look for available IRQs, DMA, and ports. To list the available resources, you should use the proc file system information in the `/proc/interrupts`, `/proc/dma`, and `/proc/ioports` virtual files.

Issue the following command to list the available free interrupts:

```
bash#cat /proc/interrupts
          CPU0
   0:    9780712       XT-PIC  timer
   1:      61964       XT-PIC  keyboard
   2:          0       XT-PIC  cascade
   4:     710344       XT-PIC  serial
   6:        562       XT-PIC  floppy
   8:          2       XT-PIC  rtc
  11:       9692       XT-PIC  eth0
  13:          1       XT-PIC  fpu
  14:    6119932       XT-PIC  ide0
  15:      74241       XT-PIC  ide1
NMI:
```

As the command output indicates, the following IRQs are available: 3, 5, 7, 10, 11, and 12. You can use any of them for the sound card. Note that IRQ 9 and IRQ 2 are the same interrupt and are not proper IRQs for the sound card. You should not use any IRQ listed in the command output; they are already taken. You should first try the 5, 7, and 10 interrupts. This does not mean that the other IRQs cannot be used. But, it's generally preferred that sound cards use these interrupts.

> **CAUTION**
>
> Some IRQs should not be used because they belong to motherboard resources. If you use any of them you will either slow down the performance of your Linux box or lock it up. These interrupts are 1, 6, 8, 13, and 14. IRQ sharing is nice, but not with those interrupts.

The output of the DMA list shows which DMA is taken:

```
bash#cat /proc/dma
 2: floppy
 4: cascade
```

You should not allocate DMA that is already taken. DMA 0, 1, and 3 can be used as low DMA, whereas 5, 6, and 7 can be allocated for high DMA. You are concerned with using only two of them, which will represent the low and high DMA that are used by sound cards:

```
bash#cat /proc/ioports
0020-003f : pic1
0040-005f : timer
0060-006f : keyboard
0070-007f : rtc
0080-008f : dma page reg
00a0-00bf : pic2
00f0-00ff : fpu
0170-0177 : ide1
01f0-01f7 : ide0
02e8-02ef : serial(set)
02f8-02ff : serial(auto)
0376-0376 : ide1
03c0-03df : vga+
03f0-03f5 : floppy
03f6-03f6 : ide0
03f7-03f7 : floppy DIR
df40-df5f : eth0
```

The preceding list indicates the available I/O ports. For a sound card to correctly work, you need to assign the card an unused I/O port.

Configuring Your Card to Use the Proper Resources

Sound cards are either PnP or non-PnP. This means that you will either have to set your card using isapnptools if it is a PnP card, or you will have to set it up using jumpers/DIP switches. In very rare cases where your sound card does not have jumpers/DIP switches and it is not a PnP card (like the early Sound Blaster 16 versions), you will have to use a utility that comes with the card to configure it.

A Jumpers/DIP Switches-Oriented Sound Card   You'll have to get the manual of your sound card and set up the card to use the resources that you found unused on your system. The manual should describe how to set up the card to use the proper IRQ, DMA, and I/O port. If you have another running operating system on which the sound card works, you may skip this part.

A PnP-Oriented Sound Card   If you plan to use the commercial version of OSS, skip this part. If you have any problems running it, come back to read this section or check if your sound card is supported by OSS. If you plan to use OSS lite or ALSA, you should read this part.

Understanding the PnP System and Its Use with Linux   The PnP system was made to make the user's life easier by making the assignment of resources dynamically allocated to the device. This means that the PnP device does not have a specific resource unless the system allocates the resource to the device. Each PnP device has a non-volatile memory that holds the possible configurations to which it can be set. In PnP-oriented operating systems, the operating system probes the devices and manages the allocation of resources at boot time. Unfortunately, Linux does not do that yet. What is available is a package called isapnptools. You use a part of this package called pnpdump, which is a program that scans your system for PnP devices and dumps the possible configurations stored on the PnP device. You edit the output of pnpdump to suit your system and execute the second program in the package, isapnp. This program, isapnp, reads the configuration file generated by pnpdump and configures the PnP devices.

Setting Up a PnP Sound Card   The process is a simple one once you understand what's going on. First, we will look at some information that you need to know about isapnptools. The configuration file for isapnptools is located in /etc/isapnp.conf. This file, if found, will be used by isapnp at system startup to configure the PnP devices. If the file does not exist, isapnp is not run. The other piece of information is that pnpdump can guess and write the correct PnP settings for the PnP devices without further help from the user. The bad news is that it could lock up your system in this operation.

The first step is to back up your isapnp.conf file, if it exists:

```
bash#cp /etc/isapnp.conf /etc/isapnp.conf.bak
```

If you think that setting up isapnp is going to be much trouble and you have another PnP OS installed on your system, you can do the following:

1. Start your computer, enter the BIOS, and specify that you don't have a PnP OS.
2. Start your computer in the other PnP OS.
3. Set up the sound card PnP settings and make sure it's working.
4. Start your computer in Linux using loadlin.
5. Log in as root.
6. Issue the command pnpdump -c > /etc/isapnp.conf.
7. Issue the command isapnp /etc/isapnp.conf.

If you get any problems, read the following section about troubleshooting isapnp.

If you don't have another OS installed on your system, you will have to set up the sound card manually. The steps are very simple, though:

1. Log in as root.
2. Issue the command pnpdump -c > /etc/isapnp.conf. This command will search your system for any PnP devices and generate the configuration file with the current settings of each device.

3. Issue the command isapnp /etc/isapnp.conf. This command will try to configure the PnP devices specified in the configuration file with the specified parameters.

CAUTION

You might be faced with one of the following cases when applying isapnptools:

- Your system locks up when using pnpdump -c.

  You'll have to generate the file without the -c parameter and edit the isapnp.conf file yourself.

- Your system locks up on isapnp.

  You'll have to reboot. If your system locks up when you start the system, use the SuSE emergency system on the SuSE installation media, mount your Linux partition, and edit the isapnp.conf file.

- isapnp outputs a fatal error.

  The resources listed in the isapnp.conf file are already in use. In most cases, they are already used by the device you want to assign the resources to. Reboot and if you get the same error at system start, you will have to edit the isapnp.conf file manually.

 TIP   You can use the SuSE Emergency System at any time to mount a system with boot up problems. In SuSE 6.3, you should boot using the second CD (Text based).

Boot from the Linux installation media or use the setup.exe to start the installation process. Boot the SuSE Emergency System. It should boot to a login prompt. Log in as root and enter the following:

```
bash#mount /dev/(Your Linux Partition) /mnt
bash#cd /mnt/etc
bash#vi isapnp.conf or bash#mv isapnp.conf isapnp.bak
```

Editing the isapnp.conf File   Throughout this book, you'll find many sections about editing the isapnp.conf file. In each chapter that we mention isapnp.conf, we'll be interested only in setting the device discussed by the chapter. So, if you find some devices in your isapnp.conf file without configuration, either look in the file you just backed up (isapnp.conf.bak) or look up the configuration procedures of the device in the corresponding chapter.

Here is a sample section from the isapnp.conf file:

```
1 # [ Start of the configuration of the 1. logical device on the 1.
  ISAPnP card]
2 # Multiple choice time, choose one only !
3 # [ Now you are offered different configuration possibilities for
  LD 0 ]
4 # [ Each possibility is separated from the following by a blank
  line ]
```

```
 5 # [ You should only select one possibility for each logical
 6 # [ Start of the configuration of the 1. logical device on the
   1. ISAPnP card]
 7 (CONFIGURE CTL009d/66776 (LD
 8 #              ANSI string -->Audio
 9 # [ 1. Configuration possibility for the 1. logical device]
10 # [ of the 1. ISA-PnP card ]
11 # Start dependent functions: priority preferred IRQ 5.
12 # High true, edge sensitive interrupt (by default)
13 (INT 0 (IRQ 5 (MODE +E)))
14 # First DMA channel 1.
15 # 8 bit DMA only
16 # Logical device is not a bus master
17 # DMA may execute in count by byte mode
18 # DMA may not execute in count by word mode
19 # DMA channel speed in compatible mode
20 (DMA 0 (CHANNEL 1))
21 # Next DMA channel 5.
22 # 16 bit DMA only
23 # Logical device is not a bus master
24 # DMA may not execute in count by byte mode
25 # DMA may execute in count by word mode
26 # DMA channel speed in compatible mode
27 (DMA 1 (CHANNEL 5))
28 # Logical device decodes 16 bit IO address lines
29 # Minimum IO base address 0x0220
30 # Maximum IO base address 0x0220
31 # IO base alignment 1 bytes
32 # Number of IO addresses required:
33 (IO 0 (BASE 0x0220))
34 # Logical device decodes 16 bit IO address lines
35 # Minimum IO base address 0x0330
36 # Maximum IO base address 0x0330
37 # IO base alignment 1 bytes
38 # Number of IO addresses required:
39 (IO 1 (BASE 0x0330))
40 # Logical device decodes 16 bit IO address lines
41 # Minimum IO base address 0x0388
42 # Maximum IO base address 0x0388
43 # IO base alignment 1 bytes
44 # Number of IO addresses required:
45 (IO 2 (BASE 0x0388))
46 (ACT Y)
```

This example shows the configuration of an AWE32 sound card using the following information:

■ IRQ= 5 as in line

■ Low DMA (8bit)=1 as in line

■ High DMA (16 bit)= 5 as in line

- ■ I/O port = 220 as in line
- ■ I/O port midi= 330 as in line
- ■ I/O MPU port= 388 as in line

TIP You'll find all the possible combinations of configurations that your sound card can take in the file /etc/isapnp.conf. You can comment out all the configurations, and then pick up a different one that has different resources and uncomment the lines that specify the correct configuration that you want your card to be set up to.

When you're done, issue the isapnp command again and check for the output message. Try different configurations until you get no error messages. If you still get warning messages, check the conflicts using the following commands:

- ■ To check on IRQ conflicts, enter the following:

  `bash#cat /proc/interrupts`

- ■ To check on DMA conflicts, enter the following:

  `bash#cat /proc/dma`

- ■ To check on I/O ports conflicts, enter the following:

  `bash#cat /proc/ioports`

Notice that isapnp can generate an error when trying to assign the interrupt to its owner if its owner already has it. In other words, suppose that the card is already set up to use IRQ 5. If you run isapnp again, it will generate an error because IRQ 5 is already taken. Reboot and check the isapnp output at system start up; if all goes smoothly, your system is fine. If you get any fatal error conflicts, you should do one of the following:

- ■ If you are absolutely sure that the error mentioned is not fatal, then edit the isapnp.conf file and modify the conflict line from

  `(CONFLICT (IO FATAL)(IRQ FATAL)(DMA FATAL)(MEM FATAL))`

  to

  `(CONFLICT (IRQ WARNING)(DMA WARNING)(MEM WARNING))`

  In this example, you force isapnp to generate a warning message instead of a fatal error message. You also force it not to complain at all for I/O conflicts.

- ■ If there are conflicts you want to get rid of, then edit the isapnp.conf file and pick up a different configuration.

Configuration of OSS/Lite

The OSS/lite version that comes with the kernel is not hard to configure. The main configuration file for this version is /etc/modules.conf, which contains the parameters that should be assigned to the modules when they are loaded. There are more advantages to setting up the sound as a module than using it as built-in. See Chapter 8, "Installing a New Kernel," for more information on modules. If you are using a default SuSE kernel, which is a kernel that comes precompiled from SuSE, make sure that you install the modules package. The following are the packages needed in case you don't want to recompile your kernel:

Series a:

- modules
- kernmod (only if you don't want to recompile the kernel)

On the other hand, if you like compiling your kernel, you should install the following packages:

Series d:

- linclude
- linux

or

Series d:

- lx_suse

Kernel Configuration and Sound Cards

Before we discuss this part, if you do not want to recompile your kernel and you are currently using the version that comes with SuSE, you can skip this part and go directly to modifying the modules configuration file. If you are using a different kernel that you installed on your own, you are encouraged to read this part.

What Kernel Configuration Do I Need For My Sound Card?

This is the most important question that you should ask yourself. And the best way to find the correct answer is to look in the /usr/src/linux/Documentation/sound directory. In this directory, search for a file that has the same name as your sound card and read the related information. Next, start whichever kernel configuration utility you prefer (refer to Chapter 8). While running X, open an xterm and issue the following commands:

```
bash$xhost +localhost
bash$su -l
bash#cd /usr/src/linux/
bash#export DISPLAY=:0
bash#make xconfig
```

Suppose you have an SB16 card that you want to set up. First click the sound button and check what options you have:

- Sound card support
- OSS sound modules (a large list of sound cards are supported by OSS/lite)
- 100% Sound Blaster compatibles (SB16/32/64, ESS, and Jazz 16) support
- FM synthesizer (YM3812/OPL-3) support

These are all the options you need to set for your SB16 card (see Figure 10.1). They will be the same for the cards listed in the preceding list's third bullet, that is (SB16/32/64, ESS, and Jazz 16).

FIGURE 10.1

Setting up the kernel options for a Sound Blaster 16. You can click help at any time to get more information about the cards supported by the driver.

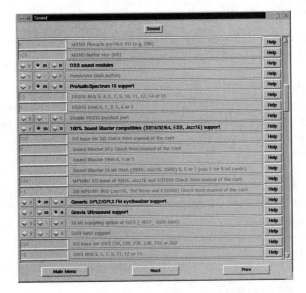

It is not difficult to pick up the correct modules. You can read the help associated with each option that you pick. Also, if you add modules that your sound card does not really need, the only harmful outcome will be an increase in the compile time. This is not a severe problem on a fast machine, although it is not a good practice.

Editing the Modules Configuration File

The modules configuration filename has changed from /etc/conf.modules to /etc/modules. conf. SuSE has prepared it all for you. The SuSE team provides you with a ready-to-edit modules.conf file that will make your life easier. First, you have to understand what this file does. The modules.conf contains the options that the modules should use when they start. Because sound is compiled as a module, when it is loaded, it uses the configuration stored in the modules.conf file to adjust to this configuration. SuSE has a modules.conf file that has a pre-setup for most sound cards that only needs to be uncommented and set to work directly. As for the SB16 that you just made, you will now set up the `modules.conf` file for its kernel configuration.

Activating the Sound Character Device   The sound module is turned off by default in the `modules.conf` file. You need to comment out the following lines:

```
alias char-major-14 off
alias sound off
alias midi off
```

thus, changing them to

```
#alias char-major-14 off
#alias sound off
#alias midi off
```

In the original `modules.conf` file that comes with SuSE, those lines should be located around line 44.

CAUTION

SuSE Linux comes with the sound character device turned off. You have to turn it on before you can use the sound. Even if you set up your sound card correctly, if you leave the sound character device turned off, your sound card will not work.

Setting Up the Sound Card Parameters   If you look in the available sound cards, you will find this section:

```
 1  #**********************************************************************
 2  #     module : sb.o                  Soundblaster 16, SB Pro + Clones
 3  #                                     Also needed for AWE32/64
 4  #
 5  #     Documentation available in
    ↪/usr/src/linux/Documentation/sound/Soundblaster
 6  #     and in /usr/src/linux/drivers/sound/sb.c .
 7  #
 8  #     Possible configuration :
 9  #
10  # alias char-major-14 sb
11  # post-install sb /sbin/modprobe "-k" "adlib_card"
12  # options sb io=0x220 irq=7 dma=1 dma16=5 mpu_io=0x330
13  # options adlib_card io=0x388
14  #
15  #**********************************************************************
```

This section, if set properly, will be the configuration for the SB16 card. Let's say that the sound card uses IRQ=5, IO=0x220, DMA= 1—the 8 bit DMA, DMA16=5—the 16 bit DMA, MPU_IO=0x300, and ADLIB_CARD_IO=0x388. These values can be obtained from the `isapnp.conf` file or from the jumper settings you made to the card.

Thus, the lines should look like the following:

```
10 alias char-major-14 sb
11 post-install sb /sbin/modprobe "-k" "adlib_card"
12 options sb io=0x220 irq=5 dma=1 dma16=5 mpu_io=0x300
13 options adlib_card io=0x388
```

Note that you removed the # sign, which means that this line is a comment. Also note that line numbers are not included but are written here for the sake of illustration.

Installing the Modules This is the simplest process of all. In this step, you will load the sound modules. After you load them with the new configuration, you will be able to listen to music. Follow these steps:

1. In another console, run the command #tail -f /var/log/messages.

2. Next you need to load the sound module. Issue the following command to probe for the sound module:

   ```
   bash#modprobe sb
   ```

   sb is the name that we gave to the module. In the /etc/modules.conf file (line 10) we called the sound character device sb.

Testing the Sound Configuration

You can test the presence of a proper sound card configuration by issuing the following command:

```
bash#cat /dev/sndstat
OSS/Free:3.8s2++-971130
Load type: Driver loaded as a module
Kernel: Linux coffin 2.2.13 #12 Sun Oct 24 07:10:02 EET 1999 i586
Config options:

Installed drivers:

Card config:

Audio devices:
0: Sound Blaster 16 (4.13) (DUPLEX)

Synth devices:
0: Yamaha OPL3

Midi devices:
0: Sound Blaster

Timers:
0: System clock

Mixers:
0: Sound Blaster
```

This shows a proper installation of a Sound Blaster 16. To test if the sound plays, issue the following command:

```
bash#cat file.au >/dev/audio
```

In this command, `file.au` is an existing sound file of the au format. If you want to listen to how your kernel sounds, try the following:

```
bash#cat /boot/vmlinuz >/dev/audio
```

Troubleshooting OSS/Lite

After I do the modprobe *and I do a* cat /dev/sndstat, *I don't find any sound devices.*

Solution: Check the configuration in the `modules.conf` file. Check the kernel module support. Maybe you didn't include your card in the kernel configuration.

The sound seems to play and freeze, then play again and freeze again.

Solution: This is an IRQ assignment problem. Make sure that the IRQ is properly set in the `conf.modules` file. Make sure that no other device is using the same IRQ. Use `cat /proc/interrupts` to check whether another device is using the IRQ you have reserved for your sound card.

I get a cannot access device *error.*

Solution: Try changing the permissions of the sound devices by using the following:

```
bash#chmod 666 /dev/dsp /dev/mixer /dev/audio
```

I get a device busy *error.*

Solution: Some program is already using the sound device. If you're running Enlightenment Window Manager for example, chances are that ESD is in control of the sound device. You can tell ESD to set the audio device free by issuing the following command:

```
#esdctl standby
```

I get errors about the conf.modules *file during system boot up. What is this?*

The change in the modules configuration file that SuSE made starting in version 6.3 can get you in trouble because of backward compatibility problems. Most programs will search for the file `/etc/conf.modules` first and then `/etc/modules.conf`. The key to solving this problem is removing the `/etc/conf.modules`:

```
bash#mv /etc/conf.modules /etc/conf.modules.old
```

Configuration of OSS

OSS configuration is the simplest configuration of all. It comes with a very neat interface that makes it very easy to install and configure.

Software Requirements

As noted before, SuSE offers you a full version of OSS. If your card is supported by OSS version 3.8, you should install the following packages. This package is already registered and you won't have to pay any extra money to 4Front.

Series pay:

- opso (for systems with one processor)
- opso_smp (for systems with multi processors kernel support)

If your card is not supported by the full registered version of OSS that SuSE offers, you might want to try the demo version of OSS. In this case, try installing the following packages. Note that this version will work only for seven days. If you like the package, you can buy it from 4Front.

Series pay:

- opsod_up (for systems with one processor—newer demo version of OSS)
- opsodsmp (for systems with multi processors kernel support—newer demo version of OSS)

Installing OSS

All you have to do is log in as root (OSS suggests that you log in and not use su, probably to use default environment variables). Then change to the directory /tmp/opso-*xxx* and run the file oss-install with the following:

```
bash#cd /tmp/opso-xxx
bash#./oss-install
```

> **N O T E** The *xxx* in *opso-xxx* refers to the package name and version that you installed in the preceding section. It will differ according to uni/smp—processor OSS and to the version of OSS that you installed. ■

A welcome message and the license agreement should appear. You will be asked the destination directory in which you want to install OSS (see Figure 10.2). We recommend that you install OSS in the /opt/oss directory to follow the SuSE Linux standards.

Part
II

Ch
10

FIGURE 10.2
OSS asks for the directory to which it should be installed when you start the installer. The recommended choice is /opt/oss.

By pressing Enter, OSS installer tries to compile the sndshiled program. It asks you for auto detection of your PnP sound cards. This process is completely safe. After this it will ask for an automatic detection of your non-PnP sound card. This might be a little unsafe if your system contains devices that use the standard sound cards resources (see Figure 10.3). It is a good idea to choose cancel and do it manually. If you have more than one sound card, you should use manual configuration.

FIGURE 10.3
OSS can auto-detect your non-PnP sound cards. It is recommended that you configure the settings for your non-PnP sound cards manually, though.

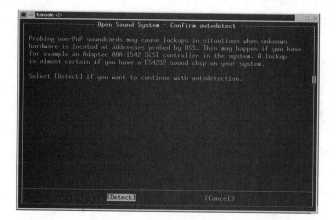

After OSS finishes detecting your system sound cards, it opens the OSS Config main menu (see Figure 10.4). From this menu, you can view and control the sound cards on your system.

If you would like to specify a special configuration to a specific sound device on your system, choose Manual Configuration from the Config main menu. The Manual Configuration menu enables you to specify the sound card setting manually as illustrated in Figure 10.5.

FIGURE 10.4
From the Config main menu you can configure all the sound devices on your system.

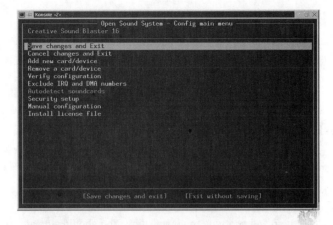

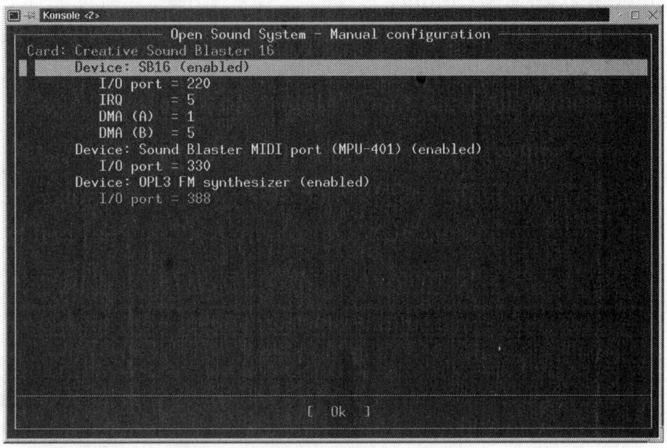

FIGURE 10.5
If you would like to specify your sound card configuration manually, you will have to use the Manual Configuration menu.

The Modules Configuration Problem

The OSS configuration will be saved to your /etc/conf.modules file instead of /etc/modules.conf. If you are running a SuSE version below 6.3, you won't have any problems. However, SuSE Linux 6.3 users have to replicate the changes made by the OSS installer from the conf.modules to the modules.conf file. Follow these steps:

1. Open the /etc/conf.modules file in your favorite text editor.

2. Check the section that was made by OSS. There should be a comment to show the start and end of the modifications made by OSS installer.

3. Append those changes to the /etc/modules.conf file.

4. Remove or rename the /etc/conf.modules file.

Activating OSS on Boot-Up

After the process of sound card setup is done, edit your `/sbin/init.rd/boot.local` and add the following line to it if you want the sound to start on system boot:

```
/usr/lib/oss/soundon
```

Troubleshooting OSS

There are a number of things that could go wrong when configuring OSS. The following are some things to look out for:

- You have sound compiled built in the kernel. If this is true, OSS will not install correctly. If you have OSS modules or OSS/lite modules loaded in the memory, OSS will unload them and continue the installation. You should stop any application that uses the sound if it's already running.

- If you have ALSA modules loaded in the memory, you probably will have to remove them yourself by issuing the following command:

  ```
  bash#/sbin/init.rd/aslsasound stop
  ```

- If you get an error that the file does not exist, reinstall the package from the SuSE source media and follow the steps again.

Configuration of ALSA

ALSA is not as easy to install as OSS, but it is very simple to configure. This might sound weird to most of us, but installation is definitely different from configuration. Installing ALSA from the source code is a different process from configuring ALSA to work on your system.

What Do You Need to Install ALSA?

You need either the source code or the binary RPMs. ALSA constitutes of a set of packages. The ALSA drivers, libraries, utilities, and the optional configuration script are named 1- `alsa-driverxxx`, 2- `alsa-libxxx`, 3- `alsa-utilxxx`, and 4- `alsaconfxyz` where *xxx* and *xyz* are version numbers. The packages should be installed in the listed sequence because they depend on each other. If you get the binary RPMs (available on the full package of SuSE), you have to install them using YaST. For more information on this, see Appendix C, "YaST." If you get the sources, refer to the installation procedures that follow.

Installing ALSA Using the Sources

To start with, assume that you have all the packages downloaded either from the Internet or from the SuSE installation media (the full version). First, you are going to untar the sources with the following command:

```
#tar xzvf  alsa-driverxxx.tar.gz -C /tmp
#cd /tmp/alsa-driverxxx

#./configure --with-isapnp=yes (Sound card is PnP. isapnptools must be installed)
#./configure    (if you don't have a PnP sound card)
#make;make install
#./snddevices  (To create the sound devices in the /dev directory)
#depmod -a  (To handle the module dependency)
#cp /tmp/alsa-driverxxx/utils/alsasound  /sbin/init.d/
```

Now you are finished installing the sound drivers. Next, you have to install the ALSA libraries with the following command:

```
#tar xzvf  alsa-libxxx.tar.gz -C /tmp
#cd /tmp/alsa-libxxx
#./configure
#make;make install
#ldconfig
```

Part
II

Ch
10

Now that the ALSA libraries are installed, you need to build the utilities. Enter the following:

```
#tar xzvf  alsa-utilxxx.tar.gz -C /tmp
#cd /tmp/alsa-utilxxx
#./configure
#make;make install
```

After you're done installing the three packages, you should delete the three directories you made in the /tmp directory to save space.

Configuring ALSA Using *alsaconf*

alsaconf is a shell script that automates the sound card configuration. This shell script uses a module (snd-detect) that was built or installed during the installation process. This script should automatically detect the existence of sound cards on your system. Again, if you have the binary RPMs, you only have to run alsaconf by issuing the following command:

```
#alsaconf
```

If you have the source distribution, you'll have to untar it and then execute it:

```
#tar xzvf  alsaconf-xyz.tar.gz -C /tmp
#cd /tmp/alsaconf-xyz
#./alsaconf
```

After alsaconf starts and displays the welcome message, it starts searching for your sound card(s). In most cases, it should find the card automatically if the card supports the PnP option. You will then be asked some questions. If your sound card is a PnP card, all the answers will be found in your /etc/isapnp.conf file. The following are the options that you must provide as input to alsaconf:

- **Card Identifier**—The card ID that refers to which sound card you are configuring. Normally, the first sound card is called CARD_0, the second card is called CARD_1, and so on.

■ **IO Port**—The same I/O port that you set in your `/etc/isapnp.conf`. Check the line in your `isapnp.conf` that represents (IO 0 (BASE 0x0220)), which indicates a value of 220.

■ **MPU IO Port**—The MPU IO port of your sound card. You can get this by checking the line in your `isapnp.conf` that represents (IO 1 (BASE 0x0330)), which indicates the value 330. If your sound card does not support MPU, use -1.

■ **IRQ**—The IRQ of your sound card. Check the line in your `isapnp.conf` that represents (INT 0 (IRQ 5 (MODE +E))), which indicates a value of 5.

■ **8-Bit DMA**—In DOS and Windows it is called *low DMA*. Check the line in your `isapnp.conf` that represents (DMA 0 (CHANNEL 1)), which indicates the value 1.

■ **Max 8-Bit DMA size in KB**—You should get this from your sound card manual if you don't have a PnP sound card. If you have a PnP sound card, check your `/etc/isapnp.conf` file. If you don't find this piece of information in the manual or the `/etc/isapnp.conf`, try a value in between the range given to you and use the trial and error technique.

■ **16-Bit DMA**—In DOS and Windows it is referred to as *high DMA*. Check the line in your `isapnp.conf` that represents (DMA 1 (CHANNEL 5)), which indicates the value 5.

■ **Max 16-Bit DMA**—Use the same steps as Max 8-Bit DMA Size in KB.

■ **Mic Auto Gain Control**—Enable this if you want microphone gain control.

Pressing Enter takes you back to the main screen (see Figure 10.6). If you are finished setting up all your system's sound cards, choose no more sound cards. You will be asked if you'd like to modify your `/etc/modules.conf`. Answer Yes. The configuration is saved and you're done with the first step. Finally, start the ALSA driver by issuing the following command:

```
#/sbin/init.d/alsasound start
```

FIGURE 10.6

You can set up more sound cards and non-PnP sound cards directly from the alsaconf script menu.

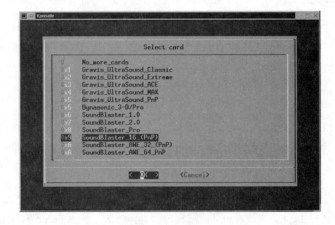

Checking if ALSA Works

ALSA uses the proc filesystem to communicate with the user. You can check which sound cards are initialized and what their current status is. ALSA created a /proc/asound/card# interface when you configured it.

The following command will print the status of your pcm device:

```
#cat /proc/asound/0/pcm0o
```

The following command will print the status of your Sound Blaster 16:

```
#cat /proc/asound/0/sb16
```

Configuring ALSA to Start on System Boot Up

This process will make ALSA start on system boot. Add symbolic links to runlevels 2 and 3 so the system will run the alsasound init script when it boots with a start message. It will run it again when it shuts down with a stop (kill) message:

```
#cd /sbin/init.d/rc2.d
#ln -s ../alsasound S70alsasound
#ln -s ../alsasound K70alsasound
#cd ../rc3.d
#ln -s ../alsasound S70alsasound
#ln -s ../alsasound K70alsasound
```

Part

II

Ch

10

Some Useful ALSA Utilities

The ALSA package comes with some useful utilities. They are used mainly for advanced functionality and sound mixing capabilities. The following utilities come with the alsautil package:

- alsactl (a mixer level control utility)
- alsamixer (a ncurses—console-based—mixer)
- amixer (a command-line mixer)
- aplay (a command-line player and recorder)
- gmix (a GTK-based mixer)
- xamixer2 (another advanced GTK-based mixer)

Note that alsactl is used to store the current configuration of your sound card volume level and then restore it back again. Each time you shut down your system, the alsasound init script executes alsactl with the store option, which stores the current mixer settings to /etc/asound.conf. When you start the system, the script calls alsactl with the restore option, which restores the mixer settings to those saved in the /etc/asound.conf. This ensures that when you return to the system, you will find the same sound settings.

Troubleshooting ALSA

ALSA is easy to troubleshoot. To correctly troubleshoot ALSA, you should use the source package and compile it using `./configure --with-debug=detect`. Install the drivers and issue the following command in a terminal or another console:

```
#tail -s /var/log/messages
```

Continue the installation process and watch for the tail window/console. Check what type of errors you get and try to fix them.

ALSA cannot work if you have sound support built in the kernel. If you cannot load the ALSA modules, check your kernel configuration.

ALSA also cannot work if OSS is already loaded. Only one of them can be loaded at a time for the same card.

Enlightenment Sound Daemon (ESD)

Enlightenment Sound Daemon (ESD) is not a sound card driver by itself. As the name indicates, ESD is a normal daemon. Why you need ESD is another story. As you might have noticed, the sound card supports only one wav file at a time. One amazing thing about Windows games is the ability to hear more than one voice at a time. This, in fact, is the gift of DirectX to Windows. Linux programmers don't like missing out on great features like this. So, they came up with ESD. ESD sits on top of the sound drivers and controls what's going in. Thus, for programs that use the ESD API, two programs can output sound (wav) at the same time.

Without getting in to technical details, ESD waits for programs that require sound output. It handles the streams sent to it and manages to *mix* them in one stream and output them to the sound card. In very simple terms, this is how ESD does it.

Remember though that you will only be able to play sounds through programs that were written to support ESD. The other programs written for OSS and ALSA, won't be able to work until ESD is terminated. When ESD is running, only ESD programs will play.

ESD is essential for Enlightenment if you want to hear sound. Sound in Enlightenment will not work if ESD is not running.

The following are some programs that use ESD:

- Enlightenment
- X Multimedia System (xmms), which has an ESD plug-in
- mpg123
- E-music
- ALSA player

To run ESD, you only need to be able to access your sound card using OSS or ALSA. ESD is not a low-level driver and is not intended to be. It will use the existing sound card driver that you're using and implement the extra functionality.

Installing ESD

The process of installing ESD is simple. You just need to set up your sound card as described in this chapter and then install the package (snd, esound).

After you're done installing the package, simply run ESD as a normal user:

```
$esd
```

ESD will automatically acquire the sound devices on your system. You'll hear a space-like sound that indicates the startup of ESD. You're done! Open XMMS or any other application that uses ESD and play sounds.

Other Programs to Control ESD

The ESD package comes equipped with some extra programs that help the user control ESD. If your system has more than one user, you might want to stop them from using the sound card while you're using it. Otherwise, they'll share it with you. Remember that because it's capable of playing two sounds at a time, when you're playing sounds, other users can be playing it, too. The output will all go to your speakers. The utility that can control this is called esdctl. The following examples show the usage of this powerful utility:

- $esd& (starts ESD)
- $esdctl lock (only the user that started esd can play sounds)
- $esdctl unlock (everybody can play sounds)
- $esdctl standby (no playing, daemon sets the audio device free. Programs that need OSS or ALSA drivers can work without killing esd)
- $esdctl resume (after standby, audio retakes control of the sound device and gets ready to play)

> **CAUTION**
>
> ESD does not give only you the ability to play more than one sound file at a time; instead it gives this ability to all the users who can access the system. If you don't want others to use ESD while you're using it, simply lock it.

Environment Variables That Can Be Used with ESD

One important environment variable that can be used with ESD is ESPEAKER. This environment variable is used by ESD to find out which host it should connect to. When using bash, try exporting ESPEAKER=localhost and then running ESD. This should be no different from using ESD without setting this variable. The only effect this may have occurs when you try to export this variable over a network. When you play sound, it might be played through the other machine's sound card. ●

Printing

Selecting a Printer for Linux

Printing is one of the most important aspects of computing. Periodically you will need a hard copy of some document. Even though the Internet has made it possible to totally get rid of paper as a medium of information exchange, the old fashioned way still is necessary sometimes. Reading something off the monitor is no match for reading it off paper.

Printing in Linux is easy to set up, provided that you have a supported printer. The number of printers supported by Linux might not be as large as those supported by other commercial operating systems, but it should be sufficient.

If you are planning to buy a printer to use with Linux, your best bet is a PostScript printer. These work well with Linux and don't require a lot of configuration effort. PostScript printers are high quality and therefore quite expensive, so purchasing one might not be an option for everybody. If that's the case, there are many other printers that work with Linux. Your best bet is a printer that is compatible to HP printers because HP printers are well supported in Linux.

One type of printer, however, never works with Linux. These are printers that are labeled "for Microsoft Windows" or "GDI Printers." These printers require special device drivers that are only available for Microsoft Windows operating systems. So, if you are planning to buy a new printer, be sure that it's not one of those and can print in MS-DOS. If it meets these two requirements, it should work with Linux just fine.

Printing from Linux

Printing in Linux requires a bit of preparation. This preparation will depend on how you want Linux to print. Printing in general can be done in various methods—for example, you can print to a printer connected to your machine or to a remote printer. We will discuss how you can do both.

Printing to a Printer Connected to Your Machine

To print to a printer connected to your machine, you will need to do three things. First, you will need to configure your kernel, then install the required packages, and finally use YaST to configure your printer. Let's get that printer working!

Configuring Your Kernel   The first step is configuring your kernel. If you have not changed anything in your kernel since you installed SuSE Linux, you won't need to do this. The kernel that is installed by SuSE is already configured to provide support for a printer. If you are not sure whether your kernel is configured to have support for printers, follow these steps:

1. Log in as root.
2. Change the directory to /usr/src/linux.

3. Run the kernel's configuration menu program by typing the following:

   ```
   # make menuconfig
   ```

4. The Linux kernel configuration program will pop up.

5. Navigate to General setup and press Enter.

6. Navigate to Parallel port support and press the space bar to enable it in your kernel. It's recommended that you make it built-in rather than a module. Press the space bar repeatedly until the feature is marked with an asterisk (*) next to it indicating that it will be built in the kernel.

7. Navigate to the next option, PC-style hardware, and make sure that it has an * next to it. Use your space bar to enable it if it doesn't.

8. Press the Esc key to exit to the upper-level menu.

9. Navigate to Character Devices and press Enter.

10. Navigate to Parallel Printer Support and use your space bar to mark it as either built-in or a module. If you are going to use your parallel port for a device other than the printer (Iomega zip drive, for example), make sure that you make this a module and not built-in. To mark it as a module, press the letter M. Otherwise, you can make it built-in.

11. Press the Esc key to exit to the upper-level menu, and press it again to exit the kernel configuration menu.

12. The program will ask you whether you want to save the new kernel configuration; choose yes and press Enter.

13. The program will exit and you will return to the command line again. Now you need to perform the actual kernel compilation.

14. Type the following commands in the exact same order they appear. Each command will take a while to finish; when it's finished, enter the next command. The commands are as follows:

    ```
    #make dep

    #make clean

    #make bzlilo

    #make modules

    #make modules_install
    ```

15. That's it, your kernel is now compiled and installed. You should reboot your system for the new kernel to be loaded.

When your system reboots, you should see a line similar to the following as the kernel boots:

```
parport0: PC-style at 0x378 [SPP,PS2]
```

This means that the parallel port has been successfully detected and initialized. Your installation was a success.

Part

II

Ch

11

Installing the Required Software   To use your printer in SuSE Linux, you will need to install a few packages from the SuSE CDs. The first one is the BSD spooling system that handles and manages all the printing jobs. The second one is the aps filter, which handles any file format conversions that need to be executed on files before they are printed. Finally, you will need to install the Ghostscript program if your printer is not a PostScript printer.

Package requirements:

Series n:

- ■ lprold

Series ap:

- ■ aps
- ■ gs_both
- ■ gs_fonts
- ■ gs_lib

Now that you have installed the required software, you will need to enable printing support in SuSE Linux. This is easily done using YaST; just follow these steps:

1. Log in as root.

2. Run YaST.

3. Navigate to System Administration, Change Configuration File and press Enter.

4. A dialog pops up; this is where you can set up all the system variables that are required to enable/disable all the services on the system.

5. Press F4 to search for the variable you want to change. A small dialog pops up; type LPD and press Enter.

6. YaST will locate the correct system variable for you, START_LPD. Press Enter to change its value to yes (see Figure 11.1).

FIGURE 11.1
Enabling printer support using YaST.

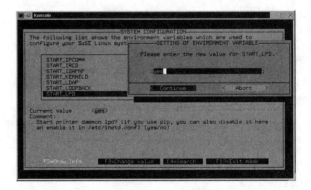

7. Press F10 to exit and save.

8. Exit YaST.

That's it; you are now ready to configure your printer using YaST.

Configuring Your Printer Using YaST If you have successfully completed the previous two steps, you now are ready to start configuring your printer using YaST. Follow these steps:

1. Log in as root.

2. Run YaST.

3. Navigate to System Administrating, Integrate Hardware Into System, Configure Printers and press Enter.

4. YaST runs the printer configuration module (see Figure 11.2).

FIGURE 11.2

YaST has an easy-to-use printer configuration module.

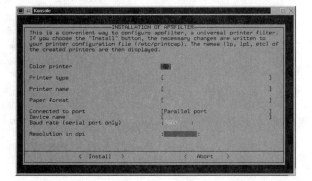

Part

II

Ch

11

5. The first option, Color Printer, asks you whether you have a color printer or not. Check this option by pressing the space bar if you do have a color printer. Press Tab to proceed to the next option.

6. In the Printer Type option, you will be presented with three choices: PostScript Printer, HP Deskjet, and Other Printer. Make your choice according to the type of printer you have. Press Enter to select one. You will be automatically moved to the next option.

7. The next option is the Printer Name. Depending on what you chose in the previous option, you will be presented with a list of printers compatible to the category you picked. Find your printer model or one that is compatible with yours and press Enter.

8. The Paper Format option sets the size and format of the paper you are going to be using. Most people use A4 paper, so you might want to choose that one.

9. The next option is Connected to Port; pick Parallel Port.

10. The Device Name option is the name of the device file to which your printer is connected. This is similar to LPT1 in MS Windows. Choose /dev/lp1 if you are running kernel 2.2.x (the default for SuSE 6.2 and up) or /dev/lp0 if you are running a 2.0.x kernel.

11. Finally, you must set the Resolution in DPI option. This is the printing resolution in dots per inch. Usually, you would get this value from your printer's manual because it differs from one printer to the other. The default of 300×300 is a safe choice in case you are not sure of what to enter here.

12. Choose Install and press Enter to install your printer. YaST will pop up a window displaying the status of the configuration (see Figure 11.3).

FIGURE 11.3
YaST displays the status of the configuration.

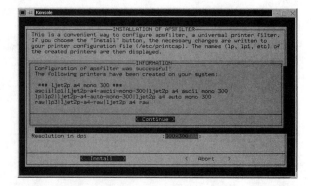

Now you have successfully installed your printer. You must do one last thing, though—make sure that the printing service is running. To do that, log in as root and run this command:

```
# /etc/rc.d/lpd restart
```

You won't need to do this again; it will be done automatically for you on every system boot up.

The printer has been installed with the name lp. We are sure that you can't wait to try it out! The simplest way is by trying to print a file from the command line. To do that, you can use the lpr command like this:

```
$ lpr file.txt
```

The contents of file.txt should be printed to your printer. If you want to try something a little more difficult than a text file, you can print from Netscape Navigator.

Your printer is now called lp, so you need to tell applications to print to that name.

Printing to a Remote UNIX Printer

If your machine is part of a network, there is a good chance that somewhere out there exists a printer you can use. This printer is considered a network printer that can be shared by more than one machine. This sure beats having to buy a printer for every machine.

You easily can set up your SuSE Linux box to print to another printer on the network. YaST enables you to do this easily. To have SuSE Linux print to a remote UNIX printer, follow these steps:

1. Log in as root.

2. Run YaST.

3. Navigate to System Administration, Network Configuration, Administer Remote Printers and press Enter.

4. A dialog window pops up—this is where you will define the remote printer (see Figure 11.4).

FIGURE 11.4

Configuring remote printers with YaST.

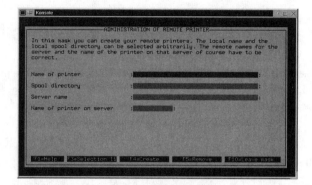

5. The first field is the Name of Printer field. You have two choices here, you can either change one of your existing printer configurations to a remote configuration, eliminating the need to adjust the rest of the system to the new configuration. Or, you can create a totally new printer configuration for the remote printer. To choose an existing configuration, press F3. A window will pop up showing you a list of the entire current printer configuration on your system; select the one you want to change and press Enter. If you are going to define a new configuration, just enter its name here—for example, `remoteprinter`.

6. Press Enter or Tab to move to the next field—the Spool Directory field. As you can see, YaST already has entered a default choice there for you. This is the directory that SuSE Linux will use to hold the files that are to be printed until the remote printer is able to process them. We recommend leaving the default value as it is. Press Enter to move to the next field.

7. The next option is where you enter the Server Name. That can be a fully qualified domain name—`printer.company.com` for example—or the IP of the server to which the remote printer is connected. You can ask your system administrator for this information if you don't know it.

8. Finally, the last field is the Name of Printer on Server option. This is the name of the printer as it is configured on the remote server. The default is usually `lp`, but you should make sure by asking your system administrator or the person who configured that machine.

9. Press F4 to apply your new configuration. YaST will attempt to verify that the server name you entered does exist. If it can't reach it, it will warn you. You can, of course, force your configuration even if YaST complains about not finding the server.

Part

II

Ch

11

Now you are finished with the remote printer configuration. If you have created a new printer name, you will have to tell your applications about it when you want to use it. If you have changed an already existing configuration to be a remote one, you won't need to change anything else. You should note, however, that you must inform the administrator of the remote printing machine that you want to use his printer. This way he will add the name of your machine to his /etc/hosts.lpd file to allow your machine to pass print jobs to his print spooler.

Printing to a Remote Microsoft Windows Printer

The previous section assumed that the network printer is connected to a UNIX machine, but what if the network is Microsoft Windows–based? That means that the printer will most likely be connected to a Windows-based PC. Printing to such a printer is easy. All the print jobs will be sent to the Windows printing system using Samba. All this can be configured using YaST.

You should, however have a working Samba configuration to successfully print to the Windows machine. Refer to Chapter 15, "Connectivity with Windows Through Samba," to learn how to set up Samba properly.

To configure your SuSE Linux box to print to a remote Windows printer using Samba, follow these steps:

1. Log in as root.
2. Run YaST.
3. Navigate to System Administration, Network Configuration, Connect to Printer Via Samba and press Enter.
4. The configuration module pops up. If you have an existing printer configuration, YaST will ask you whether you want to overwrite it or append to it (see Figure 11.5). If you are not planning to use your old settings, just overwrite them. If you want to keep your old settings and append the Samba printer configuration to them, choose Append.

FIGURE 11.5
YaST has detected that you already have a printer configuration. Should you overwrite it or append to it?

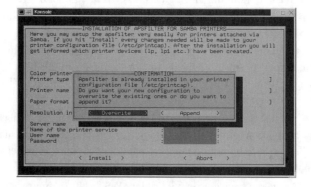

5. The first option, Color Printer, asks whether you have a color printer or not. Check this option by pressing the space bar if you do have a color printer. Press Tab to proceed to the next option.

6. In the Printer Type option, you will be presented with three choices: PostScript Printer, HP Deskjet, and Other Printer. Make your choice according to the type of printer you have. Press Enter to select one. You will be automatically moved to the next option.

7. This option is the Printer Name. Depending on what you chose in the previous option, you will be presented with a list of printers compatible to the category you selected. Find your printer model or one that is compatible with yours and press Enter.

8. The Paper Format option sets the size and format of the paper you are going to be using. Most people use A4 paper, so you might want to select that one.

9. The Server Name field is where you will enter the name of the Windows machine to which the printer is connected. This is its name as defined on the Windows network.

10. The Name of the Printer Service option is the name of the printer on that machine. This easily can be found out by browsing the Windows machine from the Network Neighborhood. The printer name is the name under the printer icon. According to Figure 11.6, this would be GCCElite.

FIGURE 11.6
You can get the name of the printer to which you want to connect from the Network Neighborhood on Windows.

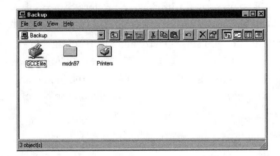

Part
II

Ch
11

11. If the printer requires a User Name, enter it here.

12. Finally, if the printer requires a Password, enter it here.

13. Choose Install and press Enter to install your remote printer configuration.

That's it; you are all set to print to the remote Windows printer thanks to Samba and YaST. All your printing jobs will be sent to the Windows print system over the network.

Printing to a Remote Printer Over a Novell Network

If your SuSE Linux box is part of a Novell Network, you still can use a remote printer. The configuration process is similar to the one you used in the previous section. YaST makes life very easy, especially when it comes to printing.

To configure your SuSE Linux box to print to a remote printer over a Novell Network, just follow these steps:

1. Log in as root.

2. Run YaST.

3. Navigate to System Administration, Network Configuration, Connect to Printer Via Novell Network and press Enter.

4. The configuration module pops up. If you have an existing printer configuration, YaST will ask you whether you want to overwrite it or append to it. If you are not planning to use your old settings, just overwrite them. If you want to keep your old settings and append the new remote printer configuration to them, choose Append.

5. The first option, Color Printer, asks whether you have a color printer or not. Check this option by pressing the space bar if you do have a color printer. Press Tab to proceed to the next option.

6. In the Printer Type option, you will be presented with three choices: PostScript Printer, HP Deskjet, and Other Printer. Make your choice according to the type of printer that you have. Press Enter to select one. You will be automatically moved to the next option.

7. The next option is the Printer Name. Depending on what you chose in the previous option, you will be presented with a list of printers compatible to the category you selected. Find your printer model or one that is compatible with yours and press Enter.

8. The Paper Format option sets the size and format of the paper you will be using. Most people use A4 paper, so you might want to choose that one.

9. The Server Name option is where you will enter the name of the machine to which the printer is connected. This is its name as defined on the Novell network.

10. If the printer requires a User Name, enter it here.

11. If the printer requires a Password, enter it here.

12. Finally, specify the name of the Printer Queue on the remote machine.

13. Choose Install and press Enter to install your remote printer configuration.

Your SuSE Linux system is now ready to print the remote printer over the Novell Network. Thanks to YaST, the configuration process was quite painless.

Allowing Others to Share Your Local Printer

So far, you have learned how to share other printers on the network. Now you will learn how to share your local printer for others to use. You can share your printer for other Linux/UNIX machines to use, and you can share it to enable Microsoft Windows machines to print to it. Let's start with Linux/UNIX machines first.

Allowing Other UNIX/Linux Machines to Use Your Printer

Thanks to the networked architecture of the printing system on Linux, this is a fairly simple process. Any machine can print to your printer if it has the correct permissions to do so.

To configure your system to allow others to print to it over the network, you will need to manually edit your system files. The good news is that you need to edit only one file, /etc/hosts.lpd. This file contains a list of hosts that are allowed to print to your printer.

The format of this file is simple; just add an entry for every host you want to allow to print on your printer. For example, if you want accounting.company.com to print to your printer, just add this line to /etc/hosts.lpd:

```
accounting.company.com
```

That's it, simple isn't it? Do the same for all the machines that you want to print to your printer.

Allowing Other Microsoft Windows Machines to Use Your Printer

If you want to enable Microsoft Windows machines to print to your printer, you will need to configure this in Samba. For detailed information about setting up your Samba server, please refer to Chapter 15.

To enable others to print to your printer via Samba, you need to define a [printers] section in your /etc/smb.conf file. The [printers] section in Samba is a special section that defines a shared printer to be exported to other Microsoft Windows machines in the network. A typical [printers] section looks like this:

```
[printers]
    comment = All Printers
    browseable = no
    printable = yes
    guest ok = no
    read only = yes
    create mode = 0700
    directory = /tmp
```

This section defines a shared printer on your machine. But, it will require a username and password to enable print jobs to be sent to it. This is because of the guest ok = no option. To enable anyone to use the printer without the need for a username and password, use guest ok = yes. Your printer share will now be visible to all other Windows machines on the network.

Crash Course on Using the Linux Printing Commands

Now that you know how to configure printing in SuSE Linux, you will need to know a bit about the printing commands. These are the commands that talk to the printing subsystem in Linux, namely lpd or Line Printer Daemon. This is the main printing server that handles all your printing jobs. The entire configuration that you have performed gets written in lpd's configuration file, /etc/printcap. lpd reads this file to understand how it's going to print your jobs.

The first command you need to know is the lpr command. This is the command that tells lpd to print something. The most common use of this command is similar to the following:

```
$ lpr filename(s)
```

This will send the file or files you specified to lpd for printing. If you have more than one printer configured on your system—for example, a local printer and a network printer—you can tell lpr which of them to print to by using the -P option. For example, if your network printer is called NETPRINT, you would print to it using the following:

```
$ lpr -PNETPRINT filename
```

Note how you enter no space after the -P option.

To tell lpr to send you an email when the print job is complete, which is useful for printing large jobs over the network, use the -m option:

```
$ lpr -m filename
```

lpr by default copies the file you want to print to the spooler directory. You can use a symbolic link instead by using the -s option. This usually will make things a bit faster because no copying takes place:

```
$ lpr -s filename
```

To print more than one copy of a file, use the -# option:

```
$ lpr -#10 file1 file2
```

This will print 10 copies of file1 followed by 10 copies of file2.

The next command is the lpq command. This command can be used to show you the status of a printer queue. You can see all the jobs that are queued for printing and who owns them. The basic form of the command is

```
$ lpq
```

This will show you all the print queues for the default printer. To specify the queue you want to see, use the -P option:

```
$ lpq -PNETPRINT
```

This will show you the print queue for the NETPRINT printer. To have lpq display as much information as possible, use the -1 option:

```
$ lpq -l
```

To remove a job from the print queue, you use the lprm command. This command takes the job number as an argument (which you can get from the output of lpq) and removes it from the queue. The following is the basic format of this command:

```
$ lprm job#
```

job# is the number of the job you want to remove. To remove all your printing jobs, type the following:

```
$ lprm -
```

This will remove all your jobs. If you run this command as root, the entire queue will be emptied. To specify the queue from which you want to delete the job, use the -P option:

```
$ lprm -PNETPRINT -
```

This will remove all your print jobs from the NETPRINT queue.

The following command enables the root user to run the lpc command. This command runs in an interactive mode to control your printer daemon. The following is a brief list of the commands supported by lpc:

- **enable**—This command takes either all (for all queues) or a printer queue name as an argument. This command will enable a previously disabled queue.

- **disable**—This command takes either all (for all queues) or a printer queue name as an argument. This command will disable an active queue from receiving any new printing jobs.

- **up**—This command takes either all (for all queues) or a printer queue name as an argument. This command reverses the effect of the down command.

- **down**—This command takes either all (for all queues) or a printer queue name as an argument. This command will put down a printer queue. You can enter (after the command's arguments) a message to be displayed by lpr when a user attempts to print to this queue—for example, down all printers are down for maintenance.

- **restart**—This command takes either all (for all queues) or a printer queue name as an argument. This command can be useful if a queue has gone down for some unexpected reason. You can restart a queue using this command.

- **start**—This command takes either all (for all queues) or a printer queue name as an argument. This command is used to start a printer queue.

- **stop**—This command takes either all (for all queues) or a printer queue name as an argument. This command will stop a printing queue after the current jobs are completed.

Part
II

Ch
11

- **status**—This command takes either `all` (for all queues) or a printer queue name as an argument. This command will report to you the status of the specified queue.

- **topq**—This command is used to reorder the print jobs. It takes the new order as an argument. The order can be in either print job numbers or usernames.

- **abort**—This command takes either `all` (for all queues) or a printer queue name as an argument. The command will terminate an active queue and disable any further printing to it. The effect is immediate.

- **clean**—This command takes either `all` (for all queues) or a printer queue name as an argument. This command will remove any of the temporary, data, or control files that are created by the printing daemon.

- **exit or quit**—Either of these commands will exit `lpc`.

That's it for the crash course on using the printer commands. Why do you need to know all this? All applications eventually use these commands to print, so you should know how to use them if you need to get the most out of your printer. Finally, all these commands will function on the default printer. You can override that using the `-P` option. To specify the name of the printer to use, just place it immediately after the `-P` option. For example, to specify NETPRINT as the printer to work on, enter the following:

```
$lpr --PNETPRINT .......
```

Alternatively, you can set the environment variable called PRINTER to the name of the printer on which you want to work. Then, all the previous commands will use that printer by default—for example,

```
$ export PRINTER=NETPRINT
```

Troubleshooting

lpd does not want to start.

This probably is because you did not configure it correctly. You probably used `/dev/lp0` as your printer device file for a 2.2.x kernel. Remember, the 2.2.x kernel uses `/dev/lp1` instead of `/dev/lp0`, which is used by the 2.0.x kernels.

lpq starts, but I can't print to it.

Make sure that you configured it. Use YaST to configure your printer daemon correctly. If you did configure it, be sure you selected the correct printer type. If you chose a compatible printer, try another one. Finally, if your printer is a Windows printer or GDI printer, it won't work.

I can't seem to print to a remote UNIX printer.

Make sure your machine name is included in the remote printer's allow list. If it's not, the remote printer will not authorize you to print to it. One other thing you should check is that you are using the correct printer name—check with the owner of the machine or the system administrator.

I can't print to a Windows machine.

Make sure that you have a correct Samba configuration. You should be able to browse the machine to which you are trying to print. Then, make sure that you specified the correct printer name to YaST. If the remote printer requires a username and password, be sure you give it the correct ones.

Printing stopped suddenly, what should I do?

Your printer daemon might have stopped for some unexpected reason; restart it using the `lpc` command. ●

Part

II

Ch

11

Configuring Peripherals

CD-ROM, CR-R, CD-RW, and DVD

Compact discs are one of the most efficient portable storage media around. It is extremely convenient to store 650MB of data on a thin plastic disc that you can take with you anywhere. Data is stored as microscopic pits on the surface of the disc and then read by a laser beam that scans the disc as it rotates. The first generation of CD-ROM drives had quite a slow data transfer rate of 150 k/s. These were soon followed by drives capable of twice that speed, then four times that speed, and so on. Now we have drives that can read up to 50 times that speed, making CDs almost as fast as your hard drive.

Compact disc technology covers several different families. A *CD-ROM* is a normal read-only drive; a *CD-R* is a recordable drive capable of writing to a CD; a *CD-RW* is a rewritable drive capable of writing to a CD more than once; and a *DVD* is a very high-capacity compact disc. Linux supports all of these drive types fairly well.

To use your CD drive, you first must configure your system. Let's see what you need to do to configure each of these drives.

CD-ROM Drives

CD-ROM drives are the easiest to configure because they have been around the longest. CD-ROM drives use either an ATAPI-enhanced IDE interface, a Small Computer Systems Interface (SCSI), or some kind of vendor-specific interface. Linux has solid support for most CD-ROM drives, so you can be confident that your drive will work. Let's start off by configuring the most common type of CD-ROM, the ATAPI-enhanced IDE CD-ROM.

ATAPI-Enhanced IDE CD-ROM   To configure an ATAPI-enhanced IDE CD-ROM, you will need to configure your kernel. In most cases, your kernel already will have such support built in, especially if you haven't changed the default kernel SuSE installed for you. If you are not sure whether you have that support or not, just follow these steps anyway. (We do assume, however, that you have installed the actual CD-ROM drive hardware.)

1. Log in as root.
2. Change the directory to the Linux kernel sources directory:
   ```
   #cd /usr/src/linux
   ```
3. Start the kernel's configuration modules by typing the following:
   ```
   #make menuconfig
   ```
4. The kernel configuration module will start; navigate to Block Devices and press Enter.
5. Use the arrow keys to highlight the Include IDE/ATAPI CDROM Support option and press Y to include it in the kernel.
6. Press the Esc key twice to exit this menu.
7. Now, you need to add support for the CD-ROM filesystem as well. Navigate to Filesystems and press Enter.

8. Highlight ISO 9660 CDROM Filesystem Support and press Y to include it in the kernel, or press M to include it as a module that will be loaded only when needed.

9. Highlight the Microsoft Joliet CDROM Extensions option and press Y to include it. This is a set of extensions Microsoft added to the CD-ROM ISO 9660 filesystem. A lot of CDs use these extensions, so you should have this.

10. Press Esc twice to exit this menu.

11. Press Esc twice again to exit the kernel configuration module. It will ask you whether you want to save your new kernel configuration; choose Yes.

12. Now you need to recompile your kernel for these changes to take effect. To do so, type in the following commands, one after the other:

```
#make dep
#make clean
#make bzlilo
#make modules
#make modules_install
```

13. Each of these commands will take some time to finish executing and a lot of text will scroll by—don't worry, this is normal. When all the commands have executed, reboot your system to load the new kernel.

When your system boots up, you should see that it detected your CD-ROM drive. Pay close attention to the device file that was assigned to your CD-ROM drive. This should be a /dev/hd? device file because this is an IDE CD-ROM drive.

SCSI CD-ROM   SCSI CD-ROMs offer better performance than the ATAPI-enhanced IDE ones. This is because SCSI is a faster interface than the ATAPI-enhanced IDE; but it also is more expensive. Installing a SCSI CD-ROM is very similar to installing an ATAPI IDE one. You will need to recompile your kernel. Just follow these steps:

1. Log in as root.

2. Change the directory to the Linux kernel sources directory:

```
#cd /usr/src/linux
```

3. Start the kernel's configuration modules by typing the following:

```
#make menuconfig
```

4. The kernel configuration module will start; navigate to SCSI Support and press Enter.

5. Use the arrow keys to highlight the SCSI support option and press Y to include it in the kernel.

6. Highlight SCSI CD-ROM Support and press Y to include it in the kernel.

7. Scroll down to the bottom of the menu, highlight SCSI Low-Level Drivers and press Enter.

8. The SCSI low-level drivers menu pops up; find your SCSI adapter from the list and press Y to include it. This is important because your SCSI CD-ROM won't work unless you perform this step.

Part
II

Ch
12

9. Press the Esc key twice to exit this menu, followed by Esc twice again to exit the SCSI support menu.

10. Now you need to add support for the CD-ROM filesystem as well. Navigate to Filesystems and press Enter.

11. Highlight ISO 9660 CDROM Filesystem Support and press Y to include it in the kernel, or press M to include it as a module that will be loaded only when needed.

12. Highlight the Microsoft Joliet CDROM Extensions option and press Y to include it. This is a set of extensions that Microsoft added to the CD-ROM ISO 9660 filesystem. A lot of CDs use these extensions, so you should have this.

13. Press Esc twice to exit this menu.

14. Press Esc twice again to exit the kernel configuration module. It will ask you whether you want to save your new kernel configuration or not; choose Yes.

15. Now you need to recompile your kernel for these changes to take effect. To do so, type in the following commands, one after the other:

```
#make dep
#make clean
#make bzlilo
#make modules
#make modules_install
```

16. Each of these commands will take some time to execute, and a lot of text will scroll by—don't worry, this is normal. When all the commands have executed, reboot your system to load the new kernel.

When your system boots up, you should see that it detected your CD-ROM drive. Pay close attention to the device file that was assigned to your CD-ROM drive. This should be a /dev/scd? device file because this is a SCSI CD-ROM drive.

Using YaST to Configure Your CD-ROM Now that you have installed the required driver for your CD-ROM, you should use YaST to configure the rest of your system to use that CD-ROM properly. To do that, just follow these steps:

1. Log in as root.

2. Run YaST.

3. Navigate to System Administration, Integrate Hardware Into System, CD-ROM Configuration and press Enter.

4. The CD-ROM setup dialog pops up (see Figure 12.1). Choose the type of your CD-ROM—for example, an ATAPI EIDE CD-ROM—and press Enter.

5. YaST gives you a list of choices for the device filename (see Figure 12.2). Pick the correct one and press Enter.

6. Exit from YaST for the changes to take effect.

Now, YaST has configured your CD-ROM drive. It created a device called /dev/cdrom that points to your CD-ROM drive.

FIGURE 12.1
YaST can be used to configure your CD-ROM.

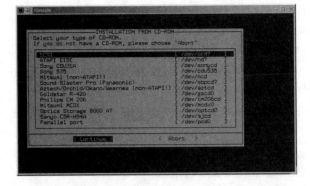

FIGURE 12.2
Choose the correct device file for your CD-ROM.

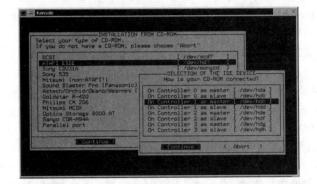

CD-Rs and CD-RW CD-Rs and CD-RW enable you to make your own CDs. CD-Rs writes only once to a CD, whereas CD-RW can write more than once on special rewritable medias. These drives come as either ATAPI EIDE or SCSI. The installation procedure for the SCSI models is exactly the same as for a SCSI CD-ROM drive. Just follow the steps listed previously for the SCSI CD-ROMs. If the drive is an ATAPI EIDE model, you will have to do a bit more work to get it running under Linux.

If you are planning not to use your ATAPI EIDE CD-R/RW under Linux for writing CDs, you can just install it as a normal ATAPI EIDE CD-ROM drive. If you want to be able to write CDs with it under Linux, you have to do some extra work. This is because Linux does not have anything called ATAPI EIDE CD-R/RW Support. Instead, it uses something called SCSI Emulation to make your CD-R/RW look like it's a SCSI model. Why would you want to do this? Well, all the CD writing software on Linux is SCSI based, and to use it with your CD-R/RW, you will have to put your drive in SCSI emulation mode.

This is not really as hard as it sounds; the actual configuration is really easy. The first part of the configuration is the kernel options, which is where you will remove built-in support for ATAPI EIDE CD-ROMS and enable SCSI emulation and support:

Part

II

Ch

12

1. Log in as root.

2. Change the directory to the Linux kernel sources directory:
   ```
   #cd /usr/src/linux
   ```

3. Start the kernel's configuration modules by typing the following:
   ```
   #make menuconfig
   ```

4. The kernel configuration module will start; navigate to Block Devices and press Enter.

5. Highlight Include IDE/ATAPI CDROM Support and press M to make it a module.

6. Highlight SCSI Emulation Support and press M to make it a module.

7. Press Esc twice to exit this module.

8. Navigate to SCSI Support and press Enter.

9. Use the arrow keys to highlight the SCSI Support option and press Y to include it in the kernel.

10. Highlight SCSI CD-ROM Support and press Y to include it in the kernel.

11. Highlight SCSI CD-ROM Generic Support and press Y to include it in the kernel.

12. Press the Esc key twice to exit the SCSI support menu.

13. Now you need to add support for the CD-ROM filesystem as well. Navigate to Filesystems and press Enter.

14. Highlight ISO 9660 CDROM Filesystem Support and press Y to include it in the kernel, or press M to include it as a module that will be loaded only when needed.

15. Highlight the Microsoft Joliet CDROM Extensions option and press y to include it. This is a set of extensions that Microsoft added to the CD-ROM ISO 9660 filesystem. A lot of CDs use these extensions, so you should have this.

16. Press Esc twice to exit this menu.

17. Press Esc twice again to exit the kernel configuration module. It will ask you whether you want to save your new kernel configuration; choose Yes.

18. Now you need to recompile your kernel for these changes to take effect. To do so, type in the following commands, one after the other:
    ```
    #make dep
    #make clean
    #make bzlilo
    #make modules
    #make modules_install
    ```

19. Each of these commands will take some time to execute, and a lot of text will scroll by—don't worry, this is normal. When all the commands have executed, don't reboot your system yet.

Ok, that takes care of the first step of the configuration. Now, you will have to tell your kernel to make your ATAPI EIDE CD-ROM act like a SCSI CD-ROM. This is done by passing an argument to the kernel when it's booting, which means you must tell LILO (the Linux Loader) to pass it to the kernel when it's booting it. To configure LILO to do that, follow these steps:

1. Log in as root.

2. Run YaST.

3. Navigate to System Administration, Kernel and Boot Configuration, LILO Configuration and press Enter.

4. The LILO Installation dialog pops up.

5. In the Append-line for Hardware Parameter field, type `hdd=ide-scsi`. Replace the `hdd` with the correct device name of your CD-ROM (see Figure 12.3).

FIGURE 12.3
The final setup for LILO.

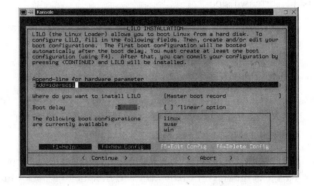

6. Press Continue to exit and save the LILO configuration.

7. YaST will apply the new settings and display a status window. Press Continue to exit.

8. Exit from YaST.

Now, LILO will pass the argument `hdd=ide-scsi` to the kernel when it boots it. This will tell the argument that the IDE device called `hdd` should be prepared for SCSI emulation. You should reboot your system now for these new settings to take effect.

When your system reboots, you have one last step to perform before you can use your CD-R/RW. You have to load the SCSI emulation module, which is done by typing the following:

```
#modprobe ide-scsi
```

Nothing noticeable will happen when you run that command. But, if you look at the file `/var/log/messages`, you will see the output of that command. It should look something like this:

```
scsi0 : SCSI host adapter emulation for IDE ATAPI devices
Feb  4 03:29:21 Shadow kernel: scsi : 1 host.
Vendor: IOMEGA  Model: ZIPCD 4x650   Rev: 1.04
Type:   CD-ROM    ANSI SCSI revision: 02
Detected scsi CD-ROM sr0 at scsi0, channel 0, id 0, lun 0
sr0: scsi3-mmc drive: 24x/24x writer cd/rw xa/form2 cdda tray
```

There, the ATAPI EIDE CD-R/RW has been identified by the system as a SCSI device called `/dev/sr0`. You now can use all the CD writing utilities that run under Linux. They will all think they are controlling a SCSI device.

Part
II

Ch
12

Just one last thing—you probably don't want to enter the modprobe command every time you reboot your system. It's a good idea to include it as part of your system boot up, for example, in the file /etc/rc.d/boot.local. Just open this file using your favorite editor and add the command modprobe ide-scsi to it. Then, save and exit.

This setup does have one glitch, though, which occurs when you have more than two CD-ROMs. You can have a CD-R/RW and a normal CD-ROM, with both being ATAPI EIDE. This causes both of them to be SCSI emulated. You can control this behavior by having only the CD-R/RW be SCSI emulated while the other CD-ROM remains an ATAPI EIDE device. To do this, you must perform two steps.

The first step is editing /etc/rc.d/boot.local again and adding the command modprobe ide-cd *before* the modprobe ide-scsi command. It should look like this:

```
modprobe ide-cd
modprobe ide-scsi
```

The second step is modifying the file /etc/modules.conf (in SuSE 6.3) or /etc/conf. modules (SuSE 6.2 and below). Open this file using your favorite editor and add this line to it:

```
options ide-cd ignore=hdd
```

You should replace hdd in the previous line with the device name of your CD-R/RW. Then, save and exit. This tells the ATAPI EIDE CD-ROM module to ignore your CD-R/RW when it loads. The modules will configure all the other CD-ROMs on your system except this one. That finalizes your CD-R/RW setup.

Crash Course in CD-Writing Tools   Now that you have configured your CD-R/RW to work with Linux, you probably want to know how to write your CDs. You must first install the required tools.

Package requirements:

Series ap:

- cdrecord
- mkisofs

CD-Writing in Linux is not really that hard. It is a two-step process in which you must create what is called an ISO image and then write it on your CD. An *ISO image* is a file that contains all the files (correctly formatted) you want to write on the CD.

The first step, in which you create the ISO file, is pretty simple. Collect all the files you want to copy to a CD in the same directory. Next, create any subdirectories you want to use and move the files to those subdirectories until you have the final setting you want. Then, run the mkisofs command:

```
# mkisofs -r -o /tmp/cdimage.iso     /myfiles
```

The previous command will create an image in /tmp called cdimage.iso, taking the files from the directory you created (which we called /myfiles). The -r option sets the permissions of all the files to be readable on the CD, whereas the -o option specifies the name of the image file. This will take some time, depending on how big /myfiles is.

When it's finished, you will find a file in /tmp called cdimage.iso. This is the file you are going to write to the CD. To check whether the ISO image is correct, you can mount it using the following command:

```
#mount /tmp/cdimage.iso /mnt -o loop -t iso9660
```

This will mount the image under the directory /mnt. You can check it to ensure that the contents of the image are correct. When you are finished, unmount the image by typing the following command:

```
#umount /mnt
```

Now, you are ready to write the image to a CD. But, before you do so, you should get some information about your CD-R/RW by running the following command:

```
#cdrecord -scanbus
```

The output of the previous command should be similar to this:

```
Cdrecord release 1.8a30 Copyright (C) 1995-1999 Jörg Schilling
Using libscg version 'schily-0.1'
scsibus0:
    0,0,0      0) 'IOMEGA  ' 'ZIPCD 4x650      ' '1.04' Removable CD-ROM
```

As you can see, it shows your CD-R/RW. The part you're interested in is 0,0,0, which is the SCSI ID of the CD-R/RW. You don't need to run this command again because this ID won't change. Now, you can start writing the image to the CD-R/RW by typing the following command:

```
# cdrecord -v speed=4 dev=0,0,0 -data /tmp/cdimage.iso
```

The -v option tells cdrecord to show verbose information while it's writing; the speed option sets the writing speed, which should be a speed that is supported by your CD writer, nothing higher. For example, if your CD writer can write at four times (4x) you would use speed=4. The dev option takes the SCSI ID you got from the previous step; and the -data option tells cdrecord that this is a data file instead of an audio file and that this is the file to write. This will start the writing process. You can remove the ISO image file when you're finished.

This technique might be a bit primitive, but it works. There are lots of graphical CD-Writing applications available for Linux, so you don't have to use the command-line interface. One such application is xcdroast, which comes with SuSE Linux—try it out; it's pretty good. If you need more information about CD-Writing, read the file /usr/doc/howto/en/ CD-Writing-HOWTO.gz by typing the following command:

```
$ less /usr/doc/howto/en/CD-Writing-HOWTO.gz
```

It has extensive information about the topic.

Part

II

Ch

12

DVD DVD is the latest development in the evolution of the CD, bringing with it massive storage capacity. A full DVD can store up to 15GB of data—that's around 25 times more than a CD! This is why DVDs currently are used to store full-length, high-quality movies. You can have a whole movie, with different languages, subtitles, different camera angles, and so on, on one DVD disc.

DVD support in Linux is quite primitive, though. You do not need any special settings to use your DVD drive; you can just treat it like an ATAPI EIDE CD-ROM. You will be able to mount it, read files from it, and so on.

Playing DVD movies in Linux is a different story, however. Linux has no DVD players available for it yet. Therefore, you will not be able to play DVD movies on your Linux box yet. Some efforts have been made by individuals to make a DVD player for Linux. And, because all these efforts were based on reverse engineering current players on other platforms, most of the code produced was removed from the Internet by court order. But, you can be sure that DVD support will make it to Linux soon; it's only a matter of time.

Zip/Jaz Drives

Most people now own hard drives at least 2.5GB in size. This is because software is bigger in size now and requires a lot of hard drive space to operate. The old 3.5-inch floppy disks just don't work anymore. These disks can hold only 1.44MB of data. Most users now find themselves needing to transfer much more data than this, thus requiring several disks. Some people instead use CDs that they make using CD-R/RW drives, but these drives are relatively expensive.

This has led to the innovation of the Zip and Jaz drives. These drives use disks that are very close in physical size to the 3.5-inch disks, only with much more capacity. A typical Zip disk can hold up to 100MB of data, and newer versions can hold up to 250MB. The Jaz disk is the real killer, though; it can hold up to 2GB of data on a small removable disk.

Both types of drives are supported on Linux, and are not very difficult to configure. Let's start with the Zip drive.

Zip Drive

The Zip drive comes in different versions: SCSI, IDE-ATAPI, and parallel port. Let's start with the most common of these drives, the parallel port model.

Parallel Port Zip Drive This model of the Zip drive is very popular because is inexpensive and very portable. You can carry the whole drive with you anywhere and use it. This model is well supported under Linux and easy to configure. It does require a kernel rebuild, though. But, the good news is that if you haven't changed the default kernel that installs with SuSE Linux, you are all set to use the drive already!

Two versions of this model exist, the normal one and the plus version. You can tell which one you have by looking at the cable; if it says Autodetect on the plug then yours is the plus version. Otherwise, it is the older version. If you bought your drive recently, you probably have the plus version.

To configure your kernel for the Zip drive, just follow these steps:

1. Log in as root.
2. Change the directory to the Linux kernel sources directory:
    `#cd /usr/src/linux`
3. Start the kernel's configuration modules by typing the following:
    `#make menuconfig`
4. The kernel configuration module will start; navigate to General Setup and press Enter.
5. Highlight Parallel Port Support and press Y to include it in the kernel.
6. Highlight PC-Style Hardware and press Y to include it in the kernel.
7. Press Esc twice to exit this module.
8. Navigate to SCSI Support and press Enter.
9. Use the arrow keys to highlight the SCSI Support option and press Y to include it in the kernel.
10. Highlight SCSI Disk Support and press M to include it in the kernel as a module.
11. Navigate to SCSI Low-Level Drivers and press Enter.
12. Highlight IOMEGA Parallel Port (PPA - Older Drives) and press M to make it a module. Pick this if your drive is an old Zip drive. If you are still not sure, it won't hurt if you make it a module anyway.
13. Highlight IOMEGA Parallel Port (IMM - Newer Drives) and press M to make it a module. Pick this if your drive is a new Zip drive. If you are still not sure, it won't hurt if you make it a module anyway.
14. The next two options are PPA/IMM Option - Use Slow (But Safe) EPP-16 and PPA/IMM Option - Assume Slow Parport Control Register. Read the help available on these two options to decide whether you need them or not (press ? to read the help for each option). We do recommend that you press Y for PPA/IMM Option - Use Slow (But Safe) EPP-16 because it's a safe option to use.
15. Press the Esc key twice to exit the SCSI low-level drivers menu.
16. Press the Esc key twice to exit the SCSI support menu.
17. Navigate to Character Devices and press Enter.
18. Highlight Parallel Printer Support and press M to make it a module.
19. Press Esc twice to exit the Character Devices menu.
20. Press Esc twice again to exit the kernel configuration module. It will ask you whether you want to save your new kernel configuration; choose Yes.

Part
II

Ch
12

21. Now you need to recompile your kernel for these changes to take effect. To do so, type in the following commands, one after the other:

```
#make dep
#make clean
#make bzlilo
#make modules
#make modules_install
```

22. Each of these commands will take some time to execute, and a lot of text will scroll by—don't worry, this is normal. When all the commands have executed, reboot your system.

Reboot your system for the changes to take effect. You can test your Zip drive by typing the first of the following commands (for the Plus version) or the next command (for the older version):

```
#modprobe imm
```

```
#modprobe ppa
```

Make sure that your drive is connected to the parallel port, is turned on, and has a disk in it before you do this. If the command is successful, your Zip drive's activity light should turn on for a brief moment. If you look at the end of the /var/log/messages file, you should see something like the following (for the imm module):

```
scsi1 : Iomega VPI2 (imm) interface
scsi : 2 hosts.
  Vendor: IOMEGA    Model: ZIP 100       Rev: J.67
  Type:   Direct-Access                  ANSI SCSI revision: 02
```

Your Zip drive is assigned the SCSI device /dev/sda4. You can mount it by typing the following command:

```
# mount /dev/sda4 /mnt/ -t vfat
```

Note that you mounted it as /dev/sda4, which is because the disk is partitioned like this by default. You can change this behavior by running the fdisk command on it like this:

```
#fdisk /dev/sda
```

Just proceed to partition it in any manner you want. You can now mount all the common files and directory commands on /mnt. The Zip driver locks the eject button when the drive is mounted. To unlock it, umount the drive like this:

```
#umount /mnt
```

This will unlock the eject button.

ATAPI/IDE Zip Drives This model of Zip drives is internal; it fits in your 3.5- or 5.25-inch drive slot and is connected to an IDE controller by a cable. These models are much faster than the parallel port. The two models for these drives are the old IDE-based model and the newer ATAPI EIDE-based model. Each is configured a bit differently from the other.

The old IDE model requires only that you have IDE support built in the kernel. Linux will then treat this drive like a normal hard drive, with no additional configuration required. The ATAPI EIDE drive requires that you have support for ATAPI floppy drive in your kernel. To configure either one of these drives, just follow these steps:

1. Log in as root.

2. Change the directory to the Linux kernel sources directory:
   ```
   #cd /usr/src/linux
   ```

3. Start the kernel's configuration modules by typing the following:
   ```
   #make menuconfig
   ```

4. The kernel configuration module will start; navigate to Block Devices and press Enter.

5. Highlight Include IDE/ATA-2 DISK Support and press Y to include it in the kernel. This is for the IDE-based model, not the ATAPI. You'll probably have this already set up if you have an IDE hard drive.

6. Highlight Include IDE/ATAPI FLOPPY Support and press Y to include it in the kernel. This is for the ATAPI-based Zip drive.

7. Press Esc twice to exit this module.

8. Press Esc twice again to exit the kernel configuration module. It will ask you whether you want to save your new kernel configuration; choose Yes.

9. Now you need to recompile your kernel for these changes to take effect. To do so, type in the following commands, one after the other:
   ```
   #make dep
   #make clean
   #make bzlilo
   #make modules
   #make modules_install
   ```

10. Each of these commands will take some time to execute, and a lot of text will scroll by—don't worry, this is normal. When all the commands have executed, reboot your system.

Reboot your system for the changes to take effect. Pay close attention to the messages the kernel displays as it boots. You should spot your Zip drive being initialized as an IDE device. It will be assigned a device file of the form /dev/hd?.

SCSI Zip and Jaz Drives

These models are internal (Zip and Jaz) and external (Jaz) and fit in your 3.5- or 5.25-inch drive slots. They are connected to a SCSI controller by a cable. Linux will treat these drives like normal hard drives. You must configure your kernel to support SCSI disks and the SCSI controller to which your drive is connected. To do that, just follow these steps:

Part

II

Ch

12

1. Log in as root.

2. Change the directory to the Linux kernel sources directory:
```
#cd /usr/src/linux
```

3. Start the kernel's configuration modules by typing the following:
```
#make menuconfig
```

4. The kernel configuration module will start; navigate to SCSI Support and press Enter.

5. Highlight SCSI Support and press Y to include it in your kernel.

6. Highlight SCSI Disk Support and press Y to include it in your kernel.

7. Navigate to SCSI Low-Level Drivers and press Enter.

8. In the list, find the SCSI controller type you have in your system and press Y to include it in your kernel. If you have a Zip Zoom, select the AHA152x driver.

9. Press Esc twice to exit the SCSI Low-Level Drivers menu.

10. Press Esc twice to exit the SCSI Support menu.

11. Press Esc twice again to exit the kernel configuration module. It will ask you whether you want to save your new kernel configuration; choose Yes.

12. Now you need to recompile your kernel for these changes to take effect. To do so, type in the following commands, one after the other:
```
#make dep
#make clean
#make bzlilo
#make modules
#make modules_install
```

13. Each of these commands will take some time to execute, and a lot of text will scroll by—don't worry, this is normal. When all the commands have executed, reboot your system.

Reboot your system for the changes to take effect. Pay close attention to the messages the kernel displays as it boots. You should spot your Zip/Jaz drive being initialized as a SCSI device. It will be assigned a device file of the form /dev/sd?.

Please note that you should read the documentation for your SCSI adapter in the SCSI How-to file found under /usr/doc/howto. It will have additional information specific to your adapter.

Crash Course in Zip/Jaz Tools

Linux comes with a set of utilities that can be used to control your Zip and Jaz drives. These utilities enable you to write protect and unprotect your disks via software.

Package requirements:

Series ap:

- ziptool

This package installs two command-line programs, ziptool and jaztool. The format of both commands is exactly the same:

```
usage: ziptool -e  <dev>    eject disk
       ziptool -s  <dev>    report protection status
       ziptool -ro <dev>    make disk read only
       ziptool -rp <dev>    make disk read only with password
       ziptool -rw <dev>    make disk full accessible
```

Let's look at some examples. To eject your disk via software, type the following:

```
#ziptool -e /dev/sda
```

To make the disk read only, type this:

```
#ziptool -ro /dev/sda
```

To make the disk read only with a password, type the following command:

```
#ziptool -rp /dev/sda
```

The program will prompt you for the password to use to write protect the disk. Be careful! If you forget it, the only way to write to the disk is by formatting it.

To report the protection status of the disk, type the following:

```
#ziptool -s /dev/sda
```

And finally, to remove the write protection, type this command:

```
#ziptool -rw /dev/sda
```

If the disk was password protected, you will be prompted to enter the password.

All these commands can be used with a Jaz drive by substituting ziptool with jaztool.

Joysticks and Gamepads

Even though Linux does not have a huge variety of games like other platforms do, support for joysticks is not ignored. Linux has support for most of the commonly used joysticks and gamepads. You must recompile your kernel to use them, though.

To configure your joystick/gamepad under Linux, just follow these steps. (Please note that if your joystick is connected to your sound card, which is the usual case, you should have your sound card working first. For more help on this topic, refer to Chapter 10, "Sound Card Configuration.") Now start with these steps:

Part

II

Ch

12

1. Log in as root.
2. Change the directory to the Linux kernel sources directory:

   `#cd /usr/src/linux`

3. Start the kernel's configuration modules by typing the following:

   `#make menuconfig`

4. The kernel configuration module will start; navigate to Character Devices, Joysticks and press Enter.
5. Highlight Joystick Support and press Y to include it in your kernel.
6. Highlight your joystick type from the list and press Y to include it in your kernel.
7. Press Esc twice to exit the Joysticks menu.
8. Press Esc twice to exit the Character Devices menu.
9. Press Esc twice again to exit the kernel configuration module. It will ask you whether you want to save your new kernel configuration; choose Yes.
10. Now you need to recompile your kernel for these changes to take effect. To do so, type in the following commands, one after the other:

    ```
    #make dep
    #make clean
    #make bzlilo
    #make modules
    #make modules_install
    ```

11. Each of these commands will take some time to execute, and a lot of text will scroll by—don't worry, this is normal. When all the commands have executed, reboot your system.

When the system reboots, your joystick should be detected as `/dev/js0`. Instruct any games you have to use this device file to access your joystick.

Fax

Even though email has proven to be a faster and cheaper method of exchanging messages and documents, people still use fax machines. You can use your SuSE Linux box to send and receive faxes if you have a fax-modem installed. SuSE Linux has a fax package called HylaFax. This is a powerful faxing server that turns your Linux box into a fax server on the network.

Configuring HylaFax can be quite complicated. However, configuring it for personal use is not that hard. First, you will need to install the packages.

Package requirements:

Series d:

- javarunt

Series n:

- ■ hylafax
- ■ susefax

Install these packages to use HylaFax. When you are finished installing these packages, you are ready to configure HylaFax.

Configuring HylaFax

Configuring HylaFax is accomplished with the program `faxsetup`. This program will take care of most of the configuration items you will need. To run it, follow these steps:

1. Log in as root.
2. Run the program by entering the following command:
   `#faxsetup`
3. The program will ask you a few questions to gather data about your system. These questions are pretty straightforward. Press Enter to accept the default answer for a question.
4. The first question asks about the Country code; enter your country code here and press Enter.
5. Now enter your Area Code and press Enter.
6. Enter your Long distance dialing prefix and press Enter.
7. Enter you International dialing prefix and press Enter.
8. The next question asks about the string rules file; accept the default of `etc/dialrules` by pressing Enter.
9. The next question is about Tracing during normal server operation; press Enter to accept the default.
10. Accept the default for Tracing during send and receive sessions by pressing Enter.
11. Enter `/etc/cover.templ` for the Continuation cover page and press Enter.
12. Accept the default for Timeout when converting PostScript documents by pressing Enter.
13. Accept the default for Maximum number of concurrent jobs to a destination by pressing Enter.
14. Enter any for Define a group of modems and press Enter.
15. Accept the default for Time of day restrictions for outbound jobs by pressing Enter.
16. Accept the default for Pathname of destination controls file (relative to `/var/spool/fax`) by pressing Enter.
17. Accept the default for Timeout before purging a stale UUCP lock file (secs) by pressing Enter.

Part

II

Ch

12

18. Accept the default for Max number of pages to permit in an outbound job by pressing Enter.

19. And finally, accept the default for Syslog facility name for ServerTracing messages by pressing Enter.

20. Faxsetup now will ask you to confirm your choices; press Enter if they are correct, otherwise, enter No.

21. Faxsetup now will restart your HylaFax server using the new configuration. Press Enter to allow it to do so.

22. Faxsetup now asks whether you want to configure a modem or not. Reply Yes and press Enter.

23. Faxsetup will ask you about your modem; enter the device file for your modem and press Enter. For example, if your modem is /dev/modem, enter modem.

24. The rest of the questions are very straightforward; you can accept all the defaults.

25. That finalizes your server setup.

Now that you are done with the server part, you will need to configure the HylaFax client.

Configuring SuseFax

SuSE created a Java client for HylaFax called SuseFax. You will use this client to send and receive faxes from HylaFax. All documents that you want to send must be in postscript format. So, when you save a document to be sent as a fax, save it as postscript.

To configure SuseFax, follow these steps:

1. Run the program from within the X Window system by typing this command in an X terminal:

   $susefax

2. The program launches for the first time. As you can see, the user interface is in German. If you speak the language then you are okay; otherwise, you probably will want to switch it to English. Click the second menu, called Extras, and click the last entry, English (see Figure 12.4). Now, you must quit the program by clicking the first menu, Program, and then clicking End.

3. Restart the program.

4. Now it runs in English.

5. Click the Main Settings icon to configure the program.

6. The SuSE Fax Settings dialog pops up (see Figure 12.5).

7. The first field is Username. Enter your username, which will be used when you create fax covers.

FIGURE 12.4
SuseFax runs in German by default.

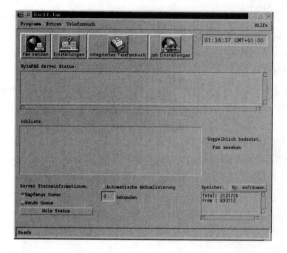

FIGURE 12.5
SuseFax's global settings.

8. The second field is Email; enter your email address here. All messages from the fax server will be sent to this email address.

9. Enter your Linux username in the User Account field.

10. Enter `localhost` in the Hostname of Faxserver.

11. The next option is Automatic Faxing. This feature enables you to automatically fax a document after you print it to a file. It acts similarly to printing to fax.

12. The Path to Spool File concerns the previous option. If you set the Automatic Faxing to on, you should enter the path to the file the server will keep checking on to fax here. A good choice might be `/tmp/fax.ps`. This way, whenever you want to print a document to be faxed, you can just save it as `/tmp/fax.ps` and it will be faxed.

13. The next field is the Path to Faxcover. This is the path to a postscript file that will be used as the cover of the fax you are sending.

14. Finally, the remaining two options have to do with your time zone and locale. Set them up correctly.

15. When you are finished configuring it, the dialog should look similar to Figure 12.6. Click OK to save your configuration.

FIGURE 12.6

An example configuration for SuseFax.

Now you should configure your jobs. A fax is considered a job, and a job has configuration parameters. To configure your jobs, follow these steps:

1. Click the Job Settings icon.

2. The Job Settings dialog pops up (see Figure 12.7).

FIGURE 12.7

Configuring the fax jobs.

3. The first parameter is the Notification Scheme, which tells the fax server when to send you an email message. You can set it to Never (only on errors), After sending, After a Re-queue, or After Re-queue and Sending. The default is fine.

4. The next option is the Resolution, which is the resolution of your fax. You can set it to high or low. It is measured in lines per inch (lpi).

5. The next option is the Priority of the job. The default is fine.

6. The Max. Tries to Send parameter tells the server how many times to try to send the fax if it fails the first time.

7. The Max. Tries to Dial parameter tells the server how many times to redial a busy number.

8. Finally, the last parameter is the Paperformat. This is the format of the paper the fax will be sent as. You have three choices, A4, A3, or North American Letter.

9. Click OK to save your settings.

That's all, you're ready to send faxes and receive faxes now. You can test whether the server is running or not by clicking the Get Status button. It should show you the state of the HylaFax server in a text box labeled HylaFax Server State. The rest of this program is easy to use; you can customize the phone book, send faxes, and so on.

Scanners

Scanners have proven to be very handy pieces of hardware, especially since they have become powerful as well as affordable. You can use a *scanner* to scan documents and send them via fax or email, scan images for your personal electronic photo album, scan images to be electronically retouched and edited, and so on—the uses are seemingly endless.

Scanners come in a variety of models, such as SCSI, parallel port, and USB-based scanners. Linux has good support for SCSI scanners, but these scanners usually are the most expensive ones because they have very high performance. Parallel port scanners offer good performance and are relatively inexpensive, but they are not very well supported by Linux. USB scanners still are not supported because USB itself is not supported by Linux.

This means that your best option is a SCSI scanner. Some parallel port scanners work well with Linux because they are internally SCSI-based, but others don't because they use a proprietary-based protocol. To get a scanner to work in Linux, you must install the package called sane (Scanner Access Now Easy).

Package requirements:

Series gra:

- ▉ sane

sane is a collection of drivers you can use to access your scanner. These drivers, along with applications that use them, form a complete scanner package.

To configure your SCSI scanner, you should have support for generic SCSI devices in your kernel. To do this, follow these steps:

1. Log in as root.

2. Change the directory to the Linux kernel sources directory:
    ```
    #cd /usr/src/linux
    ```

3. Start the kernel's configuration modules by typing the following:
    ```
    #make menuconfig
    ```

4. The kernel configuration module will start; navigate to SCSI Support and press Enter.

5. Highlight SCSI Support and press Y to include it in your kernel.

6. Highlight SCSI Generic Support and press Y to include it in your kernel.

7. Press Esc twice to exit the SCSI Support menu.

8. Press Esc twice again to exit the kernel configuration module. It will ask you whether you want to save your new kernel configuration; choose Yes.

9. Now you need to recompile your kernel for these changes to take effect. To do so, type in the following commands, one after the other:
    ```
    #make dep
    #make clean
    #make bzlilo
    #make modules
    #make modules_install
    ```

10. Each of these commands will take some time to execute, and a lot of text will scroll by—don't worry, this is normal. When all the commands have executed, reboot your system.

Now you need to check for your scanner by using the sgcheck command. Run the command like this:

```
# sgcheck
```

The command will give you a list of all the SCSI devices on your system. Your scanner should have an entry with the word Processor or Scanner somewhere in it. For example,

```
Assignment of generic SCSI devices,
device host/channel/ID/LUN type(numeric type) vendor model:

/dev/sg0 0/0/0/0 CD-ROM IOMEGA ZIPCD 4x650
/dev/sg1 0/0/5/0 Processor(3) HP C2500A
```

As you can see, the scanner here is /dev/sg1. You now can proceed to use YaST to configure that scanner. To do that, follow these steps:

1. Log in as root.

2. Run YaST.

3. Navigate to System Administration, Integrate Hardware Into System, Configure Your Scanner and press Enter.

4. The Scanner Configuration module will load. The first option is the SCSI device list. YaST will show you a list of all the generic SCSI devices on your system. Select /dev/sg1 and press Enter.

5. Next, YaST will show you a list of all the supported scanners; choose yours from the list and press Enter.

6. Press Continue to save your configuration.

7. YaST then will run SuSEConfig to finalize the configuration.

That is all you need to do to set up your scanner. You now can use xscanimage to scan images from your scanner and save them as image files. Run xscanimage from within the X Window System, from an X terminal like the following and start scanning:

```
$xscanimage
```

TV Cards

Recently, a large number of TV cards have begun appearing on the market. These cards, which are relatively inexpensive, enable you to watch TV on your computer. Linux has support for quite a few of these cards. This support is made available by the bttv kernel modules and package.

SuSE has prepared its distribution very well for TV cards. The first thing you should do is make sure that you have support for bttv in your kernel. This is not necessary if you haven't changed the kernel that is installed by SuSE. To configure your kernel, follow these steps:

1. Log in as root.

2. Change the directory to the Linux kernel sources directory:
```
#cd /usr/src/linux
```

3. Start the kernel's configuration modules by typing the following command:
```
#make menuconfig
```

4. The kernel configuration module will start; navigate to Character Devices, Video For Linux and press Enter.

5. Highlight Video For Linux and press M to include it in your kernel as a module.

6. Do the same for all the rest of the options in the list, making them all modules.

7. Press Esc twice to exit the Video For Linux menu.

8. Press Esc twice to exit the Character Devices menu.

9. Press Esc twice again to exit the kernel configuration module. It will ask you whether you want to save your new kernel configuration; choose Yes.

Part
II

Ch
12

10. Now you need to recompile your kernel for these changes to take effect. To do so, type in the following commands, one after the other:

```
#make dep
#make clean
#make bzlilo
#make modules
#make modules_install
```

11. Each of these commands will take some time to execute, and a lot of text will scroll by—don't worry, this is normal. When all the commands have executed, reboot your system.

Now, you should install the bttv package from your SuSE Linux CDs.

Package requirements:

Series gra:

- bttv

When you are finished installing the package, run the configuration tool located in /usr/doc/packages/bttv/tools:

```
# cd /usr/doc/packages/bttv/tools
# ./update
```

This command will detect your TV card and configure the system to use it. When it's finished, you can watch TV by running the xtvscreen program. Run it from within the X Window System, from an X terminal, like this:

```
$xtvscreen
```

That's it! You now can enjoy your TV.

Troubleshooting

I run cdrecord -scanbus, but I don't see my CD-R/RW.

This is probably because you did not configure your drive correctly. If it is a SCSI CD-R/RW, make sure you have support for SCSI CD-ROMs and your SCSI controller in the SCSI low-level drivers. If it is an IDE drive, make sure ATAPI/IDE CD-ROM support is a module, not built in.

I can't mount my Zip drive.

Make sure you loaded the module by running one of the following commands:

```
#modprobe imm
```

```
#modprobe ppa
```

Also, make sure that your drive is on and has a disk in it.

My joystick/gamepad is not detected!

Make sure that your sound card is configured as well. In addition, make sure that you have the correct joystick/gamepad configured in the kernel. ●

Network Configuration

## CHAPTER 13

Configuring a TCP/IP Network

In this chapter

Networking in SuSE Linux

Connected seems to be the buzzword these days. When was the last time you saw a PC that was totally disconnected from some kind of network? Being connected to a network, even if it's for a short while, is the norm these days. If you are not connected to a local area network, you most likely are connected to the Internet, or both. Linux was built with the help of the Internet. This, along with the fact that it gets its roots from UNIX, makes it a perfect platform for networks. Linux supports almost all widely used networking protocols and devices. Being on a network with Linux feels very familiar. Even when Linux is on a standalone machine, it uses networking architectures in many of its applications—for example, the X Window System.

Connecting to a network using SuSE Linux is easy. This chapter explains how to configure SuSE Linux to get connected to a local area network using TCP/IP and an Ethernet card. You should take a minute to understand how TCP/IP works; it will help when you configure your system.

Understanding TCP/IP Networking

In 1969, TCP/IP was developed by the United States Defense Advanced Research Projects Agency (DARPA). The protocol was developed for an experimental network known as ARPAnet. TCP/IP was adopted as the standard protocol to use, and ARPAnet eventually became the Internet.

The structure of a TCP/IP network is not very complex. Every machine connected to a network must have what is called an IP address. An *IP address* is a number in the format xxx.xxx.xxx.xxx—for example, 192.168.12.19—that uniquely identifies a machine on the network.

The IP address can be—but is not always—mapped to what is called a *hostname*. A hostname helps give your machine an easy-to-remember text name.

You can give your machine any name you want, as long as it is unique in the network to which you are connected. For example, you can call your machine suselinux as long as no other machine in your network is called suselinux. Please note that you can have a machine that has no hostname; it is not a necessity.

When you want to access a computer outside your network, you have to make that request to a gateway. A *gateway* is a computer or router that links different networks together, passing data packets back and forth between them.

All communication among machines is done via their IP addresses using one of the common protocols such as TCP or UDP.

It would be difficult to remember the IP address of every machine to which you want to connect. This is why we have hostnames and domains in the first place. And this is why you have a DNS server, which handles the translation of FQDN to IP addresses. The DNS server is an important machine to have around if you want to communicate with other machines on the network using their FQDN.

This was a very brief explanation of the terminology used in TCP/IP networking, which will help you understand the configuration process better. To learn more about this subject, see Chapter 14, "Configuring Domain Name Service," for a more detailed discussion.

What You Need to Know to Get Connected

You need to know a few things before you configure the networking layer in SuSE Linux. The first thing you need to know is the brand of your ethernet card. Linux supports several ethernet cards, so yours is probably supported.

You will need to know your machine's hostname, which you will give your machine. If you are connecting to a local area network, this name should be unique to your machine.

In addition, you need to know the domain name of the network of which you will be a part. Domains are a way to organize and structure big networks. An example of a domain name is infoseek.com. Don't just pick an arbitrary domain name, ask your system administrator for the correct domain name.

You need to know whether your network uses Dynamic Host Configuration Protocol (DHCP), BOOTP, or neither. This information is important because it will affect the way you configure your network.

If you are not using DHCP or BOOTP, you should know the IP address you will use on your machine. You should ask your system administrator for this information because arbitrarily picking an IP address can cause a clash with another machine using that IP.

You also will need to know which netmask to use. A *netmask* is an IP-like number that makes it clear to which network your machine belongs. Your system administrator will give you this number.

You will need to know the IP of your gateway if your network has access to the Internet. Ask your system administrator for this information. Again, if you are using DHCP or BOOTP, you won't need to know this.

You also will need the IP of the name server (DNS). This is important if you are going to address machines by their FQDN rather than their IP addresses.

You now are ready to configure your network.

Part

III

Ch

13

Using YaST to Configure Your Network

Configuring your network is easy thanks to SuSE YaST. Just be sure you have collected all the required information before proceeding with this. To configure your network, you first should configure your networking device. You will need to install the kernel modules package first.

Package requirements:

Series a:

■ kernmod

When you are finished installing this package, you can configure your Ethernet card using YaST. To do that, follow these steps:

1. Log in as root.

2. Run YaST.

3. Navigate to the System Administration, Integrate Hardware Into System, Configure Networking Device menu and press Enter.

4. The Selection of Networking Device module pops up (see Figure 13.1).

FIGURE 13.1
Configuring your
Ethernet card in YaST.

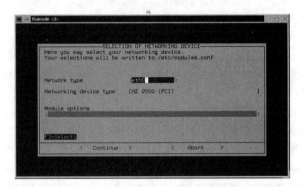

5. Press the Tab key to move to the Networking Device Type field. YaST will show you a list of supported networking cards (see Figure 13.2). Select your card from the list and press Enter.

6. If your card requires any extra module options, enter them in the Module Options field. This information is usually specific to your card, so read its documentation.

7. Press Continue to save and exit.

FIGURE 13.2

Select your Ethernet card from the list.

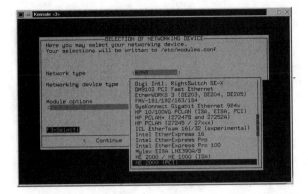

There, you have configured your networking device. Now it's time to configure the actual network. Follow these steps:

1. Log in as root.

2. Run YaST.

3. Navigate to the System Administration, Network Configuration, Network Base Configuration menu and press Enter.

4. The Selection of Network dialog appears, as shown in Figure 13.3.

FIGURE 13.3

Network configuration in YaST.

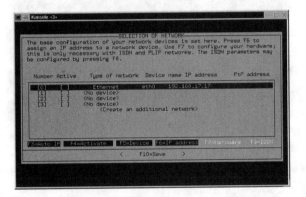

5. As you can see, you have a table that lists entries for network configuration. Currently, most of them if not all will be empty, displaying <No device>. Use the arrow keys to highlight the first free entry—this would be entry Number 0 if you haven't configured your network before—and press F5 to choose the device.

6. As you can see in Figure 13.4, YaST shows you a list of supported networking devices you can use. Highlight Ethernet and press Enter. YaST returns to the previous dialog.

Part

III

Ch

13

FIGURE 13.4
Select Ethernet from the list of network devices.

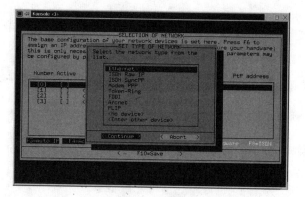

7. If your network uses DHCP or BOOTP, press F3 to configure DHCP.

8. YaST will pop up a dialog box asking you whether you are using DHCP, BOOTP, or No auto IP. Choose DHCP or BOOTP depending on what your network uses (see Figure 13.5). The remaining steps are not required for your configuration; you can exit this module by pressing F10 to save and exit.

FIGURE 13.5
SuSE Linux supports both DHCP and BOOTP protocols.

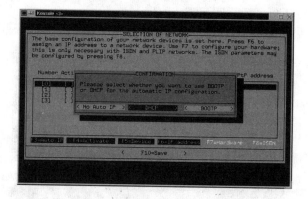

9. If you are not using any auto IP protocols (DHCP or BOOTP), press Enter to configure your network with this device.

10. YaST displays the Network Addresses dialog (see Figure 13.6). You will configure your addresses here.

11. The first field of interest is your machine's IP address. You should enter the IP address you are going to assign to your machine. Remember that this has to be unique to the network to which you are connected.

12. The next field is Netmask; enter your netmask here. This is usually 255.255.255.0, unless your administrator has told you otherwise.

13. Enter the IP of the Default Gateway Address if you have a gateway.

FIGURE 13.6

Configuration of network addresses in YaST.

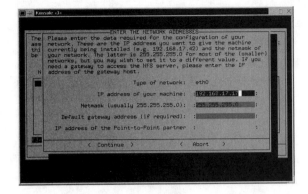

14. Press Continue to save and exit this dialog.

15. Press F4 to activate this configuration.

16. Press F10 to save your configuration and exit.

17. SuSEConfig will run to update your system.

18. In the Network configuration menu, highlight Change Host Name and press Enter.

19. YaST asks you to enter your hostname and domain name, as shown in Figure 13.7. Enter them and press Continue to save and exit.

FIGURE 13.7

Configuring your hostname and domain in YaST.

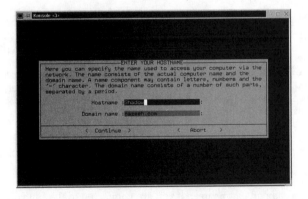

20. Finally, you will need to configure your name server (DNS). In the Network Configuration menu, highlight Configuration Name Server and press Enter.

21. YaST will ask you whether you want to access a Name Server or not; reply Yes.

22. YaST displays the Nameserver Configuration dialog (see Figure 13.8).

23. The first field is the IP address list of your name servers. You might have more than one, in which case separate them using a space.

FIGURE 13.8
Configuring your DNS servers in YaST.

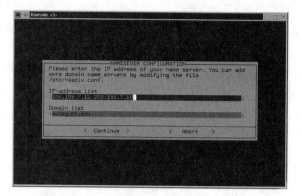

24. The next field is the domain list, which is where you enter your domain name.

25. Press Continue to save and exit.

To start your network, you can restart your system or run the following command:

```
# /sbin/init.d/network start
```

You network now should be up and running. You can see whether your network has been configured using the ifconfig command. Just type ifconfig on the command prompt:

```
#ifconfig
```

You should get an entry similar to this:

```
eth0      Link encap:Ethernet  HWaddr 00:00:1C:05:6A:34
          inet addr:192.168.17.17  Bcast:192.168.17.255  Mask:255.255.255.0
          UP BROADCAST RUNNING MULTICAST  MTU:1500  Metric:1
          RX packets:372 errors:0 dropped:0 overruns:0 frame:0
          TX packets:328 errors:0 dropped:0 overruns:0 carrier:0
          collisions:0 txqueuelen:100
          Interrupt:10 Base address:0xec00
```

This indicates that the network is up and running. You can test it further by trying to reach another machine on the network using the ping command—for example:

```
#ping www.suse.com
```

The previous command can be used if you are connected to the Internet. If you are not, just ping any other machine in your network. The ping command should give you an output similar to this:

```
64 bytes from 192.168.17.17: icmp_seq=0 ttl=255 time=0.160 ms
64 bytes from 192.168.17.17: icmp_seq=1 ttl=255 time=0.119 ms
64 bytes from 192.168.17.17: icmp_seq=2 ttl=255 time=0.117 ms
64 bytes from 192.168.17.17: icmp_seq=3 ttl=255 time=0.124 ms
```

This means that your network is running properly.

Upgrading or Changing Your Network Card

If the current kernel does not support your network card, you might need to get the latest version of the kernel (if yours is not the latest). In this case, you will need to compile that kernel with support for your network card. Some network cards work better when they are built in the kernel, instead of as modules. If this is the case, you will need to recompile your kernel to make them built in. To do that, follow these steps:

1. Log in as root.

2. Change the directory to the Linux kernel sources directory:

   ```
   #cd /usr/src/linux
   ```

3. Start the kernel's configuration modules by typing the following:

   ```
   #make menuconfig
   ```

4. The kernel configuration module will start; navigate to the Network Device Support menu and press Enter.

5. Press Y at the Network device support option. This should give you a new list.

6. Use the arrow keys to highlight the Ethernet (10 or 100Mb) option and press Enter.

7. Highlight Ethernet (10 or 100Mb) and press Y to include it in the kernel.

8. Find your card in the list and press Y to include it as built in or M to make it a module.

9. Press Esc twice to exit this menu.

10. Press the Esc key twice to exit the Network Device Support menu.

11. Press Esc twice again to exit the kernel configuration module. It will ask you whether you want to save your new kernel configuration or not; choose Yes.

12. Now you need to recompile your kernel for these changes to take effect. To do so, you have to type in the following commands, one after the other:

    ```
    #make dep
    #make clean
    #make bzlilo
    #make modules
    #make modules_install
    ```

13. Each of these commands will take some time to finish executing, and a lot of text will scroll by—don't worry, this is normal. When all the commands have executed, reboot your system to load the new kernel.

There, you're all set now. Just go through the network configuration again. If you installed your Ethernet card built in the kernel, you should skip the configure networking device step.

Part
III

Ch

13

Network-Related Configuration Files

You should be aware of a few network-related configuration files. Usually, SuSE YaST automatically modifies these files, but you can manually modify them to further meet your needs.

The first file that you might be interested in is /etc/hosts. This file is used by the system to map FQDN to IP addresses. The format of the file is simple. Each entry is made up of an IP and the FQDN that resolves to it. For example:

```
127.0.0.1        suselinux.company.com suselinux
```

This way, if you ever access suselinux, it will resolve to 127.0.0.1.

Another file of interest is /etc/networks. This file is similar to /etc/hosts in the sense that it is used to translate network names to network addresses. Its format is almost the same as /etc/hosts except that the fields are swapped. For example, the following can be an entry in this file:

```
company.com     192.186.186.0
```

The /etc/host.conf is used by the system when resolving hostnames. This file controls how the resolving process is going to occur. For example, to have your system check your /etc/hosts file first and then the DNS server when resolving a hostname, you would use the following:

```
order hosts bind
```

SuSE Linux uses Name Service Switch, which is part of the C library. Certain functions in the C library look up databases on the system. This file defines how these functions access those databases and in what order. You can get more information about this file from its man page (man 5 nsswitch.conf).

The file /etc/resolv.conf is where your DNS servers are defined. This file has a simple format. SuSE recommends that you don't edit this file manually; you should edit it using the Configure Nameserver module in YaST.

The file /etc/HOSTNAME is where the complete name of your machine is stored. This file is read on system startup to identify your hostname.

You can get more information about these files and how to configure them in Chapter 14, "Configuring Domain Name Service."

Securing Your Network Using a Firewall

Now that your network is up and running, you should start thinking about security—especially if you are connected to the Internet. One of the strongest security measures is the use of a firewall.

Firewalls are used to control the flow of data packets coming in and leaving your system. You can use a firewall to block certain packets originating from certain sources and flowing toward certain destinations. With a firewall, you can block some of the most common attacks on your system and at the same time regulate your traffic in an orderly fashion. The firewall is part of the kernel that you control with the `ipchains` package. To install `ipchains`, you need the following package:

Package requirements:

Series sec:

- `ipchains`

Installing the Firewall

To use a firewall, you must have support for both the network firewalls and IP: Firewalling options. You probably already have that support in your kernel. One way to check whether you do have it is to see whether the file `/proc/net/ip_fwchains` exists on your system. If it doesn't exist then you have to recompile your kernel with firewall support. To do this, follow these steps:

1. Log in as root.

2. Change the directory to the Linux kernel sources directory:

   `#cd /usr/src/linux`

3. Start the kernel's configuration modules by typing the following:

   `#make menuconfig`

4. The kernel configuration module will start; navigate to Networking Options and press Enter.

5. Use the arrow keys to highlight the Network Firewalls option and press Y to include it in the kernel.

6. Highlight IP: Firewalling and press Y to include it in the kernel.

7. Press Esc twice to exit the Networking Options menu.

8. Press Esc twice again to exit the Kernel Configuration module. It will ask you whether you want to save your new kernel configuration or not; choose Yes.

9. Now you need to recompile your kernel for these changes to take effect. To do so, you have to type in the following commands, one after the other:

   ```
   #make dep
   #make clean
   #make bzlilo
   #make modules
   #make modules_install
   ```

Part
III

Ch
13

10. Each of these commands will take some time to finish executing, and a lot of text will scroll by—don't worry, this is normal. When all the commands have executed, reboot your system to load the new kernel.

When your system reboots, you can make sure that it worked by checking for the existence of the file `/proc/net/ip_fwchains`; you should find it now.

Configuring the Firewall

The firewall is configured using the `ipchains` command. The configuration is pretty simple; you just need to know what you want to do. Using a firewall, you can control access to certain IP addresses, ports, and protocols. You can block their access or allow it, depending on what you want.

The firewall intercepts every packet that flows through your machine. The firewall then reads the packet's header, which contains information about where this packet came from and where it's going. Then, using some rules, the firewall decides what to do with this packet. These rules are what you will configure, and by doing so, you will be able to tell the firewall something like "all packets coming from `www.badsite.com` should not be allowed to get through," or "do not answer any ping requests, ignore them."

The firewall has three main families of rules: input, forward, and output. The *input* rules are first processed when a packet is being inspected; if any rule matches that packet, action is taken. Otherwise, the packet makes it to the *forward* family of rules, where again, if it matches any of its rules, action is taken. Finally, if the packet makes it through the forward family of rules, it is inspected by the *output* family. If all rules fail to match, a default action is executed. On well-configured firewalls, this default action is usually to reject the packet, just to be safe.

Let's look at some examples of how you can configure a firewall. You use the `ipchains` command to dictate rules to the firewall. Let's use blocking ping requests as an example. A ping request uses a protocol called *ICMP*—when someone pings your machine, they send you a certain type of ICMP packet. After your machine receives the packet, it replies with another type of ICMP packet. *Ping* is used to determine whether a remote machine is alive or not. You can block such ping packets from ever reaching your machine using the following command:

```
# ipchains -A input -p icmp -j DENY
```

The command looks cryptic, doesn't it? Not to worry; enlightenment is on the way. The first argument to the command `-A input` tells `ipchains` to add a rule to the input family of rules (`-A` is add). The second argument is `-p icmp`, which tells `ipchains` the ICMP protocol is being used (`-p` for protocol). Finally, `-j DENY` sets denying the package as the action to be taken (`-j` for jump to). In other words, this command is saying "Here's a rule to add to the input family of rules: If you ever see a packet that uses the ICMP protocol, get rid of it".

The following is the output of the `ping` command *before* you set this rule:

```
# ping localhost
PING localhost (127.0.0.1): 56 data bytes
64 bytes from 127.0.0.1: icmp_seq=0 ttl=255 time=0.149 ms
64 bytes from 127.0.0.1: icmp_seq=1 ttl=255 time=0.124 ms
--- localhost ping statistics ---
2 packets transmitted, 2 packets received, 0% packet loss
round-trip min/avg/max = 0.124/0.136/0.149 ms
```

The following is the output *after* you apply the rule:

```
PING localhost (127.0.0.1): 56 data bytes
--- localhost ping statistics ---
2 packets transmitted, 0 packets received, 100% packet loss
```

As you can see, this causes 100 percent packet loss. Here's what happens inside the firewall. The firewall is looking at the packets on your machine. It picks up a packet, looks at its header, and tries to match it with the rules it has. You ping the machine, causing ICMP packets to be sent to your machine. The firewall picks up these packets, reads their headers, and finds out that these are ICMP protocol packets. The firewall then inspects the input family of rules and finds a rule for dealing with these packets. The rule tells the firewall to get rid of them, so the firewall simply gets rid of these packets and does not allow them to pass through to your network. Therefore, ping never gets a reply to the packets it sent because your machine never even received them, thanks to the firewall.

To remove this rule, just replace the `-A` with `-D` (for delete):

```
# ipchains -D input -p icmp -j DENY
```

If you ping yourself now, your machine will reply normally.

Let's see how you can enhance this rule. Say that a friend of yours is pinging your machine constantly with large packets. This will slow down your network connection because your machine will just sit there replying to the ping requests. You can block any incoming ICMP packets from only his IP. The following is the command for that, assuming his IP is 111.222.111.222:

```
#ipchains -A input -s 111.222.111.222 -p icmp -j DENY
```

The `-s 111.222.111.222` argument tells `ipchains` to block from this source IP address. The rest of the arguments are the same as the previous command. What this rule is saying is "if you get any ICMP protocol packets from the IP address 111.222.111.222, get rid of them." If someone else pings you, she will get a reply, but your friend is going to sit there wasting his network bandwidth trying to ping you, and you will never pay attention to him.

You also can control the packets' destination. For example, if you have a lot of users on your machine, you might not want them to be able to communicate with a certain machine. You can do this with the following command, assuming the machine is called badmachine.domain.com:

```
#ipchains -A input -d badmachine.domain.com -j DENY
```

All connections to this machine will be disallowed because you just told your firewall "do not accept any packets with the destination of (-d) badmachine.domain.com."

The -s and -d options can take IP address ranges as well as single IP addresses. You can use the IP address/netmask combination to define entire networks. For example, -s 123.123.123.0/255.255.255.0 signifies all IP addresses that start with 123.123.123—the 0/0 means everything, or all IP addresses.

You can specify ports and port ranges as well. For example, to define all ports from 1000 to 6000 for the IP address 123.123.123.123, the format would be as follows:

-s 123.123.123.123 1000:6000 -p TCP

To specify all ports up to 1000, you would use :1000, and to specify all ports starting with 1000 and up, you would use 1000:.

You can use ! (NOT) to inverse a match. For example, -s ! 123.123.123.123 signifies all IP addresses *except* 123.123.123.123. You can use ! in all the options—for example:

-d 123.123.123.123 ! 8080 -p TCP

This designates the IP address 123.123.123.123 and all ports *except* port number 8080. On the other hand, the following

-d ! 123.123.123.123 8080 -p TCP

means all IP addresses on port 8080 *except* IP address 123.123.123.123.

You must specify the protocol you want using the -p option. As you can see, the previous examples all dealt with the TCP protocol.

You even can specify the interface on which the rule will act by using the -i option. For example, to block ping requests that come to you through your dial-up connection, you use the following:

ipchains -A input -i ppp0 -p ICMP -j DENY

This rule will act on the PPP interface called ppp0. If you have multiple interfaces that begin with the same name—for example, eth0 and eth1—you can use the plus sign (+) to group them:

ipchains -A input -i eth+ -p ICMP -j DENY

This rule will apply to all interfaces that begin with eth.

The -j option can take DENY, ACCEPT, REJECT, MASQ, REDIRECT, and RETURN as options. You can get more information about each one of these from the ipchains man page (man ipchains).

Saving Your Firewall Rules

All the rules you set will be lost when you reboot. You probably will want to save them and have them restored when the system boots up. This is easy; you can use the `ipchains-save` and `ipchains-restore` scripts. To save the firewall settings, add this line to your `/sbin/init.d/halt.local`:

```
ipchains-save > /etc/firewall.rules
```

And to restore them on boot up, add this line to `/sbin/init.d/boot.local`:

```
ipchains-restore < /etc/firewall.rules
```

That's it. Your firewall settings will be saved and restored on boot up.

Crash Course in *ipchains* Command-Line Arguments

The command `ipchains` has several command-line arguments you can use. The following is a brief list of the most common ones and what they mean:

- **-A**—This argument is followed by the name of a chain. It is used to append a new rule to the chain.

- **-D**—This argument is followed by the name of a chain. It is used to delete rules from the chain.

- **-R**—This command is used to replace a rule at some position in the chain. *Position* is the number of the rule you want to replace in that chain. For example, `ipchains -R input 2 ....` will replace rule number 2 in the input chain with the rule you are about to define.

- **-L**—This command can take the name of a chain and will list all the rules defined in that chain. If no argument is given, it will list all the chains, empty or not.

- **-N**—This command is used to create a new chain. This is a user-defined chain other than the default INPUT, OUTPUT, and so on. You can create your own chain of rules and use the `-A` to append rules to that chain. Then you can use that chain as a target for the `-j` argument.

- **-X**—This will delete a user-defined chain. The chain has to be empty, though. Delete all the rules you set in it.

- **-F**—This command takes the name of the chain as an argument. It then deletes all the rules in that chain.

- **-j**—This argument takes the name of an action of the chain. If the packet matches that rule, control is passed to that action of chain. You can, for example, enter the name of a user-defined chain. In that case, if the packet matches the rule, control will be passed to your chain.

Part
III

Ch
13

■ **-P**—This command takes a name of a chain as an argument. It then sets an action as the default action (and only action) in this chain. For example, `ipchains -P input ACCEPT` will allow everything to pass.

These were the most commonly used command-line options for `ipchains`. You can get more detailed information from the man page (`man ipchains`).

Troubleshooting

I configured my network but I can't access any other machines.

First check the physical side of the process. Are you sure that your network cable is properly connected? If you have another operating system installed, does it have network access? Are you sure that your network card is properly detected and running? You can find out from the output of the `ifconfig` command. Does it show an `eth0` device? If it doesn't show you one, restart the network and run the command `/sbin/init.d/network restart`. If you are using DHCP or BOOTP, check that their respective servers are up and running. Finally, is your route table properly configured? If the host you are trying to reach is on another network, you must have a gateway to that network.

My network card doesn't seem to be supported. I can't find it in the list of cards.

You might not find the exact name of the card in the list, so look for compatible cards. You should check the chipset of the card and try to find an entry that works for it. You can try the NE2000 family of cards because most cards are compatible with them. If none of them work, you can check to see whether there is a new release of the kernel; if there is, install it and try again.

Now that my network is up, people can't access me using my hostname.

You have to register your hostname with the network's DNS server. Ask your system administrator to do that for you. Hostnames are not like machine names in MS Windows—you must register them with a DNS machine.

People can't telnet or FTP to my machine.

Make sure that you turned on these services from YaST. Running the network service configuration module in YaST does this. You will find it in the menu choice System Administration, Network Configuration, Configure Network Services. ●

## CHAPTER 14

Configuring Domain Name Service

In this chapter

A Briefing on Domain Name Service

Most people have a hard time remembering numbers. If you're not convinced, try to remember how much money you have in your wallet right now or what your license plate number is. Now, imagine something even more difficult—imagine that every time you want to access an Internet site, you must do so using its IP rather than its name. So, instead of typing in the address as http://www.yahoo.com, you'll have to type in an IP. How many IPs will you be able to remember? It's hard enough remembering your spouse's birthday, your dentist's appointment, and (most importantly) your appointment with the psychiatrist after you finish reading this book! It's impossible to remember all of these plus the IPs of your favorite Internet sites. Hence, the idea of naming machines and networks. *Naming* simply means giving the network a name that describes the institution and giving the machines and hosts names that describe their sub-sections of the institution. This is the same idea as the root/sub hierarchy that you see everywhere. In this chapter, we will discuss the importance of Domain Name Service (DNS) and how you can configure it on your SuSE Linux. But, first we'll look at the origins of the Internet and the DNS system.

Internet History

In the early days of its existence (the late 1960s), the Internet was a project of the U.S. Department of Defense's Advanced Research Projects Agency (ARPA), and was therefore known as ARPANET. In the early 1980s, the TCP/IP protocol was developed and became the Internet standard. Up until this time, ARPANET had been the backbone of the Internet. But in 1988, the Department of Defense abandoned the project. The National Science Foundation (NSFNET) took over and replaced ARPANET with its NSFNET, which is the backbone of today's Internet.

DNS History

DNS's history is a part of the Internet's history because both grew up together. In the 1970s, the number of hosts on the ARPANET was small. Therefore, a single file named HOSTS.TXT was sufficient to represent all the information anyone would need to know about all the hosts on the network. All the member hosts of the ARPANET would send any changes to the Network Information Center (NIC) administrator to be applied to the HOSTS.TXT. Periodically, the hosts would grab the HOSTS.TXT file and apply it to the /etc/hosts file. As the number of hosts on the ARPANET began to increase tremendously in the 1990s, the HOSTS.TXT file increased in size, name collisions started to occur, and consistency became a problem. A DNS database had to be implemented to eliminate the problems of the old HOSTS.TXT file.

DNS Database   It wasn't until Paul Mockapetris presented the first drafts of the DNS system in 1984 that the NIC realized the new system would help them manage the huge number of hosts that they had to maintain. DNS is a *distributed database*, which means its main portion lies on NIC's servers and the extensions lie on the other DNS servers on the Internet.

DNS was based on the fact that management control belonged to zone masters, which in turn introduced the authority concept. With the introduction of the DNS database, NIC was no longer responsible for all the addresses on the Internet. NIC's role now was to control the top-level names and maintain a stable and complete DNS database. In addition, all authoritative domain name servers had a full copy of the DNS database, which reduced the load on the NIC servers and assured faster name lookup for all hosts.

Zones Versus Domains   Many people confuse zones with domains. A *zone* is a subset of a certain domain in which the name server of this zone has authority over a subset of this domain. For example, say there are six name servers: A, B, C, D, E, and F. A is the top-level name server; B and C are at the next level; D and E are sub-domains of C; and F is a sub-domain of E (see Figure 14.1).

FIGURE 14.1
In zone C, the C administrator manages the whole C branches and the C domain encompasses all the hosts in the C branches.

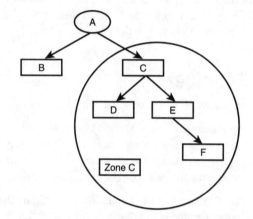

If the C domain administrator manages the branches of the C domain, C can be considered a zone. In other words, zones are hosts rooted to a higher-level domain in which they share administration privileges.

DNS Clients   DNS plays an important role in your daily Internet life. If you want to access Yahoo, for example, you write http://www.yahoo.com in the address bar of your browser and the browser opens the site. This might seem simple, but a lot had to happen for this to occur. When you typed the address and pressed Enter, the browser first tried to resolve the address you typed in. This process is called *hostname resolution* and is executed through the standard C library with which your SuSE Linux comes equipped. A special routine in the C library contacted your name server and the following scenario happened:

The browser used a gethostbyname() C function and queried the IP address of http://www.yahoo.com. The resolver scanned the configuration file /etc/resolve.conf to find out where it would locate the IP. If the resolve.conf file specified a name server to be looked up, the resolver would query the name server. The name server would then pass the query to the authoritative name server of the yahoo.com zone searching for the www host. The IP of the www host would be passed back to the name server, which would pass it to the resolver that first queried for it. Now that your resolver has resolved the IP, it can access the http://www.yahoo.com Web site.

DNS Servers   DNS servers are not all the same. A general rule says that all name servers are caching servers, but a variety of types exists:

- **Master or Primary servers**—The authoritative servers of some zone. They are responsible for finding the information for all the hosts inside their zones.

- **Slave or Secondary servers**—Servers in the next level after the master servers. They know some of the information within their domain, but are not authoritative.

- **Caching only servers**—Servers that cache the information for themselves so they do not ask too much. They build their cache through the queries that are sent to them. When this query is repeated, they have the address cached.

Configuring the Resolver

You need to configure the resolver if you want to be able to access any host by name.

You have to perform the configuration in this section to enable your applications to use names instead of IPs. Despite what most people think, the resolver is not a standalone program or daemon; rather, it is a part of the C system library. This means programs that need to access hosts by name need only to issue a call to the C functions, which will return the IP.

The simplest example of performing resolver configuration is adding the hosts in the /etc/hosts file. The format of this file is as follows:

```
IP [host address] [nick]
```

Hosts entered in the /etc/hosts file can be resolved using either the host address or the nick. This configuration works fine if your SuSE Linux machine is in a LAN with a small number of machines. As a matter of fact, you can server as a DNS if you have a good configuration of the /etc/hosts file. The following is an example of a /etc/hosts file:

```
192.186.186.126 badrlinux.itworx.com  badrlinux
192.186.186.1    mail.itworx.com   mail
192.186.186.4    badrnt.itworx.com    badr
208.159.7.2      mail.aucegypt.edu    aucmail
208.160.129.97 huss2000.aucegypt.edu huss
```

For a more sophisticated configuration that relies on the existence of a DNS, you should move on to the following section of this chapter.

What the Configuration Files Are

At the very least, you need to configure the following files for the resolver to take effect:

- `/etc/host.conf`
- `/etc/resolv.conf`

These files can be modified either manually or through YaST. In the following section, we will discuss how to configure these files using YaST and the advanced functionality that one can get through editing the files manually.

Using YaST If you do not want to edit files manually, YaST provides quick and efficient results. You should edit files manually only if you want to check for spoofing or perform host-name trimming. In other words, you do not have to edit files unless you are running a LAN and want a tweaked configuration. Home users on single machines do not need to edit files manually, unless they want to learn how to do it manually.

Using YaST, open the System Administration, Network Configuration, Configuration Nameserver. You will be asked if you want to access a name server. Answer Yes and the Nameserver Configuration window will appear (see Figure 14.2). In the IP address list, enter the primary and secondary name servers' IPs separated by a space. In the Domain list field, enter the name of the name server.

FIGURE 14.2
By choosing to configure the resolver through YaST, you don't have to edit any files. The IP address list specifies the domains to be contacted, and the Domain field represents the search list in the `/etc/resolv.conf` file. The `/etc/host.conf` file is generated automatically depending of the values you insert here.

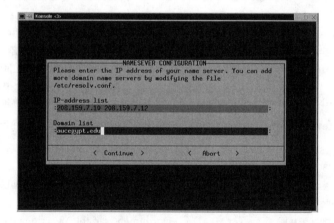

The /etc/host.conf File   This file is concerned with the options that control the behavior of the resolver. It tells the resolver what to do and how to do it. The few available options for this file are simple:

- `order [hosts|bind|nis]`—This option indicates the order in which the resolver should try to resolve the hostnames. The following parameters are available for the `order` option:
  - `hosts` tells the resolver to look first in the `/etc/hosts` file.
  - `bind` tells the resolver to query the name server.
  - `nis` tells the resolver to use NIS lookup.

  Here is an example of how this line could look:

  `order hosts bind`

  This example instructs the resolver to look in the `/etc/hosts` file. If it fails, it should resort to using the name server.

- `multi [on|off]`—When turned on, this option enables you to have multiple IP addresses in the `/etc/resolve.conf` file. It is a good idea to have it turned on.

- `nospoof [on|off]`—This option enables the resolver to check for spoofing. *Spoofing* is the attempt of a name server to supply a false hostname for a specified IP address. When this option is turned on and a case of spoofing is detected, the resolver returns an error.

- `alert [on|off]`—This option is also made for spoofing. If spoofing is detected and this option is turned on, the resolver logs the case to your system log.

- `trim [domain]`—When you supply a domain name to this option, the domain name will be removed from the hostname prior to lookup. When using this option with the `/etc/hosts` entries, it enables you to have hostnames without local domains.

The `/etc/host.conf` entries can be overridden by the following environment variables:

- `RESOLV_HOST_CONF [file path]`—This environment variable specifies a file to be used instead of the `/etc/host.conf` file.

- `RESOLV_SERV_ORDER [hosts|bind|nis]`—This environment variable overrides the `order` option in the `/etc/host.conf` file.

- `RESOLV_MULTI [on|off]`—This environment variable overrides the `multi` option in the `/etc/host.conf` file.

- `RESOLV_SPOOF_CHECK [on|off]`—This environment variable overrides the `nospoof` option in the `/etc/host.conf` file.

- `RESOLV_OVERRIDE_TRIM_DOMAINS [domains]`—This environment variable overrides the list of domains specified by the `trim` option in the `/etc/host.conf` file.

- `RESOLV_ADD_TRIM_DOMAINS [domains]`—This environment variable adds the specified domains to the trim domains list.

The following is an example of using the environment variable RESOLV_MULTI to override the one used in /etc/host.conf:

```
bash#export RESOLV_MULTI=off
```

The /etc/resolv.conf File   The /etc/resolv.conf file has the following options:

- nameserver [IP]—This option specifies the IP of the name server you would like to contact. If this option is not specified, the resolver assumes that the name server is the localhost.

- domain [domain]—This option enables you to define a shortcut local domain name. If you add this option, this domain will be appended to the hostname that you want to access locally.

  For example, if you add the statement domain aucegypt.edu in the /etc/resolv.conf file, you can access auc.aucegypt.edu by #telnet auc.

- search [domain]—This option acts exactly like the domain option. This option can be used to define a list of domains to be appended to the hostnames. Note that this option should be used with care because it can lead to confusion when resolving names.

Setting Up the Domain Name Server

After all the theoretical information on DNS, it's time to set it up. We will discuss inserting some hosts on your domain and also registering your domain name to be accessible via the Internet.

Software Requirements

This chapter explains only the use of BIND version 8.x. If you are running BIND 4.x, we advise you to upgrade to 8.x because the 4.x versions have several security bugs.

Series n:

- BIND

BIND Configuration

Even if there isn't another host connected to your SuSE Linux box, you should set up a caching only server. This will reduce your queries to the name server, which you access primarily to get the IPs of the servers you most frequently access. After you finish setting up the caching only name server on your box, for a certain length of time, your SuSE Linux will remember the IPs you accessed and will not query your ISP name server for them. If your machine is a gateway to other machines on the network, it also can easily function as a name server for these machines.

Part
III

Ch
14

Configuration Files

The main configuration file for BIND 8.x is located in `/etc/named.conf`. You should be using this file primarily to get any of the name server types that are discussed in this chapter. As mentioned earlier, this book deals only with BIND version 8.x and not version 4.x. The configuration filename is different and there are differences in its formats.

> **CAUTION**
>
> This chapter does not discuss the setup of BIND version 4.x. BIND version 8.x is considered the default for SuSE Linux, starting with version 6.2. If you are upgrading from SuSE 6.1 to SuSE 6.2 or 6.3, you have to install BIND version 8.x manually or by using YaST. It is does not get upgraded by default when you choose to update the existing system. You should consider upgrading this package because of the many security problems BIND 4.x has.

The *named.conf* Statements   The `named.conf` file has a unique syntax that is easy to understand. The file is made up of comments, statements, and sub-statements (*sub-statements* are blocks of statements from the main statements):

- **Comments**—The comment style in the `named.conf` file can be any of the following:
  - C style—`/* This is a C style comment*/`
  - C++ style—`//This is a C++ one line style comment`
  - Shell style—`#This is a shell one line style comment`

> **CAUTION**
>
> The semicolon (`;`) is not considered a comment. Semicolons are used to terminate a statement. Watch out for errors caused by semicolons.

- **Main Statements**—Every statement should end with a semicolon (`;`). The following statements are supported by BIND:
  - `acl`—This statement must be used to create a name address match list. Before using this statement, you have to define a match list name in order for `acl` to use it.
  - `include`—Includes another configuration file at the point where this statement appears. It is considered a good style if you cut the configuration file in more than one piece to have control over them.
  - `key`—To use the server definition, you must create a `key ID` for it using the `key` statement. The `key` statement creates a special key that stores associated information for authentication methods for a specified name server.

- `logging`—This statement should appear only once in the `named.conf` and include files. It controls the level of logging and the log file path.
- `options`—The global named server options are configured in this section. Note that this section should appear only once in the `named.conf` and include files.
- `server`—This statement defines the information and behavior of a particular name server.
- `zone`—This statement defines a zone and the particular behavior and information about this zone.

■ **Sub-statements**—As noted previously, sub-statements are the blocks used within a main statement. In this chapter, we will define only the sub-statements that will be used within this chapter. For a complete reference of all the sub-statements, launch your favorite Web browser and open `file:/usr/doc/packages/bind/html/config.html`, which is locally stored on your Linux partition if you have BIND 8.x installed.

The *named.conf* Syntax Look at the following example, which uses the `options` statement and the `directory` sub-statement:

```
// An example of using the options statement
options {
    directory "/var/named";
};
```

In this example, the brackets `{}` are used to create the `options` statement block. Inside this block, the `directory` sub-statement, which instructs BIND to use `/var/named` as the default directory for its output files, is defined. The following is an example that uses the `zone` statement. In this statement, the root level zone from the `/var/named/root.hints` file is defined:

```
zone "." IN{
        type hint;
        file "root.hints";
};
```

The previous section indicates that when the name server starts, it should cache the name servers that are found in the `root.hints` file. This file should be located in the path specified by the `options` section, which is `/var/named/root.hints` in this example. The `root.hints` file should look like the following:

```
G.ROOT-SERVERS.NET.      5w6d16h IN A    192.112.36.4
J.ROOT-SERVERS.NET.      5w6d16h IN A    198.41.0.10
K.ROOT-SERVERS.NET.      5w6d16h IN A    193.0.14.129
L.ROOT-SERVERS.NET.      5w6d16h IN A    198.32.64.12
M.ROOT-SERVERS.NET.      5w6d16h IN A    202.12.27.33
A.ROOT-SERVERS.NET.      5w6d16h IN A    198.41.0.4
H.ROOT-SERVERS.NET.      5w6d16h IN A    128.63.2.53
B.ROOT-SERVERS.NET.      5w6d16h IN A    128.9.0.107
C.ROOT-SERVERS.NET.      5w6d16h IN A    192.33.4.12
D.ROOT-SERVERS.NET.      5w6d16h IN A    128.8.10.90
```

Part
III

Ch
14

```
E.ROOT-SERVERS.NET.      5w6d16h IN A     192.203.230.10
I.ROOT-SERVERS.NET.      5w6d16h IN A     192.36.148.17
F.ROOT-SERVERS.NET.      5w6d16h IN A     192.5.5.241
```

You always can obtain a list of these servers from the NIC by connecting to the Internet and issuing the following command:

```
bash#dig @rs.internic.net . ns >root.hints.new 2>&1
```

This command will obtain a list of the root level master servers and place them in a file called `root.hints.new`.

Now, the second zone entry in the `/etc/named.conf` is the following:

```
zone "0.0.127.in-addr.arpa" IN{
        type master;
        file "127.0.0.zone";
};
```

In this example, `0.0.127.in-addr.arpa` defines a new zone, which is your localhost. The address of your localhost should be put in reverse order. Note that the left-most digit was not included when defining the zone. Again, the configuration file that describes the behavior is the file named `/var/named/127.0.0.zone`. This file should look like the following:

```
1-   $ORIGIN 0.0.127.in-addr.arpa.
2-   @               1D IN SOA    localhost. root.localhost. (
3-                       42          ; serial
4-                       3H          ; refresh every 3 hours
5-                       15M         ; retry every 15 minutes
6-                       1W          ; expiry of cache is 1 week
7-                       1D )        ; minimum time is one day
8-           1D IN NS    localhost.
9-   1       1D IN PTR   localhost.
```

The format for this file is simple even though it looks horrifying at first glance. This file should start with $ORIGIN and each domain should end with a dot. If a dot is not typed, BIND will attach the origin address to it, which is `localhost.` in the file = `localhost` as BIND interprets it, but `localhost` in the file = `127.0.0.localhost` as BIND interprets it. The following is a dissection of the format for this file:

- ■ **Line 1**—The $ORIGIN statement defines the hierarchy of the DNS belongs.

- ■ **Line 2**—The @ is a special notation meaning the origin. The origin domain for this file is `0.0.127.in-addr.arpa` because it is called from the `named.conf` file. The line is translated in the following:

    ```
    0.0.127.in-addr.arpa.   IN      SOA localhost. root.localhost.
    ```

    This line signifies the start of the localhost server's authority. `root.localhost.` is the email address of the host master of the localhost server and should be read as `root@localhost`.

- **Lines 3**—The serial number, also known as the version number, is used when secondary servers check for zone changes. If you make any changes to the zone that this file controls, you have to increase this number to reflect an update in the zone information.

- **Lines 4–7**—These lines define the behavior of BIND against the cached addresses.

- **Line 8**—Using the NS resource record, which defines the domain name of the origin, this line defines the name as local host.

- **Line 9**—The digit 1 at the start of the line will be appended to the IP address of the origin. The whole new IP address will be set to the name local host.

> **N O T E** The most important three resource records (RR) that a zone file can contain are SOA, NS, and PTR. The first is the Start Of Authority resource record (SOA). This record defines the origin from which the hosts or domains branch. The second resource record is the Name Service (NS). The NS tells the DNS the domain name of the origin. The third is the pointer resource record (PTR), which defines subnets and hosts from the origin. ■

Setting Up a Caching Only Name Server

Now that you have built a knowledge base, it's time to make use of it. Setting up a caching only name server is a good way to lessen the name lookup time. If your machine is on a LAN, it will lessen the load on the existing name servers if you tell the other people on the LAN to use it as a domain name server, too.

Setting Up the Server

You should start by setting up the main configuration file /etc/named.conf. Open the file in your favorite editor and enter the following configuration:

```
1   options {
2       directory "/var/named";
3       check-names master warn;
4       pid-file "/var/run/named.pid";
5       datasize default;
6       stacksize default;
7       coresize default;
8       files unlimited;
9       recursion yes;
10      multiple-cnames no;
11      // forwarders {          //This section would enhance the performance
12      //    xxx.xxx.xxx.xxx;    //uncomment those and add your primary DNS
13      //    xxx.xxx.xxx.xxx;    //and secondary DNS
14      // };
15  };
```

Part
III

Ch
14

```
16  zone "." IN {
17     type hint;
18     file "root.hint";
19  };
20  zone "0.0.127.in-addr" IN {
21     type master;
22     file "127.0.0.zone";
23     check-names fail;
24  };
```

Lines 11–14 are only important for tweaking. They lessen the load on your machine. If you have another machine that works as a name server, include its IP in the forward list. If you don't have one, add your primary and secondary DNS. If you are connected to the Internet using a modem, you should enter the DNS addresses of your ISP in the forward list.

The second file to configure is the /var/named/root.hints. Luckily, this file comes with SuSE Linux pre-prepared. However, you should update this file periodically. While connected to the Internet, issue the following command to grab a new copy of the root name servers:

```
bash#dig @rs.internic.net . ns >root.hints.new 2>&1
```

This command will grab a copy of the latest root name servers and save it to a file called root.hints.new. After you get this file, you can overwrite the original root.hints file and therefore ensure that you always have the latest version of the root name servers. It is a good idea to perform this operation on weekly basis.

The third file to configure is the /var/named/127.0.0.zone. This file should be responsible only for the localhost machine. This file comes pre-configured with SuSE Linux and should contain the following:

```
$ORIGIN 0.0.127.in-addr.arpa.
@            1D IN SOA   localhost. root.localhost. (
                42          ; serial
                3H          ; refresh
                15M         ; retry
                1W          ; expiry
                1D )        ; minimum

             1D IN NS    localhost.    ;127.0.0 is a name server
1            1D IN PTR   localhost.    ;localhost = 127.0.0.1
```

Now, you should be finished configuring a caching only name server. Restart the named so it can use the new configuration by issuing the following command:

```
bash#/sbin/init.d/named restart
```

Using the Caching Only Name Server

To use the newly configured server, you should tell the resolver to use your localhost as the primary name server. Using YaST, open the System Administration, Network Configuration,

Configuration Nameserver. In the name server field, type in `127.0.0.1`. If you want to add any advanced functionality to the resolver, refer to the first sections in this chapter to find out how to do so.

A Simple Domain Configuration

The purpose of this section is to configure a domain name server. You can start off by making a caching only name server, as you learned in the previous section. Then, you will configure a simple domain configuration.

First, you should select a name for the name server. Select a name that does not conflict with the name server of your ISP hosts or any other domain name in general. In the following example, you will be using `sampledomain.com` as your domain name.

Concerning the configuration files, you should start by adding an entry for the zone in the `/etc/named.conf` file. The entry should look like the following:

```
zone "samplecomaind.com" IN {
    type master;
    file "sampledomain.com";
    notify no;     //When you make sure everything is fine, turn this to on..
};
```

The next step is to edit the `/var/named/sampledomain.com` file. This file should contain all the information about the hosts on this domain. Although this is a simple configuration example, it might look a bit large. The following is a listing of the `/var/named/sampledomain.com` file:

```
1 $ORIGIN sampledomain.com.
2 @          IN      SOA     ns.sampledomain.com. root.sampledomain.com. (
3                            43        ; serial
4                            8H        ; refresh
5                            2H        ; retry
6                            1W        ; expire
7                            1D )      ; minimum
8 ;
9                  TXT      "Sample Domain Configuration"
10                 NS       ns                 ; Inet Address of name server
11                 NS       ns.otherdomain.com.
12                 MX       10 mail         ; Primary Mail Exchanger
13                 MX       20 mail.otherdomain.com. ; Secondary Mail Exchanger
14 gw              A        192.168.0.1
15                 HINFO    "Cisco" "IOS"
16                 TXT      "The router"
17 ns              A        192.168.0.2
18                 MX       10 mail
19                 MX       20 mail.otherdomain.com.
20                 HINFO    "K6-3" "SuSE Linux 6.3 - Kernel 2.4"
21 www             CNAME    ns
22 printer         A        192.168.0.3
```

Part
III

Ch
14

```
23                   MX      10 mail
24                   MX      20 mail.otherdomain.com.
25                   HINFO   "P6"  "SuSE Linux 6.2 - Kernel 2.2"
26                   TXT     "The print server"
27 mail              A       192.168.0.4
28                   MX      10 mail
29                   MX      20 mail.otherdomain.com.
30                   HINFO   "P5/133" "NT/4"
31 ftp               A       192.168.0.5
32                   MX      10 mail
33                   MX      20 mail.otherdomain.com.
34                   HINFO   "P6" "Corel Linux 2.0 - Kernel 2.4"
```

There are some new resource records in this file, which will be discussed one by one in the following section:

- A—An A record directly allocates the IP specified to the hostname. In this context, A is short for address.

- CNAME—Canonical naming is a way to give each machine more than one name. In this example, www is an alias for ns. You should not make an MX, CNAME, or SOA record refer to a CNAME record. CNAME records always should refer to A records only. Many system administrators recommend not using CNAME at all.

- HINFO—This resource record is meant for host machine information. The first part of it is the CPU type and the second is the OS that the machine is running.

- MX—The mail exchanger tells the mail systems where to send mail that is addressed to user@sampledomain.com. The RR with the lowest number has the first priority. In this example, line 10 indicates that mail.sampledomain.com is the primary mail server. If that fails, the secondary mail server is used.

- TXT—This is a comment that you want to add to comment on the host machine.

As you might have noticed, the file manages all the other hosts on sampledomain.com. However, you will have a problem if you have the hostname but not the IP. In this case, you will need a reverse file that maps the hosts to the IP numbers:

```
$ORIGIN 0.168.192.in-addr.arpa.
@               IN      SOA     sampledomain.com. root.sampledomain.com. (
                        43          ; serial
                        8H          ; refresh
                        2H          ; retry
                        1W          ; expire
                        1D )        ; minimum
                        NS          sampledomain.com.
1       PTR     gw.sampledomain.com.
2       PTR     sampledomain.com.
2       PTR     www.sampledomain.com.
3       PTR     printer.sampledomain.com.
4       PTR     mail.sampledomain.com.
5       PTR     ftp.sampledomain.com.
```

Finally, you will have to add an entry for this reverse file in the /etc/named.conf file:

```
zone "0.168.192.in-addr.arpa" {
        type master;
        file "192.168.0";
};
```

After you're finished editing the file, restart the named for the configuration to take effect.

Your Role

As the administrator of the DNS, your role is to keep track of the changes that occur on your network. You should check the integrity of the hosts and ensure that no two hosts have the same name. You might want to name the hosts yourself and check for the updates that take place on your network.

Registering the Domain Name from NIC   If you want a top-level domain name, you have to register it from within the NIC. It is easy to register a domain name if it is not already taken. All you have to do is visit http://www.internic.com and follow the steps on the site. One important fact you should be aware of is that this is a pay service. If you don't remember to pay your bill, no one will be able to reach you through your site name.

> **N O T E**   A funny situation occurred when Microsoft forgot to pay the bill for the hotmail domain name. Millions of people were unable to access their email. Michael Chaney, an Antioch, Tennessee-based programmer and Linux fan, paid the bill for Microsoft so that he could check his mail! ▨

Black Market in Domain Names   It can be surprising when you try to register a domain name you think is unique and find it is already taken. You might try to contact the owner of the domain name and find that she is willing to sell it—at a very high price. Some people have made big profits selling their domain names because big companies and institutions new to the Internet are willing to pay high prices to register their commercial names. If you will be using the Internet in your business at any point in the future, consider registering your domain name as soon as possible.

Troubleshooting BIND

BIND seems to stall for a long time. Sometimes it goes down without any reason. What is going on?

It has been reported that BIND 8.0 has some problems when communicating with a Windows 2000 OS that has active directories. You have to update to at least BIND 8.2. You can download the latest BIND from the SuSE FTP or from the BIND homepage at http://www.isc.org/products/BIND/.

Part
III

Ch
14

I would like to upgrade from BIND 4.xx to BIND 8.xx, but I have large configuration files and do not want to reconfigure all this.

A utility that comes with SuSE Linux called `named-bootconf` can help. This script will change your settings automatically to the new ones.

I need to know everything about BIND. Where can I find more information about BIND?

The `http://www.isc.org/services/training/` site offers training for system administrators wanting to learn more about BIND. You also can check the documentation that comes with SuSE Linux for more information. ●

Connectivity with Windows Through Samba

How to Connect to Windows Machines

Users frequently find themselves installing SuSE Linux in a network that contains Microsoft Windows–based PCs. Situations arise in which the user would want to exchange files and printing services with those PCs. The user always can use FTP to exchange files from a Linux machine to a Windows machine and back, but that isn't very convenient. Windows machines use a special networking protocol that enables them to share files and printers with each other. This protocol used to be called Server Message Block (SMB) but is now referred to as *Common Internet File System* (CIFS). If you have ever used a Windows machine in a network, you are familiar with the Network Neighborhood. The Network Neighborhood enables you to see all the Windows-based PCs that are on the network, connect to them, and exchange files and services.

Microsoft Windows PCs use the SMB protocol to communicate with each other. Andrew Trigdell started a project in 1991 that is currently known as Samba. *Samba* is the result of reverse engineering the SMB protocol by Andrew and others. Samba runs on UNIX machines to enable them to share files and printers with Microsoft Windows–based PCs on a network.

Samba is considered one of the most prominent projects produced by the open source community. It enabled the integration of Microsoft Windows PCs with the rest of the UNIX world and vice versa. Samba provided the missing link between the two worlds, and did a good job at it, too.

Even though SMB has been renamed CIFS, the rest of the UNIX world still refers to it as SMB. Therefore, to accommodate both worlds, we will refer to it as SMB/CIFS.

 TIP If you are wondering how in the world Samba got its name, you might be surprised by the answer. Andrew Trigdell initially called it SMB server, but an existing product already had that name. So, he ran a command that searched the dictionary to find all the words that contained the letters S.M.B. A list of words came out, and he picked Samba.

Installing Samba

Installing Samba should not be too difficult because it already comes pre-packaged with SuSE Linux. Chances are that it's already installed on your system. The package requirements for running Samba are as follows:

Package requirements:

Series n:

- Samba

Kernel requirements:

- Filesystems, Network filesystems, SMB filesystem support (only if you are planning to access Windows shares)

TIP Modifying the kernel to include SMB filesystem support is required if you want to be able to connect to Windows shares from your Linux box. If all you need is to have Windows machines access shares on your Linux box, you won't need to have SMB filesystem support in the kernel. But we recommend that you do have it.

Now that you have Samba installed on your system, it's time to configure it. Configuring Samba for basic functionality is a pretty straightforward process.

Configuring Samba

Samba is configured through a text file, `/etc/smb.conf`. For those who edited `win.ini` under Windows, `/etc/smb.conf` is very similar in format to that file.

Samba's configuration file is made up of two types of sections—the `global` section and the `shares` section. The `global` section carries configuration parameters that apply to Samba's behavior. The `shares` section defines the actual shares that are being made available to other PCs on the network.

Samba's `smb.conf` can get quite complex, so let's start with a simple scenario and add to it. Let's say you want to integrate your Linux box in a Windows network that has a workgroup called HOME. The first thing you will need to tell Samba is the name of the workgroup of which you want it to be a part. To do that, follow these steps:

1. Log in as root.
2. SuSE Linux comes with an example `smb.conf` file. Rename it `smb.conf.suse` for now. Start a new file from scratch so you can learn the format of the file. To rename the file, type the following:

   `# mv /etc/smb.conf /etc/smb.conf.suse`

3. Now you need to create a new `smb.conf` file using your favorite editor.
4. The first line you need to enter is the `[global]` identifier. So, type `[global]` and then press Enter for a new line.
5. You want to set the name of the workgroup, so type `workgroup = HOME`. You should, of course, replace HOME with the name of the workgroup that you have on your network.
6. Now, give your machine a description using the `server string` parameter. Type the following:

   `server string = Linux Box - Samba`

7. Now, you need to define a share on your Linux box to be viewed by others. Start a new section that is named after that share. For example, define a share called *temp* by typing `[temp]` and pressing Enter.

8. You need to give Samba more information about that share. The first parameter is where that share is on your local disk. Use the `path` parameter to tell Samba where the share is, as in the following:

   ```
   path = /tmp
   ```

9. Next, you need to tell Samba to set permissions on this share. Type `read only = no`. This tells Samba to let users write to this share. The next parameter is `guest ok = yes`. This parameter tells Samba to let anybody open this share.

10. Finally, give the share a string as a comment to describe it:

   ```
   comment = My first share
   ```

11. That's it! You have successfully created your first `smb.conf` file. Your next task is to test it.

This is what your final `smb.conf` file should look like:

```
[global]
    workgroup = HOME
    server string = Linux Box - Samba
[temp]
    path = /tmp
    read only = no
    guest ok = yes
    comment = My first share
```

To test your configuration, you have to start Samba. Use YaST to turn it on and then follow these steps:

1. Log in as root.

2. Run YaST.

3. Navigate to System Administration, Change Configuration File.

4. YaST opens up a dialog that lists system parameters. Set START_SMB to `Yes`, as shown in Figure 15.1.

FIGURE 15.1

Using this dialog, you can control all the various system variables, such as the Samba start flag.

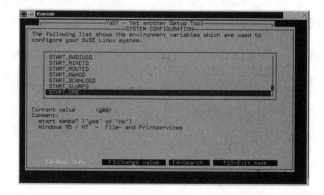

5. Press F10 to exit.

6. Exit from YaST.

Now, to start Samba, change the directory to /sbin/init.d and run the following command:

```
# ./smb start
```

 TIP You might want to run smb stop and then smb start in case Samba was already running. This way you can be sure that it will read the new configuration. This assumes that you've never configured Samba before and therefore are not breaking any existing connections.

That's it. If you switch over to a Windows machine, you should see that your machine now appears in the Network Neighborhood. The machine will be named after its hostname. As shown in Figure 15.2, the SuSE Linux machine is called Shadow, which is its hostname. Now, if you double-click the machine, Windows will prompt you to enter a password. What password?! Don't panic, this occurs simply because you didn't tell Samba what security level to use—in which case it will default to the security level user. This level demands a password to let you browse the Samba shares. For the meantime, let's loosen security by adding security = share in the global section of smb.conf. The file should now look like this:

```
[global]
    workgroup = HOME
    server string = Linux Box - Samba
    security = share
[temp]
    path = /tmp
    read only = no
    guest ok = yes
    comment = My first share
```

FIGURE 15.2

Shadow, which is a SuSE Linux box, appears just like a Windows machine in the Network Neighborhood.

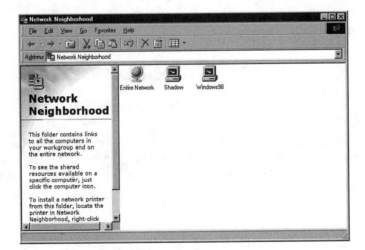

TIP When you are finished setting up your smb.conf file, it's good practice to run the utility called testparm. This small utility will inspect your smb.conf file and report to you any errors you might have made in it. In addition, it will give you a dump of all the options that this smb.conf file is going to set along with all the shares that will be declared. testparm is a great way to catch mistakes before updating Samba with the new configuration file.

You now need to tell Samba that you changed the configuration file. To do that, just run the following command:

```
#/sbin/init.d/smb reload
```

Whenever you change smb.conf, run this command to update the Samba software with the new changes. Run it now to propagate the changes to Samba. When finished, check the Windows machine to see whether you can browse the Linux machine or not. If everything was performed correctly, you will see your SuSE Linux machine on the Windows network (see Figure 15.3).

FIGURE 15.3
After setting the security option to share, you can view the shares provided by your SuSE Linux box.

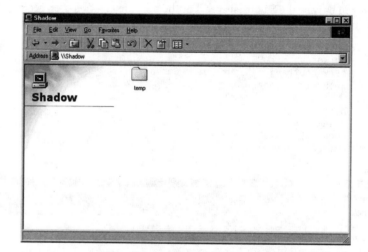

CAUTION
Please note that the current Samba configuration is extremely insecure. You should *never* use this configuration in a real network where you have users you don't trust. This configuration is purely experimental and serves the purpose of understanding the basics of smb.conf. Read on to learn how to make things more secure.

To review, you now know how to write a basic smb.conf file, add a simple share, and tell Samba that you changed the configuration. Let's learn even more about smb.conf.

The file `smb.conf` has some special sections:

- global
- homes
- printers

The *global* Section

As stated earlier, this section contains all the basic configuration parameters that apply to Samba. You have already seen three of them—the workgroup, server string, and security. Let's look at some other parameters you can use.

The *netbios name* Parameter   As you have seen, Samba by default uses your machine's hostname as its network name. You easily can change this behavior by using the netbios name parameter. To call your machine SuSELinux for example, you would add netbios name = SuSELinux to the global section of your smb.conf file. As you will see later, this option can be used in other, more advanced ways.

The *keep alive* Parameter   When a client machine connects to a Samba server, an open connection is established, which consumes resources. If the client machine crashes, this connection remains open. It can take Samba a considerable length of time before it finds out that this open connection is not actually being used, which wastes more resources. To force Samba to check on its clients, set keep alive = 30.

The *security* Parameter   This option defines the security used by Samba. As you saw earlier, when this option was not set, Samba defaulted to user security, forcing the connecting clients to enter a password to use the server. Setting this option to share allows anyone to browse the machine. As will be discussed later, you can have a mixture of both—needing a password and not needing one.

The *interfaces* Parameter   This parameter tells Samba which networking interface to use. By default, Samba uses all the available interfaces on the machine. You won't really need this option if you have just one interface, for example an Ethernet card. But, if you have more than one, and you don't want Samba to listen on all of them, you can force it to listen to just the ones you want. To use this parameter, you need to give it the IP and netmask of the interfaces to use. Use a space as a separator between the different interfaces. The final form of the parameter is interfaces = xxx.xxx.xxx.xxx/xxx.xxx.xxx.xxx xxx.xxx.xxx.xxx/xxx.xxx. xxx.xxx. The following is an example:

```
interfaces = 192.168.17.17/255.255.255.0
```

The *hosts allow* and *hosts deny* Parameters   You can use these options to control which machines can connect to your Samba server. For example, to allow all machines to connect to your server except for those that come from the subnet 192.168.121, you would enter hosts allow = ALL EXCEPT 192.168.121.. This will deny access to any machine coming from that specific subnet. The parameter hosts deny is the opposite of hosts allow. Parameters are separated by a space. The following is the supported identification format:

- **Hostnames of the machines**—For example, ftp.sales.com
- **Domain names**—For example, .yahoo.com
- **IP of subnet ending with a dot**—For example, 192.168.121.
- **Full IP**—For example, 192.168.121.17
- **Netgroups (for NIS/NIS+)**—For example, @netgroup
- **The ALL and EXCEPT keywords**—For example, ALL EXCEPT .yahoo.com

CAUTION

It's good practice to make sure that localhost is in the allow list. If it is not, certain programs, for example smbpasswd, will have to communicate with the Samba server in order to work. And, if localhost is not in the allow list, Samba will not answer these programs. Samba version 2.0.5 and up have localhost in the hosts allow list by default. If you are not sure which version you have, just add localhost to the hosts allow list.

The *guest account* Parameter   When a guest logs on to a Samba controlled server, Samba needs to map that user to a user that it already has. On SuSE Linux, this is the user nobody. So, when a guest accesses the machine, anything she does on the system is regarded to be under the ownership of the user nobody. This is relatively secure because this user has no privileges or home directory. To tell Samba to use nobody as the user, enter guest account = nobody in the global section of smb.conf.

The *homes* Section

The homes section is a special section because it represents the homes of the users as a share. To further understand this, you need to understand a bit about how Samba treats users.

Users in Samba belong to one of two groups, users or guests. *Guests* are those who do not have an account on the machine. *Users*, on the other hand, are those who have actual accounts on the machine. This means that a guest would not have a /home/ directory, but a user would. For example, if John is a user on the system, he has a directory /home/john. And, if Andrew is just browsing the Linux box as a guest, he doesn't have a /home/andrew on the physical machine because he isn't a user on it.

The homes section tells Samba what to do with the homes of the users. You can tell Samba to show the home of the user connecting to the server as a share. This way, when the user browses the machine, he gets to view the contents of his home directory. This does require the user to enter his password, even if the security = share.

The format of the homes section is very simple; it starts with the [homes] tag. The next tag you should enter is the comment tag. This is a text comment that can be used to describe the share. So far it should look like this:

```
[homes]
     comment = User homes
```

This setting will work fine, but it won't look very good when you browse the machine. When you browse the machine, you will find a share called homes, and if you are a user, you also will find your home directory as a share. For example, a user named John will find two shares, one called homes and another called john. Whereas, a guest user will see only a share called homes. For a user, both shares will point to the same directory—his home directory. If you enter the parameter browseable = no in the homes section, Samba will not show a share called homes. If a user is browsing the machine, he will see a new share that is his home. Guest users will see nothing.

Another decision you need to make is whether you want the users to be able to write to their homes or not. This is accomplished using the read only parameter. Setting this parameter to yes, which is its default, will prevent users from writing in their home directory through Samba. Setting it to no allows them to write to it.

Another useful parameter is case sensitive. Setting this to yes forces Samba to treat file-names as being case-sensitive. This is useful because Windows is not case-sensitive, and if Samba treats the filenames as case-sensitive, conflicts will arise. Setting this parameter to no will prevent such conflicts.

To hide the share homes, allow users to write to their home directories, and ignore case sensi-tivity, the code section would look like the following:

```
[homes]
     comment = User homes
     browseable = no
     case sensitive = no
     read only = no
```

The *printers* Section

This section tells Samba about your printers. You can have Samba put your printer on the net-work to be shared by others.

This section starts with [printers], followed by a comment that describes it. The next para-meter, which is the most important one, is printable. This parameter tells Samba that this share is not a disk share but a printer share. Even though section printers is a special sec-tion, you still have to enter printable = yes in it.

If you want guests to be able to print from this printer, you should include guest ok = yes in this section. Another parameter of interest is directory. When Samba receives a print request, it needs to put the file to be printed somewhere so it puts it in the directory defined by directory. Note that this directory has to be writeable to all. /tmp is usually a good choice for this directory.

A typical printers section looks like the following:

```
[printers]
    comment = All Printers
    browseable = no
    printable = yes
    public = no
    guest ok = yes
    read only = yes
    create mode = 0700
    directory = /tmp
```

Your printers should appear in Windows, as shown in Figure 15.4.

FIGURE 15.4
With the modifications you made to Samba, your printers are now shared to the rest of the network.

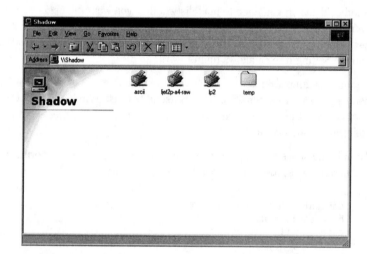

Defining Disk Shares

Now that you are familiar with the special shares, it's time to learn more about disk shares. Defining disk shares in Samba is simple. Say you want to define a new disk share called pictures so you can share your image files with the other users on the network. To do this, you would need to enter the following in your smb.conf file:

```
[pictures]
    path = /pictures/jpg
    comment = My Image files
    browseable = yes
    read only = yes
    guest ok = yes
```

The first part of this is the name of the share, `pictures`. The next parameter is the path for that share, which is the directory that you want to share. In this example, we assumed that your image files are under the directory `/picture/jpg`.

Because you want people to be able to see that share, you set the `browseable` parameter to yes. You want people to have only `read only` access, so you set that parameter to yes. Finally, you want to enable everyone on your network to see it, so you set `guest ok = yes`. Now you just need to update Samba:

```
#/sbin/init.d/smb reload
```

What if you want only a specific user to be able to view this share? Say you have a user called Sarah on your network, and you want her to be the only one who can view this share. You can do this by using the `valid users` parameter:

```
[pictures]
    path = /pictures/jpg
    comment = My image files
    browseable = yes
    read only = yes
    valid users = sarah
```

As you can see, the `guest ok` was replaced with `valid users = sarah`. Update Samba to reflect the new changes by running the following command:

```
#/sbin/init.d/smb reload
```

Now only Sarah will be able to view this share. You can add even more users to this parameter by separating each with a space.

Finally, what if you want to define more than one disk share? You will have to create a list of parameters for each one, just as you did for the `pictures` share. However, another way you can do this is by creating a template of parameters and then telling Samba to copy the template to the new share—for example:

```
[template]
   writable = yes
   browsable = yes
   valid users = andy, dave, peter
[backup]
    path = /usr/backups
    copy = template
```

The share called `template` will contain your common parameters. Whenever you create a new share, just include the `path` parameter and enter the line `copy = template`.

Advanced Samba

So far, you have learned the basics of getting Samba up and running. But several other options exist that you can use.

Encrypting Passwords

Prior to Windows 98 and Windows NT Service Pack 3, passwords were sent across the network without any encryption. This behavior was changed by Microsoft and initially broke Samba because users were unable to connect to Samba-controlled servers. To fix this problem, two solutions exist—either you force Windows machines to send text passwords to Samba, or you enable Samba to deal with encrypted passwords.

Changing the behavior of the Windows machines can be quite tedious, depending on the size of your network. For example, if you have only three Windows machines on the network, you can just change their default behavior without much hassle. But, if you have a huge network of Windows machines, changing their behavior to suit yours would be quite difficult. To disable encrypted passwords on Windows machines, you have to change a value in their registry.

If you look in `/usr/doc/packages/samba`, you will find the following files:

- `NT4_PlainPassword.reg`
- `Win95_PlainPassword.reg`
- `Win2000_PlainPassword.reg`
- `Win98_PlainPassword.reg`

Copy the file that suits your system onto a floppy and double-click it from Windows. This will edit your registry and update it to disable encrypted passwords. You also should add the parameter `encrypt passwords = no` in the `global` section of your `smb.conf`. Samba should now work fine.

The second solution is to force Samba to use encrypted passwords. The first thing you need to do is set `encrypt passwords = yes` in the `global` section of `smb.conf`. Then, for every user you want to connect to non-guest shares, add him to Samba using the `smbpasswd` command. For example, to add user John to the allowed users, type the following:

```
# smbpasswd john
```

The command will ask you to enter a password for that user twice. That's it, John can connect to Samba using this password, which will be sent encrypted. Remember that you should do this for all the users on your system.

TIP   You can use the `smbpasswd` command to add more users to your Samba. The added users do not have to be part of your system; you can add a new user to Samba and not to your SuSE Linux system. Therefore, the new user won't have a home directory like a real user will.

OS Level, Local Master, and Preferred Master

In order to understand these options, you need to learn several concepts. In a SMB/CIFS network, each machine has a NetBIOS name that defines it to other machines. For example, our machine is called Shadow. When a machine wants to know the names of all the other machines currently online, it usually sends a request to a machine that is playing the role of a local master. The *local master* is a machine that keeps a list of the names of all the machines currently online. This list is sent to any machine that needs to know this information. The local master maintains that list and continually updates it with any changes that occur on the network.

You can have your Samba server act as a local master. But, in order for a machine to be a local master, it has to win an election. When this machine joins the network, it has to challenge the current local master for an election, and the machine that wins that election gets to be a local master. Any machine on the network can call for an election at any time. When a machine calls for an election, it needs to broadcast some information about itself:

- The version of the election protocol it is using
- The version of the operating system on the machine
- Whether the machine has the preferred master bit set or not
- The amount of time that the machine has been online for
- The hostname of the machine

When a machine calls for an election, it wins only if the following are true:

- The machine uses the highest version of the election protocol. This is not that important now because all Windows machines use protocol version 1. So, this would be a tie and it would proceed to the next option.
- The machine has the highest OS version. If there is a tie, it proceeds to the next option.
- The machine has the preferred master bit on. If there is a tie, it proceeds to the next option.
- The machine has a longer online time than the challenging one. If there is a tie, it proceeds to the next option.
- The machine's hostname comes first alphabetically.

Now that you know how an election happens, let's see how you can prepare your Linux box to win, or lose, an election. The first option, as you can see, won't help because all machines will tie on the protocol version. The next option is the OS version. OS versions have special codes, as shown in Table 15.1.

Table 15.1   The OS Versions Announced by the Different Types of Windows Operating Systems

Operating System	OS Version
Microsoft Windows NT 4.0	33
Microsoft Windows NT 3.51	32
Microsoft Windows NT Workstation 4.0	17
Microsoft Windows NT Workstation 3.51	16
Microsoft Windows 98	2
Microsoft Windows 95	1
Microsoft Windows 3.1 for Workgroups	1

To enter an election, you should tell Samba to be a local master. This is done by adding `local master = yes` in the `global` section of `smb.conf`. Now, if you want Samba to *always* win an election, enter `os level = 34` in the `global` section of `smb.conf`. This way, Samba will never lose because it will have the highest OS version. If you want Samba not to act as a local master if a Windows NT machine happens to be online, set `os level = 31`. This way, Samba will beat all machines except those that run Windows NT. And, if you want Samba to lose most of the time, set `os level = 1`.

Finally, if you want to compete head-to-head with Windows NT, you can set the `os level = 33` and the `preferred master = yes`. This way, if the Windows NT machine is not a preferred master, Samba will win for sure.

Creating Multiple NetBIOS Aliases for the Same Machine

Samba gives you the ability to create more than one machine on the Windows network. This can be useful if you need to create separate machines for organization purposes. You can, for example, create a machine called Backup in addition to your main machine. Users who need to back up files can use Backup, while others who need to access their homes on your machine can use the original machine.

For example, say that your machine is called Shadow, and you want to create two other machines called `Machine1` and `Machine2`. The first thing you need to do is create a separate `smb.conf` file for each of the new machines. These files would be `smb.conf.machine1` and `smb.conf.machine2`. In your main `smb.conf` file, modify your `global` section:

```
[global]
    workgroup = HOME
    netbios aliases = machine1 machine2
    include = /etc/smb.conf.%L
    ... Rest of smb.conf file unmodified ...
```

The first thing you tell Samba is the NetBIOS aliases that you want it to use. The next entry tells Samba to include an extra `smb.conf` file to your configuration. The name of the file will depend on which NetBIOS alias was accessed. The %L will be replaced with the alias. So, if the user accesses Machine1, the include line will resolve to include = /etc/smb.conf.machine1. This is the file that you have previously created for that alias.

You now need to restart your Samba daemons:

```
# /sbin/init.d/smb reload
```

That's it. As you can see in Figure 15.5, when you browse the network using a Windows machine, you should see three machines, Shadow, Machine1, and Machine2. Each of them has its own separate configuration, but all of them are on the same physical machine.

FIGURE 15.5
Thanks to NetBIOS aliases, you are able to create more than one machine on the network. These are called virtual machines.

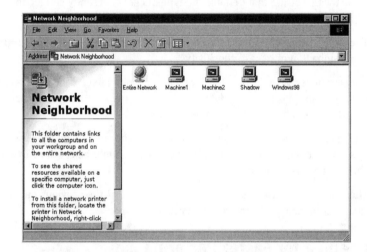

Dealing with Older Windows Clients

Old Windows clients, such as Windows for Workgroups (WFWG), are quite different from the new versions. One major difference is the way filenames are stored. In WFWG, filenames are eight characters long followed by a dot and three characters that denote the extension of the file, for example command.com. If you use Samba with these machines, you could face some problems. The most basic problem is that Linux uses long filenames that will confuse the WFWG clients. However, this problem can be fixed easily.

First, you should create a new smb.conf file called smb.conf.WfWg (please note the case of WfWg). In this file, type the following:

```
[global]
  case sensitive = no
  mangle case = yes
  mangled names= yes
  default case = upper
  preserve case = no
  short preserve case = no
```

Then, in your main `smb.conf` file, add this line to the beginning of the `global` section:

```
[global]
    include = /etc/smb.conf.%m
```

Restart your Samba daemons for these changes to take effect:

```
# /sbin/init.d/smb restart
```

That's it! Windows for Workgroups won't suffer from the problem of filenames because you told Samba that whenever a WFWG machine connects, it should load up the `smb.conf.WfWg` file. This is accomplished by the line `include = /etc/smb.conf.%m`. The `%m` is replaced by Samba with a string that denotes the type of client currently connecting. WFWG is reported by Samba as WfWg.

The new `smb.conf.WfWg` file adds new parameters, called *mangling parameters*. The first one tells Samba to ignore case sensitivity.

The parameter `mangle case` tells Samba to change mixed case filenames to either uppercase or lowercase. This is the `default case` option. If `default case = upper`, filenames with mixed case will be mangled to uppercase.

The `preserve case` parameter tells Samba whether to change the case of the filename that was supplied by the client or not. In this case, it should be set to `no` to allow `mangle case` to change the case of the filename.

The `short preserve case` parameter is the same as the previous one, but works on 8.3 character filenames. Again, set the parameter to `no`.

Tuning Samba for Faster Performance

After your Samba server is running smoothly and has all the functionality you want, you should tune your server. Tuning Samba helps to increase its performance, making it faster and more responsive. You can perform several tweaks to Samba to increase its performance. We'll discuss the most common ones.

The global parameter `socket options` is perhaps the most widely known performance parameter. You use this option to define socket options that increase performance. The first of these options is the `TCP_NODELAY` option. This option causes Samba to send as many packets as possible to decrease the delay. This option alone can increase performance by 30–50%! `IPTOS_LOWDELAY` is an option that you should use with the `TCP_NODELAY` option.

Another option that you can use is the `SO_SNDBUF`. This option tells Samba how big in bytes the packets should be before Samba sends back an acknowledgment packet. The larger this number the better the performance because time won't be wasted waiting for acknowledgments for small packets. Setting this number to 16384 and higher will give you quite a bit of performance gain. You should experiment with this option to get the best size. Don't just throw in a huge number and expect things improve—at some point, the higher the number, the worse things will become.

Finally, to speed up Samba, enter the following in your `global` section:

```
[global]
    ...
    socket options = TCP_NODELAY IPTOS_LOWDELAY SO_SNDBUF=16384
    ...
```

Restart your Samba daemons for this change to take effect.

Printing to a Windows Machine Using Samba

Just as you can enable users to print to your printer, you can use Samba to print to shared printers on Windows machines. This is a relatively simple step thanks to YaST. To configure SuSE Linux to print to a shared printer, follow these steps:

1. Log in as root.
2. Run YaST.
3. Navigate to System Administration, Network Configuration, Connect to Printer via Samba.
4. YaST brings up the setup dialog (see Figure 15.6).

FIGURE 15.6

You use YaST to configure your Linux system to print to a shared printer over the network using Samba.

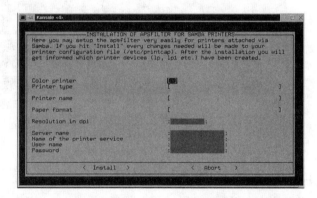

5. The first option is Color Printer; check this option if the printer to which you are trying to print is a color printer. Otherwise, leave it unchecked.
6. Press the Tab key to proceed. The next option is Printer Type, where you get to choose between Postscript Printer, HP Deskjet, or Other Printer. Make your selection.
7. The next option is the Printer Name. Select the name of your printer. If you can't find it, select the name of a printer that is compatible to yours.
8. Now YaST asks you about the Paper Format. Pick the format of the paper you use.

9. Enter the resolution in dpi that you want your printer to use in the Resolution in DPI field. You can press Enter to accept the default value.

10. Enter the name of the server that has the printer in the Server Name field. This is the name of the machine on the network.

11. In the Name of the Printer Service field, enter the name of the printer as it appears on the machine to which you are trying to connect.

12. Next, enter the username and password to use to connect to the printer in their respective fields. If the printer does not require a password, leave these fields empty.

13. Click Install to install the printer.

14. YaST will pop up a window that shows you the configuration that was created (see Figure 15.7). Your new printer can be accessed as lp1. Check the information that is in the window to find the exact name.

FIGURE 15.7
YaST has succeeded in creating your network printer link. You can now print to the shared printer on the Windows machine.

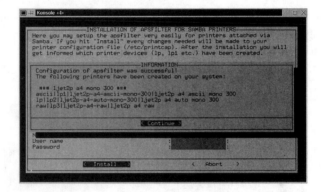

That's it, you now can use the new shared printer from any application.

Using Swat to Configure Samba

Now that you know how to configure Samba, you must be wondering if there is an easier way to do all this. The answer is yes! The Samba team provided a very powerful and user-friendly Web-based setup tool called Swat. Now that you understand the underlying system, you'll be able to use Swat effectively.

Swat is already installed with Samba, so you only need to activate it. You easily can do this by editing the file /etc/inetd.conf. Follow these steps:

1. Log in as root.

2. Open the file /etc/inetd.conf using your favorite editor.

3. Search for Swat in the file. You should find a line like the following:

```
# swat    stream  tcp     nowait.400      root    /usr/sbin/swat  swat
```

4. Remove the hash mark (#) at the beginning of the line, save the file, and exit.

5. Now you should tell inetd to re-read its configuration file and activate the changes. Type the following command:

```
# /sbin/init.d/inetd reload
```

6. Ok, you're all set now.

To use Swat, just run your Web browser and point it at `http://localhost:901`, which connects it to your machine on port 901. A small window will pop up asking you to enter a username and password. Enter `root` as the username and the root password as the password; click on OK. As you can see in Figure 15.8, your browser will load Swat. You can use it to configure and control Samba. And you don't even have to be sitting at the machine Samba is running on. It is an amazing tool to use, especially now that you understand how to configure Samba.

FIGURE 15.8

Swat runs in your browser and enables you to fully configure and control your Samba setup.

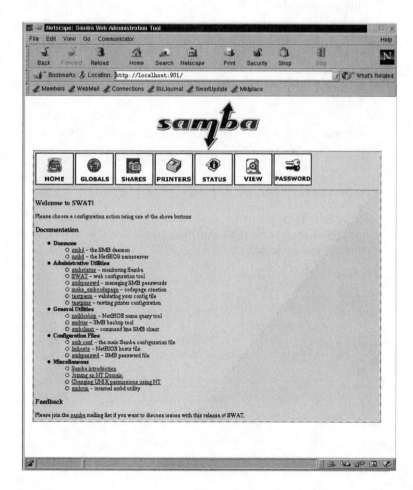

Troubleshooting

I can't seem to find any of the files you are referring to.

Are you sure that you installed Samba? If not, check the package requirements for Samba listed previously. After Samba is installed, you should be able to find all the files we are talking about.

I turned Samba on, but I can't see my machine on the network.

Check that you are on the same workgroup as the one you are looking in. If you told Samba to be part of workgroup WORK, and you are searching in workgroup STAFF, you won't see your machine. Also, check that you have Samba turned on and that it is working properly. To check whether Samba is working or not, type this command:

```
# /sbin/init.d/smb status
Checking for service smb: OK OK
```

If the command does not return OK OK as in the previous code, Samba is not running. Check your smb.conf file using testparm. Fix any errors reported and restart Samba.

People can't connect to my SuSE Linux box.

Check your security level. Also, check whether the connecting user has a valid password on the machine or not.

I am never the local master on the network; what should I do?

Make sure that you have os level = 34 in smb.conf.

I need more help; where should I look?

The primary place to look for more information is the Samba Web site at http://www.samba.org. You can submit questions and search the archives for solutions to the problems you are having. ●

Connectivity with Other Operating Systems

A Briefing

Linux primarily is used for its powerful networking capabilities. This power enables integrating Linux in two famous networking arenas: Apple networks and Novell NetWare networks. This chapter discusses how to set up and configure SuSE Linux to integrate with those two networks.

This chapter also tells you how to configure an Apple file and print server and how to print to Apple-shared printers from your SuSE Linux box. Although mounting Apple volumes is still in its pre-alpha stages, a description of mounting Apple volumes is included. This chapter teaches you how to mount Apple HFS disks and CD-ROMS.

In the Novell NetWare arena, you will learn how to configure your SuSE Linux to act as a NetWare file and print server. In addition, you will learn how to mount NetWare volumes and print to NetWare-shared printers.

Integrating with Apple Macintosh Networks

SuSE Linux talks to Apple networks using the `netatalk` package. `netatalk` is an implementation of the AppleTalk Protocol suite. It includes support for routing AppleTalk, serving UNIX and AFS filesystems over AFP (AppleShare), serving UNIX printers, and accessing AppleTalk printers over PAP.

Software Requirements

To integrate your SuSE Linux with Apple networks, you will need the following packages:

Series n:

- `netatalk`

You also will need the following kernel requirements:

Networking options:

- Appletalk DDP

Filesystems, network filesystems:

- Apple Macintosh filesystem support (experimental)

You do not have to recompile your kernel if you do not want to; you can safely use the precompiled kernel that comes with SuSE Linux if you have installed all the packages as specified previously.

You need only HFS support (filesystem support) to be able to access Apple shares and devices. Note that this kernel module is still in the alpha phase, so it is not safe to use it.

However, this chapter discusses the use of this module for people who really need it and in the hope that this code will be completed soon.

You must have a TCP/IP network up and running before you can configure `netatalk`.

> **N O T E**   Netatalk is the package used to enable Apple-based networks to see through your machine. You can't set up `netatalk` without having a working TCP/IP network. Refer to Chapter 13, "Configuring a TCP/IP Network," for more details on how to set up a TCP/IP network. ■

Acting as Server

SuSE Linux comes with most of the prerequisites for `netatalk` fulfilled. All you must do is perform a little bit of configuration and gain some knowledge of the Apple environment.

Setting Up *afpd*   The Apple Filing Protocol is supported under SuSE Linux using a daemon known as `afpd`. The configuration file for `afpd` is located in `/etc/atalkd/afpd.cond`, which is the main configuration file used to establish a server.

The `afpd.conf` file is the first file read when the `atalkd` starts. You should define the server(s) you want to use. To define a server, include only its name. If you want to establish a server that has the same name as your hostname, use the minus sign as the first entry on a new line, as in the following example:

```
-
```

The server name can include spaces. If you want the server name to contain spaces, place quotes around the server name. The following is an example:

```
"Linux Server"
```

You can have more than one server entry, which enables your SuSE Linux to act as more than one server. This is beneficial because it gives you more control over your connections. Let's look at the following example:

```
- -loginmesg "Welcome to my server"
"Guest Volume" -nocleartxt -loginmesg "Welcome guest!"
"User Volume" -noguest -uservolfirst -port 12000
"Controlled Volumes" -noguest -nouservol
"special" -notcp -ddp -defaultvol <path> -systemvol <path>
```

This example establishes three servers. The following is a discussion of the options available to users connecting to each of the servers:

■ `-`—This server has the same name as your hostname. Users connecting to your system will see the statement `Welcome to my server` as they log in to your system.

■ `"Guest Volume"`—This server will not prompt users for passwords because you used the `-nocleartxt` option. Users will see the statement `Welcome guest!` as they log in.

■ `"User Volume"`—No guest is supposed to log in to this server, as the `-noguest` option indicates. The `-uservolfirst` indicates that the `.AppleVolume` or the `AppleVolume` in the users' home directories is to be read before the systemwide `/etc/atalk/AppleVolume.default` is read. This server will accept only connections from the port 12000.

N O T E Volumes are controlled through default files stored in `/etc/atalk/AppleVolumes.system` and `/etc/atalk/AppleVolumes.default`. If the user has in his home directories either the `.AppleVolume` or `AppleVolume` file, the settings in that file override the systemwide settings by default. The section "Adding Apple Volumes on Your SuSE Linux" explains in detail the format of those files. ■

■ `"Controlled Volumes"`—This server accepts no guests and allows users to see only the systemwide volumes. If users have `.AppleVolume` or `AppleVolume` in their home directories, all the entries in these files are ignored.

■ `"special"`—This server does not allow TCP connections (`-notcp` option); instead, it allows only Apple DDP connections (`-ddp` option). You can reverse this by using the `-tcp -noddp` option. The `-defaultvol` option followed by the path to a file causes `afpd` to read a specific file for `AppleVolume.default`; whereas, the `-systemvol` option causes `afpd` to read a specific file instead of `AppleVolumes.system`. This option is very important for restricting user logins and managing security for users connecting from Apple clients.

What SuSE Already Has Done   The SuSE team has performed some configurations so that your `afpd` works out of the box. The SuSE team has added the following entries to your `/etc/services` file:

```
rtmp  1/ddp   # Routing Table Maintenance Protocol
nbp   2/ddp   # Name Binding Protocol
echo  4/ddp   # AppleTalk Echo Protocol
zip   6/ddp   # Zone Information Protocol
```

Those lines are important because they ensure that the services used by `afpd` start at boot time. The SuSE team has added the following line to your `/etc/atalkd/atalkd.conf`:

```
eth0
```

You should modify this line to the name of the network card connected to the Apple network. After you run the `atalkd` service and finish configuring the `netatalk` package, the `atalkd` daemon will add more lines to this file.

Adding Apple Volumes on Your SuSE Linux   After you have set up the `atalkd.conf` and `afpd.conf` files, which are network configuration files, you have to manage the Linux shares that appear as Apple volumes on your Apple network. The three main volume configuration files are as follows:

- `/etc/atalk/AppleVolumes.system`—This file is where you should set up user logins and the volumes that system users can see. This file also contains the settings for the guest account.

- `/etc/atalk/AppleVolumes.default`—This file is where you set up user access and the volumes the system user can see.

- `AppleVolumes` or `.AppleVolumes` in the user's home directory—If any user has either of these files in her home directory, the settings in that file will override the ones in the `AppleVolume.defatult` file.

Managing Users' Volumes   When the `afpd` starts, it first will read the configurations in the `/etc/atalk/AppleVolumes.system` for systemwide settings. It then will read the `/etc/atalk/AppleVolumes.default` file for user login information. If the user has an `AppleVolumes` or `.AppleVolumes` file in his home directory, it will be read instead of the default file.

The `AppleVolumes.default` file that comes with SuSE Linux includes only the ~ path. In other words, it shows only the home directory of a user at login time.

N O T E   For more on system security when managing users' volumes, refer to the section "Setting Up `afpd`." Most of the security tweaks are done by managing the `/etc/atalk/afpd.conf`. In addition, the user must have `AppleVolumes.default` and `AppleVolumes.system` files for each group of users as well as an entry in the `/etc/atalk/afpd.conf` for each group of users. ▨

The `AppleVolumes.default` syntax format is as follows:

```
path [name] [casefold=x] [codepage=y] [options=z,1,j]
path [name] [access=a,@b,c,d] [dbpath=path] [password=p]
```

To set up an entry for a volume, you must enter each entry on a separate line.

- `path`—This is the path to the volume on your SuSE Linux box. It can be any path the user can access through her user privileges.

- `casefold`—This option is used to set the letter case of files and directories. The casefold options can accept the following values:
  - `tolower`—lowercases names at both client and server sides.
  - `toupper`—uppercases names at both client and server sides.
  - `xlatelower`—lowercases at client side, uppercases at server side.
  - `xlateupper`—uppercases at client side, lowercases at server side.

- `access`—This option is used to restrict volume access to the listed users and groups. The list uses commas to separate usernames and group names. Users and groups are listed by their Linux usernames. An at sign (@) is pre-appended to the group name. An example of this option is `user1,@group,user2`.

- options—These are other options you might want to set:
  - prodos—This option makes volumes compatible with AppleII clients.
  - crlf—This option enables crlf translation for text files.
  - noadouble—This option is important if you do not want to waste your time cleaning. The afpd creates two directories called .AppleDesktop and Network Trash Folder. Each directory you access will create a .AppleDouble below it so that it can store resource forks. You need this option to tell the afpd not to create .AppleDouble unless a resource fork needs to be created.
- codepage—This option loads the nls codepage filename from the directory. In this option, you need to enter only the path to the filename.
- dbpath—This option tells the afpd where to store the volume database files. You must specify a path.
- password—If you want to protect the volume with a password, you can do so by creating a password the user must enter before she can access the volume.

The following is a simple example of three user volumes in the /etc/AppleVolumes.default file:

```
#The following entry specifies that a user
#can see his home directory.
~ "HOME"

#The following entry specifies that a user can see
#the mp3 directory on the server
#On the Apple side, the volume name will be
# MUSIC DIRECTORY
/usr/local/share/mp3 "MUSIC DIRECTORY"

#The following entry specifies that a user can see
#the downloads directory on the server if he belongs
#to the root group
/usr/local/share/downloads "DOWNLOADS" @root
```

CAUTION

If the user edits her .AppleVolume of AppleVolume file so that she cannot see her home directory, she will not be able to access those files again and thus will not be able to fix this problem or apply any settings. Tell your users to be careful when editing these files and to always remember their home directory as an entry.

File Types and Systemwide Settings   Apple filenames are different in style from Linux filenames. A Mac filename or directory entry is made up of two parts, a data fork and resource fork. Filenames and directory entries on Linux consist of only one part. This will cause the Linux filenames to appear as unknown documents when users view the volume shared on

Linux. To solve this problem, you must edit the entries in the `/etc/atalk/AppleVolumes.system` file, where you can register programs with Apple to get an official creator mapping. The following example maps the files with the extension `.moov` (`*.moov` files) to MooV files on the Apple client. It also associates this file type with the mMPG player, so it has the program icons and appears as a movie file.

```
.moov     MooV     mMPG
```

SuSE Linux comes with a large `/etc/atalk/AppleVolumes.system` file that has several file types already mapped. You can add or modify those file types according to your existing programs on the Apple client side.

The default `cr-lf` conversion takes place on the text file type. All text file types are modified when they are opened from the Apple client so that the cr-lf differences are fixed. However, an option on the `/etc/atalk/AppleVolumes.system` file tells `afpd` how to treat unknown file types. Do not set this option to treat unknown file types as text or you will end up destroying your files if you open them and save them again. You should have the following line in your `/etc/atalk/AppleVolumes.system` file:

```
.         BINA     UNIX
```

This line tells `afpd` to treat unknown file types as binary files that should not pass through any conversion.

Managing Guest Volumes   Guest volumes are easy to manage if you understand how to manage users' volumes. The same options that apply on the `/etc/atalk/AppleVolumes.default` file apply on the `/etc/atalk/AppleVolumes.system` file. In `/etc/atalk/AppleVolumes.system`, you can add volumes that the guest user can use passing through the same conditions that apply on the `AppleVolumes.default`—except for those that have to do with usernames and groups.

Exporting a Printer to the Apple Network   By default, all the printers available on your SuSE Linux are exported so that Apple clients can see them. But, only users who are allowed to print on your SuSE Linux can print here. Guest users can't print by default.

To export a printer to the Apple Network, you first must make sure that your SuSE Linux can print. Follow the instructions in Chapter 11, "Printing," to set up printing on your SuSE Linux.

After you have the printing service configured and started, Linux users connecting from any Apple client can use the printer, as long as they are allowed to print using your SuSE Linux. For more on print privileges, refer to Chapter 11.

You can turn off the print in background option in the Apple client because SuSE Linux will spool anyway.

If the print facility does not work out of the box when Apple clients try to print, some configuration might be needed. The configuration file you need is in `/etc/atalk/papd.conf`. This file is the primary configuration file for your SuSE Linux box and causes it to act like an Apple print server. The format for this file is as follows:

```
Name
pd: Pathname to ppd file.
pr: LPD printer name.
op: Operator name, needed for spooling.
```

You do not have to use all the previous statements. The most important statements are `Name` and `pr`. Other settings usually are made when you configure your printer as described in Chapter 11. The following is an example of sharing a printer called `lp` as it appears in the `/etc/printcap` file with your current Apple zone:

```
HP Deskjet 610c:\
        :pr=lp:
```

In this example, the LPD printer name is `lp`, but the Apple clients connecting from your zone will see this printer's name as `HP Deskjet 610c`.

If you want Apple clients connecting from other zones to see your printer, the file would look a bit different. If you want Apple clients connecting from `ZONE2` to see your printer, the configuration file would look like the following example:

```
Deskjet@ZONE2:\
        :pr=lp:
```

Now, clients connecting from `ZONE2` can use the printer on your SuSE Linux box.

Playing the Client Role

Not only is it important that Apple clients can access your SuSE Linux volumes and printers, but it is also important that your SuSE Linux is set up to see the Apple volumes and printers. In the following sections, you will learn how to mount Apple devices and volumes on your SuSE Linux. You also will learn how to use the Apple shared printers.

Mounting Apple Devices   After you have Apple filesystem support in the kernel, you can mount any storage media formatted with the Apple HFS format. For instance, you can mount a floppy disk that was formatted on an Apple machine by issuing the following command:

```
bash#mount /dev/fd0 -t hfs /floppy
```

Finding Out to Which Zone You Belong   It is important that you find out to which zone you belong before you mount Apple volumes or use a shared Apple printer. You can check the name of your zone by issuing the following command:

```
bash#getzones -m
```

The output of the previous command will be your Apple zone, from which you can use the available resources—volumes and printers. You can use a resource by using the resource name directly. In addition, you can list all the available zones on the network by issuing the following command:

```
bash#getzones
```

The previous command lists all the zones on the network. You can use resources from the other zones as well as your zone if you have the privileges to do so. You can use the resources on other zones by post-appending the @other_zone_name to the resource name.

Mounting Apple Volumes   Mounting Apple volumes is not supported by SuSE Linux because the package is still in the early stages of development and is not yet safe to use. It is highly recommended that you do not use this package. If you must mount Apple volumes, be warned that for the package to work, you need to install part of it as a kernel module. Because the module is still in the early stages, it might crash. If a kernel module crashes, your whole system will crash and you'll end up losing data. If you still must use it, make sure you have backups of all your important data. Also, make sure that you unload the module after you have what you need from the Apple volume. And, as a general rule, *never* attempt to run unstable kernel modules on SuSE Linux servers that must be up all the time.

Part
III
Ch
16

The package is available from http://www.panix.com/~dfoster/afpfs/. Search for the package source and download it. After you have downloaded the package, untar it and compile it using the following commands:

```
bash#tar xzvf <package_name.tar.gz>
bash#cd <package_name>
bash#make
```

You must have netatalk configured before you can actually mount Apple volumes.

You also will need to load the afpfs module, which you can do by using the following command:

```
bash#/sbin/insmod ./afpfs.o
```

After you have loaded the modules, you can mount the Apple volume by using the afpmount command. The command accepts the following arguments:

```
afpmount -u <username> -p <password> mount-point servername[@zone] volume-name
```

The following is an example of mounting a volume called Shared from an Apple machine called Joe (which belongs to a zone called ZONE1) to a mount point /mnt/mac:

```
afpmount -u joeadlib -p mypass /mnt/mac 'Joe@ZONE1' 'Shared'
```

Another way you can mount Apple shares is by using the normal mount command.

Printing to an Apple Shared Printer   First, you should look for the name of the shared printer. You can search for the printers available on your zone by issuing this command:

```
bash#nbplkup
```

This returns a list of all the resources available on the zone. Say, for example, you find that the output contains the following line:

```
Shared Printer:LaserWriter            12398.73:191
```

Shared Printer is the name of the printer you want to use. Next, you should make an entry in your /etc/printcap file for this printer. For now, the new entry should look like the following:

```
lp|Printer LaserWriter|Shared Printer:\
        :sd=/var/spool/lpd/Printer:\
        :lp=/dev/null:\
        :lf=/var/spool/lpd/Printer/log:\
        :if=/usr/lib/atalk/filters/ifpap:\
        :of=/usr/lib/atalk/filters/ofpap:
```

Note that you must have netatalk configured before you can actually print to Apple shared printers.

Troubleshooting Macintosh Networks

I have tried everything, but I cannot get afpfs *to compile.*

afpfs is still in its first stages and might not compile on all systems. You might want to contact some Linux developers to assist you with compiling it. We hope it becomes a stable package and joins the kernel source tree soon.

When I print to an Apple shared printer, the quality of the printing is really bad or blank paper comes out.

Change the line in the printcap file that says :if=/usr/lib/atalk/filters/ifpap:\ to the path of your specific printer filter. You can download your printer filter from the Adobe Web site at http://www.adobe.com.

Where are the nls *files I can use for* netatalk?

They are located in /usr/lib/atalk/nls.

The volumes on my HD all have AppleDouble files. What should I do?

Those files have to be created in order for the Apple Filing System to work. However, you can include the noadouble option for each entry in the AppleVolume.default file so that those files are created only when needed.

Integrating with NetWare Networks

Your SuSE Linux easily can integrate with NetWare Networks by using the IPX protocol. The most important integration aspects introduced in this chapter are mounting Novell shares and printing to a Novell server.

Software Requirements

To integrate SuSE Linux with NetWare networks, you will need the following packages:

Series a:

- `kernmod` (if you don't want to recompile a kernel)

Series n:

- `ncpfs`

You also will need the following kernel requirements:

Networking options:

- The IPX protocol
- IPX: Full internal IPX network
- IPX: SPX networking (experimental)

Filesystems, network filesystem:

- NCP filesystem support (to mount NetWare volumes)

You do not have to recompile your kernel if you do not want to; you can safely use the precompiled kernel that comes with SuSE Linux if you have installed all the packages as specified previously.

Introduction to IPX

Unlike IP-based networks, the IPX protocol uses network numbers instead of IP interfaces. In a specific LAN, hosts are connected using the same frame type. If other hosts that use different frame types are on this LAN, they are treated as if they are on a different network. Each network has a unique number, which is usually allocated by the NetWare server. The IPX clients obtain this number when they start up. By specifying the frame type that it wants to use, a client is automatically given the network number.

Each client needs to have at least one primary IPX interface, which it usually gets when IPX is initialized.

Configuring the IPX Interface

There are two ways to configure the IPX interface. You can manually configure the IPX interface or use the `ipx_configure` command to automatically configure it. Issue the following command to automatically configure your IPX interfaced:

```
bash#ipx_configure --auto_interface=on --auto_primary=on
basl#slist
```

The last command, `slist`, lists the Novel file servers on your IPX network.

Alas, `ipx_configure` works only in a Microsoft Windows 9x clean network. By *clean* we mean that there should not be any clients running Microsoft Windows 95/98. If there is, you will have to configure the IPX interface manually using the `ipx_interface` command. The `ipx_interface` command can be used as follows:

```
bash#ipx_interface add -p eth0 802.2 0x39ab0222
```

The previous command adds an interface to your (`eth0`) Ethernet card with a primary IPX interface (`-p`). `802.2` is the frame type the interface will use, and `0x39ab0222` is the IPX network address.

The `ipx_interface` command can add, delete, and check interfaces by using the following commands: `add`, `del`, `delall`, and `check`. Check the man page of the `ipx_interface` command for further information.

If you have not configured a TCP/IP network as described in Chapter 13, issue the following command to activate the Ethernet interface:

```
bash#ifcongig eth0 up
```

Working as a NetWare Client

In this section, you will learn how to mount NetWare network volumes and use a NetWare network printer.

Mounting NetWare Volumes   Using the command `ncpmount`, you can mount NetWare volumes to your SuSE Linux mount points. The following are the command-line arguments for this command:

- `-S SERVERNAME`—the `-S` argument is used to specify the server name you want to mount.

- `/MOUNTPOINT`—The *mount point* is where you want to mount the NetWare volume on your SuSE Linux box. An example of this argument is the `/mnt` directory.

- `-U USERNAME`—Using this argument, you can specify to the NetWare server the username with which you log on to the server.

- `-P PASSWORD`—This directive, followed by your password, is used to specify your password to the NetWare server.

- `-n`—If you want to log in as a guest to a NetWare server, you must use the username of the guest user along with this argument.

If you do not specify a `-P` argument to the `ncpmount` command, you will be prompted to enter one as you log in to the NetWare server.

The following is an example of the `ncpmount` command:

```
bash#ncpmount -S AUC_CS /mnt -U joe -P mypass
```

N O T E   When mounting NetWare volumes, ncpmount does *not* set gid or uid on the files
mounted in the volumes. The permissions on these files are the same as the permissions
of the mount point—in our example the mount point was the /mnt directory. Furthermore, the
NetWare server applies more trustee restrictions. You have to manage the permissions before
enabling your users to use this mount point or exporting this mount point through NFS. ■

Printing Through a Novell Server   To print through a Novell Server, you first must run
YaST. Then, select System administration, Network configuration, Connect to a remote
printer via Novell network. The printer setup module in YaST starts and queries for the
printer information. Fill in the fields for the printer information and Novell server information.
For more details on setting up printing, please refer to Chapter 11.

Working as a NetWare Server

To work as a NetWare server, you must install the following package:

Series n:

■   marsnwe (for making a NetWare server)

This package enables you to start your system as a NetWare server. The configuration file of
this package is located in /etc/nwserv.conf.

Mars NetWare Emulator Configuration

The file marsnwe is a very interesting package. It lets your SuSE Linux act as a NetWare
server. You can set up NetWare users, shares, and printers using this package. Clients can
access your SuSE Linux using the IPX protocol and communicate with you as if you were running a NetWare server. The main configuration file for marsnwe is located in
/etc/nwserv.conf. Using this file, you can set up the NetWare users, shares, and printers. In
this chapter, you will find the information you need to set up a basic server with a few tweaks.

Understanding the Configuration File Format   The Mars NetWare Emulator configuration
file is an example of the ultimate in format simplicity. It is based on sections that begin with
numbers. In other words, each line in the configuration file must start with a number unless it
is a comment. Comments in this file are shell-style comments. The # sign is used to signify
that the following is a comment. Any hexadecimal value in the file is written in C-style hexadecimal format, meaning it has the two-digit 0X pre-appended to it. The following shows an
example of a line in the Mars NetWare Emulator configuration file:

```
4   0x22   eth0   ethernet_ii   1 #Starting here, this is a comment
```

Mars Configuration   The required sections in the file must exist to ensure that the emulator
has the basic functionality it needs to run. The sections are described in the following list.
The required sections must be configured so that Mars can run. The recommended sections
are those used for important tweaking:

- **Required Section #1: Volumes**—This section identifies the share name as seen by the client, the share on the Linux machine, the share options, the directory create mask, and the file create mask. You can define more than one section of this type using the same section number. Here is how the format of this line should look like:

```
1  VOLUMENAME  DIRECTORY  [OPTIONS]  [UMASKDIR UMASKFILE]
```

The options are used to define the behavior against the shares on your Linux box. A list of the available options appears in the configuration file itself. The following is an example of creating a share called joe of the /use/local/share/joe with lower filenames (k option) and trustee rights (t option). The directory create mask is 711 and the file create umask is 600:

```
1  joe /usr/local/share/joe/ kt 711 600
```

- **Recommended Section #2: Server Name**—This section is used to give your server a name. The following example names the machine Sue:

```
2 Sue
```

- **Required Section #3: Internal Network Number**—This number should be set to your SuSE Linux IP number. To do so, simply set this section to auto, as in the following example:

```
3 auto
```

- **Recommended Section #4: IPX Devices**—Although this section is not required, it is strongly recommended that you configure it. This section takes the net number, device, frame, and ticks of data transfer. If the net number is set to 0x0, it will try to scan all network numbers available. The following example shows a net number of 0x22 on the first Ethernet interface using the ethernet_ii protocol, with ticks set to 1. Using the ethernet_ii protocol is better than using the 802.2 protocol if your network is running TCP/IP as well as IPX:

```
4    0x22    eth0    ethernet_ii
```

- **Section #5: Special Device Flags**—This section indicates how Mars should handle routing. Set this section to 0x0 unless you're testing your configuration.

- **Recommended Section #6: Version Spoofing**—Use this section to lie to the clients and tell them that you are running a certain version of NetWare. Use existing NetWare version numbers or some clients will not believe you! A list of the correct values is found in the configuration file that comes with SuSE Linux. The following configuration tells the clients that you are running NetWare version 3.11:

```
6    1    0x0
```

- **Required Section #7: Password Handling**—This section describes the password encryption method that Mars should use. The default and recommended value is 0.

- **Required Section #12: Supervisor Login**—The format of this section is as follows:

```
12    NW_LOGIN    LINUX_LOGIN    [PASSWORD]
```

In this format, NW_LOGIN is the NetWare server login name and LINUX_LOGIN is the Linux NetWare administrator's username. [PASSWORD] is the password you want to set to the NetWare server.

This section is used only once. Use this section to set up your root NetWare account and start the server. After the server has started, remove the password of this section.

- **Recommended Section #13: User Logins**—For users to have files, you must designate those users as normal SuSE Linux users. If you don't want those users to use their accounts, but do want them to use the Mars server, you can do so by making an account for each of them as described in Chapter 4, "Managing Users and Groups," and then disabling the account. The syntax for users is as follows:

```
13   NW_LOGIN   [LINUX_LOGIN]   [PASSWORD]   [FLAGS]
```

  The only flag currently available is 0X1, which disables the user's ability to change his password. Here is an example of using this section:

```
13   JOE    joe    0x1  #joe has no password...
```

- **Recommended Section #21: Print Queues**—This section should contain all the printers you want to make available to the clients. For more information regarding printing on SuSE Linux, refer to Chapter 11. The format for this section is as follows:

```
21   QUEUE_NAME   [QUEUE_DIR]    [PRINT_COMMAND]
```

  In the previous line, QUEUE_NAME is the name the clients will see as the printer name, QUEUE_DIR is the printer spooling directory, and PRINT_COMMAND is the command that should be used with this printer. Use the minus sign (-) to replace a default spooling directory. The following is an example of sharing a printer:

```
21   HPDJ610C    -    lpr
```

The other sections of the file are intended for tweaking. You can modify their values to better suit your network or improve performance. In most cases, the default values specified in the file will provide the best results.

Troubleshooting NetWare Networks

ipx_configure *doesn't seem to work. What's the problem?*

You probably have Microsoft Windows 95/98 running IPX on the network. You should use the ipx_interface command instead of ipx_configure in this case. For example, use the following:

```
ipx_interface add -p <device> <frame>
```

I cannot log in to the NetWare version 4.x server as was described in this chapter. The ncpmount *command always fails. What's wrong?*

Try passing the -b argument to the ncpmount command. ●

## CHAPTER 17

Configuring a Usenet News Service

In this chapter

Understanding Usenet

The Internet was created as a medium of exchange. Computers use it to connect to each other and exchange data and information. The transfer of information across the Internet takes different forms. Information can be exchanged via the HTTP protocol to your browser, via email messages, and so on. One of the earliest forms of communication over the Internet was news.

News is a form of communication in which people can post and read articles and messages in one common place. A special program, called a *news client*, is used to connect to that common place—known as a *news server*—and browse all the articles and messages on it. Articles and messages are sorted into categories, which span almost all aspects of discussion. These categories include programming, cooking, guitar playing, music, books, art, and others that are too numerous to mention.

Newsgroups, formally know as *Usenet*, are one of the most efficient forms of communication on the Internet. Many projects have been designed and built by groups of people who communicated using newsgroups. Linux itself was built this way, as was most of the software that runs on it.

To read news, you must have a news client and access to a news server. Access to a news server is obtained from your ISP. You can set up your own local news server for offline reading. A local news server can automatically fetch all the articles on the news groups in which you are interested and store them locally on your hard drive. You then can browse them at your own convenience instead of staying online to read them.

Configuring a local news server for offline browsing is not difficult with SuSE Linux. This server can be used as a small news server for a small network, as well.

Configuring a Local News Server

To set up your machine as a small news server for offline browsing, you must install the news server, which is called *leafnode*. Please note that you will need a large amount of empty hard disk space to run a news server because hundreds of articles will be stored on your hard drive. The amount of space you need depends on how many newsgroups you will be reading.

Installing leafnode

The package requirements for leafnode are as follows.

Package requirements:

Series n:

- leafnode

After you have installed the required package, you will use YaST to set up the first part of the news server. Just follow these steps:

1. Log in as root.
2. Run YaST.
3. Navigate to System Administration, Change Configuration File and press Enter.
4. A dialog pops up in which you can set up all the system variables required to enable/disable the system's services.
5. Press F4 to search for the variable you want to change. A small dialog pops up; type NNTPSERVER and press Enter.
6. YaST will locate the correct system variable for you, which is NNTPSERVER. Press Enter to change its value—you should enter localhost if you have a standalone machine. If you are in a networked environment, you must enter your real hostname here. Your setup should look similar to Figure 17.1.

Part
III

Ch
17

FIGURE 17.1
Setting up the news
server with YaST.

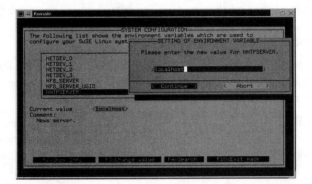

7. Press F10 to exit and save.
8. Exit YaST.

Next, you should configure leafnode.

Configuring leafnode

You now need to set up leafnode itself. leafnode uses a text configuration file, /etc/leafnode/config. Open the file using your favorite editor. You will need to configure some common parameters for leafnode.

The first parameter is the most important one—the server parameter. This is the news server from which leafnode will read the news. If you connect to the Internet via a dial-up connection, you should ask your ISP about their news server. If you are on a local network, check with your administrator about a news server that you can use.

Another parameter, expire, tells leafnode how long it should wait in days before deleting unread discussion threads. The default for this parameter is 20 days. This parameter must exist.

Some news servers require that you log in using a username and password. If your news server requires this, you can specify the username and password using the username and password parameters like this:

```
username = mike
password = secret
```

Standard news servers use port 119 to communicate with the receive requests. If the news server you are connecting to uses another port, you can tell leafnode by using the port parameter—for example, port = 9020.

You can use the supplement parameter to define to leafnode another news server to be used along with your first one. The most common use for this parameter is when one news server hosts newsgroups that are not found on the other one. Follow this parameter with the username and password parameters if your supplement server requires them. You can enter more than one supplement server by defining each one with a supplement, username, and password block.

If one of the supplement servers has a slow connection, you can tell leafnode to give it more time using the timeout parameter right after the supplement parameter. The timeout parameter takes the number of seconds to wait as a value.

You can use the groupexpire parameter to define newsgroup expiration times—for example, if a specific newsgroup is very interesting and you want to keep its articles longer than others. This parameter takes the name of the newsgroup followed by the number of days to keep the articles on your machine as a value. The following is an example:

```
groupexpire    comp.os.linux =
```

You can control how many articles leafnode is going to fetch from a newsgroup using the maxfetch parameter. This is useful because some newsgroups have hundreds of articles. The parameter takes the number of articles to fetch in one run as a value. Entering a number below 1,000 here is not recommended.

When you subscribe to a newsgroup, you can tell leafnode to fetch only a few articles the first time. This will give you a taste of what the group is all about so you can decide whether to get all the articles. To do this, use the initialfetch parameter, giving it the initial number of articles to fetch as a value.

Usually, you don't read all the articles that leafnode fetches for you. Therefore, you can save bandwidth by telling leafnode to download only the article headers. Then, when you want an article, leafnode will fetch the body text for you. This is done by setting the delaybody parameter to 1.

You can tell leafnode not to fetch old articles using the maxage parameter. If you give it a value in number of days, any articles older than that number of days will not be fetched.

These are the most common and interesting parameters for leafnode. However, the only ones that you *must* configure are the server and expire parameters. The rest can all be left at their default values.

Running leafnode

The final step is running leafnode. The first thing you must do is tell your SuSE Linux to run leafnode whenever a news client connects to your machine. You will need to edit /etc/inetd.conf manually.

Open /etc/inetd.conf using your favorite editor. Note that you have to be logged in as root to edit the file. Find the following line:

```
# nntp    stream tcp    nowait news    /usr/sbin/tcpd /usr/sbin/leafnode
```

To enable leafnode, remove the hash sign (#) at the beginning of the line:

```
nntp    stream tcp    nowait news    /usr/sbin/tcpd /usr/sbin/leafnode
```

Save the file and exit. To tell the inetd daemon to reread its configuration file, run the following command as root:

```
# rcinetd restart
```

To test your configuration, do a telnet on port 119, like this:

```
$ telnet localhost 119
Trying 0.0.0.0...
Connected to 0.
Escape character is '^]'.
200 Leafnode NNTP Daemon, version 1.9.4 running at Shadow.nazeeh.com
```

There! Your installation was a success; leafnode answered your request for a connection. Just type quit to exit this test.

To truly finalize your installation, you should edit the file /etc/crontab to make sure that the article expiration program will be scheduled to run by your system on a regular basis.

Open /etc/crontab using your favorite editor. Again, you have to be root to be able to edit this file. Find the following line:

```
#5 22 * * *    root test -x /usr/sbin/texpire && /usr/sbin/texpire
```

Remove the leading hash (#) to enable this entry to be processed by your system scheduler:

```
5 22 * * *    root test -x /usr/sbin/texpire && /usr/sbin/texpire
```

Now that you have fully configured and installed leafnode, it is time to run it. Every time you want leafnode to get the latest articles from your news server and save them locally on your machine, you must run the command fetchnews as root.

This command has to be run the first time you run leafnode. Connect to the Internet if you are using a dial-up connection and run `fetchnews` as root:

```
# fetchnews
```

This first time you run it, `fetchnews` will get you a list of all the newsgroups available on the remote news server. The `fetchnews` command should be run every time you want to update your articles. If you are on a dial-up connection, you should run `fetchnews` every time you connect to your ISP. If you are on a network, you should have your scheduler run it on a regular basis to update your articles.

TIP   The command `fetchnews` is called `fetch` in SuSE Linux 6.2 and below. It was renamed `fetchnews` in SuSE 6.3.

Now, you need a news client with which to read your news. Let's configure one.

Reading News

You can use Netscape Communicator as a news client. You need to tell it where your news server is, which easily can be done by following these steps:

1. Run Netscape.
2. Navigate the menus to Edit, Preferences.
3. Netscape's preferences menu pops up; navigate to Mail & Newsgroups, Newsgroups Servers.
4. Click Add (see Figure 17.2).

FIGURE 17.2
The Netscape
Communicator
Preferences dialog.

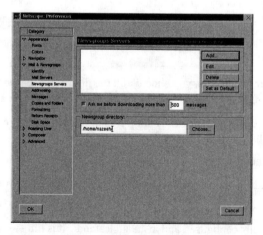

5. A small dialog will pop up asking you for the name of the news server you want to add (see Figure 17.3). Enter `localhost`; or, if you are setting up Netscape from another machine, enter the hostname of the machine on which you installed leafnode.

FIGURE 17.3
Enter the name of the
news server here.

6. If you have more than one news server set up, highlight the one you want to use as your default and click the Set as Default button.

7. Click OK to exit the preferences dialog and save your settings.

8. Now you are ready to read news using Netscape Communicator.

Just use the Newsgroup reader component of Netscape Communicator to subscribe to the newsgroups that you are interested in.

> **CAUTION**
>
> The first time you subscribe to a newsgroup, you must open it. It will be completely empty except for one message from leafnode itself—this is ok. Now that you've opened it, leafnode has registered that it will collect the articles in this newsgroup the next time `fetchnews` is run. That's why you should open the newsgroups you subscribed to in order to tell leafnode to fetch their articles. This is only needed the first time you subscribe to a newsgroup.

You now can use any news client on any platform to access your news server. Multiple connections to the server also are allowed, of course.

Troubleshooting

When I attempt to connect to my news server, using either telnet or a news client, the connection fails.

Make sure that you did install leafnode from the SuSE CDs and that you enabled it in `/etc/inetd.conf`.

I connected to the news server using my news client, but I see no newsgroups at all.

You have to run `fetchnews` before any clients connect to leafnode for the first time. This command fetches the newsgroups listing from the remote news server. Any clients who connected to leafnode before this command was run won't see any newsgroups.

I subscribed to some newsgroups, but they are all empty, except for one message from leafnode.

You need to run `fetchnews` so that leafnode will fetch the articles for you.

Do I have to run `fetchnews` everyday?

`fetchnews` is the program responsible for updating your local copy of news articles. So, how often you run `fetchnews` depends on how often you want that repository updated. Generally speaking, you should run `fetchnews` every time you connect if you are on a dial-up connection, and at least daily if you are on a network. ●

Setting Up the Apache Web Server

The Apache Web Server

The Web server is probably one of the most important pieces of software on which the Internet depends. A *Web server* is a program that enables users to connect to it using Web clients and receive information from it. If you have ever used a Web browser then you have dealt with Web servers. *Web browsers* are the clients that connect to a Web server and get information from it. This information is usually in the form of text and graphics, commonly know as *Web pages*.

The Web server is responsible for making Web pages available to users upon request. The job of a Web server in theory is really very simple. A Web server just sits there waiting for a Web browser to connect to it. After the connection has been made, the Web browser asks the Web server to send it a certain Web page or file. The Web server finds that page or file and sends it to the Web browser. The Web browser then displays the contents of the page to the user. This is the basic idea, but it can get more complicated than this, of course.

Apache is the Web server bundled with SuSE Linux. It is free software developed and maintained by a group of volunteer programmers on the Internet. Apache is being developed in very much the same fashion as Linux and most of the other free software projects. And just like Linux and the others, Apache was developed because a need for it existed.

Before the days of Apache, the most commonly used Web server was called httpd from NCSA. This server had a few problems, especially in the field of security. Soon enough, a group of programmers came together on the Internet and started to add to the NCSA server's code to fix the bugs. The additions soon included improvements to the server itself. These additions included patches to the NCSA code to make it work better and more securely. In time, the NCSA code was being so heavily changed that it started to lose all resemblance to its original unpatched code. Apache was born from the new code base; in fact, that is where it got its name. The new server was simply a patchy server, hence the name Apache (a patchy server).

Apache very quickly surpassed the performance of NCSA and became popular in the UNIX community. It was completely free, which was one of the original intentions of the project. This has enabled the UNIX community to always have a free and powerful Web server. Apache performed much better than all other servers on the market and soon gained the largest market share. This was helped largely by the fact that Apache is very portable and can be run on virtually all UNIX-based systems. OS/2 and Windows NT ports also are available.

At the time of this writing, Apache still owns the biggest market share among Web servers. It is very powerful, reliable, extensible, scalable, and customizable. Installing and configuring an Apache Web server is a relatively simple task that does not require a high level of UNIX understanding. All you need is a text editor and some patience.

Installing Apache

Apache comes packaged with SuSE Linux. The following are the package requirements for installing Apache:

Package requirements:

Series n:

■ apache

When you are finished installing Apache, you need to know how to configure it.

Configuring the Apache Web Server

Apache, like most of the software on Linux, is configured via text configuration files. These files are found in the Apache configuration directory located in /etc/httpd. Apache is configured by editing three files: access.conf, httpd.conf, and srm.conf. This enables Apache to be backward compatible to the NCSA server because it uses the same configuration files. SuSE Linux already has these files in /etc/httpd, and they contain a basic sample configuration you can use for a quick start.

The configuration files are made up of several configuration directives. A *configuration directive* is a line that starts with a tag and a list of options. The tag tells Apache what option is being configured by this line and the trailing options are the parameters to set. For example:

```
ServerAdmin webmaster@mysite.com
```

This a common example of a directive. It starts with the ServerAdmin tag, which tells Apache that this line configures the Server Administrator option. The email address is the value to set for this tag.

Directives can be grouped in sections that look very much like HTML code. A section starts with a section name between angular brackets (<>) and is terminated with a forward-slashed tag. Directives are entered in between the first tag and the terminating tag. The following is an example of a section:

```
<Directory />
    Options -FollowSymLinks
    AllowOverride None
</Directory>
```

This section configures the options for the directory /. As you can see, it starts with <Directory /> and ends with a forward slashed tag </Directory>. In between the two tags, there are two directives that define options for this entire block.

Now that you have a basic idea of how directives and sections work, let's configure a basic Apache server.

Part

III

Ch

18

Basic Server

We will now configure a basic server. You will learn how to start and stop the Apache server and actually see something on your Web browser. The file you will want to edit is /etc/httpd/httpd.conf. The other two files, access.conf and srm.conf, are left empty. The SuSE team recommends that you leave these this way and deal only with httpd.conf.

Open /etc/httpd/httpd.conf using your favorite editor. The file is already full of text. Any line that starts with a hash mark (#) is a comment and will be ignored by Apache. The SuSE team already has preconfigured this file for you. You will just check that the tags are configured correctly for your system.

The first directive you want to edit is ServerAdmin. This is the email address that will appear on the Web browser when Apache reports an error. Find this option and set it to your email address. It should look something like the following:

```
ServerAdmin nazeeh@shadow.com
```

The next options you want to configure are User and Group. These are the user and group with which Apache will run. When Apache runs, it creates child processes for the incoming requests. The master Apache process always runs with root permissions, but the child processes are set to run with the User and Group options you set here. This keeps any badly written CGI scripts from harming the system because they aren't running with root privileges. Setting these options is integral to good system security.

The User option takes a valid username or user ID (entered as #uid) for a parameter. The Group option takes a valid group name or group ID (entered as #gid) as a parameter. The SuSE team has set this option to user wwwrun and group nogroup. This choice is a safe one and should be left as is. Just make sure that this is the setting on your system. It should look like the following:

```
User wwwrun
Group nogroup
```

The ServerName tag is responsible for giving your server the correct name. This tag takes a hostname for a parameter. This name must be a valid hostname; you can't just invent any name. The name you use must have a valid DNS entry, so ask your network administrator about this. If you do not have a DNS entry, you can enter your IP instead. If you decide not to set this option at all, put a # in front of it or don't include it in the file altogether. If you don't set this option, Apache will attempt to figure it out for you. For testing purposes, you can set it to localhost. The following is an example of a configuration for this tag:

```
ServerName localhost
```

The next option is ServerRoot. This tells Apache where to find its configuration, error, and log files. The SuSE team has set this option to the correct path of /usr/local/httpd. You should make sure that your configuration looks like the following:

```
ServerRoot "/usr/local/httpd"
```

Note that the path you enter must *not* end with a slash.

The final option you will configure in this file is `DocumentRoot`. This tells Apache where to find the HTML pages that make up your Web site. Again, this option is correctly set by the SuSE team to the default directory of `/usr/local/httpd/htdocs`. Check to make sure you have the following line in your configuration file:

```
DocumentRoot "/usr/local/httpd/htdocs"
```

Ok, that's all you need for now; let's see if it really works.

Starting the Apache Server

Now that you have configured your Apache server, you probably want to give it a try. To start the Apache server, type the following on the command line as root:

```
# rcapache start
```

If you use SuSE 6.2 or earlier, you should run this command instead:

```
# /sbin/init.d/apache start
```

The Apache server will be started by your system. To try it, point your Web browser to `http://localhost`. You should see the default Web page for SuSE Linux (see Figure 18.1).

Part
III

Ch
18

FIGURE 18.1
The default page on the Apache server.

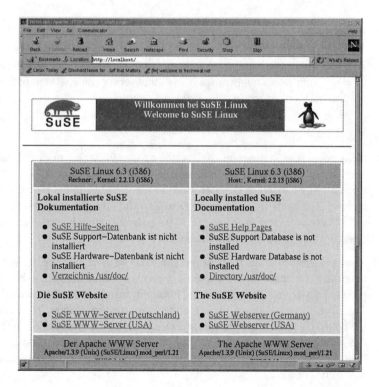

To ensure that Apache runs on every boot, you must modify your system files. This is easily done using YaST; just follow these steps:

1. Run YaST.

2. Navigate to System Administration, Change Configuration File and press Enter.

3. Use this dialog to configure system parameters. You need to find the httpd parameter. Press F4. A small dialog will pop up; type HTTPD and press Enter to make YaST search the system variables for httpd.

4. YaST has found the httpd variable, which is called START_HTTPD. Press Enter to change its value to yes.

5. Press F10 to save your changes.

Now Apache will be run automatically on system boot up.

You now can start using your Web server. Just make sure that if you use the ServerName directive, that it uses a valid hostname or IP. If you are not sure of the hostname or IP, don't use the directive and let Apache figure it out. All your HTTP pages should be stored under the directory declared by the DocumentRoot directive. You can create subdirectories under that directory if you want.

Advanced Functionality

The Web server you configured in the previous section is a pretty basic yet efficient server. However, your needs might surpass what that server can give you. In this section, you will learn more about Apache's advanced functions.

Using CGI

Many people use Web servers to host their pages for others to view. Usually in simple Web sites, all that a person on the Internet is allowed to do is view the page. It is a one-way line of communication in which the user wants to see the site and the server sends it to the user's browser. The contents of the page are exactly the same for all users—nothing changes per user. Therefore, these sites are said to have *static* content because the content does not change unless the site creator changes it.

Another approach exists that enables you to serve dynamic page content. *Dynamic* content is not exactly the same for every user; it depends on some interaction between the user and server. This interaction can be in the form of a search query the user submits to the server. Then, based on that query, the server returns different content. You must have used this at least once if you have ever used a search engine on the Web. Filling in forms on a Web page and seeing your information displayed on the site afterwards is another example of dynamic Web content. The Web server is on a communication channel with you, sending you content based on your input.

Dynamic content is possible thanks to Common Gateway Interface (CGI). CGI enables your server to run a program and display its output to the user in the form of HTML, which is how dynamic Web pages work. When you work with them, you really are working with a program, not static content. The program is executed by the Apache server, the program then outputs some text in HTML format, and the server takes that and sends it back to you. Next, you respond to the page by choosing an option, entering text, pressing a button, clicking on a link. Finally, Apache takes your input, feeds it to the program, and sends the output back to you.

CGI programs can be written in any language, scripted or compiled, such as C/C++, Perl, shell scripts, and so on. These programs are initiated by the server and are possibly passed some parameters. Your programs then should respond in exactly the same manner as a normal program, with the only exception being that they format their output in HTML so the browser can render it.

Apache on SuSE Linux is already configured to run CGI programs and scripts, and it even includes some example CGIs to illustrate the idea for you. CGIs are all placed in the directory `/usr/local/httpd/cgi-bin/`. Calls to a CGI script are part of the URL; for example, `http://www.myserver.com/cgi-bin/test-cgi` would execute a program named `test-cgi` in your CGI directory.

Apache should be configured to enable CGI execution if you want to use them. To enable CGI execution, you must uncomment one line in the Apache configuration file `httpd.conf`:

```
ScriptAlias /cgi-bin/ "/usr/local/httpd/cgi-bin/"
```

This directive tells Apache that the directory `/usr/local/httpd/cgi-bin` contains executable scripts. Chances are this directive is already enabled on your machine because SuSE Linux uses CGIs for the system online manual and help database. Restart the Apache server for the changes to take effect by typing the following command:

```
# rcapache restart
```

If you use SuSE 6.2 or earlier, you should run this command instead:

```
# /sbin/init.d/apache restart
```

To test your CGI configuration, point your browser to `http://localhost/cgi-bin/test-cgi`. This script resides in your CGI directory and is used for testing purposes. If your CGI configuration was successful, you should get an output similar to the one shown in Figure 18.2.

Part

III

Ch

18

CAUTION

You should be careful when you use CGI scripts. These are, after all, programs running on your machine upon the request of people on the Internet. Even though Apache in itself is a pretty secure server, it cannot control the security of the CGI programs and scripts. Go through any scripts and programs you are planning to use on your server to ensure they cannot be exploited in any way. A weakly designed or implemented CGI can be a very serious security hole in your system.

FIGURE 18.2
Running the
test-cgi CGI on
Apache.

Allowing Users to Have Personal Web Pages

So far, any Web pages you want to add to the server Web site must be placed in the
DocumentRoot, which is /usr/local/httpd/htdocs/ in SuSE Linux. If your users want to have
their own Web pages, they must ask you to post them. You can do this by creating a subdirectory for every user under /usr/local/httpd/htdocs and placing their Web content in it. This
is very time-consuming, especially if you have many users and they update their Web pages
frequently.

Apache solves this problem by allowing your users to put Web pages in their home directories. This enables them to control the content and update it without your help, removing quite
a load off the system administrator. The SuSE team has already configured Apache for this,
so all you need to do is uncomment a few lines in /etc/httpd/httpd.conf. The lines are as
follows:

```
UserDir public_html
<Directory /home/*/public_html>
    AllowOverride FileInfo AuthConfig Limit
    Options MultiViews Indexes SymLinksIfOwnerMatch IncludesNoExec
    <Limit GET POST OPTIONS PROPFIND>
        Order allow,deny
        Allow from all
```

```
        </Limit>
        <Limit PUT DELETE PATCH PROPPATCH MKCOL COPY MOVE LOCK UNLOCK>
            Order deny,allow
            Deny from all
        </Limit>
</Directory>
```

If you do not have the previous lines in your file, just add them. Save the file and exit. Restart your Apache server by typing the following command:

```
# rcapache restart
```

If you use SuSE 6.2 or earlier, you should run this command instead:

```
# /sbin/init.d/apache restart
```

Your users will now be able to build Web pages in their home directories and Apache will display them. The way this works is very simple. The first directive is `UserDir`, which tells Apache the name of the directory in the user's home directory in which to look for HTML content. In SuSE Linux, this is `public_html`. If a user wants to host a Web site in his home directory, he must create a directory called `public_html` in his home directory. For example, if a user named John wants to host a Web site in his home directory, he would create `/home/john/public_html`. All the HTML pages and Web content should be stored in that directory. In addition, both the user's home and `public_html` directories must have read permissions to all. This is accomplished by running the following commands:

```
$ chmod a+rx /home/john
$ chmod a+rx /home/john/public_html
```

To access a user's home page, point the Web browser to `http://www.site.com/~username`. For example, if John wants to see his page, he would load `http://www.site.com/~john`. Users now can use FTP to upload files to their home directories to update their Web sites frequently.

Virtual Servers

So far, you know how to configure Apache to serve one user as well as multiple users. For multiple users, you used the idea of having one name for the server, with each user having a URL to her Web site, which is the name of the server appended by her username. For example, user Mary's Web site on your machine would be `http://www.server.com/~mary`. If you were hosting a Web site for a company, you would use the same idea. The company's Web site would be `http://www.server.com/~company`.

What if the company whose Web site you are hosting required that you supply it with a www.company.com name? You probably would set up another machine with Apache server on it, register its name to be `www.company.com`, and host the site on it. But, what if another company wants to do the same thing? Would you run off again and set up another machine? That is not a very convenient solution, in either effort or cost. You now have more than one machine to administrate, which in itself is a headache. At the same time, the load on all three sites is so low that one machine is more than enough to serve them all. However, you have three machines that are just sitting there wasting CPU cycles you pay for.

The answer to your dilemma is *virtual* servers. Using virtual servers, Apache is capable of hosting more than one site on the same machine running the same server. All you need to do is to register the same machine IP with all the domain names you need. This causes all the domains you host to resolve to your machine's IP. Apache then checks the URL the browser sends to it and decides which pages to send back.

This enables you to host two Web sites on your machine—one using the address `http://www.company.com` and the other using `http://www.school.com`. Apache will know which one the browser connecting to it is requesting and deliver the correct page. This reduces the amount of hardware needed by half and the administration effort as well.

To build a virtual host on Apache, you construct a `<VirtualHost>` section for each Web site. Let's build one that answers to `http://www.company.com`. Just enter the following lines in your `httpd.conf` file:

```
<VirtualHost www.company.com>
DocumentRoot /usr/local/company/
</VirtualHost>
```

That's it. Although, you must make sure that `www.company.com` resolves to your machine's IP for this to work. Apache will answer any requests to `www.company.com` by reading from its document root at `/usr/local/company`. You can put any valid directives inside the virtual server section; these will override any external ones. This makes it very easy to administer the servers because they all share the directive, unless overridden inside.

Tuning Apache

After you successfully install your Web server and it has been running for a while, you might want to tune it. Getting the most from a Web server can be accomplished by approaching the problem from two ways: from the hardware and organization side and from Apache itself. You can tune both and get even better throughput.

Hardware Side

Because Apache runs on your PC, it uses your resources. To increase the performance of your server, increase the performance of the hardware on which it is running.

The CPU is one aspect that most people think of. Increasing the speed of the CPU is not always the best answer, though. Web servers do not use up as much CPU as you might think. Web servers that serve static pages, not CGIs, are very conservative in CPU usage. Increasing the speed of the CPU will increase the performance of your CGI, but this again depends on how much CPU your server uses.

Web servers love RAM; the more the better. Increasing the amount of RAM on your machine will most definitely increase your server's performance. By having more RAM, you decrease the amount of hard disk swapping needed to manage the virtual memory. This will boost the performance of your Web server. Having 32MB of RAM is sufficient for limited traffic. If you are expecting a lot of traffic, however, you should start at 128MB of RAM or more. If you can't afford to buy more RAM, at least decrease the amount of services that share the machine with your Web server. Turn off any service you are not using, such as SMTP, FTP, NNTP, and so on. Give as much memory to Apache as you can.

Your hard drive is one of the biggest performance bottlenecks. However fast your hard drive is, it is still years slower than the access time in RAM. Apache uses your hard drive frequently because this is where all the Web pages are stored. For heavy traffic sites, you should try to use SCSI hard drives because they are usually faster than IDE drives. For optimal performance, you should consider using a RAID system.

Your network card can be a bottleneck, depending on its speed. If you are running on a network card that is slower than the possible bandwidth of your network, it will slow you down. Use a network card that is at least as fast as your network's bandwidth.

Networking

If you are running a site with very heavy traffic, you might consider running a *distributed* Web server. The idea behind distributed servers is really very simple. Two servers can do more than one, and three can do even more. Instead of using just one machine as your Web server, you can use several. All the machines run a copy of Apache servicing the same content. All incoming requests are distributed on the machines, thus increasing the performance.

Implementing the idea of distributed servers is not very difficult—it just requires knowledge of DNS. You need to configure your DNS so that when a client connects requesting the IP of the server, it answers with a rotating list of IPs. This enables two connecting clients to receive two different IPs, each for a different server.

The IPs are different, but the fully qualified domain name is the same. Big sites such as www.yahoo.com use this. The name www.yahoo.com resolves to more than one IP, each running a Web server on it. Incoming connections are distributed among several servers, thus increasing the performance drastically.

Another important performance factor is the speed of your network. Generally, the faster your connection to the Internet, the faster the performance of your server. This is, of course, applicable only if your server is running at optimal speed.

Software Tuning

How you configure your Apache server is probably the most important aspect in the tuning process. A badly configured Apache server is going to perform poorly regardless of the hardware or network on which it is running. The default configuration that is set on SuSE Linux is already pretty good and well-tuned. You might not need to play around with it a lot, but you should keep the following tips in mind to achieve maximum performance for your HTTP server.

Apache uses log files to log its activity, which can be a bottleneck. Don't let Apache log anything not directly useful to you; it will just be a waste of performance because logging takes time and resources. You can configure what Apache logs and does not log using the following directives in the `httpd.conf` configuration file:

- `LogLevel`—This is the level of logging the server will use. You can set it to `debug`, `info`, `notice`, `warn`, `error`, `crit`, `alert`, and `emerg`. A good setting is `warn`, which happens to be the default on SuSE Linux.

- `HostnameLookups`—This directive, if set to on, will cause Apache to look up the hostnames of the connecting clients. This is an expensive operation, so if you do not need it, set it to off. Remember, log only what you need.

A final word on logging: Try to log on a different hard drive. Don't try to log on the same partition or another partition on the same hard drive, but log on a separate hard drive on another IDE controller if you are using an IDE system. This will enable the server to log and process requests simultaneously.

Apache forks a new process for every request it receives. To improve performance, a process that is performed with its request does not die instantly. Apache keeps it around to serve another request. You can control how long Apache lets a process live before killing it and forking another one. This is necessary if a process starts eating up too much memory because of bugs and so on. Killing children processes helps keep the server running in a healthy fashion because it refreshes its processes. To improve performance, increase the lifetime of these processes. This helps because forking is a very expensive operation, and gets even more expensive if your server is under heavy load. The directive to use for controlling process lifetime is `MaxRequestsPerChild`, which takes a number as an argument. This is the number of requests a child process is allowed to serve before it is killed. Setting it to `0` enables the child process to live forever.

The Apache server, if sent a request to display a directory on the server, first looks for a file called `index.html`. If it finds that file, it displays its contents to the user. If it can't find it, it will create an index file that contains a list of all the files found in the directory. This index generation is a rather expensive operation. Avoid making Apache do it by providing `index.html` files.

CGIs are especially heavy on the system, so use them only if you must. If you do not need CGIs, do not use them; they will just slow down your server. If you do use them, though, try to use compiled programs rather than scripts. Compiled programs run more quickly than a script. You can test how much faster a certain program is versus a script version performing the same function. To test how much time a certain program or script takes, use the `time` command:

```
$ time program
```

The previous command executes the program and when it is done, shows you how much time it takes to process.

Another thing you might want to do is to use a distributed server solution in which you have servers that are used only for CGI execution.

In normal server operation, the Web server opens a connection for every request it receives. After the request is satisfied, the connection is closed again. This is not very efficient if your client is requesting more than one item from the server because the server will initiate a connection for every request. Another method uses something called *keepalive*. This enables a browser to request a prolonged open connection with the server so it can retrieve more than one item from it. This increases the server's responsiveness because it doesn't open a new connection for every item. To enable this, set the KeepAlive directive to on:

```
KeepAlive On
```

Other related directives can control the properties of keepalive mode. MaxKeepAliveRequests controls how many keepalive connections are allowed. For example:

```
MaxKeepAliveRequests 100
```

will allow only 100 keepalive connections. KeepAliveTimeout controls how long the server waits before terminating an idle open connection. For example:

```
KeepAliveTimeout
```

will timeout an idle connection after 15 seconds.

Apache uses preforked processes to increase performance. This means it forks a few processes in preparation for incoming requests. Therefore, when a request arrives, it won't have to waste time forking a process, it just passes it to one of the free processes in the pool. This enables Apache to adapt to the load on it by controlling the size of that pool automatically.

You can control this behavior using the MinSpareServers and MaxSpareServers directives. If there are fewer than MinSpareServers, Apache will create a new spare. If there are more than MaxSpareServers, Apache kills some of the spares. The default values for SuSE Linux are as follows:

```
MinSpareServers
MaxSpareServers
```

These defaults will probably be sufficient, but experimentation and experience will decide this for sure.

Apache enables you to configure the maximum number of clients that can connect to it. After the number of clients exceeds this value, all incoming request are refused until current requests go below that number. The directive that controls this behavior is MaxClients. For example:

```
MaxClients 150
```

will allow a maximum of 150 clients to connect at one time.

Troubleshooting

I can't connect to the server on my machine.

Are you using the correct URL? Try connecting to `http://localhost` and see what happens. You should have an entry like the following in your `/etc/hosts` file:

```
127.0.0.1        localhost
```

If this does not work, make sure that the server is already installed and is running. Restart the server by typing the following command:

```
# rcapache restart
```

If you use SuSE 6.2 or earlier, you should run this command instead:

```
# /sbin/init.d/apache restart
```

If the server startup fails, check your configuration file for any typos or mistakes.

The server runs fine, but I want to change the default page.

Apache reads the HTML pages from the directory pointed to by the `DocumentRoot` directive in `/etc/httpd/httpd.conf`. This directory is `/usr/local/httpd/htdocs` by default on SuSE Linux. Place the HTML for your Web site in this directory.

I can't run CGI. What am I doing wrong?

Make sure that the `ScriptAlias` directive is uncommented in the configuration file and points to the correct CGI directory, which is `/usr/local/httpd/cgi-bin` in SuSE Linux.

I enabled user-owned Web pages, but users keep getting `Access Forbidden` messages when they try to load their pages.

This is a common permissions problem. Your users' home directories must be readable by everyone for this to work. You should run the command `chmod a+rx` on their home and the `public_html` directory inside them to make them readable by all. Another thing you can do is to create all the Web users as part of the `nogroup` group, which is the same group as Apache. Apache will then be able to see the files. To learn how to create groups and assign users to them, refer to Chapter 4, "Managing Users and Groups."

The server is running, but I don't like the performance.

Read the previous section "Tuning Apache" and try some of the tuning tips; they should help increase the performance of your server. ●

Configuring the FTP Server

File Transfer and FTP Servers

The Internet has enabled us to connect our machines together regardless of our geographical location. As a result, we can transfer all types of data from one machine to another. The Internet has defined several protocols for data transfer, one of the most famous of which is the File Transfer Protocol. *File Transfer Protocol*, commonly known as *FTP*, is a protocol that enables people to send and receive all types of files across the Internet. And because the Internet is the transfer medium, ftp is not operating system–specific. All you need to have to transfer files using FTP is an FTP client.

FTP uses what is known as *client/server architecture*. This means that for an FTP session to exist, two entities must be involved—an FTP server and an FTP client. The *FTP server* is a program that waits for a *client* to connect to it. After a client connects, and is authorized, the FTP server executes any file transfer commands issued to it by the client. These commands can make the server send and receive files to and from the client.

So, if you want FTP clients to perform file transfers on your machine, you will need to install an ftp daemon program that can communicate with them. Having an FTP server can be use-ful. Users on your system can use it to transfer files from and to their home accounts and from any operating system. You can use the FTP server to host any files or programs avail-able for download on the Internet. SuSE, for example, uses an FTP server to enable anyone to download its distribution for free. Almost all the programs available for Linux can be down-loaded from FTP sites.

You're probably wondering whether or not you can have an FTP server on your machine—the good news is, of course you can! SuSE Linux has a good FTP server packaged with it called proftpd. proftpd, which stands for *Professional ftp daemon*, is one of the best FTP servers available. Let's see how you can install and configure proftpd on your SuSE Linux.

Installing proftpd

Installing proftpd is very straightforward. The package requirements are as follows.

Package requirements:

Series n:

- proftpd
- ftpdir

Kernel requirements:

- none

When you're finished installing it from the SuSE CDs, you must tell your system to load it when it's needed. To do this, you will have to edit the file `/etc/inetd.conf`. This is the configuration file for `inetd`, which is the program responsible for starting all the network services when they are in demand. So, when an ftp client connects to your machine, `inetd` will run proftpd to handle it. To tell `inetd` about proftpd, follow these steps:

1. Log in as root.

2. Open the file `/etc/inetd.conf` with your favorite editor.

3. You should find an entry for proftpd, which will look similar to the following:

   ```
   ftp     stream tcp    nowait root    /usr/sbin/tcpd  proftpd
   ```

4. If you find an entry similar to the previous example, activate it by removing the hash mark (#) at the beginning.

5. Make sure that this is the only entry in the whole file that starts with `ftp`. If you find others, be sure that they start with a #, and are therefore deactivated.

6. If you did not find the proftpd entry, add it to the file, again making sure that it is the only activated FTP entry in the whole file.

7. Save and exit.

8. Force `inetd` to reread its configuration file by typing the following command:

   ```
   #rcinetd reload
   ```

9. That's it, you're all set now.

To quickly test your setup, type the following command:

```
# ftp localhost
```

You should get an output similar to the following:

```
Connected to localhost.
220 ProFTPD 1.2.0pre9 Server (powered by SuSE Linux) [Shadow.nazeeh.com]
Name (localhost:nazeeh):
```

Now, your FTP server is all ready for you to use. Although the default configuration is simple, you can configure proftpd to further meet your demands and style.

Configuring proftpd

proftpd reads its configuration from the file `/etc/proftpd.conf`, which is, as usual, a text file you must edit. SuSE Linux comes with a sample proftpd configuration file that you can look at to get a general idea of how to configure proftpd. Let's create your own `proftpd.conf` file, for a basic server configuration.

Basic Configuration

The configuration language used by proftpd consists of option tags that take the following form:

```
Option   value or list of values
```

Part
III

Ch
19

Back up the existing /etc/proftpd.conf file because you are about to create your own version. Open your favorite editor and read on to see how you can create your own proftpd configuration file.

Let's define some options that describe the server. Write the following in your configuration file:

```
ServerName          "powered by SuSE Linux"
ServerType          inetd
ServerAdmin         ftpadm@localhost
AllowOverwrite      on
```

The first tag, ServerName, is the string displayed to connecting FTP clients. ServerType tells proftpd how it is being started. This option takes one of two values—inetd or standalone. In your case, it takes inetd because you are using inetd to run your proftpd server. If you were going to run proftpd manually by directly executing it, you would enter standalone as the value for ServerType.

The next option is ServerAdmin, which is the email address of this server's administrator—you. It doesn't really matter what you enter for the email address because it won't affect how the server runs.

Finally, the option AllowOverwrite, when set to on, tells proftpd to allow files to be overwritten. This enables your users to overwrite files they previously uploaded. The default behavior for this option is off, so if you want it on, you should specify that explicitly. Generally, it's recommended you have it on.

You now can save this file and attempt to connect to your server. You will find that the server is functioning pretty well, even though the configuration file is very small. This is because proftpd is using defaults for all the other options.

Let's take things a step further. Open the configuration file again using your favorite editor. Suppose you want your server to display a message to anyone who connects to it, maybe with some text that tells people about your server. Use the DisplayConnect tag and give it a file as a value:

```
DisplayConnect          /etc/myftpmessage
```

Every time a client connects to your server, the contents of the file you specified will be displayed to the user. Make sure that you do create this file and put some text in it.

Now you need to define some timeouts. Use the TimeoutIdle tag to tell proftpd how long to wait before disconnecting an idle connection. An idle connection could be an FTP client connected but not doing anything, or a client that was connected but crashed without disconnecting first. Either way, your server will use up system resources for that useless connection. If you set TimeoutIdle to some value in seconds, an idle connection will be terminated when the time is up. The default for this tag is 600 seconds, but if you enter 0 seconds, you turn off this feature. It's a good idea to have it, though, so add this to your configuration file:

```
TimeoutIdle    500
```

Another timeout tag is `TimeoutLogin`, which is the number of seconds proftpd will wait until a client enters the username and password. The default for this option is 300 seconds, so add it to the file:

```
TimeoutLogin    300
```

An ftp server's sole purpose is to transfer data. So, if a client connects and does not perform any data transfer, it's wasting your resources. Use `TimeoutNoTransfer` to disconnect a client that connects to your server and does not issue any command to initiate data transfer. The default for this option is 600 seconds:

```
TimeoutNoTransfer    600
```

Now your configuration file should look something like this:

```
ServerName          "powered by SuSE Linux"
ServerType          inetd
ServerAdmin         ftpadm@localhost
AllowOverwrite      on
DisplayConnect      /etc/myftpmessage
TimeoutLogin        300
TimeoutNoTransfer   600
```

This is good configuration file for a basic FTP server. It will allow all your users to use ftp to transfer files to and from their accounts. In addition, this configuration allows *only* your users to log in. To find out how to allow non-users or anonymous people access to your machine, proceed to the next section.

Anonymous FTP

If you are familiar with FTP, you've probably noticed that the current configuration does not allow anonymous users. FTP servers allow users who have accounts on your system to log in, but no one else. However, you might want to allow other non-system, or *anonymous*, users access to your FTP server. Having an anonymous user enables you to expose certain files to the public to download—for example, the SuSE Linux FTP site uses anonymous login to allow anyone to download SuSE Linux.

For proftpd to allow anonymous users to log in, you must edit its configuration file. Add the following to the configuration file:

```
<Anonymous /usr/local/ftp>
    User        ftp
    Group       public
    UserAlias   anonymous ftp
    MaxClients
    DisplayLogin        msgs/welcome.msg
```

```
       DisplayFirstChdir      .message
       <Directory *>
           <Limit WRITE>
               DenyAll
           </Limit>
       </Directory>
</Anonymous>
```

The anonymous user has a special grouping tag called <Anonymous>, which groups all the options specific to the anonymous user. The first option is the location of the directory at which the anonymous user will be positioned after he or she is logged in. For SuSE Linux, this is configured as /usr/local/ftp, making the tag <Anonymous /usr/local/ftp>.

SuSE has prepared the directory /usr/local/ftp to be used by anonymous connections. If you view the contents of that directory, you will see that it uses the standard layout:

```
drwxr-xr-x  10 root      root         4096 Jan 26 02:44 .
drwxr-xr-x  20 root      root         4096 Jan 21 11:57 ..
drwxr-xr-x   2 root      root         4096 Dec 12 10:03 bin
drwxr-xr-x   2 root      root         4096 Dec 12 10:03 dev
drwxr-xr-x   2 root      root         4096 Dec 12 10:03 etc
drwxr-xr-x   2 root      root         4096 Nov  9 09:29 lib
drwxr-xr-x   2 root      root         4096 Dec 12 10:03 msgs
drwxr-xr-x   2 root      root         4096 Nov  9 09:29 pub
drwxr-xr-x   3 root      root         4096 Dec 12 10:03 usr
```

The next two tags, User and Group, tell proftpd what user or group to run when an anonymous user logs in. This provides security because proftpd will run with the permissions made available to user FTP, group public, which SuSE Linux has configured to have very little power in the system.

The UserAlias tag tells proftpd that anonymous and ftp are the same user. This enables people to log in using either the username anonymous or ftp—both will be treated as anonymous in the end.

The MaxClients tag is an important tag. You don't want your system resources to be totally consumed by hundreds of anonymous users logging in to your server. Setting this tag to a certain number will limit the amount of anonymous connections allowed to that number. In your case, only 10 anonymous connections will be allowed.

DisplayLogin defines a file whose contents proftpd will display to anonymous users when they connect. As you can see, the file we specified is msgs/welcome.msg, which is in /usr/local/ftp/msgs. You can use any file you want, and, if it's inside /usr/local/ftp, you can use the relative pathname.

DisplayFirstChdir takes .message as a parameter. Therefore, the first time a user changes his directory to a directory containing that file, its contents are displayed to the user. This file can be used to hold text describing what the user will find in that directory.

The next block of options start with the <Directory> tag. This tag sets options for a specific directory. You set the options for the directory *, which is all the directories in /usr/local/ftp here. To control what the connecting user can do with these directories, use the <Limit> tag. To understand how this works, let's look at the <Directory> block and how <Limit> is used in it.

The <Directory> block indicates to proftpd that you are about to set options specific to the directory *. In this particular configuration, use the following:

```
<Limit WRITE>
    DenyAll
</Limit>
```

This denies all (DenyAll) clients from being able to write to those directories. Clients can read because you said nothing about READ, but they can't write anything. This is a good configuration to use for anonymous users because it prevents them from dumping files on your hard drive. If you are still unsure about how the <Limit> tag works, don't worry; we'll talk more about it soon. Just make sure that you understand what it is doing in this specific configuration.

Finally, the </Anonymous> tag ends the anonymous section.

Setting Up User Ratios

FTP servers can be set up for a variety of purposes. You can set up an FTP server to enable your users to transfer files to and from their home accounts, therefore making life easier for them. You can set up a server to enable users to download data from your machine, making it a data repository. Sometimes, you might want to control how people transfer files from your server. Consider the following scenario.

Suppose you created an FTP server that hosts artistic images, and you want people to exchange their art using your server as the grounds of exchange. People interested in art can log on to your server to download images other artists have uploaded. After a while, you noticed that a lot of people just log in, download images, and don't ever upload anything. Your server has lost its basic purpose—facilitating the exchange of art. How can you force users to stop abusing your server and start uploading some images. You could use the DisplayConnect tag to display a message at the time of connection, but that's probably not forceful enough. This is where ratios come in.

Ratios enable you to set rules on how people are going to download and upload files to your server. You can, for example, set a rule that forces a user to upload a file for every file she downloads. This should preserve the exchange of art on your server. Ratios are pretty flexible, and very useful in helping to control abuse.

To set ratios, you must turn on the feature in proftpd. To do so, set the tag Ratios to on in your configuration file:

```
Ratios    on
```

Part
III

Ch
19

Four different types of ratios exist: UserRatio (used to set ratios on a user or all users), HostRatio (used to set ratios for specific hosts), GroupRatio (used to set ratios for groups), and AnonRatio (used to set a ratio for anonymous users). Each of these ratios takes five parameters in the following form:

```
RatioType    String FileRatio FileCredit ByteRatio ByteCredit
```

String can be a user or * for UserRatio, a hostname (including wildcards) for hosts, a group name for GroupRatio, or an email address to be matched for AnonRatio.

The remaining four parameters are all integers. FileRatio is the number of files the user has to upload in order to download a file. The FileCredit is the initial number of file credits the user gets upon connection. The ByteRatio is the ratio of upload/download in bytes. And, finally, the ByteCredit is the initial number of bytes the user gets as credit.

To understand ratios, look at the following example:

```
Ratios      on
UserRatio   art    1    1    1
```

This tells proftpd to turn on Ratios and set the following rule. A user can download one file for every file he uploads, and he gets an initial credit of one file when he logs in. Therefore, when someone logs in with the username art, he can download one file without having to upload one, but any further downloading requires him to upload files in a 1:1 ratio.

The byte limit follows the same rule as the file ratio. The user gets one byte for every byte he uploads. Having a byte ratio is useful as a secondary controlling mechanism.

Let's look at another example:

```
HostRatio   *.xyz.com   5   1   0
```

This rule says "For anyone connecting from xyz.com domain, set a file ratio of five to one (5:1) with an initial file credit of one file, and don't enter any byte ratio for them." Entering zero as a value will disable checking it.

To tell proftpd to enter a byte ratio of three to one (3:1) with 50,000 bytes initial credit and no file ratio for all users belonging to group staff, use the following command:

```
GroupRatio   staff   0   0   3   50000
```

Thanks to ratios, you are now able to control all the file transfers that occur on your FTP server. If a user attempts to break any of these rules, the server will not allow it.

Using the <Limit> Tag

The <Limit> tag is one of the most important tags in proftpd. It enables you to set limits on directories. This can be helpful in controlling how users interact with the directories being configured.

The `<Limit>` tag can be used to control the following operations:

- The ability to change the current working directory (CWD)
- The ability to make new directories (MKD)
- The ability to rename files (RNFR)
- The ability to delete files (DELE)
- The ability to remove a directory (RMD)
- The ability to retrieve a file from the server (RETR)
- The ability to transfer a file to the server (STOR)
- The ability to execute any of the reading command groups, such as RETR and STAT (READ)
- The ability to execute any of the writing command groups, such as MKD and RMD (WRITE)
- The ability to execute any of the directory listing command groups, such as LIST (DIRS)
- The ability to execute any ftp command (ALL)

As you can see from the previous list, you can set limits on individual commands or on a group of them all at once. The `<Limit>` is frequently used within a `<Directory>` context, but can be used in other contexts.

To fully understand how this tag works, let's look at an example. Suppose that you do not want your users to be able to see any part of the system other than their homes using FTP. You should first deny them the ability to see any directory in the whole system:

```
<Directory />
    <Limit DIRS>
        DenyAll
    </Limit>
</Directory>
```

Then, you should allow them to see their own homes:

```
<Directory ~>
    <Limit DIRS>
        AllowAll
    </Limit>
</Directory>
```

Now your users will be able to list only the contents of their own homes. If they try to change the current working directory to anything other than their homes, they will get a `permission denied` message.

This setup does have one flaw, though. If a user wants to transfer a file from another directory other than her home, she can do so if she knows the exact path to it. For instance, if a user knows that there is a file called `passwords.txt` in `/usr/local/data`, she will be able to download it by explicitly using the full path to the file. To fix this flaw, you should add READ WRITE to the first limit:

```
<Directory />
    <Limit DIRS READ WRITE>
        DenyAll
    </Limit>
</Directory>
```

And add it to the second one:

```
<Directory ~>
    <Limit DIRS READ WRITE>
        AllowAll
    </Limit>
</Directory>
```

There, now it's more secure.

You should be careful of how you order your rules. If you were to switch the positions of the previous <Directory> blocks, the effect would be that your users couldn't see, read, or write anything in their homes. The idea is to block global access and then allow certain paths.

> **TIP**
>
> Denying your users the ability to browse beyond their homes using the method we just explained can be accomplished using one tag. Using the DefaultRoot tag, you can jail your users within the boundaries of their home directories. For example, entering DefaultRoot ~ users in your configuration file will cause the root directory of any user in the group users to become that user's home directory. When that user logs in, he will not be able to move outside his home directory. It should be noted, however, that this method is not 100% secure—there are ways for a user to escape from this jail. This is why the method we explained previously is more secure.

So far, you have used the AllowAll and DenyAll tags to tell <Limit> what to do. You also can use AllowUser, AllowGroup, DenyUser, and DenyGroup to be more flexible. Each of these tags takes a user, a group, or a list of them as parameters. For example, the following allows the user john *and* the user mary:

```
<Limit READ>
    AllowUser john, mary
</Limit>
```

In contrast, the following code allows the user john but not the user mary. The ! is a logical NOT:

```
<Limit READ>
    AllowUser john, !mary
</Limit>
```

Miscellaneous Options

The following are some of the common tags that can be used to further define how proftpd works:

- **AllowRetrieveRestart**—This option, when set to on (default), allows clients to resume interrupted file retrievals. It's recommended that you set this option to on.

- **AllowStoreRestart**—This option, when set to on, allows clients to resume interrupted file uploads to the server. We don't recommended that you set it to on because this will allow various users to corrupt existing files. Its default setting is off.

- **CDPath**—This is exactly like the shell's CDPATH environment variable. It takes a path as an argument, allowing the user to directly change her working directory to any directory inside that path by just specifying its name. For example, suppose you have a directory called /usr/local and inside it you have /usr/local/files. Setting CDPath to /usr/local/, as in the following:

```
CDPath /usr/local/
```

will allow any user to change her working directory to /usr/local/files by just typing the following regardless of where that user is currently positioned on the filesystem:

```
cd files
```

- **DefaultTransferMode**—ftp uses one of two modes of transfer—ASCII for text files and Binary for others. Usually, ftp clients tell the server which one to use, depending on the type of file being transferred. You can tell proftpd which to use by default just in case. The following is an example:

```
DefaultTransferMode    binary
```

- **HiddenStor**—Setting this option to on will cause proftpd to store incoming files as hidden files until the transfer is complete. When the file is fully transferred, proftpd will unhide it. This is useful if you want to ensure that no one attempts to download a file that is still being uploaded to the server.

- **HideNoAccess**—Entering this option in your configuration file will tell proftpd to hide any directories that the currently logged in user has no permission to see. What is meant by permission here is the Linux filesystem permission. Because the user will be unable to access the directories anyway, you might as well tell proftpd to hide them using this option. This option applies to <Directory> and <Anonymous> sections.

- **MaxLoginAttempts**—This is how many times proftpd will let the user attempt to log in incorrectly before disconnecting him.

- **ShowDotFiles**—Setting this option to on will cause proftpd to show hidden dot files.

Troubleshooting

I can't connect to the FTP server.

This can be due to various reasons. Are you sure you enabled ftp in `/etc/inetd.conf`? If not, then do so now. Check that you are connecting to the correct machine IP and port—FTP uses port 21.

I connected but I can't log in.

To log in, you have to be a valid user on the machine. Use your valid username and password. If you don't have one, ask your system administrator to create an account for you.

Anonymous logins are not allowed.

You have to allow anonymous logins in the configuration file. Refer back to the previous section "Anonymous FTP" for more information on how to do this.

I can't see the contents of my home directory.

If you attempted the `<Limit>` example we used earlier, be sure that you entered the commands in the exact same order as the example. If you switch the `<Directory>` tags, the final effect will be a `DenyAll` for everything. Otherwise, check all your `<Directory>` and `<Limit>` tags, especially their order.

I can't see any of my dot files.

Make sure that the `ShowDotFiles` tag is set to on in your configuration file.

Some directories are hidden when I use FTP, even though I can see them when I telnet to the machine.

This is because you have the `HideNoAccess` tag set to on. proftpd will then hide any directories you do not have permission to see. ●

Configuring the Mail Server

sendmail: The Mail Server

Email has been and still is one of the main functions of the Internet. *Email*, which stands for electronic mail, enables you to send mail messages to anyone on the Internet from your computer. The mail will reach that person in a matter of minutes, meaning it's high speed communication.

Sending an email message requires you to have a mail program and mail server. Contrary to what most people think, you don't really need to have an email account or even an email address to send an email message. You need these if you want to receive mail, but to send email, you need only a mail server and mail program. When you write an email and instruct your mail program to send it, the mail program will contact the mail server. The mail server will receive the message from your mail program and, using the email address or addresses included in the message, will send it to your recipient(s).

To be a mail server, your machine must be running a *Mail Transport Agent* (MTA), which is the program that runs on the mail server and gets contacted by the mail program. The MTA is then responsible for delivering your message to its correct recipients, or bouncing it back at you if it can't deliver it. It acts much like the postal worker in real life.

The most commonly used MTA is sendmail, written by the University of Berkeley. It has been around for quite a while and has proven to be very reliable and stable. sendmail is included with SuSE Linux along with a configuration module in YaST.

Installing sendmail

sendmail is part of SuSE Linux and is usually installed by default. But, just in case it wasn't, here are the package requirements.

Package requirements:

Series n:

■ sendmail

When you are finished installing it, you should start configuring it as discussed in the next section.

Configuring sendmail

sendmail is configured via its configuration file `/etc/sendmail.cf`. If you look at that file, you might realize that you don't understand a lot of what's in it. The format of this file is very complex, which usually makes configuring sendmail a task not for the faint hearted. It takes time, patience, and a *lot* of reading to understand how to configure this file. Even worse, sendmail's definitive reference happens to be 792 pages long.

So, do you have to deal with this mess? You will be happy to know that the answer to this question is no. SuSE Linux has taken care of all this for you—thanks to the sendmail configuration module in YaST. Using the module, you can configure sendmail without having to know anything about /etc/sendmail.cf. SuSE has prepared a few common configurations that should fit your needs just fine. To configure your mail server using YaST, follow these steps:

1. Log in as root.

2. Run YaST.

3. Navigate to System administration, Network configuration, Configure sendmail and press Enter.

4. As you can see in Figure 20.1, the sendmail configuration module appears.

FIGURE 20.1

The sendmail configuration module in YaST.

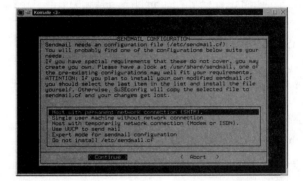

5. You can choose from four presets or you can choose Expert mode to manually enter the values for sendmail.

6. The first preset is Host With Permanent Network Connection. You can use this if your system has a permanent connection to the Internet.

7. Use the preset Single User Machine Without Network Connection if your machine doesn't have a network connection. You might be wondering why in the world you would set up an MTA in that case. Well, several of your applications send you internal mail messages to report progress and errors. Remember, even when Linux is not connected to a network, there is a network inside it.

8. Use the preset Host With Temporary Network Connection (Modem or ISDN) if you have a dial-up connection. This enables you to use your machine as a mail server; and when you connect, your email will be sent.

9. If you use UUCP to connect to a network, choose Use UUCP To Send Email.

10. Finally, when you encounter the Expert Mode For sendmail Configuration, proceed with caution. Be sure you know what you're doing. Try this if none of the presets work for you.

11. If you want a total manual configuration for your sendmail, choose Do Not Install /etc/sendmail.cf. This will prevent YaST from interfering with your configuration.

Part
III

Ch
20

12. Press Continue to save and apply your changes.

13. An `/etc/sendmail.cf` file will be created for you. Start sendmail by typing the following:

```
#/sbin/init.d/sendmail start
```

sendmail now should be all configured and running. You must attempt to manually configure sendmail to feel the amount of pain that using YaST avoided! Just use any mail program and have it use your machine as the mail server.

Expert Mode for Configuring sendmail

So, you tried the presets, but you now want more. This is where the expert mode comes in handy. You will be asked to enter the parameters that will be used to configure sendmail for you. To use the expert mode, follow these steps:

1. Log in as root.

2. Run YaST.

3. Navigate to System administration, Network configuration, Configure sendmail and press Enter.

4. The sendmail configuration module pops up (refer to Figure 20.1).

5. Highlight the expert mode and press Enter.

6. The sendmail Expert Mask appears (see Figure 20.2).

FIGURE 20.2
Expert mode for configuring sendmail with YaST.

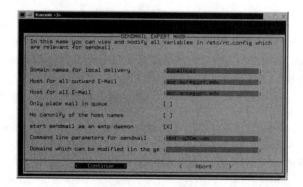

7. The first field is the Domain names for local delivery. sendmail needs to know which email is to be sent locally, and therefore should be stored locally. Enter a list of all the domains that are considered local. This usually is localhost and your hostname.

8. The next field is the Host for all outward Email. If you are on a slow connection, you can have your outgoing emails delivered to another email server that handles sending them for you. This could be your ISP's mail server. Just enter the address of that server here. You should define the protocol to be used, as well. For example, if your ISP's mail server is SMTP and is called `mail.isp.com`, the entry would be `smtp:mail.isp.com`.

9. The next field is Host for all Email. This is exactly like the previous option, except that it will handle *all* your email, even if it's local.

10. The Only place mail in queue is used if you don't have a permanent connection. This option enables any email you send to be queued only until you run the command `sendmail -q` to send it.

11. sendmail always will attempt to resolve the addresses of the recipients in the message to fully qualified domain names before it sends it. If you do not have a DNS server set up, this will not work. In that case, you should check the option No canonify of the host names to turn off this resolving mechanism.

12. The next option should be checked to start sendmail as an smtp daemon. This is recommended.

13. You can enter any command-line arguments you want to be used when sendmail is launched in the Command Line Parameters for sendmail field.

14. Press Continue to save and apply your changes.

15. An `/etc/sendmail.cf` will be created for you. Start sendmail by typing the following:

```
#/sbin/init.d/sendmail start
```

You now can test your configuration by trying to send an email using your new server as your mail server.

Manual Configuration of sendmail

If you still want more control over the configuration files, you will need to generate `/etc/sendmail.cf` by yourself. This will be a totally manual process and will not be easy. First you should make sure that YaST will not interfere with your configuration process. To do so, follow these steps:

1. Log in as root.

2. Run YaST.

3. Navigate to System administration, Network configuration, Configure sendmail and press Enter.

4. The sendmail configuration module appears (refer to Figure 20.1).

5. Highlight Do Not Install `/etc/sendmail.cf` and press Enter.

6. SuSEConfig will launch and update your system. YaST will not interfere with your sendmail configuration from now on.

Part
III

Ch
20

To generate your own `/etc/sendmail.cf` file, you can use the `/etc/mail/linux.mc` as a template with which to start. This file uses m4 macros to configure sendmail. When you are finished configuring this file, just run this command to have it generate `/etc/sendmail.cf` for you:

```
# m4 /etc/mail/linux.mc > /etc/sendmail.cf
```

The m4 macro preprocessor will use `/etc/mail/linux.mc` to generate sendmail's configuration file for you. It is still better than having to configure `/etc/sendmail.cf` directly.

Troubleshooting

I can't send any emails, and the server is not responding.

Make sure that sendmail is running. You can check this by running the following command:

`#rcsendmail status`

If it is not running, start it by entering the following:

`#rcsendmail start`

I have a dial-up connection and when I queue my mail, it doesn't get sent when I connect.

You must run the command `sendmail -q` when you connect so that your queued mail gets sent. You can enter this command in your dial-up connection scripts or in Kppp. ●

## CHAPTER 21

Configuring the Dial-In Server

A Briefing on Dial-In Servers

One of Linux's most important features is its capability to act as a fully functional ISP. Over the past two years, Linux has become one of the cheapest fully functional ISP servers. Many ISPs in Europe have replaced their old servers with Linux to give their customers better accessibility at lower costs. In addition, most new ISPs use Linux as their main dial-in server. In this chapter, you will learn how to set up dial-in on your SuSE Linux. You also will learn how to set up a full ISP if you plan to use SuSE Linux as a fully functional ISP with users who can have full access to the Internet and others who are restricted to fewer services, such as only email or only FTP.

Why Would I Set Up Dial-In on My SuSE Linux?

When you set up your SuSE Linux as a dial-in server, you get the advantage of being able to access it wherever you are. For example, you can dial in to your SuSE Linux from a laptop and have access to all the facilities it provides. Not only will you be able to access the files on the system, but you also will be able to run the programs on SuSE Linux. In addition, you can run X Windows and export the display to the machine from which you are dialing. In other words, you will be able to access your SuSE Linux as if you were sitting right in front of it.

Why Would I Use SuSE Linux in My ISP?

Using SuSE Linux in ISPs lowers the cost required to make up the ISP. SuSE Linux can be configured to provide the best performance for a dial-in server. You can tweak the configurations that apply to each group and even increase the user level. For example, you can have a user group that can access only email, another group that can access only FTP, and another that has full access to the Internet.

Hardware Requirements

Hardware requirements for a home user who wants to access his SuSE Linux are simple. You need only to have a modem connected to your computer and a phone or ISDN line. You can use the same modem you use to dial out.

Software Requirements

Package requirements:

Series n:

- mgetty

Kernel requirements:

- Network Device Support
- PPP (point-to-point) support
- SLIP (serial line) support

Configuration Basics

Before you start setting up the system for dial-in, you must configure and set up your hardware. To set up the modem or ISDN equipment, see Chapter 23, "Connectivity to the Internet." After you have set up your modem and made sure that it can dial out, you can start configuring your SuSE Linux for dial-in.

The following are the three steps for configuring SuSE Linux for dial-in:

1. Set up mgetty.
2. Set up the authentication method.
3. Set up pppd.

In practice, these are the only steps required to configure either a simple dial-in server or a full ISP dial-in server. One difference does exist, however—the privileges and security issues you must be aware of if you are configuring a full ISP.

getty and *mgetty+sendfax*

getty is a special program invoked by `init` to enable users to log in. It opens a `tty` line and sets its mode. An example of a `tty` line is your console. It then prints the login prompt, reads the username, and starts a login process for the user.

On the other hand, mgetty is a getty replacement with hayes-compatible data and data/fax modems. Using these capabilities, mgetty enables system logins over `ttyS`, therefore enabling users to log in over serial connections. mgetty can be set up to receive fax as well as voice. In this chapter, we will cover only the capabilities that cause your computer to act as a dial-in server.

mgetty Configuration Files

Older versions of mgetty required that you configure it through the source code definitions. Luckily, this has changed and all the configurations for mgetty can be done through the configuration files located in `/etc/mgetty+sendfax`. The directory contains various configuration files:

- `dialin.config`—If you have installed a caller ID service, you can tell mgetty to (or not to) answer certain phone numbers by configuring the entries in this file.

Part

III

Ch

21

- `login.config`—This file describes how mgetty should behave if the user who dials in logs in successfully.
- `mgetty.config`—In this file, you should specify to which modems/ports mgetty should listen. Each modem or port can have its own configuration that should be used by mgetty.
- `voice.conf`—This file is used to configure your SuSE Linux as a voice answering machine.

In this chapter, we will discuss the first three files. In addition, one more configuration file exists that you should edit. You should add an entry to the `/etc/inittab` file to cause mgetty to start on system boot.

N O T E   mgetty is not a normal program that is run by hand. For mgetty to function correctly, it must be called by `init`. This requires mgetty to have an entry in the `/etc/inittab` file. ■

Preparing *inittab*

As root, open the `/etc/inittab` in your favorite editor. SuSE Linux has prepared a default entry for mgetty around line 85 in SuSE Linux 6.3. The default entry is commented out; remove the comment hash and save the file. If you have lost the entry, it should look like the following:

```
mo:23:respawn:/usr/sbin/mgetty -s 38400 modem
```

The `modem` in the previous line represents the modem port on your system. If you have set up your modem using YaST as described in Chapter 23, you will have a `/dev/modem` symbolic link to your mode port. You can specify other ports to use by changing `modem` to the port your modem uses. The `-s` option sets the speed of this modem to 38400. In fact, setting up options for the modem in `inittab` is not recommended; you should use the `/etc/mgetty+sendfax/mgetty.config` to set options instead.

After you have edited the entry in `/etc/inittab`, you should activate this entry by issuing the following command as root:

```
bash#kill -1 1
```

Preparing *mgetty.config*

The `mgetty.config` configuration file is organized with one global section followed by per port configuration sections, with the global configuration section coming first. A simple `mgetty.config` file should look like the following:

```
speed 38400    #set the speed to 38400 for all modems
rings 3        #answer after the third ring
port modem     #modem on port /dev/modem
```

In this configuration, mgetty will answer calls on the port modem after three rings. modem should be a symbolic link to your modem if you have set up your modem using YaST. It will set the speed of the modem to 38400bps.

mgetty.config can be used to configure more than one port. The following example shows a more complicated setup:

```
speed 38400    #set the speed to 38400 for all modems
port-owner uucp
port-group uucp
port-mode 0664
rings 3        #answer after the third ring
port modem     #modem on port /dev/modem
port ttyS1     #another modem at /dev/ttyS1
rings 1        #this modem answers after one ring
```

In this example, the modems are owned by the uucp user, which belongs to the uucp group. The port mode is set to 0664. Remember that devices on SuSE Linux are treated as normal files in which you can write and read data. By setting the mode to 0664, you give permission to users belonging to the uucp group to use the modems. The system has two modems, one that is a symbolic link, modem, and another that is at /dev/ttyS1. The modem on modem will answer an incoming call after three rings, while the modem on ttyS1 will answer after one ring.

More on *mgetty.config* mgetty can be configured and tweaked to suit a large number of modems and faxes. It also can use chat scripts to set up the modem configuration to suit all the modems that work on Linux. The default mgetty.config file that comes with SuSE Linux contains examples of how to make several configurations for modems. If you use a specific initialization string to initialize your modem, you should configure mgetty to use it.

Preparing *login.config*

Using the login.config file, you can determine what mgetty should do after a successful login. In fact, if you have followed the approach that was discussed in the previous examples, you already have made what is called a SLIP account. You can call your computer from another computer and you will log in to a terminal.

This happens because the login.config file contains two lines that come pre-configured with SuSE Linux and are not commented out:

```
/AutoPPP/ -    a_ppp   /usr/sbin/pppd auth
*    -    -    /bin/login @
```

If the file is missing or empty, the second line is executed by default. The first line automates the connections made from a Windows 9x box. If you are connecting from a Windows9x box, you don't have to make it show a terminal after dialing. Instead, you can fill in the User Name and Password fields in the main connection dialog. If the file is missing, you need to show a terminal after dialing so that you can log in to your SuSE Linux.

Part

III

Ch

21

The format of this file is as follows:

```
username userid utmp_entry login_program [arguments]
```

The following are the format options:

- username—This is the login name first sent by the dialing users. You can use an asterisk (*) to specify a default behavior. If the user first sends /AutoPPP/, you can redirect the login program to the pppd program and have it perform the authentication.
- userid—This is a valid SuSE Linux username. You must use a hyphen (-) to not set a login user id and keep the uid/euid root for /bin/login.
- utmp_entry—This will appear when a user executes the who command to list users currently logged in. Use - to not set a utmp_entry. You should not set a utmp_entry if you are executing /bin/login. Use the at sign (@) to set it to the username. The utmp_entry should not exceed eight characters.
- login_program [arguments]—The program that will be executed, with the arguments passed in [arguments]. You have to use @ to send the username entered to the login program.

For example, the following line makes mgetty wait for a connection from a Windows 9x box, which will eventually send an AutoPPP request:

```
/AutoPPP/  -    a_ppp    /usr/sbin/pppd auth
```

When a connection is established, mgetty will keep the root uid/euid and write a utmp_entry of a_ppp. The authentication is performed entirely through the pppd. This is why mgetty did not send a @.

Preparing *dialin.config*

If you have installed a caller ID, you can filter the calls mgetty should answer and those it should not answer. For example, say you have a mobile phone and notebook and, to increase security, you want to restrict the calls your SuSE Linux should answer to only calls you make through your mobile phone. To do this, you use the dialin.config, which has a very simple format. The grammar of this file is as follows:

- *number* or *prefix*—This is the number or prefix to allow.
- !*number* or !*prefix*—This is the number or prefix that will not be answered.
- none—These are the callers whose numbers could not be identified.
- all—This designates all numbers.
- OUT_OF_AREA—These are numbers that are out of the area.

The following example allows only numbers we know and disallows answering for out-of-area numbers:

```
#disallow all numbers
!all
#disallow calls whose numbers couldn't be identified
!none
#disallows out of area
!OUT_OF_AREA
#allow the following numbers
4186813
2436371
#allow this prefix
456
```

N O T E To restart mgetty, issue the following command:

bash#kill -9 `ps aux|grep mgetty`

In actuality, this command kills mgetty, and then whenever init finds that mgetty is down, it spawns it again.

Preparing PPP

Initiating a PPP connection between your SuSE Linux and a client is one of the most important factors for establishing an ISP. As you have learned in the previous sections, you can have pppd handle the authentication. This is important for two authentication protocols: PAP and CHAP. In this section and the following ISP example, we will set up pppd without pap and CHAP. The next sections will set up PAP and CHAP.

N O T E For people with ISDN connections, the same rules that apply on pppd should apply on ipppd. Whenever the options file is mentioned, the ioptions file should be used instead.

The /etc/ppp/options File   If you use your modem to dial out and want to use it to dial in as well, you must ensure that the /etc/ppp/options file works for both. The options to prepare this file to dial out are discussed in Chapter 23. In general, you need to have only the following lines:

```
modem
-detach
proxyarp
lock
```

For this example, assume that your SuSE Linux has only one modem to which you're dialing in using terminal login.

The /etc/ppp/options.ttySxx Files   Each serial port on your SuSE Linux can have its own configuration file. For example, you can have a /etc/ppp/options.modem in which modem is a symbolic link to your modem serial port. If you have a multi-port board—a board that has more than one serial board designed for ISPs—each serial port can have its own options file, too. This configuration is integral to assigning IPs to users dialing in to this serial port.

Part
III

Ch
21

The following is an example of a `/etc/ppp/options.modem` that will assign the caller an IP of 192.168.1.2 while assigning SuSE Linux an IP of 192.168.1.1:

```
# server   : client
192.168.1.1: 192.168.1.2
```

If you have more than one modem or a multi-port board, you can assign IPs to callers by modifying the files. You can accomplish this using the following example, which assumes you are on a class C network with IPs starting from 208.159.7.0 to 208.159.7.255:

```
/etc/options/ttyC0

# server    : client
208.159.7.100:208.159.7.101


/etc/options/ttyC1

# server    : client
208.159.7.100:208.159.7.102


/etc/options/ttyC2

# server    : client
208.159.7.100:208.159.7.103


/etc/options/ttyC3

# server    : client
208.159.7.100:208.159.7.104
```

A Dial-In Server Example

In this example, you will learn how to apply the configurations discussed in the previous sections. The following are assumed:

- The SuSE Linux server is connected over a LAN—SuSE Linux has the IP 192.186.1.24 over this LAN. The DNS servers of the LAN are 192.186.1.1 and 192.186.1.2.

- The SuSE Linux server has only one modem, which has a symbolic link `/dev/modem` that points to the correct serial port—You use this modem to dial to the Internet, and now you want to use it to dial in. The phone line to which SuSE Linux is connected supports caller ID, as does the modem.

- You will be connecting to SuSE Linux using Windows 9x—Throughout this example, the machine dialing in and its OS will be called the *client*. You will be dialing in to this server from the following number: 4186813. All other numbers will be disallowed.

Your goal is to contact the SuSE Linux server, log in to it, and view shares of the LAN on your Windows 9x Network Neighborhood.

The following steps are required to perform such an operation:

1. Set up Samba on your SuSE Linux server. This is important if you want to enable your clients to see the Windows shares on the LAN. Check whether your SuSE Linux server can see the shares.

2. Set up the workgroup in your Windows 9x to be the same workgroup as in your LAN. This step and the previous one are discussed in more detail in Chapter 15, "Connectivity with Windows Through Samba."

After you have set up these prerequisites, you can move on to configuring the dial-in facility.

The Configuration for the Simple Dial-In Server

All the settings in the following section must be performed as root.

Add the following entry in the /etc/inittab:

```
mo:23:respawn:/usr/sbin/mgetty -s 38400 modem
```

After you have added the entry, issue the following command:

```
bash#kill -1 1
```

Then, add the following lines to the /etc/mgetty+sendfax/mgetty.config file:

```
speed 38400    #set the speed to 38400 for all modems
rings 3        #answer after the third ring
port modem     #modem on port /dev/modem
```

Check whether your /etc/mgetty+sendfax/login.config file has the following entry. Because it is a default, it's not important that the file has this entry; however, you should make sure that it is not overridden:

```
*    -    -    /bin/login @
```

Add the following lines to your /etc/mgetty+sendfax/dialin.config:

```
#disallow all numbers
!all
#allow the following numbers
4186813
```

Next, add the following lines to the /etc/ppp/options file:

```
ms-dns 192.186.1.1
ms-dns 192.186.1.2
modem
proxyarp
-detach
lock
```

Then, add the following lines to the /etc/ppp/options.modem file:

```
# server   : client
192.186.1.24: 192.186.1.xxx
```

Part
III

Ch
21

In the previous code, xxx replaces the IP number you want to assign to your client when she logs in. You should not assign an IP that is used by another client on the network.

Setting Up the Windows 9x Client

To set up the Windows 9x side of the connection, follow these steps:

1. Double-click My Computer to open it.

2. Double-click Dial-Up Networking.

3. Double-click Make New Connection.

4. In the Make New Connection dialog, enter a name for the new connection. In this example, call it SuSE Linux. Now, you need to configure your modem to show a terminal window from which you can log in to your SuSE Linux. Click Configure to open the Modem Properties dialog. Click the Options tab and check the Bring up Terminal Window after Dialing checkbox. Click OK to accept the changes. In the Make New Connection dialog, click Next to begin setting up the phone number.

5. Enter the phone number to which your SuSE Linux is connected. When you have completed filling in the information, click Finish.

After you have made the new connection, double-click it to make a new connection to your SuSE Linux. When you connect to your SuSE Linux, a terminal window should pop up asking for your username and password. Enter your username and password to log in to your SuSE Linux.

When you see the bash prompt, enter pppd. This will start pppd with the configuration you previously set up. Click the Continue button in your terminal window to start the PPP connection.

What You Can Do

Using this simple configuration, you should be able to view all the Windows shares on the LAN from your Network Neighborhood. Click the Network Neighborhood on your desktop to access them. You also can download your SuSE Linux local mail. As you can see, you have access to all the facilities SuSE Linux provides as if you were sitting right there in front of it.

To run SuSE Linux commands, you must telnet to it and run those commands. Click Start, Run and enter telnet 192.186.1.24 in the Run dialog box.

SuSE Linux comes with freeware and shareware X servers for Windows 9x. You can install these packages if you want to run X programs on your Windows 9x. The X server for Windows 9x is on the first CD in the path cdrom:\dosutils\mix. You must telnet to your SuSE Linux and export the display to your IP. While running the X server for Windows 9x, issue the following command to the bash prompt in the telnet session:

```
bash#export DISPLAY=192.186.1.xxx:0
```

In the previous command, xxx is the last three digits of the client IP. Now, you can start X-Windows programs that will run on your Windows 9x. Enter the following command:

```
bash#xmessage "Hello from SuSE Linux Dial-In Server"
```

Setting Up PAP

Password Authentication Protocol (*PAP*) works almost the same way as the normal login procedure. The client sends a username and password, which might be encrypted in some cases, to the server. The server checks the username and password and authenticates the client accordingly.

PAP authentication is performed through the pppd. In fact, what makes PAP such a widely used protocol is that it does not require a terminal window for a user to log in. Also, in cases in which the password is sent encrypted, the client can ensure that her password is always safe.

To set up PAP, make sure you do the following:

- Include an entry in /etc/ppp/options for PAP.
- Set up users in /etc/ppp/pap-secrets.

The entry in /etc/ppp/options should be the following:

```
require-pap
```

Add the following entry in the /etc/ppp/options to enable your SuSE Linux users to connect using their SuSE Linux usernames and passwords for PAP authentication:

```
login
```

You should bear in mind that pap-secrets works for both incoming and outgoing connections. SuSE Linux comes with a pap-secrets file that contains some pre-configuration for most of the ISPs in Germany.

To configure the pap-secrets file for inbound connections, add the entries as follows:

```
# User         Server         Secret         Address
```

The fields in this file are explained in the following list:

- User—The username the connecting client should use.
- Server—The server name, mainly, your hostname.
- Secret—A secret word or sentence in quotes.
- Address—IP address or host address of the caller.

Part
III

Ch
21

The `pap-secrets` file is used in SuSE Linux to decide which users to block from using the pppd. So, you can decide which users you want to keep from using the `pppd` and add them to a list in the following format:

```
username          hostname          "*"
```

In the previous code, `username` is the SuSE Linux username you want to block from using pppd and `hostname` is your SuSE Linux IP address or hostname.

Setting Up CHAP

Challenge Handshake Authentication Protocol (*CHAP*) ensures better security because passwords always are encrypted. CHAP is more powerful than PAP in the sense that it sends requests to the client to solve the challenge sent to it during the connection time. The server sends the hostname along with a random string to the client. The client looks up the hostname and checks for the secret associated with the hostname. After the client has found the secret, it combines it with the string that was sent and encrypts them both. The client then sends them back to the server, which tests whether the results are correct. The server continues checking the client every now and then to see whether the client changed.

Setting up CHAP is as easy as setting up PAP. The secrets file for CHAP is located in `/etc/ppp/chap-secrets` and has the same rules as the PAP secrets file. Read the previous section "Setting Up PAP" for more information on how to set up this file:

```
require-chap
login
```

You will also have to set up the `/etc/ppp/chap-secrets` file as described previously.

Limiting Services

To establish an ISP using SuSE Linux, you must set up either one of the previous configurations. We recommend that you use CHAP instead of PAP for your PPP users. An ISP usually offers more than just PPP service; some users might want to have email accounts as well. This requires different levels of configuration for each type of user.

To limit users connecting to SuSE Linux to using only email or FTP, make sure your `/etc/options` file does not contain the following options:

```
defaultroute
proxyarp
```

Instead, make sure it includes the following lines:

```
nodefaultroute
noproxyarp
```

Eliminating the `defaultroute` and `proxyarp` options ensures that users will be able to access only the SuSE Linux server—meaning they will only be able to grab their emails or FTP to the SuSE Linux server.

For users whom you want to be able to access the Internet through SuSE Linux, add the following lines to the `.ppprc` that resides in their home directories:

```
defaultroute
proxyarp
```

Troubleshooting

I can't dial in to my SuSE Linux. It does not answer. Why is that?

This might be due to several reasons:

- mgetty isn't running or was run by hand. Make sure that mgetty has an entry in the `/etc/inittab` file as discussed in this chapter.
- mgetty isn't configured on the correct modem port. Review your configuration and make sure that mgetty is listening to the correct port.
- Make sure the number you are dialing in isn't one of the disallowed numbers if you have a caller ID installed.

I'm trying to establish a connection through the terminal. The connection dies when I start pppd.

This is an `/etc/options` misconfiguration. Some people need to have the `-detach` option in this file.

I can't see any machine beyond the server. Why is that?

The `/etc/options` file needs to have the following lines to make a route entry for the client:

```
defaultroute
proxyarp
```

## CHAPTER 22

Setting Up SuSE Linux as a Proxy Server

In this chapter

What Is a Proxy Server?

The Internet is growing day by day, and is becoming more of a necessity to our lives than ever before. Speed is the buzz word these days—we all want faster Internet connections. Several techniques and technologies are currently available to meet this demand. One of these technologies is the proxy server.

A *proxy server* is a program that you can use to speed up the retrieval of frequently visited material on the Internet. To understand what a proxy server is, let's look at a common scenario. Let's assume that your system is configured to use a proxy server. When you attempt to visit SuSE's Web page at http://www.suse.com, your browser will send the request to the running proxy server. The proxy server will then make the connection to SuSE's Web site and retrieve the page. The server will send your browser a copy of that page and save another copy on the hard disk. The next time you want to view SuSE's Web site, the proxy server will simply send your browser a copy of the page it already has on the hard disk. The Internet connection will seem much faster to you because the page will almost immediately pop up when you send the request.

This process of keeping a copy of the pages you visit on a hard disk is known as *caching*. Proxy servers cache requested pages on a hard disk in case they are requested again. Proxy servers handle most of the common protocols used on the Internet, of which the most important are HTTP and FTP.

Proxy servers are used not only to speed up Internet connections, but to perform a lot of other functions, too. You can use a proxy server to allow machines that have no Internet connection to browse the Web by using a proxy server installed on one machine that does have Internet access. For example, say you have two PCs at home, and they are connected together via a network cable. One of them has a modem, but the other one doesn't. You could connect to the Internet and run a proxy server and then configure the other machine to use that server. With this configuration, both machines can browse the Web using one Internet connection.

Well-configured proxy servers can be used as a controlling mechanism for your users. A large company might be interested in setting up a proxy server that blocks access to certain non–work-related Web sites from their employees. This ensures that working hours are not wasted browsing irrelevant Internet sites.

Proxy servers have a wide spectrum of uses that are limited only by your imagination. SuSE Linux comes with one of the best proxy servers available—squid. Squid is an open source proxy server that offers very good performance and includes support for multiple proxy server uses.

Installing the Squid Proxy Server

To install squid, you will use YaST. The package requirements for squid are the following:

Package requirements:

Series n:

- squid2

Kernel requirements:

- none

When you are finished installing squid, you will need to modify your system to run squid at boot up. Again, use YaST to do this:

1. Run YaST.
2. Navigate to System Administration, Change Configuration File and press Enter.
3. You use this dialog to configure system parameters. You need to find the squid parameter. Press F4 and a small dialog will pop up. Type squid and press Enter to have YaST search the system variables for squid. Make sure you type SQUID in SuSE 6.2 and below since these are not case insensitive like in SuSE 6.3.
4. As you can see in Figure 22.1, YaST has found the squid variable, which is called START_SQUID. Press Enter to change its value to Yes.

FIGURE 22.1

Using this dialog, you can control all the various system variables, such as the squid start flag.

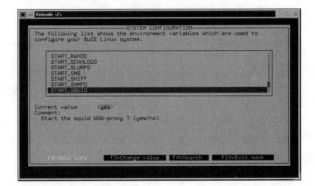

5. Press F10 to save your changes.
6. Exit YaST.

Now squid will run automatically on system boot up. It is not running now, so you will have to either start it manually now or reboot the system. Before you attempt to start it, you should first configure it.

Running Squid for the First Time

Now that you have successfully installed squid, you will want to test it. Simply running it and trying to connect to it using your Web browser will not work, however. This is because squid's default configuration does not allow for clients to connect to the proxy server.

Basic Configuration

Squid is configured through the configuration file /etc/squid.conf. As is the case with most of the configuration files, this is a text file that you will need to edit. This file can actually be considered a manual because of the vast amount of documentation it contains. Every option is preceded with detailed text on what it's supposed to do and how to configure it.

You're probably very eager to test your proxy server, so we'll start with a minimal configuration. The default configuration does not allow clients to connect to the proxy server. This is good, though, because if you turn on your proxy server by mistake, no one will abuse it and share your connection with you.

Let's learn how to configure your proxy server to allow clients to use it, and how to configure your browser to use it. Log in as root and open /etc/squid.conf using your favorite editor.

All the documentation in the file is in the form of comments. Comments start with a hash (#). The first section of the file is called NETWORK OPTIONS. The first option here is the http_port, which is the port that squid will use to receive connections. By default, this is 3128. If you want to change it to another port, just uncomment the line #http_port 3128 and change the number of the port. Do not use a port number that is less than 1024 because these ports are reserved for the system to use.

TIP

In Unix, all ports up to 1024 are inaccessible to anyone but root. So, any user program that attempts to use one of those ports to receive connections on will fail. The only way for that program to take hold of a port below 1024 is if it is run by root. You can change the permissions of the program to always run with root ownership regardless of who runs it by using the chmod +s program command. You have to run this command as root *and* the program must be owned by the root user. This is not recommended, however, because it causes security problems and breaches. Consult the program's manual before changing its permissions to be setuid root.

The next thing you want to do is to have squid allow all clients to connect to it. Scroll down the file until you find a tag called http_access. You should find it somewhere around line number 1029. The tag reads:

```
http_access deny all
```

You should change this to the following:

```
http_access allow localhost
```

Save the file and exit. Now it's time to try out your proxy server. First of all, start it. To do that, follow these steps:

1. Log in as root.
2. Change the directory to /sbin/init.d.
3. Start squid by running the following command:
   ```
   # ./squid start
   ```
4. That's it, squid is now started.

The next thing is to configure your browser to use the proxy server. You can easily do this by following these steps:

1. Run your Netscape browser.
2. Click the Edit menu, and click Preferences at the bottom of the menu.
3. The Preferences dialog appears. Click Advanced, Proxies.
4. Click Manual Proxy Configuration.
5. Click the View button. The View Manual Proxy Configuration dialog appears.
6. Enter 127.0.0.1 in the HTTP Proxy field.
7. Enter 3128 in the Port field (see Figure 22.2). If you changed the default port number in squid's configuration file, enter the new one instead.

FIGURE 22.2

Setting up Netscape to use the proxy server.

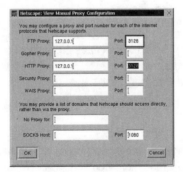

8. Repeat the previous step with the FTP Proxy fields.
9. Close all the dialogs.

Your browser is now ready to use the proxy server. Test it by typing in any URL. The browser will contact the proxy server, asking it to fetch that URL. The server will then fetch it, save a local copy, and return another to the browser. As time passes and your use of the proxy server increases, the pages will load more quickly. This is because squid has cached them on your local disk drive for fast access.

If everything works fine, you might want to have the rest of your applications use the proxy server. Some applications such as GNU wget use a proxy if certain system variables are declared. Other applications use the same behavior. The variables are `http_proxy` and `ftp_proxy`. To set them up, enter the following declarations in `/etc/profile`:

```
export http_proxy=http://localhost:3128
export ftp_proxy=http://localhost:3128
```

Now all applications that use these variables will use the proxy server.

Access Control in Squid

The configuration that you just made is simple but good enough for home use. You told squid to allow all clients that are connecting from localhost. Localhost is your machine, which means that if another machine on the network attempts to use your proxy server, squid will not allow it to do so. Squid uses Access Control Lists (ACL) to define the entities that have access to its services. ACLs are an important concept to understand if you are to properly configure squid.

Actually, you have already used ACLs without knowing it—when you modified `/etc/squid.conf` to include the line `http_access allow localhost`. How do you suppose squid understood what `localhost` is? From a previous ACL. If you look at the section prior to the tag you modified, you will see the following line:

```
acl localhost src 127.0.0.1/255.255.255.255
```

An ACL statement starts with the tag `acl`, followed by the name of the access list you are defining. In this case, it's `localhost`. The `src` tag defines the sources of the access list, which are `127.0.0.1/255.255.255.255` in the case of `localhost`. So, this statement is saying "Define `localhost` as a machine that comes from `127.0.0.1/255.255.255.255`."

Another important ACL is the `all` ACL. This is defined as the following:

```
acl all src 0.0.0.0/0.0.0.0
```

As you can tell by now, this ACL defines `all` to be any machine that matches the IP 0.0.0.0 with netmask 0.0.0.0, which is any machine. So, when you say `http_access deny all`, you are telling squid to deny all machines.

Squid uses ACL statements to know what to do with connecting clients. ACL statements are in the following form:

```
acl-name acl-type string
```

You can define many different ACLs that behave differently. The following are the most common source definition types:

- **src**—These ACLs are used to define client sources by using IPs. For example, you can define an ACL statement for one IP/Netmask like this:
  ```
  acl someone src 192.186.168.17/255.255.255.255
  ```

This defines someone as the client with IP 192.186.168.17. You specify a whole subnet like this:

```
acl mynetwork src 192.186.168.0/255.255.255.0
```

This ACL defines `mynetwork` to be all machines with IP 192.186.168.x. If you wanted to create an ACL for just a few of these machines, the ACL would be as follows:

```
acl friends src 192.186.168.5-192.186.168.56/255.255.255.0
```

Now `friends` is defined as all machines from IP 192.186.168.5 to 192.186.168.56.

- **srcdomain**—This ACL type uses domains rather than IPs to define clients. For example, to define an ACL for all clients coming from `mycompany.com` domain, you would use the following:

```
acl mycompany srcdomain mycompany.com
```

- **srcdom_regx**—This ACL type defines source ACLs using patterns. You can enter a regular expression to define a pattern. The following defines a source ACL for any machine with the word `friend` as part of its domain name:

```
acl friends srcdom_regx friend
```

This ACL is case sensitive, however. To make it case insensitive, use the `-i` option:

```
acl friends srcdom_regx -i friend
```

These were the source definition types; you also can define destination types, such as the following:

- **dst**—To define an ACL for requests to a specific IP, enter the following:

```
acl companyserver dst 192.186.168.17/255.255.255.255
```

This ACL defines `companyserver` as a destination ACL with IP 192.186.168.17.

- **dstdomain**—This is used to define domains. The following creates an ACL for the `infoseek.com` domain:

```
acl searchengine dstdomain infoseek.com
```

- **dstdom_regx**—Destinations also can be patterns. This is particularly useful if you want to block access to a certain genre of sites. You use the `dstdom_regx` type to use patterns. To create an ACL for destinations that contain the word "music" in them, type the following:

```
acl musicsites dstdom_regx music
```

And just like the `srcdom_regx` type, you can use `-i` to make the pattern case insensitive:

```
acl musicsites dstdom_regx -i music
```

- **url_regex**—The previous ACL type blocks domains, but what if you want to block URLs with a specific word in them? You use `url_regex`. To block the "music" from any URL, enter the following:

```
acl music url_regex music
```

■ **time**—This can be used to define time ACLs. You can use this to control when the server is to be used. The format of the time ACL is as follows:

```
acl workhours time [day] [time-range]
```

day can be S (Sunday), M (Monday), T (Tuesday), W (Wednesday), H (Thursday), F (Friday), or A (Saturday). Time range is in the format *start_hour*:*start_minute*-*end_hour*:*end_minute*. The following is an example:

```
acl timeslot time s,a 00:00-08:00
```

This ACL defines timeslot to be on Saturday and Sunday from midnight to 8 a.m.

■ **port**—This can be used to define connections that specify the port. For example, use the following to create an ACL for the common Internet ports such as HTTP and FTP:

```
acl commonports port 80
```

You also can specify a range of ports:

```
acl portrange port 360-1024
```

■ **proto**—This is used to define protocols. To define an ACL for common Internet protocols, type the following:

```
acl commonprotocols proto HTTP FTP
```

The commonprotocols ACL corresponds to HTTP and FTP.

TIP

In all the ACL statements, you can replace the defining statement with a path to a file that has the pattern you want. This is useful if you want to maintain a list of domains without having to edit /etc/squid.conf every time you add a new domain. The format of the ACL is as follows:

```
acl domains destdomain "/etc/domainlist.txt"
```

/etc/domainlist.txt is a file containing a list of domains, with each on a separate line.

These are the most common ACL types. Now that you know them, how can you use them? ACLs are made to define how squid reacts to a connection request. When a client attempts to connect to a squid proxy server, squid checks its access list to see whether this client is allowed to connect or not. This access list is a set of ACLs that define the different entities, but this list alone does not do anything. ACLs are used by another tag called http_access. The http_access tag is responsible for telling squid what to do with connecting clients and their requests.

So, when a client connects, squid goes through the http_access tags to see whether this client is allowed to connect or not. If the client is allowed access, squid checks whether the request the client has made is allowed or not, again by checking the http_access tags. This might sound a bit confusing at first, but a good example will clear up all that confusion.

Say that you have the following section in your /etc/squid.conf file:

```
acl localnetwork src 192.186.168.0/255.255.255.0
acl protocols proto HTTP FTP
```

```
acl localhost src 127.0.0.1/255.255.255.255
acl all src 0.0.0.0/0.0.0.0
http_access allow localnetwork
http_access deny !protocols
http_access deny all
```

The section starts off by defining a few ACLs. It defines localnetwork as the subnet 192.186.168.x, protocols as HTTP and FTP, localhost as the IP of the machine, and all as all IPs.

Then it starts to define access rules using http_access. It tells squid to allow all clients from localnetwork to connect to the server, to deny any protocols other than protocols (the ! means NOT, so the http_access statement says to deny all protocols that are not HTTP and FTP), and finally to deny all IPs.

You might be confused by the last http_access statement, but hold on; enlightenment is on the way. When squid checks for access rules, it goes through the list of rules and tries to match the request with a rule. If it fails with a rule, it checks the next one. So, if a client from localnetwork connects, squid will find a match for it in the first access rule and allow it. When that client requests a Web page, squid will match the protocol with the second access rule and allow it. If squid fails to match to any of the access rules, it will do the opposite of the last rule in the list. Therefore, if the last rule happens to be an allow, it will become a deny and vice versa. This is why it's good practice to enter http_access deny all as your last line. This way, if a matching rule is not found, the last rule will always match and prevent squid from reversing the last rule—whatever it may be—and do something wrong.

CAUTION

Don't ever enter http_access deny all as the first rule. If you do, no one will be able to connect to your proxy because all checks will match to this rule and squid won't proceed to check the rest of the rules. It will simply deny the connection. The same applies for http_access allow all; if you enter it as the first rule, everyone will be allowed to connect regardless of any other rules you have later in the section.

You can get really creative with ACLs and http_access rules. You are limited only by your imagination. You can put ACLs together on the same http_access rule to come up with more complicated rules. For example, to allow friends to use your proxy on Sundays only:

```
acl timeslot time s 00:00:23:59
acl friends src 192.186.160.0/255.255.255.0
acl all src 0.0.0.0/0.0.0.0
http_access allow friends timeslot
http_access deny all
```

Clients connecting from the subnet 192.186.160 will have access to the proxy server only on Sundays.

You can get more information about ACLs and `http_access` rules by reading `/etc/squid.conf`. It has a lot of documentation and examples.

Controlling How Squid Will Use Your System Resources

As is the case with very active programs, you should have a way of controlling the amount of resources that they will attempt to devour. Squid is quite an active program, and it will take whatever amount of resources you give it. Fortunately, you can tell squid how much of your valuable resources to use.

The first parameter that you will want to adjust is the `cache_mem`. This is how much memory squid is going to use for its operations, not how much memory squid is going to use overall. The amount of memory that you specify in this parameter will be exceeded if the need arises. This might happen if the requests to the server are more than the designated memory can handle. Squid will free the extra blocks as soon as the load decreases, however. The following is the format of this parameter:

```
cache_mem      8 MB
```

Of course, you would replace the 8 with the amount of RAM you want squid to use. A good estimate is 5 MB for every 1 GB of cache.

The `maximum_object_size` is used to tell squid the maximum size of an object to save on disk. Any objects larger than the value you set here will not be saved on disk. The following is the format of this parameter:

```
maximum_object_size    4096 KB
```

This is set to 4MB, which is squid's default value for this parameter. This is a reasonable size, but it really depends on your network and surfing habits.

The `cache_dir` parameter tells squid where your cache is and how big it should be. Squid usually has built it values for this, but you can override them with this parameter. The following is the format of this parameter:

```
cache_dir      /var/squid/cache    100    16    256
```

The parameter takes four options. The first is the path to the directory to use as cache— `/var/squid/cache` is the default for SuSE Linux. The second parameter is the size in megabytes of the cache. A reasonable value for starters is 100 MB, but again, this depends on your network and amount of users who will be using the cache. The third option is the number of directories that squid will create under /var/squid/cache to store the caches object in. Squid creates a hierarchy of directories in its cache directory; using the default value of 16 is good enough. The last option is the number of directories that squid will create in each of the 16 directories it creates. You can think of it as a level 1 and level 2 of directories. Using 256 means that in each of the 16 directories, squid will create 256 directories inside it. Again, the defaults are good enough.

Creating a Cache Hierarchy

A *cache hierarchy* is a process in which you have more than one proxy server running with a line of communication between them. Cache hierarchies enable you to connect a network of proxies together to achieve the fastest response possible.

A typical scenario for cache hierarchies is when a user requests a URL from your proxy. If your proxy does not have the page on local disk, it will go ahead and download it from the origin server. If your server is part of a cache hierarchy, it will proceed to ask the other proxies whether they have that URL cached or not. If they do, it downloads it from them and gives it to you; otherwise, it gets it from the origin server.

Caches in cache hierarchies are one of two types—a parent or a sibling. When a proxy fails to find a page in its local cache, it will first ask the sibling caches whether they have it or not. If none of the siblings have it, the server doesn't get the page itself; it asks the parent to get it. If the parent has it cached, it passes it down to your server; if not, it proceeds to ask other servers on its level for it or gets it itself. The whole process is very much like a tree—parents are siblings to each other but parents to their children and so on.

Creating a Cache Hierarchy of Siblings

To have two or more proxies communicate together in a sibling fashion is quite easy. It just requires a few modifications to their configuration files.

Let's say that you have two proxy servers on your network and you want them to communicate together as siblings. The first server is called server1 and the second one is called server2. Here's what you would enter in each of the servers' configuration files:

- In server1:

  ```
  cache_host server2.company.com sibling 3128 3130 proxy-only
  ```

- In server2:

  ```
  cache_host server1.company.com sibling 3128 3130 proxy-only
  ```

That's it; now both servers will communicate together if they can't find a request in their caches. The `cache_host` parameter takes the name of the other server as the first option, followed by the `sibling` keyword. The third option is the HTTP port of the other proxy server followed by the ICP port. The ICP port is the port that the server uses to communicate with other servers. Finally, the last option, the `proxy-only`, tells squid not to keep a copy of the requested page so it doesn't have a duplicate on all the servers. This option virtually doubles the size of your cache because you never have more than one copy of a page in all the caches.

This setup is useful if you have a large network and need a big proxy but don't have the resources to invest in huge machines. You can just use more than one machine to create a virtually big cache server.

Creating a Parent Cache

In big networks, you might have a big proxy server on a fast link, and other smaller ones that are used to take the load off that big server. The big server is a parent to the others. The smaller servers can be siblings to each other, and when they can't find a page in their cache, they can consult the big server for it.

Configuring the small servers to use a parent cache is not much different from the sibling configuration. The only difference is that you don't perform any configuration to the parent server.

Say you have one big parent server called `parent`, and you want your server to use it when it fails to find a request. The configuration file of your server would include this entry:

```
cache_host parent.company.com parent 3128 3130
```

There, now your server will query the parent server for the request. But before it does that, it will first send packets to that server to check whether it's online or not. If you are sure that the parent always will be online, you can have squid skip that step:

```
cache_host parent.company.com parent 3128 3130 no-query default
```

The `no-query` option tells squid not to query for the server, to just use it. As for the `default` tag, that's another story.

You can have more than one parent server. Your server would ask each one whether it had the page or not. If none of the parents had the page, your server would ask the `default` server to get the page for it. Usually the default server is the one that your server will ask to get the page. You usually would choose the fastest server as the default server.

Troubleshooting

When I attempt to connect to the proxy server, I get an `access denied` *message.*

The most common reason behind such a message is that the access rules are denying your access to the server or to the request that you made. Check your ACLs and `http_access` rules.

I am having problems connecting to Hotmail from the proxy server; I get the error `Intrusion Logged, Access Denied.`

This is because Hotmail requires that all connections be made from the same IP. To fix that, add the line

```
hierarchy_stoplist hotmail.com
```

to your `squid.conf` file.

I get an error message saying `Too many files open.`

This probably means that you are running out of file descriptors. To open a file, you need a file descriptor, and if you run out of them, you can't open new files. You can fix this by increasing the number of file descriptors on your system by typing the following command:

```
# echo 4024 > /proc/sys/fs/file-max
```

I want to ban a long list of sites, but putting them all on the same ACL statement is a pain. Any ideas?

Yes, just put them all in a file, with each on a line of its own. Then pass the name of the file to the ACL. ●

Connectivity to the Internet

A Briefing on Connectivity to the Internet

When we talk about connectivity to the Internet, we actually talk about a whole generation. For in the previous 10 years, the Internet has become a way of life, a must-know technology, a profession, and much more. Connectivity to the Internet can be achieved through many methods. Using a modem or ISDN stand are the most common ones. Linux supports both. In this chapter we are going to discuss how to connect to the Internet using these dial-up services.

Connectivity Using Modems

The modem has long since been known as the main device to connect computers to the Internet. Despite the proliferation of other connectivity devices, modems are still widely used in most countries. One reason for this is that many countries lack ISDN support. Even if the phone company supports ISDN, many ISPs do not support it.

Using a Modem to Connect to the Internet

What do you need in order to set up Internet connectivity using modems on Linux?

- A modem, of course
- An Internet account
- A serial port
- PPP/SLIP support
- YaST setup
- PPP daemon

What Is a Modem?

Modems are devices that can be used to transfer digital signals over phone lines that do not support digital signals. What you actually do when dialing up your ISP is dial to an existing modem at the ISP that is waiting for your call. Your modem converts the digital signal to an analog signal and sends it through the phone line to the other modem. The other modem converts the signal back to digital and feeds it to the server to which you're connecting. When the other modem sends you data, the roles swap. Therefore, a *modem* is a device that is used to transport digital data over an analog phone line by first converting it to analog and then restoring it back to digital.

Types of Modems

Modems come in two basic types—internal and external. The significant difference between the two is that *internal* modems are built into either the motherboard or normal ISA/PCI cards, whereas *external* modems are devices that reside outside the machine, such as a printer or scanner. External modems connect to the serial port through a serial cable. All external modems work on Linux whether they are PnP or non-PnP.

What Are Win-Modems?

Win-modems are not modems in the sense that they do not have some chips that were originally found on normal modems; instead, win-modems use software capabilities to implement the functions of those chips. One advantage of this technique is the fact that win-modems are easy to upgrade because they're software-oriented. However, one disadvantage is that replacing hardware functions with software puts more overhead on your processor.

Does Linux Support Win-Modems?

Up to the writing of this book, we had heard of only two win-modems that are supported (Alpha Stage). This means that Linux can run those modems. The only problem facing programmers is that the manufacturers would not release the source of their drivers for those modems, nor would they release a comprehensive design sheet. Therefore, if you asked any Linux user, he'd tell you to avoid win-modems. For more information on the level win-modem support has reached, check the following site: http://www.linmodems.org.

Does Linux Support PCI Modems?

The 2.2.x series of the Linux kernel does *not* support serial ports on PCI devices at the time of this writing. In other words, the 2.2.x series does not support PCI modems. However, the 2.3.x series partially supports serial interfaces on PCI devices. This means that the next stable 2.4.x series will have good support of PCI modems. Although, we might get some support for the PCI serial port in 2.2.x after this book has been published. In general, stick to the external and ISA modems for the time being.

Plug-and-Play Modems

Linux does not support PnP devices by itself; rather it does so through a special package called *isapnptools*. The only problem with PnP devices in general is that you have to go through the process of setting up everything that has to do with the device. The program isapnp is very comprehensive and easy to use, so you should not have any trouble setting up all the PnP devices on your system.

How Modems Communicate with the Computer

Modems communicate with the computer through the serial port. Internal modems have a built-in serial port, whereas external modems use an existing serial port on your machine through a serial cable. Still, like any normal device on the system, modems have I/O ports and IRQs. You should not confuse the serial port with the I/O port—these are two different things.

TIP   To communicate with the computer, modems require a serial port, an I/O port, and an IRQ.

Serial Ports and Linux

As a POSIX-compatible OS, all the devices in Linux are found in the /dev directory. Thus, you will find all the serial ports in this directory. Linux maps the serial ports starting from ttyS0. Table 23.1 shows the mapping of the serial ports when using DOS/Win9x/WinNT and Linux.

Table 23.1 DOS/Win9x/WinNT and Linux Ports Mapping	
DOS/Win	**Linux**
com 1	/dev/ttyS0
com 2	/dev/ttyS1
com 3	/dev/ttyS2
com 4	/dev/ttyS3

As mentioned in the previous section, internal modems have a built-in serial port. This built-in serial port can be changed either through jumper/DIP switch setting in the case of a traditional card or through software in the case of a PnP card. External modems will use an existing serial port just as mice do.

Setting Up a New Modem

The process of setting up a new modem involves the following steps:

1. Setting up software requirements
2. Configuring the modem
3. Configuring the serial port
4. Telling YaST where the modem is
5. Testing and troubleshooting

Modem Connection Software Requirements

Package requirements:

Series a:

- modules
- net_tool
- netcfg

- ▪ kernmod (only if you don't want to recompile your kernel)
- ▪ isapnp (for PnP modems)
- ▪ pciutils (for automatic configuration of PnP cards)
- ▪ nkita (Packages nkita and nkitb have security holes in all SuSE versions up to 6.2. You might want to upgrade them from the SuSE FTP site. The new secure version is available on the accompanying CD.)
- ▪ nkitb

Series n:

- ▪ ppp
- ▪ wvdial (only for SuSE 6.1 and earlier; 6.2 users use YaST)
- ▪ minicom
- ▪ inetcfg

Kernel requirements:

- ▪ Character devices, standard/generic (dumb) serial support
- ▪ Network device support, dummy net driver support
- ▪ Network device support, PPP if you use a PPP connection
- ▪ Network device support, SLIP if you use a SLIP connection

You can have those kernel requirements installed as built in or as modules if you don't know the type of your ISP connection. For SLIP type connections, you can include the CSLIP for SLIP compression. Another option for slow SLIP connections is the Keep Alive and Linefill. This option ensures that your connection is not accidentally terminated.

Configuring the Modem

Setting up the modem is an easy task, yet you have to consider which type of modem you're currently using. Internal and external modems are generally set up using one of the following methods:

- ▪ Traditional jumper/DIP switch setting
- ▪ PnP setup

Setting Up the Modem

At this point, you want to direct the modem to use the available resources on your computer. You want the modem to pick up a free serial port, IRQ, and correct port. Here you'll learn about the two types of internal modems—the traditional jumper/DIP switch setting and the PnP modems.

Part

III

Ch

23

To find out where the available resources are on the machine, you have to use the `proc` filesystem that holds all of your computer's information.

To pick a free IRQ, do the following:

```
bash#cat /proc/interrupts
```

The previous command will list the used IRQs on your system, so you can pick up a free one. The following example illustrates how to find an unused IRQ:

```
bash#cat /proc/interrupts
          CPU0
   0:     167388        XT-PIC  timer
   1:       5185        XT-PIC  keyboard
   2:          0        XT-PIC  cascade
   5:          1        XT-PIC  soundblaster
   8:          2        XT-PIC  rtc
  11:      12237        XT-PIC  eth0
  13:          1        XT-PIC  fpu
  14:     335341        XT-PIC  ide0
  15:          6        XT-PIC  ide1
```

In this example, notice that interrupt 4 is free. Tell the serial port to use this free interrupt.

N O T E   Note that the PCI system allows interrupt sharing; for example, two serial ports can use the same IRQ but with different I/O ports. This means that even if IRQ 4 is already taken by another serial port, it is still possible to share it with the modem serial port. ▪

CAUTION

The following IRQs should not be used because they belong to motherboard resources. If you use any of them you will either slow down the performance of your Linux box or lock it up. Those interrupts are 1, 2, 6, 8, 9, 13, and 14.

Setting Up the Modem's Jumper/DIP Switch Settings   In some cases, this process might require that you have the modem's manual. If you have an internal modem, then you will need to change the placement of some jumpers/DIP switches. If you have an external modem, it's more likely that the changes will be made through buttons or DIP switches. You will have to change the serial port to a suitable and free one through the jumpers/DIP switches. Also, in most cases, you will have the ability to change the IRQ and I/O port.

Setting Up a PnP Modem   This is a simple process once you know what you're doing. First, you have to know that Linux by itself does not support PnP auto device configuration. You have to do this manually, which means that you won't get the full advantage of PnP devices. You will get only the ability to control the PnP device via software. This might be a curse instead of a blessing. PnP devices do not save the settings that you make to them. So, when you shut down your system and start it again, the settings might change. This was causing Linux users problems until a very important package was implemented: `isapnptools`. This package, when configured properly, sets the PnP devices to the setting specified in the configuration file each time you start Linux.

The configuration file for `isapnptools` is located in `/etc/isapnp.conf`. You need an understanding of what is going on and how to use this package. The package consists of two main commands: `isapnp` and `pnpdump`. The `isapnp` command configures the settings provided in the `/etc/isapnp.conf` file; in other words, it looks in the configuration file and assigns to the PnP device the settings specified in it. The `pnpdump` command searches through your system for all available PnP devices and outputs all the combinations that would be applicable for this device. There is a special switch `-c` that causes `pnpdump` to make the decision by itself—that is, check the current configuration of the device and save it. If you think that setting up `isapnp` is going to be too much trouble and you have another PnP OS installed on your system, you can do the following:

1. Start your computer, enter the BIOS, and specify that you don't have a PnP OS.
2. Start your computer in the other PnP OS.
3. Set up the modem PnP settings and make sure the modem is working.
4. Start your computer in Linux using `loadlin`.
5. Log in as root.
6. Issue the following command:

   ```
   bash#pnpdump -c > /etc/isapnp.conf
   ```

7. Issue the following command:

   ```
   isapnp /etc/isapnp.conf
   ```

If you get any problems, check out the "Troubleshooting `isapnp` Output" section later in this chapter.

If you don't have another OS installed on your system, you will have to set up the modem manually. The steps are as follows:

1. Log in as root.
2. Issue the following command:

   ```
   pnpdump -c > /etc/isapnp.conf
   ```

   This will search your system for any PnP devices and generate the configuration file with the current settings of each device.

3. Issue this command:

   ```
   isapnp /etc/isapnp.conf
   ```

   This will configure the devices specified in the configuration file with the specified parameters.

Part

III

Ch

23

Editing the `isapnp.conf` ***File***   The `isapnp.conf` file is easy to understand once you get to know the hierarchy of it. It starts by a general configuration section. This section is actually `isapnp`-specific; it controls the behavior of `isapnp`. You will be interested in this part only if you don't have any conflicts and `isapnp` gives you a fatal error. In this case, you'll be searching for a line that contains the following:

```
(CONFLICT (IO FATAL)(IRQ FATAL)(DMA FATAL)(MEM FATAL))
```

In fact, this line forces `isapnp` to stop and generate a fatal error if it finds any conflict in the resources specified in the previous code. You can cut the part that generates the fatal error. Suppose that the fatal error is due to I/O conflict. To make `isapnp` generate a warning, but also set up the resources, the line should look like this:

```
(CONFLICT (IRQ FATAL)(DMA FATAL)(MEM FATAL))
```

Now that you've completed the general configuration section, let's move on to device configuration. This section includes each PnP device found on your system with the available configurations that can be assigned to each device. Here is an example of a modem configuration. Note that line numbers are used here only to make it easy for you to read the configuration file and are not included in the `isapnp.conf` original file:

```
1    (CONFIGURE CTL3013/4206 (LD
2    #       ANSI string -->Modem<--
3
4    # Multiple choice time, choose one only !
5
6    #       Start dependent functions: priority preferred
7    #       IRQ 3, 4, 5, 7, 9, 10, 11 or 15.
8    #       High true, edge sensitive interrupt (by default)
9    (INT 0 (IRQ 3 (MODE +E)))
10   #       Logical device decodes 16 bit IO address lines
11   #           Minimum IO base address 0x03e8
12   #           Maximum IO base address 0x03e8
13   #           IO base alignment 1 bytes
14   #           Number of IO addresses required:
15   (IO 0 (SIZE 8) (BASE 0x03e8) (CHECK))
```

This example shows that the modem will occupy IRQ 3- (IRQ 3 (MODE +E))- (line 9), I/O 3e8- (BASE 0x03e8)- (line 15). Let's suppose that this IRQ is actually occupied by another device and you want to use IRQ 4 instead. In this case, you'll have to modify line 9 from the following:

```
(INT 0 (IRQ 3 (MODE +E)))
```

to the following:

```
(INT 0 (IRQ 4 (MODE +E)))
```

Hint

You'll find all the possible combinations of configurations that your modem can take in this file. You can comment out this configuration and then pick up a different one that has IRQ 4 and uncomment the lines that specify the correct configuration to which you want your card to be set up.

When you're finished, issue the `isapnp` command again and check for the output message. Try different configurations until you no longer get error messages. If you still get warning messages, it is safe to ignore them.

Troubleshooting `isapnp` ***Output***   Consider the following output that can be generated by `isapnp`:

- **All boards enabled, no warning or fatal errors**—You're such a lucky person!

- **Warnings**—Some resources conflict; in most cases these messages can be ignored. To check whether they can be ignored or not, see what resources conflict.

  The following message shows that the conflict occurs where port is 2E8:

  ```
  /etc/isapnp.conf:11 -- Warning - resource conflict
  ➥allocating 8 bytes of IO at 2E8 (see /proc/ioports)
  ```

  Issue the following command:

  ```
  bash:#cat /proc/ioports |grep 2e8
  02e8-02ef : serial(set)
  ```

  The output shows that the resource is taken by the serial port. In fact, this is what you are going to do later. The modem is actually assigned to this port, so there is no problem. The same goes for IRQ conflicts, except that the command issued will change to the following:

  ```
  bash#cat /proc/interrupts
  ```

  Also, remember that if you have a PCI-oriented system, IRQ sharing is applicable. Two different serial ports can use the same IRQ at the same time.

- **I/O port or IRQ fatal error**—If you get a fatal error, most likely the current settings are false, or `isapnp` is making a little problem look like a big one. First, check the conflicts as described in the section "Editing the `isapnp.conf` File." If things look fine (if there are no other devices trying to use the same I/O port or IRQ other than the serial device), then `isapnp` is magnifying a minor problem. However, if there is a device occupying any of the IRQs or the I/O port, you will have to edit the configuration file. In fact, you'll have to edit the configuration file in both cases.

Configuring the Serial Port

This process involves notifying the serial port driver of the new setting for the device connected to it. You normally set it up through the setserial command, but the SuSE team has provided a script called serial that can be used instead. This script is located in /etc/rc.d/serial and configures all the serial ports on the system startup. By default, this script is written to do nothing. The script has to be modified to set the correct corresponding values to set the serial ports. You get those values from the isapnp.conf if you have a PnP modem or from the settings you made to the jumpers/DIP switches if you have a traditional modem.

Modifying the */etc/rc.d/serial* Script

Modifying the serial script can be done two ways. You can let the script try to guess the serial port configuration, or you can force it to use a certain configuration. We'll call the first the *automatic* method and call the latter the *manual* method.

The Automatic Method   The script primarily uses the setserial command to configure the serial ports. The first part of the script is designed to automatically configure the serial ports, whereas the second part is designed to enable manual configuration. To enable the automatic configuration you have to uncomment the following lines:

```
run_setserial /dev/ttyS0 ${AUTO_IRQ} skip_test autoconfig
run_setserial /dev/ttyS1 ${AUTO_IRQ} skip_test autoconfig
run_setserial /dev/ttyS2 ${AUTO_IRQ} skip_test autoconfig
run_setserial /dev/ttyS3 ${AUTO_IRQ} autoconfig
```

You might want to uncomment only the proper serial port that your modem acquires. You can now save the file and run the script for the changes to take effect:

```
bash#/etc/rc.d/serial stop
bash#/etc/rc.d/serial start
```

Or, simply enter the following:

```
bash#/etc/rc.d/serial restart
```

In most cases this will immediately work. Be warned that this might cause your system to lock up in some cases—read the following Caution. Read the output of the serial script; if the values are correct for the corresponding serial port, you're done! If not, you'll have to comment out the lines you just uncommented and proceed to the manual configuration. Here we explain how to read the serial script output:

```
bash# /etc/rc.d/serial stop
bash# /etc/rc.d/serial start
Configuring serial ports
ttyS0 at 0x03f8 (irq = 4) is a 16550A
ttyS1 at 0x02f8 (irq = 3) is a 16550A
ttyS2 at 0x02e8 (irq = 3) is a 16550A (spd_vhi)        done
```

Part

III

Ch

23

CAUTION

If you are using the IBM 8514 or compatible adapter, it is much safer if you configure your modem manually and at a serial port other than `ttyS3`. If you have to use `ttyS3` because you're running out of serial ports, you should be careful when doing so and use only the default serial port settings as specified in Table 23.2. Do not by any means try the automatic configuration part in the serial script; it will immediately lock up your system. Because it's a boot script, the next time you start your computer, it will lock up, too. Use the manual method as described in the next section "The Manual Method."

Table 23.2 shows an explanation of the serial script output. Note that the Device column is based on what we know about the system but is not generated in the script output.

Table 23.2   Explanation of the Serial Script Output

Serial Port	Device	IRQ	IO	Speed
ttyS0=com1	Mouse	4	0x03f8	16550A
ttyS1=com2	None	3	0x02f8	16550A
ttyS2=com3	Modem	3	0x02e8	16650A

If the modem is the owner of `ttyS3`, you can verify whether the resources allocated to it are true or false by checking either the settings made in the `isapnp.conf` file or the settings you made to the modem jumpers/DIP switches. If your modem does not have a jumper/DIP switch for setting the I/O port, you should be using the default I/O port for the serial ports. Table 23.3 shows the default IRQ and I/O port for their corresponding serial ports.

Table 23.3   The Default Serial Port Resources

Serial Port	Default IRQ	Default I/O
ttyS0	4	0x3f8
ttyS1	3	0x2f8
ttyS2	4	0x3e8
ttyS3	3	0x2e8

The Manual Method   When editing the `serial` script, you might notice that the file is mainly a combination of `setserial` commands written in an organized way. Consider the following line that exists in the manual configuration part of the serial script:

```
bash#run_setserial /dev/ttyS2 uart 16550A port 0x2E8 irq 3 spd_vhi
```

The previous line directs the serial port `ttyS2` to use IRQ 3 and I/O 0x2E8. By modifying the values, you can configure the serial port to use other IRQ and other I/O. Refer to the previous table or to your `isapnp.conf` file to get the correct values. Adding `spd_vhi` to the line will give you better performance on 33.6bps and higher modems.

Telling YaST Where the Modem Is

Start YaST by issuing the command yast as root. From the YaST menu, choose System Administration, Integrate Hardware Into the System, Modem Configuration. YaST's Modem Configuration window opens (see Figure 23.1).

FIGURE 23.1
YaST's Modem Configuration Window.

In the Modem Configuration window, you find the serial ports that can be assigned to the modem. Pick up the applicable port that you set your modem to use.

Now that you have told YaST where the modem is, YaST will keep in mind that the modem is on the specific serial port and will create a symbolic link in the /dev directory. The symbolic link will be /dev/modem, where modem points to the modem's serial port. From now on, you can use /dev/modem and don't have to worry about remembering the serial port.

> **CAUTION**
>
> There is a disadvantage to giving the modem a symbolic link. Two users could try to use the modem at the same time. One of them could use /dev/modem while the other uses /dev/ttyS3. This would result in a problem that is usually solved by locking the device to one user at a time. But, this could not be done because the users call the same device two different names. Thus, when ttyS3 is locked and the other user tries to use the modem symbolic link, he'd find it unlocked.
>
> If you're the only user of the machine, you should try to use either the modem symbolic link all the time or the original device name. If the system has many users with access to the modem, you might consider deleting the symbolic link and telling the users to use the modem serial port directly.

Establishing Your Connection

To establish a PPP/SLIP connection to the Internet you need to dial in, log in, and then pass the control to the PPP daemon. We will be discussing three different ways to do this. Using WvDial, which is a package that comes with SuSE Linux, is considered the SuSE standard. However, using minicom is essential for testing and troubleshooting. The third method, kppp, is considered an advanced and easy application to use if you are a KDE user. But, before you use any of these programs, you have to set up the nameserver section in YaST (DNS).

Setting Up YaST (Domain Name Server)

After you connect to the Internet, you need to access a nameserver. This is important if you don't want to access servers only with their IPs. For example, if you start Netscape and type http://www.suse.com, Netscape will generate an error even though you are connected to the Internet. *Domain Name Server* (DNS) is a special server program that resides in your ISP. When you type the URL address, DNS will resolve it to the corresponding IP. To set up the DNS you need to perform the following steps:

1. Start YaST by issuing the command yast as root.

2. From the menu, select System Administration, Network Configuration, Configuration Nameserver. The Nameserver Configuration dialog box appears (see Figure 23.2).

FIGURE 23.2
YaST Domain Name
Server configuration.

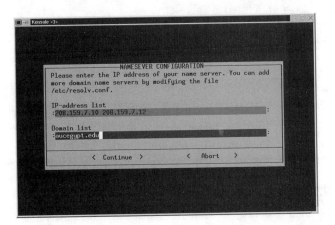

In the IP address list, type the primary DNS followed by the secondary DNS. In the domain list, type the ISP domain name.

If you don't have this information, call your ISP to get it because it's important that you have this information. If you use other OSes on the same machine, you might consider checking the values using the other OS. For example, in Windows you can use the nslookup command, which prints the DNS server when it starts. The following example illustrates how `nslookup` starts when run on a Windows NT platform:

```
C:\>nslookup
Default server: dns.wayout.net
Address: 163.121.142.2
```

The primary DNS of the ISP used in this example is 163.121.142.2.

Modifying the *pppd* Options

`pppd` is the PPP daemon, which is responsible for negotiating the PPP protocol over a TCP/IP network. After you have dialed to your ISP and logged in, you have to pass control to `pppd`. This is done by issuing the command `pppd`. When `pppd` is started, it looks in the `/etc/ppp/options` directory, which is the `pppd` configuration file. To save time, the following are situations in which you do not have to edit this file:

- You plan to use `wvdial` because it outputs a correct `/etc/ppp/options` file.
- You plan to use `kppp`.

Should you be editing this file, this section tells you the most important options of the `pppd` and how to include them in the file. The `/etc/ppp/options` file that comes with SuSE is heavily documented and easy to understand.

The main options are listed in Table 23.4.

Table 23.4	Main Options in the *pppd* Configuration File
Option	**Meaning**
Noipdefault	Your ISP allocates IPs dynamically
Lock	Only the `pppd` should use the modem while connected
Modem	Usage of modem control lines
115200	The connection speed. (230400/115200/57600/38400/19200/9600)

Using WvDial

WvDial is an intelligent application. It is intelligent in that it has a special auto configuration, searches for the modem technology, and has a built-in database of login strings. This makes the configuration of `wvdial` very simple and straightforward. The package consists of the following programs:

- **wvdialconf**—Responsible for searching for the modem and creating a configuration file for WvDial. The default configuration file is stored in `/etc/wvdial.conf`.
- **wvdial.tcl**—Responsible for modifying the configuration file to insert your account-specific information (your account name, ISP phone number, and so on).
- **wvdial**—Responsible for connecting to the Internet using the configuration file created by the previously listed programs.

Luckily, SuSE Linux includes a YaST module that configures WvDial. The next section explains how to configure WvDial manually and by using the YaST module.

Configuring WvDial Using YaST   You can use YaST to configure a modem connection without having to go through the trouble of editing files and configuring devices. YaST uses interactive menus to set up a connection from the ground up. To set up a connection using YaST, follow these steps:

1. Start YaST.
2. Open System Administration, Network Configuration, Configure a PPP Network. This will bring up the SuSE WvDial Configuration window (see Figure 23.3).

Part

III

Ch

23

FIGURE 23.3
SuSE WvDial
Configuration window.

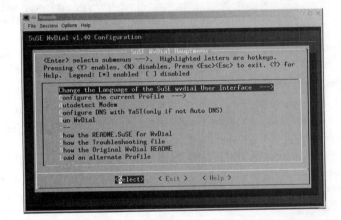

SuSE WvDial Configuration   The first step in WvDial configuration is to configure it to detect your modem. To do so, highlight the Autodetect Modem option and press Enter. WvDial will attempt to scan your serial ports looking for a modem. After it finds one, WvDial will attempt to communicate with the modem and find the best `init` and `dial` strings to use with the modem. Scroll down the output window to check the output of the `wvdialconf` program.

Next, you must edit the connection profile by highlighting the Configure the Current Profile option and pressing Enter. Once in the Configure the Current Profile menu, fill in the following values (see Figure 23.4):

- **Phone number**—Your ISP phone number.
- **Area code**—The area code of your ISP. You can leave this field empty if you are dialing from the same area.
- **Account name**—The username you use to connect to this ISP.
- **Password**—Your password.

FIGURE 23.4
You can configure the new connection using the Current Profile Window.

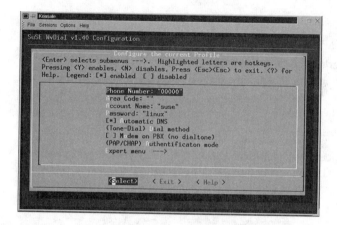

- ■ **Automatic DNS**—Check this box if your DNS supplies you with the DNS when you connect.

- ■ **Dial method**—Select the dialing method from Tone dial or Pulse dial.

- ■ **Modem on PBX (no dialtone)**—Check this box if your modem is on a PBX or you get an error saying there is no dialtone. Note that your modem will not complain if the phone line is not connected if you check this box.

- ■ **Authentication mode**—Select the authentication mode your ISP uses. WvDial recognizes most of the authentication modes used by many ISPs. You have the following options:
    - ● PAP/CHAP
    - ● Compuserve
    - ● Germany:T-Online
    - ● Non-Standard-Login

- ■ **Expert menu**—Using this menu, you can change the type of modem you are using (see Figure 23.5). You can also change the init strings that are sent to the modem when initializing the modem.

- ■ **Modem type**—You can use this menu to change the modem type. You have the following options in this menu:
    - ● Standard-Analog-Modem/non-ISDN, which you can use if you use a normal analog modem.
    - ● The rest of the choices apply to ISDN cards. If you are going to use WvDial with an ISDN modem, select your ISDN modem from the list.

- ■ **Init String 1**—This string will be sent to the modem when WvDial attempts to open the serial port.

FIGURE 23.5
Using the Expert menu, you can set up the modem type and modem advanced settings.

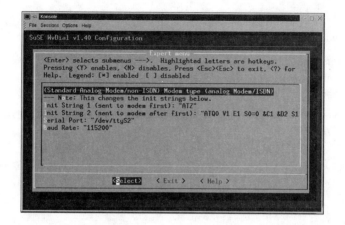

- **Init String 2**—This string will be sent to the modem when WvDial receives an OK reply for the first initialization string.

- **Serial port**—If WvDial failed to correctly detect your modem port, you can specify it manually using this field.

- **Baud rate**—You can edit the default baud rate you want to use in this field.

If your ISP does not assign you a DNS automatically, you should configure the DNS by highlighting the Configure DNS with YaST (Only if not Auto DNS) option and pressing Enter. This will bring up the YaST DNS configuration, which was discussed previously in the section "Setting Up YaST (Domain Name Server)."

After you have finished configuring WvDial, test your new connection by highlighting the Run WvDial option and pressing Enter. If your connection goes flawlessly, press Esc. You will be prompted to save your settings. Save your settings and exit.

Later, when you want to establish a connection, enter the following command:

```
bash$wvdial
```

Your modem will start dialing your ISP and establish a connection.

Configuring WvDial Manually   To configure WvDial, you must log in to X session (through xdm or startx). After you're inside X, start an xterm and follow these steps:

1. Enable connectivity to the X server from the localhost by issuing the following command in an xterm:

   ```
   xhost +localhost
   ```

2. Change to a superuser, such as the following:

   ```
   su -l
   ```

3. Issue the following command:

```
wvdialconf /etc/wvdial.conf
```

You should get output that looks like this:

```
bash# wvdialconf  /etc/wvdial.conf
Scanning your serial ports for a modem.

Port Scan<*1>:  Ignoring ttyS0 because /dev/mouse is a link to it.
ttyS1<*1>: AT -- AT -- AT -- nothing.
ttyS2<*1>: AT -- OK
ttyS2<*1>: ATZ -- OK
ttyS2<*1>: ATQ0 -- OK
ttyS2<*1>: ATQ0 V1 -- OK
ttyS2<*1>: ATQ0 V1 E1 -- OK
ttyS2<*1>: ATQ0 V1 E1 S0=0 -- OK
ttyS2<*1>: ATQ0 V1 E1 S0=0 &C1 -- OK
ttyS2<*1>: ATQ0 V1 E1 S0=0 &C1 &D2 -- OK
ttyS2<*1>: ATQ0 V1 E1 S0=0 &C1 &D2 S11=55 -- OK
ttyS2<*1>: ATQ0 V1 E1 S0=0 &C1 &D2 S11=55 +FCLASS=0 -- OK
ttyS2<*1>: Modem Identifier: ATI -- 33600
ttyS2<*1>: Speed 2400: AT -- OK
ttyS2<*1>: Speed 4800: AT -- OK
ttyS2<*1>: Speed 9600: AT -- OK
ttyS2<*1>: Speed 19200: AT -- OK
ttyS2<*1>: Speed 38400: AT -- OK
ttyS2<*1>: Speed 57600: AT -- OK
ttyS2<*1>: Speed 115200: AT -- OK
ttyS2<*1>: Speed 230400: AT -- OK
ttyS2<*1>: Max speed is 230400; using 115200 to be safe.
ttyS2<*1>: ATQ0 V1 E1 S0=0 &C1 &D2 S11=55 +FCLASS=0 -- OK

Found a modem on /dev/ttyS2.
ttyS2<Info>: Speed 115200; init "ATQ0 V1 E1 S0=0 &C1 &D2 11=55
+FCLASS=0"
```

With this, `wvdialconf` has found your modem, guessed the dial string, guessed the speed, and wrote the corresponding configuration file.

4. Export the DISPLAY of the super user to be equal to the current X session, for example:

```
export DISPLAY=:0
```

5. Start `wvdial.tcl` and fill in the information in the configuration dialog box (see Figure 23.6).

6. Press Save to save the current configuration file. You can also click Dial to test the connection. If it says you have a connection, skip ahead to the section "Testing an Existing Connection."

The next time you try to connect, you'll have to open a terminal or a normal console and start `wvdial`. To disconnect, activate the window/console and press Ctrl+C.

FIGURE 23.6

The `wvdial.tcl`
script. Using this script
makes it easy to mod-
ify the `wvdial` config-
uration file.

Using minicom

minicom is considered one of the main programs for testing and troubleshooting modems. In
fact, you might find yourself using minicom in cases where you find your modem stuck and
unable to hang up, or you might use it as your main dial-in program. When you first start
minicom, you should start it as root with the -s parameter (see Figure 23.7). This parameter
brings up the setup menu for minicom in which you should specify the serial port to be used
for the modem.

FIGURE 23.7

Starting `minicom` with
the –s command-line
parameter brings up
the configuration
screen for minicom.

As noted before, the serial port of the modem has become `/dev/modem`. You might want to
change the Modem and Dialing settings to suit your modem configuration, in which case you
will be referring to your modem manual. After you're finished setting up minicom, you
should save the settings. By saving the settings, minicom will change to the terminal screen
at which you can send commands directly to the modem or bring up minicom facilities.

You can look up the mini modem commands in Table 23.5. The minicom help dialog box can
be brought up by Alt+Z, which shows a menu with the available commands.

To establish a connection using `minicom`, use the following steps:

1. Press Alt+D to bring up the dialing directory.
2. Press Add by moving the cursor using the left and right arrows.
3. Select the new entry using the up and down arrows (see Figure 23.8).

FIGURE 23.8

Adding a new entry in the minicom dialing directory.

4. Press Edit.
5. Change the entries applicable as follows (see Figure 23.9):
   - **A**—Name of connection
   - **B**—Phone number
   - **C**—Dialing script number

FIGURE 23.9

Editing the proper entries in the new connection.

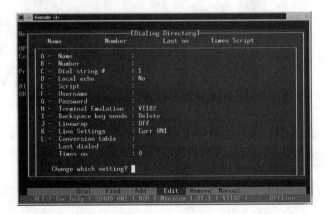

minicom can automate a connection, but this is not explained in this chapter. Refer to the minicom manual for more information about automating a connection using scripts.

6. Press Esc to go back to the dialing directory.

7. Press Dial. minicom will dial your ISP and bring up the login terminal.

8. Log in to your account.

9. After you have logged in, press Alt+Q to exit minicom without resetting the modem.

10. In the shell, start the pppd to pass control to it with the following command:

    bash#pppd

To end the connection, start minicom again and issue the command ATZ, which will reset the modem. pppd will die and the connection will be terminated. You also can use #killall pppd as root.

Using kppp

If you like KDE and use it often, you will want to use kppp. kppp is a K application that features many capabilities (see Figure 23.10). Among them are multiple accounts, docking in the panel, modem lights, not needing to set up the /etc/ppp/options, accounting, and on-line graph activity. kppp configuration is performed using the dialogs that come up when you press setup. We will discuss the main dialogs and the connectivity procedures within kppp.

FIGURE 23.10
A screenshot of kppp.

The kppp Configuration Dialog   The kppp configuration dialog is the main configuration dialog from which the hierarchy of setting up your connection starts (see Figure 23.11). The Accounts tab enables you to configure as many accounts as you might have, along with their different ISPs, login scripts, and styles of accounting. The Device tab deals primarily with the serial port and its settings. The Modem tab enables you to set up your modem-specific commands (AT commands) and troubleshoot your modem via the modem terminal. The Graph tab enables you to activate the online graph. And lastly, the About tab provides information about the authors of kppp.

The Accounts Tab   Setting up the accounts is very simple. Click New to make a new account, and then type in the connection name and phone number (see Figure 23.12). If you want to enter more than one phone number, separate the numbers with colons (:). Choose the type of authentication your ISP uses (for testing, use terminal-based). You can edit the pppd (PPP daemon) arguments by clicking the Arguments button. For more information on pppd arguments, refer to the section "Modifying the pppd Options" earlier in this chapter.

FIGURE 23.11
The main configuration
window of kppp.

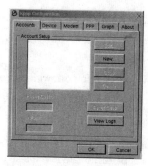

FIGURE 23.12
Setting up your
account-specific config-
uration in kppp.

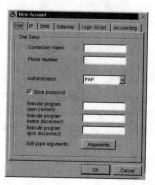

In the IP tab, specify whether you are using a dynamic or static IP. In the DNS, specify the
domain name server and the IP of the domain name server of your ISP. If you don't have this
information, refer to the section earlier in this chapter, "Setting Up YaST (Domain Name
Server)." In the Gateway tab, click assign default gateway to this gateway and edit any gateway preferences. The login script enables you to automatically log in to your ISP once you
know the specific procedure. Test the login procedure using the terminal first, then create a
login script to automate the procedure. The Accounting tab lets you enable accounting for
your online time.

The Device Tab The Device tab enables you to specify the settings for your serial port
settings. The modem device should be /dev/modem. The other settings are modem- and
serial-port specific. The following are the recommended settings:

- **Flow Control**—(CRTSCTS)
- **Line Termination**—CR/LF
- **Connection Speed**—115200 for most 33.6K and 56K modems
- **Use Lock File**—Unchecked
- **Modem Timeout**—Depends on your ISP, values higher than 50 are recommended

The Modem Tab   You set up modem-specific settings in the Modem tab (see Figure 23.13). You can adjust your modem volume with the slider. You also can edit your modem strings by pressing the Modem Commands button. If you are going to modify the pre-init and post-init fields, be sure to set the delay time high enough so your modem has time to respond (50 milliseconds is good). You might want to edit the dial string to ATX3DT if you get an error of NO DIAL TONE while your modem is properly connected to the phone line. You can always query your modem to test it by clicking Query Modem. Also, you can test your modem by clicking the Terminal button, which gives you the ability to talk directly to the modem. You have to be a modem expert if you want to do this. You might want to check some modem commands in Table 23.5, which appears later in this chapter.

Part

III

Ch

23

FIGURE 23.13
Modem configuration
can be used to set
modem-specific com-
mands.

The PPP Tab   The PPP tab contains features that control the kppp behavior for PPP connections:

- **pppd timeout in seconds**—Enter the timeout in seconds after which pppd should die if no connection is established.

- **Dock Into Panel on Connect**—When enabled, kppp will dock in the KDE panel when the connection is established.

- **Automatic Redial on Disconnect**—When checked, kppp will try to redial the connection if you get disconnected due to reasons other than clicking disconnect.

- **Show Clock on Caption**—This will show the connection time on the caption of kppp.

- **Disconnect on X-Server Shutdown**—Uncheck this option if you want to keep your connection when you close your X session.

- **Quit on Disconnect**—Check this option if you want kppp to quit when you disconnect.

- **Minimize Window on Connect**—Check this option for kppp to be minimized when the connection is established.

The Graph Tab   kppp can graph the connection time you spend in each connection. You can change the colors of the graph by clicking on the corresponding buttons in this tab.

We recommend that you read the kppp help dialog by clicking the Help button on the kppp main dialog. kppp features a very comprehensive help documentation that provides troubleshooting and script writing techniques.

Testing an Existing Connection

Now that you dialed in, logged in, and started the pppd, you're finally connected. So, let's test the connection. To test the connection, you have three main utilities that show whether everything works fine—ifconfig, route, and ping.

Using *ifconfig*

By issuing the command ifconfig without arguments, you get a list of the configured network interfaces on your system. Here is an example of the ifconfig output:

```
bash#ifconfig
dummy0    Link encap:Ethernet  HWaddr 00:00:00:00:00:00
          inet addr:192.168.0.1  Bcast:192.168.0.255  Mask:255.255.255.255
          UP BROADCAST RUNNING NOARP  MTU:1500  Metric:1
          RX packets:0 errors:0 dropped:0 overruns:0 frame:0
          TX packets:165 errors:0 dropped:0 overruns:0 carrier:0
          collisions:0 txqueuelen:0

lo        Link encap:Local Loopback
          inet addr:127.0.0.1  Mask:255.0.0.0
          UP LOOPBACK RUNNING  MTU:3924  Metric:1
          RX packets:1440 errors:0 dropped:0 overruns:0 frame:0
          TX packets:1440 errors:0 dropped:0 overruns:0 carrier:0
          collisions:0 txqueuelen:0

ppp0      Link encap:Point-to-Point Protocol
          inet addr:208.169.244.18  P-t-P:208.169.244.70  Mask:255.255.255.255
          UP POINTOPOINT RUNNING NOARP MULTICAST  MTU:1524  Metric:1
          RX packets:11 errors:0 dropped:0 overruns:0 frame:0
          TX packets:10 errors:0 dropped:0 overruns:0 carrier:0
          collisions:0 txqueuelen:10
```

What you are interested in is the ppp0 interface, which represents the connection you just made. If it doesn't appear, there is something wrong. In this case, try to start the pppd or check whether the PPP support is included in the kernel. By reading the output of this example, you find that the local IP is 208.169.224.18 and that the gateway's IP is 208.169.244.70.

Using *route*

route is a special command because it usually is used to pass arguments to the route table. Issuing the route command with no arguments lists the route table and the default gateway:

```
bash# route
Kernel IP routing table
```

Destination	Gateway	Genmask	Flags	Metric	Ref	Use	Iface
coffin.aucegypt	*	255.255.255.255	UH	1	0	0	dummy0
208.169.244.70	*	255.255.255.255	UH	0	0	0	ppp0
loopback	*	255.0.0.0	U	0	0	0	lo
default	208.169.244.70	0.0.0.0	UG	0	0	0	ppp0

The default gateway is 208.169.244.70, which corresponds to the ppp0 interface. You now can use the Internet safely.

Using *ping*

You can use ping to check whether your computer can reach a network. Ping the IP address or the full hostname of a machine on a network to ensure you can reach this network. For example, after you have connected to the Internet, use the following commands to ensure you can reach the freshmeat network:

```
bash$ping www.freshmeat.net
PING freshmeat.net (209.207.224.211): 56 data bytes
64 bytes from 209.207.224.211: icmp_seq=0 ttl=243 time=1060.2 ms
64 bytes from 209.207.224.211: icmp_seq=1 ttl=243 time=1147.5 ms
64 bytes from 209.207.224.211: icmp_seq=2 ttl=243 time=927.5 ms
^C
--- freshmeat.net ping statistics ---
4 packets transmitted, 3 packets received, 25% packet loss
round-trip min/avg/max = 927.5/1045.0/1147.5 ms
```

After you have issued the ping command, it will run until you press the Ctrl+C combination. The Ctrl+C combination terminates the ping command and writes ping statistics.

The first IP you want to ping to test a connection is your ISP IP. If you can ping your ISP, you can reach your ISP network. Second, try to ping addresses such as www.cnn.com, www.freshmeat.net, and so on. If you get an error, try to ping IPs you know because the problem might be name resolution rather than an inability to reach the network. The result can be one of the following:

- **You can access networks using both IPs and hostnames**—You have a completely configured and working connection.

- **You can access networks using IPs, but not hostnames**—You have a problem setting up the DNS. Review the DNS settings you made.

- **You can access networks using either IPs or hostnames but you can ping your ISP**—You have a routing problem. Refer to the previous section "Using route".

General Modem Connection Troubleshooting

I do not have read/write permission to ttySx.

This is a common error. SuSE offers the solution for this error by changing the group of the user to dialout or uucp. Use YaST to add your username to the users allowed to use the modem. Refer to Chapter 4, "Managing Users and Groups," for more information.

Or, you can give the user read/write permissions to the specific ttySx—for example:

```
chmod +rw /dev/ttySx
```

> **CAUTION**
>
> This might result in a security hole if the system has more than one user. Changing the group of the user to `dialout` or `uucp` is a wiser solution.

I do not have permission to execute pppd.

Again, this is a common problem. As in the previous problem, change the group of the user to `dialout` or `uucp`. Use YaST to add your username to the users allowed to use the modem. Refer to Chapter 4 for more information.

Or, again, you can give the user read/execute permission to `pppd`:

```
chmod +rs /usr/sbin/pppd
```

> **CAUTION**
>
> Again, this might result in a security hole if the system has more than one user. Changing the group of the user to `dialout` or `uucp` is a wiser solution.

The connection is slow.

The speed you specified in the serial file for the UART might be too low. Try increasing it.

Also, the problem might be that the IRQ settings might not be correct; read the section "Configuring the Serial Port" earlier in this chapter.

Another problem might be that your Maximum Receive Unit (MRU) and Maximum Transmit Unit (MTU) are incorrectly set. Slower speeds necessitate lower MRU/MTU; higher speeds necessitate higher MRU/MTU. Specify the packets that travel the link. Slow or noisy links should have a small MRU/MTU, which is inexpensive in cases where errors occur when packets are transmitted. On high-speed links where noise isn't such a problem and errors are rare, you should use high values for MRU/MTU.

The system locks up when I run the serial script.

You probably are using an IBM 8514 video adapter or compatible. You should read the section "The Automatic Method" earlier in this chapter for more information. If your system locks up the next time you start it, you should boot from the SuSE CD and start the emergency system. Then, you should mount the Linux partition and edit the serial script.

The system gets really slow or locks up when I start to access the modem.

You probably assigned a motherboard resource IRQ to the serial port. You should not assign any of the following IRQs to the serial port: 1, 6, 8, 13, and 14.

You can use the following mini-reference for the modem AT commands. The commands in Table 23.5 are understood by most modems.

Table 23.5   Modem *AT* Command Mini-Reference

Command	Meaning
ATZ	Reset modem
ATD#	Dial the number
ATDT#	Dial the number using tone dial
ATDP#	Dial the number using pulse dial
ATX3	Don't wait for dial tone
ATM0	Speaker off
ATL1–ATL3	Speaker volume level 1–3
ATDL	Re-dial last number
ATD,#	Dial number but pause seconds
ATH	Hang up modem
ATA	Answer mode
AT/	Repeat last command

The complete reference set usually comes with the modem's manual.

Part

III

Ch

23

Connectivity Using ISDN

ISDN (Integrated Services Digital Network) is considered a breakthrough in our current time. It has a big advantage over the normal analog phone lines. Using the same wires of your normal phone line, you can upgrade to ISDN. We will not get into the technical details of the ISDN, but we will list the pros and cons of ISDN.

Advantages of ISDN

The following are the advantages of using ISDN:

- The basic ISDN (BRI) supports up to two operations at a time. For example, you can connect to the Internet, use the phone, and send a fax at the same time via the same line. The advanced line (PRI) supports up to 23 operations at a time.

- Because each B-channel can get to a speed of 64Kbps, you can reach up to 128Kbps when using the BRI by bundling the two B-channels in your basic BRI setup. When using the PRI, you can get to a maximum of 23×64 Kbps.

- The dialing speed is very fast—2 seconds compared to 40 to 60 seconds on the normal phone lines. This gives you the option of dial-on-demand, which will be discussed in the section "Dial-on-Demand" later in this chapter.

Disadvantages of ISDN

The following are the disadvantages of using ISDN:

- Your phone company and ISP have to support it.
- It is more expensive than the normal phone lines.
- You might have to change the wiring of your phone line if it's old.

Dial-on-Demand

The dial-on-demand is an interesting feature of the ISDN. This feature takes advantage of the fast dial speed of the ISDN. Consider the following scenario:

1. You start Netscape, which automatically opens your start page.
2. A connection is automatically established to server Netscape.
3. After a specified period, if there is not any application that needs the connection, it gets terminated.

As you might have noticed, this method will save a great deal of your online time. This means that you're online only when you need a connection; otherwise, you're actually offline. This feature cannot be applied when using normal modems because the minimum time used for dialing and logging in is at least 50 seconds, while in ISDN it is 2–3 seconds.

ISDN Controllers/Cards

ISDN cards come in two varieties: active and passive.

The *active* cards handle ISDN connection protocols by themselves, whereas *passive* cards rely on software capabilities for doing so.

ISDN and Legalities

It is important to understand that for any ISDN connection to be legally established, there must be a hardware-software certification. The hardware must run a certified software from the manufacturer. Most of the active cards use the HiSax driver that comes with the kernel, which is certified by most manufacturers. This means that if you're running an active card using the HiSax driver, you're safe. When compiling your kernel, you should download a full kernel source. If you patch your kernel, your HiSax driver loses the certification.

ISDN and Linux

The ISDN package that comes with Linux was developed in Germany. For this reason, most of the documentation for the package is written in German, and the German national ISDN support is advanced in the package. It is important to note that only the traditional German ISDN and the Euro-ISDN are supported by Linux.

N O T E Despite the fact that the SuSE manual says that ISDN supports only the Euro-ISDN, some firms in North America wrote the drivers for their cards to work for Linux on the NI-1 protocol. Please check `http://www.spellcast.com` for more information if you are a North American user. ▨

Supported ISDN Cards

Linux supports a large number of active and passive ISDN cards. Appendix B, "Hardware Compatibility List," contains a list of the supported ISDN cards. For passive cards to work, you have to connect them to your Phone Branch Exchange (PBX), which might get them to work.

ISDN Connection Software Requirements

Package requirements:

Series a:

- ▨ modules
- ▨ `net_tool`
- ▨ `netcfg`
- ▨ `kernmod` (only if you don't want to recompile your kernel)
- ▨ `isapnp` (for PnP controllers)
- ▨ `pciutils` (for automatic configuration of PnP controllers)
- ▨ `nkita` (Packages `nkita` and `nkitb` have security holes in all SuSE versions up to 6.2; you might want to upgrade them from the SuSE FTP site. The new secure version is available on the accompanying CD.)
- ▨ `nkitb`

Series n:

- ▨ `ppp`
- ▨ `inetcfg`
- ▨ `i4l`

Kernel requirements:

- ▧ Character devices, standard/generic (dumb) serial support
- ▧ Network device support, dummy net driver support
- ▧ Network device support, PPP or SLIP

Part
III

Ch
23

Configuring the ISDN Card

Like any normal device, the ISDN can be either PnP or non-PnP. This section discusses how to configure both types of cards.

Non-PnP Controllers

Most non-PnP controllers come with their configuration utilities, which you should use to set up the controllers. You need to know the following:

- IRQ
- Memory base address
- IO port

Those controllers are recognized by the Linux drivers and need no further changes after setup. Remember that you can use dosemu to configure your controller using your controller's DOS software.

PnP Controllers

PnP cards need special attention because they are not automatically configured. Refer to the section "Setting Up a PnP Modem" earlier in this chapter. The operation should be similar, except for some values that would differ and two extra variables to set (ISAC and HSCX). You must compile HiSax as modules to use PnP controllers if the following are true:

- You don't have a PnP BIOS.
- You have another operating system on the same system.

As you might know, the kernel is the first thing that loads and starts execution. If HiSax is built in the kernel, it will try to probe the resources in its configuration files on startup. In the case of PnP cards, the settings might change. Thus, HiSax will fail. Remember that isapnp does not start until the kernel boots.

> **NOTE** Some ISDN cards cannot use IRQ 12 or 15, so avoid using these interrupts.
>
> You should not allow IRQ sharing for the ISDN controllers. This will result in improper connection or a drop in speed. ■

Configuring ISDN Hardware via YaST

SuSE Linux made ISDN launching easy using YaST. If you have an active non-PnP card, YaST will do most of the work for you. Even if you don't have one, chances are that YaST will still do the work for you. Follow these steps:

1. Log in as root and start YaST.

2. To ensure every step you are going to make during the configuration goes flawlessly, you should watch the system message log. A special command called `tail` has been designed to watch the lines that are added to a file. In another terminal or console, enter the following command to watch the system message log file changes:

```
bash#tail - f  /var/log/messages
```

3. From the menu, choose System Administration, Integrate Hardware into the System, Configure ISDN Hardware. The YaST ISDN setup window appears (see Figure 23.14).

FIGURE 23.14

YaST ISDN hardware setup menu.

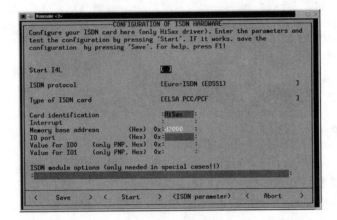

4. From this dialog, you need to enter the following details:

- **Start I4L**—Check this box if you want to activate ISDN, which you do.
- **ISDN Protocol**—This box indicates which ISDN your phone company uses. Euro-ISDN (EDSS1) is suitable for most users, but 1TR6 might be a choice for many German users. If you don't know which one your phone company uses, you should contact them or do some trial and error checks.
- **Type of ISDN Card**—Select your ISDN controller from this list. If you can not find your ISDN controller in the list, select Generic ISDN Controller.
- **Controller identification**—Leave this box as is.
- **Interrupt**—Fill in this value from the settings you obtained before. If you have a PnP card, you should get this value, along with ISAC and HSCX, from the `/etc/isapnp.conf` file.
- **Memory Base Address**—Fill in this value from the settings you obtained before. If you have a PnP card, you should get this value, along with ISAC and HSCX, from the `/etc/isapnp.conf` file.
- **IO Port**—Fill in this value from the settings you obtained before.
- **Values of IO0 and IO1**—If you have a PnP ISDN controller, you will find those values in the `/etc/isapnp.conf` file.
- **ISDN Module Options**—This box should be left empty in most cases.

After you have filled in the values, press Start. If all goes smoothly, press Save. If problems occur, check the kernel messages by looking at the terminal you opened before. You might consider the following:

- **The module might be already loaded in memory**—If you already have the HiSax module loaded in memory, you should first unload it and then start it with the new setting you just made. To do this, you have to enter the following:

  ```
  bash# rmmod hisax.
  ```

  Then press Start again.
- **The IRQ settings are incorrect**—Do *not* use IRQ 12 or 15. Do *not* allow IRQ sharing with your ISDN controller.

Other ISDN Configurations

ISDN can do a couple of things that YaST does not configure yet. One important feature that is not configured by YaST is logging. Another important feature is checking the caller ID. When combined, they are important for dialing in and troubleshooting.

Setting Up Logging

The configuration file for `isdnlog` is `/etc/isdn/isdnlog.conf`. This file has to be configured according to your phone company. The main inputs in the GLOBAL section are as follows:

- COUNTRYPREFIX—Entering this value is optional; you can leave it as it is. The default value for country prefix is = +.

  ```
  COUNTRYPREFIX = +
  ```

- COUNTRYCODE—This value is also optional.
- AREACODE—This value is the most important in this section. This value is equal to your area code after stripping the leading zero. This means that if your area code is 0111, you should enter 111.

The `isdnlog` options are located in `/etc/isdn/isdnlog/isdnctrlx.options`. You can set up the sensitivity of logging ISDN activity by setting up the options in this file. Normally, this is unnecessary.

Setting Up Caller ID

The configuration file for caller ID is `/etc/isdn/callerid.conf`. The format for this file is very simple:

```
[MSN]
Number=        #Number of the caller
Alias=         #Name of the caller
Zone=          #Zone of the caller
```

Configuring the ISDN Network Interface via YaST

After you're finished configuring the hardware part, you must configure the network layer for the ISDN interface. YaST makes it easy for you. You only have to decide which protocol you will be using. This depends on your ISP. The following are the three main ISDN protocols:

- syncPPP
- rawip-HDLC
- Terminal login (X.75)

The steps to set up the first two protocols are almost the same. Only the last part differs.

Part

III

Ch

23

The ISDN *syncPPP* Protocol

Follow these steps to set up the syncPPP protocol:

1. Launch YaST as root.
2. From the menu, choose System Administration, Network Configuration, Network Base Configuration. The Selection of Network dialog appears (see Figure 23.15).

FIGURE 23.15

ISDN network configuration via YaST.

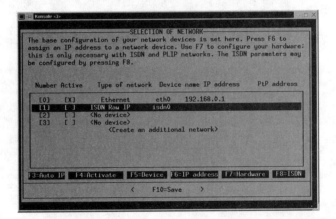

3. Choose an empty number and press F5. This will enable you to select the proper device for the network interface.
4. Select the ISDN syncPPP protocol. This is one of the protocols to be used when using ISDN connections.
5. Enter your IP and your PtP IP (partner's IP). If you don't know these IPs or you use a dynamic IP with syncIP, use any values (192.168.0.100 and 192.168.0.101 will work just fine).
6. After you test your connection, issue the ifconfig command and get your ISP's IP through its output.

7. Go back to the settings in YaST and change your ISP's IP to the correct value.

8. Press F4 to activate the network device.

9. Press F8 to enter your connection and the following ISDN information (see Figure 23.16):

- **Your Telephone Number (MSN)**—A list of MSN formats is available at the end of this chapter.

- **Number to be Called**—This is the number of the host ISP.

- **Only Given Numbers are Allowed**—No user is to call a number that is not given. This increases security.

- **Dial Mode**—This option defines how a connection should be started. You can select the dial mode to be Auto, Manual, or Off.

- **Idle Time**—How long the network should be up while no activity is noticed.

- **Name of PPP Login**—Enter your username here.

- **Password of PPP Login**—Enter your password here.

FIGURE 23.16

ISDN account information via YaST.

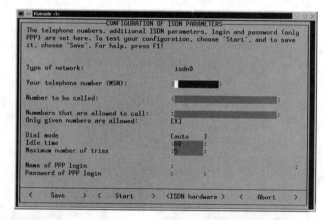

CAUTION

For people with `syncPPP`, you should turn off the BSD compression in the kernel for proper ISDN connections.

After you have set up your account, click Start to test the configuration. If you're satisfied with the configuration, click Save to save your settings.

The ISDN *rawip* Protocol

Follow these steps to set up the `rawip` protocol:

1. Launch YaST as root.

2. From the menu, choose System Administration, Network Configuration, Network Base Configuration. The Selection of Network dialog appears (refer to Figure 23.15).

3. Choose an empty number and press F5. This will enable you to select the proper device for the network interface.

4. Select the ISDN `rawip` protocol. This is one of the protocols to be used when using ISDN connections.

5. Enter your IP and your PtP IP (partner's IP). If you don't know these IPs or you use a dynamic IP with `syncIP`, use any values (`192.168.0.100` and `192.168.0.101` will work just fine).

6. After you test your connection, issue the `ifconfig` command and get your ISP's IP through its output.

7. Go back to the settings in YaST and change your ISP's IP to the correct value.

8. Press F4 to activate the network device.

9. Press F8 to enter your connection and the following ISDN information (refer to Figure 23.16):

    *   **Your Telephone Number (MSN)**—A list of MSN formats is available at the end of this chapter.

    *   **Number to be Called**—This is the number of the host ISP.

    *   **Only Given Numbers are Allowed**—No user is to call a number that is not given. This increases security.

    *   **Dial Mode**—Choose Auto, Manual, or Off.

    *   **Idle Time**—This is how long the network should be up while no activity is noticed.

    *   **Maximum Number of Tries**—This is how many trials to dial.

    *   **Name of PPP Login**—Enter your username here.

    *   **Password of PPP Login**—Enter your password here.

After you have filled in the data, press Start to test the new setup. If no problems occur, save the setup. If it gives you an error, skip ahead to the section "General ISDN Troubleshooting."

After you have saved your settings, start Netscape and open `http://www.suse.com`. After 2–3 seconds you should see the SuSE Web page. If you don't, read the section "General ISDN Troubleshooting."

Part

III

Ch

23

> **N O T E**   To correctly set a default route after a connection is terminated, you have to edit
> `/etc/ppp/ip-down`. Do this by issuing the following command:
>
> `bash#/sbin/init.d/route restart`
>
> This will set the route table to its original status. ■

The Terminal Login (*X.75*) Protocol

Setting up terminal login using the `X.75` protocol is a simple process. Let's say that your
ISDN device is `/dev/ttI0`. You can use minicom and configure it to use this device just like
you use your modem. What you get is an error message. Safely ignore it and issue the following commands:

```
ATZ
ATS14=0&Exxx     where xxx is your MSN number
```

Now dial the ISP number, which includes the area code as well as the phone number. You
should see the ISP login prompt.

Setting Up a Nameserver via YaST

To access a host by its name—for example, www.cnn.com—instead of by typing its IP, you
must set up your SuSE Linux to use DNS. This is accomplished through YaST, System administration, Network configurations, Configuration Nameserver. The steps to configure it are
fully explained in the earlier section "Setting Up YaST (Domain Name Server)."

General ISDN Troubleshooting

My ISDN card will not work when I test it when setting YaST.

Is your card supported by Linux? (See Appendix B.) Are the required packages installed?
Check whether the `kernmod` package is installed. Is the module already loaded? Check the
messages to see how the module you are trying to load reacts. Did you install the correct
driver from the kernel setup (only for people who compiled their kernels)?

How do I finish the ISDN connection?

Enter the following command as root to forcefully finish an ISDN connection:

`bash#/sbin/init.d/i4l stop;/sbin/init.d/i4l_hardware stop`

When I go offline, my default route is not correct. How should I fix this?

`Enter the following command as root:bash#/sbin/init.d/route restart`

I start the interface to test the new connection but I get an error.

Review the values you have just edited. Check the MSN list in the following section "MSN Format."

I have followed the steps described in this chapter and configured an ISDN connection. Now that I should be online, how can I test the connection?

Refer to the section "Testing an Existing Connection" earlier in this chapter for information on how to use `ifconfig`, `route`, and `ping` to test a connection.

Part
III

Ch
23

MSN Format

The following formats should be used with the corresponding countries. Table 23.6 is not complete but represents an example of what the MSN would be in some cases. If your country does not have MSN, you might want to try to see whether it would work the way it is represented in the table. Some PBXs still require a leading zero, though.

Table 23.6	MSN Formats in Some European Countries		
Country	Area Code	Phone Number	MSN
Italy	099	12345678	9912345678
Netherlands	099	12345678	9912345678
Austria	Xx	Xx	0 or none
Switzerland	Xx	123456	Rightmost digit=6
Portugal	Xx	Xx	0 or none

Configuring the Desktop

The K Desktop Environment

> "UNIX popularity grows thanks to the free variants, mostly Linux. But still a consistent, nice looking free desktop-environment is missing. There are several nice either free or low-priced applications available, so that Linux/X11 would almost fit everybody's needs if we could offer a real GUI."

The previous paragraph was the first paragraph of the posting by Matthias Ettrich in 1996. In his posting, he hit upon many important problems with the Linux desktop. At that point in time, there was nothing known as consistency in widget sets. You had to practice with each application to check the response of your Backspace key, which might work in one but not the other. Your mouse keys would behave one way in some applications but in a completely different way in others. Ettrich realized this inconsistency would make it hard for new users to switch to Linux and UNIX. In 1998, version 1.0 of the K Desktop Environment (KDE) was released. At that time, the KDE FTP contained not only the KDE base applications, but also numerous KDE-based applications. In January 1999, KDE version 1.1 was released. This version had many improvements over the 1.0 version. KDE was, and still is, progressing very quickly. The number of applications increases everyday. In late 1999, KDE released Krash, which is a developers' version of KDE 2.0 released only for testing. KDE 2.0 is considered a breakthrough in the Linux desktop over any scale.

SuSE Linux 6.3 comes equipped with KDE 1.1.2, which is the latest stable release of KDE. KDE is the primary desktop environment for SuSE Linux Snapshot, which is included on the CD that comes with this book. In this chapter, you will learn the philosophy of KDE, how to configure KDE, how to tweak it, and how to get the best performance out of it.

Understanding KDE

Before you begin configuring KDE, you should note some important points. If you are used to the Linux environment, you probably know most of these. If you are porting to SuSE Linux from the Windows 9x/NT environment, you definitely need to know these points.

KDE is not your operating system and is not responsible for configuring your system; it is only your desktop environment. In a Windows 9x/NT environment, the operating system is connected to the desktop environment, but this is not the case in SuSE Linux. Currently, some system configuration tools exist in KDE. Yet, to configure the system properly in SuSE Linux, you must use YaST. In some cases where YaST cannot configure a specific service, you might have to edit the configuration files manually.

On the other hand, many projects from the KDE team include packages that are meant to configure system services. Hopefully, we might find an alternative to editing configuration files for the services in the near future.

Installing KDE

KDE comes in two parts in the full version of SuSE Linux. The first part is the *KDE series*, which is the stable branch of KDE applications. The other part is *KPA*, which is the unstable branch of KDE. As mentioned earlier, an unstable KDE application is still usable.

KDE Integrated Framework

In the beginning, KDE was designed to offer an integrated alternative to the existing Linux programs. KDE programs understand drag and drop from and to each other. They communicate with each other and have the same look and feel. In other words, if you know how to use one KDE application, you know how to use other KDE applications.

KDE offers a Window Manager, Panel, and File Manager. These are the most important parts of KDE and make up most of its interface. In addition, numerous other applications are offered by KDE. The applications cover almost everything a normal user needs.

KDE Libraries

KDE-based applications all look and feel the same because they use what is called the *KDE Libraries*. KDE Libraries, which are free of charge, provide the basic tools for building an application. They are based on another famous library, Qt. *Qt* is a C++ library written by Troll Technologies. You can use the Qt library under the QPL restrictions, which is the Qt License. If you are going to create programs that use the Qt toolkit, you should read the Qt License. If you plan to release the programs you create under the GPL License, you can use Qt freely.

CAUTION

Although the Troll Qt Public License makes it easy for people to write applications that use the Qt toolkit freely, building commercial software using Qt requires that you buy the Qt toolkit. Please refer to the Qt Web site at `http://www.troll.no` for more information and the full listing of the license.

KDE Applications

KDE *applications* are applications that use the KDE Libraries. Accordingly, they all have the same look and feel. They also share the powerful APIs that KDE Libraries afford. KDE Libraries offer a wide variety of powerful functions that make the writing of an advanced program an easy task. Because almost all the applications that exist in the Linux world are released under the GPL license, a large number of those applications have been ported to KDE, thus offering the most powerful Linux and GNU tools to the user in a simple GUI where the user can simply point and click.

Starting KDE

Starting KDE on SuSE Linux is very easy. SuSE Linux 6.3 prepares your system to use graphical login using KDM by default. If you log in using KDM, enter your username and password, select KDE as your window manager, and click the Login button. You should log in to KDE immediately.

If you log in to your system using the normal console login, type the following:

```
bash$startx
```

If you have KDE installed, KDE should start immediately because it is the default desktop environment, if it's found on the system. For more information on how to set up graphical login using KDM, refer to Chapter 3, "Installing the X Window System."

KDE Basics

The first step in KDE is understanding the various parts of it. Your KDE interface consists of the following basic items:

- **KWM**—KWM is the KDE window manager. A window manager's importance arises from the fact that the X server does not offer any window decoration. KWM offers much more than decoration. KWM's functions will be discussed in detail in the next sections.

- **KPanel**—KPanel is the bar that contains the K button, which is normally used to start KDE applications. It also shows the current running programs to enable easy switching between them.

- **KFM**—The current KDE File Manager. KFM serves as file manager, mime-type handler, Web browser, and FTP client. Konquerer in KDE 2.0 will replace KFM.

In fact, although these are the parts you see, there are many other parts of KDE running behind the scenes to serve you. However, you should start by learning about what you can see.

KWM

KDE can use any KDE-compliant window manager. However, the default window manager that comes with KDE, KWM, works best with it. KWM is responsible for the following jobs:

- **Window decorations**—KWM draws the window decorations. Window decorations include the title bar for the windows, the window frames, and the window shape. KWM is *themable*, which means that you can apply themes to your windows instead of the default KDE theme. SuSE Linux comes with a large collection of KWM themes that can completely change the look of your KDE.

- **Window operations**—KWM is responsible for moving and resizing windows. You can move a window by holding the left mouse button on the window and moving the mouse, and you can resize a window by holding the left mouse button on the window frame and moving the mouse. KWM extends its functionality by offering the ability to do the following:

  - **Minimize a window**—You can minimize a window by clicking the minimize button. The minimize button is the dot button in the default KDE theme.

  - **Maximize a window**—You can maximize a window by clicking the maximize button. The maximize button is the box button in the default KDE theme.

  - **Close a window**—You can close a window by clicking the close button. The close button is the X button in the default KDE theme.

  - **Shade a window**—You can shade a window by double-clicking the window title bar.

  - **Make a window sticky**—You can choose to make a window sticky by clicking on the pin button. This makes the window available on all desktops.

- **Multiple desktops**—KDE offers the ability to have up to eight virtual desktops. Virtual desktops are a real blessing if you work with many opened windows. You can have some applications running on a desktop while others are open in another desktop. After you get used to the virtual desktop environment, you will be able to use it efficiently. You can make a window sticky, which will make it available on all desktops. It will move to other desktops as you move to them.

Part

IV

Ch

24

KPanel

KPanel is composed of two parts: the taskbar and the panel. Unlike the Windows 9x/NT panel, the taskbar is not embedded in the KPanel. The taskbar can be used to switch between applications, while the panel is used to start applications, move between desktops, and dock applications.

The Taskbar   The taskbar's default placement is above the panel where both of them are placed in the lower area of your desktop. The taskbar shows the names of your applications with clickable buttons next to them. You can click a minimized application to maximize it and vice versa. To show that the application is running on another virtual desktop, the taskbar puts an empty space between the windows buttons (see Figure 24.1). The following operations are supported by the taskbar:

FIGURE 24.1
While Display Settings and KDE Help are running on a virtual desktop, Konsole is running on another. You can identify this by the little space left between the KDE Help and Konsole buttons on the taskbar.

- **Left mouse click**—Opens an iconified window or iconifies an open window. It will move to the desktop that the window is in if necessary. If you are working with two open windows, it will only switch the focus from one to another.

- **Right mouse click**—Opens a pop-up window that gives you control over the window. You can maximize the window, minimize it, make it sticky, bring it to the current desktop, iconify other windows, and close the current window (see Figure 24.2).

FIGURE 24.2

A right mouse click on the taskbar buttons open up the menu for performing operations on an application.

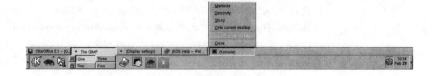

- **Middle mouse click**—Opens an iconified window or iconifies an open window. It will not move to the desktop where the window is. If you are working with two open windows, it will iconify the one you clicked. It switches the focus only when opening an iconified window.

The Panel   The KDE Panel is unique in style. It offers many capabilities to KDE users. The panel consists of seven important parts:

- **The show/hide buttons**—When you want more desktop space, you can hide the panel. If you click any of the arrow buttons at the panel corners, the panel will slide to disappear (see Figure 24.3). In this case, a small K button, a WindowList button, and a KDiskNavigator will appear in the taskbar. By clicking the arrow button that appears after you have selected to hide the panel, it will slide back and the three buttons will disappear from the taskbar.

FIGURE 24.3

Using the show/hide buttons, you can make more desktop space available to your applications.

- **The K button**—A K button with a wheel background is the default application starter button (see Figure 24.4). KDE applications add shortcuts in the K menu so it can be easily started afterwards. SuSE Linux adds a menu with many X applications.

- **Quick Launch buttons and folders**—By creating a quick launch button or folder, you can have fast access to your most frequently used applications. You can drag files or folders from the desktop over the panel to add them to your panel.

FIGURE 24.4
Use the K button to start your applications when running SuSE Linux.

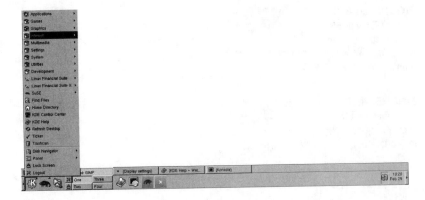

■ **Virtual Desktops**—You can switch between virtual desktops by clicking the virtual desktop number or name (see Figure 24.5). You can change the name of a virtual desktop by clicking it twice.

FIGURE 24.5
Virtual desktops help you manage your desktop more efficiently when using KDE.

Part
IV

Ch
24

■ **The Logout and the Lock Screen buttons**—Two small buttons are connected to the virtual desktop buttons (refer to Figure 24.5). The X shaped button is used to log out of the KDE, which closes all running programs. Be careful when logging out of KDE. If one of the programs you are running is not KDE-aware, you can lose any work you haven't saved manually because the program will not tell you you are closing it or give you the option to save your work. The other button on the KDE Panel has a lock icon. It locks your screen and requires that you enter your password so you can continue your KDE session. Use it when you're away from your computer.

■ **The Dock**—The dock is a special portion of the panel where KDE applications that support docking can leave an icon for quick access (see Figure 24.6). For example, you can configure kppp to dock when it connects to the Internet. It is designed so applications that do not require desktop space live in this dock, giving the user fast access to them. Try clicking, double-clicking, and right-clicking the applications that are docked to see their behavior.

■ **The clock**—The panel shows the time using a digital clock (see Figure 24.7). You can configure it to show the clock in different formats. It also can show the Internet beats instead of normal time.

FIGURE 24.6
Many KDE applications use the dock to save your panel space while running.

The dock

FIGURE 24.7
If you ever want to know what time it is, take a look at the clock.

The clock

KFM

While most file managers only offer managing local files, KFM can handle HTTP and FTP protocols. You can use KFM as a Web browser or to browse FTP sites. KFM offers the following capabilities:

- **Multitasking**—KFM does not block while copying or moving files. It is a fully multitasking file manager.

- **Drag-and-drop support**—You can drag files from KFM windows to other KFM windows. With drag-and-drop, you can move, copy, and create symbolic links.

- **Templates**—KFM enables you to create new files by using templates. You can add your own templates to the templates directory, which will cause them to appear in the New menu.

- **Directory customization**—You can customize how a specific directory looks by editing a .kde.html or index.html file and placing it in this directory. KFM will read those files instead of the directory contents.

- **Mime-Types**—KFM uses mime-types to assign each file extension to a program that is used to open it. For example, if you click a jpeg image, KView starts and opens the image.

- **System Devices**—KFM enables you to mount system devices with a simple mouse click. After you have set up your /etc/fstab as described in Chapter 5, "Managing Filesystems," you can create an icon for your CD-ROM to mount it and unmount it with mouse clicks.

- **Bookmarks**—You can add bookmarks to your KFM that are either on the Internet or local to your machine.

- **Autostart**—The Autostart folder on your desktop is where you should place programs you want to start upon login.

KDE Configuration

Earlier in this chapter, we stressed the fact that KDE is not your operating system. You should note that the systemwide configuration is performed primarily through YaST in SuSE Linux. However, KDE also offers programs that are used for system configuration.

KDE centralized configuration is accomplished through the KDE Control Center. The KDE *Control Center* offers a hierarchical configuration tree that relies on categories for quick access to what the user wants to configure.

The KDE Control Center is one of the icons on the KDE Panel by default. You also can access it by clicking K, KDE Control Center.

KDE Control Center

When the KDE Control Center starts, it shows a window that contains the following (see Figure 24.8):

- The KDE version, so you can know which KDE version you're currently running
- Your username and hostname
- Your system type and kernel information

It also shows the available KDE Control Center modules installed on the system in a tree-like hierarchy. The following sections include a node-by-node explanation of the tree branches.

FIGURE 24.8
You can get information about the KDE version, Kernel version, and hostname from the KDE Control Center.

Configuration Applications

In the Applications branch, you can control several KDE applications.

KDE su The KDE su application is used to pass the root password to some application so you can run as root for a specific period of time or while performing a specific operation.

Login Manager—KDM Configuration If you use KDM for graphical login to your SuSE Linux, you can configure KDM using this branch. To modify the KDM options, you must log in to KDE as root. This enables you to configure KDM through the following tabs (see Figure 24.9):

FIGURE 24.9
You can configure KDM by changing the Login Manager configuration in the Applications branch of the KDE Control Center.

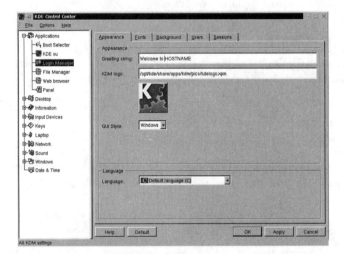

- **Appearance**—You can change the welcome message that appears on top of KDE when you log in to your system by editing the Greeting string. You also can change the KDM logo by either typing one in the path in the KDM logo field or clicking the KDM icon and browsing to select the logo you want. In addition, you can select the style of widgets KDM should use, which can be either Windows or Motif styles. The last field is the Language field, from which you can choose the language you want KDM to use.

- **Fonts**—The Fonts tab enables you to set the fonts for KDM. KDM uses three fonts. The first is the Greeting font, which it uses to write the welcome message. To change the welcome message font, select Greeting from the combo box and click Change to change the properties of the font. The second font KDM uses is the standard font, which it uses to write the usernames and default labels. To change this font, select Standard from the combo box and click Change to change its properties. The last font is the Fail font, which KDM uses to write `login failed` in case of failed logins. Select Fail from the combo box and click Change to change the properties of the Fail font.

- **Background**—You can change the KDM background by selecting one of the following options:

- **Solid color**—Check the Solid color check box and click the color button to change the color. Make sure there is no background wallpaper selected.

- **Horizontal or Vertical blends**—Check the corresponding check box and click the color buttons to change the color blends.

- **Wallpaper**—Select the wallpaper by clicking the combo box to get a list of the wallpapers that come with KDE by default. If you want to use other wallpaper, you can click the browse button to browse to the image you want to set as wallpaper. The check boxes under the wallpaper combo box control the wallpaper orientation. You can choose to tile the wallpaper or have it scaled to fill in the screen. If your wallpaper does not fill all the screen, the colors selected will fill the rest of the screen.

- **Fancy**—Check this check box to get a fancy, moving KDE logo.

Part

IV

Ch

24

- **Users**—The Users tab enables you to control the users whom you want your KDM to show or hide (see Figure 24.10). Three list boxes appear in this tab. You can move users from one list to another by clicking the arrow buttons beside the lists. The lists are as follows:

FIGURE 24.10
You can manage how KDM shows or hides users with the users interface in KDM users management.

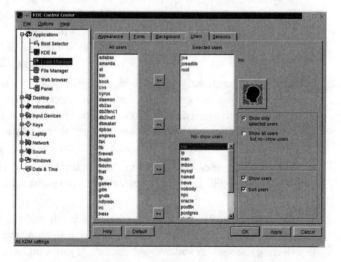

- **All users**—This list shows all the users on the system. In fact, it shows the users who are not included in either of the other two list boxes.

- **Selected users**—This list shows the users you select. If you check the Show only selected users button, only users in this list will be shown as icons in KDM. Even if a user is not shown in an icon, he can still log in to the system by entering his username manually.

- **No-show users**—Users in this list will not be shown as icons in the KDM login manager. If you check the Show All Users But No-Show Users Box, the users in the All users list will be shown as icons. Users belonging to this list will not show up as icons in KDM.

  You can uncheck the Show Users check box to hide all users and allow logins only by typing in the username and password. Also, if you check the Sort Users check box, users' icons will be sorted according to username. By selecting a user from any group and clicking the icon, you can change the icon that belongs to this user. The default KDM users icon path is `/opt/kde/share/apps/kdm/pics/ users`. If you add more icons to this path, you will be able to set up an icon for each user who can access the system. It is convenient for each user to have her icon so that she won't have to read the username or type it in. Use different icons for quick access to the system.

■ **Sessions**—KDM enables you to control the behavior of shutting down the system and session types through the Sessions tab. The groups in this tab are as follows:

- **Allow to shutdown**—You can choose which people are allowed to shut down the system using KDM with the options available in this combo box. The selections are All: All users are allowed to shut down the system; Root Only: After the user clicks shutdown, she must enter the root password to shut down the system; Console Only: Users can shut down the system using the console; and None: No user is allowed to shut down the system using KDM.

- **Shutdown command**—In this field, you must enter the command KDM should use to shut down the system. If your system supports turning off the system— most ATX motherboards do—you can choose to use the command `/sbin/ poweroff`. KDE comes with the command `/sbin/halt` by default. The latter command shuts down only the operating system, not the computer.

- **Restart command**—This field should contain the restart command. The restart command on SuSE Linux is `/sbin/reboot`. There isn't much that you can change in this field.

- **Session types**—This list contains the sessions that appear in the KDM session type combo box upon login. You can remove a session from the KDM list by selecting the session and clicking remove. If you want to add a session, type in the session name—the executable name of the window manager—and click Add. You can move sessions up and down in the list by selecting the session you want to move and using the up and down arrows next to the session list.

File Manager   The File Manager node in the Applications branch is used to configure the look and feel of KFM when it's used as a file manager (see Figure 24.11). The File Manager configuration has the following tabs:

■ **Fonts**—You can set up the default font size for the file manager to be small, medium, or large by checking the corresponding box. The Fonts tab also has the following options:

- **Standard Font**—You can change the proportional font for your KFM by selecting a proportional font from this combo box.

- **Fixed Font**—You can select a non-proportional font for your KFM by selecting a font from this list.

- **Default Charset**—You can select a default charset to be used when displaying text in KFM by selecting one of the charsets in this combo box. If you set it to Use language charset, it automatically will be set to the language you use.

FIGURE 24.11
You can change the KFM fonts to suit your preferences.

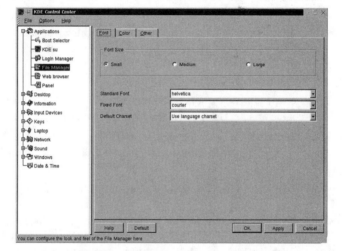

■ **Color**—From this tab, you can control the colors and configurations for your KFM. You can change the background color, normal text color, and link color by clicking the color button next to them. You can also choose to do the following:

- **Make your cursor shape change over links**—You can do this by checking the Change cursor over link check box. This is a good option to check.

- **Make links appear underlined**—You can do this by checking the Underline links check box. This is a good option to have turned on onscreen, but remember to turn off this option when printing.

- **Make KFM use the colors you specify**—You can do this by checking the Always Use my Colors check box and entering the color(s) you want in this dialog. The colors you specify will override any settings in the document.

Konquerer, the Web Browser KFM also can server as a Web browser. Just as any other powerful Web browser does, KFM enables you to set up proxy settings, HTTP settings, browser identification settings, and cookies settings. In fact, the KFM Web browser called Konquerer will be the KDE file manager name of future versions. The following tabs include the settings for Konquerer:

- **Proxy**—If you enable the Proxy check box, you will be able to edit the proxy settings for the KFM Web browser. Enter the values for your proxy settings and KFM will start using them immediately. You can enter the IP addresses you don't want to use in the No Proxy For field.

- **HTTP**—In this tab, you can enter the settings Konquerer should use when receiving documents using the HTTP protocol. The settings include the following:

  - **Accept languages**—Some Web sites can send many versions of the same HTML page in many languages. You can specify which languages you want KFM to accept by typing them here. Abbreviations are used for the languages, such as "en" for English, "fr" for French, and so forth. You can set it to * to accept all languages.

  - **Accept character sets**—You can set up Konquerer to accept or deny specific character sets. Using * will accept any character set.

  - **Assume HTML**—Some sites send HTML data without sending the correct information that specifies the document as an HTML document. This option will assume that the received document is an HTML document unless otherwise specified by the Web site.

- **User agent**—In many cases, Web sites will ask the browser to identify itself and its version before the site sends the data to the browser. In the User Agent tab, you can tell Konquerer to identify itself using other well-known browsers and browser versions so that the Web site is assured it is capable of viewing the page. Enter the Web site to which you want Konquerer to identify itself as another browser in the On Server field. Then enter how you want Konquerer to identify itself in the Login field. After you have entered the correct information, click Add to add it to the User Agent list.

  The most famous Web browsers are

  - **Mozilla**—Used by Netscape Navigator to identify itself. Append version 3 to ensure you can view frames.

  - **Internet Explorer**—Used by Microsoft Internet Explorer to identify itself. Append version 3 to ensure you can view frames.

  Note that Konquerer is not 100% compatible with either Mozilla or Internet Explorer. The page might not look the same if you see it using Netscape Navigator, for example.

- **Cookies**—Some Web sites use cookies to store information about you so that you don't have to enter this information each time you enter the site. Cookies are stored locally on your hard drive and do not require large disk space. You can control how KFM behaves with cookies. You can choose to disable cookies or have Konquerer ask you before it receives cookies. You also can delete a cookie by selecting it from the list and clicking Delete. You can choose to not accept cookies from a certain Web site by entering the Web site's address and clicking Reject.

Panel   The Panel node includes both taskbar and panel settings. In this node, you can configure how your panel should look, how it should behave, the virtual desktops settings, and the disk navigator settings. The settings are configured through the following tabs:

■ **Panel**—The Panel tab enables you to set up the look of your panel and taskbar. You can set their placements by selecting the check boxes that correspond to the location of each. For example, you can set up your taskbar to be on top by selecting the Top check box in the Taskbar group box. Or, you can move the panel to the right side of the screen by selecting Right from the Location group box (see Figure 24.12).

FIGURE 24.12
Changing the placement of the panel in KDE is as easy as checking some radio buttons. You also can access this dialog by right-clicking the panel and selecting Configure.

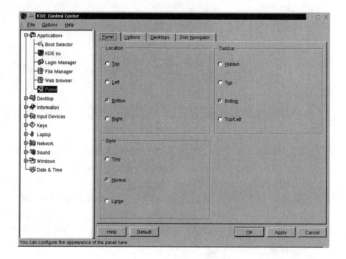

In addition, you can set the icon size of the panel to be Tiny, Normal, or Large by selecting the appropriate check box in the Style group. If you are running KDE on a high resolution, it's a good idea to configure this option to show large icons. People with KDE running on low resolution might prefer to have tiny icons.

■ **Options**—You can customize your panel to some extent by setting options for it. The options, as shown in Figure 24.13, include the following:

● **Show Menu Tooltips**—By showing menu tooltips, when you open the K menu, a tooltip will appear for each application in the menu. This is a good option for people using KDE for the first time. For example, if you open K, Internet and move the mouse over kppp, a tooltip will tell you this is an Internet dial-up tool.

You can customize the delay after which the tooltip should appear by using the delay slider. A small delay makes the tooltip appear after a short amount of time when the mouse pointer is placed over the application, while a large delay makes the tooltip appear after a longer period of time when the mouse pointer is placed over the application.

FIGURE 24.13

You can always change the feel of the panel by using the Panel options.

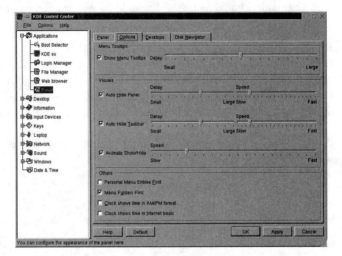

- **Visuals**—You can configure the panel, taskbar, or both to disappear when the mouse pointer is not over them by checking the Auto Hide Panel or Auto Hide Taskbar check box. For example, if you choose to auto hide the taskbar, the taskbar will scroll to disappear, leaving only a tiny line on the corner of the screen where it disappeared. When the mouse pointer touches this line, the taskbar will immediately appear again. This option is helpful because it can save desktop space.

  You can configure the properties of the Auto Hide option by using the sliders associated with the panel and taskbar. For example, if you set the delay to be short, the taskbar hides itself after the pointer has moved out of its area. If you set the delay to long, the taskbar waits for a while before it disappears. The Speed slider corresponds to the speed at which the taskbar hides itself when it starts to disappear. In other words, it is the speed at which the taskbar slides.

  The last check box in the Visuals group is Animate Show/Hide. As you might recall from a previous section in this chapter, you can click the arrow buttons on the panel to hide the panel. If you want to animate the panel while hiding it, you can check this option. You also can set the speed of the animation by moving the slider.

■ **Desktops**—If you want to increase or decrease the number of virtual desktops shown on the panel, you can do so by moving the Visible slider, which will increase or decrease the number of available desktops. On the other hand, you can increase the width of the visual desktop buttons on the panel by increasing or decreasing the width using the Width slider. This option is used when the text you set to a virtual desktop name is larger than the default space provided by KDE and is therefore chopped off.

■ **Disk Navigator**—One of the most interesting KDE features is that it adds a disk navigator to the K menu. The disk navigator enables you to navigate through your system and mount devices through the K menu. The disk navigator settings include editing the personals and shared menus that appear in the Disk Navigator branch in the K menu. It can be configured to store recent files and directories through the Max recent files and Max recent folders fields. You also can choose to not show some fields by unchecking their corresponding check boxes.

Desktop

KDE was originally created to supply UNIX and Linux users a powerful desktop. This is why you see many applications and settings created specifically to bring the power of Linux to the desktop. In the Desktop branch of the K Control Center, you can customize your KWM and KFM settings for the desktop, default language, fonts, advanced power management settings, and more. This section helps you to understand what each node in the desktop branch does:

■ **Background**—This node sets up the background of your desktop. Its settings include having a different background for each virtual desktop or having one common background for all virtual desktops. Backgrounds can be colors or wallpapers. The Background node has the following options:

- **Color**—Click the Color button to change the color of the background. You can choose to make a blend or tile of two colors by selecting the two colors check box. To set up your favorite blend or tile, click Setup and select your favorite blend or tile orientation.

- **Wallpaper**—You can choose one of the wallpapers that come with SuSE Linux by selecting it from the wallpaper combo box. SuSE Linux comes with a large number of tiles. If you want to make your own background wallpaper, you can select it by clicking Browse and browsing to your image. If you check the Random check box, KDE will randomly change your wallpaper from a list you create by clicking Setup.

When you click Setup to set up a random wallpaper list, a random mode setup dialog with an empty list appears. You can fill the dialog from a file by checking the Pick Files From Directory check box and clicking Browse to select the directory. You can add images one by one to the list by clicking the Add button, in which case you will be able to select images rather than directories. Enter the time delay between image changes in the Time Delay in Seconds field. Images will be changed randomly unless you check the In Order check box, which causes the images to be changed according to the order in which they appear in the list.

The background properties include an option that makes the desktop properties dialog dock an icon in the panel. This makes it easier for a user to quickly access the desktop settings. The *cache size* is the amount of memory the screen needs to be adjusted. This value varies according to your desktop background wallpaper or color and the size of your display. The larger the cache amount, the higher the desktop changing and loading is.

■ **Borders**—The Borders node enables you to set the behavior of your windows and desktop borders. If you enable Active Desktop Borders, when you move your mouse to the edge of the desktop, you will immediately switch to another desktop. This option is not recommended for people who are not used to it because the swapping of the desktop can get users lost between virtual desktops. An interesting feature is associated with this option—moving the pointer toward the center of the screen after a switch. You can set up the sensitivity of this active desktop feature by using the Desktop Switch Delay slider.

■ **Colors**—The Display node is used to configure the KDE color schemes. You can choose a pre-configured color scheme or create your own color scheme. If you move the mouse to click one of the objects in the mini display screen that shows a desktop with an open application, you can modify the color of the selected object. You can set up the contrast of the scheme by using the Contrast slider.

N O T E   Using a high color contrast is recommended. High contrast gives your applications more focus and is easier on your eyes. ■

■ **Fonts**—Font settings are highly configurable in SuSE Linux. You can change the font settings of the following font categories:

- **General font**—General font is the font used in normal windows. This is the most frequently used font you'll see in your KDE applications.
- **Fixed font**—The non-proportional font that is used in most applications.
- **Window title font**—Window titles use this font setting.
- **Panel clock font**—The font that the clock on the panel uses.

To change any of these fonts, you must select it first and then change the font family, character set, and size.

■ **Desktop icons**—In this branch, you can customize the look of your desktop icons (see Figure 24.14). Use the Horizontal Root Grid Spacing and Vertical Root Grid Spacing fields to customize the spacing of your desktop and folder icons.

You can make the background text of your desktop icons transparent by checking the Transparent Text For Desktop Icons check box. Use the colored buttons to select the Icon foreground color and Background text color. This changes the color of the icons' text and background. If you check the Show Hidden Files on Desktop box, files that start with a dot will appear on your desktop; otherwise, they will not.

FIGURE 24.14
Use the desktop icon settings to tweak the look of your desktop.

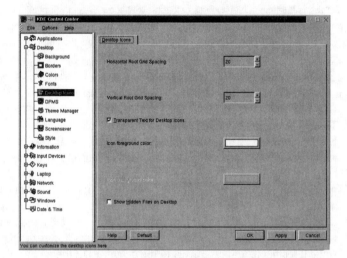

■ **DPMS**—This node is used to configure the advanced power management of your PC. Check the DPMS Enabled check box to activate this functionality. The DPMS node contains the following options:

- **Standby Time**—Use this slider to set the delay after which the monitor will go to standby mode if the system is not used.

- **Suspend Time**—Use this slider to set the delay after which the monitor will go to suspend mode if the system is not used.

- **Off Time**—Use this slider to set the delay after which the monitor will go to off mode if the system is not used.

Hint

You can configure DPMS to your KDM so that your monitor can use the standby, suspend, and off modes if no one logs on to the system for a long time. To do so, open your /etc/XF86Config file and add the following lines to it.

In the Device section, add the following line:

```
Option      "power_saver"
```

continues

continued

In the Screen section, add the following lines:

```
BlankTime    5
SuspendTime  10
OffTime      15
```

`BlankTime` is the time in idle minutes before the X Window System will blank the screen. `SuspendTime` is the amount of idle time in minutes before the monitor is put into suspend mode. Finally, `OffTime` is the amount of idle time in minutes before the monitor is turned off.

The `/etc/XF86Config` file usually contains more than a screen section. If you find yourself confused as to which one you should add the lines to, add the lines to all of them. If you have used SaX to set up your X Window, you will find only two screen sections.

■ **Theme Manager**—To completely change the look of your KDE, you can use themes. KDE themes can change the window borders, colors, and so on. SuSE Linux comes with a reasonable number of KDE themes that will appear in the theme list when you click the Theme node in the Desktop branch (see Figure 24.15). If you click a theme, a preview of the theme appears in the preview window with a short description underneath it. You can customize which theme content you want to apply to the selected theme by using the Contents tab. After you have selected a theme and the contents you want to apply to the theme, click Apply to test your settings or OK to use the theme without testing it. You can revert to the default KDE theme by selecting Default from the theme list and selecting all the contents on the Contents tab.

FIGURE 24.15
You can easily change your KDE theme using the KDE Theme Manager.

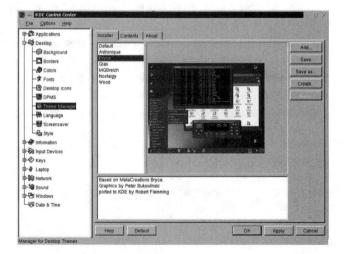

■ **Languages**—KDE supports many languages, and KDE programmers come from many countries. This is why KDE programs have many translations. In some cases, the program might come with translations for only a few languages. You can set your language preference by selecting the first language to be your preferred language. If the program does not have support for your default language, KDE will try to find a translation for your second preferred language. The same goes for the third preferred language. You can customize your language preferences by selecting them from the three combo boxes or leaving them at their default setting, which is English.

■ **Screensaver**—The Screensaver node is used to configure the settings of the screensaver. You can select the screensaver you want to use from the Screensavers list. After you have selected a screensaver, a preview of the screensaver appears in the preview monitor. You can configure the selected screensaver settings by clicking the Setup button located under the Screensaver list (see Figure 24.16). Or, you can test your screensaver settings by clicking Test.

FIGURE 24.16
You can configure your screensaver to be active when clicking the corners of the preview monitor.

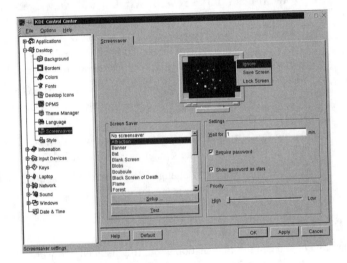

The general settings for the screensaver are as follows:

- **Wait for**—This field sets the delay after which the screensaver starts.
- **Require password**—If you check this check box, you will have to enter your password after the screensaver has started.
- **Show password as stars**—If you must enter a password because your screensaver requires a password or if you have locked the screen, the password will appear as stars if this check box is enabled.
- **Priority**—This slider is used to indicate the priority of the screensaver to the system. Screensavers will look good in high priority, but other processes are usually more important. We recommend that you set this to the minimum.

The preview monitor in the Screensavers node is used not only for previewing the selected screensaver, but you can also use it to set the corners of the screen at which you want to invoke the screensaver or lock the screen immediately. If you use the left mouse button to click one of the corners, a pop-up menu appears with the following values:

- **Ignore**—If you move the mouse pointer to this corner, nothing happens.
- **Save screen**—If you move the mouse pointer to this corner, the screensaver will start.
- **Lock screen**—If you move the mouse pointer to this corner, the screen will lock.
- **Style**—This node enables you to configure the look of the widgets, the style of non-KDE applications, and the panel icon style.
- **Draw widgets of the style of Window 95**—Qt widgets can use the Windows 95 style or Motif style. Set this check box to your preferred widget set. KDE 1.1.x uses the Qt 1.42+ libraries, which support only the Motif and Windows 95 look and feel. KDE 2.0, however, uses Qt 2.0 libraries, which enables you to apply themes to the widgets. KDE 2.0 will be completely themable.
- **Menubar on top of the screen in the style of MacOS**—This option puts a menu at the top of the screen. If you are used to MacOS, you will feel at home with this option.
- **Apply fonts and colors to non-KDE applications**—KDE will try to make non-KDE applications look as similar as possible to KDE applications.

The icon style enables you to change the size of the icons used in the Panel, KFM, and Other. Change the size to your preference by selecting the corresponding check box.

Information

In this branch, you can get information about the installed and working devices on the system. Most of the information in this branch is read from the /proc filesystem. Use this branch to query information about your devices, system memory, Samba status, and so on.

Input Devices

KDE enables you to control the behavior of the system's input devices. Input devices in this branch include the International Keyboard, Joystick, Keyboard, and Mouse. More devices will definitely be added in the future, but so far, these are the only ones. An explanation of each node follows:

- **International Keyboard**—This node enables you to change the language to your native language (see Figure 24.17). Clicking Add causes a list of the available languages to appear. Select the language you want to add and then click OK. You can arrange the languages in the list by clicking the Up and Down buttons.

In the StartUp tab, set International Keyboard to Autostart to ensure that it starts the next time you start KDE. You can make it iconify itself as a dock icon to enable fast access to it.

FIGURE 24.17
To localize your KDE, use the International Keyboard to quickly change the settings from one language to another. This also will apply to the language of your KDE applications.

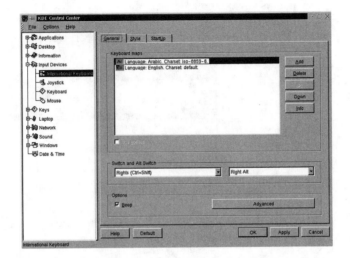

- **Joystick**—This node enables you to calibrate your Joystick axis. It will load the Joystick driver, if present.
- **Keyboard**—This node enables you to set up your keyboard auto repeat and key click volume.
- **Mouse**—In this node, you can configure the mouse settings. You can set up the mouse acceleration and mouse threshold using the sliders. After you have set the mouse speed settings, you can swap the mouse buttons to your preference by checking the Right Handed or Left Handed check boxes.

Keys

You can set the key combination defaults that come with KDE to your preferences using this branch. You also can define new combinations to perform some KDE-specific operations, start programs, or send signals to running programs:

- **Global keys**—These are the KDE desktop management–specific key bindings (see Figure 24.18). You can modify them to your preferences. For example, if you have a Microsoft Natural Keyboard or compatible, you might want to assign the Windows key to open the K menu instead of Alt+F1. To do so, follow these steps:
    1. Select the Pop-up System Menu from the Action list.
    2. Click the Custom Key radio button.

3. Uncheck the Shift, Ctrl, and Alt check boxes.

4. Click the key-shaped button to activate it and press the Windows key on your keyboard. The key text will change to Super_L or Super_R according to the Windows key you pressed.

FIGURE 24.18
The KDE global keys are used to create key combinations that will be used in Windows Management.

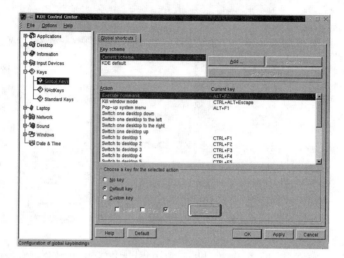

■ **KHotKeys**—This node enables you to configure the KHotKeys program settings (see Figure 24.19). You can run programs or send a signal to a running program using KHotKeys. Click Add Action to create a new entry and edit the settings for the action you want to perform when you press the hotkey.

FIGURE 24.19
Using KHotKeys, you can create shortcuts to start your favorite programs.

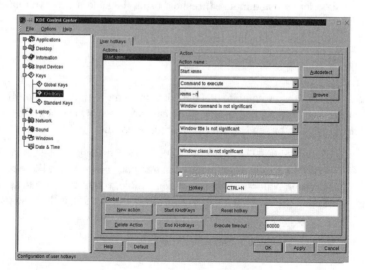

■ **Standard Keys**—Use this node to configure standard key bindings that are not specific to KDE management but are applied on all KDE applications. They follow the same methodology used to configure the Global Keys.

Laptop

This branch is specific to laptop machines, as you might have realized. You can configure KDE to warn you of a low or critical battery if you are running KDE on a laptop. You also can check your PCMCIA by using the PCMCIA node. If you want to enable auto suspend/standby, you must use the Power Control node, which requires that you have a running apmd.

Network

The Network branch is used to control the networking facilities on the system. Most of the configuration performed in this branch requires root privileges and that you run KDE Control Center as root. Using the Network branch, you can do the follwing:

■ Configure BIND.

■ Configure DHCP.

■ Configure kISDN, a KDE application used to automate ISDN connections.

■ Configure Talk.

■ Configure PGP settings.

Sound

KDE enables you to associate actions with events. The Bell node is used to configure the system speaker settings, whereas the System Sounds node enables you to configure the sounds you hear along with a KWM event.

To configure System Sounds, check the Enable System Sounds check box, select the event for which you want to set a sound, and select the sound from the Sounds list, as shown in Figure 24.20.

Part

IV

Ch

24

FIGURE 24.20

Using KDE system sounds, you can associate KWM events with sounds.

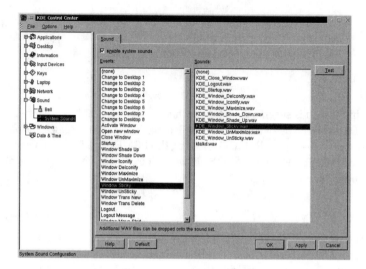

Windows

The Windows branch enables you to configure KWM. The customization enables you to tweak KWM to your optimal preferences. The nodes in this branch are as follows:

- **Advanced**—The Advanced tab contains two main groups (see Figure 24.21):
  - **Keyboard and Mouse**—This group enables you to configure KWM's response to keyboard and mouse events.

    You can configure the Ctrl+Tab binding to switch desktops by enabling the Ctrl+Tab Walks Through Desktops check box. If you enable the check box Alt+Tab Is Limited to Current Desktop, when you press Alt+Tab, it will show only the applications on the current desktop. Otherwise, it will show all the applications on all the desktops. The Alt+Tab mode can be set to either KDE or CDE mode. The KDE mode pops up a graphical, borderless dialog that shows the application names and icons before you can switch to one of them. The CDE mode switches between open windows directly. The last option in the Keyboard and Mouse group is a check box in which you indicate whether or not you want to make the right mouse button available to KWM. Some applications do grab this mouse button—for example, GIMP. Uncheck this option if you've had any trouble with the right mouse button in any application.

  - **Filters**—Using this option, you can start an application in a special decoration mode. For example, if you want Kicq to start as a sticky application, follow these steps:

    1. Select Start as Sticky from the Windows Will combo box.

2. Enter `kicq` in the Classes field; the + button will be enabled.

3. Click the + button.

The next time you start Kicq, it will be started as a sticky application.

FIGURE 24.21

Advanced KDE configurations for Alt+Tab behavior and filters for windows.

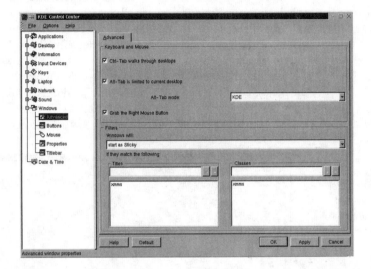

■ **Buttons**—KWM enables you to control which buttons you want in the windows title. You also can choose where those buttons should be placed. For example, if you select the Off radio button in front of Sticky, the sticky button will not appear in the window's title bar.

■ **Mouse**—This option enables you to control the behavior of all mouse actions. KDE default settings are compatible with Windows 9x/NT mouse click settings. You can change the settings by selecting the behavior you want from the corresponding combo box.

■ **Properties**—From this node, you can configure the properties of windows and the placement of new windows (see Figure 24.22). The settings are separated into three groups:

  • **Windows**—In this group, you can configure the behavior of your windows when you maximize, move, or resize windows. Uncheck the Vertical Maximization Only by Default box to make your windows fill the whole area of the desktop when you click the Maximize button. If your system is not fast, it is recommended that you uncheck the Display Content in Moving Windows and Display Content in Resizing Windows check boxes. The Resize Animation slider controls the speed of the maximization or minimization action of a window.

- **Placement policy**—You can select where the newly opened windows will appear. Select one of the methods in the combo box. The KDE team recommends the Smart policy.

- **Focus policy**—The Focus policy combo box determines which window gets activated. Microsoft Windows' focus policy is Click to Focus, in which a user must click the application to activate the window. Focus Follows Mouse activates the window in which the mouse pointer is located. The focus changes only when the mouse pointer enters another window. Classic Focus Follows Mouse is similar to Focus Follows Mouse, but it allows the Alt+Tab combination to switch focus. If the mouse pointer is not over a window, no window is in focus. The last option is the Classic Sloppy Focus, which is similar to Classic Focus Follows Mouse, except that the Alt+Key combination doesn't switch focus.

FIGURE 24.22
Using Windows properties, you can control Window movement and resize, placement, and focus policies.

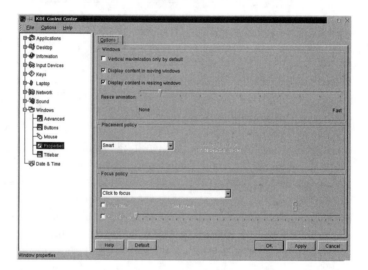

- **Titlebar**—The Titlebar node gives you control over the titlebar's look and feel. You can choose the placement of the titlebar text and appearance by selecting one of the Title Alignment radio buttons. You also can choose a title or image for the titlebar in its active or inactive states from the Appearance group. The Mouse Action group determines what KDM does when you double-click the titlebar; KDE's default is to shade the window. If you want to change the action to Microsoft's default, which is maximizing/minimizing the window, select (Un)Maximize from the Left Button Double Click Does combo box. KDE text title animates if the window title width is not wide enough to display the whole text. You can set the animation speed by using the Title Animation slider.

KDE Applications

KDE is most famous for its large number of applications. It is not possible to list them all because there is an application released everyday! However, this section will mention the most important KDE applications.

KOffice

KOffice is a fully integrated office suite based on the KDE Libraries. Unfortunately, it does not come with SuSE Linux 6.3 because the latest versions of KOffice require KDE 2.0 Libraries. It is worth mentioning that KOffice will be released with SuSE Linux at the same time that KDE 2.0 is distributed with it.

KOffice is made up of 10 components:

- **KWord**—A professional word processor.
- **KSpread**—A powerful spreadsheet program.
- **KPresenter**—An advanced presentation program.
- **KIllustrator**—A vector drawing program for KDE.
- **KImageShop**—A professional bitmap image editor.
- **KAtabase**—A desktop database application that supports forms, reports, and scripting.
- **KFormula**—A formula editor for the KOffice project.
- **KChart**—The KOffice chart drawing application.
- **KImage**—The KOffice image viewer.
- **Filters**—This makes the other parts of KOffice support as many file formats as possible.

Others

In this section, we will discuss a few more KDE applications. If you have installed the full version of SuSE Linux 6.3 and have chosen to install the whole KDE branch and KDE alpha branch, your K list will be full of applications. Take your time to experiment and see what those applications can do. You will definitely find most of them useful. The following are applications that most people use:

- **KMail**—A very powerful email client. KMail comes with SuSE Linux 6.3. To start KMail, click K, Internet, KMail. KMail integrates with KAb, which is an address book application for KDE. You will be able to manage your email as well as your contacts by using a combination of these two applications.
- **kppp**—The Internet dial-up utility for KDE. Kppp makes connectivity to the Internet using SuSE Linux very easy. Refer to Chapter 23, "Connectivity to the Internet," for information about how to set up kppp to connect to the Internet.

Part

IV

Ch

24

- **KWrite**—A text editor for KDE. KWrite can highlight syntax when used as a development environment. It is integrated in the KDevelop application, which is mainly used for C/C++ application development.

- **KNotes**—A small dock application that is used to store sticky notes in your dock.

- **Konsole**—Your KDE terminal application program. Konsole is highly configurable compared to most terminal emulation programs. It supports a wide range of terminal emulation protocols and manages sessions that can be used quickly. You can open more than one terminal emulation session in the same window so you don't fill up your desktop with consoles.

- **KBiff**—A small dock application that docks in your KPanel and checks whether you have new email.

- **KIcq**—An ICQ client for KDE. It has most of the features that come with the AOL ICQ client for Windows.

- **KPm**—A process management program that enables you to send signals to running processes. Use this program to kill applications that halted and wouldn't close.

- **KDevelop and the upcoming Kstudio**—Used for software development (see Figure 24.23). They provide full project management for a development environment. These two applications, especially KDevelop, have done a lot to increase the speed at which other K applications are created.

FIGURE 24.23

The development of new KDE applications is expected to quicken in pace thanks to KDevelop and other KDE development programs that were created to make the lives of KDE programmers easier.

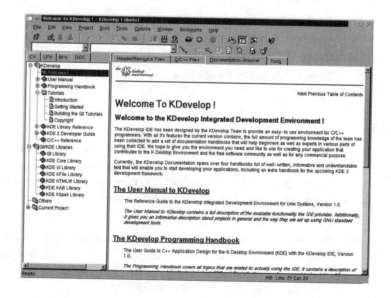

Troubleshooting KDE

I just installed a KDE application but it won't show up in my K menu.

Right-click the panel and click Restart to update the changes.

KDM keeps flashing and I can't use the system.

Try to reboot the system by pressing Alt+Ctrl+Del until the system catches the reboot signal. At the LILO prompt, type Linux 2 to enter your system in console mode. Reconfigure your X Window System and make sure you can start it using the startx command.

GNOME

GNOME (GNU Network Open Model Environment) is the result of a project by the same name to create a user-friendly desktop environment for flavors of UNIX. As Linux started to gain ground with new users, the need for a user-friendly desktop was undeniable. This need was the inspiration behind the creation of GNOME, a completely free desktop environment. KDE was created for the exact same purpose; however, it's not entirely free because it uses the QT user interface library that is not under the GPL license. GNOME, on the other hand, is entirely made up of GPL modules and libraries, so it is sometimes favored over KDE.

To understand what GNOME has achieved, you need to understand the graphical world of Linux. Linux uses the X Window System to display graphics. The X Window System in and of itself is not very usable; its sole purpose is to provide applications with the capability to display graphics. A window manager runs on top of the X Window System to enable the user to interact with the running applications. This interaction includes moving, resizing, minimizing, and maximizing the application windows. The X Window System does not handle that for you, the window manager does.

For a long time, Linux only had window managers. Some of these window managers had extra features such as application launch panels that could be used to create icons for applications and launch them without using the command line. Others used menus that popped up when you clicked the desktop and had shortcuts to the most common applications on the system. Running applications seldom involved any interaction between the applications. You couldn't really drag a file from one application and drop it in another one. Every application was detached from the others, unless it was explicitly programmed to communicate with others.

GNOME offers the user a desktop environment, not a window manager. A *desktop environment* is different from a window manager in the sense that it offers integration among the running applications. Applications can exchange data among themselves using drag-and-drop. GNOME has brought integration and collaboration of applications to the user.

The GNOME team achieved this by building a framework a developer can use to create his application, and this framework is the core of GNOME. This enables the application to use all the user-friendly features GNOME has to offer. This includes session management, which restores your desktop to the same look you left it in when you last logged out. Drag-and-drop among applications is now possible because applications are all developed using the GNOME framework, which uses drag-and-drop.

The GNOME user interface is built using the GNOME core framework, enabling all GNOME components to work together very well. GNOME is a highly configurable desktop environment; you can control almost every aspect of how it looks and feels. You are not tied to simple themes that just change your background and scheme colors; you can control everything. You can change the look of the widget set (buttons, scrollbars, check boxes, and so on) to make them look completely different. GNOME is not only productive and user-friendly, it's also a lot of fun to use and watch.

GNOME is made up of a few core components—the Panel, File Manager, and Control Center. Figure 24.24 shows a fresh installation of GNOME. You can see the Window Manager, File Manager, Control Center, and Panel in the figure.

FIGURE 24.24
A fresh installation of GNOME (first run).

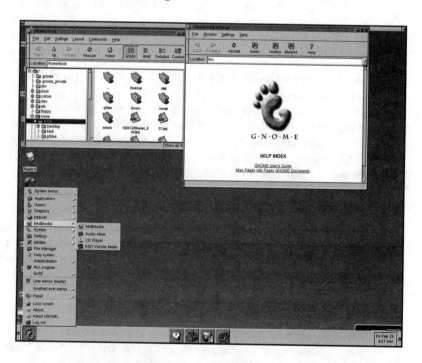

The *Panel* is the bar at the bottom of the screen. The About dialog of the panel defines it as "...responsible for launching other applications, embedding small applets within itself, world peace, and random X crashes." The panel might not really be responsible for world peace, but it does launch other applications and embed small applets within itself. The panel is used to house the GNOME menu, which contains shortcuts to applications on your system. The GNOME menu is very similar in function to the Start menu in the Microsoft Windows operating system. You can embed small applets in the panel as well, which can be anything from clocks to CD players. These applets are usually very small and are quite handy if you use them frequently.

The File Manager is built on the famous Midnight Commander text-based file manager. Midnight Commander is known for being one of the best file managers available on the shell. The GNOME File Manager stems from the same source base as Midnight Commander, thus resembling quite a bit of its functionality. You can use it to copy, move, delete, and rename your files. Double-clicking an application will launch it, whereas double-clicking a file will open it in the correct application. The File Manager is also responsible for any icons that are placed on the desktop.

The Control Center is where you configure most of GNOME's behavior. You can change the widget's theme, background, screensaver, dialog behavior, sounds, events, keyboard and mouse settings, and so on.

It is important that you understand that GNOME in itself is not an operating system. It is a mere shell that runs on the X Window System to make it easy to work with the desktop. Thanks to its very powerful framework, developers can build complex and user-friendly applications both quickly and easily.

GNOME still needs a window manager to be running, though. GNOME does not manage windows by itself, it is made up of windows itself. You still need to have a window manager running so you can control the positioning of your applications on the desktop. GNOME will work with any window manager, but it works best with GNOME-compliant window managers, which can talk with GNOME and its applications. This gives GNOME more control over the positioning of its windows and components on the screen. Currently, the best window manager to use with GNOME is Enlightenment.

Enlightenment is a 100% GNOME-compliant window manager. Enlightenment is considered one of the most powerful window managers available for Linux and is so highly configurable that you can give it whatever look and feel you want. It uses themes that completely change both its look and behavior. Seeing Enlightenment in two different themes can fool you into thinking they are two different window managers altogether.

GNOME, GNOME-compliant applications, and a GNOME-compliant window manager create a very user-friendly and powerful desktop environment. Even though GNOME applications tend to work best within GNOME, there is no problem whatsoever when you run them from within KDE or anything else. They might lose some of the GNOME-specific features, but that's all. In addition, non–GNOME-compliant applications won't be affected when they run with GNOME. GNOME is integrated, but it is not restrictive. Work is currently underway to make GNOME- and KDE-based applications communicate together, which will bring the best of both worlds together under one desktop.

GNOME comes prepackaged with the SuSE Linux complete distribution, but not the evaluation snapshot. SuSE 6.3 comes with the latest version of GNOME, called October GNOME. This is considered the most stable release of GNOME at this moment. The GNOME team is working very hard to bring GNOME 2.0 to life. It is expected to have several more powerful features and its own office suite, GNOME Office.

Installing GNOME

Installing GNOME is a simple matter thanks to the SuSE team. SuSE has packaged GNOME as well as most of its applications for your convenience. To install GNOME, you need to install the following packages. Make sure that you use YaST because these packages depend on a lot of other packages. YaST will automatically resolve these dependencies for you and install the required packages, as well.

Package requirements:

Series gnm:

- All packages for complete GNOME installation
- Or these packages for the minimal installation:
    - gmc
    - gncontr
    - gncontrd
    - gncore
    - gncored
    - gnlibs
    - gnlibsd

Again, we recommend using YaST to install these packages so it will resolve all the package dependencies that might arise. GNOME is quite a large environment and uses a large number of libraries and programs that must be installed for it to work properly.

Running GNOME

Now that you have installed GNOME, you will want to run it. You can run it using one of two methods, either through KDM (the graphical login manager) or via the shell.

Running GNOME from KDM is very simple. You just enter your username and password and select GNOME from the list of environments available on the system; the default is usually KDE.

If you are going to run GNOME from the shell, you will need to set an environment variable called WINDOWMANAGER to gnome. To do this, type the following command:

```
$ export WINDOWMANAGER=gnome
$ startx
```

The X Window System will start and GNOME will be launched. It will start off with the Enlightenment window manager loading up with a progress bar. The next screen will be split in two sliding halves, one sliding upward and the other downward. This is Enlightenment announcing that it has loaded up and is revealing the GNOME desktop.

Configuring GNOME

Now that you've installed GNOME, it's time you learn how to configure it. GNOME is made up of more than one core component, each with its own configuration. The following sections, explain how to configure each of these components and then how to use the GNOME Control Center to configure the overall behavior of GNOME.

Part

IV

Ch

24

Configuring the GNOME Panel

The GNOME Panel is probably the most frequently used component in GNOME. You can use it to launch applications, navigate the GNOME menu, and embed small applets within it.

The default position of the panel is at the bottom of the screen. You easily can change that by dragging it with the middle mouse button to any of the screen's four sides.

The default panel setup has five buttons on it. The first button is the GNOME menu button, which has an icon of a foot on it. This button opens the GNOME menu. The other four buttons are application launchers. The first one launches the GNOME help browser, the second launches the GNOME Control Center, the third launches the Netscape Web browser, and the last one launches a terminal. The clock at the far right is a good example of an embedded applet.

 TIP You can move the launchers and applets that are on the panel at any moment in time by dragging them using the middle mouse button.

Adding Launchers to the Panel The panel can be used as an application launcher by creating a launch icon. The launch icon lives on the panel at all times and when clicked on, will launch the application it is configured to run. The GNOME Panel has three default application launchers configured on it; you can create your own very easily, though.

Say you want to create a launcher for StarOffice on the panel. To create the launcher, follow these steps:

1. Right-click the panel to bring up the panel menu.
2. Click Add New Launcher.
3. The Create Launcher Applet will pop up (see Figure 24.25).

FIGURE 24.25
The Create Launcher
Applet is used to
define the properties
of your launcher.

4. In the Name field, type the name you want to assign to this launcher. For this example, type `StarOffice`.

5. In the Comment field, type `Launches StarOffice`.

6. In the Command field, type the path of the StarOffice binary. For this example, it is `/home/nazeeh/Office51/bin/soffice`.

7. Finally, you can choose an icon for the launcher by clicking the Icon button. It brings up a window of icons you can use; choose the one you want and click OK to use it.

8. Figure 24.26 shows the final look of the launcher properties dialog for our example; yours should look similar to it. Click OK to create the launcher.

FIGURE 24.26
The final look of the
launcher properties
applet.

The launcher will be created on the panel. Click it to run StarOffice. You can create more launchers using the previous method.

Another way you can create launchers on the panel is by dragging application shortcuts from the GNOME menu on the panel. To do this, just open the GNOME menu, find the application you want to add to the panel as a launcher, and either right-click it and click Add This Launcher to Panel or drag it on the panel. Both methods will create the launcher on the panel.

You can add a logout button on the panel by clicking the Add Log Out button from the panel's menu. This button will log you out of GNOME when you click it.

Adding Drawers to the Panel   As you have probably noticed by now, the size of the launchers is pretty large. You can't really put a lot of launchers on the panel because sooner or later you will run out of space. This is where drawers come in handy.

A *drawer* is a special kind of launcher on the panel. A drawer can be used to hold any number of launchers that are accessed by first clicking on the drawer and then the launcher you want. When you click a drawer, it extends outside the panel to reveal all the launchers within it (see Figure 24.27). This enables you to have one drawer containing all your Internet-related launchers, another containing music application launchers, and so on.

FIGURE 24.27
An example of an extended drawer.

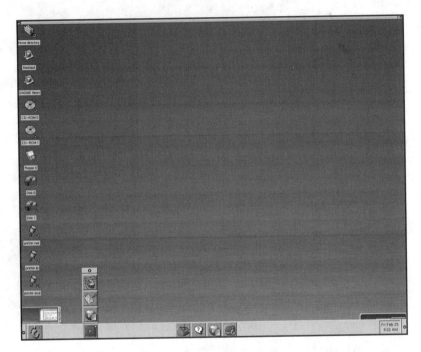

To create a drawer on the panel, just right-click the panel to bring up the Panel menu. Next, click Add Drawer to create a new drawer. The new drawer will take its place on the panel and will be open by default initially. Adding launchers to the drawer is done in the exact same way as adding launchers to the panel. You can drag any launcher from the panel or GNOME menu onto the extended part of the drawer to add it there. Clicking the drawer toggles its state from opened to closed and vice versa.

Drawers are very useful and you are encouraged to use them to organize your launchers.

Adding Embedded Applets   The panel has support for embedding small applications—known as *applets*—within it. These can be virtually anything from system monitors to clocks to CD players and so on. A good example of such an applet is the clock on the far right of the

Part

IV

Ch

24

panel, which is a small application that tells the time. The panel accepts only GNOME-compliant applets. GNOME comes with a set of applets you can embed on the panel.

To add an applet on the panel, follow these steps:

1. Right-click the panel to bring up the Panel menu.
2. Navigate to Add Applet.
3. The Add Applet submenu will branch out of the Panel menu (see Figure 24.28).

FIGURE 24.28
You have a variety of applets you can embed on the panel.

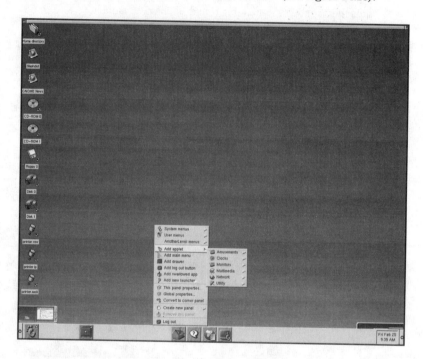

4. The applets are grouped into the following six categories:
   - **Amusements**—These are for fun applets; they do not do anything really useful, but are fun to have.
   - **Clocks**—These are applets that tell time in one way or another.
   - **Monitors**—These are quite useful applets. They give you a visual report on the current state of the system. This can be CPU and memory usage, disk usage, and so on.
   - **Multimedia**—These are multimedia-related applets. You will find a CD player applet here, for example.
   - **Network**—These are networking-related applets such as network status monitors and dialers.
   - **Utility**—These are applets that perform certain utility-like tasks.

5. Choose the applet you want to use and click it to add to the panel.

6. Repeat these steps to add other applets.

Adding Another Panel   You can have more than one panel on your screen. This is useful if you need more panel space and don't like having to open drawers to find the launchers you want. A panel in GNOME is one of two types, either an edge panel or a corner panel. An *edge* panel is one that extends from one end of the screen to the other—for example, the default GNOME panel. A *corner* panel is one that resizes as you add launchers and applets on it. Therefore, it might not stretch from one end of the screen to the other like an edge panel.

When you add a new panel, you probably want it to be a corner panel because having more than one edge panel tends to consume a lot of screen space. To create a new panel, follow these steps:

1. Right-click the panel to bring up the Panel menu.

2. Click the Create New Panel submenu.

3. Click Edge Panel or Corner Panel to create the new panel.

Part
IV
Ch
24

If you choose an edge panel, it will be created on the top part of the screen. If you choose a corner panel, it will be created on the top right corner of the screen as two small arrows facing opposite each other. A new corner panel looks like a normal panel but is empty, therefore the edge arrows are close together.

You can start adding launchers and applets to the new panel by either creating them or dragging them from the original panel. When you drag a launcher or applet from one panel to another, you should drag using the middle mouse button, not the left mouse button.

You can convert any edge panel to be a corner panel and vice versa at any time you want. This is done by right-clicking the panel to bring up the panel menu and choosing either Convert to Corner Panel for edge panels or Convert to Edge Panel for corner panels. The change will take effect immediately and is reversible using the same procedure.

Panel Properties   You can configure each panel you have independently. This enables each panel to behave in a different manner from the others. To configure a panel, follow these steps:

1. Right-click the panel to bring up the panel menu.

2. Click This Panel Properties.

3. The Properties dialog pops up (see Figure 24.29).

4. The first page on the dialog has two sets of options to configure, the Position and Minimize options.

5. The Position is where on the screen this panel should be positioned. You have four choices: Left, Right, Top, or Bottom.

FIGURE 24.29

The panel's properties dialog.

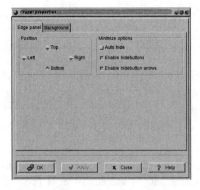

6. The Minimize options configure the hiding of the panel. You can choose Auto Hide to have the panel hide when the mouse pointer is not over it. You can enable or disable the hide buttons at the edges of the panel by toggling the Enable Hidebuttons options. Finally, you can toggle having arrows on the hide buttons or not via the Enable Hidebutton Arrows option.

7. The second tab in the configuration is the Background tab (see Figure 24.30). This is the background of the panel. You have three options here: You can either have the panel use the Standard background, a Pixmap, or a Color. If you choose Pixmap, you must specify the path of the pixmap you want to use for the panel's background. If you choose Color, you can select the color you want to use from the Background color button at the bottom of the tab.

FIGURE 24.30

The panel's background settings.

8. Click OK to apply and save your settings to the current panel.

Global Properties So far, you have configured each panel independently. The global properties configuration applies to all the panels you have. To configure the global properties of all the panels, follow these steps:

1. Right-click the panel to bring up the panel menu.
2. Click Global Properties.
3. The Global Panel Configuration dialog pops up (see Figure 24.31).

FIGURE 24.31
The Global Panel Configuration dialog is used to configure all the panels.

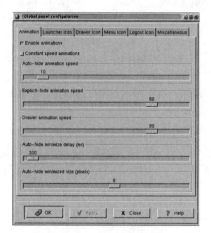

4. The first tab is the Animation tab. This is where you configure the parameters that apply to the panel's animation sequences. You can
   - Enable/disable animation.
   - Set the Auto-hide animation speed.
   - Set the Explicit-hide animation speed. This is when you use the arrows at the end of the panel to hide it.
   - Set the Drawer animation speed.
   - Set the Auto-hide minimize delay in milliseconds. This is how much time the panel will wait before it hides itself when the mouse pointer is no longer above it.
   - Set the Auto-hide minimized size in pixels. This is how much of the panel will be visible in pixels when it is minimized.

5. The next four tabs have to do with icons on the panel. They configure the Launcher icon, Drawer icon, Menu icon, and Logout icon. Each tab configures the following options:
   - **Tiles enabled**—This will enable/disable having a tile for the icon.
   - **Image files**—These are the images to use for the tiles if they are enabled. You must choose a tile for when the button is clicked and when it is released.
   - **Border width**—This is the width of the border between tiles in pixels. It's only applicable if you enabled use of tiles.
   - **Depth**—This option sets how deep the icon will be displaced when you click it.

Part
IV

Ch
24

6. The final tab is the Miscellaneous tab. This has the following options for the behavior of the panel:

   - **Tooltips enabled**—This will toggle the use of tooltips on the panel.
   - **Menus**—This section sets the options for the pop-up menus on the panel.
   - **Movement**—This section defines how icons will behave when you move them around the panel.
   - **Miscellaneous**—This section has options for raising the panel, keeping it below other windows, and closing drawers after a launcher inside them is pressed.
   - **Applet padding**—This is how many pixels should be maintained between applets.

7. Click OK to apply and save the changes.

The GNOME Menu Editor   To configure the GNOME menu, a special program is available for you to use. This is the GNOME menu editor, which is found in the GNOME menu and is used to organize the GNOME menu to your preference. To configure the GNOME menu using the menu editor, follow these steps:

1. Navigate the GNOME menu to Settings, Menu editor.
2. The Menu Editor pops up (see Figure 24.32).

FIGURE 24.32

The GNOME Menu Editor is used to edit the panel's menu.

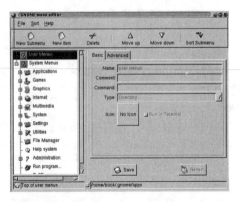

3. The left side of the program displays the current menu in a tree form. The right side displays the properties of the currently selected item on the menu.
4. You cannot change much in the System Menus section because you don't have the permissions to do so, unless of course you are running GNOME as root.
5. To start adding entries to the menu, add them to the User Menus section.
6. To add a new item to the menu, click New Item from the toolbar at the top of the editor. Fill in the properties of the item you are adding in the right side of the program. When you are finished, just click Save to save the new item to the menu.

7. You can create submenus by clicking New Submenu from the toolbar at the top of the editor. Fill in the properties for the new submenu on the right side of the editor. Again, click Save to save the new submenu.

8. You can drag icons from one section of the menu tree to another to move things around.

9. When you are finished, you can sort your submenu by clicking the Sort Submenu button on the toolbar.

10. Finally, you can exit the editor by clicking Exit from the file menu.

The GNOME menu will now reflect all the changes you made using the menu editor.

Configuring the GNOME File Manager

The GNOME File Manager is an integral part of GNOME. Apart from being a very powerful file manager, it also handles all the icons you can place on your desktop. Because it was built on Midnight Commander, the GNOME File Manager is very good with file manipulation. You can use it to copy, move, rename, delete, and change permissions of files and directories on your system.

The GNOME File Manager is composed of two sections (see Figure 24.33). The left side contains a tree of the directories on your hard drive. The right side shows the contents of the currently selected directory.

Part IV

Ch 24

FIGURE 24.33
The GNOME File Manager.

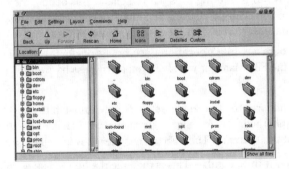

The GNOME File Manager is configured in the Preferences dialog. To bring up this dialog, click Settings, Preferences from the menu. The Preferences dialog pops up (see Figure 24.34).

FIGURE 24.34
The GNOME File Manager Preferences dialog.

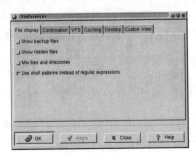

The first tab is the File Display. This is where you configure which files the File Manager will display. You can enable or disable the following options:

- **Show backup files**—These are files created by some programs as backups of files they are about to modify. These usually end with tilde (~).

- **Show hidden files**—These are files that start with a dot. These files are meant to be hidden, and are usually settings or directories containing settings and configuration files for applications. It is recommended that you do not enable this option because you might end up deleting one of those files by mistake if you can see it.

- **Mix files and directories**—This will mix files and directories in the display rather than list the directories first and then the files.

- **Use shell patterns instead of regular expressions**

The Confirmation tab has the following options:

- **Confirm when deleting file**—When enabled, the File Manager will ask you to confirm file deletions. This is a good option to have because it can save you from deleting files by mistake.

- **Confirm when overwriting files**—If you enable this, the File Manager will ask you to confirm a file overwrite operation. This happens if you attempt to copy a file in a directory that already includes a file of the same name. Again, it is recommended that you enable this option.

- **Confirm when executing files**—If you enable this option, the File Manager will ask you before it executes a binary you double-clicked. This is a good option to enable because it can save you from accidentally double-clicking the wrong binary.

- **Show progress while operations are being performed**—When this option is enabled, the File Manager will show you a progress bar when it is performing lengthy operations.

The VFS tab configures the virtual filesystem feature found in the GNOME File Manager. This feature is inherited from Midnight Commander and enables you to use the File Manager as an FTP client transparently. The VFS tab has the following options:

- **VFS timeout in seconds**—This is the time the File Manager will wait before giving up on trying to establish an FTP connection.

- **Anonymous FTP password**—This is the email address the File Manager should use when performing anonymous FTP. This should be your valid email address.

- **Always use FTP proxy**—If this option is enabled, the File Manager will always make the FTP connection through an FTP proxy.

The next tab is the Caching tab, which configures how the File Manager caches data for quick retrieval. It has the following options:

- **Fast directory reload**—If you enable this option, the File Manager will cache the contents of visited directories for fast retrieval. This will make the File Manager work faster because it doesn't have to rescan visited directories. But the listing you see might not be updated with what's actually on disk.

- **Compute totals before copying files**—If you enable this option, the File Manager will find out how much space the files you are about to copy need. This is necessary if you want to see a correct progress bar in copy operations.

- **FTP directory cache timeout**—This sets the amount of time in seconds before the File Manager will reload an FTP directory to get an updated listing.

The Desktop tab configures the desktop icons' behavior. The first option is the Icon position. This is a small picture showing you the position of the icons on the desktop. You can move the position of the icons by clicking the corners of the picture. For example, you can place all desktop icons on the right side of the desktop instead of the left. The remaining options are as follows:

- **Automatic icon placement**—If enabled, icons will be automatically positioned on the desktop.

- **Snap icons to grid**—If enabled, icons will be snapped to a virtual grid on the desktop. This helps a lot if you want to position the icons in an orderly fashion.

- **Use shaped icons**—If enabled, the icons will have a transparent background that shows the underlying desktop.

- **Use shaped text**—If enabled, the icon text also will have a transparent background.

Finally, the last tab is the Custom View. This is where you define what fields should appear for files and directories when you switch the File Manager to use Custom View from the toolbar. This tab has two lists, the one on the right is a list of all the Possible Columns and the one on the left lists all the Displayed Columns. To add one of the possible columns to the displayed columns, highlight it and click the Add button.

Click OK to save your preferences to the File Manager.

The GNOME Control Center

The GNOME *Control Center* is where you configure how GNOME and its applications behave. It is the central configuration module for all of GNOME. The GNOME Control Center is made up of capplets. *Capplet* stands for control applet, which is a mini application. The Control Center loads up all the available capplets when it starts. By using capplets, the Control Center can be extended to configure other things by simply adding a new capplet to it.

To start the Control Center, navigate the GNOME menu to Settings, GNOME Control Center. The Control Center pops up (see Figure 24.35). As you can see in the figure, the Control Center has a tree on the left side, which lists all the available capplets in an orderly fashion. By clicking one of the titles in the tree, the proper capplet is loaded in the right side of the Control Center.

Part
IV

Ch
24

FIGURE 24.35

The GNOME Control Center is where you configure the overall behavior of GNOME and its applications.

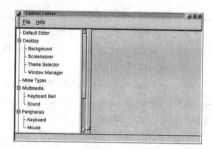

The first configuration in the tree is the Default Editor capplet, which configures the editor that will be used when you attempt to edit a file from the GNOME File Manager. A list of editors from which you can choose is provided.

Next is the Desktop section of capplets, which configures the desktop. The first of these is the Background capplet. As you can see in Figure 24.36, this capplet configures the desktop background. You can choose a solid color or gradient color for the background from the Color section of the capplet. If you would rather use an image for the background, you can browse for it and configure it in the Wallpaper section. If you do not want GNOME to handle your background—for example, if you are letting Enlightenment do that for you—you can keep it from interfering by selecting the Disable Background option.

FIGURE 24.36

The Desktop configuration capplet.

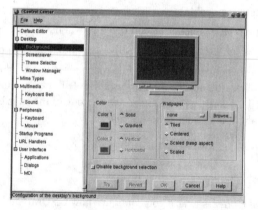

The Screensaver capplet configures GNOME's screensaver (see Figure 24.37). You can choose the screensaver you want to use from the Screen Saver list; a small preview is displayed in the Screen Saver Demo square. The Screen Saver Settings section is where you will configure when GNOME will start the screensaver, whether it requires a password to switch off the screensaver, and the priority of the screensaver. If you do not want the screensaver to take too much CPU, set its priority to Low. You can turn on power management by enabling the Use Power Management option. This will turn off the monitor after a specific time of inactivity after the screensaver starts. This is a good option to have because it saves electricity.

FIGURE 24.37

The Screensaver configuration capplet.

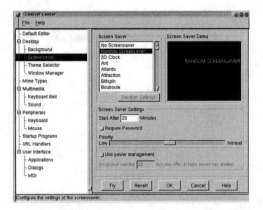

The Theme Selector has got to be the most fun to use of all the capplets in the Control Center (see Figure 24.38). This is where you get to select the themes that will be used for the user interface. Select the theme you want to use from the list of Available Themes and you will get a preview of what your buttons and widgets will look like when you use this theme. Each theme changes the look of your interface completely. You can set the font you want to use for your widgets from the User Font section.

FIGURE 24.38

The theme configuration capplet.

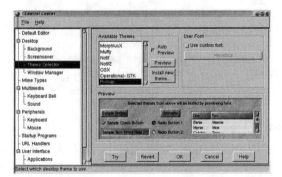

The Window Manager capplet defines which window manager GNOME will use (see Figure 24.39). This tab contains a list of window managers; just highlight the one you want to use with GNOME and when you click OK, the current window manager will be substituted with the new one. You won't need to restart GNOME for the change to take effect. You can add window managers to the list using the Add button.

Now that we've discussed all the Desktop capplets, let's look at the next capplet, which is not part of any category. The Mime Types capplet is used to configure the applications to be used to open different types of files (see Figure 24.40). A list of all the supported file types appears on this tab. Double-click the extension you want to edit to configure it. A small configuration dialog pops up, which you can use to dictate to GNOME which programs to use to open, view, and edit this file type (see Figure 24.41). Click OK to save this association.

Part
IV

Ch
24

FIGURE 24.39

The Window Manager configuration capplet.

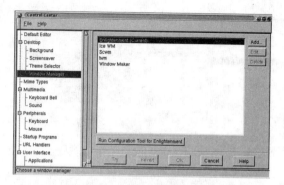

FIGURE 24.40

The MIME Types configuration capplet.

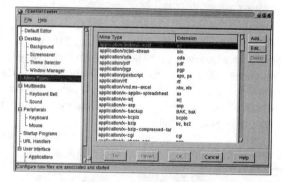

FIGURE 24.41

Associating file types with a program.

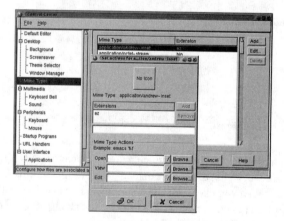

The next section is the Multimedia set of capplets. The first of these is the Keyboard Bell capplet, which configures the sound of the keyboard bell. You can control the Volume, Pitch, and Duration of the beep.

The Sound capplet configures the sounds in GNOME. To have sound support in GNOME, you must enable the Enable Sound Server at Startup option and Sounds for events. The second tab in this capplet is the Sound Events. As you can see in Figure 24.42, you can associate a sound with many events that occur in GNOME.

FIGURE 24.42

The Sounds configuration capplet.

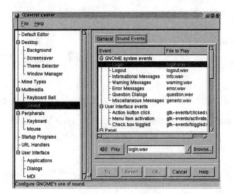

The next section of capplets is the Peripherals section. The first capplet here is the Keyboard capplet. You can use this capplet to configure how the keyboard behaves in terms of Auto Repeat and Keyboard Click Volume.

The Mouse capplet configures your mouse in GNOME. You can switch the mouse to be left-handed or right-handed. You also can set the Mouse motion in terms of acceleration and threshold.

The Startup Programs capplet is not part of any category. It configures which programs you want GNOME to run on startup. To add a program to be started when GNOME starts, click the Add button. A small dialog pops up in which you can enter the command to run and the priority by which to run it. Programs with lower priority run before those with higher ones. By setting priorities, you can tell GNOME to run one program before another one. You can get a list of all the currently running programs by clicking the Browse Currently Running Programs button. You can then choose to remove any of these programs from being restarted by GNOME, and shut them down, on the next log on. Be very careful with this dialog; if you remove the panel, it won't start with GNOME the next time.

The URL Handlers capplet configures how GNOME handles calls to open URLs. For example, if you double-click an HTML file, GNOME will know that it should open it using Netscape.

The User Interface section configures how applications built using the GNOME framework behave. The first of these capplets is the Applications capplet (see Figure 24.43). You can configure most of the application's behavior with the following options:

Part
IV

Ch
24

FIGURE 24.43
You can configure the
behavior of GNOME-
compliant applications
using this capplet.

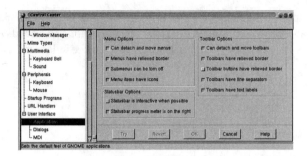

■ **Menu Options**—This selection box contains the following options:

- **Can detach and move menus**—Menus in GNOME can be detached from the application and placed anywhere. You can enable or disable this feature from here.

- **Menus have relieved border**—This is the default setting in GNOME; you can disable it from here.

- **Submenus can be torn off**—Submenus in GNOME can be torn off to be separate small movable menus. You can disable this feature from here.

- **Menu items have icons**—If a GNOME application uses icons in its menus, you can disable that from here.

■ **Statusbar Options**—This selection box contains the following options:

- **Statusbar is interactive when possible**—Some applications in GNOME can detach the statusbar to be a window by itself. You can control this behavior from this option.

- **Statusbar progress meter is on the right**—This is the default option for GNOME; you can disable it if you don't like it.

■ **Toolbar Options**—This selection box contains the following options:

- **Can detach and move toolbars**—If enabled, you can detach the toolbar from its position and place it somewhere else.

- **Toolbars have relieved border**—This is the default for GNOME; you can disable it from here.

- **Toolbar buttons have relieved border**—The default for this option is off, but you can turn it on from here.

- **Toolbars have line separators**—If enabled, the toolbars will have line separators between them.

- **Toolbars have text labels**—If you do not want the toolbars to have text labels, you can disable that from here.

The next capplet is the Dialogs capplet (see Figure 24.44). This is where you configure the dialog in GNOME applications. The first section in the capplet is the Dialog Layout. You can set how buttons on the dialogs are justified from the dialog Buttons list.

FIGURE 24.44

You can configure the behavior of the dialogs in GNOME-compliant applications using this capplet.

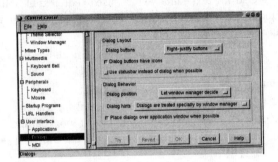

If you want the dialogs buttons to have icons, enable the Dialog Buttons Have Icons option.

Enable Use Statusbar Instead of Dialog When Possible to have GNOME make more use of the statusbar.

The Dialog Behavior section configures how dialogs behave. You can control the Dialog Position, Dialog Hints, and whether to Place Dialogs Over Application Window When Possible.

The last capplet is the MDI capplet. MDI stands for *Multiple Document Interface*, which configures an application to display windows inside it in the form of tabs. You have only two options to set here (see Figure 20.45). The Default MDI Mode has three settings: Modal, Notebook, and Toplevel. The MDI notebook tab position has four settings: Right, Left, Top, and Bottom.

FIGURE 24.45

Configuring the MDI behavior of GNOME-compliant applications.

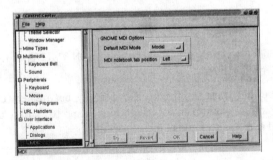

GNOME Applications

GNOME comes with a variety of applications that were designed and built using the GNOME framework. This section will mention some of these applications and explain what they do. We will assume here that you have a full installation of GNOME.

Part
IV

Ch
24

Applications Submenu

The Applications submenu contains the following GNOME-compliant applications:

- **gEdit**—This is a strong text editor you can use to edit text files. It uses plug-ins to extend its functionality. You can use it to write code, edit configuration files, or perform just about any task that requires text editing.

- **gnotepad+**—This is an HTML editor you can use to author Web pages. It does not use a visual approach, though it helps you in writing HTML code by offering an interface to the most common tags.

- **Calendar**—This is probably one of the most useful applications available for GNOME. This is an organizer you can use to put some order into your life. You use it to maintain your appointments and tasks. It has a built-in calendar with daily, weekly, monthly, and yearly views.

- **Address Book**—You can use this application to organize your addresses. You can store addresses of people and retrieve them very easily using a graphical user interface.

- **Gnumeric Spreadsheet**—This is part of the upcoming GNOME office suite. It is a user-friendly spreadsheet program that utilizes plug-ins to extend its functionality. This program is under heavy development, but most of the useful functions are already there.

- **GHex**—This is a hex editor for GNOME. You can use it to edit files in hex.

- **Time tracking tool**—This is a simple application you can use to keep track of tasks you need to do. It is similar to a to-do list.

- **Pharmacy**—This is a graphical front-end for the Concurrent Versioning System (CVS), which is used by developers to organize teamwork in programming projects. This is a useful tool for programmers.

Games Submenu

This submenu includes several games you can play in GNOME. They range from card games to puzzles and other fun games.

These games are nowhere near sophisticated graphically, but are very entertaining if you want to take a break from work. Some of the puzzles are pretty hard to solve or beat, so you might find yourself addicted to some of these games!

Graphics Submenu

The graphics submenu includes the following graphics-related applications:

- **The GIMP**—This application is not really built using the GNOME framework. In fact, this is the application that was the result of the birth of the widget set used in GNOME.

GIMP (GNU Image Manipulating Program) is similar to Adobe Photoshop in many ways. You can use it to retouch images, create new images, and so on. It is a highly mature piece of software that is considered to be one of the best applications developed by the open source community. It is definitely worth a look.

- **Electric Eyes**—This is an image viewer. It supports viewing a large variety of image formats.

- **PostScript file viewer**—This program displays PostScript files. It is very powerful and complete, and comes in handy when you need to view a PostScript file.

Internet

This submenu contains all the Internet-specific applications:

- **XSitecopy**—You can use this program to publish your Web site to a remote server.
- **Balsa**—This is *the* GNOME email client.
- **PPP dialup utility**—This is the GNOME dial-up connection dialer. You can use it to configure your system to dial in to any ISP using your modem.
- **Talk**—This is GNOME's version of the famous console talk command. You can use it to open a chat session with other users on your system or on another system.

Part

IV

Ch

24

Multimedia Submenu

This submenu contains all the multimedia-specific applications, which are as follows:

- **Audio Mixer**—You can use this application to control the volume of the various multimedia devices you have.
- **CD Player**—You can use this application to play your audio CDs in GNOME.
- **ESD Volume Meter**—You can use this to see a spectrum analyzer for ESD, the sound daemon.

System Submenu

This submenu contains all the following system-specific applications:

- **GnoRPM**—This is GNOME's front end to the RPM command.
- **Shut Down or Reboot**—This will shut down or reboot the machine. You must be root to use this command.

Settings Submenu

This submenu contains shortcuts to all the capplets you have in the GNOME Control Center. You can directly launch them from here instead of using the Control Center.

Utilities Submenu

This submenu contains the following utility applications:

- **Eterm**—This is a powerful X terminal variant.
- **GNOME Terminal**—This is the GNOME version of the X Terminal. It is highly configurable.
- **System log monitor**—This program is useful only if you are running it as root. It displays all the system log files.
- **Simple calculator**—This is the GNOME calculator, a simple calculator you will find useful.
- **Color Browser**—This little application displays all the colors supported by your current X display.
- **GNOME DiskFree**—This application shows you meters that display the amount of free space you have on all your hard disks.
- **Font Selector**—You can use this application to browse the currently installed fonts.
- **GNOME Search Tool**—You can use this application to search the hard disk for files.
- **System Info**—This application shows you information about your current system.

GNOME Tips

Using GNOME is one of the most entertaining things you can do using SuSE Linux. The whole desktop environment is designed to be fun to use. As you use GNOME more, you will discover how powerful it can be. To make your experience even better, we will give you a few GNOME tips.

GNOME makes extensive use of the drag and drop technology. For example, if you have a color selector open from any application, you can drag any color from it to the panel to change the panel's color. The same applies to the GNOME terminal—dragging a color on it will change its background to that color. Dragging a color on any of the text in the terminal will change the text color as well.

When you are setting up your background using the Background capplet, you can still use drag and drop. For example, you can open the GNOME File Manager and drag an image file on the Background capplet to use it for your background. The same applies when you drag an image to the panel; it will be used on the panel's background.

Most GNOME-compliant applications accept drag and drop. You can drag a file from the File Manager on any GNOME application to have it open it. For example, dragging a spreadsheet file on Gnumeric will open it. This drag and drop is Motif-compatible, which means you can drag links to Netscape and it will open them. It works with most Motif applications, as well.

You can even use drag and drop between two running instances of the GNOME File Manager. Just drag a file or folder from one to the other to perform a copy operation.

You also can drag and drop directories. You can drag a directory out of the GNOME File Manger and place it on the panel. This will create a new menu, giving you easy access to the files in that directory.

If you use the X Multimedia System (xmms), you can drag files and directories from the File Manager to it to add them to the playlist.

You should use the GNOME terminal more often because it is very powerful. If you have any text in the terminal that has any URLs, they will be underlined when you run the mouse pointer over them. If you press the Ctrl button on the keyboard and click the URL, Netscape will be launched to open this URL.

If your GNOME session won't start properly, just press Ctrl+Shift when you log in to GNOME. GNOME will then ask you if you want to start with the default programs or remove all user settings. Starting with the default programs will start you with a clean session but still preserve your settings. If you choose to remove all user settings, GNOME will be restored to its default state and you will lose all your configurations.

Troubleshooting GNOME

I can't find my panel.

Make sure that it is not hidden. Look for the small arrows at the edges of the screen. If you find any, click one to restore the panel. If you find none, then maybe the panel crashed; just open a terminal and type the following command:

```
$ nohup panel&
```

This will start the panel again and keep it running even if you close the terminal.

I can't change the GNOME menu using the menu editor.

Yes you can, it's just that you can't change the default menu because you don't have the permission to do so. You can add to the user menu section, not the system menu. To add to the system menu, you must run GNOME as root. The changes will be reflected on all users, though.

How can I stop GNOME from reloading my session?

If your GNOME session won't start properly, just press Ctrl+Shift when you log in to GNOME. GNOME will then ask you if you want to start with the default programs or remove all user settings. Starting with the default programs will start you with a clean session but still preserve your settings. If you choose to remove all user settings, GNOME will be restored to its default state and you will lose all your configurations. ●

Installing and Configuring StarOffice

StarDivision and Sun Microsystems— History and License

StarOffice is a full-featured office suite of applications. It includes common office applications such as a word processor, spreadsheet, presentations maker, graphic design utility, database, email client, news client, and a scheduler. One of the most impressive things about StarOffice is that there are versions for more than one platform. You can find a version for MS Windows, IBM OS/2, Solaris, Linux, and Java. StarOffice was developed by a German company called StarDivision. The company offered StarOffice free for personal use; a commercial license had to be bought if the suite was to be used commercially.

Very recently Sun Microsystems acquired StarDivision and gave away StarOffice for all platforms and all types of uses, commercial or personal. You can either download it from Sun directly or have them send it to you on a CD along with a manual for a small fee. SuSE Linux 6.3 (full version) comes with the latest version of StarOffice, version 5.1a. StarOffice is truly a great piece of software, and the fact that it is included with SuSE makes it a great value.

Soon after its purchase of StarOffice, Sun Microsystems started the StarOffice NOW program. This is a program for partners and other third parties interested in providing StarOffice to their subscribers, customers, or students. You can access this program from the Sun Microsystems Web page at `http://www.sun.com/products/staroffice/starofficenow/`.

StarOffice Features

Not only does StarOffice serve as an office suite, but also as an integrated desktop environment. By using StarOffice, you can do your daily business work without having to use any other application or a file manager. This is because StarOffice can serve as a file manager by itself while at the same time it has the capabilities of serving most of the home and business users' needs.

By using StarOffice, you can edit and manage your documents easily. The full suite that comes with SuSE Linux includes all of StarOffice's *modules*. Modules are the file manager, word processor, spreadsheet editor, presentation designer, and so forth.

StarOffice Modules

StarOffice is a very complete office suite. It is built around the philosophy of *do everything in one place*. The idea behind this is that instead of having a separate application for word processing and another for spreadsheet editing, you have all of them under one environment that is StarOffice.

StarDesktop and StarExplorer

You can manage your files With StarExplorer. When you open StarOffice, the first thing you see is the StarDesktop. This interesting feature of StarOffice enables you to quickly manage your documents in folders and to have direct access to all the files that your SuSE Linux can access. Review Chapter 15, "Connectivity with Windows Through Samba," for connectivity with Windows, Chapter 16, "Connectivity with Other Operating Systems," for connectivity with other OSes, and Chapter 5, "Managing File Systems," for managing file systems. You can also access all of StarOffice's modules via StarDesktop (see Figure 25.1). With StarExplorer, you get a tree view of all of StarOffice's modules along with the features of StarOffice. Use StarExplorer for quick access to your documents and folders.

FIGURE 25.1
StarDesktop enables you to have quick access to all the StarOffice components and your folders and documents.

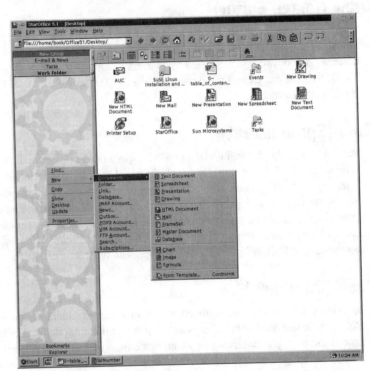

Part
IV

Ch
25

StarWriter (Word Processor)

StarWriter offers very sophisticated word processing capabilities. You can expect to find all you want from a word processor in StarWriter. As an integrated environment, all the objects that are created by using the other modules of StarOffice can be embedded in the StarWriter document. You can use StarWriter to save HTML files that are ready to be published to the Internet. StarWriter supports a large variety of document formats, including Mircosoft Word documents, Rich Text format, WordPerfect, and many others.

StarImpress (Presentation)

StarImpress can create elegant presentations for you in no time, thanks to the available wizards and templates. You can quickly create presentations by using the existing templates or create your own theme. StarImpress offers you advanced control over your presentation; you can embed documents made by other StarOffice modules. You can open and save presentations in Microsoft PowerPoint. You can also export a presentation to a wide variety of image formats. The most important exportation feature is the ability to export a presentation in HTML format, which enables you to easily publish any presentation that you make directly to the Internet.

StarDraw (Image Editor)

StarDraw serves the other modules of StarOffice. StarDraw features easy editing of drawings that serve the business user. You can easily add text boxes, connectors, trees, and others to a drawing. Any drawing that is made by StarDraw can be directly used in the other modules of StarOffice. You can export the drawing made by StarDraw either to HTML or to a wide variety of image formats.

StarCalc (Spreadsheet)

StarCalc offers the capabilities of a powerful spreadsheet program. It includes all the functions needed for business use, including financial and statistical functions, StarCalc database functions, and much more. Like all the other StarOffice modules, you can embed StarChart charts, StarDraw drawings, or StarWriter documents. Thanks to the autopilot and wizard capabilities, you can now easily create powerful and professional spreadsheets. StarCalc can load and save a large variety of spreadsheet formats, including Microsoft Excel. You can also save your spreadsheet in HTML format to publish it directly on the Internet.

StarBase (Database)

By using StarBase, you can easily create a fully featured database. You do not need to be an SQL guru to use StarBase; rather, you can can use the autopilot capabilities to make a sophisticated and complete database. By using StarBase, you can manage your work, your collections, your budget, or anything that you want to manage. An example of using StarBase is the address book that comes with StarOffice. Queries and reports can be easily created by using the autopilot.

StarScheduler (Scheduler)

StarScheduler is very helpful in managing your tasks and events. This is where your reminders and appointments should go. You can categorize your reminders or appointments. StarScheduler can manage your life. You can export your StarScheduler in vCalender format so you can import it from other programs that support this format.

StarOffice Internet Capabilities: Browsing, Email, and News

The most powerful feature of StarOffice is its Internet capabilities. StarOffice was designed to integrate with the Internet. All StarOffice modules can export HTML-formatted documents. On the other hand, StarOffice can work as a Web browser, an email client, and a news client. StarOffice can use the system Java library so that it can view Java applets. By using StarOffice as an email client, you can access your POP3 and IMAP accounts.

Other Interesting StarOffice Modules

StarOffice comes equipped with other powerful modules. StarBeamer can serve as a quick access to your multimedia files so that you can quickly include them in your document. The Help Agent enables you to get help on functionality that StarOffice supports. The Navigator enables you to navigate the document modules while the Stylist enables you to quickly apply general or custom styles to your document.

Installing StarOffice

StarOffice comes with SuSE Linux 6.3, which makes installing it very easy. If you have the evaluation version of SuSE 6.3—this book comes with the evaluation version of SuSE Linux 6.3—you can download StarOffice from the Sun Microsystems Web site or order a copy of the StarOffice CD which is very inexpensive. StarOffice can be downloaded free of charge from `http://www.sun.com/staroffice`. We advise you to order the StarOffice CD from the Sun Microsystems Web site because their CD contains a copy of StarOffice for each supported platform. If you have the full version SuSE Linux 6.3, make sure that you install the following package:

Series pay:

- so_en

Part
IV
Ch
25

Starting the Installation Process

Starting the installation process of StarOffice differs according to the version of SuSE Linux that you have. This book only discusses the installation of StarOffice 5.x for SuSE Linux version 6.x. Follow one of these methods according to source media from which you want to install StarOffice:

- **A package on the full version of SuSE Linux**—In this case you will find a StarOffice icon on your KDE or GNOME desktop. Click this icon and move on to the next section.

- **A downloaded StarOffice tar file**—In this case, all you have to do is extract the file to a temporary directory and start the installation. To extract the file, follow these steps:

```
bash$tar xzvf <staroffice.tar.gz> -C /tmp/staroffice
```

Now the installation binaries have been extracted to the `/tmp/staroffice/` directory. You can start the installation by changing the current directory to the path where you untarred—extracted—StarOffice and executing the `setup` script. You can do this by issuing the following command in an `xterm` while in X Windows:

```
bash$cd <staroffice path>;./setup
```

■ **An ordered CD from Sun Microsystems**—All you have to do in this case is to mount the CD-ROM and change the working directory to the Linux version of StarOffice and run the `setup` script. While you're in X Windows, issue the following commands in an `xterm`:

```
bash$mount /cdrom
bash$cd /cdrom/<Linux version of StarOffice path>
bash$./setup
```

The Setup Process

Setting up StarOffice is graphical from A to Z, so there is no need to panic; you're done with the hard part already.

When the welcome dialog box appears, click the Next button to move to the next step (see Figure 25.2). During the whole installation process, you can use the Next button to move to the next step while you can use the Back button to go one step back to fix some setting that you want to change.

FIGURE 25.2
The StarOffice installation process is typically a fully graphical installation. You can easily prepare StarOffice on your system or user account after you finish this installation.

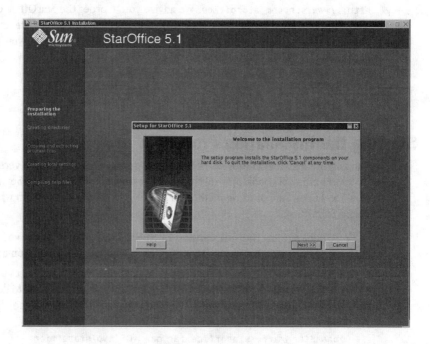

After the welcome dialog box comes the Important Information dialog box. This chapter handles most of the important information that you are concerned with; you can safely click Next to move ahead to the License dialog box. Read the license carefully and click Next when you agree to the license.

The Enter User Data dialog box is an important dialog box (see Figure 25.3). Be sure you fill in your information completely. The most important information that StarOffice needs is your name and your email address. Although you can leave all fields empty, it is highly recommended that you fill in all the fields that apply to you. This will save you time later when you need to set some services that StarOffice offers.

FIGURE 25.3
StarOffice needs to know some information about you to set up some services for you later. You will need to enter at least your name and email address. If you do not have an email address, you can safely leave the field blank.

Part
IV

Ch
25

Depending on the media where you have started the installation of StarOffice, the installation path would take two branches this time:

- If you install StarOffice from the SuSE 6.3 full version, you will be asked if you want a Standard Workstation Installation or a Standard Local Installation. The Standard Workstation Installation is your best shot because it will save you a large amount of disk space. Note that in this case, only the root user will be able to add printers and fonts to StarOffice. It is highly recommended that you use the Standard Workstation installation.

- If you install StarOffice from a downloaded tarball file or from the StarOffice CD, you can customize the installation by selecting the modules that you want to install from the StarOffice package. Note that there are some features that you might not need that will be installed by default. Check the Modules tree and decide which to install and which not to install.

The next step is selecting the path where you want StarOffice to be installed. The default directory that StarOffice offers is Office51 in your home directory. You will be prompted to create this directory if it does not exist. Press Complete when you finish this step to start the installation process.

Java Auto Detection When the StarOffice installation starts, StarOffice tries to detect the existing Java libraries on your system to use them for Java-based scripts, applications, and applets (see Figure 25.4). If you have installed Java runtime libraries or the Java Development Kit, you will find them in a list so that you can select which one StarOffice should use. StarOffice supports the 1.1.5 and 1.1.7 versions of Java. You can disable Java's use in StarOffice by clicking the No support for Java or JavaScript in StarOffice radio button.

FIGURE 25.4
If you are not going to use StarOffice as a browser, you might want to disable the use of Java in StarOffice. However, you will be missing a lot of interesting Internet features if you use StarOffice as a browser without Java support. You can easily direct StarOffice afterwards to use Java if you do not set it up in this dialog box.

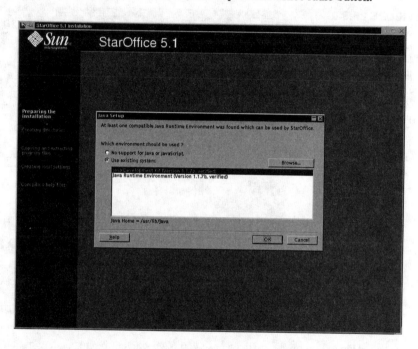

This was the last step in StarOffice installation. Remember to register so that you can get special offers and attention when you query about StarOffice at Sun Microsystems. When StarOffice starts for the first time, you can register electronically if you are connected to the Internet.

Installing New Printers

Printing documents is a very important concern when we consider an office suite. It is very important that your office suite be able to easily access printing. In fact, setting up printing on StarOffice is simple if your printer is supported by Linux.

Prerequisites

Installing new printers requires that you have already set up printing on your system. To enable printing on your system, please refer to Chapter 11, "Printing," where you learn to set up printing on your SuSE Linux machine. To sum up, what you need is a working printer port (lpr) that points to a local or network printer.

Printer Setup on StarOffice

After you have ensured that printing works with other applications, you can begin setting up your printer on StarOffice. To start the printer setup process, double-click the Printer Setup icon on you StarDesktop. This launches the Printer Setup program, which will help you set up your printer (see Figure 25.5). If you do not have an icon called Printer Setup on your StarDesktop, open an xterm window and run the command /opt/Office51/bin/spadmin.

FIGURE 25.5
By using the Printer Installation program, you can ensure that StarOffice uses your printer settings. This enables StarOffice to have control over the printing speed and quality.

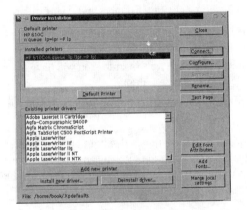

Part
IV

Ch

25

Printer Drivers   The Printer Installation program enables you to select your printer-specific driver from a list of printer drivers. If you can't find your printer's name in the list, you can ask your printer manufacturer if they have released a driver. You can always use the Generic Printer if you do not have access to your printer-specific driver. Please note that using your printer-specific driver makes printing faster and gives you more options in the printing dialog boxes. If you have access to your printer driver, click the Install new driver button and browse to the path where you have the driver. Drivers are usually *.PS or *.PCL files. After you have installed your driver, click the Add new printer button to move it to the Installed printers list.

Connecting Your Printer   The next step is to select the printer that you assign to the driver. If you have carefully followed the steps of setting up a printer in Chapter 11, you probably have more than one printer setting now. Click the Connect button to connect your printer driver to the correct printer queue. From the queue list that appears, select the printer queue that you want the printer driver to use. After you have selected the corresponding queue, click OK and move to the next step.

Configuring the Printer   This step involves configuring the printer to its default settings. This includes the default paper size, the paper orientation, and so on. Click Configure to open the Configure dialog box. From the Configure dialog box, press the Default values button to apply the default values that your printer should use, according to the driver information. If you are using your corresponding printer driver, those values are likely to be the best to use with your printer. If you are using the Generic Printer driver, you might want to change those values a bit so that they best suit your printer. You can get the best settings for these values from your printer manual or your printer manufacturer. After you have checked the values in the Configure dialog box, press OK to save your settings.

Testing Your Settings   The moment of truth has come; turn on your printer. From the Printer Installation main dialog box, press the Test Page button to try your printer settings. What was the result of Test Page?

- **Nothing came out of the printer**—You might be connecting the printer to a wrong queue. Change the queue by clicking Connect and trying again.
- **The printing is very slow**—If other applications can print faster than this speed, you might want to get your printer-specific driver.
- **The page is chopped or some text is cut**—You will have to change the setting of the page by clicking the Configure button.
- **A full test page without errors**—Congratulations, you can use StarOffice for printing from now on.

Making It Default   Now that you have finished setting up your printer, you might want to make it the default printer for StarOffice so that you can print by mouse clicking the printer icon. Select the printer that you want to set as default if you have installed more than one printer—or select your printer from the Installed printers list—and click the Default printer button.

Installing New Fonts

Although the Printer Installation program also offers the ability of installing new fonts StarOffice can use, we greatly recommend that you do not use this option but rather install the fonts to your X server global fonts directory. Refer to Chapter 3, "Installing the X Window System," for more about installing fonts to your X server global fonts directory. After you have installed the fonts to your X server global fonts directory, follow these instructions:

1. Run the Printer Installation program as described in the printer installation section. Even if you do not have a printer, this is where you add new fonts to StarOffice.
2. Press the Initialize font path button.
3. Press OK so that the system will be searched for new fonts. Some fonts cannot be used with StarOffice; you will be prompted when those files are found. Note that TrueType

fonts cannot be directly used with X Windows or StarOffice. You will need to do some extra work to get them to function. This book does not discuss how to get StarOffice to use TrueType fonts, but Chapter 3 discusses how to get TrueType fonts to work under X Windows.

4. You will be prompted when the fonts to be installed are scanned and found. You can modify these fonts' properties by selecting the font and editing the properties and clicking Apply when you are done.

5. Generate a font metrics for all the fonts by clicking the Convert All Metric Files button.

6. Click Close to apply the changes to StarOffice.

Setting Up StarOffice as a Web Browser

StarOffice can serve as an enhanced Web browser. You can navigate the Web by using StarOffice simply by typing the URL in the address bar and clicking Enter. The settings you use to make StarOffice behave as a Web browser are accessed by opening the Tool, Options menu and then selecting the Browser branch from the Options dialog box.

Setting Up a Cache

Caching documents is important for speed when accessing the Internet. You can configure how StarOffice treats cacheing by selecting Cache from the Browser branch (see Figure 25.6).

FIGURE 25.6
StarOffice enables you to control the size of cached documents on your drive. Cache is important for navigation speed but it eats up disk space.

The caching options for StarOffice include the following:

- **Memory Cache**—This option indicates how many documents—Web pages— StarOffice should cache in memory. Caching documents in memory drastically enhances the speed of Internet navigation. You can clear the memory cache by clicking the Clear button next to it.

- **Disk Cache**—You can decide how many megabytes StarOffice should use for caching documents. It is important to note that you should not allow StarOffice to use a large amount of hard disk space if your system administrator sets up quotas or you'll run out of disk space sooner that you may think.

- **Verify Document**—This option indicates the behavior that StarOffice should take against documents in cache. If you set it to Once per session, StarOffice checks to see whether the document on the Web site matches the one in your cache once for each time you run StarOffice and try to access this site. If set to Never, StarOffice never checks and always loads the page stored in the cache. If you set this option to Always, StarOffice always compares the document in cache with that on the Web site.

- **Save Expired Document in Cache**—Cache has an expiration time. When documents get "old," StarOffice attempts to delete them automatically. If you set this option, StarOffice will not delete the expired documents.

- **No Cache For**—Some sites on the Internet are updated very regularly. You might want to turn off caching for these sites because caching those pages will not save you speed. In this edit box, enter the sites for which you don't want StarOffice to cache their pages. For example, you can enter `www.freshmeat.net` or `www.linuxtoday.com`.

File Types

StarOffice enables you to control the action that it takes when you click links to files on a Web page by defining a MIME type to the file extension and associating it with a StarOffice module, plug-in, or external application. You can access this option from the Browse, File Types menu. Figure 25.7 shows the Options File Type dialog box that appears.

FIGURE 25.7

By setting up the File Types, you can bind the click on a link of a specific file type to an action that StarOffice takes.

To configure the MIME types, select the file type that you want to modify from the File Types list. After you select a file type, you can modify its settings. The settings that can be assigned to a file type include the following:

- **Clipboard ID**—By using this option, you can give the file type a clipboard ID so that your SuSE Linux can handle the file if you decide that the file should be handled through an external application.

- **Extension**—Here you can change the extension through which a file type is identified. A file type can have more than one extension. You can use wildcards in this field. Separate the extensions with a semicolon.

- **Open With**—An action is associated with the file type through the Open with combo box. If you select a StarOffice module to handle the file, you have also to select the filter that should apply to this module. For example, if you specify that a file type should be opened through StarCalc, you should also specify the filter that StarCalc should use—StarCalc document version, MS Excel document version, or others. If you select to open the file using a plug-in, you also have to specify the filter that the plug-in should use. StarOffice comes only with one plug-in, the StarDownload plug-in. If you select to open the file using another plug-in, you have to specify the filter that the other should handle. Those include treating the file as a Java applet, as an executable, and others. If you decide that this file type should be handled through an external application, you can browse and enter the full path of the external application in the line edit box that appears instead of the filter combo box.

After you have modified a file type, you have the option either to add it to the list or to over-write the original file type that you modified.

Scripting

You can tweak StarOffice's behavior against scripts from the Browser, Scripting menu. In this dialog box you can enable or disable running Java scripts. StarOffice supports StarBasic, which is an advanced scripting language that is quite similar to Visual Basic scripts. Beware that some StarBasic scripts might be designed to do some damage to your system. You can turn on and off StarBasic scripting from the Internet by selecting Always Execute or Never Execute. If you trust that a site doesn't have a script that will damage your system, you can add it to the Execute StarBasic Scripts Form site list. After you have done so, you can select the From list to enable StarOffice to execute StarBasic scripts only from those sites.

Cookies

Many sites on the Internet use cookies to set some preferences or information about you. You can set up the behavior that StarOffice should take against cookies from the Browser, Cookies menu. You can select whether to always accept cookies, to never accept them, or to have StarOffice alarm you on receiving a cookie. You can manage your cookies by clicking the Confirm button. After you have clicked the Confirm button, you can select the cookies that are available in the list (see Figure 25.8).

Part

IV

Ch

25

FIGURE 25.8
StarOffice gives you absolute control over cookies. You can control the reception of cookies from a specific server to be totally ignored or always accepted. You can also manage the existing cookies on your hard drive.

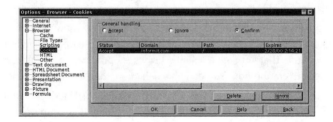

After you have selected a cookie, you can choose to ignore all the cookies that this domain sends, including the selected cookie, by clicking Ignore. You can also click Accept to accept all the cookies that this domain sends by clicking Accept.

HTML

In the HTML Settings dialog box, you can configure how StarOffice should handle all HTML files. You can reach the HTML Options dialog by selecting Browser, HTML (see Figure 25.9).

FIGURE 25.9
The most important StarOffice feature is that it is Internet ready. HTML imports and exports are highly advanced in StarOffice. Even if StarOffice does not understand some point in an HTML file, it would still keep what it didn't understand as is when it saves the file.

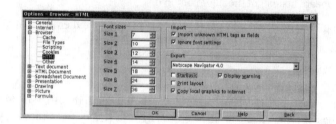

The following are the options in this dialog:

- **Font Sizes**—The Sizes fields are special HTML tags that define the font sizes. You can change the font sizes of HTML documents by changing the sizes in these fields.

- **Import**—The fields in this group box are used to define how an HTML document should be treated when StarOffice imports it. You can choose to Import Unknown HTML Tags as Fields, which enables you to save the documents using the same tags that were first loaded if StarOffice does not recognize those tags. The Ignore Font Settings option is useful if you want to save your HTML document using the page style defaults.

- **Export**—In this group box are all the options that you might want to use if you want to export StarOffice documents to HTML format. The options include exporting HTML documents that support a specific browser optimization which can be selected from the browsers combo box. You can also select one of the following options for exporting.

  - **StarBasic**—Check this box if you want your HTML documents to include StarBasic scripts. Note that those scripts will not run unless the viewer is using StarOffice as a Web browser.

  - **Display Warning**—Check this box to be warned if the StarBasic scripts are to be removed when exporting HTML documents.

- **Print Layout**—Check this box to enable your exported HTML pages to have print layout.
- **Copy Local Graphics to Internet**—Check this option to copy any graphics that the document contains to the selected Internet server when you save your document as HTML.

Other

The Other branch of the Browser tree is where you can configure Java applications' and applets' behavior, plug-ins, start page, and browser identification. The following are the Other dialog box's options:

- **Java**—This group is concerned with enabling the Java applications to run using StarOffice. You must have Java installed on your system for Java to run. You can specify the Java library location through browsing to the class path location on your system. Java is usually installed in `/usr/lib/jre1.1.7/lib/i686/green_threads`. You have to make sure that you installed the `jre` package before you enable Java. It is advised that you check the Enable Security Checks option and set the Net Access to Host (see Figure 25.10). You can enable StarOffice to load and run Java applets and plug-ins by checking the corresponding check boxes.

Part
IV
Ch
25

FIGURE 25.10
To enhance security, you can turn on and off the Java support. You can also control the level of security while using Java by using the options in this dialog.

- **Homepage**—Set the URL field to your starting home page so that you can directly access it by clicking the home icon on the Function bar.
- **Browser Identification**—Some Web servers ask the Web browser for its identification so that they can supply it with a browser-specific Web page. In other words, if your browser is identified as Netscape 3.0, the server would send a page that is optimized for Netscape 3.0; if your browser is identified as Internet Explorer 4.0, the server would supply the same page but with Internet Explorer 4.0 optimization. By clicking the default button, StarOffice describes itself as a Netscape browser. You should be getting the best results by keeping the default settings.

Proxy Settings

If you use a proxy server, you can tell StarOffice to use the proxy server from the Internet, Proxy branch. Change the proxy server from None to manual and fill in your proxy server settings.

If you do not want to use proxy for specific servers, you can avoid this by listing the servers in the No proxy For edit box. Each server should be separated from the following one by a semicolon.

Setting Up StarOffice as an Email Client

StarOffice can manage your emails effectively even if you have multiple email accounts. Setting up StarOffice as an email client requires that you identify yourself first; then you can set up email accounts.

Preparing Outgoing Email Settings

If you haven't already configured this during your StarOffice setup, you can set up your personal information through the Tools, Options menu and selecting General, User Data. Fill in your information to be able to send email messages. You should fill in the email address field or you will get an error message if you try to send an email.

Next, you have to setup the outgoing email server. The outgoing email server is the server that you use to send your emails. You can set this up through the Internet, Mail/News branch. Fill in the outgoing email.

When you are done with those settings, you can use StarOffice to send email messages by simply clicking the New Mail icon on the StarOffice desktop.

Managing Email Properties

You can access the email settings through the Internet, Mail/News branch. In this dialog, enter your email settings—your incoming email server, your username, and your password. This dialog enables you to control the message format. You can set it to HTML format, rich format, or StarOffice format. The most common email formats are the plain text and HTML formats.

The Extra group defines the behavior of StarOffice when you click an incoming message. When you click an incoming message, StarOffice automatically opens it in a preview window. If you want to read your email in the preview window, you can set StarOffice to mark the message as read after a specified amount of time. You can enable this option and set the time that StarOffice should consider the message as read from this group box. If you choose to disable this option, you will have to mark the message that you read manually.

Managing Email Accounts

StarOffice can communicate with the most commonly used email protocols. You can create a new email account by right-clicking the StarDesktop and selecting New. From the pop-up menu, select the email account protocol that your email provider uses. In the email proprieties dialog box that appears, fill in all the needed information. After you save the settings that you made by clicking OK, you will find a new item with the name that you specified when setting up the email account on your StarDesktop. You can create as many email accounts as you want using the same method.

Setting Up StarOffice as a News Reader

To use StarOffice as a News Client, you have to fill in your identification information. Refer to the previous section on preparing outgoing email settings.

News Settings

As a matter of fact, news settings do not differ from email settings except for the account setup. Open the Tools, Options menu and select Internet, Mail/News branch. Fill in your news server address in the server field.

Check the boxes next to the message formats that you want to be able to use from the text format group. This will enable you to send messages using those text formats. Note that if the receivers do not have StarOffice, they will not be able to read your messages. In most cases, people use plain text and HTML-capable news clients.

The messages group describes how StarOffice should treat your incoming messages if you view/preview them. Refer to the previous section "Managing Email Properties" for further details.

Managing News Accounts

You can create a news account simply by right-clicking the StarDesktop and selecting New. From the pop-up menu, select News. Fill in the information required to prepare the news account. Select the Subscribe tab and search for the newsgroup to which you want to subscribe. When you're finished, click OK to save the news account. An icon with the name you selected for the news account should appear on your StarDesktop. The next time you want to check your news messages, all you have to do is double-click this icon. You can have as many news accounts as you want by using the same procedure previously described.

Part
IV

Ch
25

StarOffice General Configuration

Because it is almost impossible to discuss configuring StarOffice in one chapter, this chapter touches on only the most important features. StarOffice is highly configurable and customizable. The key to configuring StarOffice is using the Tools, Options menu. The Options dialog box makes it easy for a user to modify her StarOffice component settings through a tree hierarchy that has a category/sub-category configuration. This tree hierarchy enables the user to quickly access her configurations. Most users who are used to other office suites will find this method better than having several sub-menus or tab dialogs.

You customize StarOffice by setting up your options first; then you customize the menus, keyboard shortcuts, status bar, and so on. You can access those custom settings from the Tools, Configure menu. You can customize StarOffice to use your preferences through the Customization dialog box that appears (see Figure 25.11).

FIGURE 25.11
Configure StarOffice to suit your preferred shortcuts from the Configuration dialog box. Add your touch!

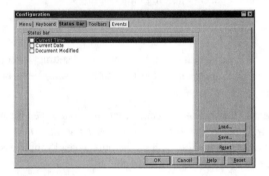

StarOffice Look and Feel

StarOffice's standard look and feel is close to that of Microsoft Windows. Yet, you can change this by choosing the Tools, Options menu, General, View branch. From this dialog box, you can set the way StarOffice looks and feels. You can see how other OSes feel by changing the StarOffice look and feel. StarOffice look and feel can be set to Standard, Macintosh, X Windows (motifish), or OS/2.

Other settings concerning how StarOffice looks can be set from this same dialog box. You can set the button sizes, the mouse interaction with new dialogs, and so on.

Your File Paths

StarOffice standard folders can be changed from the Tools, Options menu, General, Paths branch. If you want to change the path of the standard StarOffice work folder, select it from the list and click Browse. Browse to the path you want to set as the work folder and click OK. You can think of the standard work folder as the My Documents folder in the Microsoft Windows environment.

Auto Save

One of the most important features a word processor must have is the auto save functionality. Although StarOffice can restore the latest open dialog box in case it crashed, it is highly recommended that you enable this option so you do not lose your documents. It is better to restore the document as it was a minute ago rather than losing it at all. You can set this option through the Tools, Options menu General, Save branch.

On Your Own with the Help Agent

You can navigate through the Options dialog box to see if there are any tweaks that you want to apply to StarOffice. You can turn on the Help Agent at any time by clicking Help. The Help Agent will always explain what options are available to you at any time. The Help Agent follows your mouse clicks or keyboard focus on any button, edit box, and so on and informs you what it is for. You can rely on the Help Agent for getting good information on StarOffice configuration.

Troubleshooting

Part
IV

Ch
25

I'm having some trouble printing my documents.

Is the printer turned on? If so, check these solutions:

- Does the printer print garbage? In this case, you need to review Chapter 11.
- The printer does not print at all? Again, you need to review Chapter 11.
- The text or graphic on the printed paper is chopped out. In this case, you have to get your printer driver and install it or you will have to set up the paper size by using your printer manual.

Whenever I try to set up a printer or install a new font, I get an access denied error about my permissions to some files.

This always happens if you installed StarOffice with the Workstation option. Only root can have access to setting up printers and adding new fonts.

My machine is very slow and StarOffice takes forever to load.

If you installed StarOffice from a tarball downloaded file or the StarOffice CD, you can customize your installation to only the modules you will be using. This drastically decreases the loading time. It is noted, though, that only the StarOffice startup takes time. After it is loaded, it is fast.

I is bad on grammar. Do StarOffice repair mine document?

StarOffice can only check for spelling mistakes. If your document contains grammatical mistakes, you will have to fix them yourself. They won't even be underlined. ●

Installing and Configuring WordPerfect

Corel WordPerfect 8.0 Features

Corel WordPerfect is one of the leading and highly featured word processors in the market. WordPerfect runs on several platforms, namely all Microsoft Windows versions, Unix, and Linux. For a long time, WordPerfect was available for Linux, but it was not free. With the introduction of version 8.0, Corel decided to give away its award-winning word processor to the Linux community. This was a highly regarded and appreciated move. Now anyone can download the fully functional WordPerfect 8.0 for Linux for free personal use. A deluxe version is also available for purchase. This version includes more features than the download version such as a complete manual, clipart, photos, fonts, and so on.

WordPerfect 8.0 has a lot of features that make it an amazing word processor:

- The ability to open most of the commonly used file formats (40 formats), including Microsoft Word 97 files.

- It incorporates the Shadow Cursor technology, enabling you to point and click anywhere in the document and start typing. This feature is simply amazing when it comes to inserting text in unusual places in the document. To insert text in the same place without this tool you would normally need to use lots of spaces and new lines or even tables. With Shadow Cursor, just point, click, and type! This can make filling in forms very easy.

- It is fully compatible with all previous versions of WordPerfect. This way, you won't lose any documents you previously had; this includes all versions of WordPerfect since version 1. WordPerfect uses the same file format across platforms, so you can exchange documents very easily.

- By using the Corel Versions technology, you can keep track of document revisions. This helps if you are working on the same document with more than one person. You can then keep track of who changed what in the document.

- Corel's Grammar-As-You-Go technology checks your text for any grammatical errors as you type. Suggestions are also provided to you; these show how you can better phrase your sentence. You can even set the level of grammar check to suit the type of document you are writing.

- Corel's Spell-As-You-Go technology checks your text for any spelling errors as you type. Misspelled words are clearly underlined for you and a list of correct words is provided.

- File management is a breeze thanks to WordPerfect File Manager.

- WordPerfect has an extensive functionality for charting and drawing. Images can be moved, rotated, and sized. Text can be wrapped around and beside them. Graphics can be placed on top of text, and then gradients applied to them, 3D objects and lines inserted, and so on.

- All table modifications are point and click. This includes changing the size of the table, splitting and joining cells, and so on.

- You can create your own Web documents to be published on your Web site. You can use WordPerfect to create HTML documents full of hyperlinks and bookmarks. Existing HTML documents can be converted to WordPerfect format for further editing.

- You can insert hyperlinks in your documents to connect them together or to other documents on the Web.

- A complete online help system is available.

- Over 90 built-in spreadsheet functions aid you in numerical documents.

- All this for free...

As you can see, WordPerfect 8.0 is an excellent and very complete word processor. Corel graciously offers it to the Linux community for free.

WordPerfect 8.0 is not bundled with SuSE Linux. This, however, is not a problem because you can easily download it free from the Internet.

Getting WordPerfect 8.0

As mentioned previously, WordPerfect 8.0 is not bundled with SuSE Linux. Therefore, you will need to get it yourself. This is not much of a problem. There are two ways you can get WordPerfect 8.0; one is by downloading it from the Internet for free and the other is by purchasing the deluxe version. If you do a lot of word processing, you may want to consider purchasing the deluxe version because it offers many more fonts and graphics than the download version.

The primary place to get Corel WordPerfect 8.0 for Linux is from Corel's Web site, `http://linux.corel.com`. You can also find it on `http://www.downloads.com`. The file is approximately 20 MB in size. You can download it all in one piece or in smaller pieces in case you have a slow or unreliable connection. If you want support for other languages, make sure that you download their language modules as well.

Part

IV

Ch

26

Installing WordPerfect 8.0

Installing WordPerfect 8.0 is very easy thanks to its graphical installation screens. To install WordPerfect 8.0, just follow these steps:

1. Log in as root and start X Windows.

2. The first thing that you have to do is to unpack the files you downloaded. If you downloaded the program as one file, it will be called GUI00.GZ; if you downloaded the separate files, they will be called GUI00.GZ to GUI06.GZ.

3. Create a directory to unpack WordPerfect 8.0 in, for example, `/tmp/corel`:
   ```
   #mkdir /tmp/corel
   ```

4. Now start to unpack the files into that directory. If you downloaded the program as one file, the command is the following:

```
# tar xvfz GUI00.GZ -C /tmp/corel
```

5. If you downloaded the separate files, run this command for each of the six files:

```
# tar xvfz GUIXX.GZ -C /tmp/corel
```

6. If you downloaded any language modules, extract them by using the same method you used for the previous files. They should all end up in the same directory as the installation file, /tmp/corel.

7. When you're done unpacking the files, you should end up with these files in /tmp/corel (including the language modules):

```
-rw-r--r--   1 424      users         46 Feb 10   2000 Moves
-rw-r--r--   1 424      users          6 Feb 10   2000 Name
-rw-r--r--   1 424      users        850 Feb 10   2000 Readme
-rwxr-xr-x   1 424      users       5818 Feb 10   2000 Runme
-rw-r--r--   1 424      users    4177920 Feb 10   2000 b_ins00
-rw-r--r--   1 424      users     153600 Feb 10   2000 b_ins01
-rw-r--r--   1 424      users    4065280 Feb 10   2000 b_req00
-rw-r--r--   1 424      users     849920 Feb 10   2000 b_req01
-rw-r--r--   1 424      users     133120 Feb 10   2000 b_us00
-rw-r--r--   1 424      users    4259840 Feb 10   2000 g_req00
-rw-r--r--   1 424      users    4188160 Feb 10   2000 g_req01
-rw-r--r--   1 424      users    4208640 Feb 10   2000 g_req02
-rw-r--r--   1 424      users    2334720 Feb 10   2000 g_req03
-rw-r--r--   1 424      users    4075520 Feb 10   2000 g_us00
-rw-r--r--   1 424      users     184320 Feb 10   2000 g_us01
drwxr-xr-x   7 424      users       4096 Feb 10   2000 linux
drwxr-xr-x   2 424      users       4096 Feb 10   2000 readme
drwxr-xr-x   2 424      users       4096 Feb 10   2000 shared
```

8. Change the directory to /tmp/corel:

```
#cd /tmp/corel
```

9. Run the installation command:

```
#./Runme
```

10. The installation program first asks you whether or not you unpacked the files you downloaded. Answer yes by typing y.

11. The install program starts to extract its files. This will take some time; be patient.

12. The installer will complain that your kernel is not certified. Should it go on or not? Answer yes. This is not a problem; it's just that WordPerfect 8.0 was not built on the Kernel 2.2.x series, but it works fine.

13. The first screen in the graphical installation appears (see Figure 26.1). Select the language in which you want to read the license agreement and click OK.

FIGURE 26.1

The first screen in the Corel WordPerfect installation.

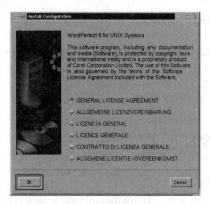

14. The next screen is the license agreement. Read it carefully, and if you choose to accept it, click Accept.

15. In the next screen the installer asks you where you want to install WordPerfect 8.0. A good, common place is /opt/wp8. You could use any other directory, of course; it's up to you. Click OK to move to the next screen.

16. The Installation Size screen is where you specify how big the installation should be. You have three choices: Full installation (61–70MB), Medium Installation (44–50MB), and Minimum Installation (36–40MB). To know what each of them will install for you, click the Help button for more information. We recommend the Full or at least the Medium installation. The minimum installation does not even have grammar check. Make your choice and click OK to move to the next screen.

17. The Existing Application screen is useful if you already have an older installation of WordPerfect on your machine. Just give the installer the path to that installation and it will take all of the settings and defaults from it and apply it to the new installation. If you don't have an older installation, just leave the path field empty and click OK.

18. The next screen asks you whether or not you want the installer to edit your /etc/magic file. The file command uses this file to identify file types. If you want file to correctly identify WordPerfect files, choose Update the Magic File. This is recommended; it won't hurt if you do it. Click OK.

19. The next screen is the language selection screen. Here you should select the languages you want to install. If you have not downloaded any extra language modules, you will only find English. Otherwise, you will find a list of all the languages that are now available. Choose the ones you want to install and click OK.

20. This screen is for printer driver selection. To select a printer, find it in the list of printers either by looking through the list or by using the Name Search field below the list. To select a printer driver, highlight it and click Select. Repeat the same process to select more than on printer driver. When done, click OK.

Part

IV

Ch

26

21. Now you have to assign each printer driver you selected to a printing destination. Just highlight the printer driver from the list and click Assign. A small window pops up, showing you all the system printer configurations that exist. Choose the one you want to use and click OK. When you are done assigning all the printers you selected to printing destinations, click OK. For more information about setting up your system to use a printer, see Chapter 11, "Printing."

22. The next screen gives you the option of installing extra CDE (Common Desktop Environment) specific features. Because SuSE Linux does not ship with CDE, you don't need this. Click OK.

23. The next screen, shown in Figure 26.2, shows you a summary of what has happened so far; this is a Review List. You can go back to any installation step by highlighting it and clicking OK. When you are ready to start the installation, click OK.

FIGURE 26.2
Here's a jump point to any of the installation steps in case you want to modify anything before starting the installation.

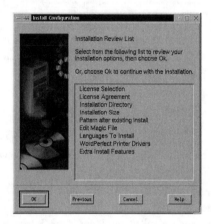

24. WordPerfect starts the actual installation using the options you've set up. This may take some time, so be patient.

25. When it's done, The README Review screen pops up. You can view any one of the listed documents by highlighting it and clicking View. When you're done, click Done to exit the installer.

That's it; WordPerfect is now successfully installed. You may remove the installation directory; you don't need it anymore. Issue the following command:

```
#rm -rf /tmp/corel
```

Running and Configuring WordPerfect 8.0

Now that you have installed WordPerfect 8.0, no doubt you are eager to run it and play with it. To run it, execute this command from an X terminal:

```
$ /opt/wp8/wpbin/xwp
```

You should of course use the correct path that you used in the installation. You can create an icon on your desktop in KDE or GNOME for WordPerfect so that you don't have to type this command every time you want to launch WordPerfect.

WordPerfect launches for the first time as in Figure 26.3. As you can see, it asks you for a registration number. That's okay; don't panic. You don't have to enter it now; click Enter key later. Just make sure that you visit `http://linux.corel.com` and register your copy of WordPerfect. It won't cost you anything, but you do need the registration key that the site gives you. Every time you run WordPerfect, it asks you to enter this key; when you finally do, it won't ask again. If you don't enter this key within 90 days, you won't be able to use WordPerfect until you do enter it.

FIGURE 26.3
You see this the first time you run WordPerfect.

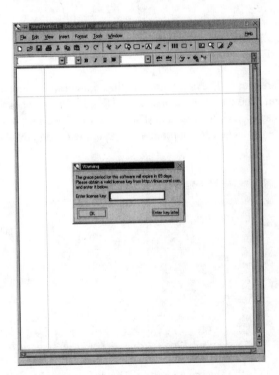

The Configuration Module

If you frequently use a word processor, you will feel right at home with WordPerfect. All of the tools that you expect to find in a quality word processor are there, along with some extra features. The main configuration module for WordPerfect can be called from the Preferences menu (see Figure 26.4). The Preferences configuration dialog box pops up when you click that menu (see Figure 26.5). The configuration module is where you find most of the interesting parameters that you can tweak.

FIGURE 26.4

Click Preferences to
get the Preferences
dialog box.

FIGURE 26.5

The WordPerfect
Preferences
dialog box.

The Display Preferences   The first button on the configuration module is Display. This is
where you configure the display parameters. The Display Preferences dialog box pops up
when you click Display, as in Figure 26.6. The top row of the dialog box contains a group of
radio buttons; when you click any of them, the rest of the dialog box shows this options configuration.

FIGURE 26.6

The Display
Preferences
dialog box.

The first radio button is the Document button. The dialog now shows you all of the document-
specific options. Starting from the top left to bottom right, they are Show, Scroll Bars, Shadow
Cursor, and Measurement. Here's a brief description of most of these options:

■ The Show block contains options for what to show in your document window. Toggle
  Show Table Gridlines; this shows tables as a grid in case you have turned off table
  lines. This way, you can still see the table, but the lines won't show up when you print.
  The Graphics option toggles the display of images and other graphics. The Blinking
  Cursor button toggles the display of a blinking cursor. The Hidden Text button toggles
  the display of special hidden text. Finally, the Comments button toggles the display of
  embedded comments in your text.

- The Scroll Bars block defines how you want the scroll bars to behave in the document window. Click Vertical and Horizontal to enable or disable having vertical and horizontal scroll bars. The remaining two options are radio buttons—Show Always and When required. These control when scroll bars appear. You can show them all the time (Show Always) or when the text runs beyond the display (When Required).

- The Shadow Cursor block button sets the options for WordPerfect's Shadow Cursor feature. This feature enables you to point anywhere in the document with your mouse, click, and start typing there. To change the color of the cursor, click the Color button. You get a color palette to choose a color from. Click the Shape button to choose a shape for your shadow cursor. You can have the shadow cursor snap to Margins, Tabs, Indent, or Spaces from the Snap to block. Finally, you can choose to have the shadow cursor active in Text, White space, or both from the Active in block.

- The last block in the Display Preferences is the Measurement block. You have two options to configure here. Units of Measure allows you choose the unit system of measurement you are most comfortable with. The Application Bar/Ruler Display sets the measurement units that are to be used for the application bar and the ruler on the top of the document.

The View/Zoom radio button shows viewing and default zoom options. You can set the default view of the document to be either Draft or Page in the Default View block. The Default Zoom block sets the zoom value for the default view of the document. You can choose from any of the presets or you can enter your own value.

The Ruler Bar buttons shows the ruler's configuration. You can toggle whether or not you want the ruler to appear on new and current documents. The Ruler Bar Options button sets whether or not you want tabs to snap to the ruler's grid (Tabs Snap to Ruler Bar Grid) and whether or not you want to show the ruler bar grids (Show Ruler Bar Guides).

The Show ¶ radio buttons shows the configuration for hidden formatting texts. You can toggle whether or not you want to see this text. It won't come out in printing even if you do show it. The Symbols to Display block gives you options of which hidden symbols to display.

The Reveal Codes radio button shows you the configuration for the revealed codes. You can toggle whether or not you want to show the codes. The Font Face lets you choose the font and font size to be used for the revealed codes. Finally, the Options enable you to set how revealed codes behave, whether they should wrap at the ends of lines, show spaces as bullets, and so on.

The Merge radio button shows the merge codes configuration options. You can set merge codes to be displayed as text (Display Merge Codes), as markers (Display Merge Coded As Markers), or to hide them altogether (Hide Merge Codes).

That's it for the Display Preferences. Click OK to save your settings and exit.

The Environment Preferences   When you click the Environment button, the Environment Preferences dialog box appears (see Figure 26.7).

Part

IV

Ch

26

FIGURE 26.7

The Environment Preferences.

This is where you configure options that affect your environment:

- The User Info for Comments/Summary blocks concerns your name and initials. That information is used in comments and the document summary.

- The Beep On block defines when audible beeps should be heard. WordPerfect can beep on an Error, Hyphenation, and Find Failure.

- The Formatting block deals with formatting issues. You can control the Hyphenation Prompt to be When Required, Always, or Never. You will find that it's best left as When Required so that it doesn't annoy you all the time. The remaining two options in the block are toggle options that deal with confirmations.

- The Menu block configures how the menus should behave. Click Display Last Open Filenames to have the menus show you a list of the most recently opened files. Click Display Shortcut Keys to have the menus display the corresponding shortcut keys for each option. Finally, you can set the time, in seconds, that WordPerfect waits before showing you the quick tip for an option from the Show Quick Tips.

- The Save Workspace option defines when your workspace should be saved. This can be Always, Never, or Prompt on Exit.

- The Save block shows document saving options. The first one is Set QuickMark on Save; if you enable this, WordPerfect inserts a visible mark in the text where you saved so that you can see at which point in the text you were when you last saved. The Reformat Documents for Default Printer on Open option, if enabled, reformats any document you open to best suit your printer configuration.

- Click Activate Hyperlinks on Open if you want any of a document's hyperlinks to be active. Hyperlinks links are links to other documents, either locally present or on the Web.

- Click Graphical Banner and Startup Screen if you want to see the splash screen when you start WordPerfect.

- Click Select Whole Words Instead of Characters if you want text selection to be word by word rather than character by character.

That's it for the Environment Preferences. Click OK to save your settings and exit.

The Files Preferences   When you click the Files button, the Files Preferences dialog box pops up, as in Figure 26.8. This is where you set the paths to the important files WordPerfect uses. This dialog box is very similar to the Display Preferences dialog box because it has radio buttons at the top, each with its own configuration options.

FIGURE 26.8
The Files Preferences dialog box.

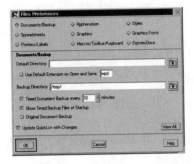

The following are the options for the Files Preferences dialog box:

- The Documents/Backup button configures where your documents are usually kept and where to back them up. You just need to fill in the paths for these values.
- The Hyphenation button configures the path where you want to keep the hyphenation files.
- The Styles button configures the path where you want to keep your personal style files.
- The Spreadsheet button configures the path where you want to keep your personal spreadsheet files.
- The Graphics button configures the path where you want to keep your personal graphics files.
- The Graphics Fonts button configures the path where you want to keep your graphics fonts data files.
- The Printers/Labels button configures the path where you want to keep your printers and labels files. You can set the Default Labels to Display to Laser, Tractor-Fed, or Both.
- The Macros/Toolbar/Keyboard button configures the path where you want to keep your macros, toolbar, and keyboard settings files.
- The ExpressDocs button configures the path of the ExpressDocs. These are template documents that aid you in creating standard documents quickly.

    As you might have seen, some of the paths are grayed out. These mainly define paths to be shared by everyone. You should configure WordPerfect as root if you want to change any of these paths.

■ You can click the View All button any time to view all the paths that have been set. Please note that for any paths that you set in this dialog you must have write permissions on. A good place to do this is anywhere inside your home directory.

That's it for the Files Preferences. Click OK to save your settings and exit.

The Document Summary Preferences When you click the Summary button, the Document Summary Preferences dialog box appears (see Figure 26.9).

FIGURE 26.9

The Document Summary Preferences dialog box.

This is where you specify the options for the document summary:

■ The first option is Default Subject Text. This is the text that is put before the subject in the summary. The default value is RE:, which is fine in most cases.

■ Default Descriptive Type defines the descriptive type that you want to use.

■ Click Use Descriptive Names to show descriptive file names in the file manager and file dialogs.

■ Click Create Summary on Save/Exit to have WordPerfect create a summary when you save and when you exit.

That's it for the Document Summary Preferences. Click OK to save your settings and exit.

The Application Bar Preferences When you click the Application Bar button, the Application Bar Preferences dialog box appears, as shown in Figure 26.10. Here you can customize the application bar by using drag and drop.

FIGURE 26.10

The Application Bar Preferences dialog box.

First, select what items you want to appear on the application bar at the bottom of the document from the list of available items. Each item has a corresponding icon that appears on the document bar. You can move those icons around by dragging them with the mouse pointer. To remove an icon, just drag it off the application bar.

That's it for the Application Bar Preferences. Click OK to save your settings and exit.

The Keyboard Preferences   When you click the Keyboard button, the Keyboard Preferences dialog box appears (see Figure 26.11). This where you can edit and create the keyboard's behavior. You already have presets, such as EquationEditor, which sets the keyboard in the Equation Editor mode.

FIGURE 26.11

The Keyboard
Preferences dialog box.

Click Create to create your own keyboard behavior. Click Edit to edit an existing keyboard behavior. Click Delete to delete a keyboard behavior. Finally, click Copy to make a copy of the currently selected keyboard behavior. This is useful if you want to fine tune one of the existing keyboards.

That's it for the Keyboard Preferences. Click OK to save your settings and exit.

The Font Preferences   When you click the Font button, the Font Preferences dialog box appears (see Figure 26.12). This dialog box has two option blocks—the Redline and the Size Attribute Ratios:

FIGURE 26.12

The Font Preferences
dialog box.

- The Redline block sets the options for the redline. You can set it to any of the following modes:
  - Printer Dependent, which usually is a shaded background
  - Mark Left Margin, which marks redline text with a vertical bar in the left margin

Part

IV

Ch

26

- Mark Alternating Margins, which marks redline text with a vertical bar in the left for even numbered pages and on the right for odd numbered pages

- Mark Right Margin, which marks redline text with a vertical bar in the right margin.

■ The Redline Character is activated if you click any of the margin settings. Specify the character that you want to use as a marker.

■ The Size Attribute Ratios section defines the size of certain text in relation to your text. The value is a percentage of the size of your font. Set the ratios you want for Fine, Small, Large, Very Large, Extra Large, and Super/Subscript text in your document.

That's it for the Font Preferences. Click OK to save your settings and exit.

The Convert Preferences   When you click the Convert button, the Convert Preferences dialog box pops up, as in Figure 26.13. This dialog box configures how WordPerfect converts files to its format. You have two option blocks—Delimiters, which defines the delimiter character to use when reading other formats and the Character block of options, which specifies encapsulated characters and such. This is a bit of an advanced topic. You can get more information about it from WordPerfect's user manual.

FIGURE 26.13
The Convert
Preferences
dialog box.

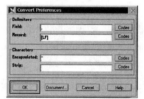

That's it for the Convert Preferences. Click OK to save your settings and exit.

The Color Preferences   When you click the Colors button, the Color Preferences dialog box appears (see Figure 26.14). By using this dialog box, you can customize all the colors WordPerfect uses. This is a very simple dialog box to use. You can choose a preset color from the Color Scheme List if you don't want to create your own.

FIGURE 26.14
The Color Preferences
dialog box.

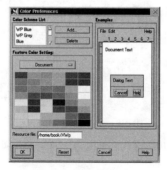

Creating your own scheme is very simple; just choose the item for which you want to change its color from the Feature Color Setting block and pick a color for it.

You will have to restart WordPerfect for your changes to take effect.

That's it for the Color Preferences. Click OK to save your settings and exit.

The Print Preferences   When you click the Print button, the Print Preferences dialog box appears (see Figure 26.15).

FIGURE 26.15
The Print Preferences
dialog box.

This dialog box has all the options for your printing:

- The Copies block of options tells WordPerfect how many copies of every document to print. Put the number of copies you want in the Number of Copies text box. You can decide what will generate the copies in the Generated By list. You can have WordPerfect, the spooler, or the printer deal with multiple copies.

- The Document Settings block of options configures the printing quality and color. You can set the Print Quality to High, Medium, or Draft. To disable color printing, set the Print Color to black. The last option is Do Not Print Graphics; enable it if you don't want any graphics to be printed.

- The WPApp Destination Options sets the printing priority for you.

- The Spool Command Settings block configures any options that you want to send to the underlying printing system, usually LPR. For more information regarding this option, see Chapter 11. The Secure Print Files option should be enabled; it prevents security problems with printing.

That's it for the Print Preferences. Click OK to save your settings and exit. ●

Part
IV

Ch
26

Installing GIMP

What Is the GIMP?

The GIMP (GNU Image Manipulation Program) is a program for manipulating images in a variety of ways. For those who have worked with applications such as Adobe Photoshop, you will feel right at home with the GIMP. The GIMP is a free, open source application. This means that you do not pay anything to get it, and you get the source code as well.

The GIMP was initially developed by Spencer Kimball and Peter Mattis, two students at the University of California, Berkeley. It started off as a project for the compiler class in Lisp. Due to a lot of crashes and dislike for the project, it started to move in a totally different direction, and the GIMP was born. Kimball and Mattis decided to code an image manipulation program in C. They didn't have much knowledge about how to do this, but they didn't let that stop them. That small project kept growing until it became a full-fledged and extremely powerful application.

Initially, the GIMP used Motif for its GUI. Soon enough, the two students did not feel comfortable with Motif, and they decided to make their own GUI toolkit. GTK+ (The GIMP Toolkit) was born. GTK+ was primarily developed for GIMP, but is now the *defacto* standard GUI toolkit for Linux.

The GIMP is a true masterpiece. It was built on the image of the famous Macintosh and Windows Adobe Photoshop. The GIMP has a lot of the features available in Adobe Photoshop, along with some extra ones. The following are some of GIMP's main features:

- The GIMP includes all of the basic drawing tools such as brushes, pencils, airbrushes, cloning tools, and so on. You can even create your own brushes.
- The GIMP incorporates the famous idea of layers and channels for better control over your project. Using layers, you can easily control different aspects of your standalone images and then merge them into the final image.
- The GIMP is capable of dealing with very large images. This is because of the method it uses to manage its memory. The GIMP uses a tile-based memory management algorithm that enables you to create images with sizes that are limited only by the amount of available disk space. So, the more free space you can afford, the larger the size of the images you can deal with.
- Antialiasing technology is used with all the paint tools using sub-pixel sampling. This gets rid of all those rigid edges and makes them smooth and natural. You can create natural-looking images with little effort.
- Using its own Lisp-based scripting language, script-fu, gives GIMP extremely advanced scripting capabilities. The GIMP has a procedural database for calling internal GIMP functions from external programs. This, along with script-fu, creates an excellent engine for rapid graphic generation. For example, you can use this to create logos and such in mere seconds.

■ When you are doing creative work such as art, you are bound to change your mind a lot and make mistakes along the way. Therefore, the GIMP has a strong Undo/Redo algorithm. You have unlimited Undo/Redo commands and are only limited by your amount of free disk space.

■ Working with an image, you might need to have multiple image windows open at the same time. The GIMP developers understand that, which is why you do not have a limit on the number of image windows you can have open at any time.

■ Gradients are used extensively by most artists. They use them to achieve a natural effect. The GIMP has a powerful gradient editor that comes with several prebuilt gradients for immediate use. If you need to build your own gradient, you can use this editor to do so very easily. Your gradients can use any available colors as well as transparency—you are limited by only your own imagination.

■ The GIMP was initially developed for Web graphics. This is obvious in the amount of tools available for that task. Animated graphics are a breeze to create using the GIMP. It is all a matter of drawing several frames and telling GIMP to animate them.

■ The GIMP has all the required transformation tools available. You can stretch, shear, flip, and rotate any image in seconds using the GUI. Every transformation has a set of parameters you can use to fine tune it to your preference.

■ The GIMP can be integrated into any project without any problems. It supports virtually every graphic file format out there. You can use gif, jpg, png, xpm, tiff, tga, mpeg, ps, pdf, pcx, bmp, and many others. You can even use Adobe Photoshop's file format (psd). New file formats are constantly being added as the need for them arises. Because GIMP supports all those different file formats, you easily can convert an image from one format to the other in no time.

■ The GIMP offers a set of good selection tools, which are used to select a region of the image. You can use the usual rectangle or ellipse selection tools. Or, if you need to select nonregular regions you can use the free, fuzzy, or bezier tools. An intelligent scissors selection tool also is available.

■ Adobe Photoshop uses plug-ins to extend its functionality. The GIMP uses the exact same idea by using a good plug-in architecture. The GIMP has more than 100 different plug-ins that range from simple drawing functions to complex lens and lighting effects. Plug-ins are being developed rapidly for the GIMP.

The GIMP has more features than what is listed here. But these are the ones that are of interest to most people. The GIMP is one of the best image manipulation programs out there. It is being used for professional graphics and Web site graphics, and as a backend engine for automated graphics generation. You name it, it's used for it.

Part
IV

Ch

27

Installing the GIMP

Now that you know all about the GIMP, you probably want to try it out. SuSE comes with a copy of the latest version of GIMP. To install GIMP on your machine, you need to install the gimp package in the gra series using YaST.

This is the easiest and fastest way to install the GIMP. To run it, just type the following command in an xterm while you are in the X Window System:

```
bash$gimp
```

The first time you start the GIMP, it needs to install some important user-specific files. Figure 27.1 illustrates the first time a user runs GIMP. Just click the install button and the GIMP will load when it's done.

FIGURE 27.1

The first time the user runs GIMP it installs some specific files in her home directory.

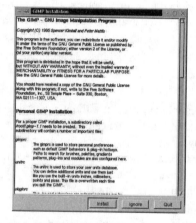

How can you tell whether you have the latest version of GIMP? This is easy—when the GIMP loads, you can see the version number in the splash screen. If you have missed that, you can find out from the File, About option in the menu. An About dialog appears giving credit to the people who made GIMP, a nice logo, and the version number (see Figure 27.2). The GIMP uses a versioning system that is similar to that used by the kernel.

FIGURE 27.2

The About dialog shows the current GIMP version.

The version is three digits, as in *x.x.x*. You have two branches of development—the stable branch and the development branch. The stable versions of the GIMP always have an even number for the second digit (for example, 1.0.4); whereas the unstable development versions have an odd second number (for example, 1.1.3). You are better off with the stable version if you intend to use the GIMP frequently. The development versions have more features and might be faster in some parts, but overall are less stable and reliable than the stable versions.

To check for the latest versions of both branches, you can check the GIMP site at `http://www.gimp.org`. Load the page using your browser, and click Download. When the download page loads, you will see the latest versions available for both branches (see Figure 27.3). At the writing of this book, the latest stable version is 1.0.4 and the latest development version is 1.1.11.

FIGURE 27.3
The GIMP download site.

After you find out that there is a new version available, you have to remember the golden rule of upgrading. If it's working fine, and you don't need more, don't upgrade. You can check the ChangeLog in the package's files to see what changed. If you really don't need it, then you don't have to upgrade.

Before you attempt to download the latest package, you might want to check whether SuSE is offering an RPM of the new version. See Chapter 7, "System Upgrade," for more information on upgrading your SuSE system. If SuSE does not have an RPM for the latest version, you will have to get it yourself, which is really not a problem at all.

System Requirements for GIMP

You need to have the X Window System installed to run GIMP. If you haven't installed X Windows yet, see Chapter 3, "Installing the X Window System," for instructions on how to do that. To use the GIMP comfortably, you will want to run it on a relatively fast machine. It works fine on Pentium 100Mhz machines, but the more demanding you are, the faster the hardware you should use. If you are planning to work with large image sizes, you will need to have a lot of RAM and disk space.

To compile and run GIMP, you need to have GTK+ and Glib libraries installed—again, these come with SuSE. So if you installed SuSE and you are upgrading your GIMP, you need to get only GIMP, nothing else. If you need to upgrade your GTK+ and Glib libraries, you can do so by getting them from `http://www.gtk.org`. To compile and install them, refer to the section "Installing a New Library" in Chapter 7.

To use the GIMP, you should have at least 256-color–capable display equipment. Of course, the more colors and the higher the resolution you have, the better the GIMP experience will be. For serious work using the GIMP, you should have at least 16,000 colors and 1024×768 resolution. Any less and you will suffer.

Obtaining and Compiling the GIMP

To compile the GIMP, you need to download the source code for it. You can get this from `ftp://ftp.gimp.org/pub/gimp/`. After you are here you have two choices—you can download either the stable version or the development version. The stable version is located under a directory named after the version number. In your case, this is v1.0, which makes the URL for the latest stable versions `/pub/gimp/v1.0/latest`.

As for the latest development versions, you will find those under a directory called `/unstable/latest`, which makes the URL for it `/pub/gimp/unstable/latest`.

It's up to you which version you want to get—the stable or the development. The compilation process is identical for both. In our case, we will get the latest development version because it is supposed to be somewhat stable. At the writing of this book, it is v1.1.11.

You need to download two files—the GIMP source code and the gimp-data file. The latter has all the files required for the brushes and patterns used by GIMP; if you are upgrading your GIMP, you won't need that package. The first file is the actual program. We choose to get the bzip2 compressed package that is around 6 MB. The name of the file is `gimp-1.1.11.tar.bz2`.

Before you start compiling the program, if you already have a previous version of GIMP installed using RPM, remove it first. To start compiling the program, follow these steps:

1. Unpack it somewhere, for example `/tmp/sources`.
2. Enter the following command to create a temporary directory to extract the sources in. This is really for the purpose of neatness:

   ```
   # mkdir /tmp/sources
   ```

3. Enter the following command to extract the source in the newly created directory:

```
# tar xvfI gimp-1.1.11.tar.bz2 -C /tmp/sources
```

4. A new directory will be created as /tmp/sources/gimp-1.1.11. Next, you configure the source.

5. Enter the following command to change the directory to the extracted source:

```
# cd /tmp/sources/gimp-1.1.11
```

6. Enter the following command to start configuring the source for compilation:

```
# ./configure
```

7. Configuration of the source takes some time; GIMP tends to check for quite a lot of things. If the script fails for any reason, check the error message and see if it tells you that you need to have another package installed. When the script is done executing successfully, move on to compiling the program.

8. Enter the following command to start compiling the source:

```
# make
```

9. When it's done, install it by entering the following command:

```
# make install
```

10. Enter the following command to update the system for any new libraries that GIMP might have installed:

```
# ldconfig
```

That's it. GIMP is installed now. Before you run it, be sure that you remove the old GIMP setting from your home directory, especially if your previous version was from a different branch (stable branch, for example). You might want to let all your users know that they should remove their old GIMP settings file from their home directories. This is a fairly simple thing to do. Run the following command at the root of your home directory—for example, /home/john:

```
$ rm .gimprc
```

Run GIMP, which will ask to install the new settings for you; let it do so. You now should have a new version of GIMP running. The next time you upgrade it in the same way, you won't need to remove the current version to install a new one because the files will be replaced by the make install command.

Getting the CVS Version

If you plan to do some development work on the GIMP, or you are just one of those people who love to be on the cutting edge, you will want to get the Concurrent Versions System (CVS) version. CVS is the repository that holds the latest version of the GIMP code base. The development versions are recent, but not as recent as the CVS versions. So, if you want to get the latest code, this is where you will get it. But you have to know that this code is not meant for releasing at all, and it might not even compile. Development versions are basically work-ing snapshots of the CVS, and the code in them changes frequently.

To get the CVS version, the first thing you need to have installed on your machine is the CVS program. This comes with SuSE, but you might not have installed it. You will need to use YaST to install cvs, which is found in series D on your SuSE CDs.

After you install the cvs.rpm, you are ready to access the GIMP CVS. You do not have to be root to do this. Follow these steps:

1. Create a directory to store the files:

   ```
   $ mkdir /tmp/cvs
   ```

2. Enter the following command:

   ```
   $ cd /tmp/cvs
   ```

3. Prepare to make the CVS connection:

   ```
   $ export CVSROOT=':pserver:anonymous@anoncvs.gimp.org:/cvs/gnome'
   ```

4. Log in to CVS with the following command:

   ```
   $ cvs login
   ```

5. Get the code for GIMP:

   ```
   $ cvs get gimp
   ```

This will start to download the latest source code base for GIMP in a subdirectory in /tmp/cvs. This will take some time, depending on the speed of your connection.

When it's done, you might attempt to compile the code you just received. Be sure you read any documents regarding the installation and compilation of this code before you start. It might not even compile; so if that happens, don't be surprised. This version is the latest of the latest and it certainly is not finished. You can get other modules if you want, such as the fol-lowing available GIMP-related modules:

- gimp
- gimp2 (no code here, just a holding place for ideas)
- gimp-data-extras
- gimp-plugins-unstable
- gilb
- gtk+

You can get any of these in the same way you got the GIMP code—by entering the following code:

```
$ cvs get gtk+
```

Getting and Installing Plug-Ins

The GIMP uses plug-in architecture to expand its functionality. This is similar to how Adobe Photoshop uses plug-ins. There are a lot of plug-ins available, and quite a few of them come with the GIMP pre-installed. To get the latest plug-ins for the GIMP, check `http://registry.gimp.org/`. This is the main site for GIMP plug-ins.

To install a new plug-in for GIMP, you have two choices:

- If the plug-in is packaged as an RPM, you might want to try that first.
- If it doesn't work, you will want to find the source code package. When you download the source code package, all you have to do is compile. This never takes a lot of time because plug-ins are usually small in size.

For example, we chose to download a new version of the Nova plug-in for the GIMP 1.1 series. The plug-in is packaged in a file called `nova.tgz`. Unpack it with the following commands:

```
# cd /tmp/sources
# tar xvfz nova.tgz
```

You have two ways of going about this—the plug-in either has a configure script or it does not. If it has a configure script, run it:

```
# ./configure
```

If it does not have a configure script, it is probably ready to be compiled without further adjustment, so run a make:

```
# make
```

And then enter the following command:

```
# make install
```

That is all you need to do to install a new plug-in. Restart GIMP and check whether that plug-in is installed.

Obtaining and Installing Script-Fu Scripts

Script-fu is the scripting language used by GIMP to automate it. It is a Lisp-based language that enables you to call internal GIMP functions. GIMP comes with many script-fu scripts that do a lot of different things, such as drop shadow, create logos, and so on.

You can download additional script-fu scripts from the Internet and add them to your GIMP. You can find links to pages of scripts at `http://www.gimp.org/links.html`. Scripts come as text files, and installing them is simply a matter of placing them in the correct location.

Part
IV

Ch

27

When you download a new script, you either can install it so that everyone on the system can use it, or you can install it locally in your home. To install a script for global usage, you need to copy the script file in `/usr/share/gimp/scripts` (if you installed GIMP from an RPM). If you compiled GIMP using its defaults, then the directory to copy the file to is `/usr/local/share/gimp/scripts`. Copy the script file there with the following:

```
# cp script /usr/share/gimp/scripts
```

To install it locally in your home, you need to place it in `.gimp-1.1/scripts` (please note the dot preceding `gimp-1.1`). So, if your username is `john`, you would place it in `/home/john/.gimp-1.1/scripts/`, as shown in the following:

```
$ cp script  ~/.gimp-1.1/scripts
```

The `~/` is replaced by `/home/john`. The script is now installed—restart GIMP and check it out.

Troubleshooting

I can't compile the GIMP.

Are you sure that you have all the required libraries installed? Make sure that you have the GTK+ Development library installed.

GIMP doesn't run correctly after I upgraded.

Did you remove the `.gimprc` in your home directory? If not, then do so using the procedure that was described earlier. The reason you should do this is that GIMP attempts to read the current configuration file, which was built by another version.

I can't open some of the common image formats, why?

GIMP supports all the image formats as long as the corresponding image library is found. For example, for GIMP to support JPEG images, you should have `libjpeg` installed. Make sure that you have the required library for the image you are trying to open.

I just installed a new plug-in/script-fu but it is not working.

Did you restart the GIMP? For script-fus, are you sure you placed the script in the correct place? Put it inside your home directory first to make sure that it's working.

Script-fu is not working correctly, and displays an error message. This happens especially with the logos.

If you are using GIMP 1.0 series, and a script-fu fails with an error message, this usually means that the font you are trying to use cannot be found. Change the name of the font. Otherwise, make sure that the script you are running is compatible with your GIMP version. ●

Installing and Configuring Netscape Communicator

A Briefing on Netscape

Soon after it was founded in 1994, Netscape released what was to become the most famous Internet graphical browser—Netscape Navigator. When Navigator was first released in 1995, its ease-of-use and powerful capabilities made it one of *the* major breakthroughs of the Information Age. It wasn't long before subsequent releases of Netscape products started to incorporate the new HTML technologies.

Netscape and Linux

It wasn't long before Netscape was ported to Linux. As a matter of fact, when Netscape was ported to Linux, it wasn't only used in Internet navigation. Some of the various uses were in printing! Some users would write their documents in HTML, use Netscape Navigator to view them, and then print them out! This is in the past, of course. Thanks to StarOffice, WordPerfect, and some other word processing suites, we don't need Netscape Navigator for this purpose now. Netscape continued providing the Linux community with new versions of Netscape Communicator, thus making Internet navigation as simple as possible through interactive menus, a clear interface, and helpful tools. Netscape's browser comes in two flavors: the stand-alone Navigator and Netscape Communicator. The difference in size is not large, but the capabilities differ between each flavor.

Software Requirements

Package Requirements:

Series xap:

- Netscape
- plugger

Series snd:

- xMP
- sidplay

Series gra:

- xanim

Series pay:

- acroread
- MpegTv

Obtaining the Latest Netscape Version

The simplest way to get the latest Netscape version is getting the package through the Netscape FTP. But, before you get the latest version of Netscape, you have to decide which flavor you want.

Choosing Which Netscape Package to Get

As mentioned before, Netscape comes in Navigator stand-alone and Communicator packages. By getting the Navigator stand-alone version, you get only the Web browser. The Communicator package has Netscape Messenger and Netscape Composer in addition to the Netscape Navigator.

Connecting to the Netscape FTP Site

Due to the load on the Netscape FTP site, Netscape made some mirrors from which users can get free Netscape products. The mirrors start from `ftp.netscape.com` to `ftp20.netscape.com`. You can start the download process with the following:

```
bash#ftp
ftp>open ftp20.netscape.com
```

You will be asked for a username and password. Use anonymous as the username and your email address as the password. If you don't have an email address, enter any string. After you are connected, you can get to the package you want. In this chapter, you should be getting the Communicator package. Therefore, issue the following command:

```
ftp>cd /pub/communicator/
```

In this directory you will find the Communicator package in several different languages. In this example you will be getting the English version of Communicator, with the following command:

```
ftp>cd english
```

Now the time has come to see what is the latest version of Netscape. List the available directories on the FTP:

```
ftp> ls
200 PORT command successful.
150 Opening ASCII mode data connection for /bin/ls.
total
drwxr-xr-x    4 888      999          34 Sep 28 14:14 .
drwxr-xr-x   14 888      999        4096 Jun 15 16:26 ..
drwxr-xr-x    5 888      999          50 Jun 14 16:01 4.61
drwxr-xr-x    5 888      999          50 Sep 28 17:31 4.7
226 Transfer complete.
```

The listing shows that 4.7 is the latest version. It's easy to figure out because 4.7 is greater than 4.61. Enter the following command to get version 4.7:

```
ftp>cd 4.7
```

Part
IV

Ch
28

Then, to get the Linux version of Netscape, change to the following directory where the Linux binaries of Netscape are found:

```
ftp>cd unix/unsupported/linux22/
```

This directory has a listing of `complete_install` and `navigator_standalone`. Netscape Communicator is located in the `complete_install` directory, while Navigator is located in the `navigator_standalone` directory. To get to the `complete install` directory, enter the following:

```
ftp>cd complete_install/
ftp>lcd /tmp
ftp>bin
ftp>get communicator-v47-export.x86-unknown-linux2.2.tar.gz
```

The preceding `ftp` commands download Netscape Communicator into the `/tmp` directory. After the download is complete (12+ MB), proceed to the installation process.

Installing the Latest Netscape Version

Now that you have downloaded the latest version of Netscape off its FTP site, you can start installing it. The installation process is done by first removing the old version of Netscape and then installing the new version.

The following command will uninstall the Netscape package that comes with SuSE:

```
bash#rpm -e netscape
```

You then start unpacking the Netscape version that you just downloaded and start the installation program:

```
bash#cd /tmp
bash#tar xzvf communicator-v47-export.x86-unknown-linux2.2.tar.gz
bash#cd communicator-v47-export.x86-unknown-linux2.2
bash#./ns-install
```

The installation program starts and asks you for the location of the installation. The default is `/opt/netscape`. Press Enter to accept the default or enter a new path to install the Netscape files to. The last step is to delete the old files from the previous installation, if they exist.

Configuring Netscape's Appearance (Netscape Navigator)

Because Netscape is customizable through menu-driven commands, it's not strange that customization is easy in Netscape. Open the Edit menu and choose Preferences. The Preferences window appears and you can start configuring the appearance of Netscape. Netscape has built a hierarchy tree of the preferences that can be set. By clicking the arrow next to the section name, you can expand or collapse the tree. In the Appearance section, you can choose the module that should be launched first when you start Netscape and the button interface. Figure 28.1 shows the Netscape preferences tree with appearance settings selected.

FIGURE 28.1
Setting up Netscape's
Appearance.

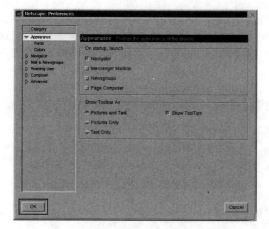

Fonts

Netscape can use your default X fonts. In the Fonts section you can set the default fonts that
Netscape should use and their default size. You can add more fonts to the menu by adding
more fonts to your X.

Colors

You can change the colors of Netscape by choosing the appropriate colors from the Colors
section. The default colors (Black and Gray) can be changed here. You can choose whether to
underline links or not. Also, you can override the document colors with the ones you choose.

Configuring Netscape Browser (Netscape Navigator)

Follow the same steps as mentioned in the previous section to open the Preferences window
of Netscape (that is, choose Edit, Preferences). Click the Navigator arrow to expand the
Navigator configuration tree as shown in Figure 28.2. The Navigator options include the start
page setup, which is the page that automatically opens when you start Navigator and the history expiration period.

Languages

Internet documents, or Web pages, are usually written using different languages. In the
Languages section, you can choose which language decoding you prefer to use while viewing
Web pages.

Applications

It is important that you set up the Applications section to get the best of the Web. Web pages
do not only include text and images. There are pages that have animation, movies, and sound.

Part
IV

Ch

28

Even though Netscape by itself cannot view or play these extensions, it can use the available programs on your system that can. But, you have to set these up! The plug-in will make use of the available software on your system automatically, enabling you to start using Netscape at full capability.

FIGURE 28.2

Setting up Netscape Navigator.

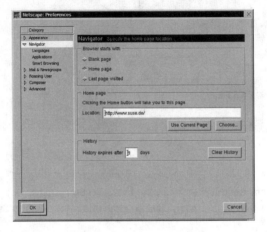

Plug-Ins *Plug-ins* are programs the Netscape browser can use to play extensions that the browser by itself cannot play. Take for example the Flash plug-in provided by Macromedia. This plug-in can play a special format with animation and video after your system is set up. You can get the Flash plug-in by downloading it from the Macromedia Web site at http://www.macromedia.com. You can find more plug-ins for Netscape at http://www.geggus.net/sven/netscape-plugins.html.

Plugger Plugger is a special plug-in. It is special in the sense that it does nothing by itself, yet it makes use of what you already have and makes it available to Netscape. For Plugger to work, you have to install the following software as well.

- **MpegTv**—For playing DAT and MPEG video files.
- **Xanim**—For playing a wide variety of video and animation extensions.
- **TiMidity++**—For playing midi files.
- **mpg123**—For playing MPEG audio files (mp3 files).
- **XMP**—For playing mod files.
- **Sidplay**—For playing Commodore audio files.

Smart Browsing

Smart browsing is an interesting feature of Netscape Navigator. When enabled, it shows a little button beside the location bar. When you click this button, it loads a list of the sites related to the current site you are viewing. The options for this feature include the following:

- Enabling or disabling this feature.

- The Automatically Load What's Related option sets the behavior of this feature. If your Internet link is fast, you might want to turn it to Always; otherwise, After First Use can be a good choice.

- The domain names that you do not want to see when searching should be included in the edit box. You can limit the smart browsing features using this box. An example of domain names that you might want to discard when using the smart browsing feature are `www.microsoft.com`, `www.hotmail.com`, and `home.microsoft.com`. When you click the What's Related button, it will not list any URL on these sites.

- Check Enable Internet Keywords if you want to see names instead of URLs in the What's Related list.

Configuring Netscape Messenger (Email Client and News Reader)

Netscape Messenger is considered a very powerful email and news client. Click the Edit menu, choose Preferences, and select Mail and News Groups, as shown in Figure 28.3. The main section identifies the behavior of Messenger.

FIGURE 28.3
Setting up Netscape Messenger.

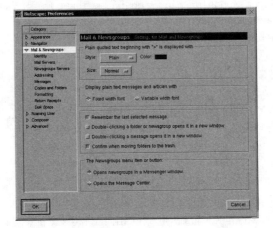

Identity

The Identity section is self-explanatory. You need to fill your information in the boxes listed in this section. If you like to attach your v.card to your outgoing email, you can set it up by clicking the Edit Card button. V.cards enable the receiver to easily add you to his/her address book.

Part
IV

Ch
28

Mail Servers

Editing the Mail Servers options is essential if you want to use Netscape as an email client. You have to add the servers from which you get your email. You can have only one POP email server, whereas you can have more than one IMAP server. Click Edit to edit the proprieties of your email server. You must enter an outgoing email server to be able to send messages.

News Groups Servers

In the News Groups Servers section, you have to enter the news groups servers that you're using. You can list as many news servers as you want.

Addressing

The Addressing section is mainly for your address book settings. You can configure local address book settings and enable contacting a directory server for looking up people. Settings of how names should be displayed in the Messenger address bar can be configured through this section, too.

Messages

Through the Messages section you can set up the way that messages should be treated. You can configure the way forwarded messages are treated and the way plain text messages that exceed the window boundary are treated.

Copies and Folders

In the Copies and Folders section you can set up the management of your messages. You can store a message locally after sending it. Also, you can send this message to yourself as well as the receiver. You can configure the drafts and templates folders by clicking the corresponding buttons.

Formatting

As the name suggests, the Formatting section enables you to configure the format of a new message. It specifies whether or not to use HTML and the way in which outgoing HTML messages should be formatted.

Return Receipts

Setting up receipts is accomplished in the Return Receipts section. You can set up your preferences for receiving receipts, where to store them, and how Messenger should treat a requested receipt.

Disk Space

From the Disk Space section you can set up the disk usage of the message. You can choose whether to keep large messages or to automatically compact folders. You also can configure how news groups messages are treated when stored locally.

Configuring Composer (HTML Editor)

Using Netscape Composer, you can edit and publish HTML files. Composer is a powerful HTML editor. It is a WYSIWYG (what you see is what you get) application. The configuration for Composer can be called through Edit, Preferences, Composer (see Figure 28.4). Here, you'll find the following fields:

FIGURE 28.4

Setting up Netscape Composer.

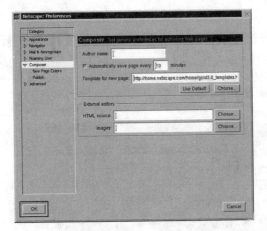

- **Author Name**—Fill this field with the default editor name, in other words, your name.
- **Automatically Save Page Every xx Minutes**—To protect yourself against losing work, check this field and type in a reasonable period. Two to five minutes is considered a reasonable period. On the other hand, you might make some changes that you find you don't like and lose your original work. It's a double-edged sword.
- **Template**—This is the default page that is used as a template.
- **External Editors**—These are the editors used to edit the HTML source and the image editor. Use your preferred editors for these fields. You might consider editors such as `nedit` for HTML source and GIMP for images.

New Page Colors

In the New Page Colors section you set the defaults that the new page in Composer should use. These settings are applied whenever you click File, New in Composer.

Part
IV

Ch
28

Publish

One option of Netscape Composer is publishing your Web page to the server. Other options include the following and are found in the Publish section:

- **Maintain Links**—This option will make the links relevant to the document's location instead of absolute links. This option is very important. For example, an image location would be `../images/image1.gif` instead of `/home/joe/web_page/images/image1/gif`.

- **Keep Images with Document**—This option will create a copy of your images in the current document location. You should disable this option if you have a special Web page hierarchy in mind.

- **Default Publishing Location**—These boxes indicate the server to which you will be uploading your Web page.

Configuring Netscape's Advanced Options

Netscape gives you the ability to configure advanced options that can be turned on and off. These are called through Edit, Preferences, Advanced as shown in Figure 28.5. In this section, you can configure the following:

FIGURE 28.5
Setting up Netscape's advanced options.

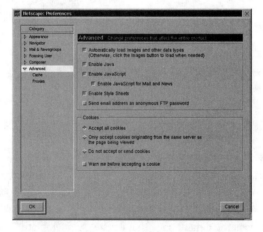

- **Automatic Loading of Images**—If enabled, Netscape will load all the images in the document. If disabled, Netscape will not load images unless you press the load images button in your browser.

- **Enabling Java/Java Scripts**—You can enable Netscape's Java applets/Java Scripts capabilities through this option.

- **Style Sheets**—Most HTML pages have style sheets that control the way the page looks and feels. You can turn on and off the style sheet capabilities of Netscape.

- **Anonymous Password Set to Email**—When you log in to FTP as anonymous, Netscape will use your email address as your password. You can turn off this feature, forcing Netscape to not use your email address as the password.

- **Cookies**—Many sites on the Internet use cookies to set some preferences or information about you. Cookies are stored in files in your home directory.

Cache

Using the Cache section, you can set up the amount of cache you want Netscape to use. Cache is important because it lessens the network load. In other words, if you want to visit a page that you visited before, Netscape will look in the cache first for a cached version of the page and try to get the cached page instead of trying to get it again from the Internet. This option is great on slow connections. Decide the size of the cache by considering your hard drive space and the amount of memory available on your machine.

Proxies

If you are connected to the Internet through a proxy server, you have to configure Netscape to use the proxy settings. In the Proxies section you can select that you have either a direct connection to the Internet or a connection through a proxy. Proxies can be configured with a special URL you can request from your ISP, or through manual settings that you can request from your network administrator.

Netscape Tips and Tricks

Most Netscape users know about only the front interface and do not make use of Netscape's advanced facilities. The following are some of the advanced facilities that Netscape provides:

- The What's Related button that appears next to the location bar is rarely used, maybe because most users already are used to the old way of searching. This button is a powerful tool. It searches for the keywords that the current document has and searches the Internet for documents with the same keywords. Don't be shocked if you find that it works better than the manual search.

- Sometimes you type in the URL, press Enter, and nothing happens for a long time. You can click the location bar and press Enter again to make the process faster. It is advisable that you use this method instead of clicking the Reload button because this method causes Netscape to resume instead of restart.

- If you are willing to learn the absolute address of a page in a framed Web site, try clicking the link of the page using the middle mouse button or right-click and choose Open Link in New Browser.

- If you are using a slow link, set the start page as a blank page.

Part
IV

Ch
28

- Arrange your bookmarks using File Bookmark instead of Add Bookmark. Arranging your bookmarks in folders can save you a lot of time.

- If you lose a site that you visited recently, use Communicator, Tools, History to review which pages you visited.

- If Netscape stops functioning, terminate it using the `kill` command while sending signal 12. This should save the updates that you made to it. Do not worry about bookmark updates—they take place immediately.

  To send signal 12 to netscape, use:

  ```
  bash$ killall -12 netscape
  ```

- If you do not want to get underlined links when printing a document, you can choose not to underline links by choosing Edit, Preferences, Appearance, Colors and unchecking Underline links.

- You can clean the Netscape cache when you need disk space. An amount of 10MB of cache sounds reasonable if you use the Internet daily. Use the menu Edit, Preferences, Advanced Options, Cache and click the Clear Disk Cache button to clear the Netscape cache.

Troubleshooting Netscape Communicator

Netscape freezes each time I start a page with a Java applet.

On some systems, enabling Java causes some problems. You can disable Java on your browser or look for the latest Netscape version.

I get a message saying: server has no DNS entry or Netscape is unable to locate server.

In most cases, the problem is solved by clicking reload or clicking on the location bar and pressing Enter. If you continue to get this error, contact your network administrator for TCP/IP problems (maybe the Internet link is down in your ISP). If the problem persists, check your pppd options. (See Chapter 23, "Connectivity to the Internet," for more information.)

Netscape wouldn't start at all. I get a segmentation fault message.

Maybe you installed the wrong version of Netscape (glibc/libc). SuSE Linux is glibc based starting with version 6.0.

Netscape wouldn't start. I get no error message or problem with linked libraries missing.

Issue the command `ldd /opt/netscape/netscape`. It will issue the libraries that Netscape needs. If any of them does not exist or you have other versions, try making a symbolic link to the newer version first. If it still doesn't work, try linking it to the older version. An example of this would be the following:

```
bash#ln -s libstdc++.so.2.8  /usr/lib/libstdc++.so.2.8
```

Configuring MySQL

A Briefing on MySQL

MySQL is a database package that was made to be a fast and robust SQL server. The package features a daemon that represents the server part, a shell that features powerful capabilities, and some extra command-line programs that enable you to easily control and administer the database. MySQL features multithreading, C, C++, Java, Perl, Python, and TCL API interfaces, which make the development of programs that interface with the database possible. It also supports ODBC interface with Windows 9x.

MySQL is very stable, which means that it can and actually does handle huge and important databases. MySQL is Y2K-compliant and should not exhibit any problems in the new millennium. One important feature of MySQL is that is can be used on the Web. Many important sites have been using MySQL without any problems. One example is http://www.filewatcher.com, which has gotten more than 1,000,000 requests to its MySQL file database.

One of the main reasons you should consider using MySQL is its license. You can use MySQL for free as long as your development and use of it is internal. You have to pay for MySQL only if your use of it results in a monetary profit. Read the MySQL FREE PUBLIC LICENSE for new updates and changes. We do encourage you to buy a license if you decide to use MySQL as your main database engine.

Software Requirements

Package requirements

Series pay:

- ◼ mysql
- ◼ mysqbnch
- ◼ mysqclnt
- ◼ mysqldev

Using the MySQL Shell

The MySQL shell is very powerful. It features auto completion, aliases, command history, and many other features. You primarily will be concerned with some important commands that are unique to MySQL.

Creating a New Database

Creating a new database is simple when it comes to MySQL. The user can create a new database in two ways:

- **Using the system shell**—Log in as root and enter the following at the command line:
  ```
  $mysqladmin create university
  ```

- **Using the MySQL shell**—To log in to the MySQL shell, issue the command `mysql` in your shell and it will launch immediately. Read the section "Administering MySQL" later in this chapter for further information about logging in.

When you run the MySQL shell, your prompt will be `mysql>`. At this prompt, you can enter SQL commands and MySQL-specific commands. When you run the MySQL shell, you get a welcome message and some information such as the connection ID and MySQL version. At the MySQL prompt, enter the command `create database` followed by a database name to create a database. The following example shows how you can create a database called university:

```
bash$ mysql
Welcome to the MySQL monitor.  Commands end with ; or \g.
Your MySQL connection id is 18 to server version: 3.22.21
Type 'help' for help.
mysql>create database university;
```

Creating Tables

Creating tables is accomplished by using normal SQL commands. Before you can create a table, you have to be connected to a database. Consider that you created a database called university:

```
mysql>connect university;
mysql>create table student (ID char (30) NOT NULL ,Name char (30) NOT NULL);
mysql>create table course (Number char (30) NOT NULL ,SID char (30) NOT NULL);
```

You have created two tables. The first table is called `student` and contains students' names and IDs. The second table is called `course` and contains course numbers and IDs of students who are registered in the course.

The *show* Command

The `show` command is an important command in MySQL. You can use the `show` command to check which databases exist, which tables exist, what the database status is, and other important information. For example, issue the following command:

```
mysql>show tables;
+---------------------+
| Tables in university |
+---------------------+
| course              |
| student             |
+---------------------+
2 rows in set (0.01 sec)
```

Using this command, you can view the tables that exist in the database space. In most cases, this is not enough. Sometimes you will want to know what the fields are in a specific table. To get that information, you can use the show command again:

```
mysql> show columns from course;
+---------+----------+------+-----+---------+-------+
| Field   | Type     | Null | Key | Default | Extra |
+---------+----------+------+-----+---------+-------+
| Number  | char(30) |      |     |         |       |
| SID     | char(30) |      |     |         |       |
+---------+----------+------+-----+---------+-------+
2 rows in set (0.03 sec)
```

As you can see, the show command neatly presents the available fields in the course table. A synonym to columns in this example is fields. Both can be used to get the fields in a table. In other words, you could have used the command

```
mysql> show fields from course;
```

instead of using

```
mysql> show columns from course;
```

Another important use of the show command is showing the current variables of MySQL. MySQL variables are set up specifically and can be changed to fine-tune the MySQL server. By entering the show variables from within the mysql shell, you can view the current MySQL configuration:

```
mysql> show variables;
+----------------------------+----------------------------+
| Variable_name              | Value                      |
+----------------------------+----------------------------+
| back_log                   | 5                          |
| connect_timeout            | 5                          |
| basedir                    | /usr/                      |
| datadir                    | /var/mysql/                |
| delayed_insert_limit       | 100                        |
| delayed_insert_timeout     | 300                        |
| delayed_queue_size         | 1000                       |
| join_buffer                | 131072                     |
| flush_time                 | 0                          |
| key_buffer                 | 8388600                    |
| language                   | /usr/share/mysql/english/  |
| log                        | OFF                        |
| log_update                 | OFF                        |
| long_query_time            | 10                         |
| low_priority_updates       | OFF                        |
| max_allowed_packet         | 1048576                    |
| max_connections            | 100                        |
| max_connect_errors         | 10                         |
| max_delayed_insert_threads | 20                         |
| max_join_size              | 4294967295                 |
| max_sort_length            | 1024                       |
```

```
| net_buffer_length       | 16384            |
| port                    | 3306             |
| protocol-version        | 10               |
| record_buffer           | 131072           |
| skip_locking            | ON               |
| socket                  | /tmp/mysql.sock  |
| sort_buffer             | 2097144          |
| table_cache             | 64               |
| thread_stack            | 65536            |
| tmp_table_size          | 1048576          |
| tmpdir                  | /tmp/            |
| version                 | 3.22.21          |
| wait_timeout            | 28800            |
+-------------------------+------------------+
34 rows in set (0.00 sec)
```

Table Optimization   It is important to optimize a table after you have performed large updates or deleted a large number of records. Optimization is necessary only if the table contains columns with fields of variable sizes, such as varchar, blob, or text. Optimization will maintain the unused space generated by the delete operation. Let's suppose that the course table contains a column called name of type varchar. If you deleted a large amount of rows, it would be nice if you optimized the table to save disk space. The following example shows how to optimize the course table:

```
mysql>optimize table course;
```

Table Locking   Despite the fact that all operations in MySQL are atomic, you might want to lock the table for some operations to be performed in sequence. MySQL is not a transactional environment, so you should be careful when your updates are dependent. You can invoke a read lock or a *write* lock on a table by entering the following command:

```
mysql> lock tables student read, course write;
```

Do whatever you want to the tables, and then unlock the tables using the following command:

```
mysql> unlock tables;
```

Invoking the Editor

Sometimes when you want to write a long SQL script, you don't want to use the MySQL interpreter. In such a situation, you can invoke the editor. The editor can be invoked with the following command:

```
mysql>edit;
```

The default editor is the editor defined in your system shell $EDITOR variable. You can redefine this variable to pico using bash by entering the following:

```
bash$export EDITOR=pico
```

Killing a Thread

Killing a thread means disconnecting a user from the database server. Each connection uses a thread, thus, when you kill a specific thread, you're actually closing the connection, as in the following:

```
mysql>kill thread_id
```

You can obtain the `thread_id` by listing the process currently using MySQL. This is done through the `show processlist` command:

```
mysql> show processlist;

+---+--------+---------+-----+--------+-----+-----+---------------+
|Id |User    |Host     |db   | Command|Time |State|Info           |
+---+--------+---------+-----+--------+-----+-----+---------------+
| 9 |root    |localhost|mysql| Sleep  |18857|NULL |NULL           |
|17 |joeadlib|localhost|trial| Query  |0    |NULL |show processlist|
+---+--------+---------+-----+--------+-----+-----+---------------+
2 rows in set (0.00 sec)
```

Comments in MySQL

The comments in MySQL differ from those found in most database shells and are easy to use. There are two types of comments supported by MySQL:

- The hash sign (#)
- The C style comment (/* */)

The following is an example of their use:

```
mysql> select * from student;  #select all students in table
mysql>select * /*we are going to select all*/
    from student; /*the students in the table */
```

As you can see, you can insert the C style comment (/* */) inside the body of the query statement.

> **NOTE**   MySQL does not support the -- comment that is used by most databases. This comment
> style does not cope with MySQL because it is not easily interpreted by it. Due to the
> problems it might cause, there are no plans to support it. If you have an SQL file with this type of
> comment, you easily can change it to the MySQL comment style by using the `replace` command
> that comes with MySQL:
>
> ```
> bash$replace " --" " #" -- file.sql
> ```

Parsing a MySQL File

You can write all the queries you want in a single text file and parse it to be executed by MySQL all at once. This is done by first editing the file and saving it, and then executing the following command:

```
bash$mysql < mysql_file.sql
```

Stuff That You'll Miss

Unfortunately, MySQL lacks some important features that are not yet implemented. Most of these are on MySQL's to-do list, but until they are implemented, you will have to work around them:

- **Sub selects**—You cannot use anything of the following type:

  ```
  select ..from .. where .. in (select .. from .. where ..)
  ```

  In most cases, you can work around this by using `join` or `logical and`. Here is an example of using `join` to perform a sub-select:

  The following query
  ```
  select * from course where sid in (select id from student);
  ```

  can be written as
  ```
  select course.* from course left join student
  on course.sid=student.id where student.id is not null;
  ```

- **Selection into table**—You cannot use anything of the following type:
  ```
  select ..from .. into table ..
  ```

  MySQL does not support this format. However, this can be performed through the use of the following:
  ```
  insert into table select .. from ..
  ```

- **Transactions and roll back**—These are not supported. The work-around for transactions is locking the tables manually whenever you need to update a table without interference from other users' updates. MySQL soon will support atomic transactions, which means that you will not have to perform locking by yourself. It seems that rollback is not on their future schedule.

- **Foreign keys**—Unlike in other databases, foreign keys in MySQL are not used to join tables, but rather to check the integrity of references. The work-around in this case is the use of a full select statement without relying on the foreign key.

- **Procedures and triggers**—Neither are supported in MySQL, but procedures are on the to-do list. There are no plans to implement triggers soon and they are not on the to-do list because they slow down the database. (A primary goal of the MySQL development team is speed.)

- **Views**—This superior feature is not yet supported by MySQL. However, it is on the to-do list with a very high priority and is likely to be implemented very soon. Views are very important in privileges and administration issues, so it's a big disadvantage to not have them.

Administering MySQL

This process of administering MySQL is not as hard as one might think—it's just a matter of editing the values of the MySQL privileges. Note that in this case we will not be considering administration in its fullest sense (as in the Database Management System). Instead, we'll focus on authentication and privileges.

MySQL presents an easy-to-use but non-standard system of authentication. This might look horrible at first glance, but after you see how simple the system is, you will get used to and possibly prefer to use it. The authentication system of MySQL checks the host from which the user is connecting. It then checks which privileges the user has. MySQL supports anonymous users, which also can have privileges. You can set the privileges for any user, including anonymous, using hostnames and supporting different privileges depending on hostnames.

Logging In

MySQL uses usernames and passwords to connect to a database. These are completely different from the Linux username or password of the user. In fact, if you connect to a database without using a username, your Linux username will be used by default.

In the following examples, we will assume that your Linux username is john and that the MySQL database allows connections for the users john and joe. We also will assume that you have logged in to your Linux box as john.

If you directly run the MySQL shell as in the following example, MySQL will try to log in using the username john:

```
bash$mysql
mysql>connect university;
```

Otherwise, if your Linux username is john but your MySQL username is joe, you should be adding the -u parameter that tells the MySQL shell you want it to run with a different username:

```
bash$mysql -u joe
mysql>connect university;
```

To include a password, you will use the following command:

```
bash$mysql -u joe -p
Enter password:
```

You can include the password on the command line, but this is not good practice. After all, anyone can scroll up the text and get your password.

You can connect to other hosts using the MySQL shell. This is very simple. Consider the following command:

```
bash$mysql -h some.host.com -u joe -p
```

In this example you will be connecting to some.host.com that runs mysqld, which is waiting for your connection.

You can automate the login by using the .my.cnf file. Simply create a .my.cnf file in your home directory and edit the following:

```
[client]
host=hostname
user=username
password=password
```

Save the file and issue the command chmod 400 .my.cnf to secure your password. This step is important to ensure the file permission will not be read to your group.

Changing a User's Password, Namely the Root Password

MySQL does not come with the user password set, which makes most database administrators very uneasy. The first thing that any administrator should do is set up a secure password. Next, you must set up secure passwords for your users, and ensure that they do not share their passwords with anyone. These two steps will help ensure that you don't get complaints from your users about the weak security level of the database (and that you get to keep your job!).

One way of setting the password is to enter the following:

```
bash$ mysql -u root mysql
mysql> update user set Password=password('new_password') where user='root';
mysql> flush privileges;
```

Another way is

```
bash$ mysqladmin -u root password new_password
```

However, the following method is preferred and should be recommended to your users:

```
bash$ mysql -u root mysql
mysql> set password for root=password('new_password');
```

> **CAUTION**
>
> When MySQL is first installed, the root has no password. Make sure that the first thing you do is set the root password.

The Privilege System in MySQL

To use the privilege system in MySQL, your control panel must be the MySQL database. The MySQL database contains three tables: `host`, `user`, and `db`. From these three tables you can control which user can log in, from which host she can log in, and what privileges she can have. Let's start with the basics.

First, each database has a root. In other words, the user root is the database administrator. You should log in to MySQL as root if you are going to change privileges. Type the following:

```
bash$ mysql -u root -p
```

Isn't that convenient? The most important thing that you should do is make sure that the root has a password. MySQL's default root password is not set—be sure to set it.

After you have logged on to your MySQL shell, it is time to connect to the database. You will be connecting to the database called MySQL.

In the following example, you start by connecting to the MySQL database and are shown the tables that live in this database:

```
mysql>connect mysql;show tables;
Reading table information for completion of table and column names.
You can turn off this feature to get a quicker startup with -A
Connection id:    12
Current database: mysql

+-----------------+
| Tables in mysql |
+-----------------+
| columns_priv    |
| db              |
| func            |
| host            |
| tables_priv     |
| user            |
+-----------------+
6 rows in set (0.01 sec)

mysql>show columns from host;
```

Field	Type	Null	Key	Default	Extra
Host	char(60)		PRI		
User	char(16)		PRI		
Password	char(16)				
Select_priv	enum('N','Y')			N	
Insert_priv	enum('N','Y')			N	
Update_priv	enum('N','Y')			N	
Delete_priv	enum('N','Y')			N	
Create_priv	enum('N','Y')			N	

```
| Drop_priv        | enum('N','Y') |       |      |  N       |        |        |
| Reload_priv      | enum('N','Y') |       |      |  N       |        |        |
| Shutdown_priv    | enum('N','Y') |       |      |  N       |        |        |
| Process_priv     | enum('N','Y') |       |      |  N       |        |        |
| File_priv        | enum('N','Y') |       |      |  N       |        |        |
| Grant_priv       | enum('N','Y') |       |      |  N       |        |        |
| References_priv  | enum('N','Y') |       |      |  N       |        |        |
| Index_priv       | enum('N','Y') |       |      |  N       |        |        |
| Alter_priv       | enum('N','Y') |       |      |  N       |        |        |
+------------------+---------------+-------+------+----------+--------+--------+
17 rows in set (0.00 sec)
```

As you can see, the host table contains the host from which the user can connect, the user (which is the username), and the privileges that belong to the user. Let's create a user that can connect from host.somewhere.com and who has a username of john. Enter the following command:

```
mysql>insert into user values('host.somewhere.com','john',
password('secret_word'), 'Y','Y','Y','Y','Y','Y','Y','Y',
'Y','Y','Y','Y','Y','Y')
```

The user that has just been created can connect only from host.somewhere.com and has all the privileges on the tables. The user also has the password secret_word. It is important that you use the function password() because this is a direction to encrypt the password into the user table. If you don't use it, the user will get an access denied error because MySQL uses encryption in the authentication process.

If you have another user named john who will be logging in from anywhere other than host.somewhere.com and you want to create another account for him, you would use the following command:

```
mysql>insert into user values('%','john',password('secret_word'),
'Y','Y','Y','Y','Y','Y','Y','Y','Y','Y','Y','Y','Y','Y')
```

The % means anywhere. It's a wild card that means any value is accepted. If it is used on usernames, it also means anonymous or anybody. The john in the last example is a different user from the first one. They are two different entities.

You also can use the famous grant command to create a new user. Consider the following example:

```
mysql> grant all privileges on *.* to john@localhost identified
 by 'secret_word' with grant option;
```

This example creates a new user john who has all privileges on all operations. This user is as powerful as the database administrator. To set up a user with no privileges at all, use the keyword usage instead of all privileges, as in the following example:

```
mysql> grant usage on *.* to john@localhost identified by 'secret_word';
```

This example creates a user john who can connect from localhost and literally do nothing more than this. All privileges are set to N.

The db and host tables are used together to allow or deny a user's access to a specific database and are split to allow one user to work on multiple databases. They are checked when a user tries to connect to a specific database and check her privileges on the tables inside this database. They easily can be used with some basic SQL commands, just like the user table. Note that when creating a new user, you don't have to touch those tables unless you need to set some privileges or restrictions on a specific database.

For an intensive reference on the MySQL privilege system, please consult your manual, which will be located in the `file /usr/doc/packages/mysql/html/manual.html` if you have installed the MySQL.

When the Server Gets the News

`mysqld` reads the privileges only once. This one time is done on startup, so your changes will never take place if you don't do something. In fact, you can flush the changes that you made in two ways:

- Through the MySQL shell:
  ```
  mysql>flush privileges;
  ```

- Through the normal bash shell (as the user who started `mysqld`):
  ```
  bash$mysqladmin flush-privileges
  ```

Notice that you don't have to be root to start `mysqld`. It is actually better that you don't start it as root.

Backing Up a Database

A good administrator always keeps a backup. Rule number one in computers says that anything that can go wrong, will go wrong! So, if a hard disk crash can occur, it eventually will. It is very likely that your database will be the first victim of a hard disk crash, cracker attack, or any other variable that is likely to affect your system. Therefore, because your database is so essential, the keyword is *backup*. You should back up as often as possible. If your database is updated weekly, a weekly backup is a good idea. If your database is updated daily, a daily backup is needed. If it is updated hourly or continually, backing up somewhere between every 6–12 hours will do. It all depends on the size and the type of the database you're running and the data you're using. Check the importance of the data your database holds and how easy it is to restore it. From this information, you can decide how often you need to back up your database.

How Can I Back Up a Database?

The steps involved in backing up a database are very simple. The first step in the process is locking the database tables so no one can update right at the moment you are performing your backup—this ensures consistency. Then, you back up the database files. And finally, you unlock the tables and replicate the updates in the log files.

Step 1: Locking the Tables As stated earlier, the first step you should perform when backing up a database is locking the database. Locking the database will temporarily stop the ability of your users to update the database fields. It's a good practice to back up when the database is not heavily used. If the database is running in a company, a good time to back up is after office hours, during lunch breaks, and so on. This way, locking the database won't have an effect on the users who are currently logged on. Finding a time to perform the backup shouldn't be too difficult because backups don't take much time (depending on the size of your database).

If `university` is the database name that you want to lock, you can lock it by issuing this command:

```
bash$mysqldump  --lock-tables --quick university
```

or

```
bash$mysqldump -l -q university
```

where `university` is the name of your database.

Step 2: Backing Up the Database Files The second step involves copying the database files to the backup media. The default path for MySQL database files is `/var/mysql/db_name`. In fact, to keep a consistent backup of the database, you have to back up all `*.frm`, `*.ISD`, and `*.ISM` files. You can perform a copy operation or make a tarball file of all those files. If you are not sure which MySQL data files are in the default directory, issue the following command:

```
bash> mysqladmin variables|grep datadir
| datadir                      | /var/mysql/
```

The output of this command shows that the `datadir` of MySQL is `/var/mysql/`, which is the default directory.

Step 3: Unlocking the Database and Replicating Changes After you're finished copying the files to the backup media, you need to unlock the database and replicate the changes that occurred during the locking period. This operation is very simple and straightforward.

In the following example, the commands stop the MySQL daemon, replicate the changes to the database, and then start the server again:

```
bash$/sbin/init.d/mysqld stop
bash$mysqld --log-update
bash$/sbin/init.d/mysqld start
```

How Can I Restore a Database?

Say you need to restore a corrupted database. Your first step is to not panic. It is important that you do not panic because this might impair your ability to fix your database, putting your job at risk. Database administrators are the backbone of the database and if anything goes wrong, they are the target at which all fingers point. Managers are not concerned with hardware or software crashes; they are concerned only with outcomes. So, keep in mind that you need to perform this task correctly or you could end up in trouble.

First, shut down the mysqld if it is still running. Some users still might be connected and trying to update, but the database is already at an inconsistent state so there's no need to make matters worse. Second, shut down all network activities. Sometimes the problem can be that someone has cracked into the system. Third, back up the state at which the database is at right where you are. Of course, do not use the same media on which you have the last consistent backup—that's a treasure that might now equal your job!

Step 1: Fixing a Corrupt Database   If the database becomes inconsistent or database files become corrupt, before you try to restore the backup copy, you should try fixing the database. Several utilities exist that will help you do this. One such command is isamchk, which checks and repairs ISAM tables. As MySQL documentation states, this command works 99.9 percent of the time. Remember to shut down mysqld first and then issue the following command:

```
bash$cd /var/mysql/university
bash$isamchk -r *.ISM
```

This command should fix all the problems associated with your database files, as long as they exist in the first place. In other words, this command cannot fix files that have been lost because of a disk crash, for example.

Step 2: Restoring a Database from Backup   This step requires that you already have made a backup. You should restore a database only after you have tried the first step unsuccessfully. Follow these steps:

1. Copy the files of your backup to their original place. This step restores the last consistent state of the database that you have. In other words, it will restore your database to the state it was in when you performed the backup.

2. If you didn't lose the log files of your database that are called hostname.n, where hostname refers to the hostname from which the connection was made and n refers to the number of logins, you can restore the database to the last state before which it was corrupted. The following command will replicate the changes that were lost:

```
bash> ls -1 -t -r hostname.[0-9]* | xargs cat | mysql
```

CHAPTER 30

Installing and Configuring Oracle

In this chapter

A Briefing on Oracle

Founded in 1978, Oracle has been widely known for its Database Management System, also called Oracle. Oracle, the DBMS, was first offered for UNIX in 1984 and has been the most widely used DBMS in critical databases ever since. Oracle did not originate in UNIX, but when it integrated with it, Oracle took advantage of the system and went to higher advances in security and stability. When it was first manufactured, Oracle developers had compatibility in mind. Oracle was compatible with IBM DB2, making the portability of the applications that used DB2 to Oracle quite an easy task. It wasn't long before Oracle realized a need in the Linux world for a full, powerful DBMS. When Oracle for Linux was first released, everyone favored the power of SQL at full gear. With its intense facilities provided in the various software packages that come with the full distribution of Oracle, we can proudly say that Linux now can serve large and critical company database systems. In this chapter, we will discuss the installation of Oracle 8.1.5 Standard Edition and Enterprise Edition on SuSE Linux 6.3 and 6.2. Keep in mind that the installation process will differ if you have another version of Oracle or SuSE.

One important point about installing Oracle on SuSE Linux 6.3 is that most of the steps discussed in this chapter are already done; that is, the SuSE Linux team has prepared them for you. However, if you are a SuSE Linux 6.2 user, you will have to follow the steps discussed in this chapter. Even if you are using SuSE Linux 6.3, you should still read what the SuSE team has done so that you can follow the flow of the installation and understand what is going on. To avoid any confusion, we will mention what method of installation applies to each SuSE Linux version.

Hardware Requirements

Hardware requirements for Oracle are not strict. In fact, Oracle can install even if all the hardware requirements aren't present, except for the required disk space, of course. The hardware requirements for Oracle simply ensure that the system will be able to run Oracle at an optimal speed. With the required hardware, you'll get good performance, and with better hardware than what is required, you'll get even better performance. The Oracle documentation suggests the following minimum hardware requirements (shown in Table 30.1), though they're not very strict.

Table 30.1   Oracle Minimum Hardware Requirements

Device	Requirements
Memory	128MB required, 256MB recommended
Swap Space	Double the size of your memory
CD-ROM	Only if your installation media is a CD

The next hardware requirement is the disk space needed to install Oracle. The required disk space varies according to the type of installation used. Table 30.2 shows the required disk space by the different types of installation.

Table 30.2   Oracle Minimum Disk Space Requirements

Installation Type	Minimum Space Required
Minimum	660MB
Typical	811MB
	+ Oracle8*i* Client= 306MB
	+ Programmer/2000= 276 MB
Custom	660MB at least

Part

IV

Ch

30

Software Requirements

This section is different from most of the chapters in this book when it comes to Oracle. As a matter of fact, the software requirements vary according to the Oracle version that will be installed and the SuSE version you are running. The Oracle installation in this chapter explains installing Oracle 8.1.5 EE|STD on SuSE Linux 6.3 or 6.2. If you have other versions of Oracle or SuSE Linux, you might want to look at `http://www.suse.de/en/support/oracle/`, which is a Web page developed by SuSE to make the installation process of Oracle easier for you.

The packages needed to install Oracle are not distributed with SuSE Linux 6.3 CD. They are available on the following ftp site: `ftp://ftp.suse.com/pub/SuSE-Linux/suse_update/Oracle/`.

Also, those files are included on this book's accompanying CD in `/suse_update/Oracle/oracle815-suse62.tar.gz`.

These files include the following:

- ■ `Oracle8i-EE-patch.tar.gz`—A patch to Oracle Enterprise Edition to make installation easier and flawless (SuSE version 6.3 and 6.2).

- ■ `Oracle8i-STD-patch.tar.gz`—A patch to Oracle Standard Edition to make installation easier and flawless (SuSE version 6.3 and 6.2).

- ■ `orarun.rpm`—An init script to bring up the Oracle server on system boot (SuSE version 6.3 and 6.2).

- ■ `tcl75lib.rpm`—Only needed for Oracle Intelligent Agent (SuSE version 6.3 and 6.2).

- ■ `javarunt.rpm`—Java run-time libraries. You should replace this package with the one that comes with the original SuSE installation (SuSE version 6.3 and 6.2).

You must be using a 2.2.x kernel to install Oracle 8.1.5, which is the default kernel that is installed by SuSE 6.3 and 6.2.

Pre-Installing Oracle 8.1.5 EE|STD on SuSE Linux 6.3/6.2

Installing Oracle can be a difficult task if you don't know what's going on. It is highly recommended that you have this chapter as well as the Oracle manual at hand when you install Oracle.

Extracting and Installing the Software Provided by SuSE (Version 6.3 and 6.2)

You need to extract the file you downloaded from the SuSE ftp site. As a matter of fact, this file includes packages and patches that should be applied before you install Oracle. As a root user, issue the following commands to install the software that SuSE provides:

```
bash#cp oracle815-suse62.tar.gz /tmp
bash#cd /tmp
bash#tar xvzf oracle815-suse62.tar.gz
bash#cd oracle815-suse62
bash#rpm -Uvh orarun.rpm
bash#rpm -Uvh tcl75lib.rpm
bash#rpm -Uvh javarunt.rpm
bash#ln -s /usr/local/jre /usr/lib/jre
```

Applying the Patch (Version 6.3 and 6.2)

This step is necessary, though irritating, if you have the installation CD. You will have to copy the contents of the CD to your hard drive. The fact that this step is a must arises when you consider the patch that SuSE made to Oracle. This patch should be applied so that the installation executes flawlessly. Do not bypass this step; the Oracle installation contains errors that will be fixed by this patch:

```
bash#mount /dev/cdrom /cdrom
bash#cp /cdrom /tmp/oracle -R
bash#cd /tmp/oracle
```

- For the Enterprise Edition:

  ```
  bash#tar xzf ../oracle815-suse62/Oracle8i-EE-patch.tar.gz -C /tmp/oracle
  bash#cd Oracle8i-EE-patch
  bash#./INSTALL.sh
  ```

- For the Standard Edition:

  ```
  bash#tar xzf ../oracle815-suse62/Oracle8i-STD-patch.tar.gz -C /tmp/oracle
  bash#cd Oracle8i-STD-patch
  bash#./INSTALL.sh
  ```

Creating Mount Points (Version 6.3 and 6.2)

You must create mount points to use them for Oracle. Mount points are used to ensure that no I/O bottlenecks occur and are an important part of the Oracle installation. As the root user, create the following directories to be used as mount points for Oracle:

```
bash#mkdir /u02    (Database mount point)
bash#mkdir /u03    (Another Database mount point)
bash#mkdir /u04    (Yet another Database mount point)
```

Creating Groups (Version 6.2)

This step involves creating the corresponding groups that are able to administer, operate, or use Oracle. Bear in mind that those groups are important to both the installation process and the usage process.

NOTE Database administrators are known by their membership in the DBA group. This group must be created to install or administer Oracle. ■

Use YaST to create the groups dba and oinstall. Refer to Chapter 4, "Managing Users and Groups," for further information on creating groups.

Creating Users (Version 6.2)

In this part, we will discuss the default Oracle user, who is able to start the installation process, and prepare for the first steps of use. The default username for this process is oracle. This user should be created using YaST as mentioned in Chapter 4. After you have created this user, you should ensure that she belongs to the group oinstall in order for this user to start the installation process. Not only will this user perform the installation process, but she also will own the Oracle software after the installation process is completely finished.

Setting the Environment Variables (Version 6.2 and 6.3)

In this section, you will set the environment variables that will be used during the installation and that will be used as long as you use Oracle on your system. The variables that you should set in this section vary from the Oracle directories to the languages used. The following variables should be set:

- ORACLE_BASE—This variable contains the root directory of the Oracle software installation. It is not required to specify this directory, but it is highly recommended.

- ORACLE_HOME—This variable contains the directory of the Oracle software. This variable is required.

- NLS_LANG—This variable holds the information on which language is used. It contains which character set to use. The default value is US7ASCII. You should use the default value during the installation process.

- ORA_NLS33—This variable contains the storage character information. It is important only if you use a storage character other than US7ASCII, which is the default value.

Table 30.3 shows the default values for all the environment variables needed to install and run Oracle.

Table 30.3	Default Variable Values
Variable	**Default Value**
ORACLE_BASE	/u01/app/oracle (Oracle Standard)
	/opt/oracle (SuSE Standard)
ORACLE_HOME	/u01/app/oracle/product/8.1.5 (Oracle Standard)
	/opt/oracle/product/8.1.5 (SuSE Standard)
NLS_LANG	US7ASCII
ORA_NLS33	$ORACLE_HOME/ocommon/nls/admin/data

As the root user, edit your /etc/profile file and append the following lines to it:

```
export ORACLE_BASE=/opt/oracle
export ORACLE_HOME=/opt/oracle/product/8.1.5
export NLS_LANG=US7ASCII
export ORA_NLS33=$ORACLE_HOME/ocommon/nls/admin/data
```

After you are done editing the file, save it and execute the following command for the changes to take effect:

```
bash$source /etc/profile
```

Installing Oracle 8.1.5 EE|STD on SuSE Linux 6.3/6.2

Now, the groups are there, the installer user is there, and the environment set—all the preconditions are completed. Now, you need to start the installation. Enter one of the following code snippets:

If you happen to be using the Enterprise Edition, enter the following:

```
bash$ cd /tmp/Oracle8i-EE-patch
bash$ ./runInstaller
```

Or, if you are using the standard edition, enter the following:

```
bash$ cd /tmp/Oracle8i-STD-patch
bash$ ./runInstaller
```

The Oracle Universal Installer (OUI) starts, showing you a welcome message and prompting you to press Next (see Figure 30.1).

FIGURE 30.1
The first start of the Oracle Universal Installer is Java AWT-based, a graphical installation instead of the old text-based one.

File Locations

The next window—the File Locations window—asks for the default locations for the installation and the inventory files (see Figure 30.2). This is simply the source and destination path. If you have set the environment variables as previously mentioned in this chapter, you'll have them filled in with the correct values by default.

FIGURE 30.2
The OUI will get the source location by using the path from which it started. The destination file location is read from the environment variables that you have exported before.

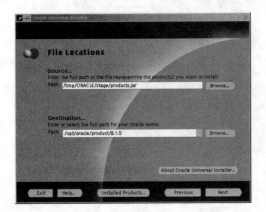

The UNIX Group

Next, the OUI asks for the UNIX user group that can have access to the installation and installation update. Enter the group name `oinstall`. The OUI will prompt you that some actions have to be taken using the root permissions. Open another terminal, `xterm` or `rxvt` for example, and type in the following commands:

```
bash$su -l
Password:
bash#cd /tmp/OraInstall
bash#./orainstRoot.sh
```

The output of this script should look like the following:

```
Creating Oracle Inventory pointer file (/etc/oraInst.loc)
Changing groupname of /opt/oracle/oraInventory to oinstall.
```

In other words, the script has made a file in the /etc directory, which contains the path of the Oracle Inventory. It also has given privileges to the oinstall group to have control over the Oracle Inventory directory in /opt/oracle/oraInventory. After you have run the script, go back to the OUI and press Retry.

Oracle Products

The Available Products dialog that appears next asks about which Oracle product you want to install (see Figure 30.3). The Oracle CD comes with three products:

- Oracle Enterprise Edition
- Oracle Client
- Oracle Programmer

FIGURE 30.3
You can choose which product you want to install by clicking the corresponding radio button and then clicking Next.

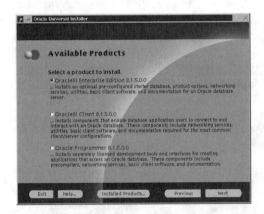

This chapter deals mainly with installing the Oracle Enterprise Edition. You can still install the other products on the CD by selecting the product and clicking Next. In our case, we chose the Oracle Enterprise Edition and clicked Next.

Installation Types

The next step is the selection of the installation type. You must choose whether you want to have a Typical, Minimal, or Custom installation. A short description of each installation type appears beneath them, as Figure 30.4 shows.

N O T E Oracle recommends that you choose a Custom installation because some errors exist in the Typical and Minimal installation types. ▪

FIGURE 30.4
The OUI offers three types of installation for the Oracle Enterprise Edition. You must choose with which method you prefer to install the product.

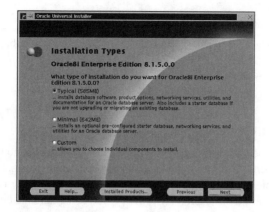

Creating a Database

After you have selected a Custom installation, the OUI suggests that you create a new database. Click Yes to create a new database and fill in the Database Identification dialog that follows. You can stick to the default values of the Database Identification or change them to your preferences (see Figure 30.5). The next question is the location of the database files. You can use browse to pick up a directory to store the database files. The Oracle standard suggests that you use directories on other disks for the best performance. Use the mount points that you previously created on /u02, /u03, and /u04 for locations to store your database files.

FIGURE 30.5
The OUI offers the ability to create a database. You can change the proprieties of this database using the Database Identification dialog.

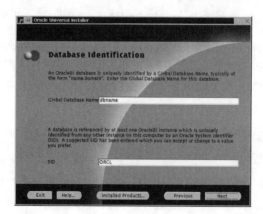

Creating a Database During the Installation

The OUI enables you to create a database during the installation. During this process, you'll fill in the identification of this database and the location of the database files. The location of the database files is the mount points of the database. The standard mount points suggested by Oracle are /u02, /u03, and so on. Oracle suggests that you keep the database files on hard drives other than the system hard drive.

Network Protocols

Now, you need to select the network protocols that you want to use when using the Oracle server. You can choose which network interfaces you want to use when using the Oracle server from the list supplied by the OUI. If none exists, you might want to buy a full Oracle distribution or check for Oracle updates.

Installation Summary

The next step is an installation summary. This is your last chance to go back and make any modifications. Click the Next button and wait for the installation to finish. The installation can take quite a long time depending on the options you selected and your machine's configuration and load. A moderate installation on a PII 300, 128 RAM can take up to 50 minutes. In other words, there are many things that you can do other than watching the progress bar!

N O T E The Oracle installation process relinks several binary files during the installation; this leads to very high use of the CPU for quite a while. If you plan to do some real work in a short while, consider starting the installation sometime later. ■

Post-Installing Oracle 8.1.5 EE|STD on SuSE Linux 6.3/6.2

Even though you are finished installing Oracle, there are still some other things left to do. When the installation process is complete, the OUI generates a file called `root.sh`, which sets the correct permissions for all the files that you installed. This file should be executed before you start using Oracle. Log in as root and execute the following commands:

```
#cd $ORACLE_HOME
#./root.sh
```

Automating Database Startup and Shutdown (Version 6.2 and 6.3)

This is the easiest part in this chapter. All you have to do is follow these steps:

1. Edit the `/etc/rc.config`.
2. Search for `START_ORACLE="no"` and change it to `"yes"`.
3. Search for `ORA_HOME=""` and change it to the correct value of `$ORACLE_HOME`.
4. Save your file.

The second file to edit is the `/etc/oratab`. Edit this file and change the value of `ORACLE_SID:ORACLE_HOME:N` to `ORACLE_SID:ORACLE_HOME:Y`.

Now, the next time you start the system, Oracle will start automatically with run levels 2-console- and 3 -xdm or kdm.

Configuration of SQL*Plus

It is important that database administrators master SQL*Plus. SQL*Plus provides commands for data definition, data manipulation, and database administration. While it can be used as a basic database interface, its main use should be setting up the database and privileges of the database users. To master SQL*Plus, you must master the SQL language.

SQL*Plus Configuration Files

The configuration files for SQL*Plus are located in
$ORACLE_HOME/sqlplus/admin/glogin.sql and the home directory of the user
($HOME/login.sql). The first is known as the global SQL*Plus configuration file and is the first to be read when SQL*Plus is started, while the latter is read second. These two files contain the settings for SQL*Plus.

> **CAUTION**
>
> The User Profile (login.sql) should be saved in the home directory of the user. A problem arises in two cases:
>
> - If there is a file called login.sql in the current directory, it will be used instead of the file in the home directory.
> - If the environment variable SQLPATH has a path in which the home directory comes last and there exists a directory in which there is a file, it will be used instead of the one in the home directory.

Basics of Oracle on Linux

The database administrator has quite a heavy load. An administrator is responsible for managing users, databases, security, and system load. Mostly, this is done through SQL and some well-known parameters. Administering a large Oracle database can be looked at as both an art and a science. We will not get into the details of administering an Oracle database because it is beyond the scope of this book. However, you might want to look at the references that come with the full commercial Oracle package. This section will discuss some important notes for the newbie administrator.

Who Is Who?

One big question many new administrators of Oracle have is "Who are those users that we just created?" The primary users of the Oracle database that were created belong to the DBA group. Those users have administration control over the database. Any normal Linux user can belong to the DBA group. Therefore, a user can be a normal system user and also a database administrator. Be warned!

> **CAUTION**
>
> You must be careful about who belongs to the DBA group. A user can be a normal system user, but by being a part of the DBA group, she also can be a database administrator.

Database Users

In most cases, users should log in using the `oracle` user that you created first. By connecting to the database using an application or SQL*Plus, users will identify their Oracle usernames and passwords.

Troubleshooting Oracle

I can't log in to Linux as the user `oracle` *(SuSE 6.3).*

In SuSE 6.3, the user `oracle` already exists and belongs to the correct groups. The password for this user is disabled by default. You can change it to any value you want by following these steps:

1. Log in as root.
2. Issue the command `passwd oracle`.
3. Change the password to the value you want. Do not leave it empty during the installation—this can threaten your database security later.

I can't start the installation for some reason.

This problem could be due to many reasons, such as the following:

- Did you follow the procedures described exactly as mentioned in this chapter?
- Check the dependencies of the system libraries.
- Check the Java installation on your system. The OUI is Java based, so you might have to uninstall the Java, which is already installed on your system. Then, you will have to install the one supplied on the accompanying CD or the one on the SuSE ftp site.

■ Did the patch process execute flawlessly? If not, re-patch Oracle.

■ Are you using the versions described in this chapter? Other versions need different procedures. Check the Web page `http://www.suse.de/en/support/oracle/` and the Oracle documentation.

I get an error during the installation.

Do you have enough disk space? Did you set the environment variables as mentioned in this chapter? Do you have write permissions to the directories—mount points—you want your database on?

You might want to turn off the network if the CPU load is high on your machine. You might as well close all the programs that require high usage of CPU. The Oracle installation requires very high CPU usage.

I'm finished installing, but I get an error about missing shared libraries.

This is because the shared libraries that come with Oracle are not listed in the `/etc/ld.so.conf` file. To add them to the shared libraries path, follow these steps:

1. Log in as root.
2. Edit the file `/etc/ld.so.conf`.
3. Add the line `/opt/oracle/product/8.1.5/lib` to the file, where `/opt/oracle/product/8.1.5/` is the `ORACLE_HOME` on your system.
4. Run `ldconfig` to update the library database.

I get the following error when I try to run sqlplus:

```
Message file sp1<lang>.msb not found
Error 6 initializing SQL*Plus
```

The environment variables are not correctly exported. Check the pre-installation procedures described in this chapter. Exporting the correct environment variables should solve this error along with any error concerning missing language files. ●

Using the Shell

The Command-Line Interface

Even though SuSE Linux offers you a graphical user interface, you will have to learn how to use the command line. Linux, built on the image of UNIX, has inherited all the power available for the UNIX command line. To get the most out of Linux, you should know how to use the command line. The more familiar you are with it, the more power you will be able to get out of Linux.

The command-line interface in Linux is very strong and flexible, much more so than other command lines such as MS-DOS. It will take you some time to truly master it, but once you do, your whole experience with Linux will be easy and efficient. Most of the powerful features in Linux are accessible only through the command line. So, if your whole interface to Linux is through the X Window system, you will be missing a lot.

Using the Shell

SuSE Linux comes with a variety of shells. A *shell* in Linux is a command-line interpreter you use to issue commands to the operating system. When you type the ls command, you are typing it in a shell, which then executes that command by interacting with the operating system.

As mentioned previously, SuSE Linux ships with more than one type of shell. All shells work similarly, but some shells do have slight differences. However, these differences are apparent only to the experienced user. The most commonly used shells are bash (Bourne Again Shell) and csh (C Shell).

In this chapter, you will learn about the shell independent commands, the bash and csh shells, and how to write small shell scripts to automate tasks. But first, you will learn about the most common shell operations.

Navigating Directories

One of the most basic operations a user performs is navigating through his filesystem. *Navigating* means moving from one directory to another, creating directories, removing directories, listing files, and so on.

To move from one directory to another using the shell, you use the cd command. This command stands for Change Directory. To change the current working directory to another directory, just type the following:

```
$ cd new directory
```

For example, if you are in /home/john and you want to change the directory to /home/john/doc, you could type the following command:

```
$ cd /home/john/doc
```

Or, if you are changing to a directory that is a child of the current directory, you could just type

```
$ cd doc
```

The shell then would assume that doc is a directory inside the one in which you are currently. To change the directory to the parent directory, you would type this command:

```
$ cd ..
```

In the previous command, the two dots (..) point to the parent directory of the directory in which you are currently. So, if you are in /home/john/doc and you run the previous command, you would end up in /home/john again. Type the command again and you would move to /home and so on.

To create a new directory, you use the mkdir command, which stands for Make Directory. For example, to create a directory called files in /home/john, you could type

```
$ mkdir /home/john/files
```

Again, if you are currently in /home/john, you could just type the following command:

```
$ mkdir files
```

The previous command causes the shell to assume you want to create this directory right here. If you want to create a whole family of directories in one step, you can use the -p option. For example, if you want to create the directory /home/john/files/pics, the command

```
$ mkdir -p /home/john/files/pics
```

creates the directory pics and all its parent directories if they don't already exist. This is easier than first creating /home/john/files and then creating /home/john/files/pics.

To remove a directory, you can use the rmdir command, which stands for Remove Directory. For example, to remove the directory called pics, you could type the following:

```
$ rmdir /home/john/files/pics
```

The directory must be empty, though. So, you should use the rm command to delete all the files in it first:

```
$ rm -r /home/john/files/pics
```

In the previous command, the -r option tells rm to delete recursively, removing any internal directories in pics and pics itself.

You can list the files in a directory using the ls command. For example

```
$ ls
```

shows you a listing of all the files in the current directory. In addition,

```
$ ls -l
```

shows you a long listing of all the files. The long listing will show you the size of each file, the date each was last modified, and so on.

The following command includes all the hidden files in the directory listing:

```
$ ls -a
```

Copying, Moving, and Renaming Files

Manipulating files and directories is a frequently preformed task for most users. You will surely find yourself needing to copy a file here, move a file there, rename a file, and so on. Most of these operations are easily accessible from graphical desktop environments such as KDE or GNOME. But, knowing how to perform them using the shell is definitely beneficial because you will not need to switch to a graphical desktop environment to copy some files.

To copy a file using the shell, you use the cp command. In its simplest form, if you want to copy a file from one place to another, you type the following:

```
$ cp filename destination
```

For example, to copy the file mail.txt to /tmp, you use the following command:

```
$ cp mail.txt /tmp
```

You also can use wildcards; for example,

```
$ cp *.doc /tmp
```

copies all files that end with the extension .doc to /tmp. You can copy entire directories using the -R option:

```
$ cp -R /usr/ /mnt/backup
```

The previous command copies all the contents of /usr recursively to /mnt/backup.

To move files from one place to another, you use the mv command. This command is quite similar to the cp command. For example, to move a file from one place to another, you would use this command:

```
$ mv mail.txt /tmp
```

This moves the file called mail.txt to /tmp. The original file will no longer exist where it was; it will be moved to /tmp. You can consider this a copy operation followed by a delete operation on the file at its original location.

You can move entire directories using the mv command, for example:

```
$ mv documents/ /tmp/backup/
```

This moves the directory called documents/ to /tmp/backup. Note that you cannot move directories across filesystems. The mv command also is used to rename files. For example, to rename the file called mail.txt to oldmail.txt, you would type the following:

```
$ mv mail.txt oldmail.txt
```

The same applies for directories. The following command renames the directory called documents/ to olddocuments/:

```
$ mv document/ olddocuments/
```

Using Symbolic Links

Symbolic links are one of the most useful features of the Linux filesystem. A *symbolic link* is a shortcut to another file or directory. You create symbolic links using the ln command. To understand what a symbolic link is, let's look at an example.

Say you have a file called MyEverSoLongDocument.txt. You can create a shortcut to it named longdoc.txt by typing the following command:

```
$ ln -s MyEverSoLongDocument.txt longdoc.txt
```

The previous command creates a symbolic link to the file called MyEverSoLongDocument.txt. This link is called longdoc.txt. You now can access the file using either name because they both refer to the same file on disk.

You can create symbolic links to multiple files in a directory. For example

```
$ ln -s /home/john/* /tmp/links
```

creates a symbolic link to all the files and directories in /home/john in /tmp/links.

Symbolic links are very useful for directories. Say you have a directory you use often and it is not inside your home. You can create a link to that directory in your home so that you can access it directly. For example, if your system has a directory called /usr/local/src that includes files you access frequently, you can create a symbolic link to that directory in your home. To do this, type the following:

```
$ ln -s /usr/local/src sources
```

Next, you can type the following command:

```
$ cd sources
```

and you will be taken to /usr/local/src. Your system will treat sources as a directory of its own, but you know that it is just a pointer to /usr/local/src.

So far, you have been creating symbolic, or soft, links. These links do not affect the actual files to which they are pointing. If you delete a symbolic link that points to a file, the file itself won't be deleted. But this is not the same for symbolic links to directories. If you run the command

```
$ rm -r sources
```

you will delete all the files in /usr/local/src, provided you have the permission to write to that directory. Hard links are another type of link. *Hard links* are a bit different from soft links in the sense that the file and its hard link become one. If you hard link a file and delete the original file, the link will still contain the information in that file. For example:

```
$ ln test.txt oldtest.txt
```

creates a hard link to `test.txt` called `oldtest.txt`. If you delete `test.txt`, the file will still be accessible as `oldtest.txt`. Basically, a hard link is just another name for the file, not a pointer to it. You can hard link directories, but you have to be root to do that.

File Ownership and Permissions

In Linux, you can use file ownership and access permissions to enable users to own their files and set whatever access permissions on those files they want. Access permissions also are used to tell the system which users may or may not read and write to a file.

To control a file's permissions, you must own it. Root is the only user who is allowed to change the ownership of files. Files and directories have two fields of ownership, the user and the group. You can change the ownership of a file by using the `chown` command. For example, to change the ownership of the file called `secrets.txt` to belong to user `john` of the group `users`, you would type the following:

```
# chown john.users secrets.txt
```

Now, user `john`, who belongs to the group `users`, owns the file. He can change its permissions and read, write, and delete the file. You can use the `-R` option to recursively change ownership of directories to another user. For example,

```
# chown -R john.users /usr/local/src
```

changes the ownership of the directory `/usr/local/src` and all the files and directories inside it to the user `john`, who's a member of the group `users`.

File permissions are controlled using the `chmod` command. To understand how to use this command, you will need to know how permissions work. Every file and directory on the system has three sets of permissions: Owner, Group, and Others. You set the read, write, and execute permissions for each of these entities. This means that you can set the permissions of a file to be read/write by owner, read by group, and no access by others. Therefore, the owner of the file will be able to both read and write to the file, anyone belonging to the same group as you will be able to read the file, and anyone from other groups will not be able to read or write to the file.

Permissions are represented by the `ls` command like this:

```
rwxrwxrwx    filename
```

As you can see in the previous command, there are three sets of `rwx`. The `r` stands for read, the `w` stands for write, and the `x` stands for execute. The first set is the owner's permissions, the second is the group's permissions, and the last is others' permissions. For example:

```
rw-r----- test.txt
```

gives the owner read/write permissions on the file (`rw-`), the group read permission (`r--`), and others no access to the file (`---`). The execute permission when set on files makes them executable, meaning they are programs you can run—provided the file is really a program. When it is set on a directory, you can enter that directory. So, a directory with (rw-) permissions is one that you cannot enter because it is not executable.

Changing permissions using the chmod command is very simple. Let's look at an example. Say you want to allow read/write permissions for yourself on the file called manual.txt, read access to the group, and no access to others. The command would be as follows:

```
$ chmod u+rw,g+r,o-rwx manual.txt
```

The previous command says to allow the owner (u) to have read/write access (+rw), the group (g) to have read access (+r), and others (o) to have no access (-rwx) to the file. The plus sign (+) enables permissions and the hyphen (-) disables permissions. In addition, you must enter a comma between the fields. The u signifies the owner of the file, the g signifies the group, and the o signifies others.

Using Pipes and Redirection

Part
IV

Ch

31

Linux has inherited both the tools and philosophy of UNIX. This philosophy is that every tool should perform a certain function, and should perform it well. Then, you can put these tools together to do something more complex. You put them together by taking the output of one tool and making it the input of another and so on—it works like a chain of events. This is where pipes come into play; you use pipes to redirect the output of one program to the input of another.

The simplest example of this is piping the output of the ls command to a pager tool such as less. If you are listing the contents of a large directory, you can have the luxury of paging to see all the files at your own pace. To do this, you type the following:

```
$ ls | less
```

In the previous command, the vertical bar (|) between the two commands is called a *pipe*. When the shell sees this, it directs the output of one command to the input of another. The effect of this line is that the output of ls will be fed to less to page it. The following is another example:

```
$ ls -l | sort +4n | less
```

This command will pipe the output of ls to the sort utility, which sorts it. Then, its output is piped to the less command to page it.

Another method of redirection is file redirection. You can use this to redirect the output of a command to a file. For example:

```
$ ls > listing.txt
```

stores the output of the ls command in the file called listing.txt. In this command, the greater than symbol (>) means redirect the output of the command to this file. If you use >>, the shell will append the output to the file you specified. If you want to redirect error messages that are sent to the standard error, type the following:

```
$ command 2> file.txt
```

In the previous command, 2> redirects the standard error to the file you specify. You can combine both pipes and redirecting in the same command:

```
$ ls   -l | sort +4n > sortedlist.txt
```

The previous will store the output of the piped commands in the file called `sortedlist.txt`.

The Bash Shell

Bash is one of the best shells available for Linux and is the default shell in SuSE Linux. Bash offers several features that are available in other shells, and some features that are specific to Bash. Bash has features that were inspired by other shells such as the Korn shell, C shell, and Bourne shell. This makes bash a very powerful shell because it takes the best of all the shells and adds to it.

Initialization Files

The bash shell reads special configuration files when it begins to configure itself: `/etc/profile`, `.bash_profile`, and `.bashrc`. Which files are read depends on how you run bash.

The first of these files is `/etc/profile`, which is discussed in earlier chapters. This file is the systemwide configuration file and is read by all users' shells when they start. This file is only writeable by root, which uses it to declare system variables and scripts root wants to apply to all users in the system. Bash will read and execute all the commands found in `/etc/profile` whenever you run it as a login or interactive shell. An *interactive* shell is a shell you use to type commands in.

The second configuration file is `.bash_profile`, which resides in your home directory. This file is read by bash whenever you run it for login or interactive use. You can set any configurations for the shell you want in this file. In SuSE Linux, this file is named `.profile`. Despite its different name, it is the exact same file as `.bash_profile`.

The third configuration file is `.bashrc`, which also resides in your home directory. This file is read whenever bash is run, interactive or not. Running bash in non-interactive mode occurs when you run any program from the shell. When you execute a program from the shell, another copy of the shell gets created for the program to run in. This second copy of the shell is not interactive, it exists only to run your program. This non-interactive shell will read `.bashrc` when it is launched.

We haven't yet mentioned the final configuration file—`.bash_logout`. This file is called whenever you exit the shell by calling the `logout` command. You can enter any commands in it that you want executed when you exit the shell, such as clean up commands or a good-bye message.

The SuSE team has done such a professional job with these initialization files. They have prepared a very detailed and powerful /etc/profile for you. You can learn a lot by just reading this file because it uses well constructed scripts and commands. In addition, they have put all the configuration in the .bashrc file, which can be called from .profile using the following command:

```
if test -f ~/.bashrc; then
        . ~/.bashrc
fi
```

This small construct checks whether you have a .bashrc file in your home directory; if one exists there, it executes it. This ensures that no duplication of the configuration occurs between the two files. The .bashrc file contains all the shell configuration parameters for the shell.

Environment Variables

Now that you know which files get read by the shell to configure it, you need to know how you can configure the shell. Bash is configured by using system variables. A *system variable* is a word you define to have a certain value. You can get that value by asking about that word. For example, you can define a variable called NAME to hold the value MARY; then, whenever you ask about NAME, MARY will be returned by the system. To set a variable, you use the export command in bash:

```
$ export NAME=MARY
```

The previous command creates a variable called NAME, if it doesn't already exist, and gives it the value MARY. To access the value of the variable, you must enter a dollar sign ($) before its name. The following is an example:

```
$ echo $NAME
MARY
```

To remove a variable, you use the unset command in bash:

```
$ unset NAME
```

This removes the variable called NAME and its value. Trying to access that variable now will not be successful because it will return an empty value.

Some variables are declared for you by the system, while others can be declared by you. The following is a list of the system-declared variables:

- HOME—This is the path to your home directory, for example, /home/john.
- LOGNAME—This is the name you use to log in, or your login name.
- USER—This is the name of the user currently logged in.

The following are variables that either configure Bash or are used by some programs on your system:

- ■ PATH—This is a colon-separated list of paths the shell is going to search for executables. This is probably already defined for you by /etc/profile. If you want to add your own paths, you should add them as demonstrated in the following so you don't lose the current value:

  ```
  $ export PATH=$PATH:/home/john/mybins
  ```

- ■ PS1—This is the prompt you get from the shell. You can declare whatever you want here. For example, if you set it to yes?, the shell prompt look like the following:

  ```
  yes? cd /usr
  yes? ls
  ```

- ■ PS2—This is the secondary shell prompt.

- ■ MAILCHECK—This is the interval for checking your mail. It is used by some mail programs, but not all.

- ■ TERM—This is the name of your terminal type. It is used by some programs to determine how they should display themselves.

- ■ CDPATH—This is probably one of the most useful shell variables you can set. This is a colon-separated list of paths that the cd command will search for directories. For example, if you have a directory called /usr/local/src and you set CDPATH to /usr/local, typing cd src from anywhere on your system will directly take you to /usr/local/src. It is recommended that you enter the current directory in the CDPATH as well. This is accomplished by declaring it like this (the dot indicates the current directory):

  ```
  $ export CDPATH=.:/usr/local
  ```

- ■ PWD—This variable will always hold the present working directory's path as its value. You can use it in either a program or script to find out where you are on the filesystem.

- ■ OLDPWD—This variable holds the path to the directory you were in before changing to another directory.

- ■ UID—This is the ID of the user currently logged in.

- ■ BASH—This is the full path to bash.

- ■ BASHVERSION—This is the version of bash you are running currently.

- ■ HOSTTYPE—This is a string describing the type of machine on which bash is running.

- ■ OSTYPE—This is a string that holds the name of the operating system on which bash is running.

- ■ TMOUT—This variable takes a number as a value, which is the number of seconds of inactivity before the shell will terminate.

Scripting in Bash

A *script* is a text file that contains commands for bash to execute. It is similar to writing a program, but is on a higher level. Bash scripts are similar to batch files in MS-DOS, for example.

To write a shell script, you must write the commands you want to execute in a text file and run that file. Let's look at an example of the simplest possible shell script to see how one is constructed. Using your favorite editor, enter the following in a new text file:

```
#!/bin/bash
ls
```

Save the file as myls and exit. Now, you can run this shell script in two ways—either by feeding it to bash or by making it executable. The following is an example of the first method:

```
$ bash myls
```

The previous command starts a new bash that will read your script and execute it. You can, however, make the script executable so you can run it as a normal program. To do that, you must change the permission of the file to be executable:

```
$ chmod u+x myls
$ myls
```

Now, the shell script will run as a normal program. When you run it, the first line in the file, #!/bin/bash, indicates that this file is a bash shell script. This is why you should make sure this line is the first line in the script. The actual script is really simple, it just runs the ls command.

You can add to the shell script to make it more complex, for example:

```
#!/bin/bash
clear
ls
```

The previous command causes the script to first clear the screen and then execute the ls command. You can add more commands if you want and you can use pipes and redirection operators. You can even have the shell script read arguments from the command line. For example:

```
#!/bin/bash
clear
ls $1 | less
```

takes the path to a directory as its argument. Then, it lists the contents of that directory and pipes it to the less command to page it. In the command

```
$ myls /usr/
```

$1 is replaced by the first command-line argument you have. Command-line arguments begin with $0, which is the name of the actual shell script. In our example, myls is the shell script's name, $1 is the first argument, $2 is the second argument, and so on.

Part
IV

Ch
31

You can use environment variables in your shell script to read user input. For example, modify the script like this:

```
#!/bin/bash
clear
echo "Which directory do you want to view?"
read DIR
ls $DIR | less
```

This script uses the read command in bash. It reads input from the user and assigns it to the environment variable called DIR. The ls command takes the value in DIR as its argument.

Scripts use control structures, which enable you to execute certain parts of the shell based on a value of something. For example, let's extend our simple script to give us a nice menu:

```
#!/bin/bash
clear
echo "Simple Script"
echo "1- Normal ls"
echo "2- Paged ls"
echo "3- Exit"
echo "Please make your choice"
read CHOICE
case $CHOICE in
    1) ls $1
        ;;
    2) ls $1 | less
        ;;
    3) exit
        ;;
    *) echo "Unknown choice...Aborting"
        exit
        ;;
esac
```

The previous script brings up a menu with three options. It uses the read command to read the user's input and then it uses the case construct to determine which part to execute based on that choice. The case construct has the following format:

```
case variable in
    value1) commands
    value2) commands
    *) default command
esac
```

In the previous code, you must enter the terminating esac, which is a reversed case. The asterisk (*) is the default and will be executed if none of the previous choices match.

Another interesting control structure is the for structure. To understand how it works, let's look at the following example:

```
#!/bin/bash
for i in $1/*
do
    file $i
done
```

The previous script takes a directory as an argument. It then loops on all the files in that directory and executes the `file` command on each entry. This script will show you information about each file in that directory. If you enter `/usr` as the argument, `$1/*` will be expanded to `/usr/*` by the shell, thus indicating all files in the directory. The main execution body of the `for` loop is between the `do` and `done` keywords. You can enter as many commands as you want between them.

As you can see, this script will run the `file` command on everything, even directories. What if you want it to run it only on files? You can have the script check whether that entry is a file. The modified script is as follows:

```
#!/bin/bash
for i in $1/*
do
    if [ -f "$i" ]
        then
            file $i
    fi
done
```

This script will first check whether the entry is a file, and if it is, it will run the `file` command on it. The testing is caused by the `[ -f "$i" ]` construct, which returns true if `$i` is a file. In this construct, the `-f` indicates to ask whether this is a file. You must maintain the spaces between the brackets or the contained condition `[-f "$i"]` won't work. You then can check on the return value of this construct using an `if..then..fi` block. If the expression between the brackets is true, which means it is a file, then the `file` command runs. If you run the new script now, you will notice that it checks only files, not directories.

The following is a listing of all the options you can use instead of `-f`:

Option	Meaning
-b	The file exists and is block special.
-c	The file exists and is character special.
-d	The file exists and is a directory.
-e	The file exists.
-f	The file exists and is a regular file.
-g	The file exists and is set group id.
-k	The file exists and has its stick bit set.
-l	The file exists and is a symbolic link.
-p	The file exists and is a named pipe.
-r	The file exists and is readable.
-s	The file exists and is larger than zero bytes.

continues

Part

IV

Ch

31

continued

Option	Meaning
-s	The file exists and is a socket.
-t	The file exists and is open on a terminal.
-u	The file exists and is set uid bit.
-w	The file exists and is writeable.
-x	The file exists and is executable.
-O	The file exists and is owned by the current user.
-G	The file exists and is owned by the current group.
-z	The file exists and is zero bytes in length.
-n	The file exists and is not zero bytes in length.

This was a brief crash course in shell scripting. Shell scripts are one of the most powerful aspects of Linux. A discussion on how to fully master them is beyond the scope of this book, but is something you should definitely seek. So much can be accomplished using a shell script, you'd be amazed. A good starting place for more information is the scripts that are available in SuSE Linux. Read /etc/profile and for more scripts, check the init scripts in /sbin/init.d—these are works of art!

TCSH Specifics

The TCSH is another shell you can use with SuSE Linux. It is similar to bash in many ways because bash has inherited a bit of TCSH. TCSH is an improvement over the older C shell and is particularly appealing to programmers because it uses syntax that is similar to the C language. You don't have to be a programmer to know how to use the shell, but if you are, you will enjoy it even more. As an interactive shell, the TCSH is almost exactly the same as bash, but when it comes to scripts, the two differ greatly.

Initialization Files

The TCSH has three configuration files, .login, .tcshrc, and .logout. These files work the same in TCSH as they do in the bash shell.

The .login file is executed every time you run TCSH as a login shell. This file corresponds to the .profile file used by the bash shell. The .login file should contain any environment variables you want declared when you log in. The SuSE team does not supply you with a .login file because bash is the default shell for SuSE Linux. So, you don't really have to start with this file like you do with bash's .profile.

The .tchsrc file is executed every time the shell is run, regardless of whether it's a login shell or subshell. This file is the same as the .bashrc file in bash. In this file you enter all the environment variables you want to have in *all* instances of the TCSH. If you want to follow the SuSE method here, you can enter all the environment variables you want in your `.tcshrc` file and then call this file from the `.login` file.

The last configuration file is `.logout`. This is similar to the `.bash_logout` file in bash. In this file you enter any commands you want to execute when you exit the shell.

Environment Variables

The TCSH is configured using environment variables just as bash is. But, instead of using the `export` command as in bash, you use the `set` command in TCSH to configure variables. To cancel a variable, you use the `unset` command. The following paragraphs discuss the options you can configure for the TCSH.

If you want TCSH to echo the command you entered before executing it, you set the `echo` variable. To do that, you type the following command:

```
> set echo
```

The default behavior of the TCSH is to allow users to exit the shell by pressing the Ctrl+D key combination. To disable this, you type the following:

```
> set ignoreeof
```

If you want the TCSH to avoid overwriting a file when you are redirecting the output of a command, you type this command:

```
> set noclobber
```

The previous command causes the shell to check whether the file to which you are redirecting the output already exists. If it does, it will give you an error instead of overwriting it.

If you want the shell to notify you that a background job has terminated, set the `notify` variable:

```
> set notify
```

The following is a list of the significant TCSH environment variables:

- `home`—This is declared by the shell and its value is the path to your home directory.
- `user`—This is declared by the shell and its value is the name of the current user.
- `cwd`—This is declared by the shell and its value is the current working directory.
- `path`—This is the list of directories in which the shell will search for binaries.
- `shell`—This is the path of the current shell binary.
- `prompt`—This is the primary shell prompt.
- `cdpath`—This is a list of paths in which the `cd` command will search for directories.

Scripting in TCSH

A script is a text file that contains commands for TCSH to execute. It is similar to writing a program. A TCSH script functions the same as batch files do in MS-DOS, for example.

To write a shell script, you must write the commands you want to execute in a text file and then run that file. Let's look at an example of a simple shell script to see how one is constructed. Using your favorite editor, enter the following in a new text file:

```
#
ls
```

Save the file as myls and exit. You have two choices of how to run this shell script, by either feeding it to TCSH or making it executable. The following is an example of the first method:

```
>tcsh myls
```

The previous command starts a new TCSH that will read your script and execute it. You can make the script executable so you can run it as a normal program, though. To do that, you must change the permission of the file to be executable:

```
> chmod u+x myls
> myls
```

The shell script now will run as a normal program. When you run it, the first character in the file, #, indicates that this file is a TCSH shell script. For this reason, you should enter this character as the first character in the script. The actual script is quite simple; it just runs the ls command.

You can add to the shell script to make it more complex, as in the following:

```
#
clear
ls
```

Now, the script first clears the screen and then executes the ls command. You also can add more commands and use pipes and redirection operators if you want. You can even make the shell script read arguments from the command line. The following is an example:

```
#
clear
ls $1 | less
```

The previous script takes the path to a directory as its argument. Then, it lists the contents of that directory and pipes them to the less command to page it. In the command

```
> myls /usr/
```

$1 is replaced by the first command-line argument you have. Command-line arguments start with $0, which is the name of the actual shell script. In our example, myls is the shell script's name, $1 is the first argument, $2 is the second argument, and so on.

You can use environment variables in your shell script to read user input. For example, modify the script like the following:

```
#
clear
echo "Which directory do you want to view?"
set DIR = $<
ls $DIR | less
```

Unlike bash, TCSH does not have a read command, instead it redirects the standard input to the variable using the $< special character. It reads input from the user and assigns it to the environment variable called DIR. The ls command takes the value in DIR as its argument.

Scripts use control structures to enable you to execute certain parts of the shell based on a value of something. For example, let's extend our simple script to give us a nice menu:

```
#
clear
echo "Simple Script"
echo "1- Normal ls"
echo "2- Paged ls"
echo "3- Exit"
echo "Please make your choice"
set CHOICE = $<
switch ($CHOICE)
    case 1:
        ls $1
        breaksw
    case 2:
        ls $1 | less
        breaksw
    case 3:
        exit
        breaksw
    default:
        echo "Unknown choice...Aborting"
        exit
endsw
```

This script will bring up a menu with three options. It uses standard input redirection to read the user's input and then it uses the switch construct to determine which part to execute based on that choice. As you can see, it is very similar to programming in the C language.

Scripting in TCSH is quite an advanced matter, even more advanced than scripting in the bash shell because it uses programming language syntax and constructs. For a programmer, though, it shouldn't be a problem.

Part

IV

Ch

31

A Briefing on Midnight Commander

Midnight Commander is an advanced visual file manager for UNIX-compatible operating systems. As a matter of fact, Midnight Commander can replace the shell for novice and experienced users. You can use Midnight Commander to browse your directories, manage your files, browse FTP and network directories, browse compressed files, and much more. The most interesting feature of Midnight Commander is that you don't have to enter a command. Although it offers a mini command-line input in which you can still enter the shell commands, you can use the file view it offers to navigate through the filesystems it supports. Midnight Commander uses your mouse to enable you to quickly access almost everything within it, including your files.

Midnight Commander comes with some extra programs such as an internal viewer for text files. It also can use the existing programs on your system to better format the file to be viewed. For example, if you choose to view an HTML file, the Midnight Commander viewer (mcview) will use lynx to view the file within mcview. Midnight Commander also comes with a good text editor called mcedit. mcedit is a powerful editor that supports syntax highlighting, cut and paste capabilities, and many other options. If you are familiar with the Norton Commander program that is used under Windows 9x/NT operating systems, you will probably find Midnight Commander easy to use.

Midnight Commander Software Requirements

Midnight Commander comes with SuSE Linux in the following packages:

Package requirements:

Series ap:

- mc

Configuring Midnight Commander

Midnight Commander is easily configured through menus and dialogs. Midnight Commander's ease of configuration makes it a perfect choice for users who do not have the time to learn the shell and shell commands.

The Left/Right Menus

You can customize the look of each of the panels by changing the following options within the Left/Right menus:

- **The Listing Mode**—The listing mode specifies what each panel should contain. You can set up the panels to predefined configurations listed in the Listing mode box (see

Figure 31.1). You also can set up your own configuration for the panel by typing in the fields you want to appear in the panel. The following possibilities can be added to the panel:

FIGURE 31.1

By customizing the listing mode, you can change the fields the panels view to give you the best results while managing your files.

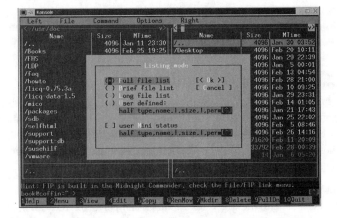

- **Full/Half**—Should be the first option in the line. It specifies the size of the panel.
- **name**—Displays the filename.
- **size/bsize/bf**—Displays the file size. Try each of them to see which one you like.
- **type**—Displays the file type.
- **mtime**—Displays the file's last modification time.
- **atime**—Displays the file's last access time.
- **ctime**—Displays the file's creation time.
- **perm**—Displays the file's permissions.

The previous are the most widely used options for viewing files. Other modes can be used in this field. For more information on those modes, read the Midnight Commander manual page.

You can set up Midnight Commander to show a mini status field that explains the properties of the currently highlighted file. To do so, you check the user Mini Status check box and enter the setting for the mini status. The following are the options you can set:

■ **Sort Order**—You can set up Midnight Commander to sort files in any order you want from the sort order dialog. You can access this dialog from Left/Right, Sort Order.

■ **Network Link**—You can use Midnight Commander to copy files across NFS by selecting Left/Right, Network Link. In the dialog that appears, enter the machine name or IP address of the machine to which you will be connecting. You can enter a username for the machine in the following form: joe@192.187.186.1. When connected, Midnight Commander will prompt you for a password. If you enter the correct password, Midnight Commander can be used to copy files from the server.

■ **FTP Link**—Alternatively, you can use Midnight Commander as an FTP client. Select Left/Right, FTP Link to bring up the FTP dialog. In the dialog that appears, enter the machine name or IP address of the machine to which you will be connecting. If you do not want to connect as an anonymous user, you can enter a username and password to connect to an FTP using the following format: `joe@192.187.186.1`. When connected, Midnight Commander will prompt you for a password. If you enter the correct password, Midnight Commander can be used to copy files from the server.

The Midnight Commander Options

Midnight Commander *options* are the settings that can control the Midnight Commander file manager's look and feel. Using the Options menu, you can configure the panel settings, file listing view settings, layout settings, confirmation settings, and virtual filesystem settings. The following section is a step-by-step guide to each of the options found in the Midnight Commander Options menu.

The Configuration Dialog   Using the Configuration dialog, you can set up how Midnight Commander reacts to the major operations it can perform. You can open this dialog by selecting the Options, Configuration menu. The following are the items that can be configured using this dialog (see Figure 31.2).

FIGURE 31.2

You can set up almost all the configuration settings available in Midnight Commander using the Midnight Commander Configuration dialog.

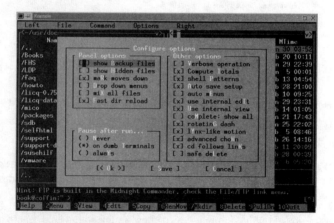

■ **Panel options**—This group box contains the options for the panel file view. To activate an option in this dialog, highlight the option and press the spacebar. If you are using the mouse, simply click on the check box to check the option. The following options are available in the Panel options group:

• **show Backup files**—If you choose to show backup files, Midnight Commander will show the backup files in the panel; otherwise, Midnight Commander will not show them. If you work on projects that require you to have many backup files, which are usually generated by editors, you probably will want to check this option to quickly access your backup files. If you do not need to view the backup files regularly, disable this option. Backup files normally end with a tilde (~) on SuSE Linux.

- **show Hidden files**—By checking this box, you force Midnight Commander to show the files that start with a dot. Files that start with a dot are not shown if this check box is not checked. Note that on SuSE Linux, files that start with a dot are usually configuration files.

- **maRk moves down**—This option will cause the highlight bar used to select files to move down to the following file or directory when you press Insert to mark a file as selected.

- **Drop down menus**—Midnight Commander can hide the upper menu if you do not use it regularly. You can save display space by unchecking this option. You will still be able to access the menu by pressing the F9 shortcut key or left-clicking the upper side of the screen.

- **miX all files**—When this option is not checked, Midnight Commander will show the directories first and then the files arranged by names. If you check this option, Midnight Commander will sort the files and directories using their names and neglecting their types, so they will be merged together and sorted only by name.

- **Fast dir reload**—If you check this option, Midnight Commander will not try to reload the directory listing unless files are created or deleted. Note that enabling this option is not recommended in most cases. If you have made changes to the files in the directory and want to update the changes in Midnight Commander panels, use CTRL+R to re-read the directory listings.

- **Pause after run**—If you use Midnight Commander to run your programs, you can make it pause after a program is terminated if you want to read the output of the program. You can set up the pause after settings by selecting one of the radio button options listed.

- **Other options**—Midnight Commander displays a long list of options that can be used to configure Midnight Commander to your preferences. The list includes the following:

  - **Verbose operation**—This option indicates whether the file operations are verbose. When checked, a dialog of the file operation's progress pops up. If you have a slow terminal, you might want to disable the verbose operation. This option is automatically turned off if the speed of your terminal is less than 9600bps.

  - **Compute Totals**—If checked, Midnight Commander will compute the total byte sizes and total number of files before performing any operation on files. This makes the progress bar more accurate. If Verbose Operation is disabled, this option does not have any effect.

Part

IV

Ch

31

- **shell Patterns**—Check this option to easily select and deselect files using the shell patterns and wild cards.

- **Auto save setup**—If this option is set, Midnight Commander will save its current settings when you exit it. Then, the next time you start Midnight Commander, it will use the last setting you left it on.

- **auto mEnus**—If set, when you start Midnight Commander the user menu will immediately pop up.

- **use internal edIt**—This option controls the default editor invoked when the F4 key is pressed over a file. If you do not want Midnight Commander to use its internal editor, uncheck this option and export the EDITOR environment variable to your preferred editor. For example, the default editor could be set to nedit: export EDITOR=nedit.

- **use internal view**—If you want to setup Midnight Commander to use its internal viewer, you can do so by checking this option. If you want to declare an external viewer to be used by Midnight Commander, you can do so by deselecting this option and exporting the PAGER environment variable to your desired viewer.

- **coMplete: show all**—This option is important for users who use the mini command line provided by Midnight Commander. When set, Midnight Commander will show all the available completion patterns possible for your search if you press the Alt+Tab keys.

- **rotatinG dash**—When enabled, Midnight Commander will show a rotating dash in the corner of the screen to represent activity when running a command.

- **lYnx-like motion**—This option makes directory navigation easier by enabling you to use the left/right arrow keys to enter and exit directories.

- **advanced choWn**—When enabled, the Advanced chown dialog will be invoked if you use the chown or chmod commands.

- **cd follows linKs**—If this option is enabled, Midnight Commander follows the logical chain of directories. If you uncheck this option, Midnight Commander follows the real directory structure. It is recommended that you set this option so you will return to your original directory when you enter a link; otherwise, you will be taken to the parent directory of the link instead of the directory that contains the link.

- **safe deLete**—If enabled, the delete confirmation dialog will require you to type in your confirmation on the delete operation. This is different from the Yes/No dialog that is set up in Layout Options.

The Layout Dialog   You can change the layout of Midnight Commander using the Layout dialog (see Figure 31.3). You can access this dialog through Options, Layout.

In the Layout dialog, you can specify how the file view should be split in the Panel split group. You can specify whether you want the split to be vertical or horizontal by selecting one of the radio buttons in the options box. You also can set up the width and height of each panel. If you decide they should be equally split, you can select the Equal split check box.

In the Highlight section, you can select to highlight the file permissions or file types. It is recommended that you check both boxes.

In the Other options group box, you can specify other layout options such as the following:

- **menuBar visible**—Using this option, you can set the menubar on top of Midnight Commander to always be visible.

- **show Mini status**—If you check this box, when you move the selection bar over a file, the file information you selected to show in the right/left menus will be shown in a bar called mini status.

- **command Prompt**—If this check box is checked, Midnight Commander will show a one-line mini command prompt that you can use to enter shell commands. To view the output of this command, press the Ctrl+O combination.

- **Keybar visible**—This option shows a list of buttons at the bottom of the screen with the important shortcut command. The buttons are Norton Commander–style buttons. This option is recommended if you are going to use the mouse with Midnight Commander. It also is recommended for novice Midnight Commander users.

- **hIntbar visible**—Midnight Commander shows a random hint under the file list view. If you want to disable this hintbar to gain more display space, you can disable this option.

- **Xterm hintbar**—If you open Midnight Commander using terminal emulator in X Windows, the window title bar will show the Midnight Commander hints. This option is great for saving display space and showing Midnight Commander hints at the same time.

Part
IV

Ch
31

FIGURE 31.3
Using the Layout menu, you can control the look and feel of Midnight Commander.

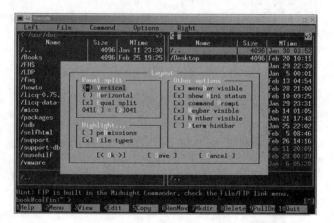

The Confirmation Dialog Midnight Commander can be configured to verify a specific command. Suppose that you pressed F8, which deletes a file, by mistake. Following the better-safe-than-sorry philosophy, Midnight Commander gives you the ability to confirm such critical commands. You can reach the Confirmation dialog by Options, Confirmation. The following are its options:

- **Confirm delete**—Check this box to ensure you don't delete a directory or file by mistake.

- **Confirm overwrite**—Check this box to ensure you do not overwrite a file by mistake.

- **Confirm execute**—If you want Midnight Commander to confirm before it runs an executable file, check this box.

- **Confirm exit**—If checked, Midnight Commander will ask for a confirmation if you press F10. It will not ask for confirmation if you issue the exit command on the command line.

Display Bits Midnight Commander runs on a wide range of UNIX-compatible operating systems. The display bits on each of these systems vary. SuSE Linux is capable of using Full 8 bits output. You should check this box along with the Full 8 bits input. This option is very important if you are going to use Midnight Commander with programs such as acon, which can be used to edit and view Arabic language text within Midnight Commander.

Learn Keys On many systems, the terminal keys do not work. Fortunately, with SuSE Linux, you will not have to worry about broken terminal keys. On the other hand, some terminal emulation programs under X Windows might be broken. To ensure that you correct the settings for those terminal emulation programs, start the Learn Keys dialog from the Options, Learn Keys menu and enter your keyboard mapping.

Virtual Filesystem Settings Midnight Commander uses a virtual filesystem of its own to store information it needs to configure to make navigation local and remote directories faster for the user. You can tweak the settings for the Midnight Commander virtual filesystem using the Options, Virtual File System Setting menu (see Figure 31.4). The dialog contains the following options:

FIGURE 31.4
Using the Virtual File System Setting menu, you can set up the preferences that determine how Midnight Commander should treat caching.

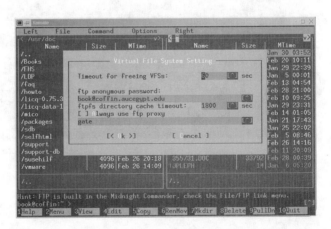

- **Timeout for freeing VFSs**—This is the timeout in seconds after which Midnight Commander will forget the cached information it has about local directory listings or a compressed file's contents.

- **FTP anonymous password**—When logging in as an anonymous user on FTP, you can change the password to be anything you enter in this field. You should make sure that the entry in this field is a valid email address. Some FTP sites require the password to be in a valid email address format even if the email address does not exist.

- **ftpfs directory cache timeout**—This is the timeout in seconds after which Midnight Commander will forget the cached information it has about a remote directory listing on an FTP.

- **Always use FTP proxy**—If you check this box, you must enter the gateway of the proxy server in the gateway field. Midnight Commander will use the proxy server settings when requesting remote files.

Saving the Settings   After you have set up the layout configuration for Midnight Commander, you should save your settings by choosing the Options, Save Setup menu item. If you do not save your settings, you will have to reconfigure Midnight Commander the next time you start it. ●

Part

IV

Ch

31

Appendixes

Getting More Information

In this chapter

The SuSE Help System

SuSE Linux comes with a Help system created by the SuSE team. The Help system for SuSE Linux is a program that consists of a large online database with an additional support database.

The SuSE Help system can run on any Web browser. If you have just installed Linux, you can start the SuSE Help system by issuing the following command:

```
bash$hilfe
```

You also can start it easily by passing the correct address of the SuSE Help system index page to a browser. Here is an example:

- In X Windows, run one of the following applications:
  - Netscape—Run it by typing `bash$netscape`.
  - Arena—Run it by typing `bash$arena`.
  - KFM—To run it while in KDE, open any file manager window.

  Type `http://localhost` in the address bar and press Enter.

- In the SuSE Linux console, it's sufficient to just issue the `hilfe` command. Although, you can specify the `-nox` parameter to force it to use lynx as a browser:

  ```
  bash$hilfe -nox
  ```

The SuSE Help system is a page that supports keyword searches. Choose the file you want more information about from the categories or enter your query to search the whole documentation that comes with SuSE for your keyword.

Software Requirements

It might seem a bit weird that this appendix requires special software packages. However, you need to install certain packages and applications to get more information and functionality. For example, the SuSE Help system must be run over a Web server to be compatible with any Web browser. In addition, to access any application's documentation, you first must have the application installed. You also can get more information by installing the documentation and HOWTO packages. The following are the documentations available on the SuSE Linux CDs.

Package requirements:

Series doc:

- `allman`—All manual pages for all packages.
- `books`—Some books.
- `dns_faq`—Domain Name System Frequently Asked Questions (and answers).

- `elispint`—Programming in Emacs Lisp.
- `elispman`—GNU Emacs Lisp Reference Manual.
- `fhs`—Filesystem Hierarchy Standard.
- `gawkdoc`—Documentation for gawk. You need this only if you are going to develop shell scripts.
- `gccinfo`—GNU info pages for gcc. You need this only if you are going to develop Linux applications.
- `ge_info`—Info files for GNU Emacs. You need this only if you are going to use Emacs as your editor.
- `gppinfo`—Documentation for libg++. You need this only if you are going to develop Linux applications.
- howto series—The howto series that comes with SuSE Linux comes in more than one format and in more than one language. Select the language and format you want to use when reading HOWTOs. Note that HTML is used when using the SuSE Help system.
- `inf2htm`—info2html, which converts info pages to HTML pages. This package enables the SuSE Help system to generate HTML files from info pages.
- `javadoc`—Java JDK1.1.3 documentation and demos. You need this only if you are going to develop Java applications.
- `ldp`—Linux Documentation Project HTML archive.
- `ldpman` series—Man pages from the Linux documentation project. Again, this package comes in several languages. Select the language you want from the ldpman series.
- `libcinfo`—Info files for the GNU C library and GDBM library. You need this only if you are going to develop Linux applications.
- `lx_docu`—Kernel documentation. You need this only if you are going to hack into the kernel. Good luck!
- `man9`—Some man pages from section 9.
- `manyfaqs`—A collection of frequently asked questions.
- `odshtml`—HTML pages from Offenes Deutsches Schulnetz.
- `perlref`—Perl 5 Reference Guide. You need this only if you are going to develop Perl scripts.
- `ppp_nt`—Linux connection to Windows NT.
- `pyth_doc`—Python Documentation (HTML).
- `rfc`—The RFCs (requests for comments).
- `sdb`—SuSE Support Database. You must install this package along with one of the following packages to run the SuSE Support Database, which has a lot of information on how to configure and troubleshoot problems on SuSE Linux:

- `sdb_XX`—The language of the sdb. You must install at least one language to get the SuSE Support Database running properly.
- `susehilf`—SuSE Help system (base).
- `suselxen`—SuSE Linux Manual (English). This is the SuSE Linux manual that comes with the full distribution of SuSE Linux. It is available in other languages, as well.
- `susepakXX`—SuSE Help system. You must install this package in one of the available languages to run your SuSE Help system. The Help System is available in English, German, and French.

- `uucpdoc`—Taylor UUCP Documentation.
- `xe_info`—Info files for X Emacs. You need this only if you are going to use X Emacs as your editor.
- `xf86html`—HTML Pages from Xfree86.

Series n:

- Apache—The Apache Web server. The SuSE Support Database System requires that you run a Web server to search for a keyword within the Support Database.

Chapter-by-Chapter Walkthrough

This section guides you through, chapter by chapter, how to find the proper documentation for the software discussed in each chapter in this book. Most of the documentation mentioned in this section comes with SuSE Linux.

Each of the packages listed in the following sections has its own documentation in the `/usr/doc/packages/<package name>` directory. You can read the files in this directory as well as the listing beside each package in the chapter-by-chapter listing.

Chapter 1, "Pre-Installing SuSE Linux"

- FIPS—The documentation is located in the FIPS package located on the first SuSE Linux CD in `CDROM:\dosutil\fips`
- Partition Resizer—The documentation for PResizer is on the CD that comes with this book, located in `CDROM:\extra\presizer`
- Power Quest Partition Magic—`http://www.powerquest.com`

Chapter 2, "Installing SuSE Linux"

- The SuSE Linux manual

Chapter 3, "Installing the X Window System"

- XFree86-HOWTO
- XFree86-Video-Timings-HOWTO
- XWindow-User-HOWTO
- The XFree86 Web site at `http://www.xfree86.org`
- The X consortium Web site at `http://www.x.org`

Chapter 4, "Managing Users and Groups"

- User-Group-HOWTO
- Man pages of the commands used in the chapter (`bash`, `passwd`, and so on)
- YaST documentation and help page

Chapter 5, "Managing Filesystems"

- Various man pages for mkfs, mkswap, and fstab
- NFS-HOWTO

Chapter 6, "Backing Up the System"

- YaST—The YaST manual page. You can read Appendix C, "YaST," as well
- tar—The tar info page
- cpio—The cpio manual and info pages
- Time Navigator—`http://www.quadratic-software.com`

Chapter 7, "System Upgrade"

- The KDE Web site at `http://www.kde.org`
- The GNOME Web site at `http://www.gnome.org`
- Various README and INSTALL files in the packages

Chapter 8, "Installing a New Kernel"

- Kernel-HOWTO
- Kernel Documentation at `/usr/src/linux/Documentation`
- Kernel help in the kernel configuration modules

Chapter 9, "Configuring the System Boot Up Sequence"

- The Linux Documentation Project at `http://www.linuxdoc.org`
- LILO documentation

Chapter 10, "Sound Card Configuration"

The `Sound-HOWTO.gz` and `Sound-Playing-HOWTO.gz` HOWTOs are great sources of information:

- `isapnptools`—The isapnp and pnpdump manual pages.
- pciutils—The pciutils home page at `http://atrey.karlin.mff.cuni.cz/~mj/pciutils.html`
- OSS—The OSS documentation. You also should take a look at the 4Front Web site at `http://www.4front.com` for more information
- OSS/Lite—The kernel documentation
- ALSA—`http://www.alsa-project.org`
- ESD—The enlightenment Web site at `http://www.enlightenment.org`

Chapter 11, "Printing"

- Printing-HOWTO
- Printing-Usage-HOWTO

Chapter 12, "Configuring Peripherals"

- Kernel documentation at `/usr/src/linux/Documentation`
- CD-Writing-HOWTO
- Hardware-HOWTO
- PCI-HOWTO
- Fax-Server-HOWTO
- ZIP-Drive-HOWTO

Chapter 13, "Configuring a TCP/IP Network"

- Firewall-HOWTO
- NET-3-HOWTO
- NET3-4-HOWTO
- Networking-Overview-HOWTO

- Firewall-Piercing-HOWTO
- IP-Masquerade-HOWTO
- IP-Subnetworking-HOWTO
- UNIX-Internet-Fundamentals-HOWTO

Chapter 14, "Configuring Domain Name Service"

- The DNS-HOWTO.gz
- The BIND makers Web site at `http://www.isc.org`
- There is a large FAQ on the `http://www.intac.com/~cdp/cptd-faq/` Web site

Chapter 15, "Connectivity with Windows Through Samba"

- SMB-HOWTO

Chapter 16, "Connectivity with Other Operating Systems"

- netatalk—You should read the AppleTalk section in the NET-3-HOWTO.gz
- ncpfs—You should read the IPX-HOWTO.gz
- marsnwe—The full documentation of this package is located in the `/usr/doc/packages/marsnwe`

Chapter 17, "Configuring a Usenet News Service"

- News-Leafsite-HOWTO

Chapter 18, "Setting Up the Apache Web Server"

- The Apache Web site at `http://www.apache.org`

Chapter 19, "Configuring the FTP Server"

- The full documentation for proftpd is found in the `/usr/doc/packages/proftpd` directory
- The ProFTPD Web site at `http://www.proftpd.net`

Chapter 20, "Configuring the Mail Server"

- The sendmail Web site at `http://www.sendmail.org`
- sendmail documentation in `/usr/doc/packages/sendmail`

Chapter 21, "Configuring the Dial-In Server"

- mgetty—http://alpha.greenie.net/mgetty/
- pppd—The pppd manual page

Chapter 22, "Setting Up SuSE Linux as a Proxy Server"

- The full documentation for Squid2 is found in the /usr/doc/packages/squid2 directory
- The Squid Web site at http://squid.nlanr.net/Squid

Chapter 23, "Connectivity to the Internet"

The ISP-Hookup-HOWTO.gz, Modem-HOWTO.gz, and PPP-HOWTO.gz HOWTOs are very important for the interested reader:

- isapnptools—The isapnp and pnpdump manual pages. You also should read the Plug-and-Play-HOWTO.gz
- pppd—The pppd manual page
- pciutils—The pciutils home page at http://atrey.karlin.mff.cuni.cz/~mj/pciutils.html
- minicom—Full information on Minicom is located in /usr/doc/packages/minicom
- wvdial—wvdial is integrated in YaST, so you should use YaST help for wvdial. Check the /usr/doc/packages/wvdial, which has complete information on wvdial in many languages

Chapter 24, "Configuring the Desktop"

- KDE—The KDE help, KDE Quick Start Guide, and KDE user's guide
- GNOME—The GNOME help, GNOME Quick Start Guide, and GNOME user's guide

Chapter 25, "Installing and Configuring StarOffice"

- StarOffice—The StarOffice Help and StarOffice Sun Microsystems Web page at http://www.sun.com/products/staroffice
- Printing in StarOffice—See Chapter 11

Chapter 26, "Installing and Configuring WordPerfect"

- The Corel WordPerfect Help
- The Corel WordPerfect Web site at http://linux.corel.com

App
A

Chapter 27, "Installing GIMP"

■ The GIMP Web site at `http://www.gimp.org`

Chapter 28, "Installing and Configuring Netscape Communicator"

■ Netscape Help—The Netscape Help and Netscape online help

■ The Netscape Web site at `http://www.netscape.com`

Chapter 29, "Configuring MySQL"

■ MySQL documentation stored locally on your system in
`/usr/doc/packages/mysql/html/index.html`

■ The MySQL Web site at `http://www.mysql.com`

Chapter 30, "Installing and Configuring Oracle"

■ Oracle documentation

■ SuSE online Oracle Installation

Chapter 31, "Using the Shell"

■ bash—The bash manual and info pages

■ csh—The csh manual and info pages

■ Midnight Commander

Appendix B, "Hardware Compatibility List"

■ The SuSE hardware listing online database

Appendix C, "YaST"

■ The SuSE hardware listing online database

Appendix D, "Tips and Tricks on Tuning Your Linux Box"

■ The tricks HOWTO at `/usr/doc/howto/en/Tips-HOWTO.gz`

■ The Linux tuning Web site at `http://tune.linux.com`

Appendix E, "Various Utilities"

■ tar—The tar info page

Hardware Compatibility List

This appendix attempts to list most of the hardware supported by SuSE Linux. If your hardware does not appear in this list, please check for the latest updates of this list on SuSE's Web site at `http://cdb.suse.de/cdb_english.html`. You will find a huge hardware database with searching capabilities that is updated very frequently.

Supported Motherboards, CPUs, and Memory

Linux has support for most motherboards in existence today. It is very unlikely that you will find a motherboard that has problems with Linux. ISA, VLB, EISA, and PCI buses are all supported. PS/2 and Microchannel (MCA) are supported in the standard, as well. Support also exists for MCA in the 2.2.x kernel and above, but this code is still a little buggy.

Linux supports a wide variety of x86 processors. Intel/AMD/Cyrix 386SX/DX/SL/DXL/SLC and 486SX/DX/SL/SX2/DX2/DX4 are supported. In addition, Intel Pentium, Pentium Pro, and Pentium II are supported. And, AMD K5 and K6 work well, although older versions of K6 should be avoided because they are buggy. However, setting the internal cache to disabled in the BIOS setup can be a workaround for this problem. IDT Winchip C6-PSME2006A processors also are supported under Linux. Plus, Linux has built-in FPU emulation if you don't have a math coprocessor.

Linux supports systems that use multiple processors, which are also known as SMP systems. Linux has supported these systems since the 2.0.x branch of the kernel. The 2.2.x branch offers better support in this area, and the upcoming 2.4.x branch is promising even better support.

Linux supports all the memory types in existence. All memory such as DRAM, EDO, and SDRAM can be used with Linux. On some systems, you might need to tell the kernel how much memory you have if you have more than 64MB. This also is necessary for the 2.0.x branch of the kernel. To tell the kernel how much memory you have, just add the following line to your `/etc/lilo.conf` file:

```
append="mem=96M"
```

Then, run `lilo`. Make sure that you enter the right size of the memory. Do not enter a value that is more than what you physically have because it will cause the kernel to crash.

Supported Video Graphics Cards

Linux has good support for most of the video graphics cards that are available today. This support does not come from Linux, though; it comes from the XFree86 that gave Linux a port of the famous X Window system.

XFree86 supports the following cards:

- 2 the Max MAXColor S3 Trio64V+
- 3DLabs Oxygen GMX
- 928Movie
- AGX (generic)
- ALG-5434(E)
- 3Dexplorer
- ATI Mach64 GT (264GT), aka 3D RAGE, Int. RAMDAC
- ATI Mach64 VT (264VT), Internal RAMDAC
- ATI Mach64 with AT&T 20C408 RAMDAC
- ATI Mach64 with ATI68860 RAMDAC
- ATI Mach64 with ATI68860B RAMDAC
- ATI Mach64 with ATI68860C RAMDAC
- ATI Mach64 with ATI68875 RAMDAC
- ATI Mach64 with CH8398 RAMDAC
- ATI Mach64 with IBM RGB514 RAMDAC
- ATI Mach64 with Internal RAMDAC
- ATI Mach64 with STG1702 RAMDAC
- ATI Mach64 with STG1703 RAMDAC
- ATI Mach64 with TLC34075 RAMDAC
- ATI Pro Turbo+PC2TV, 3D Rage II+DVD
- ATI Ultra Plus
- ATI Video Xpression
- ATI Video Xpression+
- ATI WinBoost
- ATI WinBoost with AT&T 20C408 RAMDAC
- ATI WinBoost with ATI68860 RAMDAC
- ATI WinBoost with ATI68860B RAMDAC
- ATI WinBoost with ATI68860C RAMDAC
- ATI WinBoost with ATI68875 RAMDAC
- ATI WinBoost with CH8398 RAMDAC
- ATI WinBoost with Mach64 CT (264CT)
- ATI WinBoost with STG1702 RAMDAC
- ATI WinBoost with STG1703 RAMDAC

App

B

- ATI WinBoost with TLC34075 RAMDAC
- ATI WinCharger
- ATI WinCharger with AT&T 20C408 RAMDAC
- ATI WinCharger with ATI68860 RAMDAC
- ATI WinCharger with ATI68860B RAMDAC
- ATI WinCharger with ATI68860C RAMDAC
- ATI WinCharger with ATI68875 RAMDAC
- ATI WinCharger with CH8398 RAMDAC
- ATI WinCharger with Mach64 CT (264CT)
- ATI WinCharger with STG1702 RAMDAC
- ATI WinCharger with STG1703 RAMDAC
- ATI WinCharger with TLC34075 RAMDAC
- ATI WinTurbo
- ATI WinTurbo with AT&T 20C408 RAMDAC
- ATI WinTurbo with ATI68860 RAMDAC
- ATI WinTurbo with ATI68860B RAMDAC
- ATI WinTurbo with ATI68860C RAMDAC
- ATI WinTurbo with ATI68875 RAMDAC
- ATI WinTurbo with CH8398 RAMDAC
- ATI WinTurbo with Mach64 CT (264CT)
- ATI WinTurbo with STG1702 RAMDAC
- ATI WinTurbo with STG1703 RAMDAC
- ATI WinTurbo with TLC34075 RAMDAC
- ATI Wonder SVGA
- ATI Xpert
- ATI Xpert XL
- ATI Xpert@Play PCI and AGP, 3D Rage Pro
- ATI Xpert@Play
- ATI Xpert@Work, 3D Rage Pro
- ATI integrated on Intel Maui MU440EX motherboard
- ATrend ATC-2165A
- AccelStar Permedia II AGP
- Actix GE32+ 2MB
- Actix GE32i
- Actix GE64

- Actix ProStar
- Actix ProStar
- Actix Ultra
- Acumos AVGA3
- Alliance ProMotion 6422
- Ark Logic ARK1000PV (generic)
- Ark Logic ARK1000VL (generic)
- Ark Logic ARK2000MT (generic)
- Ark Logic ARK2000PV (generic)
- Avance Logic 2101
- Avance Logic 2228
- Avance Logic 2301
- Avance Logic 2302
- Avance Logic 2308
- Avance Logic 2401
- Binar Graphics AnyView
- Boca Vortex (Sierra RAMDAC)
- COMPAQ Armada 7380DMT
- COMPAQ Armada 7730MT
- California Graphics SunTracer 6000
- Canopus Co. Power Window 3DV
- Canopus Total-3D
- Cardex Challenger (Pro)
- Cardex Cobra
- Cardex Trio64
- Cardex Trio64Pro
- Chips & Technologies CT64200
- Chips & Technologies CT64300
- Chips & Technologies CT65520
- Chips & Technologies CT65525
- Chips & Technologies CT65530
- Chips & Technologies CT65535
- Chips & Technologies CT65540
- Chips & Technologies CT65545
- Chips & Technologies CT65546

App

B

- Chips & Technologies CT65548
- Chips & Technologies CT65550
- Chips & Technologies CT65554
- Chips & Technologies CT65555
- Chips & Technologies CT68554
- Chips & Technologies CT69000
- Cirrus Logic GD542x
- Cirrus Logic GD543x
- Cirrus Logic GD5446 (no-name card) 1MB upgraded to 2MB
- Cirrus Logic GD544x
- Cirrus Logic GD5462
- Cirrus Logic GD5464
- Cirrus Logic GD5465
- Cirrus Logic GD5480
- Cirrus Logic GD62xx (laptop)
- Cirrus Logic GD64xx (laptop)
- Cirrus Logic GD754x (laptop)
- Colorgraphic Dual Lightning
- Creative Blaster Exxtreme
- Creative Labs 3D Blaster PCI (Verite 1000)
- Creative Labs Graphics Blaster 3D
- Creative Labs Graphics Blaster Eclipse (OEM Model CT6510)
- Creative Labs Graphics Blaster MA201
- Creative Labs Graphics Blaster MA202
- Creative Labs Graphics Blaster MA302
- Creative Labs Graphics Blaster MA334
- DFI-WG1000
- DFI-WG5000
- DFI-WG6000
- DSV3325
- DSV3326
- DataExpert DSV3325
- DataExpert DSV3365
- Dell S3 805
- Dell onboard ET4000

- Diamond Edge 3D
- Diamond Fire GL 1000
- Diamond Fire GL 1000 PRO
- Diamond Fire GL 3000
- Diamond Multimedia Stealth 3D 2000
- Diamond Multimedia Stealth 3D 2000 PRO
- Diamond SpeedStar (Plus)
- Diamond SpeedStar
- Diamond SpeedStar 24X (not fully supported)
- Diamond SpeedStar
- Diamond SpeedStar A50
- Diamond SpeedStar HiColor
- Diamond SpeedStar Pro (not SE)
- Diamond SpeedStar Pro 1100
- Diamond SpeedStar Pro SE (CL-GD5430/5434)
- Diamond SpeedStar64 Graphics 2000/2200
- Diamond Stealth
- Diamond Stealth
- Diamond Stealth 3D 2000
- Diamond Stealth 3D 2000 PRO
- Diamond Stealth 3D 3000
- Diamond Stealth 3D 4000
- Diamond Stealth 64 DRAM SE
- Diamond Stealth 64 DRAM with S3 SDAC
- Diamond Stealth 64 DRAM with S3 Trio64
- Diamond Stealth 64 VRAM
- Diamond Stealth 64 Video VRAM (TI RAMDAC)
- Diamond Stealth II S220
- Diamond Stealth Pro
- Diamond Stealth VRAM
- Diamond Stealth Video 2500
- Diamond Stealth Video DRAM
- Diamond Stealth64 Graphics 2001 series
- Diamond Stealth64 Graphics 2xx0 series (864 + SDAC)
- Diamond Stealth64 Graphics 2xx0 series (Trio64)

- Diamond Stealth64 Video 2001 series (2121/2201)
- Diamond Stealth64 Video 2120/2200
- Diamond Stealth64 Video 3200
- Diamond Stealth64 Video 3240/3400 (IBM RAMDAC)
- Diamond Stealth64 Video 3240/3400 (TI RAMDAC)
- Diamond Viper 330
- Diamond Viper 550
- Diamond Viper PCI 2Mb
- Diamond Viper Pro Video
- Diamond Viper VLB 2Mb
- Digital 24-plane TGA (ZLXp-E2)
- Digital 24-plane+3D TGA (ZLXp-E3)
- Digital 8-plane TGA (UDB/Multia)
- Digital 8-plane TGA (ZLXp-E1)
- EIZO (VRAM) AGX
- ELSA ERAZOR II SVGA
- ELSA Gloria Synergy 3DLabs
- ELSA Gloria-L 3DLabs
- ELSA Gloria-L/MX 3DLabs
- ELSA Gloria-S 3DLabs
- ELSA Gloria-XL 3DLabs
- ELSA Gloria-4 S3
- ELSA Gloria-8 S3
- ELSA VICTORY ERAZOR SVGA
- ELSA Victory 3D SVGA
- ELSA Victory 3DX SVGA
- ELSA Winner 1000/T2D S3
- ELSA Winner 1000 R3D SVGA
- ELSA Winner 1000AVI (AT&T 20C409 version) S3
- ELSA Winner 1000AVI (SDAC version) S3
- ELSA Winner 1000ISA S3
- ELSA Winner 1000PRO with S3 SDAC S3
- ELSA Winner 1000PRO with STG1700 or AT&T RAMDAC S3
- ELSA Winner 1000PRO/X S3
- ELSA Winner 1000TRIO S3

- ELSA Winner 1000TRIO/V S3
- ELSA Winner 1000TwinBus S3
- ELSA Winner 1000VL S3
- ELSA Winner 2000 S3
- ELSA Winner 2000/Office 3DLabs
- ELSA Winner 2000AVI S3
- ELSA Winner 2000AVI/3D SVGA
- ELSA Winner 2000PRO-2 S3
- ELSA Winner 2000PRO-4 S3
- ELSA Winner 2000PRO/X-2 S3
- ELSA Winner 2000PRO/X-4 S3
- ELSA Winner 2000PRO/X-8 S3
- ELSA Winner 3000 SVGA
- ELSA Winner 3000-L-42 SVGA
- ELSA Winner 3000-M-22 SVGA
- ELSA Winner 3000-S SVGA
- EPSON CardPC (onboard) SVGA
- ET3000 (generic) SVGA
- ET4000 (generic) SVGA
- ET4000 W32i, W32p (generic) SVGA
- ET4000/W32 (generic) SVGA
- ET6000 (generic) SVGA
- ET6100 (generic) SVGA
- ExpertColor DSV3325 SVGA
- ExpertColor DSV3365 S3
- Generic VGA-compatible VGA16
- Genoa 5400 SVGA
- Genoa 8500VL(-28) SVGA
- Genoa 8900 Phantom 32i SVGA
- Genoa Phantom 64i with S3 SDAC S3
- Genoa VideoBlitz III AV S3
- Hercules Dynamite SVGA
- Hercules Dynamite 128/Video SVGA
- Hercules Dynamite Power SVGA
- Hercules Dynamite Pro SVGA

App

B

- Hercules Graphite HG210 AGX
- Hercules Graphite Power AGX
- Hercules Graphite Pro AGX
- Hercules Graphite Terminator 64 S3
- Hercules Graphite Terminator 64/DRAM S3
- Hercules Graphite Terminator Pro 64 S3
- Hercules Stingray SVGA
- Hercules Stingray 128 3D SVGA
- Hercules Stingray 64/V with ICS5342 SVGA
- Hercules Stingray 64/V with ZoomDAC SVGA
- Hercules Stingray Pro SVGA
- Hercules Stingray Pro/V SVGA
- Hercules Terminator 3D/DX SVGA
- Hercules Terminator 64/3D SVGA
- Hercules Terminator 64/Video S3
- Hercules Thriller3D SVGA
- Integral FlashPoint SVGA
- Intel 5430 SVGA
- Interay PMC Viper SVGA
- JAX 8241 S3
- Jaton Video-58P SVGA
- Jaton Video-70P SVGA
- Jazz Multimedia G-Force 128 SVGA
- LeadTek WinFast 3D S600 SVGA
- LeadTek WinFast 3D S680 SVGA
- LeadTek WinFast S200 SVGA
- LeadTek WinFast S430 S3
- LeadTek WinFast S510 S3
- Leadtek WinFast 2300 3DLabs
- MELCO WGP-VG4S SVGA
- MELCO WGP-VX8 SVGA
- MSI MS-4417 SVGA
- Matrox Comet SVGA Matrox Marvel II SVGA
- Matrox Millennium 2/4/8MB SVGA
- Matrox Millennium (MGA) SVGA

- Matrox Millennium G200 4/8/16MB SVGA
- Matrox Millennium G200 SD 4/8/16MB SVGA
- Matrox Millennium II 4/8/16MB SVGA
- Matrox Millennium II AGP SVGA
- Matrox Mystique SVGA
- Matrox Mystique G200 4/8/16MB SVGA
- Matrox Productiva G100 4/8MB SVGA
- MediaGX SVGA
- MediaVision Proaxcel 128 SVGA
- Mirage Z-128 SVGA
- Miro Crystal 10SD with GenDAC S3
- Miro Crystal 12SD S3
- Miro Crystal 16S S3
- Miro Crystal 20SD PCI with S3 SDAC S3
- Miro Crystal 20SD VLB with S3 SDAC (BIOS 3xx) S3
- Miro Crystal 20SD with ICD2061A (BIOS 2xx) S3
- Miro Crystal 20SD with ICS2494 (BIOS 1xx) S3
- Miro Crystal 20SV S3
- Miro Crystal 22SD S3
- Miro Crystal 40SV S3
- Miro Crystal 80SV S3
- Miro Crystal 8S S3
- Miro Crystal DVD SVGA
- Miro miroCRYSTAL VRX SVGA
- Miro miroMedia 3D SVGA
- Miro MiroVideo 20TD SVGA
- Miro Video 20SV S3
- Neomagic SVGA
- Number Nine FX Motion 331 S3
- Number Nine FX Motion 332 SVGA
- Number Nine FX Motion 531 S3
- Number Nine FX Motion 771 S3
- Number Nine FX Vision 330 S3
- Number Nine GXE Level 10/11/12 S3
- Number Nine GXE Level 14/16 S3

App

B

- Number Nine GXE64 S3
- Number Nine GXE64 Pro S3
- Number Nine GXE64 with S3 Trio64 S3
- Number Nine Imagine I-128 (2-8MB) I128
- Number Nine Imagine I-128 Series 2 (2-4MB) I128
- Number Nine Imagine-128-T2R I128
- Number Nine Revolution 3D AGP (4-8MB SGRAM) I128 S3 86C260 (generic) SVGA
- S3 86C280 (generic) SVGA
- S3 86C325 (generic) SVGA
- S3 86C357 (generic) SVGA
- S3 86C365 (Trio3D) VGA16
- S3 86C375 (generic) SVGA
- S3 86C385 (generic) SVGA
- S3 86C391 (Savage3D) VGA16
- S3 86C764 (generic) S3
- S3 86C765 (generic) S3
- S3 86C775 (generic) S3
- S3 86C785 (generic) S3
- S3 86C801 (generic) S3
- S3 86C805 (generic) S3
- S3 86C864 (generic) S3
- S3 86C868 (generic) S3
- S3 86C911 (generic) S3
- S3 86C924 (generic) S3
- S3 86C928 (generic) S3
- S3 86C964 (generic) S3
- S3 86C968 (generic) S3
- S3 86C988 (generic) SVGA
- S3 86CM65 S3
- S3 911/924 (generic) S3
- S3 924 with SC1148 DAC S3
- S3 928 (generic) S3
- S3 964 (generic) S3
- S3 968 (generic) S3
- S3 Aurora64V+ (generic) S3

- S3 Savage3D VGA16
- S3 Trio32 (generic) S3
- S3 Trio3D VGA16
- S3 Trio64 (generic) S3
- S3 Trio64V+ (generic) S3
- S3 Trio64V2 (generic) S3
- S3 Trio64V2/DX (generic) S3
- S3 Trio64V2/GX (generic) S3
- S3 ViRGE (generic) SVGA
- S3 ViRGE (old S3V server) SVGA
- S3 ViRGE/DX (generic) SVGA
- S3 ViRGE/GX (generic) SVGA
- S3 ViRGE/GX2 (generic) SVGA
- S3 ViRGE/MX (generic) SVGA
- S3 ViRGE/MX+ (generic) SVGA
- S3 ViRGE/VX (generic) SVGA S3 Vision864 (generic) S3
- S3 Vision868 (generic) S3
- S3 Vision964 (generic) S3
- S3 Vision968 (generic) S3
- SHARP 9080 S3
- SHARP 9090 S3
- SNI PC5H W32 SVGA
- SNI Scenic W32 SVGA
- SPEA Mercury 64 S3
- SPEA Mirage S3
- SPEA/V7 Mercury S3
- SPEA/V7 Mirage P64 S3
- SPEA/V7 Mirage P64 with S3 Trio64 S3
- SPEA/V7 Mirage VEGA Plus SVGA
- SPEA/V7 ShowTime Plus SVGA
- STB Horizon SVGA
- STB Horizon Video SVGA
- STB LightSpeed SVGA
- STB LightSpeed 128 SVGA
- STB MVP-2 SVGA

App

B

- STB MVP-2 PCI SVGA
- STB MVP-2X SVGA
- STB MVP-4 PCI SVGA
- STB MVP-4X SVGA
- STB Nitro (64) SVGA
- STB Nitro 3D SVGA
- STB Nitro 64 Video SVGA
- STB Pegasus S3
- STB Powergraph 64 S3
- STB Powergraph 64 Video S3
- STB Powergraph X-24 S3
- STB Systems Powergraph 3D SVGA
- STB Systems Velocity 3D SVGA
- STB Velocity 128 SVGA
- STB Velocity 64 Video S3
- STB nvidia 128 SVGA
- SiS 3D PRO AGP SVGA
- SiS 5597 SVGA
- SiS 5598 SVGA
- SiS 6326 SVGA
- SiS SG86C201 SVGA
- SiS SG86C205 SVGA
- SiS SG86C215 SVGA
- SiS SG86C225 SVGA
- Sierra Screaming 3D SVGA Sigma Concorde SVGA
- Sigma Legend SVGA
- Spider Black Widow AGX
- Spider Black Widow Plus AGX
- Spider Tarantula 64 S3
- Spider VLB Plus SVGA
- TechWorks Thunderbolt SVGA
- TechWorks Ultimate 3D SVGA
- Toshiba Tecra 540CDT SVGA
- Toshiba Tecra 550CDT SVGA
- Toshiba Tecra 750CDT SVGA

- Toshiba Tecra 750DVD SVGA
- Trident 3DImage975 (generic) SVGA
- Trident 3DImage975 AGP (generic) SVGA
- Trident 3DImage985 (generic) SVGA
- Trident 8900/9000 (generic) SVGA
- Trident 8900D (generic) SVGA
- Trident Cyber 9382 (generic) SVGA
- Trident Cyber 9385 (generic) SVGA
- Trident Cyber 9388 (generic) SVGA
- Trident Cyber 9397 (generic) SVGA
- Trident TGUI9400CXi (generic) SVGA
- Trident TGUI9420DGi (generic) SVGA
- Trident TGUI9430DGi (generic) SVGA
- Trident TGUI9440 (generic) SVGA
- Trident TGUI9660 (generic) SVGA
- Trident TGUI9680 (generic) SVGA
- Trident TGUI9682 (generic) SVGA
- Trident TGUI9685 (generic) SVGA
- Trident TVGA 8800BR VGA16
- Trident TVGA 8800CS VGA16
- Trident TVGA9200CXr (generic) SVGA
- Unsupported VGA-compatible VGA16
- VI720 SVGA
- VL-41 S3
- VidTech FastMax P20 S3
- VideoLogic GrafixStar 300 S3
- VideoLogic GrafixStar 400 S3
- VideoLogic GrafixStar 500 S3
- VideoLogic GrafixStar 550 SVGA
- VideoLogic GrafixStar 560 (PCI/AGP) SVGA
- VideoLogic GrafixStar 600 SVGA
- VideoLogic GrafixStar 700 S3
- ViewTop PCI SVGA
- WD 90C24 (laptop) SVGA WD 90C24A or 90C24A2 (laptop) SVGA
- Weitek P9100 (generic) SVGA

- WinFast 3D S600 SVGA
- WinFast S200 SVGA
- WinFast S430 S3
- WinFast S510 S3
- XGA-1 (ISA bus) AGX
- XGA-2 (ISA bus) AGX

Hard Drive Controllers

Linux supports most of the hard drive controllers available today. Linux will work with standard IDE, MFM, and RLL controllers. Enhanced IDE (EIDE) interfaces also are supported, with up to two IDE interfaces and up to four hard drives and CD-ROM drives. Linux successfully detects and uses the following controllers:

- CMD-640
- DTC 2278D
- FGI/Holtek HT-6560B
- RZ1000
- Triton I (82371FB) (with busmaster DMA)
- Triton II (82371SB) (with busmaster DMA)
- Tekram D690CD IDE PCI Cache Controller (with RAID level 1 mirroring and caching)

As for SCSI device controllers, Linux has very good support for them. The following cards are supported:

- AMI Fast Disk VLB/EISA (BusLogic-compatible)
- Adaptec AVA-1502E (ISA/VLB) (AIC-6360) (Use the AHA-152x driver)
- Adaptec AVA-1505/1515 (ISA) (Adaptec AHA-152x-compatible)
- Adaptec AHA-1510/152x (ISA/VLB) (AIC-6260/6360)
- Adaptec AHA-154x (ISA) (all models)
- Adaptec AHA-174x (EISA) (in enhanced mode)
- Adaptec AHA-274x (EISA) (AIC-7771)
- Adaptec AHA-284x (VLB) (AIC-7770)
- Adaptec AHA-2920 (PCI) (Use the Future Domain driver. LILO parameters are needed when used for hard disks.)
- Adaptec AHA-2940AU (PCI) (AIC-7861)
- Adaptec AHA-294x/U/W/UW/D/WD (AIC-7871, AIC-7844, AIC-7881, AIC-7884)
- Adaptec AHA-3940/U/W (PCI) (AIC-7872, AIC-7882) (since 1.3.6)
- Adaptec AHA-398x/U/W (PCI) (AIC-7873, AIC-7883)

- Adaptec PCI controllers with AIC-7850, AIC-7855, AIC-7860
- Adaptec on board controllers with AIC-777x (EISA), AIC-785x, AIC-787x (PCI), AIC-788x (PCI)
- Advansys 5140 (ISA)
- Always IN2000
- BusLogic (ISA/EISA/VLB/PCI) (all models)
- DPT PM2001, PM2012A (EATA-PIO)
- DPT Smartcache/SmartRAID Plus, III, IV families (ISA/EISA/PCI)
- DTC 329x (EISA) (Adaptec 154x-compatible)
- Future Domain TMC-16x0, TMC-3260 (PCI)
- Future Domain TMC-8xx, TMC-950
- Future Domain chips TMC-1800, TMC-18C50, TMC-18C30, TMC-36C70
- ICP-Vortex PCI-SCSI Disk Array Controllers (many RAID levels supported)
- ICP-Vortex EISA-SCSI Controllers (many RAID levels supported)
- Media Vision Pro Audio Spectrum 16 SCSI (ISA)
- NCR 5380 generic cards
- NCR 53C400 (Trantor T130B) (use generic NCR 5380 SCSI support)
- NCR 53C406a (Acculogic ISApport / Media Vision Premium 3D SCSI)
- NCR chips 53C7x0
- NCR chips 53C810, 53C815, 53C820, 53C825, 53C860, 53C875, 53C895
- Qlogic / Control Concepts SCSI/IDE (FAS408) (ISA/VLB)
- Quantum ISA-200S, ISA-250MG
- Seagate ST-01/ST-02 (ISA)
- SoundBlaster 16 SCSI-2 (Adaptec 152x-compatible) (ISA)
- Tekram DC-390, DC-390W/U/F
- Trantor T128/T128F/T228 (ISA)
- UltraStor 14F (ISA), 24F (EISA), 34F (VLB)
- Western Digital WD7000 SCSI
- AMD AM53C974, AM79C974 (PCI) (Compaq, HP, Zeos onboard SCSI)
- Adaptec ACB-40xx SCSI-MFM/RLL bridgeboard
- Always Technologies AL-500
- BusLogic (ISA/EISA/VLB/PCI) (new beta driver)
- Iomega PC2/2B
- Qlogic (ISP1020) (PCI)
- Ricoh GSI-8

App
B

The following are not supported:

- Parallel port SCSI adapters
- Non–Adaptec-compatible DTC boards (327x, 328x)

Hard Drives

Linux supports all hard drives, as long their controllers are supported. All direct access SCSI devices with a block size of 256, 512, or 1024 bytes should work. Other block sizes will not work. Large IDE (EIDE) drives work fine with newer kernels, but the boot partition must lie in the first 1024 cylinders because of PC BIOS limitations.

Some Conner CFP1060S drives might have problems with Linux and ext2fs. The symptoms are inode errors during e2fsck and corrupt filesystems. Conner has released a firmware upgrade to fix this problem, though.

Tape Drives

Linux supports several tape drives. The following is a list of supported drives:

- SCSI tape drives
- Seagate Sidewinder 50 AIT (on ICP 6527 RAID-controller)
- QIC-02 drives
- Iomega DITTO internal (ftape 3.04c and newer)
- * QIC-117, QIC-40/80, QIC-3010/3020 (QIC-WIDE) drives

In addition to those drives listed previously, most tape drives using the floppy controller should work with Linux.

ATAPI Tape Drives

The following tape drives are supported:

- Seagate TapeStor 8000
- Conner CTMA 4000 IDE ATAPI Streaming tape drive

The following are not supported:

- Emerald and Tecmar QIC-02 tape controller cards
- Drives that connect to the parallel port (For example, Colorado Trakker)
- Some high-speed tape controllers (For example, Colorado TC-15)
- Irwin AX250L/Accutrak 250 (not QIC-80)
- IBM Internal Tape Backup Unit (not QIC-80)
- COREtape Light

CD-ROMs

Linux supports a variety of CD-ROMs, including the following:

- SCSI CD-ROM drives
- EIDE (ATAPI) CD-ROM drives (IDECD)
- Mitsumi FX400
- Nec-260
- Sony 55E
- Aztech CDA268-01A, Orchid CDS-3110, Okano/Wearnes CDD-110, Conrad TXC, CyCDROM CR520ie/CR540ie/CR940ie (AZTCD)
- Creative Labs CD-200(F) (SBPCD)
- Funai E2550UA/MK4015 (SBPCD)
- GoldStar R420 (GSCD)
- IBM External ISA (SBPCD)
- Kotobuki (SBPCD)
- Lasermate CR328A (OPTCD)
- LMS Philips CM 206 (CM206)
- Longshine LCS-7260 (SBPCD)
- Matsushita/Panasonic CR-521/522/523/562/563 (SBPCD)
- MicroSolutions Backpack parallel port drive (BPCD)
- Mitsumi CR DC LU05S (MCD/MCDX)
- Mitsumi FX001D/F (MCD/MCDX)
- Optics Storage Dolphin 8000AT (OPTCD)
- Sanyo CDR-H94A (SJCD)
- Sony CDU31A/CDU33A (CDU31A)
- Sony CDU-510/CDU-515 (SONYCD535)
- Sony CDU-535/CDU-531 (SONYCD535)
- TEAC CD-55A SuperQuad (SBPCD)
- LMS/Philips CM 205/225/202
- NEC CDR-35D (old)
- Sony SCSI multisession CD-XA
- Parallel Port Driver

App
B

CD-Writers

The following is a list of all the supported CD-Writers in Linux:

- Grundig CDR 100 IPW
- HP CD-Writer+ 7100 and 8100
- HP SureStore 4020i
- HP SureStore 6020es/i
- JVC XR-W2010
- Mitsubishi CDRW-225
- Mitsumi CR-2600TE
- Olympus CDS 620E
- Philips CDD-522/2000/2600/3610
- Pinnacle Micro RCD-5020/5040
- Plextor CDR PX-24CS
- Ricoh MP 1420C
- Ricoh MP 6200S/6201S
- Sanyo CRD-R24S
- Smart and Friendly Internal 2006 Plus 2.05
- Sony CDU 920S/924/926S
- Taiyo Yuden EW-50
- TEAC CD-R50S
- WPI(Wearnes) CDR-632P
- WPI(Wearnes) CDRW-622
- Yamaha CDR-100
- Yamaha CDR-200/200t/200tx
- Yamaha CDR-400t/400tx

Removable Drives

Linux supports all SCSI drives as long as the controller is supported, including optical (MO), WORM, floptical, Bernoulli, Zip, Jaz, SyQuest, PD, and others. The following is a list of those supported:

- Panasonic MO (combines a CD-ROM drive and an optical removable disk)
- Parallel port Zip drives
- Parallel port Avatar Shark-250

- Fujitsu magneto-optical disk drives M2513
- LS-120 floptical
- PD-CD

Mice

Linux supports the following mice:

- Microsoft serial mouse
- Mouse Systems serial mouse
- Logitech Mouseman serial mouse
- Logitech serial mouse
- ATI XL Inport busmouse
- C&T 82C710 (QuickPort) (Toshiba, TI Travelmate)
- Microsoft busmouse
- Logitech busmouse
- PS/2 (auxiliary device) mouse

Controllers (I/O)

Linux will support any standard serial/parallel/joystick/combo cards. Linux supports 8250, 16450, 16550, and 16550A UART's. In addition, cards that support non-standard IRQs (IRQ > 9) can be used.

Controllers (Multiport)

Linux supports both types of multiport controllers, non-intelligent and intelligent. The non-intelligent cards that are supported are as follows:

- AST FourPort and clones (4 port)
- Accent Async-4 (4 port)
- Arnet Multiport-8 (8 port)
- Bell Technologies HUB6 (6 port)
- Boca BB-1004, 1008 (4, 8 port) (no DTR, DSR, and CD)
- Boca BB-2016 (16 port)
- Boca IO/AT66 (6 port)
- Boca IO 2by4 (4 serial / 2 parallel, uses 5 IRQs)

- Computone ValuePort (4, 6, 8 port) (AST FourPort-compatible)
- DigiBoard PC/X, PC/Xem, PCI/Xem, EISA/Xem, PCI/Xr (4, 8, 16 port)
- Comtrol Hostess 550 (4, 8 port)
- PC-COMM 4-port (4 port)
- SIIG I/O Expander 4S (4 port, uses 4 IRQs)
- STB 4-COM (4 port)
- Twincom ACI/550
- UseNet Serial Board II (4 port)

The following intelligent cards are supported:

- Computone IntelliPort II (4/8/16 port)
- Cyclades Cyclom-8Y/16Y (8, 16 port) (ISA/PCI)
- DigiBoard PC/Xe (ISA), PC/Xi (EISA), and PC/Xeve
- Equinox SST Intelligent serial I/O cards
- Hayes ESP 1, 2, and 8 port versions
- Stallion EasyIO (ISA) / EasyConnection 8/32 (ISA/MCA) / EasyConnection 8/64 (PCI)
- Stallion EasyConnection 8/64 (ISA/EISA) / ONboard (ISA/EISA/MCA) / Brumby (ISA)
- Comtrol RocketPort (8/16/32 port)
- DigiBoard COM/Xi
- Moxa C102, C104, C168, C218 (8 port), C320 (8/16/24/32 expandable), and C320T
- RISCom/8
- Specialix SIO/XIO (modular, 4 to 32 ports)
- Specialix IO8+

Network Adapters

Linux has good support for most network cards. The basic rule here is the newer the card, the better the performance. Linux supports the following cards:

- 3Com 3C501 (avoid this one like the plague)
- 3Com 3C503, 3C505, 3C507, 3C509/3C509B (ISA) / 3C579 (EISA)
- 3Com Etherlink III Vortex Ethercards (3C590, 3c592, 3C595, 3c597) (PCI), 3Com Etherlink XL Boomerang Ethercards (3c900, 3c905) (PCI), and 3Com Fast Etherlink Ethercard (3c515) (ISA)
- AMD LANCE (79C960) / PCnet-ISA/PCI (AT1500, HP J2405A, NE1500/NE2100)
- AT&T GIS WaveLAN

- Allied Telesis AT1700
- Allied Telesis LA100PCI-T
- Ansel Communications AC3200 EISA
- Apricot Xen-II / 82596
- Cabletron E21xx
- Cogent EM110
- Crystal Lan CS8920, Cs8900
- Danpex EN-9400
- DEC DE425 (EISA) / DE434/DE435 (PCI) / DE450/DE500 (DE4x5 driver)
- DEC DE450/DE500-XA (Tulip driver)
- DEC DEPCA and EtherWORKS
- DEC EtherWORKS
- DEC QSilver's (Tulip driver)
- Fujitsu FMV-181/182/183/184
- HP PCLAN (27245 and 27xxx series)
- HP PCLAN PLUS (27247B and 27252A)
- HP 10/100VG PCLAN (J2577, J2573, 27248B, J2585) (ISA/EISA/PCI)
- ICL EtherTeam 16i / 32 EISA
- Intel EtherExpress
- Intel EtherExpress Pro
- KTI ET16/P-D2, ET16/P-DC ISA (work jumperless and with hardware-configuration options)
- NE2000/NE1000 (be careful with clones)
- Netgear FA-310TX (Tulip chip)
- New Media Ethernet
- PureData PDUC8028, PDI8023
- SEEQ 8005
- SMC Ultra / EtherEZ (ISA)
- SMC 9000 series
- SMC PCI EtherPower 10/100 (Tulip driver)
- SMC EtherPower II (epic100.c driver)
- Schneider & Koch G16
- Western Digital WD80x3
- Zenith Z-Note / IBM ThinkPad 300 built-in adapter
- Znyx 312 etherarray (Tulip driver)

App

B

ISDN

Linux supports many of the popular ISDN cards. The following is a list of all the cards Linux supports:

- 3Com Sonix Arpeggio
- ASUSCOM Network, Inc. ISDNLink 128K PC adapter (HiSax)
- AVM A1 (HiSax)
- Combinet EVERYWARE 1000 ISDN
- Compaq ISDN S0 (ISA) (HiSax)
- Creatix PnP S0 (HiSax)
- Dr. Neuhaus Niccy PnP/PCI (HiSax)
- Dynalink IS64PH (HiSax)
- Eicon.Diehl Diva 2.0 ISA and PCI (S0 and U interface, no PRO version) (HiSax)
- Eicon.Diehl Diva Piccola (HiSax)
- Elsa Microlink PCC-16, PCF, PCF-Pro, PCC-8 (HiSax)
- ELSA QuickStep 1000/1000PCI/3000 (HiSax)
- HFC-2BS0–based cards (HiSax)
- IBM Active 2000 (ISA) (act2000)
- ICN ISDN cards (icn)
- Ith Kommunikationstechnik GmbH MIC 16 (ISA) (HiSax)
- ITK ix1-micro Rev.2 (HiSax)
- Octal PCBIT (pcbit)
- Sedlbauer Speed Card (HiSax)
- Teles 8.0/16.0/16.3 and compatible ones (HiSax)
- Teles 16.3c (HiSax)
- Teles S0 (HiSax)
- Traverse Technologies NETjet PCI S0 (HiSax)
- USR Sportster internal TA (HiSax)

Pocket and Portable Adapters

The following is a list of all the pocket and portable adapters that are supported in Linux:

- Accton parallel port ethernet adapter
- AT-Lan-Tec/RealTek parallel port adapter
- D-Link DE600/DE620 parallel port adapter

Slotless

The following is a list of all the slotless ports that are supported in Linux:

- SLIP/CSLIP/PPP (serial port)
- EQL (serial IP load balancing)
- PLIP (parallel port) (using LapLink cable or bi-directional cable)

ARCnet

SuSE Linux works with all ARCnet cards.

Token Ring

Linux supports the following token ring cards:

- Any IBM token ring card not using DMA
- IBM Tropic chipset cards
- Madge TokenRing OCI 16/4 Mk2

FDDI

Linux supports the following FDDI card:

- DEFEA (EISA) / DEFPA (PCI) (kernel 2.0.24 and later)

Amateur Radio (AX.25)

Linux supports the following Amateur Radio cards:

- Gracilis PackeTwin
- Ottawa PI/PI2
- Most generic 8530-based HDLC boards

Ethernet

Linux supports the following Ethernet cards:

- Racal-Interlan NI5210 (i82586 Ethernet chip) (Avoid this card. It does not function properly with the current driver.)
- Racal-Interlan NI6510 (am7990 lance chip) (Starting with kernel 1.3.66, more than 16MB RAM is supported.)
- Racal-Interlan PCI card (AMD PC net chip 97c970)

ISDN

Linux supports the following ISDN card:

- SpellCaster's Datacommute/BRI, Telecommute/BRI (ISA) (sc)

ATM

Linux supports the following ATM adapter:

- Efficient Networks ENI155P-MF 155 Mbps ATM adapter (PCI)

Frame Relay

Linux supports the following frame relay card:

- Sangoma S502 56K Frame Relay card

Wireless

Linux supports the following wireless technology:

- Proxim RangeLan2 7100 (ISA) / 630x (OEM mini-ISA)

Sound Cards

Linux has good support for most sound cards. The following is a list of the supported sound cards:

- 6850 UART MIDI
- Adlib (OPL2)
- Audio Excell DSP16
- Aztech Sound Galaxy NX Pro
- Crystal CS4232/CS4236 (PnP)-based cards
- ECHO-PSS cards (Orchid SoundWave32, Cardinal DSP16)
- Ensoniq SoundScape
- Gravis Ultrasound
- Gravis Ultrasound 16-bit sampling daughterboard
- Gravis Ultrasound MAX
- Gravis Ultrasound ACE (No MIDI port and audio recording)
- Gravis Ultrasound PnP (with RAM)
- Logitech SoundMan Games (SBPro, 44KHz stereo support)

- Logitech SoundMan Wave (Jazz16/OPL4)
- Logitech SoundMan 16 (PAS-16–compatible)
- MediaTriX AudioTriX Pro
- Media Vision Premium 3D (Jazz16)
- Media Vision Pro Sonic 16 (Jazz)
- Media Vision Pro Audio Spectrum
- Media Vision Pro Audio Studio
- Microsoft Sound System (AD1848)
- OAK OTI-601D cards (Mozart)
- OPTi 82C924/82C925 cards (Use the MSS driver and isapnp tools)
- OPTi 82C928/82C929 cards (MAD16/MAD16 Pro/ISP16/Mozart)
- OPTi 82C931 cards
- Sound Blaster
- Sound Blaster Pro
- Sound Blaster
- Sound Blaster 32/64/AWE (Configure it like Sound Blaster 16)
- Sound Blaster AWE63/Gold and 16/32/AWE (PnP cards need to be activated using isapnptools)
- Turtle Beach Wavefront cards (Maui, Tropez)
- Wave Blaster (and other daughterboards)
- Cards based on the ESS Technologies AudioDrive chips (688, 1688)
- AWE32/64 support starts in kernel series 2.1.x (check the SoundBlaster AWE mini-HOWTO by Marcus Brinkmann for installation details)
- MPU-401 MIDI
- Sound Blaster Live!
- MPU-401 MIDI (intelligent mode)
- PC speaker / Parallel port DAC
- Turtle Beach MultiSound/Tahiti/Monterey

Modems

Linux supports all internal modems and external modems connected to the serial port. Alas, some manufacturers have created Windows 95–only modems. A small number of modems come with DOS software that downloads the control program at runtime. Loading the program under DOS and performing a warm boot normally enables the use of these. Such modems are probably best avoided, though, because you won't be able to use them with non-PC hardware in the future.

All PCMCIA modems should work with the PCMCIA drivers.

Printers

Linux supports a large variety of printers. One subset of printers, however, is designed for only MS Windows and doesn't work with Linux. The following is a list of supported printers:

- Apple Imagewriter
- C. Itoh M8510
- Canon BubbleJet BJ10e (bj10e)
- Canon BubbleJet BJ200, BJC-210 (B/W only), BJC-240 (B/W only) (bj200)
- Canon BubbleJet BJC-600, BJC-610, BJC-4000, BJC-4100, BJC-450, MultiPASS C2500, BJC-240, BJC-70 (bjc600)
- Canon BubbleJet BJC-800 (bjc800)
- Canon LBP-8II, LIPS III
- DEC LA50/70/75/75plus
- DEC LN03, LJ250
- Epson 9 pin, 24 pin, LQ series, AP3250
- Epson Stylus Color/Color II/500/800 (stcolor)
- HP 2563B
- HP DesignJet 650C
- HP DeskJet, DeskJet Plus (deskjet)
- HP DeskJet 500, DeskJet Portable (djet500)
- HP DeskJet 400/500C/540C/690C/693C (cdj500)
- HP DeskJet 550C/560C/600/660C/682C/683C/693C/850/870Cse (cdj550)
- HP DeskJet 850/870Cse/870Cxi/680 (cdj850)
- HP DeskJet 500C/510/520/5540C/693C printing black only (cdjmono)
- HP DeskJet 600 (lj4dith)
- HP DeskJet 600/870Cse, LaserJet 5/5L (ljet4)
- HP DeskJet 500/500C/510/520/540/550C/560C/850C/855C
- HP DeskJet 720, 820, and 1000 series
- HP PaintJet XL300, DeskJet 600/1200C/1600C (pjxl300)
- HP LaserJet/Plus/II/III/4
- HP PaintJet/XL

- IBM Jetprinter color
- IBM Proprinter
- Imagen ImPress
- Mitsubishi CP50 color
- NEC P6/P6+/P60
- Oki OL410ex LED (ljet4)
- Okidata MicroLine 182
- Ricoh 4081/6000 (r4081)
- SPARCprinter
- StarJet 48 inkjet printer
- Tektronix 4693d color 2/4/8 bit
- Tektronix 4695/4696 inkjet plotter
- Xerox XES printers (2700, 3700, 4045, and so on)
- Canon BJC600/800 color printers

Scanners

Linux supports scanners using the SANE package. This package supports the following scanners:

- A4 Tech AC 4096 / AS 8000P
- Adara Image Star I
- Conrad Personal Scanner 64, P105 handheld scanners
- Epson GT6000
- Fujitsu SCSI-2 scanners (contact Dr. G.W. Wettstein)
- Genius ColorPage-SP2
- Genius GS-B105G handheld scanner
- Genius GeniScan GS4500, GS4500A handheld scanners
- HighScreen Greyscan 256 handheld scanner
- HP ScanJet II series SCSI
- HP ScanJet IIc, IIcx, IIp, 3c, 4c, 4p, 5p, 5pse, plus
- Logitech Scanman+, Scanman 32, Scanman 256 handheld scanners
- Microtek ScanMaker E3, E6, II, IIXE, III, and 35t models
- Mustek M105 handheld scanner
- Mustek HT800 Turbo, Matador 105, and Matador 256 handheld scanners

- Mustek Paragon 6000CX
- Nikon Coolscan SCSI 35mm film scanner
- Pearl 256 handheld scanner
- UMAX SCSI scanners
- Genius GS-4000, ScanMate/32, ScanMate/GS handheld scanners
- Mustek HT105, M800 handheld scanners
- Voelkner Personal Scanner 64 handheld scanner

The following scanners are not supported:

- Acer scanners (Acer is not releasing any programming information.)
- Escom 256 (Primax Lector Premier 256) handheld scanner
- Genius ScanMate/256, EasyScan handheld scanners
- Mustek CG8000 handheld scanner
- Trust AmiScan handheld scanner

Amateur Radio

Linux supports the following cards:

- KISS-based Terminal Node Controllers
- Ottawa PI card
- Gracilis PacketTwin card
- Other Z8530 SCC-based cards
- Parallel and serial port Baycom modems
- Sound Blaster cards
- Soundcards based on the Crystal chipset

Terminals on Serial Port

Old terminals easily can be used under Linux by connecting them to your system's serial port. The following terminals are supported:

- VT52
- VT100
- VT220
- VT320
- VT420

Joysticks

Joystick support exists in the latest XFree86 distributions (3.3.x) and kernel versions 2.2.xx and above.

Video Capture Boards/Frame Grabbers/TV Tuners

Linux has support for the following video capture cards:

- CMOS Video Conferencing Kit (The video capture card has a BT849 chipset. It comes with a CCD camera.)
- Data Translation DT2803
- Data Translation DT2851 Frame Grabber
- Data Translation DT3155
- Diamond DTV2000 (based on BT848)
- Dipix XPG1000/FPG/PPMAPA (based on TI C40 DSP)
- Epix SVM
- Epix Silicon Video MUX series of video frame grabbing boards
- FAST Screen Machine II
- Hauppage Wincast TV PCI (based on BT848)
- Imaging Technology ITI/IC-PCI
- ImageNation Cortex I
- ImageNation CX100
- ImageNation PX500 (being worked on) (Ask for current status.)
- Imaging Technology, Inc. IC-PCI frame grabber board
- Matrox Meteor
- Matrox PIP-1024
- MaxiTV/PCI (based on ZR36120)
- Miro PCTV (based on BT848)
- MuTech MV1000 PCI
- MuTech MV200
- Philips PCA10TV (not in production anymore)
- Pro Movie Studio
- Quanta WinVision B&W video capture card
- Quickcam
- Sensus 700

- Smart Video Recorder III (based on BT848)
- STB TV PCI Television Tuner (based on BT848)
- Tekram C210 (based on ZR36120)
- Video Blaster, Rombo Media Pro+
- VT1500 TV cards

UPS

Linux supports the following UPS models:

- APC SmartUPS
- APC-BackUPS 400/600, APC-SmartUPS SU700/1400RM
- UPSs with RS-232 monitoring port (genpower package)
- MGE UPSs

YaST

In this appendix

SuSE YaST: An Introduction

SuSE Linux has excelled on most other distributions primarily because of its setup tool, YaST. *YaST*, which stands for *Yet Another Setup Tool*, is the heart of SuSE Linux. You have already been introduced to YaST through the installation process. You also might have used it to configure various parts of your system. YaST is the control center for SuSE Linux; it can be used to control and configure the various parts of your system.

YaST is made up of a group of modules, each of which has a specific task. For example, there is a module for managing the users and groups on your system, a module for configuring your network, another for configuring your hardware, and so on. YaST is a menu-driven interface you use to access these modules.

To use SuSE Linux efficiently, you should be aware of what YaST can and cannot do. This appendix will walk you through the various parts of YaST, giving you a brief explanation of what each module does and how to use it.

To use YaST, type the following command as root:

```
# YaST
```

YaST will start with its opening screen (see Figure C.1).

FIGURE C.1
YaST's main screen.

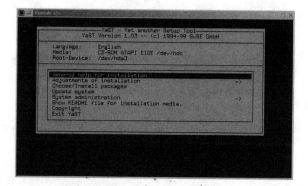

The Opening Screen

When you first run YaST, you are presented with its opening screen. As you can see in Figure C.1, YaST uses a completely menu-driven interface. You use the arrow keys to navigate the menu and press Enter to select an item. Submenus branch out of certain menu items, enabling modules to be organized by category. Pressing the Esc key takes you to a previous state. The following is a list of the items in the main menu, with an explanation of what each one does:

- **General help for installation**—This menu item displays text that contains general help information on the installation process.

- **Adjustments of installation**—This menu item will pop up a submenu that contains all the modules used to configure YaST for an installation. You can define things such as the language to be used, the keyboard mapping, and so on.

- **Choose/Install packages**—This menu item loads up the package manager module in YaST, in which you can install and uninstall packages from your system.

- **Update System**—This menu item loads up the SuSE update module. You use it to update your system to a new version of SuSE Linux.

- **System administration**—This menu item pops up a submenu that contains all the modules used to configure and administer your SuSE Linux system. This is probably one of the most important and frequently used sections of YaST.

- **Show README for installation media**—This menu item displays the README file found on your installation medium.

- **Copyright**—This menu item displays copyright information.

- **Exit YaST**—This menu item exits YaST.

App

C

Adjustments of Installation

The Adjustments of Installation menu is used to prepare YaST for an installation session. You can configure the following (see Figure C.2):

FIGURE C.2

The Adjustments of Installation menu.

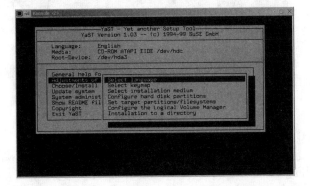

- **Select language**—This is where you will select the language YaST will use.

- **Select keymap**—This is where you can select the keyboard key mapping that matches your keyboard.

- **Select installation medium**—This is where you tell YaST what to use as your installation medium. This can be your CD-ROM, hard drive, network via NFS, or FTP.

- **Set target partitions/filesystems**—This is where you can create, delete, and configure your partitions. You can change their type, mount point, and so on.

- **Configure the Logical Volume Manager**—This is where you can configure all the options and settings of your logical volume manager, if you use one. This is an advanced section that should not be tampered with unless you know what you are doing.
- **Installation to a directory**—This is probably one of the coolest features of YaST. You can tell it to install a whole Linux system on the directory of your choice using this module. So, you can install another copy of SuSE Linux on another partition or hard drive while your system is up and running normally.

Let's get more acquainted with each of these modules.

Select Language

In the Select Language menu, you choose the language YaST will use for the installation process. This is helpful because having YaST speak your native language eliminates any misunderstandings or misinterpretations. Use the arrow keys to highlight the language you want to use for the installation and press Enter to activate it (see Figure C.3).

FIGURE C.3
Selecting the language.

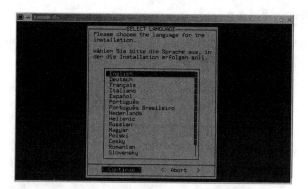

Select Keymap

This module configures the keyboard mapping YaST will use to interpret your keystrokes. This is very important because if you use the wrong mapping for your keyboard, characters you type will be incorrectly interpreted by YaST. Use the arrow keys to highlight the keymap you want to use for the installation and press Enter to activate it (see Figure C.4).

Select Installation Medium

This module configures YaST to install from a specific medium. As Figure C.5 shows, you can install from a CD-ROM, NFS, a reachable directory, a hard drive, and an FTP site.

FIGURE C.4

Selecting the keyboard mapping.

FIGURE C.5

Selecting the installation medium.

If you choose to install from a CD-ROM, YaST will pop up a dialog requesting you to define your CD-ROM (see Figure C.6). Find your CD-ROM in the list and press Enter to select it as your installation medium.

FIGURE C.6

Selecting your CD-ROM.

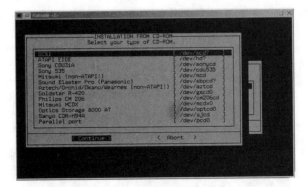

If you choose to install via NFS, YaST will pop up a dialog requesting you to enter the IP of the machine that has the SuSE Linux packages and the directory in which they reside (see Figure C.7). Enter the required information and press Enter to use it.

FIGURE C.7

NFS installation settings.

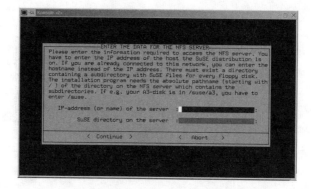

If you choose to install from a reachable directory, YaST will pop up a dialog requesting you to enter the path of that directory (see Figure C.8). Enter the required information and press Enter to use it.

FIGURE C.8

Settings for installing from a reachable directory.

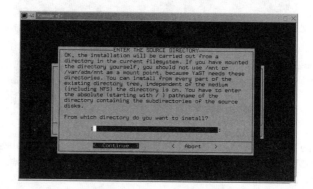

If you choose to install from a hard drive, YaST will pop up a dialog requesting you to select the partition that contains the installation files (see Figure C.9). After you choose the partition, YaST will prompt you for the name of the directory that contains the installation files and packages. Enter the required information and press Enter to use it.

FIGURE C.9

Settings for installing from a hard drive.

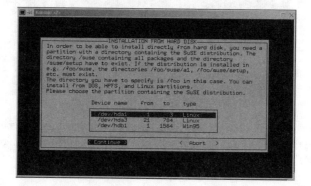

If you choose to install via FTP, YaST will pop up a dialog requesting you to enter the address of the FTP site to use. As shown in Figure C.10, YaST has filled in most of the information for you. Of course, you can change any information you want. Press F10 to accept the current configuration.

FIGURE C.10

Settings for installing from FTP.

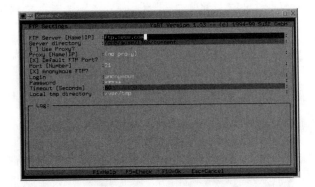

Configure Hard Disk Partitions

This module is used to configure the partitions on your hard disks. You can create, delete, and modify partitions to your heart's desire. If you have more than one hard disk on your machine, YaST will ask you which one of them you want to configure. Select the one with which you want to work and press Enter.

As you can see in Figure C.11, YaST will display all the partitions found on your hard disk. You can manipulate your partitions in any fashion you want. Nothing will be physically changed on your hard drive until you click Continue. Take your time to check what you have changed before you click Continue. Configuring a partition incorrectly can damage it, and a damaged partition is not a very pleasant thing to have—trust us on that one!

FIGURE C.11

Viewing and modifying your partitions from YaST.

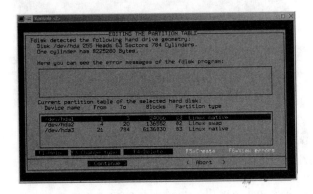

Set Target Partitions/Filesystems

This module is used to configure the target partitions for the installation. You use it to tell YaST where to install the packages on your hard disk. You also can use it to configure the mount points for the various partitions on your system. This module is self-explanatory and very easy to use (see Figure C.12).

FIGURE C.12

Setting the target partitions and mount points using YaST.

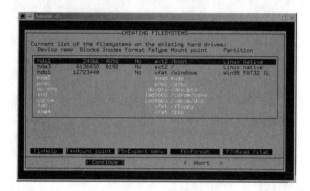

Installing to a Directory

This module enables you to set a directory to be used by YaST as the installation destination. You can install SuSE Linux on another partition or hard disk while your system is still running. Just enter the path to the directory to which you want to install (see Figure C.13).

FIGURE C.13

Installing to a directory.

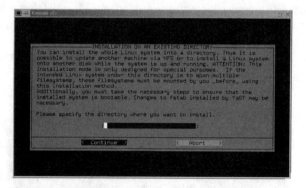

Choose/Install Packages

The Choose/Install Packages section is one of the most important sections in YaST; it is the package manipulation center. You frequently will come here to install new packages, remove unwanted packages, and so on. The module is menu driven, as you can see in Figure C.14. The following lists the items in this menu:

- **Load configuration**—This menu item enables you to load one of the preset package configurations for quick installations, so you can skip the process of manually choosing the packages.

- **Save configuration**—If you have manually selected some packages, you can save this configuration so you can load it up later using the Load configuration option.

- **Change/create configuration**—This is where you browse all the packages that come with SuSE Linux to select which ones you want to install and which you want to remove from your system.

- **Check dependencies of packages**—Some packages in SuSE Linux depend on the presence of other packages for proper functioning. This menu item will show you whether you have any packages that are missing some dependencies. You can have it resolve these dependencies for you by installing the required packages.

- **What if**—You can use this menu item to have YaST tell you what is going to happen if you proceed to install with the current configuration. This enables you to know what is going to change in your system so you can then prevent any unwanted deletions or additions.

- **Start installation**—After you are finished configuring the packages, you can install them using this option. YaST then starts installing the packages to your hard disk.

- **Index of all series and packages**—This option shows you an index of all the packages and the series to which they belong.

- **Package information**—You can use this module to search all the packages using patterns, enabling you to locate a package when you don't know its actual name.

- **Install packages**—This menu item launches a general package installation module. You can use it to install packages from a variety of different sources, not just the SuSE Linux CDs. This is very useful if you have downloaded some packages and want to install them.

App

C

FIGURE C.14

The package configuration and installation menu.

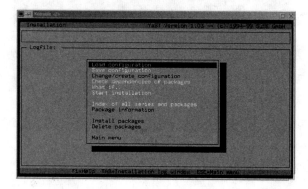

■ **Delete packages**—This menu item launches a general package management module. You can use it to delete any of the packages on your system regardless of where they came from.

■ **Main menu**—This menu item takes you back to the main menu.

Let's take a closer look at the important modules.

Change/Create Configuration

You will probably use this module frequently in SuSE Linux. In most of the chapters in this book, you have had to install certain packages from the SuSE distribution. This is the module you use to install those packages.

YaST shows you a list of all the series found on your SuSE distribution (see Figure C.15). Packages are ordered according to series; for example, the Apache Web server package is found under series n (network). To select a package, highlight the series to which it belongs and press Enter. Packages can have one of the following five states:

■ **[ ]**—The package is not installed on your system.

■ **[i]**—The package is already installed on your system.

■ **[X]**—The package is now selected for installation on the system.

■ **[R]**—The package is already installed but will be reinstalled.

■ **[d]**—The package is selected for removal.

FIGURE C.15

Changing the configuration of packages.

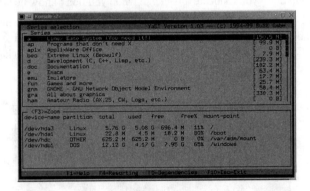

You can change the state of a package by pressing the space bar to cycle through all five states.

To exit from a series, press F10 (the same applies if you want to exit the whole module). Next, you must install the packages by selecting the Start installation option from the main menu and pressing Enter.

Install Packages

The Install Packages module is a general package installer. You can use it to install packages from a variety of different sources, including your source medium. The first thing you must do is to tell the module where to find the packages you want to install by selecting the correct source from the Source field (see Figure C.16).

FIGURE C.16

General package installation.

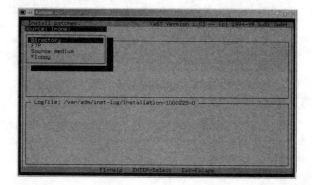

When you select the source of the packages, which can be a directory, the source medium, FTP, or a floppy disk, you will see a list of all the available packages. A common scenario for this is that you downloaded a few packages in RPM format and want to install them. Say you downloaded them in a directory called /tmp/downloads. You would tell YaST that your source is a directory and then enter /tmp/downloads as the path of that directory. YaST then would scan the directory and list all the packages in it. The packages can have one of the following four states:

- **[ ]**—The package is not installed on your system.
- **[i]**—The package is already installed on your system.
- **[X]**—The package is now selected for installation on the system.
- **[o]**—Another version of the package is installed on your system.

When you are finished selecting the packages you want to install, press F10 to install them on your system.

Delete Packages

This menu item launches a general package management module. You can use it to delete any of the packages on your system regardless of where they came from. This module will show you a lengthy list of all the installed packages on your system (see Figure C.17). To delete a package, mark it with an X by pressing the spacebar. Press F10 to delete the selected package(s).

App

C

FIGURE C.17
General deletion of
packages.

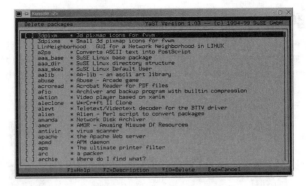

System Administration

The System Administration menu item branches out to another submenu. This submenu contains all the modules relevant to administering your SuSE Linux system. The following is a brief list of these items (see Figure C.18):

- **Integrate hardware into system**—This item branches out into another submenu in which you can add hardware to and remove hardware from your system.

- **Kernel and bootconfiguration**—This item branches out into another submenu in which you can install new kernels to the system and all the system boot up–related configurations.

- **Network configuration**—This item branches out into another submenu in which you can configure your network.

- **Configure Live-system**—This item branches out into another submenu in which you can configure the SuSE Linux live system. The live system is a complete Linux system available in installed form on a CD.

- **Login configuration**—This is where you can configure how your SuSE Linux will handle logins. You can set SuSE Linux to start a graphical login manager or a console-based login manager.

FIGURE C.18
The System
Administration menu.

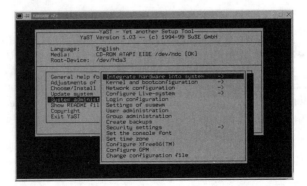

■ **Settings of susewm**—This module enables you to configure the various window managers available on your system. You can use it to set the default window manager for your system.

■ **User administration**—This module is used to manage all the users on the system. You can add, remove, and modify users here.

■ **Group administration**—This module is used to manage all the groups on the system. You can add, remove, and modify groups here.

■ **Create backups**—This module can be used to back up your system.

■ **Security settings**—This item branches out into another submenu that contains your system's security settings.

■ **Set the console font**—You can set the console's font in this module.

■ **Set time zone**—You can set your time zone using this module.

■ **Configure XFree86**—This module launches one of the three configuration programs that can be used to configure your X Window System.

■ **Configure GPM**—This module configures your mouse for use in the console.

■ **Change configuration file**—You can change many of the system variables using this module.

Let's take a closer look at the submenus and the rest of the menu items.

Integrate Hardware into System

You will use this menu whenever you want to configure your hardware. YaST cannot configure all of your hardware, but it does a good job with the common types. This menu has the following modules:

■ **Mouse configuration**—This module configures your mouse (see Figure C.19). YaST asks you about your mouse type. Use the arrow keys to locate your mouse type and press Enter for SuSE to configure it. If your mouse is a serial mouse, YaST will prompt you for the COM port it uses.

FIGURE C.19
Configuring your mouse.

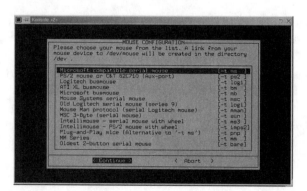

■ **Modem configuration**—This module configures your modem. YaST asks you about the COM port your modem uses (see Figure C.20). Highlight it using the arrow keys and press Enter for YaST to configure it.

FIGURE C.20

Configuring your modem.

■ **CD-ROM configuration**—This module configures your CD-ROM. YaST asks you about your CD-ROM's model (see Figure C.21). Highlight it using the arrow keys and press Enter for YaST to configure it.

FIGURE C.21

Configuring your CD-ROM.

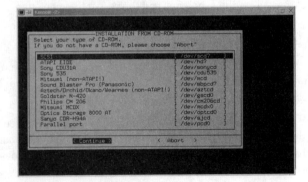

■ **Configure printers**—This module configures your printer. YaST asks you for information about your printer (see Figure C.22). Enter that information and click Continue for YaST to configure your printer.

■ **Configure ISDN hardware**—This module configures your ISDN. YaST asks you for information about your ISDN hardware (see Figure C.23). Enter that information and press Enter for YaST to configure it.

■ **Configure your scanner**—This module configures your scanner. YaST asks you for information about your scanner (see Figure C.24). Enter that information and press Enter for YaST to configure it.

FIGURE C.22

Configuring your printer.

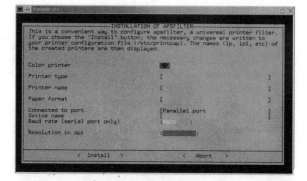

FIGURE C.23

Configuring your ISDN.

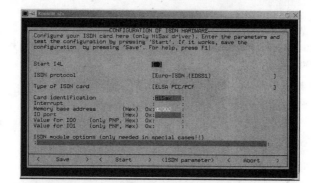

FIGURE C.24

Configuring your scanner.

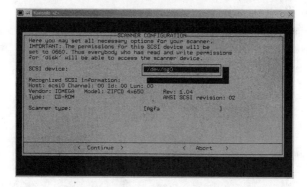

■ **Configure networking device**—This module configures your networking device. YaST asks you for information about your networking device (see Figure C.25). Enter that information and press Enter for YaST to configure it.

FIGURE C.25
Configuring your networking device.

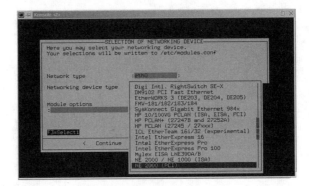

Kernel and Bootconfiguration

This menu contains all the modules related to your kernel and system boot up. It contains the following three modules:

- **Select boot kernel**—This module can be used to install another one of the preinstalled kernels packaged with SuSE Linux.
- **Create rescue disk**—You can use this module to create a rescue disk for your system.
- **LILO configuration**—This module configures the Linux loader (LILO).

Let's take a closer look at these important modules.

Select Boot Kernel

You can use this module to install one of the precompiled kernels packaged with SuSE Linux. To install any of these kernels, highlight the one you want with the arrow keys and press Enter to install it (see Figure C.26).

FIGURE C.26
Selecting the boot kernel.

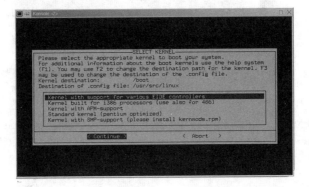

LILO Configuration

You can use this module to configure your Linux loader (see Figure C.27). You must fill in the information required for LILO and press Enter to install it.

FIGURE C.27
Configuring the Linux loader (LILO).

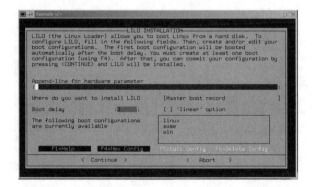

Network Configuration

This menu contains all the modules that configure different aspects of networking in SuSE Linux. The following lists these modules:

- **Network base configuration**—This module configures your basic networking in SuSE Linux.

- **Change host name**—You can use this module to change the hostname of the machine.

- **Configure network services**—This module helps you configure which networking services are to be started on system boot up.

- **Configuration nameserver**—This module is used to configure the name servers your SuSE Linux will use to resolve domain names.

- **Configure YP client**—This module configures your system to be integrated in an NIS+ network.

- **Configure sendmail**—This module configures your sendmail.

- **Configure ISDN parameters**—This module configures your ISDN interface.

- **Configure a PPP network**—You can configure your PPP network using this module.

- **Administer remote printers**—You can configure your system to print to remote printers using this module.

- **Connect to a printer via Samba**—You can configure your system to print to a remote MS Windows printer using this module.

- **Connect to a printer via a Novell network**—You can configure your system to print to a remote Novell printer using this module.

The following sections examine these modules more closely.

Network Base Configuration

This module is used to configure your network in SuSE Linux. It is used to configure all the networking devices on your system and has a user-friendly interface (see Figure C.28).

FIGURE C.28
Basic network
configuration.

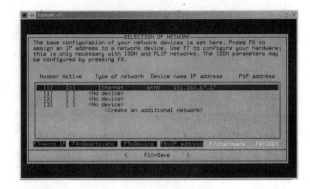

Configure YP Client

If your machine is part of an NIS+ network, you can integrate into it using this module. YaST will ask you to enter the YP domain and IP of the YP server to which you will connect (see Figure C.29). Click Continue for YaST to configure your system.

FIGURE C.29
NIS client
configuration.

Configure sendmail

This module configures your mail system in SuSE Linux. sendmail is known for its difficult configuration process, but that's not a problem in SuSE Linux thanks to this module. As you can see in Figure C.30, the module asks for simple information and YaST takes care of the rest.

FIGURE C.30
Configuring sendmail.

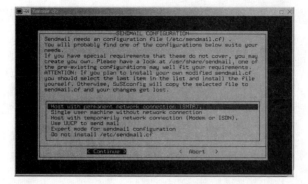

Configure ISDN Parameters

This module configures your ISDN system in SuSE Linux. To get your ISDN up and running, you just have to fill in the information that YaST requests in the module (see Figure C.31). When you are finished, click Continue and YaST takes care of the rest.

App

C

FIGURE C.31
Configuring ISDN.

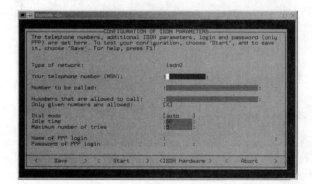

Configure a PPP Network

This module configures your PPP networking in SuSE Linux. To get your PPP network up and running, you must fill in the information that YaST requests in the module (see Figure C.32). When you are finished, click Continue and YaST takes care of the rest.

Administer Remote Printers

If you want to print to a remote UNIX/Linux printer, this module is for you. It configures your system to print to a remote printer by asking you for some simple information, such as the address of the print server (see Figure C.33).

FIGURE C.32

Configuring PPP.

FIGURE C.33

Configuring a remote UNIX/Linux printer.

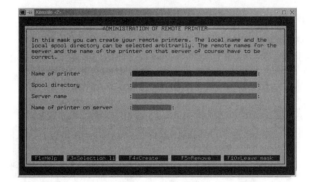

Connect to a Printer via Samba

This module enables you to print to a remote MS Windows printer. It configures your system to print to a remote printer by asking you for some simple information, such as the address of the print server (see Figure C.34).

FIGURE C.34

Configuring a remote MS Windows printer using Samba.

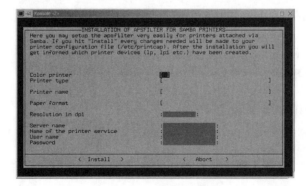

Connect to a Printer via Novell Network

You can use this module to print to a remote Novell network printer. It configures your system to print to a remote printer by asking you for some simple information, such as the address of the print server (see Figure C.35).

FIGURE C.35
Configuring a remote
Novell network printer.

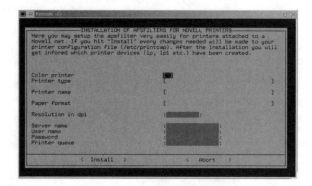

System Administration: Continued

Now that you are finished with all the submenus, let's take a look at the rest of the modules in the System Administration menu.

Login Configuration

This module is used to configure whether you want SuSE Linux to start the login manager as graphical or text-based. All the settings are easily configured (see Figure C.36).

FIGURE C.36
Configuring the login
manager.

Settings of susewm

This module is used to configure the default window manager that will be initiated when you run the X Window System. Several window manager–specific configurations are available in this module (see Figure C.37).

FIGURE C.37

Configuring your window manager's settings.

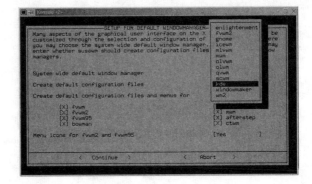

User Administration

This module is your control center for managing your users and their attributes. As you can see in Figure C.38, the module is very easy and self-explanatory.

FIGURE C.38

User administration using YaST.

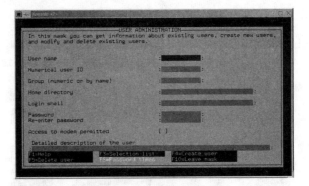

Group Administration

This module is your control center for managing your groups and their attributes. This module is also very easy and self-explanatory (see Figure C.39).

FIGURE C.39
Group administration
using YaST.

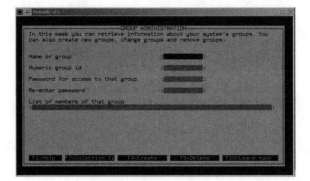

Create Backups

YaST also can be used as a system backup tool. This is achieved by using this module. You can exclude filesystems from being backed up, you can add and remove directories, and so on. We cannot stress enough the importance of backups; it is a highly recommended practice.

App
C

Troubleshooting

When I run YaST, it tells me the screen is not big enough.

This usually happens when you run YaST in an X terminal. To solve this problem, resize the X terminal to make it bigger. Run YaST again and it should work correctly. ●

Tips and Tricks on Tuning Your Linux Box

In this appendix

Tuning Your SuSE Linux

Installing and configuring your SuSE Linux is one thing, tuning it is another. Linux is so flexible that the same task can be accomplished in several ways—some efficient, some not. Different people like to approach a problem in different ways.

This appendix includes a collection of the best tips and tricks found on the Linux Web site (http://www.linux.com). These tips and tricks are posted here by the Linux community to be shared by all. They are the result of personal experiences and tested methods. Some of these tips are for tuning purposes, while others help make your experience with Linux both easier and more fun!

Filesystem Tips

The following set of tips are filesystem-specific. These tips should help speed up any file operations.

Speeding Up Your Hard Drive

Most new IDE hard drives use Ultra DMA technology. This technology enables you to free the CPU from handling any large file transfers on your hard drive. Usually, the CPU has to be involved when you use your hard drive, but when using Ultra DMA technology, the CPU just issues the commands and the hardware works on it. This causes your system to be more responsive and file transfers to be faster.

Ultra DMA usually is not enabled by default because some hard drives fail when Ultra DMA is on. To check whether it's on, use the hdparm command as root:

```
# hdparm /dev/hda
/dev/hda:
 multcount     =   0 (off)
 I/O support   =   0 (16-bit)
 unmaskirq     =   0 (off)
 using_dma     =   0 (off)
 keepsettings  =   0 (off)
 nowerr        =   0 (off)
 readonly      =   0 (off)
 readahead     =   8 (on)
 geometry      = 784/255/63, sectors = 12594960, start =
```

As you can see, the command lists all the hardware-specific properties of your hard drive. In the previous example, Ultra DMA is not enabled, as evidenced by the line using dma   = 0 (off). To turn it on, issue the following command:

```
# hdparm -d 1 /dev/hda
```

Now, Ultra DMA is on. You should see the difference now, especially when you are performing huge file transfers. If you are running a database of some sort, you should use this option.

Another good option is I/O support. In our example, it is set to 16 bit. The hardware in most new machines is capable of 32-bit I/O support, which provides better performance. To set your hard drive to use 32-bit I/O, use the following:

```
# hdparm -c 1 /dev/hda
```

You should enter these two commands in /sbin/init.d/boot.local so they will run every time you reboot. One final note, though, this works only for IDE drives, not SCSI ones.

Detecting Changed Files

Have you ever wanted to know which files were changed by a certain program? Sure, you can get the source code for the program and see for yourself. But let's get real here, no one is really going to do that. Instead, there is a really easy way to do that.

Let's say you want to see which files in your home have been modified by the program you are about to run. Create a list of all the files you have in your home by running the following command:

```
$ ls -Rl /home/john > before.txt
```

This generates a lengthy file named before.txt. This file has a list of all the files in your home directory (assuming it is called /home/john). Now, run your program and repeat the previous step, but on a different file:

```
$ ls -Rl /home/john > after.txt
```

Now use diff to see the differences between the two files:

```
$ diff before.txt after.txt
```

The diff utility shows you the names of all the files that were modified and the modifications made to the files.

Protecting Your Files

If you have some files or directories you want to protect from any changes, you can use the chattr command. This command must be run by root, though. If you run the command

```
# chattr +i myfile
```

no one, not even root, will be able to delete, rename, move, or modify that file. The command works on directories as well. To revert its effect, type the following:

```
# chattr -i myfile
```

Please be careful when you use this command. Files affected by it will be totally immune to any changes, which can drive you crazy when troubleshooting a problem. Make sure that you don't apply it to files or directories that will be changed in any way.

App
D

Gaining More Hard Drive Space

Running out of hard drive space is usually not a pleasant experience. Linux's ext2 filesystem makes it quite easy to expand your space by adding new hard drives to the system. You can expand your hard drive space by adding a new hard drive or partition to the system.

After your new partition is ready and formatted, you must copy a heavily populated part of your drive to it. A good choice is the /usr directory. Mount the new partition and copy the contents of /usr to it:

```
cp -a /usr/ /mnt/new
```

Now remove /usr:

```
# rm -rf /usr
```

Then, create a link called /usr/ to the new partition:

```
# ln -s /mnt/new /usr/
```

You now have more space on your original drive. Just make sure that you add the new partition to your /etc/fstab file to be mounted automatically on boot up.

Freeing Up More Space

Do you need more space but can't afford throwing in a new hard drive or partition? How common! We have a trick, though, that you can use to give you some more space. Most programs in Linux are compiled with debugging symbols enabled so they can be debugged very easily. The symbols tend to enlarge the size of the binaries considerably. You can remove them using the strip command. For example,

```
# strip /usr/bin/program
```

removes the debugging symbols from the program you specified. You can run this on most of your binaries to reduce their size.

Locating Big Files

Keeping track of where your space has gone can get quite difficult. You might have a useless file somewhere on your system that is taking up space for no reason. To list all the files on your system in descending order of size, run this command as root:

```
# ls -Rl / | sort +4n > files.txt
```

You can inspect the contents of files.txt to see the result of this command, which will help you find the really big files on your hard drive.

Can't Unmount a Device?

It happens to all of us: You attempt to unmount a device and it gives you a device busy message. It can take quite a while to find the program that is using that device. You can use the lsof utility to get some help, though. For example, if you are unable to unmount your CD-ROM that is mounted on /mnt/cdrom, type the following command:

```
# lsof  /mnt/cdrom
```

The previous command shows you which processes are using your CD-ROM. You then can choose to kill them or close them gracefully.

Spreading Your IDE Drives

The IDE architecture does not allow two devices connected to the same IDE controller to be active at the same time. Therefore, if you have a hard drive and a CD-ROM both connected to the same IDE controller, only one of them can be active at one time. For this reason, you should avoid putting drives on the same IDE controller. If you have more than two drives, you should at least avoid putting the CD-ROM on the same IDE with another hard drive because it will slow it down whenever you use it.

Jailing Programs

If you are worried about a program damaging your files, you can jail it. *Jailing* it means limiting its view of your hard drive, which in turn limits its damage. Use the chroot command to jail a program. For example, to jail a program called funny to be able to see only /tmp and the underlying directory and file structure, use the following command:

```
# chroot funny /tmp
```

When you issue the previous command, the program will not be able to see anything but /tmp. Just make sure that any files it needs are available inside that jail or else it won't work.

App

D

Safe Transfers

If you want to verify that a file you just transferred to your machine is the same file as the original one, you can use the md5sum utility. Run the utility on the original file to cause it to generate a checksum for that file. Then, when you transfer it, run the command on the new copy and compare the checksums to ensure nothing changed in the file. You can post md5sums of your files to people so they can be sure that what they are getting is what you posted originally.

Identifying File Types

You can identify the type of a file using the file command. This command scans files and attempts to recognize their type. The following is an example:

```
$ file test.ps
test.ps: PostScript document text conforming at level 3.0
```

Tips for Using Your System

The following set of tips help make your everyday experience with Linux easier and more efficient.

Reading Binary Files

If you have a binary file you want to read, you can use the `strings` command. This command shows you a list of all the strings inside the binary file. This command comes in very handy for developers. You can use it to see all the strings in a binary file or library. Its general format is as follows:

```
$ strings filename
```

Viewing All Running Processes

To view all the currently running processes, you can use the `ps` command. This command lists your own processes by default, but to make it list all processes, type the following:

```
$ps aux
```

If the listing seems to go beyond the edge of the screen, use the `w` option to cause the lines to wrap around:

```
$ps auxw
```

Recursive *grep*

You can use the `grep` command to search for text in a group of files. For example,

```
$ grep linux *.txt
```

searches all files with the `.txt` extension for the word `linux`. This will not search subdirectories, however. You should use `rgrep` if you want to search recursively.

Easy Downloading

SuSE Linux includes a utility that is considered one of the best downloaders available for Linux, wget. You can use wget to grab whole Web sites or single files. To grab a whole Web site, use the following command:

```
$ wget -r http://www.suse.com/
```

To grab a single file, type the following:

```
$ wget ftp://ftp.somewhere.com/file.tar.gz
```

Give wget a try; you will surely find it very handy and useful.

Using the Manual Pages

Linux has a set of manual pages that explain most of the commands and programming API available. You can access this manual using the man command. For example, to find the manual page for the ls command, type the following:

```
$man ls
```

Manual pages are in sections. The following are the available sections:

- Section 1: User Commands
- Section 2: System Calls
- Section 3: Subroutines
- Section 4: Devices
- Section 5: File Formats
- Section 6: Games
- Section 7: Miscellaneous
- Section 8: System Administration
- Section n: Tcl/Tk

To access a section, just type its number after the man command. For example, the following searches section 1 for the command you enter after the 1:

```
$ man 1 command
```

You can use the -k option if you want man to search all the sections for the command you want.

Changing the Priority of Your Processes

Processes in Linux get CPU time according to their priority. The higher the priority, the more CPU time the process will get. To change the priority of a process, use the nice command. Priorities are a numerical value that ranges from –20–19, with 0 as the default. The lowest priority is 19, whereas the highest priority is –20.

To change the priority of a process, type the following:

```
$ nice 10 pid of process
```

You should note that a normal user cannot change the priority of a process to a number below 0, only root can do that. You can only change the priority of a process you own.

Viewing Files in Pieces

You can use the head command to view the top 10 lines of a file. You can do the opposite using the tail command, which will show you the last 10 lines in a file. You can use the -f option in tail to cause it to continuously list the last 10 lines of a file as it grows in size.

This is very handy when tracking your log files. For example, enter the following to continuously see the latest log messages:

```
$ tail -f /var/log/messages
```

Killing Processes

To kill a process, use the `kill` command. You must know the ID of the process you want to kill; you can use `ps` to get it. Alternatively, you can use the `killall` command, which takes the name of the process you want to kill rather than its ID. For example, the following kills all the Netscape processes that belong to you:

```
$killall netscape
```

Be very careful with this command when you are running as root. You can easily kill other users' processes by mistake!

X Window System Tips

If you use SuSE Linux as a desktop operating system, you will be using the X Window System quite often. We will discuss several tips to enhance your X Window experience in the following sections.

Speeding Up Your X Window System

The 2.2.x kernel uses a feature present in Pentium Pro and later processors called *Memory Type Range Registers*. You must enable them in your kernel configuration, in the Processor Type and Features section.

Using MTRR, you can tell the kernel to enable write combining on a block of memory, which increases the speed of data transfers. This is useful if you have a PCI or AGP display card. You can enable write combining on the card's memory, thus speeding up your graphics. This in turn will speed up your X Window System quite considerably.

To use MTRR, you need to know the beginning of your card's memory address space. You can find this information by looking at the `/proc/pci` file:

```
# cat /proc/pci
```

The previous command gives you a list of all the PCI devices you have on your system. You are interested only in the part that has to do with your graphics card. The following is an example of such a section:

```
Bus  1, device   0, function  0:
   VGA compatible controller: NVidia Unknown device (rev 21).
      Vendor id=10de. Device id=2d.
      Medium devsel.  Fast back-to-back capable.
      ➥IRQ 11.  Master Capable. Latency=64.  Min Gnt=5.Max Lat=1.
      Non-prefetchable 32 bit memory at 0xf5000000 [0xf5000000].
      Prefetchable 32 bit memory at 0xfc000000 [0xfc000008].
```

The part you are interested in is the line `Prefetchable 32 bit memory at 0xfc000000` `[0xfc000008]`. In this example, this tells you that our card's memory starts at `0xfc000000`.

To tell the kernel to enable write combining on this memory, type the following as root:

```
# echo "base=0xfc000000 size=0x2000000 type=write-combining" >> /proc/mtrr
```

The size field takes the size of the RAM on the card in hex. In the previous example, it's `0x2000000`, which is 32MB. You can calculate it on any calculator.

That's it, restart your X Window System to see the difference. You should notice an overall increase in speed, especially if you are using GNOME and have a lot of themes applied.

You should enter the previous line in `/sbin/init.d/boot.local` if you want it to take effect when you reboot.

More Acceleration to Your X Window System

If your graphics card and X Server support acceleration, you can turn it on using the `Accel` option. Just edit `/etc/XF86Config` and add the following option to the `device` section:

```
Option "accel"
```

The final section should look something like the following:

```
Section "Screen"
    Driver "svga"
    Device    "RIVA TNT2"
    Monitor   "DELL"
    Option    "accel"
```

App
D

You will see the rest of the section, but it's not included because it's not relevant here. Restart your X Window System for the changes to take effect. Please note that this will work only if *both* the server and the card support acceleration.

Using the Geometry Option

You can make an application start in a specific spot on your screen using the `-geometry` option, which tells the application where to position itself on the screen. The option's form is `-geometry WxH+X+Y`, where W is width, H is height, and X and Y are the coordinates. For example, the following causes xclock to position itself in the top left corner of the screen:

```
$ xclock -geometry 100x100+0+0
```

It will have a height of 100 pixels and width of 100 pixels.

If you replace the plus sign (+) with a hyphen (-) in the X,Y coordinates, it will start from the right side of the screen for the X and the bottom for the Y. For example, the following places xclock in the top right corner of the screen:

```
$ xclock -geometry 100x100-0+0
```

This occurs because the X coordinate `-0` indicates 0 pixels from the right of the screen.

Starting More Than One X Session

More than one instance of the X Window System can run on the same machine. To do this, type the following:

```
$ startx -- :1
```

The new X Window session will start alongside the currently running one. The first one can be accessed by pressing Ctrl+Alt+F7 and the new one by pressing Ctrl+Alt+F8. For example, you can run KDE in one and GNOME in the other.

Getting the Most Out of a Netscape Crash

If your Netscape hangs on you, the usual solution is to kill it using the `killall` command:

```
$ killall -9 netscape
```

This, however, will not save your session (bookmarks, preferences, history, and so on). For Netscape to save the session, use the following:

```
$ killall -12 netscape
```

The previous command keeps you from losing any new bookmarks.

Menus in X Terminals

You can bring up menus that configure your X terminal using the Ctrl key and a mouse button. Each of the three buttons on the mouse will bring up a different menu. Just press Ctrl+Mouse button 1 to see one of them.

Networking Tips

The following sections discuss a few network-specific tips.

Listing All Open Connections

If you are wondering who is connected to your machine, wonder no more. You can use the `netstat` command to list all the open connections to and from your machine. For example, the following shows you a detailed list of all the open connections to and from your machine:

```
$ netstat -na
```

The previous command is very useful for monitoring your network for efficiency and security reasons.

Speeding Up Your TCP/IP

The following will not really speed up your TCP/IP, but it will enable it to handle more connections. Just run these commands, which set some parameters for TCP/IP:

```
echo 30 > /proc/sys/net/ipv4/tcp_fin_timeout
echo 1800 > /proc/sys/net/ipv4/tcp_keepalive_time
echo 0 > /proc/sys/net/ipv4/tcp_window_scaling
echo 0 > /proc/sys/net/ipv4/tcp_sack
echo 0 > /proc/sys/net/ipv4/tcp_timestamps
```

You might want to enter the previous commands in `/sbin/init.d/boot.local` for them to take effect every time you reboot.

Disabling Ping Responses

If you don't want your machine to answer any ping requests, type the following command:

```
echo 1 > /proc/sys/net/ipv4/icmp_echo_ignore_all
```

Now your machine will not answer any ping packets. This is easier than establishing a firewall for the same purpose.

Changing Your MAC Address

Ethernet cards each have a unique Machine Address (MAC) that identifies them on the network. This is how packets find their way to your machine. On the hardware level, IPs are mapped to that MAC address so the hardware can communicate together.

You can change your card's MAC address using the `ifconfig` command:

```
#ifconfig eth0 hw ether ddaabaaf1001
```

Now your card will answer to the MAC address `ddaabaaf1001` instead of its original one. Software is used to change the address, which is why it will be slower than using your hardware MAC address. You should be careful with this because you can conflict with someone else on the same network ●

App

D

Various Utilities

In this appendix

Your Toolbox

Linux inherits almost all the tools found on UNIX. These tools are small programs, each of which specializes in a certain task. You use these programs either standalone or by grouping them together to achieve a bigger and more specific task. You can think of them as tools in your toolbox. Each tool performs a certain job, and performs it well. You can use all the tools together to build something big.

To be comfortable using Linux, you have to be familiar with the most commonly used tools. You usually can get away with using the GUI equivalents, but these are never as powerful or complete as the command-line versions. Throughout this book, you have been using quite a few of these tools; now it's time you get to know them better.

Compression and Data Archiving Tools

Linux has a wide variety of programs that compress and decompress files. This can be very helpful in reducing the size of files to save disk space or bandwidth if you are going to be transferring these files over a network. Some of these programs work on individual files and others work on multiple files.

compress

compress is one of the oldest file compression tools in existence. It works on individual files, compressing them using the adaptive Lempel-Ziv coding. To compress a file, just type the following:

```
$ compress filename
```

This will compress the file and add the extension .z at the end of the file. So, if the file is called funds.sdw and you compress it, it now will be called funds.sdw.Z.

To decompress a file, you use the uncompress command. This command takes the name of the compressed file as input, as in the following:

```
$ uncompress filename.Z
```

This will uncompress the file and remove the .z extension. So, if you have a file called funds.sdw.Z and you uncompress it, it now will be called funds.sdw.

Compressed files are not readable or usable unless you decompress them. Loading a compressed document file into StarOffice won't work because it won't be able to read it. You have to feed it the decompressed version.

You can use the -r option to cause compress to dive into subdirectories and compress the files inside them as well. This is useful if you want to compress all the files in a directory including the subdirectories.

You can use the -v option to cause compress to print out the compressing ratio that was achieved for the current file. This ratio depends on the type of the file—some files compress better than others.

compress uses magic numbers to decide whether to compress a file or not. *Magic numbers* are headers in different types of files that declare their type. For example, certain headers in jpeg image files identify these as jpeg files. Image files such as jpeg are already compressed, and trying to compress them further will not decrease their size. compress tries to be smart in that manner; it checks the magic number of a file and compresses it only if it will decrease its size.

You can use the zcat utility to see the contents of a compressed file. This is obviously useful if the compressed file is a text file. Then, you can view its contents without the need to decompress it first. For example, the following will dump the contents of `notes.txt.Z` on your display without decompressing it:

```
$ zcat notes.txt.Z
```

gzip

One of the best compression programs is GNU zip, or gzip. *gzip* is an older program, but it has a very good reputation. gzip is powerful because it can compress and decompress its own files as well as others. You can use it to decompress files that were created by gzip, compress, and pack.

gzip works in almost the same manner as compress. It takes the name of a file as an argument and produces a compressed version with an extension of `.gz`. To compress a file, type this command:

```
$ gzip filename
```

This will produce a file called `filename.gz`. To decompress this file, type the following:

```
$ gzip -d filename.gz
```

In the previous code, -d signifies to decompress the file. Alternatively, you can use the gunzip command to get the same result as gzip -d.

gzip identifies a file to be decompressed from its extension. It can identify `*.gz`, `*.tar.gz`, `*.tgz`, and `*.Z`. If you have a compressed file, but it does not use any of the previous extensions, gzip won't decompress it.

You can use the zcat utility with gzip in the same fashion as you use it in the compress program. It will dump the contents of the compressed file to your display without decompressing it.

You can use the -l option to cause gzip to dump information about the file you are querying, such as compressed size, uncompressed size, compression ratio, and so on.

For gzip to act recursively, use the -r option, which causes it to dive into subdirectories, compressing all the files inside them.

App

E

The -t option is used to test the integrity of a compressed file, ensuring that it wasn't corrupted. This can be handy if you want to make sure the file you are about to transfer is not corrupted, especially if it is a big file that will take some time to transfer.

The -v option causes gzip to show verbose information, such as the name and percentage reduction for each file on which it's working.

The -# option sets the speed of execution for gzip. You replace the # with a number from 1–9, with 1 being the fastest and lowest compression ratio and 9 being the slowest and highest compression ratio. -6 is a good choice in most cases.

bzip2

bzip2 is a newcomer in the scene of compression programs. This program, however, has a *very* high compression ratio. It will almost always compress files more than gzip and compress can, but is slower than them. The bigger the file you are compressing using bzip2, the bigger the difference between its size and that of a file compressed by gzip. For example, some bzip2 compressed files are 10MB, while their gzip equivalents are 12MB.

bzip2 works in exactly the same way as gzip. It takes the exact same arguments and options, which makes it very easy to replace gzip with bzip2 without modifying how you use them. bzip2 gives its compressed files a .bz2 extension.

You can use the bzcat utility in the same manner as the zcat utility is used with compress and gzip. It will dump the contents of the compressed file to your display without decompressing them.

bzip2 has a useful utility called bzip2recover, which attempts to recover as much data as possible from corrupted compressed files. It won't fix a corrupted file, but it will do its best to extract as much data from it as possible.

tar

tar, which stands for *tape archive*, is one of the most commonly used archiving programs in Linux. So far, all the programs discussed in this chapter work on single files. They compress them on an individual basis. tar, on the other hand, groups files together in one single file or archive. This enables you to move more than one file by tarring them into a single file. tar, however, does not compress the files; it only archives them.

To archive a group of files, use the c and f options, as in the following:

```
$ tar cf filename.tar [list of files]
```

list of files can be anything, such as a list of individual files, wildcards, or directories. The c option tells tar to create a new archive. In addition, the f option tells it that the name of the archive, which is filename.tar, is coming next. Let's look at some examples:

```
$ tar cf presentation.tar funds.sdw logo.jpg graph.jpg
```

The previous command will create an archive called `presentation.tar` that includes the files `funds.sdw`, `logo.jpg`, and `graph.jpg`. The following will create an archive called `backup.tar` that includes all the files that end with the extension `*.sdw` or `*.jpg`:

```
$ tar cf backup.tar *.sdw *.jpg
```

The following will create an archive called `backup.tar` that includes all the files from the directory called `documents`:

```
$ tar cf backup.tar documents/
```

This will be recursive; `tar` will dive into all the subdirectories inside `documents`.

You can unpack archives by using `tar`, as well. To do this, use the `x` (for extract) option. For example, the following will extract the contents of `backup.tar` into the current directory, building any internal directory structures in the archive:

```
$ tar xf backup.tar
```

The following will extract the contents of `backup.tar` to the directory specified after the `-C` option:

```
$ tar xf backup.tar -C /tmp
```

`tar` is a very useful tool when it comes to making backups. Its only drawback is that it doesn't compress the files. But, no one said *you* can't compress them. You can easily compress tar archives using compress, gzip, or bzip2. For example, if you create an archive called `backup.tar` and compress it using bzip2, you end up with `backup.tar.bz2`. To do this, just run the following command on the archive:

```
$bzip2 backup.tar
```

And, when you want to unpack the archive, reverse the operation by first decompressing the archive with the following command:

```
$bzip2 -d backup.tar
```

And then run the `tar` command to extract it:

```
$tar xf backup.tar
```

The good news is you don't even need to do this in two separate steps. You can use the `z` option for gzip and the `I` option for bzip2. For example, the following will first tar them and then compress the archive using bzip2 automatically:

```
$ tar cfI backup.tar.bz2 [list of files]
```

The reverse is also true—the following will decompress the archive and unpack it all in one command:

```
$tar xfI backup.tar.bz2
```

App
E

zip

zip is the compression program most users, especially MS Windows users, are familiar with. It uses the same compression algorithm as WinZip and PKZip; therefore, it can handle files compressed by these utilities.

The `zip` command is very convenient in the sense that it both archives and compresses files all in one step using one program. It does not rely on gzip or bzip2 to function like tar does.

To create a zip archive of some files, use the following command:

```
$ zip backup.zip file1 file2 file3 ...
```

This will create an archive called `backup.zip`, which contains compressed copies of the list of files you specified. You can specify a directory and use wildcards.

If you want to password protect your archive, use the `-e` option:

```
$zip -e backup.zip file1 file2 file3
```

The program will then prompt you to enter the password twice. Make sure you don't forget that password or you won't be able to unpack the archive.

To unpack an archive, you use the `unzip` command like this:

```
$unzip backup.zip
```

This will unpack the contents of the archive in the current directory. If you want to specify a different directory, use the `-d` option:

```
$unzip backup.zip -d /tmp
```

The previous command unpacks the contents of the archive in `/tmp`.

Editors

Throughout this book, we have been asking you to use your favorite editor to edit this and edit that. Which editor are you going to make your favorite? SuSE Linux bundles several editors—more than you can imagine. The three main editors you will find on most if not all Linux distributions are pico, Emacs, and the infamous vi.

pico

The *pico* editor is part of the pine email client package. It is a good editor and is quite easy to use. pico is a visual editor that runs in the console. To run the program, just type `pico` on the command line:

```
$pico
```

This starts pico, and as you can see, it lists all its commands in the bottom part of the window. All the commands contain a carat (^) followed by a letter. Commands in pico all follow the form Ctrl+letter, which means you press the Ctrl key on your keyboard along with a letter to execute a command.

The first command you'll want to try is the `Read File` command. This command's shortcut is Ctrl+R, or `^R` in pico notation. Pressing Ctrl+R will cause pico to ask you to enter the name of the file you want to open. If you want pico to bring up a directory listing for you to navigate to find the file, use Ctrl+T. Just find the file you want to open and then press Enter to open it.

Editing in pico is very easy because you can use the cursor keys to move around the document. Any text you type will be inserted wherever the cursor is. You can display the position of the cursor by using the Ctrl+C command. You will get detailed information about where the cursor is in the text relative to line numbers and characters.

To cut a line of text, use the Ctrl+K shortcut. The line will be removed from the text and copied to the clipboard. You then can paste it anywhere in the document by using Ctrl+U.

Searching within the text is easily done by using the Ctrl+W shortcut. pico will ask you for the word for which you want to search; type it in and press Enter. pico then will show you the first occurrence of that word in your document. To search again, just press Ctrl+W and then Enter. pico will remember the last word for which you were searching and will search for it again.

To save the contents of the document, use the Ctrl+O shortcut. pico will ask you to enter the name of the file you want to save this document as. Just press Enter to use the original name of the document. You can press Ctrl+T if you want pico to bring up a file listing so that you can select a file. You also can use the Tab key to complete a name of a file just like on the shell.

Finally, to exit pico use Ctrl+X. If the document you have open is still modified, you will be prompted to save it first. At any point in time, you can call pico's help by pressing Ctrl+G.

Emacs

Emacs is one of the most powerful editors in existence. Emacs is not only an editor; it also can be used as a mail reader, news reader, Web browser, organizer, code compiler, code debugger, and so on. Some people use nothing but Emacs everyday to do everything for them. Because of Emacs's extensibility, you can make it do anything you want by using a lisp-like configuration language. Users usually either totally love Emacs or totally hate it.

Discussing how you can get the most out of Emacs is beyond the scope of this book, but we will explain how it can be used as your favorite editor.

Emacs works both in the XWindow System and console. To run Emacs, just type the following:

```
$ emacs
```

App

E

Depending on whether you are running the X Window System or not, either the X version of Emacs will run or the text version will. The X version of Emacs is a bit more user-friendly because it uses menus and such for its interface. The text version is a bit less user-friendly. However, both use the exact same shortcuts, which brings us to the subject of shortcuts in Emacs—if you want to call them "short." Emacs uses not-so-short shortcuts, which have been a subject of holy war among Emacs lovers and haters. A typical Emacs shortcut is Ctrl+X Ctrl+F, which means you press Ctrl+X followed by Ctrl+F. Emacs shortcuts really aren't that bad once you get used to them.

The Emacs window has three main sections, the menu bar at the top, the document section below it, and the minibuffer at the bottom of the window. The minibuffer is where all messages and prompts from Emacs are shown.

To open a file for editing in Emacs, use the Ctrl+X Ctrl+F shortcut. Emacs will prompt you for the name of the file you want to open in the minibuffer at the bottom of the window. You can press the Tab key to complete a partial name or press it twice to have Emacs show you a directory listing.

Emacs will open your file in the document editing section. You can use the arrow keys to move around the document. Typed text will be inserted wherever the cursor is.

You can split Emacs' window into sections so you can view more than one file at the same time. To split the current section into two horizontal halves, use Ctrl+X 2. To split it vertically, use Ctrl+X 3. To move from one partition to the other, use either your mouse or the shortcut Ctrl+X o. To delete a section, use Ctrl+X 0. To delete all partitions except the one you are currently in, use Ctrl+X 1. Every command you execute will apply to the partition you are currently in.

To search within your text, use Ctrl+S to search forward and Ctrl+r to search backward. Emacs will prompt you in the minibuffer for the word for which you want to look. Emacs will interactively search the text as you type each letter. To repeat the search, just press Ctrl+S again.

To search and replace, you use the M+% shortcut. The M key is the meta key; on PCs you can use the Esc key instead. Emacs will prompt you for the name of the word you want to replace and for the word with which you want to replace it. Emacs will stop at every occurrence of the word and ask you whether you want to replace it or not; type Y to replace it. To undo a change, use the Ctrl+X U shortcut.

To save a file in Emacs, use the Ctrl+X Ctrl+S shortcut and to save all open files, use Ctrl+X S. To save a file by another name, use Ctrl+X Ctrl+W; you will be prompted to enter the name of the file in the minibuffer.

To exit Emacs, use Ctrl+X Ctrl+C. At any point in time, you can cancel a partially typed command in the minibuffer by using the Ctrl+G shortcut.

There is a lot more to Emacs than what we have explained here. You can do so much more with it, but it takes a while to get used to it. After you get used to it, however, you will find it hard to use anything else.

vi

vi is one of the most popular editors within the UNIX/Linux community. You will not find a lot of newcomers using it, but the old-timers use nothing else!

vi appears to be a very primitive editor at first. It uses a different concept from most editors and is quite difficult to get used to and become comfortable with. Nevertheless, it is a must to learn because wherever you go, on any flavor of UNIX/Linux, you surely will find vi. You might not find Emacs or pico, but you will find vi. In certain situations, your system could be so crippled and damaged that the only editor that will work is vi. If you don't know how to use it, you will be stuck trying to edit files.

vi uses two modes of operation—command and insert mode. The *command* mode is used to issue commands to vi, and the *insert* mode is used to type in and edit the actual text. To start vi, just type `vi` on the command line followed by the name of the file you want to edit or create:

```
$ vi file.txt
```

vi will open with the content of `file.txt` in the editing field. To create a new file, type the following:

```
$ vi
```

vi will start with a blank screen. You will see a vertical line of tilde characters (~) on the right of the screen. Each ~ denotes an empty line. vi is now running in command mode; to switch it to insert mode type `i`.

vi is now in insert mode; start typing your text normally. To issue a command, just press the Esc key to get back in command mode. To save the file, type `:w`, which will write the file to disk. To quit, type `:q`; if you want to save and quit at the same time, type `:wq`. If you want to quit without saving, type `:q!`.

As you can see, the whole idea behind using vi is to know when to use the command mode and when to use the insert mode. The command mode is used to execute commands on the text and vi itself. The following is a list of the most commonly used commands in vi:

- `a`—This means append; use it to start writing after the cursor. (The cursor will move one character to the right before you start typing.)
- `i`—This means insert; use it to start writing where the cursor is now.
- `x`—Pressing this key will delete the character under the cursor.
- `r`—This replaces the current character with another one you type.
- `dd`—This cuts the current line to the clipboard.
- `yy`—This copies the current line to the clipboard.
- `p`—This pastes the text from the clipboard.
- `u`—This undoes the latest change.
- `U`—This undoes all the changes in the current line.

App

E

- ■ /—This searches the text for a string. For example, /models will search the text for the word models.
- ■ :q—This quits vi.
- ■ :w—This saves the file.
- ■ :wq—This saves and exits.
- ■ :q!—This saves without exiting.
- ■ zz—This is equivalent to :wq.

These are the most commonly used commands in vi. Most of these commands can be executed more than once by entering a number before them. For example, to delete four characters, you could type 4x, which executes the x command four times in a row. The same can be accomplished with the cut/copy commands. For example, to copy five lines, you would type 5yy, which copies five lines to the clipboard. You would then type p to paste the contents of the clipboard to your current location.

These commands should be good enough to get you through a session of vi safely, although vi supports many more commands and extensions. vi is a very powerful editor after you learn all its shortcuts and commands. It doesn't have to be your favorite editor, but you should know how to use it well because it makes a great tool in times of need.

Other Tools

This section deals with all the tools that are not editors or achievers. These are the small programs that are very handy to have around.

grep

grep is one of the most useful utilities in Linux. It enables you to search for strings in a file or group of files. Say you're looking for a file, but you can't find it. But you know it contains the word Alfred. You easily can locate the file using grep. All you have to do is type the following:

```
$ grep Alfred *.doc
```

grep will go through all the files that end with .doc searching for the string Alfred in each one. If it finds it, it will display the name of the file along with the full line containing the search word.

find

The find command is used to find files. It will search a given path recursively for the name of the file for which you are looking. For example, to find the file called inetd.conf, enter the following command:

```
$ find / -name "inetd.conf"
```

The previous line will search for the file called `inetd.conf` starting from the root directory (/). You can search for patterns or extensions using wildcards. For example,

```
$ find / -name "*.doc"
```

will find all the files that end in `.doc`. While the command

```
$ find / -name "*net*"
```

will find all the files that contain the string `net` in their name.

`find` can execute a command on the files it finds. For example, to place a copy of all the document files you have on your drive in one directory, use the following command:

```
$ find / -name "*.doc" -exec cp {} /tmp/docs/ \;
```

The previous line copies all the found files to the directory called `/tmp/docs`. This is achieved by the `-exec` argument; you enter the command you want to run on the files after it. The `{}` is replaced by the full path of the file that was found. The `\;` is the terminator of the command. If you want it to ask you for a confirmation on every found file, replace `-exec` with `-ok`.

Pagers

You can use *pagers* to view files quickly. Pagers are helpful when all you want to do is view the contents of a file. You can use either the `more` command or `less` command. Both perform the same basic job of viewing files; however, `less` is a bit more powerful than `more`.

The basic use of these command is either of the following:

```
$ more filename
```

```
$ less filename
```

You are probably better off using `less` because it has more features than `more`. You can view text files, gzipped files, tarred files, and so on with the `less` command.

You can pipe the output of a command to either one of these commands. For example, the following will page the output of the `ls` command:

```
$ ls -l | less ●
```

App

E

Index

The IT site
you asked for...

It's
Here!

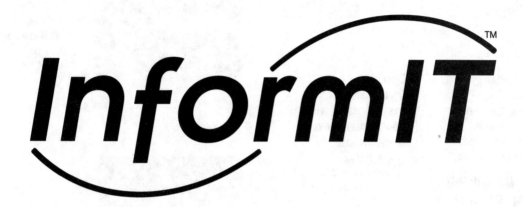

InformIT is a complete online library delivering
information, technology, reference, training, news
and opinion to IT professionals, students
and corporate users.

Find IT Solutions Here!

www.informit.com

Other Related Titles

CD-ROM Installation Instructions

Installing from a Bootable CD-ROM

Before you begin an installation, it is advised that you make backups of your valuable data. Please read "suselxen.pdf" in the "docu" directory on the CD-ROM.

These instructions assume that you will choose English (US) as your language of choice.

1. Place CD-ROM in the CD-ROM drive.
2. Restart your computer. The SuSE Linux installation program will start if you have a CD-ROM drive that can autoboot. If Linux does not start up, you may have to change your BIOS boot-order or boot from a floppy. See below for instructions on how to install SuSE Linux from a boot floppy.
3. In a few moments you should see a screen allowing you to change the language of the screens that follow. The default language is German, which you will need to change to your desired language.
4. Change column labeled "Sprache" (Language) to the desired language.
5. Change column labeled "Tastaturlayout" (Keyboard Layout) to the desired language.
6. Change column labeled "Zeitzone" (Timezone) to desired timezone.
7. Click the button labeled "Ubernehman" (Apply) to effect your selections. Click the "Weiter" (Next) button.
8. Choose either Automatic Installation (default) or Guided Installation. Click the "Next" button.
9. Follow the onscreen prompts to finish the installation of the SuSE Linux 6.3 Evaluation Version.

Installing from a Boot Floppy

You will need a blank, DOS-formatted 1.44MB floppy to set up a boot floppy.

These instructions assume that your CD-ROM drive is "D." If your drive letter is not "D," please substitute this letter with the corresponding drive letter for your system.

Insert the floppy into the floppy drive on your computer. If you are in Windows, open up a DOS prompt.

Insert the companion CD-ROM into the CD-ROM drive on your computer.

Using the DOS prompt, go to the CD-ROM drive and type:

```
D: <ENTER>
```

Navigate to the directory DOSUTILS on the CD-ROM by typing

```
cd \DOSUTILS\RAWRITE <ENTER>
```

Start the floppy creation process by typing

```
rawrite <ENTER>
```

When prompted for the boot image, type

```
\disks\bootdisk <ENTER>
```

When prompted for the destination drive, type

```
a <ENTER>
```

Make sure that the floppy is inserted in the drive and press <ENTER>.

When the process is finished, leave the floppy in the floppy drive and restart the computer.

Follow the onscreen prompts to finish the installation.

Read This Before Opening the Software